W9-BYR-829

THE BRONZE HORSEMAN

THE BRONZE HORSEMAN

FALCONET'S MONUMENT TO PETER THE GREAT

ALEXANDER M. SCHENKER

YALE UNIVERSITY PRESS
NEW HAVEN AND LONDON

Set in Garamond type by Achorn Graphic Services, Inc.
Printed in the United States of America by Sheridan Books.

Library of Congress Cataloging-in-Publication Data

Schenker, Alexander M.
    The Bronze Horseman : Falconet's monument to Peter the Great /
Alexander M. Schenker.
        p.   cm.
    ISBN 0-300-09712-3 (cloth : alk. paper)
    1. Falconet, Etienne, 1716–1791. Peter the Great. 2. Peter, I, Emperor of Russia, 1672–1725—Statues. 3. Equestrian statues—Russia (Federation)—Saint Petersburg. 4. Monuments—Russia (Federation)—Saint Petersburg.   I. Title.
NB553 .F2A73   2003
730′.92—dc21

                                                            2003000244

A catalogue record for this book is available from the British Library.

The paper in this book meets the guidelines for permanence and durability of the Committee on Production Guidelines for Book Longevity of the Council on Library Resources.

10 9 8 7 6 5 4 3 2 1

For Fred, Michael, and Cathy

Contents

Illustrations

ILLUSTRATIONS

Preface

This book is an outgrowth of a lecture given in 1996 to a group of Yale alumni during a ten-day boat trip from St. Petersburg to Moscow. To transform a cursory presentation into a study of considerable scope was an undertaking that had to draw on the help of a number of institutions and individuals. It is a pleasure gratefully to acknowledge them all.

The magnificent holdings of the Sterling, Beinecke, Arts and Architecture, and Lewis Walpole libraries at Yale enabled me to do much preliminary research without leaving my familiar grounds. I am especially beholden to Vincent Giroud, Curator of Modern Books and Manuscripts at Beinecke, whose unfailing readiness to put his erudition at my service was a boon throughout my work on the book. I also owe thanks to Tatjana Lorković, Curator of Yale's Slavic and East European Collection, Fred Musto and Margit Kaye of the Map Collection, and Karen Duval of the Yale Benjamin Franklin Papers for their help, always graciously extended.

My other Yale colleagues whose advice was particularly valuable to me are the historian Paul Bushkovitch, the art historian Maria Georgopoulou, the economist and art historian John Michael Montias, and Tomas Venclova, whose official designation as historian of Slavic literatures covers but a segment of his intellectual domain.

Much of what Yale's collections could not provide became available to me in the Library of Congress, which I visited in 1997 on a short-term grant from the Kennan Institute.

Three weeks of research in the State Archives of Venice in 1997 allowed me to discover the circumstances of Marin Carburi's ignominious flight from Venetian justice. My wife and I had the good fortune to be guests of the Hellenic Institute of Byzantine and Post-Byzantine Studies of Venice, whose gracious hospitality was placed at our disposal by its late director, Professor Nikolaos Panagiotakis. In my work on Carburi I received much timely help from Professor Nikolaos Chrissidis of Southern Connecticut State University in New Haven. I also had an opportunity to speak to Professor Virgilio Giormani of the University of Padua about his work on the Carburi brothers.

In 1998 I undertook a research trip to Russia and France on a travel grant from the American Philosophical Society. In the Russian State Archives of Ancient Documents in Moscow I benefited from the help and advice of

Svetlana Dolgova, Ekaterina Gerasimova, and Dr. Sergei Karp. Also in Moscow I pursued my quest for a likeness of Prince Dmitry Alekseevich Golitsyn, Falconet's devoted friend. I was assisted in that endeavor by Dr. Georgy S. Golitsyn of the Institute of Atmospheric Physics in Moscow and by the Moscow painter Vladimir Illarionovich Golitsyn, who allowed me to examine family portraits in his own collection and directed me to the gallery of other family portraits on the Golitsyn estate in Bol'shie Viazëmy near Moscow. I am grateful to Dr. Nikolai Vsevolodovich Kotrelev and his family for making my stay in Moscow as fruitful as possible.

My archival sources in St. Petersburg were the Russian State Historical Archives, the Russian State Naval Archives, the archive of Jakob Stählin in the Manuscript Division of the Russian National Library, the Hermitage Museum, and the Russian Museum. At the Russian State Historical Archives I received much help from Serafima Varekhova; at the Hermitage I had the good fortune to meet and become friends with Sergei Olegovich Androsov, Curator of Modern Sculpture, who guided me through the eighteenth-century holdings of the museum and shared with me his profound knowledge of Italian Baroque and Russian eighteenth-century art. Professor Michael Pesenson of Bowdoin College was kind enough to assist me in various ways during my stay in St. Petersburg.

While in St. Petersburg I met Ekaterina Georgievna Krupysheva, daughter of the late Georgii Ivanovich Ivanov, a well-known city architect and author of a fine book on the history of the transportation of the Thunder Rock. With the kind permission of Valentina Nikolaevna Ivanova, the architect's widow, Ekaterina Krupysheva put at my disposal Georgii Ivanov's research notes, plans, drawings, and photographs, three of which are reproduced in this book in their original or adapted form.

Viacheslav Semënovich Mozgovoi, a restorer of sculptures in St. Petersburg, acquainted me with the fascinating details of his examination of the internal structure of the monument during its major restoration in 1976–77, while his wife, Professor Elena Borisovna Mozgovaia of the Academy of Fine Arts in St. Petersburg, provided me with precious bibliographic information.

During my stay in Paris I used the collections of the Archives Nationales, which hold Falconet materials, transferred mostly from the archives of the Académie des Beaux-Arts. I am grateful to Henri Zuber, Chief Curator in charge of the Centre d'Accueil et de Recherches, for his kind assistance. The Archives du Ministère des Affaires Etrangères, Correspondance Politique, contain diplomatic dispatches to and from Russia, reflecting the tensions in Franco-Russian relations during the reign of Catherine the Great. My work on the Falconet-Diderot correspondence in the Bibliothèque Nationale de France was greatly facilitated by the advice of Annie Angrémy, Curator of the Manuscript Division of the library. In my examination of the archival files in the Louvre, I was fortunate to have the assistance and counsel of Jean-René Gaborit and Guilhem Scherf, both Curators in the Department of Sculpture, and Madeleine Pinault-Sørensen, Curator in the Department of Graphic Arts. Monsieur Scherf deserves particular thanks for encouraging my efforts during initial stages of my research.

At the Manufacture Nationale de Sèvres, Marie-Noëlle Pinot de Villechenon, Curator at the Musée de Céramique, conducted me through the gallery of eighteenth-century biscuit and terracotta production, while Tamara Préaud, the Archivist of the Manufacture, opened up to me eighteenth-century records of appointments and salaries, including those of Falconet.

Professor Georges Dulac, Director of the Centre d'Etudes du XVIIIe Siècle at the University of Montpellier, kindly shared with me the details of his projected edition of Prince Dmitry A. Golitsyn's correspondence with Vice Chancellor Prince Alexander M. Golitsyn, and sent me copies of passages pertinent to Falconet.

The *chargée* of the Musée des Beaux-Arts in Nancy, Mme Béatrice Salmon, provided me with a list of the works by Collot held by the museum, as well as of works by Falconet *père* and *fils*. I am obliged also to the curator Clara Gelly-Saldias and the documentalist Patricia Pedracini for their kind assistance.

An incidental advantage of archival research is that it may put one researcher on the trail of another working in the same general area of study. Such was the unexpected benefit of my work in the Marie-Anne Collot archive in Nancy. While leafing through it, I came across a well-focused inquiry by Marie-Louise Becker, a Paris art historian and *antiquaire,* which revealed a seasoned researcher with an abiding interest in Collot. That accidental encounter marked the beginning of a fruitful scholarly partnership and personal friendship in which much information and many insights in our common venture of studying the Falconet-Collot connection changed hands. I was the greater beneficiary in that barter. Mme Becker's reading of one of Diderot's letters to Falconet provided important corrections to the scholarship on Diderot and Collot. Her discovery of a clearly identified drawing of Prince Dmitry A. Golitsyn by Pierre-Etienne Falconet, and its confrontation with a terracotta bust by Collot, confirmed our earlier suspicions that the bust is, in fact, a portrait of the prince rather than of Friedrich Melchior Grimm, as had been thought. Her assignment of a specific author to the so-called *Eloge de Mademoiselle Collot,* which heretofore was considered anonymous, has, in my view, a good chance of being accepted by the scholarly community.

It was also thanks to Mme Becker that I had the privilege of meeting Mme Elisabeth Nénert and Count Bertrand de Warren, two descendants of the original heirs of Marie-Lucie de Jankovitz (née Falconet). Opportunities to see heretofore unknown portraits of the Falconet family and their friends, as well as to touch objects which had once been in the hands of Peter the Great and Catherine the Great, count among the most unforgettable experiences of my adventure with the Bronze Horseman, ones for which I will always be profoundly grateful.

As a reader of the manuscript for Yale University Press, Professor William Mills Todd III of Harvard University earned my gratitude for his meticulous attention to my text and for a number of thoughtful comments and suggestions.

It is natural, though regrettable, that in a book of this size not all the works and topics mentioned can be accompanied by illustrations. Fortunately, three publications are of great help in this regard. Réau's fundamental work on Falconet contains reproductions of all major and a good number of minor works of the sculptor. Falconet's models for the Sèvres Manufacture are now available in the richly illustrated catalog of the exhibit *Falconet à Sèvres, 1757–1766 ou l'art de plaire,* while a selection of reproductions of Collot's sculptures may be found in Becker, 1998, and Becker, forthcoming. For views of Falconet's monument as it appears today I am grateful to the St. Petersburg photographer Leonid Bogdanov. My daughter-in-law Kathy Schenker, a most resourceful graphic designer, and Joseph Szaszfai, photography manager at Yale's Audio-Visual Center, have earned my gratitude for their skillful work on a number of photographs.

Falconet stressed his obligation to Mademoiselle Collot for her excellent advice: "She made me throw out a number of silly things," he said in one of his letters to Diderot. That acknowledgment encompasses but a fraction of my debt to my wife Krystyna, who was a tireless critic and adviser throughout my work on this book. Another trait which links her with Collot is a remarkable understanding and forbearance for the "monumental" fixation of her *compagnon de vie.*

Incomplete as this roster is, it would have been inadmissibly so without a tribute to my learned Leningrad friend Igor Mikhailovich Vaisbein. Igor's evocations of the physical and literary landscape of his climatically disadvantaged city, narrated under the cloudless skies of Tajikistan, had all the unreal and spellbinding qualities of the tales of Scheherezade. Their seed took exactly sixty years to germinate and bear fruit.

My final words of appreciation are addressed to my agent, William B. Goodman, who spared no effort piloting my manuscript, to my copy editor, Gavin Lewis, whose learning and sharp eye helped improve it in a multitude of ways, and to my proofreader, Dan Heaton.

The book is dedicated to Fred, Michael, and Cathy. Cathy deserves special thanks for editing early drafts of the text and helping me banish from it the ghost of a Slavic philologist, my other persona in scholarship.

It is a source of particular pleasure that this book, appearing as it does in the year of St. Petersburg's tercentenary, may be regarded as a token of my personal admiration and affection for that city and a contribution to its celebration.

I should like to believe that the words with which Falconet summed up the goals of his richly annotated translation of three art-oriented books of Pliny the Elder's *Natural History* apply also to the sentiments which guided me during the seven years of work on the Bronze Horseman: "This is the fruit of knowledge which I succeeded to obtain in Art. I consider it the heritage of my Fathers. All I wanted to do was to put it to use. I did not want to distort it. On the contrary, I tried to enlarge and improve it as much as I could."

A. M. S.
Hamden, May 2003

THE BRONZE HORSEMAN

Introduction

On these deserted shores whose life, it might seem, was driven out
by nature itself, Peter set down his capital and created his subjects.
Their children, milling around his august monument, look up at
the awesome arm extended over them and wonder whether that
bronze palm protects or threatens them.
—Joseph de Maistre (1809)

The scene is St. Petersburg. It has been drizzling since morning. Now it's
close to noon, but green watery fog is still shrouding the embankment of
the Neva. Out of the fog, like the mast of an anchored ship and a buoy
bobbing in water, two golden shapes come into view. On the left, the slender
spire of the Admiralty, and in the background, the majestic dome of St.
Isaac's. A car pulls up and out come a young woman, all in white, and a
young man in a black suit. They pick up a bouquet of flowers and, with
the best man and the maid of honor holding umbrellas aloft, walk slowly
to the granite boulder on which a huge equestrian statue looms through the
fog. Once there, the newlyweds turn to be photographed and turn again to
place the flowers on the flagstones below the Bronze Horseman, as the Russian poet Alexander Pushkin named the monument to Peter the Great.
Stretched out above them, as if in a gesture of benediction, is the open palm
of Tsar Peter. A kiss, applause, good wishes, more photographs, and the
young couple depart in the company of their families and friends for the
wedding banquet.

What is it that makes young Petersburgers direct their first steps after the
marriage ceremony to the Bronze Horseman, as if wanting Peter the Protector to be a witness of their union? Why do they treat the bronze effigy on
top of a granite rock as an icon to which they turn for the blessing? How
is it that a monument to a Russian tsar, created by a French sculptor,
Etienne-Maurice Falconet, has entered the heart and gut of the city in which
it stands, so that the Bronze Horseman is as unthinkable in any other setting
as is St. Petersburg without it?[1] These are some of the questions with which
this book is concerned.

If the era known as the Enlightenment is delimited by the death of Louis XIV in 1715 and the promulgation of the Declaration of the Rights of Man and the Citizen in 1789, then the span of Falconet's life is practically coextensive with it. In 1716, when he was born, Voltaire was twenty-two, Benjamin Franklin was ten, Rousseau was four, Diderot was three, and the rule of Louis XV, who presided over the fates of France during its fifty years of *la vie douce,* was about to begin. When he died in 1791, Louis XVI was just two years away from being led up the steps of the guillotine that had replaced the grandiose equestrian statue of Louis XV on the large Paris square then called place Louis XV, but renamed later, undeservedly it would seem, place de la Concorde. The grimly serious nineteenth century was just around the corner.

It was during Falconet's lifespan that the modern world was launched, a world that was moderately skeptical and cautiously optimistic, a world in which the notions of personal freedom and the rule of reason took root in the Western mind. Happiness and scientific progress were deemed worthy goals of human pursuit, while commerce and industry were accepted as the means to achieve them. That was also the time when Russia arose from its medieval slumber and began to cast an ever-lengthening shadow over Europe, causing concern, even alarm, in major European capitals. Yet the job of Europeanizing Russia, begun so abruptly by Peter the Great, had not yet managed to penetrate much below the skin of the country. When Falconet was born, the city of St. Petersburg, the most dramatic example of Peter's efforts to redirect the destinies of Russia, was barely thirteen years old.[2] It would be another thirteen years before the woman who was to continue Peter's work was born in the Prussian port city of Stettin. And an additional thirty-seven years were needed before she, then as Empress Catherine II, summoned Falconet to St. Petersburg to "put flesh on Peter's spirit."[3]

"Does Russia belong to Europe? Perhaps it does, perhaps it doesn't, perhaps a little, just as you please." So mused Nikolai Danilevsky (1822–85), a Russian biologist of Slavophile leanings, as he considered the mixture of European and Asian elements in the Russian collective psyche.[4] One would have thought that with the same Judeo-Christian roots, Russia and the West should have had no problem finding a common ground. Yet, fuzzy similarities are often more confounding than well-defined differences, and one has to be reconciled to the fact that, despite much searching, the key to the understanding of the nature of Russia's relationship to Europe remains elusive. To a Western student of Russia's cultural identity, it is a small consolation to know that a Russian appears to be as baffled by it as he is.

Russia's geographic location, astride the Eurasian continental divide, is just one element in that persistent quandary. Much more important have been the effects of two long periods in Russia's early history. The first began in the mid-thirteenth century, when the invasions of the Mongols brought about two hundred and fifty years of political subservience to the Golden Horde and cultural isolation from Western Europe. The second extended over the sixteenth and seventeenth centuries, when the military power of Sweden, Poland, and Turkey created a virtual *cordon sanitaire* along Russia's western and southern borders. With the Baltic controlled by the Swedes and the Black Sea by the Ottoman Turks, Russia had to rely on the semi-Arctic port of Archangel as its lone sea outlet to the Western world. The four and a half centuries of isolation from the main currents of Western thought could not but force the Russians onto their own cultural and political paths. Hence Russia's introspective attitudes, its traditionalist clinging to Byzantine models, and its lingering problems with self-identification.

By the end of the seventeenth century, however, Poland's poorly functioning elective monarchy, the obsolescence of Ottoman political institutions, and Sweden's powerful push into central and eastern Europe forced Russia into assuming a more active international stance and prompted it to reach beyond its immediate neighbors for cultural leadership and political models. The lot of shaking the country out of its lethargic Muscovite conservatism and introducing it to the dynamic ways of emergent Western capitalism fell to the third monarch in the dynastic line of the Romanovs, Tsar Peter I. Peter sensed that Russia's future lay in a rapprochement with the West and that, in order to fulfill its historical destiny, Russia had to open itself to a free flow of Western ideas. Europeanization became the main goal of his reign, and he set about it with the ruthless determination of a righteous ideologue, convinced of the correctness of his ways. His Muscovite subjects, reluctant to abandon their traditions and shocked by the abruptness and brutality of Peter's ways, tried to put up resistance. But the "Westernizing" tsar, whose political and military successes earned him the designation "the Great," followed his vision unflinchingly. And to crown his efforts he marshaled all his resources in order to give his country a westward-looking center of power and made it rise like a phantasmagoric exhalation from the marshes in the estuary of the Neva River.

St. Petersburg, which even today is the world's northernmost megalopolis and Russia's cultural capital, was founded—so says the tradition—on May 16, 1703, near the place where the Neva fans out in multiple arms to form a delta that descends gently to the Gulf of Finland. The city, the most dramatic example of Peter's revolutionary ways, amazes by the very fact of its existence. Its site, a mere five hundred miles below the Arctic Circle, was ill-suited for human habitation and urban construction. It was a low-lying, desolate marsh, soaked by abundant ground water and frequent rains, mosquito-infested during the short summers, and frozen over for five months of the year. The sodden ground could not support the weight of fortifications, palaces, and larger buildings without painstaking preparations: dredging, drainage, landfill, and reinforcements with wooden piles driven into the soil. The stone which was used for the construction of houses and embankments had to be brought in by boat. In the words attributed to one of Peter's jesters, it was a place where "on one side was the sea, on the other sorrow, on the third moss, on the fourth a sigh."[5]

The Neva is only fifty miles long from its source in Lake Ladoga to its mouth in the Gulf of Finland, but during that short run it becomes a mighty river, reaching seventy-five feet in depth and well over five hundred yards in width, as it approaches the sea. A river of such dimensions is just too overpowering to blend into the urban landscape, as do, for instance, the Seine in Paris, the Vltava in Prague, or the Arno in Florence. Like the Hudson in New York, the Neva divides rather than unites. During the warmer season, the river does provide a picturesque setting for the architectural treasures lining its embankments. Yet even then, the beautiful palaces and government buildings look disproportionately small to a viewer standing on the opposite bank. And in wintertime, when the river freezes over, its lifeless white expanse clashes with the gentle warmth of the Rococo architecture. To the painter's eye of Robert Ker Porter, who visited Russia from 1805 to 1808, the frozen Neva is "one bleak, extended snowy plain [that] generalizes the views; and scarcely a trace is left to convey an idea that a river ever glided through the heart of this imperial city."[6] No, it is not the Neva that gives St. Petersburg its charm and its Bruges-like aspect, but the many canals and rivulets criss-crossing the city and the graceful bridges that span them.

In fact, the main bed of the Neva is so wide that it did not get a permanent bridge until the mid-nineteenth century.[7] During the cold months, when the Neva was frozen over, it could be crossed on ice along its full length.[8] But when the ice melted, the Petersburgers had to use ferries or pontoon bridges. The first pontoon bridge, the so-called Great Isakievsky Bridge, lay almost directly in front of the Bronze Horseman. It connected St. Isaac's Square with the academic buildings on the Vasilievsky Island. The bridge was opened every night to let the boat traffic go through. In wintertime it was stowed away.

The Neva could also bring havoc and misfortune to the people living in its delta by spilling over its low-lying banks and flooding the soggy land on which the city was founded. St. Petersburg's notoriously wet climate did not bear the sole responsibility for the dreaded floods. Had they been due to rains alone, the city would have been under water most of the time. No, for the floods to occur the river had to be barred from the Gulf of Finland by winds blowing in from the west. When the winds were so powerful as to stop the otherwise strong current, the river would swell up and flood the countryside. Between 1721 and 1756 St. Petersburg was flooded at least ten times. Two of the most damaging inundations took place in the years 1777 and 1824. The former occurred while Falconet and Collot were still in the city. Catherine the Great watched its ruinous aftermath from a window in the Winter Palace: "It looked like the destruction of Jerusalem. The unfinished embankment was covered with three-masted merchant vessels. . . . How many broken windowpanes! . . . Yes, that was something to see! And what's the point of it all?"[9]

However much one wonders about the wisdom of establishing a major city in such an inhospitable environment, one has to admit that Peter the

Great did not have much choice in selecting its site. Anxious for a seaport from which he would be able to trade with the great Western maritime powers such as Holland, England, France, and Venice, the tsar made Russia's access to the Baltic one of the goals of his foreign policy.[10] The Swedish victory at Narva in 1700 slowed down, but did not stop, his efforts. By the time St. Petersburg was founded, the Russians had managed to wrest away from the Swedes all of the Neva and a small strip of the Ingrian land along the southeastern shore of the Gulf of Finland. Then the tides of war turned in Russia's favor, Sweden's supply route to its fleet on Lake Ladoga was cut off, and Peter was finally able to start translating his dream into reality.

St. Petersburg's first major building projects, the mighty Peter and Paul Fortress on Hare Island and, diagonally across the river, the shipbuilding wharfs of the Admiralty, show that the initial impulse for the founding of the city was strategic—the Russian settlement at the mouth of the Neva was to prevent the Swedes from using the river for their incursions into the Russian hinterland.[11] Politics, however, was not long to follow. The celebrations of the Russian victory over the Swedes at Poltava in 1709 had hardly died down when Peter designated St. Petersburg the country's new capital. An insane idea, or so it seemed to many of his compatriots, friends and enemies alike. Should an entirely new capital that had so little to do with the traditional values of the land and its deeply ingrained cultural and religious sentiments and institutions be imposed upon the people by the sovereign will of the monarch? Could a slice of mosquito-infested northern marshes be turned into one of the world's political hubs? The chances of success of the tsar's venture must have seemed as chimerical as would be an attempt to turn Anchorage, Alaska, into a major metropolis.[12] As if the difficulties of building a city in such an inhospitable environment were not sufficient, Peter's hubris demanded that St. Petersburg be created ex nihilo, in a quasi-divine process that invites comparisons to the Book of Genesis.[13] Little wonder that for the Russian traditionalist, St. Petersburg was a satanic creation and its founder the embodiment of Antichrist.

Yet, the phenomenon of St. Petersburg must be judged as something much bigger and more important than the feat of "inventing" a city, of creating a capital in the midst of physical bleakness and desolation. What St. Petersburg stands for in the minds of the Russians is Peter's "cultural revolution," his attempt to change the time-honored and comfortable habits of his country in so radical a fashion as to virtually stand them on their head. In the thirty-six years of his reign this six-foot-six monarch succeeded in accomplishing what still today seems hardly possible. He yanked Russia out of its medieval backwater and sent it spinning into the modern age. He broke with the introvert ways of old Muscovy and embraced the spirit and the letter of the bustling world of eighteenth-century Europe, a world of capital accumulation, formation of colonial empires, and technological advances. And he did it so thoroughly and perdurably that ever since his name has served as the boundary line between the Russia that used to be a blank page on the political map of Europe and the Russia that has become one of the major players in the international arena, between the pre-Petrine and post-Petrine periods in Russian history.

St. Petersburg lived up to Peter's expectations and during the two centuries of its existence as the capital, it became Russia's "window to Europe," to use a phrase coined by Count Francesco Algarotti and given currency by Alexander Pushkin in the opening lines of *The Bronze Horseman*.[14] In 1739, a mere fourteen years after Peter's death, this is how St. Petersburg appeared to Algarotti as he stood on the deck of a boat coming from the Gulf of Finland and entering the mouth of the Neva:

> After having sailed some hours in the midst of this hideous and silent wood, behold, the river turns at once, and the scene changes in an instant, as at an opera. We see before us the imperial city. On either shore, sumptuous edifices grouped together, turrets with gilded spires rising every here and there like pyramids; ships, which by their masts and flying streamers, mark the separation of the streets, and distinguish the several quarters; such was the brilliant sight which struck our eyes. We were told, here is the Admiralty, there is the Arsenal, here the Citadel, yonder is the Academy, on that side the empress' winter palace.[15]

Though Peter's reforms affected just the upper crust of Russian society, they were sufficient to project a new image of Russia, not as a mysterious land beyond the rainbow, but as a country on the move, eager to assimilate as quickly as possible what the West had achieved during centuries of laborious development. By the second decade of the eighteenth century, Russia had a new Western-style capital, a Western-style army and navy, and some Western-style institutions of government. St. Petersburg, the symbol of Russia's commitment to European values, was teeming with visitors from the West, ready to help the newly refurbished country and make good money along the way. Flowing in the opposite direction were members of the Russian elite, its nobility, who succumbed to the prodding of the tsar and the lure of the unknown. They were eager to test their newly acquired social graces at some of the grandest European courts in order to see and learn what the West had to offer.

St. Petersburg was a city with many faces. A maritime harbor to some, a commercial center to others; a combination of a magnificent imperial court, attracting fashionable visitors from every country of Western Europe, and a bazaar filled with the multinational populace of Russia's immense empire; a place of fabled opulence and the lowest depths of human misery; Italianate palaces standing alongside wooden huts, muddy side streets leading to elegant granite-clad embankments, the latest Parisian fashions next to traditional belted shirts worn over homespun pants.

It was through St. Petersburg that Russia first experienced the West in all its cultural richness and heterogeneity: Italian, French, and Scottish architecture; Venetian canals and bridges; a Dutch seaport; German scientific institutions; English art collections, gardens, and articles of luxury; and French literary fashions. But St. Petersburg was not content to import styles and objects. It imported their creators—architects, artists, and city planners who designed its wide avenues, put up its buildings, laid out its squares, and filled them with monuments. In the words of the poet Joseph Brodsky, Peter the Great "did not suffer from the traditional Russian malady—an inferiority complex toward Europe. He did not want to imitate Europe, he wanted that Russia be Europe, just like he himself, at least in part was European, just like many of his friends and companions, just like the main enemies against whom he warred." And that is the image which he succeeded in imprinting upon the city to which he gave the name of Apostle Peter, his patron saint.[16]

Yet, even though the *Peter* in the name of the city is that of the apostle, the name *Sankt-Peterburg* has a built-in ambiguity, for it could be understood as either the *city of Saint Peter* or as the *holy city of Peter*. Among those who thought of their tsar as a builder, Jesus' reference to the Apostle Peter as the rock on which he would build the edifice of the church must have struck a sympathetic chord.[17] There was also a desire to legitimize the power "usurped" by St. Petersburg by associating it with the heritage of some of the holiest cities of early Christianity: Rome, whose first bishop was St. Peter; Kiev, whose legendary founder was St. Andrew, St. Peter's brother; and above all, Constantinople, whose name is associated with that of its founder. Various analogies were used to strengthen these associations and help St. Petersburg overcome the finality of Moscow's claim to supremacy among the Orthodox.[18] The coat of arms of St. Petersburg was designed with two crossed anchors which, like the two crossed keys of the Roman See of St. Peter, are turned upward. St. Andrew was "appointed" patron of the Russian navy, which was created by Peter the Great and which was, and largely is to this day, based in St. Petersburg. Finally, the founding of St. Petersburg, just like the founding of Constantinople, was said to have been accompanied by the appearance of an eagle, a symbol of imperial power.

Peter's revolution went far deeper than the external manifestations of modernization—changes in the liturgy, calendar, and alphabet, Western garb, and shaved-off beards. Following the prescription of every successful revolution, Peter unraveled the threads that made up the tissue of Russian society and replaced them with new ones of his own making.[19] The losers were the ancient boyar families; the gainers were Peter's cronies, yesterday's nobodies, today's powerful princes and counts. Peter's famous Table of Ranks created a quasi-military structure of state functionaries, a pyramid of puppets set in motion by the threads gathered in the hand of the tsar.

Another consequence of Peter's revolution was the rift that has ever since divided the Russians into those who, like their tsar, have allied themselves with Western cultural values and those who have identified with native patrimony and for whom its abandonment by Peter was an act of cultural betrayal and a sellout to the West. These two groups have been known since the mid-nineteenth century as the Westerners and the Slavophiles. To the latter,

St. Petersburg was not a "window to Europe" but an open door through which the sinful ways of the West could enter and roam freely all over Holy Russia.[20] Like its diabolical conjurer, it was a city cursed by God and fated to be swallowed up by the very waters upon which it was created.[21] They saw the fulfillment of that prophecy not only in the inundations periodically visited on St. Petersburg but in the death of Peter himself, brought on by a pneumonia, which he had caught in the freezing waters of the Gulf of Finland while trying to rescue shipwrecked seamen.

Division, duality, ambiguity. Andrei Bely found a strikingly pictorial way of bringing out that aspect of Peter's heritage in his description of Falconet's monument: "A rippling *half-shade* covered the horseman's face and its enigmatic expression was *reflected* in bronze. His palm *split* the turquoise hues. From that grave time when the bronze horseman came tearing to the banks of the Neva, from that grave and momentous time when he flung his steed onto gray Finnish granite, Russia has been *severed in half,* the very destiny of the country has been *severed in half, severed in half* is Russia, suffering and weeping until its final hour."[22]

But Catherine the Great, herself a European through and through, was not bothered by St. Petersburg's identity problems because she herself had none. As wise a monarch as Europe had seen, she was able to rise above her German birth, her adopted ethnic Russianness, and her cultural Frenchness, and skillfully combine these identities into one imperial persona that allowed her to rule almost by public acclaim. To a Muscovite traditionalist she was a Russian *matushka,* or dear mother, while to a French intellectual she was the very embodiment of an enlightened ruler, a monarch whom a Voltaire or a Diderot wished he had at home. Unlike Peter, she bore Moscow no grudge and, if needed, would stay in the ancient capital for a year at a time. At the same time, she was not bothered by St. Petersburg's maritime location and climatic peculiarities, finding in them an affinity with her native Stettin. Immensely successful in her domestic and international policies, she threw herself wholeheartedly into the business of transforming St. Petersburg into a European metropolis. Falconet became one of the tools in that grand enterprise.

Falconet was but one of the many Frenchmen who struck out from their native land in search of freedom or fortune in North America or in Russia. Leaving the soil of *la douce France* did not mean, however, that the French were leaving its spiritual climate. Eighteenth-century France stood supreme among the civilized nations as the leader in every domain of intellectual life and a trendsetter in every aspect of culture. True to its name, the French language was the lingua franca of the educated Europeans. It was the preferred language of correspondence even when another language would seem a more natural medium.[23] During the Catherinian period, all educated Russians spoke French at least as well as their native tongue, a situation which allowed a Frenchman like Falconet to spend twelve years in Russia without learning Russian and without ever complaining that this caused him the slightest discomfort.

Eighteenth-century Russia, by contrast, was a country just emerging from centuries of arrested development. It did not share in such Western institutions as knighthood and chivalrous traditions, artisanal guilds and municipal self-government, and the ideological revolutions exemplified most vividly by the thematic and stylistic innovations of the Gothic and Renaissance eras. Its models were the inflexible ways of the East, a political system that turned absolutism into despotism and serfdom into slavery. It is not surprising, therefore, that in the popular perception of the French, the seventeenth-century Russia was a land half-frozen, in the literal and figurative sense, a land in which fur-clad people dwelled in smoke-filled huts.[24]

While Louis XIV could still afford to give little thought to the lands going by the name of Muscovy, his successors could not fail to notice the stirrings in the vast country, which was being awakened after centuries of hibernation by a dramatically innovating ruler.[25] Peter the Great's Westernizing reforms, and the pro-Western policies of his daughter Elizabeth (r. 1741–62), changed the inward-directed ways of the country. The Russians stopped treating France as a fabled land "beyond the seven seas and seven rivers" and began craning their necks toward Paris as the center of learning and the arts, luxury and fashion, and the acknowledged cultural capital of the world. In Pushkin's fanciful formulation, Russia's victory at Poltava allowed "the European Enlightenment to drop anchor in the conquered Neva."[26]

May 7, 1717, the day when Peter the Great descended upon the Paris of the Regency, was perhaps the most important date in the history of modern relations between Russia and France. On that day the Russian tsar, who during his "great embassy" to Holland and England twenty years earlier could not extract an invitation from Louis XIV, was received with open arms by the regent, Philippe, duke of Orléans. For the Parisian crowds staring at the gigantic ruler of Russia and his motley retinue, self-confidently displaying Russia's power, the occasion must have had a symbolic meaning. There in front of their eyes were messengers from the new Russia, a Russia which "irrupted into Europe like a ship launched to the sound of axes and the thunder of cannon" to claim a permanent place in Europe's political consciousness.[27] Did they realize, as they watched the alternately entrancing and scandalizing behavior of their visitors, that Russia's integration into the European polity depended less on Europe's willingness to accept it into the club than on Russia's readiness to apply for membership?[28]

The door between Russia and Europe stood open, but French officialdom was not ready to take advantage of the opportunity and stepped aside with cautious reserve.[29]

Undaunted, the Russians sought other political partners. When the French did not act on Peter the Great's offer of the hand of his daughter Elizabeth in marriage to the young Louis XV, Russia's diplomatic interests shifted to

Austria and Prussia, inaugurating an era of pro-German and anti-French feelings at the Russian court. There was nothing surprising in such a disposition of sentiments, for the two countries lived by the age-old system of alliances according to which your next-door neighbor is your enemy and the enemy of your enemy is your friend. Hence the political map of Europe resembled a checkerboard on which white squares opposed black ones in a variety of alliances. Since France and Poland were enemies of Prussia, and Poland was an enemy of Russia, France was a natural ally of Poland and enemy of Russia, which in turn made it an ally of the Ottoman Empire in its conflict with Russia.

That is why Catherine looked with a great deal of suspicion on the official representatives of France in St. Petersburg. A perusal of French official documents in the archives of the Ministry of Foreign Affairs in Paris shows that her skepticism was well founded. Louis XV, alarmed by Catherine's seizure of power and a possible shift from the pro-French policy of Elizabeth, instructed Baron de Breteuil, his plenipotentiary minister in St. Petersburg, that "everything that helps throw [Russia] into Chaos and makes it retire into obscurity is advantageous to my interests," and that "the only object of my policy towards Russia is to distance it to the greatest possible degree from the affairs of Europe."[30]

After Russian military successes in Prussia, Louis XV wrote to marquis de Bausset, just appointed to succeed Breteuil: "The enlightened nations view with apprehension as Russia, barely stripped of its truly barbarous bark, profits rapidly from its new situation to extend its borders and come closer to us."[31] Ten years later, an official French dispatch from St. Petersburg painted Russia's future in dusky hues: "It is morally impossible for the Russians to form what one calls a nation. In general, they do not have any kind of character. Avarice allied with extravagance, bad faith, groveling servility, insolence, and vanity will be the eternal products of this barren land. . . . They have all our faults with none of our qualities. . . . There is practically no exception to these rules."[32]

Nonetheless, eighteenth-century Europe did not allow affairs of state to interfere with matters of culture, and regard for French arts and letters remained high in all the capitals of continental Europe, regardless of France's standing as a political ally or foe. This was particularly true of the reign of Catherine the Great, and it is a measure of the intellect and broad-mindedness of the German-born empress of Russia that she was able to rise above frustrations and reverses in her official dealings with France and emerge as a friend and protector of the best that the French Enlightenment could offer. Craving full accreditation at the intellectual courts of Europe, she saw herself, and wanted others to see her, not only as a builder of a capital filled with elegant palaces and residences, but as one of Europe's most enlightened monarchs, a patroness of the arts and letters, a supporter of learning, and a discriminating collector. To fulfill that ambition she corresponded tirelessly with the likes of Voltaire, Diderot, d'Alembert, Grimm, Mme Geoffrin, and

Marmontel, and did so in a French that has been hailed for its expressiveness, wit, and grace of style.[33]

Voltaire was rightfully at the head of the list of the *philosophes* who fascinated Catherine. She knew and admired his writings long before 1762, when she initiated their famous epistolary friendship, using as pretext her wish to correct some factual errors in Voltaire's biography of Peter the Great. Voltaire accepted the invitation by sending Catherine one of his books with a flattering inscription. In response she wrote him directly, asking him not to praise her without sufficient reason and telling him that his writings had always been her inspiration and the one reason why she had stopped reading novels. An exchange of letters followed, half serious, half tongue-in-cheek, with Catherine proving to be the more interesting and attractive correspondent. Her letters are witty and natural. Voltaire's letters, on the other hand, are full of indiscriminate flattery and misplaced admiration.

Here are a few examples of Voltaire's gushing declarations of affection for Catherine and his chimerical tributes to Catherinian Russia, written to the empress directly or to others in the enormous circle of his correspondents: "My heart is like the compass needle—it turns to the North." "I wish [Catherine] a reign that it is as long as it is glorious. Where is the time when I was only seventy? I would have run to admire her. Where is the time when I could still sing? I would have glorified her all the way from the foothills of the Alps to the sea of Archangel." "Courage, brave Russians! Victory has always come from the North. May your good sense triumph! May the beautiful and unfortunate climes, so long dominated by the inquisition and its equivalents and inhabited by so many swindlers and fools, be enlightened by the Northern Star, which shines from above the North Pole spreading the brilliance of universal tolerance."[34] Such metaphoric effusions, including the replacement of the biblical East with the Russian North as the source of all light *(ex oriente lux)* could, when taken literally, border on hallucinatory. Voltaire mused, for instance, about a trip to St. Petersburg and Taganrog in order to enjoy the Russian weather, following Catherine's promise that she "would do everything in [her] power to procure a better climate for the city of St. Petersburg."[35] In that area, however, Catherine's powers were limited.

Catherine's success with Voltaire and other figures of the European Enlightenment was due in no small measure to her skill in the game of public relations. Exploiting her own "Western" roots and intellectual curiosity, she succeeded in cultivating the crème de la crème of the French intellectual establishment and turned public opinion in her favor.[36] In Europe, exhausted by two long international conflicts, the War of the Austrian Succession and the Seven Years' War, Catherine could claim the role of a truly enlightened monarch, that is, a ruler whose intellectual and artistic interests were backed up by considerable and generously dispensed financial resources, a sui generis modern foundation.

The views of the *philosophes* clustering around Catherine in poses of worshipful reverence should not be taken, however, as being representative of the general attitude in France.[37] Despite the modern facade of its capital, Russia was still perceived as a medieval autocracy with a thin varnish of culture and all too few comforts for those accustomed to the luxury distinguishing the reign of Louis XV. Characteristic in this respect is Diderot's account of how his efforts to send two workers, a molder Simon and a sculptor Vandendrisse, to Falconet in St. Petersburg had to overcome a fierce campaign of anti-Russian tales: "There is nothing that those infernal souls would not imagine to trouble, alarm, frighten, and revolt this poor Simon. They showed him the Russians with horns, tails, and talons and Russia as the hell of Milton, where the damned were taken alternately from the abyss of ice to the abyss of fire, so as to make one extreme more stinging and cruel by the other extreme. They depicted the Russians as people without integrity, honor, or faith, ferocious jailers from whose hands one cannot be pulled if one has the misfortune of falling into them."[38]

It is true that the image of Russia was beginning to change gradually. From a country which until then was considered barbarous or, at the very least, exotic, it was now seen as a potentially dangerous major power, which had to be reckoned with and was certainly worth reconnoitering. Outside of that goal, however, Russia did not constitute an attraction in France, other than as a place of employment for legions of French teachers, governesses, artisans, and cooks. It was they who were chiefly responsible for what may appear as the Russian vogue in France.

The Russians, by contrast, visited the French capital in droves with tourism as their main object, as shown by Diderot's off-the-cuff remark that "our [Paris] residential hotels are continually filled with the Russians."[39] In the words of Aleksandr Brückner: "Having failed to become German, Dutch, or English under Peter, [the Russians] showed an ability to become half-French after Peter."[40] French tastes took over in every domain of life, from architecture to culinary art. Jakob Stählin, an attentive observer of the artistic life of the capital, remarked on the popularity of French styles of interior decoration: "By the 1750s there was not a single house of quality in St. Petersburg which would not be furnished in accordance with the latest French fashion and richly decorated with gilt carving." He singled out the mansion of Court Marshal Naryshkin, in which Diderot spent the eight months of his stay in St. Petersburg, as especially sumptuously furnished.[41] Catherine the Great's decision to entrust a French artist with the creation of a monument encapsulating her political credo is one of the most eloquent testimonies of the French domination of the Russian cultural scene.

That the French, other than the intellectual coterie of Catherine, looked at Russia's awesome riches and power with a growing feeling of malaise may be gathered from the books about Russia which began to be written by the growing number of diplomats, military men, and scientists who traveled to Russia and wished to leave for posterity an account of their impressions. All too often, the writers were ignorant of the Russian language and the native customs, and in their descriptions of the chasm between the idealized image of the country based on the splendors of the new capital and the stark realities of the traditional interior, they had to rely on observations made from a speeding coach. At the same time, they were certainly able to comment insightfully on the social views and political behavior of the French-speaking elite, which makes their accounts more reliable as a critique of the Russian government than as a study of Russian society at large. That, in turn, rendered them especially irritating to the rulers of Russia who would feel obliged to counter them with self-righteous indignation and accusations of bias.[42]

Above all, however, eighteenth-century France emerged as a hothouse of the visual arts and, politics aside, began to exert a major influence on the Russian effort to raise its own crop of painters and sculptors. Russian artists were sent to be trained in France, and many artists from France, as well as from other Western European countries, accepted invitations to work in the new Russian capital, tempted by high salaries and various benefits offered by the Russian government.

The flow of French visitors grew and became more variegated as the eighteenth century progressed. Its beginnings, however, were fairly modest, with city planners and architects leading the field during the construction-filled years of Peter the Great. The only major French city planner to be involved, however briefly, in the planning of St. Petersburg was Alexandre-Jean-Baptiste Le Blond (1679–1719), who arrived in 1716. Le Blond, however, died three years after his arrival in St. Petersburg, too short a time to leave a lasting legacy on the cityscape. The ideas which he managed to leave on paper show him a singularly unpractical man. As a result, a number of his projects, interesting as they are for the history of eighteenth-century urbanistic thought, remained unrealized. Le Blond's St. Petersburg was to be a heavily fortified oval, located principally on the right bank of the Neva, that is, on the Vasilievsky Island and in a section of the so-called Petersburg District. About one-tenth of the city was to be on the left bank, providing economic support for the existing wharfs of the Admiralty and the rest of the city. The eastern approaches to St. Petersburg were to be guarded by the Fortress of Peter and Paul. The whole was to be crisscrossed by regularly alternating ramrod-straight canals and streets.

It was a utopian plan, drafted without any consideration for the historical and topographical realities of the city. Le Blond treated St. Petersburg as one would treat a large colonial outpost, without a hinterland and without a history. He was oblivious of the huge Russian ancestral possessions that stretched for thousands of miles to the south and east of the city. Nor did he realize that practically all the inhabitants of St. Petersburg were recent settlers, who did not want to be isolated from their native towns and villages by a wide river that was still unspanned by bridges. He overlooked what no St. Petersburger could afford to forget, that the Vasilievsky Island, as the city's lowest-lying region, would always be the first to succumb to the notorious St. Petersburg floods and the last to shake off their disastrous consequences. It is not surprising, therefore, that Le Blond's plan rests as a curiosity in the archives of the Russian Academy of Sciences and that the city grew naturally on the left bank of the Neva, while the Vasilievsky Island remained virtually undeveloped until well into the nineteenth century.[43]

In the first years of its existence St. Petersburg lacked basic amenities, let alone luxuries, for the kind of living that would be conducive to the propagation of fine arts. In a city which was more a promise than a reality, neither painters nor sculptors were eager to test their skills. Still, portraits of the tsar, his family, and the officials who followed him to the northern capital had to be painted. In the absence of native talent, foreign portraitists had to be imported to St. Petersburg or the subject had to go abroad to pose for a foreign master. The most successful exploitation of the latter of these two alternatives occurred in 1717 when Peter the Great and his wife Catherine were in Western Europe and had themselves painted by Jean-Marc Nattier, the court portraitist of Louis XV. As a result, we have two excellent portraits of the tsar and tsarina. Imported from the West was Louis Caravaque, a little-known painter from Marseilles, who succumbed to the economic lures offered him by the Russians and in 1716 accepted their offer to settle in St. Petersburg.[44] He died there in 1754 after painting a number of undistinguished portraits. His main value was in the training of native Russian painters.

With the passage of time, the city began to lose its primitive aspect and gradually became an acceptable temporary option for better-known foreign masters. In that regard, the accession of the pleasure-loving and Francophile Empress Elizabeth marked a definite turn for the better. Toward the end of her reign three fine French painters arrived in St. Petersburg for brief stays. Louis Tocqué came in 1756 for a stay of two years, leaving behind a number of excellent portraits of local aristocracy. Jean-Baptiste Le Prince (1734–81) lived in Russia from 1758 to 1763 touring the Russian countryside, whence he brought a number of charming pre-Romantic paintings and sketches of rustic scenes.[45] He was also the author of a series of folkloristic engravings depicting the inhabitants of Moscow and St. Petersburg at work and in the marketplace. Louis-Jean-François Lagrenée (1724–1805) came to St. Petersburg in 1760 to assume the professorship of painting at the Academy of Fine Arts. A prolific painter, he had much success with his portraits and paintings on historical and mythological topics, but it was only after his return to Paris in 1762 that he achieved true fame, especially after the Salon of 1765 where he exhibited more than a dozen paintings, all highly praised by Diderot.

There was only one French sculptor in St. Petersburg before Falconet's arrival. He was Nicolas-François Gillet (1712–91), who was invited to St. Petersburg in 1758 as professor at the newly founded Academy of Fine Arts.[46] He turned out to be a good pedagogue, but an artist of little consequence. Among his disciples were all the best representatives of the Russian school of sculpture, Fedot I. Shubin, Mikhail I. Kozlovsky, Fedor G. Gordeev, and Ivan P. Martos. Falconet, by contrast, was a distinguished sculptor but, to the dismay of the Russians, he showed no interest whatsoever in didactic work. Yet his legacy has turned out to be of greater import to Russia than any number of disciples could have been.

Sunday, August 7, 1782, according to the Julian calendar used in Russia, or August 18, 1782, according to the Gregorian calendar used in the West, was designated as the day of the centennial of Peter's ascension to the throne. In St. Petersburg the principal attraction of the celebrations was to be the official unveiling of the monument to the monarch who founded the city and whose vision propelled Russia into the modern age.

When, to the accompaniment of martial music, rocket flares, and gun salutes, the screens shrouding the monument were pulled down, the assembled crowd saw one of the greatest works of heroic sculpture in the world and certainly the most stirring equestrian monument of all time, a work which, in the words of Falconet's most distinguished critic and biographer, is "one of those which have carried farthest the reputation of French art."[47] Its blend of the Baroque and Neoclassicism echoes the timeless spirit of the city for which it was created.

The emperor is shown astride a horse that has just charged up a large granite rock and is rearing above its edge. Calm and dispassionate, he extends his right arm in a gesture of a soothsayer casting a spell over the waters of the river flowing in front of him. The horse, by contrast, is all unbridled frenzy and fire, excitement and passion, muscular tension and condensed energy. Give it wings and it would fly off its rocky perch. The inscription, written in Russian across one face of the rock and in Latin across the other, says: "To Peter the First, Catherine the Second." It was a message rich in symbolism. It presented Catherine as a logical successor of Peter, it bridged the chasm of nearly two generations and five rulers separating their two reigns, and it affirmed that in Catherine's Russia the Byzantine East and the Latin West would be treated as equals.

The greatness of the monument, however, is not merely in its stylistic conventions, the novelty of the sculptor's conceit, or the beauty of the execution. Even more important is the reception the monument has received from the people among whom it stands. They have bestowed upon it the greatest and rarest mark of recognition with which a work of art may be graced— the warming pulse of life. Like Galatea awakening from her marble repose under the adoring eyes of Pygmalion, Peter and his mount have been quickened by the breath of public acclaim and transfused with the blood of those among whom they have found their home.

To create an emblem of such import Falconet had to comprehend the enormity of the task that Peter set before himself. He had to understand that by replacing the musty atmosphere of Muscovy with the novel ways of the West, the tsar shook Russia down to its very roots. He had to realize that Peter's so-called reforms were in fact a revolution, a war waged by the ruler against his own society. Even the founding of St. Petersburg reflects the magnitude of Peter's upheaval. Standing all time-honored notions on their head, Peter decided to have his capital not in a central, traditionally Russian setting, but on the fringes of his empire, in an area that was ethnically Finnish. Instead of building with clay on a foundation of stone, he built with stone on a foundation of mud. Instead of remaining true to the traditional Russian attachment to dry land, he turned to the sea, which had not figured in Russian consciousness since the days of the Norsemen.[48] "I've been accused of grabbing land," said the tsar, "while all I have ever sought was water."[49]

In fact, just as earth and fire are emblematic of the solidly grounded, wooden Moscow, so water and air are the elements of the ethereal and diffuse St. Petersburg. Placed in the midst of the swampy delta of the Neva and planned with the extravagance afforded by the limitless expanse of its primeval setting, St. Petersburg bears an imprint of irreality and impermanence, a vague foreboding of the day when the natural order of things will rally and exact an apocalyptic retribution for having been defied.

That sense of perplexity and menace is what Falconet succeeded in projecting through his monument. The clash between the imperious calm of the horseman and the raging furor of his mount alludes to the contrast between the quiescent and the violent, the impassive and the impassioned, which has so often colored events of Russia's history. That is why Diderot was guilty of a serious misreading of the monument's conceit when, upon first seeing the large model of the statue, he exclaimed that Falconet had fused man and beast to form a beautiful centaur. What the sculptor did, in fact, was exactly the opposite. He took advantage of the composite nature of the equestrian statue to endow the horseman and the horse with separate individualities in order better to convey the complex nature of Peter's policies and their momentous but troubling legacy.

When one approaches the monument from its western side, the side of the Senate, the statue rises up like a giant question mark. Questions have, in fact, been a major part of the monument's message. Will Peter's stewardship match his riding prowess? Will his works last longer than the horse's suspension in midair? Will the city, conceived in insolent disregard for divine and human laws, survive and keep its power and splendor?

Here is how Nikolai Antsiferov, one of the most perceptive interpreters of the myths and secrets of St. Petersburg, describes the magnetic power with which the monument holds a viewer trying to discern the destination of the horseman's gallop:

If someone happens to be near the monument on a rainy autumn evening, when the sky turns into Chaos and descends upon the earth filling it with confusion, when the river moans and strains in its granite straitjacket, when sudden gusts of wind move the street lights to and fro and their shimmering glow makes the surrounding buildings sway, let him look at the Bronze Horseman. He will see fire turned into bronze, its mighty contours standing out in sharp outline. He will sense an immense force, a passionate and stormy force, calling him into the unknown. Its sweep will make him ask fearfully: Where to? What's ahead? Victory or fall and destruction?[50]

Such questions have confounded the visitors to the monument from the moment of its unveiling. They have also made the monument a fecund subject for further artistic explorations. Two major nineteenth-century works have been particularly seminal. One is the *Monument of Peter the Great* by the great Polish Romantic poet Adam Mickiewicz. The other, written partly in response to it, is arguably the greatest Russian narrative poem, Alexander Pushkin's *The Bronze Horseman.* They, together with the monument itself, usher in the so-called "St. Petersburg theme" in Russian arts, a capacious metaphor, which alimented much of Russia's nineteenth- and early twentieth-century literature.[51]

Despite its great intrinsic value, however, a study of the symbiotic relations of different forms of artistic expression, generated by the procreative power of a potent work of art, cannot be considered within the confines of a book whose focus is that single work of art, a history of its making and the life stories of its makers—Etienne-Maurice Falconet and his disciple, collaborator, and lifelong companion, Marie-Anne Collot, two French sculptors who set out over uncharted waters en route to the creation of a masterpiece.

I

Paris: The Early Years

SCULPTOR OF THE KING

[Falconet] has finesse, taste, intelligence, delicacy, kindness, and grace in full measure; . . . he is awkward and polite, friendly and brusque, kind and harsh; . . . he reads and reflects; . . . he's amiable and caustic, serious and mocking, . . . he's a *philosophe,* who doesn't believe in anything and knows perfectly well why.
—Diderot (1765)

Etienne-Maurice Falconet came from a family of simple artisans of very modest means.[1] How plain his origins were can be seen from an entry for February 12, 1714, in the register of the church of Notre-Dame de la Bonne Nouvelle in Paris, where his parents were married. According to the church records, his father, Maurice, and his uncle Pierre Falconet were journeymen joiners; his paternal grandfather, Claude Falconet, was a peasant from Savoy; his maternal grandfather, Nicolas Guérin, was a cobbler, and his uncle François Falconet was a servant. The newlyweds settled in a modest lodging on rue de Bourbon-Villeneuve, and that was where Etienne-Maurice saw the light of day on December 1, 1716.[2]

Falconet's digital dexterity was inherited from both sides of the family. His father must have possessed an ability to carve intricate designs on the furniture of his making in order to satisfy the dictates of contemporary fashion. On his mother's side, there was an uncle, Nicolas Guillaume, who owned a stonecutting workshop and is referred to in church records as a "sculptor." That is where young Falconet was initiated into the craft of working with a chisel and mallet. He helped to make marble mantelpieces, garden furniture, and tombstones. To earn extra money he cut wooden dummies for wigmakers' shops. His heart, however, was not in commercial art. He dreamed of making sculpture "in the grand style."

There was little sympathy for such fantasies in the Falconet family. As his friend the painter Robin wrote: "if sometimes, driven by a compelling force, he tried to shape figures out of wood or clay, he was reproached for wasting his time."[3] But he was not easily discouraged. He may not have received much support from his family, but the country at large was alive with artistic creativity and was able to support a brilliant pleiad of painters, sculptors, and architects. They found their patrons not only at the court, in the nobility, or among the princes of the church, but also in the increasingly prosperous *tiers-état*. That artistic climate was all that a talented young sculptor needed to encourage him to pursue his calling.

Sculpture was best suited to reflect the glories of the times, and it was habitually called upon to do so. Every city of the realm wanted to have its own statue of the sovereign, equestrian if it could afford it, surrounded by symbolic representations of the country's achievements in war and commerce, industry and agriculture.[4] Sculptors were asked to produce freestanding allegories of provinces, cities, rivers, and seas, and to express in the language of the visual arts such abstract concepts as Wisdom, Vigilance, or Fame, and the various branches of human endeavor traditionally symbolized by the nine Muses. Demand created supply and there was no shortage of artists who were eager to offer their services to anyone willing to pay, preferably the king himself.

Of the Paris sculptors born in the eighteenth century, Jean-Baptiste II Lemoyne (1704–78) was certainly the best known. As a favorite *sculpteur du Roi,* he received many commissions and needed skilled apprentices. Since he enjoyed an excellent reputation as a teacher, it was to him that Falconet, then aged seventeen, bore a sample of clays he had made in the workshop of his uncle. Here is how Pierre-Charles Lévesque, Falconet's earliest biographer, describes their first meeting: "After trying for a long time to muster enough courage, [Falconet] takes the best of his pieces and goes to ring the bell at the door which was indicated to him. A small man in a working blouse covered with plaster, powdered marble, and clay opens the door. Falconet asks timidly for Monsieur Lemoyne. 'That's me,' answers the little man, 'Come in!' It is too late to retreat. The trembling Falconet uncovers the samples of his work. The indulgent sculptor finds them promising, and agrees to guide him in his artistic career."[5]

Denis Diderot (fig. 1.1), the greatest admirer of Falconet's art and his closest intellectual friend in Paris, offers a somewhat different version of the same episode. According to him Falconet was brought to Lemoyne's studio by the painter Dumont le Romain, who had seen a hollow torso made by Falconet. "The young Falconet offered to be Lemoyne's servant, his valet, whatever he wished. But seeing the torso, Lemoyne said: Young man, you as my valet? You, my friend, are not made for that. You'll be my colleague."[6]

Bright and hard-working, Falconet soon became Lemoyne's favorite pupil. He helped him execute several major commissions, including the *Basin of Neptune* in Versailles and a large equestrian statue of Louis XV in Bordeaux. Falconet would always recognize his debt to Lemoyne: "[He] deserves my praise and my gratitude. He has earned them by his knowledge and the excellent lessons he had taught me."[7] He was not alone in retaining such warm memories of Lemoyne. The talented group of Lemoyne's children, as the *maître* used to call them, included such sculptors as Jean-Baptiste Pigalle,

Fig. 1.1. Marie-Anne Collot, *Denis Diderot*. Marble, 1772. The State Hermitage Museum, St. Petersburg.

Jean-Jacques Caffiéri, and Augustin Pajou. They, together with Falconet, represent the best among the young eighteenth-century French sculptors.[8]

The ten years that Falconet spent with Lemoyne were an unusually long term of apprenticeship. Was he simply too comfortable in the household of the hospitable and avuncular Lemoyne? Was he apprehensive about exchanging the modest financial security his work for Lemoyne offered for the incertitude of the highly competitive art market? Or was he eager to stay in a large enterprise and use the time afforded by it to make up in independent study for what he had missed in formal education? All those reasons must have delayed his striking out on his own until well after his marriage imposed upon him serious financial obligations. When he finally left Lemoyne's atelier, he was coming up to thirty, which in those days was considered an advanced age for an artist starting an independent career.

Falconet and Anne-Suzanne Moulin, daughter of a high-class cabinetmaker (*ébéniste du Roi*), were married on November 19, 1739, in the church of St.-Eustache. She was a woman of no intellectual pretensions, preoccupied with daily domestic problems. Of the couple's four children, only the first one survived into maturity. Pierre-Etienne was endowed with modest artistic gifts, sufficient, he thought, to ensure success as a portrait painter. His father, however, did not think much of his son's abilities and diligence and did not shrink from airing this opinion in public, when he thought that the young man deserved such treatment. Nevertheless, Pierre-Etienne was persistent. He shook off his father's strict controls and demanding standards and settled in London, where he eventually achieved a measure of success as a society portraitist. At thirty-two, however, he reentered his father's life and, from then on, played an important part in it.

In order to become "accredited" a French artist had to submit an original project to the Académie Royale de Peinture et de Sculpture. If the work was judged acceptable by the jury, the artist would be allowed to initiate the process of full membership in the Académie. For sculptors, the next step was the submission of a clay or plaster model of the project. Its approval gave the applicant the title of *agréé* of the Académie, along with the right to exhibit in the biennial Salons in the Louvre. He would then proceed to the definitive version of the work, which would become his *morceau de réception* to the Académie.

An ambitious applicant could use this process to define his own artistic persona by challenging the work of his predecessors. An eighteenth-century French sculptor would have many distinguished masters to measure himself against. In the large group of sculptors born before 1700, six names at the very least stand out: Pierre Puget (1620–94), François Girardon (1628–1715), Martin Desjardins (1640–94), Charles-Antoine Coysevox (1640–1720), Guillaume Coustou, Senior (1677–1746), and Edme Bouchardon (1698–1762). They all worked in the idiom of the Baroque, the dominant style of the day, characterized by a restless line, a whirling composition, and chiaroscuro. By depicting dramatic situations with two or more participants, who displayed their sensations and emotions, the Baroque artist could present durative and dynamic aspects of action, conquering thereby the inevitable limitations imposed by inert matter and "single-frame" representation. The highest point of the Baroque is associated with the oeuvre of the Italian sculptor, architect, and urban planner Gian Lorenzo Bernini (1598–1680). His *Ecstasy of St. Teresa* (1645–52) is often cited as the most programmatic and paradigmatic example of the Baroque. It was also the inspiration of what is generally regarded as the supreme example of French Baroque sculpture, Puget's *Milo of Crotona* (1672–82).

The theme that inspired Puget was a dramatic story about a powerful sixth-century B.C. Greek athlete Milo of Crotona, who won so many laurels in military campaigns and wrestling competitions as to be considered invincible.[9] One day, while walking through a forest, Milo came upon a tree trunk which several lumberjacks had tried to split. Unable to do so, they had walked away, leaving behind a wedge stuck in the trunk. Milo, confident of his strength, decided to split the trunk with his bare hands. But as he tried to tear it asunder, the wedge slipped out and fell to the ground, while the trunk closed in on his hand. His arm now rendered useless, Milo was attacked by the animals of the forest and killed.

The bulging muscles of the athlete trying to free his trapped hand and defend himself, the anguish of pain and fear, the ferocity of the beasts—in short, all the visual aspects of the scene—offered a challenge to a Baroque artist and attracted a number of interpretations in sculpture and painting.[10] At the same time, the story of Milo's tragic death in spite of his superhuman strength had a deeper symbolic significance. In ancient Greece it referred to the inexorable powers of Fate, while in the age of the Baroque it became laden with other meanings. On the one hand, it deplored the victory of sheer strength over reason, a concern which was at the center of the intellectual debates of the times. On the other, it alluded to the conflict between the individual and the absolute monarch. That tension must have been on the mind of Puget, who was born in autonomous Marseilles and traveled extensively in Italy, where he became used to the freedom accorded the artist. When he returned, he found himself hemmed in by the authority of Versailles, which had by then been imposed on Marseilles. That is probably why Puget injected royal symbolism into his sculpture by replacing the wolves of the original story with a lion. Puget's idea appealed to Falconet, who on August 29, 1744, presented his own variant of that theme to the judges of the Académie.

The jury of the Académie, however, turned down Falconet's terracotta model of the *Milo of Crotona* on the grounds that it was too similar to Puget's piece. Not only was Falconet assigned an entirely new subject, an allegory of the *Genius of Sculpture,* but he was asked to work on it in one of the rooms of the Académie in order to prove that he did not benefit from outside help.[11] When these humiliating demands were fulfilled and it became obvious that the newly submitted work was truly Falconet's own, the jury allowed the sculptor to return to the *Milo of Crotona* theme and submit it in a different version as his *morceau de réception*. The damage, however, was done, the reception piece was delayed, and Falconet had to petition the Académie for deadline extensions. Worse than that, the experience made Falconet realize how dependent he was on the whims of his older confrères. It could not but heighten his hypersensitivity to criticism and to real or imagined threats to artistic freedom.

However unpleasant the jury's initial misgivings must have been for Falconet, they gave us two treatments of one and the same theme, *Milo* 1744 and *Milo* 1754. The difference between them can be observed in the Hermitage Museum in St. Petersburg, where their plaster models are exhibited side by side in the collection of eighteenth-century French art (figs. 1.2 and 1.3).

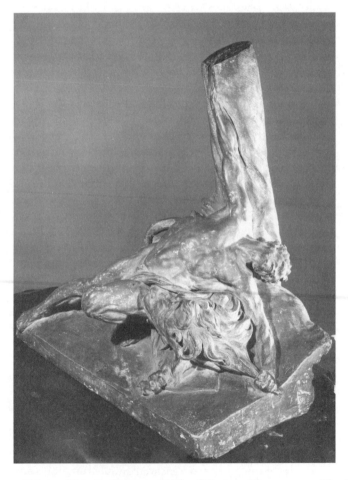

Fig. 1.2. Etienne-Maurice Falconet, *Milo of Crotona*. Plaster, 1744. The State Hermitage Museum, St. Petersburg.

Fig. 1.3. Etienne-Maurice Falconet, *Milo of Crotona*. Plaster, 1754. The State
Hermitage Museum, St. Petersburg.

The frontal view of the 1744 version shows Milo hanging by his right arm,
caught in the tree trunk. As he falls over the lion, he stretches his left hand
trying to push the lion's head away from his body. But weakened by the
struggle, all he can do is tug at the lion's mane. He looks defeated and
resigned. In fact, in the foreshortened view from top and left, Milo appears
more like the crucified Christ, in the final moment of agony. The arms are
extended, the head is inclined to the left, the eyes are turned upward, and
the parched mouth is half-open, giving the face a mysteriously smiling expression. From that vantage point the composition is not unlike the down-
ward perspective of the *Crucifixion* by Salvador Dalí.

This suffering Christ-like aspect is what Falconet's *Milo* 1744 shares with
Puget's, and it is that similarity that must have made the judges make their
original ruling against it. Puget's *Milo* is trying to stand, his disproportion-

ately small head hanging limply on his shoulder. His eyes are closed. The chiton slides down his left arm. There is an empty itinerant's bowl lying on the ground. Milo's whole figure seems resigned and impassive. Even the lion lacks the features of a beast of prey. He looks up at Milo's face with a quasi-human expression of curiosity, as if to see what effect its fangs and claws are having on the dying man. In the words of Réau, it is an animal from "a book on heraldry, not a menagerie."[12] Despite their strikingly different positions— Puget's ellipsoid composition being vertical and Falconet's early *Milo* being horizontal—the judges must have been struck by their emotional kinship.

In Falconet's *Milo* 1754 the mood changes. While Puget humanized his lion, Falconet turned his Milo into a wild animal. He gave him a plain face, an upturned nose, a hirsute aspect, and a wide-open mouth as if in a growl of anger rather than pain. Instead of a resigned victim, we see a fighter who is down, but not out. The end may be inevitable, but Milo, though fallen, has not given up the struggle. His muscular body tenses and writhes, his right leg stretches stiffly beyond the boundaries of the composition in a dynamic that brings to mind the Hellenistic group of the *Laocoön*.

As Levitine perceptively observed, the triangular shape of the composition and its flattened bas-relief aspect suggest "a Hellenistic or Baroque faun caught in the rigorous geometry of a Classical metope."[13] Falconet's predilection for triangular compositions is evident in a number of his works, especially in the small projects prepared for execution in biscuit during his employment in the porcelain Manufacture in Sèvres.[14]

There is another aspect of Falconet's *Milo* 1754 that deserves closer scrutiny. As the sculptor himself admits, the head of Milo was his self-portrait.[15] A bust made by Marie-Anne Collot in 1768 (fig. 1.4) confirms the veracity of that claim. Despite its time remove, it shows the same high forehead, deep-set eyes, upturned nose, and prominent chin. Yet, how different these two portraits are in depicting the inner essence of their subject! In the gentle Falconet of Collot's bust one would never suspect someone with a notoriously difficult character. It is a portrait of a relaxed and mildly bemused man, still quite youthful for his fifty-two years, with intelligent eyes and a light smile playing on his lips. The self-portrait in the *Milo* sculpture comes closer to the inner essence of Falconet. It shows a plain, satyr-like face, whose features may resemble those on Collot's portrait, but more as a caricature than as a likeness.[16]

But why did Falconet identify with his entrapped and suffering hero? Levitine surmises that "the sculptor found in the theme of *Milo of Crotona* a symbolical expression of his own anxiety."[17] Indeed, Falconet's writings confirm the justice of such an interpretation, for they are pervaded by a sense of loneliness and struggle against overwhelming odds. This fierce polemicist, who imagined a threat to his artistic freedom lurking behind every door, had to pay a high price for his uncompromising but all too often quixotic stands in defense of his independence. Above all, they deprived him of the pleasures of conviviality, for none but his most devoted friends could put

Fig. 1.4. Marie-Anne Collot, *Etienne-Maurice Falconet.* Marble, 1773. The State
Hermitage Museum, St. Petersburg.

up for long with the outward manifestations of the sculptor's hypersensitivity. The lonely plight of Milo of Crotona must have struck a respondent chord.

As a self-made man Falconet despised unearned success and flaunted his humble background. When someone addressed him in Russian as *vysokorodie*, he reacted with his typical flippancy: "this title suits me perfectly, since I was born in the attic."[18] Yet he must have resented the fact that his origins deprived him of schooling and handicapped his aspirations of joining the intellectual elite of the times. He did all he could to make up what he had missed in formal training when he was in the atelier of Lemoyne. He was a self-taught Latinist, learned Italian, read widely on the history and theory of art, and in the end emerged a better-educated man than any of his confrères.[19] But all that took him away from his family and professional work and magnified a sense of entrapment that must have made him feel a kinship with Milo's predicament. The years with Lemoyne contributed undoubtedly to Falconet's professional development and were a source of strength for years to come, but being apprenticed to another sculptor at the time when his younger colleagues were practicing as independent artists must have bred resentment.

Financial problems may also account for the growl on the face of *Milo* 1754. Falconet affected a lack of interest in material possessions, but the need to support his family was at least partly responsible for making him hold on to Lemoyne and for preventing him from competing for a scholarship to the Rome station of the French Académie, where most of the gifted young French artists would traditionally spend training time. Sadly, his dream of visiting Italy one day was never to be fulfilled.

Shortage of money was at least partly responsible for a contretemps which occurred in the spring of 1755, at the time when annual pensions were being assigned to deserving artists. The pensions came from a royal fund with a fixed endowment so that the monies from it became available for reassignment only when a vacancy occurred. The deaths of the sculptors Lemoyne and Vinache freed twelve hundred livres, and Marquis de Marigny, as director of the Bâtiments du Roi, whose function was to protect artists, recommended that this sum be split evenly between the sculptors Michel-Ange Slodtz and Jacques-François Saly. The king approved this recommendation on May 27, 1755. On August 4, however, Marigny had a change of heart. As he explained in a letter to the king, he had just learned from the Académie that Saly was very well paid in Denmark, where he worked on the equestrian statue of King Frederick V. Falconet, on the other hand, was in straitened financial circumstances and had not yet received any royal favors. The letter ended with a plea that the pension of six hundred livres originally earmarked for Saly "be placed much more appropriately on the head of *Sieur* Falconet."[20] This request was approved, but the incident must have thrown a shadow over Falconet's friendship with Saly.

Received by the Académie at the ripe age of thirty-eight, Falconet must have looked with envy at other sculptors of his generation who had passed him by on the road to success and who had had time to adjust to the new economic situation of mid-eighteenth century France, when the building boom that began under Louis XIV came to an end. Immense royal palaces, with their ornate interiors and elaborately laid-out gardens enlivened by fountains, ponds, bridges, and statuary, gave way to smaller-scale commissions for houses and garden pavilions of the lesser nobility and rich bourgeoisie, eager to display their newly gained fortunes. The very names of these residences, *Bellevue, Mon Repos, Sans Souci, Ermitage, Solitude,* were descriptive of their purpose, which was to assure the privacy required by the aesthetic program of the new Rococo style, with its stress on the senses. Decoration and portraiture became the dominant modes in the arts. Royal statuary was still in vogue, but there was acute competition for it, and French sculptors, eager to make up for lost commissions, had to look for employment opportunities abroad. Of the sculptors who were Falconet's direct competitors in the dwindling French market two names stand out, Jean-Baptiste Pigalle (1714–85) and Jacques-François Saly (1717–76).[21]

The artistic careers of Pigalle and Falconet do invite comparisons. Both were of humble origin, both were Lemoyne's disciples, and both were protégés of Madame de Pompadour. Yet their paths, similar in the beginning, diverged quickly. Pigalle was less inhibited and soon became the darling of the court and the public. He was only two years older than Falconet, but was received into the Académie ten years earlier. His *Mercury Fastening His Sandal* (1742) became his *morceau de réception* and was an instant success. It was followed by a number of lucrative commissions, including a monument to Louis XV in Reims. Wealth and honors were not far behind, including the award of the Cross of Saint-Michel.[22] Falconet's artistic path, by contrast, was much more arduous, and there must have been an element of envy that affected his attitude to Pigalle.

That attitude was most probably responsible for Falconet's ill-advised support of the sculptor Louis-Claude Vassé's attempt to win the commission for the completion of the equestrian monument to Louis XV by Bouchardon, despite the dying sculptor's express wish to entrust it to Pigalle. Falconet's mission was unsuccessful, but it surely angered the arts establishment with Marigny at its head. It is to the credit of both Pigalle and Falconet that they were able to rise above their personal sentiments and express respect for each other's artistry. Diderot reports in his account of the Salon of 1765 that when Pigalle saw Falconet's *Pygmalion,* he said: "I would have liked to have made that myself." Falconet returned the compliment when Pigalle's monument for Reims was exhibited: "Monsieur Pigalle, I've seen your *Citizen,* [and] I don't think that art can advance one iota farther." But, being Falconet, he added: "I don't like you and, I think, you feel the same way about me."[23]

Saly, a disciple of Guillaume Coustou, was a sculptor of lesser talent than Pigalle, and it would seem that Falconet had little reason to be envious of his progress. It is true that Saly, though slightly younger than Falconet, got into the Académie three years before him, and that his reception piece, the *Faun Holding a Goat* (1751), created such a sensation in Paris that the king demanded to see it. It is also true that Saly, like Pigalle before him, was decorated with the Cross of Saint-Michel. Yet, those were minor irritants. The main source of distress must have been Saly's good fortune in being able to fulfill "the supreme ambition of eighteenth-century sculptors, a commission to make an equestrian statue."[24] His fine monument to Frederick V of Denmark (1768) stands today on Amalienborg Square in Copenhagen, a witness to the regrettable fact that royal statuary by seventeenth- and eighteenth-century French sculptors survived outside of France only. If any incentive was needed, Saly's success in obtaining the Danish commission must have spurred Falconet to do all he could not to miss the opportunity which was soon to present itself in St. Petersburg.

Sculpture on the grand scale, the dream of every sculptor, requires major outlays of money. Despite his title of *le sculpteur du Roi*, Falconet was not one of the king's favorite sculptors and could not count on royal patronage for larger works of art. In fact, immortality would not have beckoned, had he not received a chance to gain it in Russia.[25] His one large royal commission was a fiasco. When in 1745, on the occasion of the king's recovery from a serious illness, the then director of the Bâtiments du Roi, Lenormant de Tournehem, commissioned Falconet to make an allegory representing *France Embracing the Bust of Louis XV*, the subject bored him so much that he could not bring himself to complete it. He did, however, present a plaster model of it at the Salon of 1748 after a design by the painter Coypel. It was a tastelessly sentimental group showing France as a heavily draped woman, dropping to her knees before the bust of the king mounted on a column-like pedestal.[26] In 1762, realizing that he would not be able to finish a statue which he himself considered mediocre, Falconet asked the new director of the Bâtiments du Roi, Marquis de Marigny, to allow him to abandon the project. Since he had been receiving annual up-front payments for the marble version of the statue totaling nine thousand livres, he offered to use his annual pension to repay that sum.[27] Marigny granted Falconet's request, but magnanimously allowed him to keep the money he had already received as payment for the unfinished statue.[28]

In the absence of lucrative royal commissions, Falconet had to content himself with small decorative sculptures like the *Bather* or the *Pygmalion*. In his letters to Marigny, Falconet returned over and over again to the high cost of marble and to his own straitened circumstances. In one such appeal of June 4, 1765, Falconet pleaded with Marigny to give him an order for a marble sculpture of *Winter* whose model the marquis had seen and liked: "In view of my miserable situation, it is a plant which will dry up if you don't give it life. I'm not complaining about my fortune. What I'm simply saying is that [my royal pension] won't suffice for the initial cost of a marble statue."[29]

Ironically for a man whose views on religion alternated between agnosticism and moderate Jansenism, Falconet had to rely on church commissions for a living. Not much of it has survived the anticlerical fury of the Jacobins, and the stooping figure of *Christ on the Mount of Olives* (1757, fig. 1.5) is the

Fig. 1.5. Etienne-Maurice Falconet, *Christ on the Mount of Olives.* Pierre de Tonnerre, 1757. Church of St. Roch, Paris. Courtesy Conservation des oeuvres d'art religieuses et civiles de la ville de Paris.

only major religious sculpture that can still be seen. It stands high on the left side of the nave of St. Roch's, the church whose decoration was Falconet's largest and most demanding Paris commission. It may be said, in fact, that of all of his Paris works, it was the statuary in the church of St. Roch which by its very monumentality and drama anticipated best the monument to Peter the Great in St. Petersburg. Otherwise, except for the large Glory and a marble memorial medallion of Madame La Live de Jully in one of the side chapels, Falconet's production for St. Roch's must be judged on the basis of contemporary descriptions and drawings.[30]

The Neoclassical church of St. Roch, whose large size and proximity to the Louvre made it one of the most prestigious churches in Paris, is situated on rue St. Honoré near the Tuileries. Its construction was begun in 1653 and completed in 1740, replacing two earlier versions going back to the sixteenth century.[31] In 1749 the parish of St. Roch was assigned a new curé, Abbé Jean-Baptiste Marduel, a cultivated churchman with artistic tastes, whose ambition was to refurbish the interior of the church. He chose Falconet to supervise the task, entrusting him in particular with the construction of a new altar in the chapel of the Virgin Mary and the addition of a new chapel of the Calvary. To the former Falconet contributed an Annunciation in marble, flanked by the prophets David and Isaiah in gilt lead, and a large Bernini-esque Glory in gilt stucco.[32] For the latter he designed a naturalistic rocky setting in which he set a large Crucifixion with Mary Magdalene in wood, two Roman soldiers, and a snake.[33] The altar in the chapel of the Virgin Mary was constructed under an open arcade so as to make the Crucifixion visible in the background, thus uniting the initial and final stages in the life of Jesus in one line of sight.

It has been noted that Falconet's *Christ on the Mount of Olives* owes much to Bernini's famous *Ecstasy of Saint Teresa* in the church of Santa Maria della Vittoria in Rome. That Bernini was the Baroque artist whom Falconet esteemed most and to whom he felt most indebted is unquestionable.[34] It is therefore likely that the *Saint Teresa* was on his mind when he was trying to show Christ in the moment of his greatest weakness, tired in flesh and drained of will. Like Bernini's *Saint Teresa,* Falconet's Christ is wrapped in a robe whose folds betray a slackening body, and, like in Bernini, Christ's arm hangs down limply. That, however, is where the similarities end. While Bernini's cloudborne *Saint Teresa,* with her mouth half-open in a sensuous trance, yields to a mystical force which lifts her heavenward in the company of a smiling, Cupid-like angel, Falconet's *Christ on the Mount of Olives* is earthbound and lonely, his head sinking dejectedly. Falconet departed from the usual iconography of the scene by leaving out the vision of an angel and eliminating the sleeping disciples. With his lips barely parted in a sign of lassitude, Falconet's Christ is one of the most poignant depictions of despondency in sculpture.[35] As the First Station on the Lord's road to Calvary, the statue was an object of particular veneration during Easter.

To judge by the comments of contemporaries, the work on St. Roch was successful, but no more than that. The influence of Bernini was palpable, yet the ensemble paled next to the Italian master's work in St. Peter's. Falconet himself felt dissatisfied and owned up to his feelings in a letter to Marquis de Marigny, in which he referred to his work as a "job (*besogne*) done for an enterprising priest, which did not bring me anything but bread and divine masses, . . . feeble support for the grand machine of sculpture." Whatever virtues the work had, he said, were due to his sense of professional responsibility rather than personal involvement.[36]

Falconet's last major work in Paris was the *Saint Ambrose,* commissioned for the redecoration of the church of the Invalides as one of the fourteen religious statues to be executed by the best French sculptors of the day, among them Lemoyne, Pigalle, L. S. Adam, Caffiéri, and Houdon. The model of it, showing the bishop of Milan barring the entrance to the cathedral to the penitent Emperor Theodosius, was exhibited at the Salon of 1765, where it was well received by Diderot.[37] Falconet, however, had no time to execute it in marble before his departure for Russia, and entrusted its completion to Lemoyne, who did it in 1769. In his obituary remembrance of Falconet in 1791, the painter J.-B.-C. Robin described the statue as a work showing Falconet "as truly great and worthy to walk alongside such sculptors as Legros and Algardi." In accordance with the dictates of the reigning style, he paid special attention to Falconet's treatment of the bishop's vestments, especially the folds of his loosely hanging mantle.[38] The *Saint Ambrose* was lost in the same circumstances as most of the statuary in St. Roch's, and it is only thanks to a drawing by the Antwerp sculptor Joseph Camberlain that we know its design.[39]

The Salon of 1765 was Falconet's most impressive showing. In addition to a small model of the *Saint Ambrose,* it included the *Sweet Melancholy; Friendship,* a terracotta remake of a saccharine portrait of Madame de Pompadour offering a heart, presumably her own, to the king; a terracotta model of *Winter;* and the relief *Alexander the Great Offering Campaspe to the Painter Apelles* (fig. 1.6), illustrating a story according to which Alexander the Great, having commissioned a nude portrait of his concubine Campaspe from Apelles, offered her as a gift to the painter, who was falling in love with the girl.[40] It is one of the two surviving examples of Falconet's works in relief, the other being the medallion of Mme La Live de Jully. The technique in the *Alexander the Great* consists in varying the depth of the incisions so as to obtain an illusion of perspective. Falconet employed four levels, each assigned a different function: high relief for the three protagonists of the story, low relief for two soldiers standing in the background, and flat outline for the painter's canvas and architectural detail, while the unfinished portrait of Campaspe is in intaglio. The idea was to demonstrate that relief is an intermediary genre between sculpture and painting.[41]

Atypically for a sculptor of the eighteenth century, Falconet showed little interest in portraits and programmatically cut himself off of that source of income. He doubted his skill in that domain and once smashed to pieces a

Fig. 1.6. Etienne-Maurice Falconet, *Alexander the Great Offering Campaspe to the Painter Apelles.* Marble, 1765 (Réau, 1922, p. 222). Present location unknown. Formerly in the collection of Baron Maurice de Rothschild.

head of Diderot of his making when he realized that it was inferior to one by Collot.

There are reasons, however, to question the justice of this self-criticism. There survive two busts by Falconet, both of Dr. Camille Falconet, a distinguished physician of Louis XV, but no relative of the sculptor. The two were good friends and the sculptor was a frequent user of the physician's excellent library.[42] The first bust of the physician, aged seventy-six, was shown at the Salon of 1747, that is, just three years after the sculptor left Lemoyne's atelier. His patron's influence is plainly in evidence as Falconet traces every wrinkle and every crease in the wizened, but intellectually alert face. The second bust was shown at the Salon of 1761 when the physician was ninety. The outlines of the face, the shirt and cravat, the slight turn of the head to the right, are all the same. Everything else, however, bears witness to the fourteen years that had passed. The eyes have none of their former brilliance and are deeper-set, the cheeks are hollow, the mouth is drawn, the head, formerly adorned with a resplendent wig, is now frankly bald, and the inquisitive expression of the 1747 face now gives way to a disconnected, faraway look. The busts are superb examples of portrait sculpture and a persuasive proof of the sculptor's ability to depict outer and inner changes wrought by the passage of time.[43]

It is more probable that the real cause of Falconet's unwillingness to engage in portraiture should be sought in his ideological lack of regard for that genre. He considered its popularity a diagnostic test of blight in art: "Many beautiful portraits are made when art develops vigorously. But it is a sign of decadence, when portraits alone are made. One admires nothing else, one encourages nothing else . . . and one loves and desires solely one's own image."[44] Such moralistic pronouncements may well be another symptom of Falconet's self-hate, a futile attempt to free himself from the overpowering weight of his own narcissism.

SCULPTOR OF MADAME DE POMPADOUR

And from the gate, where one may linger,
A footpath homeward will convey,
Past impish Cupid of Falconet,
Who smiles in sport and wags his finger.
—Pushkin ("Fonvizin's Shadow," 1815)

Falconet's financial fortunes took a decisive turn for the better when his works caught the eye of Madame de Pompadour. Though no longer a favorite of Louis XV, she exercised much influence at the court and used it for the promotion of the arts, with a special interest in the protection of the Royal Manufacture of Porcelain in Sèvres. In that task she was aided by her brother, Marquis de Marigny, who oversaw French fine arts from his post of director of the Bâtiments du Roi. In 1757, impressed by Falconet's work in the church of St. Roch and aware of his penchant for small-size sculpture, Madame de Pompadour appointed him *artiste-en-chef* in charge of sculpture at the Sèvres Manufacture, a new position created at the behest of Falconet's friend the painter Jean-Jacques Bachelier, who was in charge of decoration.

The idiom of the Sèvres Manufacture was the highly ornate new style that was sweeping France and the rest of Western Europe. Identified with the tastes of Madame de Pompadour, it came to be known as the Rococo, a jocular derivation from *rocaille,* the French word for "shell," which was a frequent element of Rococo ornamentation. The roots of the Rococo were in the French variety of the Baroque. While the Italian Baroque had elements of religious triumphalism, celebrating the victory of the Counter-Reformation, seventeenth-century France was a country still torn by religious strife, not only between the Catholics and the Protestants but also, within Catholicism itself, between the Jesuits and the Jansenists. In such a religiously heterogeneous situation, it was the absolute monarchy of Louis XIV, not the papacy, which played the role of the country's unifier. The arts reflected that assignment of political responsibilities, and the French Baroque, unlike the Italian one, assumed forms glorifying secular rather than religious powers. French architecture and the arts of the period were appropriately monumental and ostentatious. The opulent palace of Versailles and the towering equestrian statues of Louis XIV reminded the French that the state was the king and the king was the Sun.

The Rococo came to replace those outward marks of royal splendor and grandeur. During the dissolute period of the Regency of Duke Philippe of Orléans and *la vie douce* under Louis XV, the official and impersonal Baroque gave way to a more intimate and sensuous style, designed to serve the tastes of the rising *tiers-état*. It was marked by greater and freer social contacts and a more pleasure-seeking mode of life. The imposing Baroque palaces were now joined by small villas and pavilions set in parks embellished by fanciful arrangements of rocks, fountains, and artificial grottoes. There, the newly "entitled" could enjoy public amusements, *les fêtes galantes et champêtres* glorified by Watteau, masked balls, theater performances, and concerts. For private *divertissements* the French designed more intimate interiors, decorated with intricate ornamental designs, paintings with pastoral and floral themes, statuettes, bonbonnières, table settings, and the like. It was a style in which whimsical playfulness and sensuality were sometimes ostentatiously displayed, but more often discreetly suggested by an elaborate system of symbolic gestures and situations.

The conquest of Western markets by Rococo decorative art in the second half of the eighteenth century would not have been possible without a new arrival from China, a kind of glazed ceramic with translucent and waterproof qualities reminiscent of mother-of-pearl. The new import entranced the more affluent Europeans from the mid-sixteenth century and throughout the seventeenth. Its first specimens were brought to Europe by Venetian and Genoese merchants, who gave it the name of *porcellána.*[45] That name spread throughout Europe, either directly from Italian or in its French guise as *porcelaine.* The basic color of porcelain was white, but the glaze could be ornamented with various designs and colors, made fast by additional firings.

For many centuries China was the only country to possess the recipe for making porcelain. The Chinese owed their monopoly to their discovery and sole possession of kaolin, a pure and delicate clay, which, when heated to high temperatures, vitrified and produced a firm, glistening surface with a deep, pure white color. The term *china,* used in England, testifies to China's exclusivity in the production of hard-paste porcelain, which is how the product containing kaolin came to be known.

The porcelain-collecting craze, which spread throughout Europe, spurred investments in laboratory research aiming to duplicate the jealously guarded Chinese methods. These efforts were crowned with partial success only, because what they produced initially was a kind of ersatz porcelain, which contained ground glass instead of kaolin. In the beginning of the eighteenth century, however, Saxon chemists discovered a method of producing hard-paste porcelain from a mixture of various local clays and rocks, paving the way to the founding of the Royal Saxon Porcelain Manufacture in Meissen (1710), which soon attained the reputation of producing the finest porcelain in Europe. In France, in particular, its popularity was so great as to alarm the country's financial establishment and spur it to greater efforts to match the success of the Saxons.

Unable to come up with their own hard-paste porcelain, the French experimented with a mixture of sand, clay, and alkaline melting agents such as soda and lime, which, when heated, turned liquid and vitreous. The batch was then allowed to solidify, ground to a powder, and mixed with white clay to produce what came to be known as "soft paste." Given shape and fired again, soft paste turned into a rock-hard, milky white, and translucent faience-like substance, called "biscuit."[46] When biscuit was glazed over and fired again, it produced porcelain of remarkable subtlety of color, without the harsh brightness of the crystalline surfaces of hard-paste porcelain. This allowed its French makers not only to keep pace with the output of Meissen, Dresden, and Naples, but to outstrip it in popularity.

Of the several small, privately owned French porcelain *manufactures,* the best known was the one founded in Chantilly in 1725. Plagued, however, by mismanagement and high production costs, the Chantilly factory had to limit its operations drastically. A competing factory was started in Vincennes in 1738, but it too ran into financial problems. There arose a danger that France would be left without a major porcelain producer unless a new, well-capitalized venture could be started.

It was at that moment that Madame de Pompadour intervened. Guided by her ambition that France should be able to produce porcelain of internationally recognized quality and convinced that the demand for it was and would remain high, she appealed to Louis XV to take porcelain production under the crown's control. The king, swayed by the arguments of his former mistress, decided to restructure the Vincennes company by forming a new Société de la Manufacture with a capital of eight hundred thousand livres, of which he himself invested two hundred thousand. In 1753 the Vincennes factory was renamed the Manufacture royale de porcelaine, and three years later it was moved to the village of Sèvres near Paris, where it occupied a complex of new buildings on a large lot bought from Madame de Pompadour, whose château of Bellevue was nearby. The marquise herself was entrusted with the general supervision of the Manufacture, a task that she fulfilled until her death in 1764. Under her protection *porcelaine de Sèvres* enjoyed immense success and became known far and wide for its quality, design, and colors, especially the combination of rich gold with dark green (*vert pomme*) or turquoise blue (*bleu céleste*). Even when large deposits of kaolin were found in the vicinity of Limoges in 1768 and the production of hard-paste porcelain could begin, the demand for soft-paste porcelain from Sèvres did not slacken.

The difficulty that the French glazers experienced initially in trying to imitate the deep enamels of hard-paste Saxon porcelain turned eventually to their advantage. Jean-Jacques Bachelier (1724–1806), a well-known Paris painter who served as art director first at Vincennes and then at Sèvres, noticed that the surface of biscuit had the whiteness and satined texture of alabaster, allowing it to duplicate the subtle play of light, typical of marble sculpture, which glazed porcelain tended to efface. These remarkable qualities of unglazed soft-paste biscuit, Bachelier urged, offered the best medium to reproduce sculptures in a serial and relatively inexpensive way, without sacrificing much of a sculptor's original design.

Bachelier's revolutionary idea appealed to sculptors, who welcomed an opportunity to popularize their works. Porcelain manufacturers were hesitant at first, but hoping, correctly as it turned out, that the new product would gain acceptance among the buying public and result in higher profits, soon embraced it wholeheartedly. Besides, they must have been glad that the success of Vincennes and Sèvres biscuit freed them from the constant need to look over their shoulders to see what the Saxon and Neapolitan companies were doing. But it also placed on them a greater responsibility, because from producers of *objets de luxe,* they became producers of *objets d'art.* That is why Bachelier decided to create a new position of *artiste-en-chef* in charge of sculpture and entrusted it initially to his friend Falconet. When Falconet left for Russia in 1766, his duties were taken over first by Bachelier and, from 1774, by the sculptor Louis-Simon Boizot (1743–1809). Both were fine artists, devoted to the Sèvres biscuit, but it was Falconet who was the true creator of that graceful and expressive genre whose elegance and gentleness, enlivened by a touch of sensuality, was so much in vogue in the Rococo boudoirs and which became the company's chief product during the third quarter of the eighteenth century.

Falconet's tasks at Sèvres consisted in the supervision of the production of clay and terracotta models by such leading sculptors of the time as Pigalle, Caffiéri, La Rue, Pajou, Boizot, Clodion, and Houdon. Falconet himself led them all in the creation of clay models, making close to one hundred of them by the time he departed for Russia. His favorite subjects were children at play and work, shepherdesses and milkmaids, graceful nymphs, and mischievous cupids, often after designs by Bachelier and François Boucher. In the first year of his employment, he created a series of sixteen tiny figurines of children *(Enfants Falconet, première grandeur)* based on models by Boucher. There followed, between 1764 and 1766, a smaller series of seventeen children *(Enfants Falconet, deuxième grandeur)*. Reproductions of his own work include the *Cupid* and the *Bather,* both of 1758, and the *Pygmalion* of 1763.[47] Some of those miniatures are all that remains of Falconet's marble sculptures that have disappeared. Such is, for instance, the graceful *Erigone (La nymphe à la vigne)* of 1759, whose larger original was exhibited in the Salon of 1747. Some were created specifically for Sèvres, such as *Psyche* (1761), as a biscuit pendant to the *Cupid,* and the *Bather with a Sponge* (1762) to go with the older *Bather.* Boucher's suggestive paintings and drawings were the inspiration for several of Falconet's models, such as the *Kiss Given* and the *Kiss Received,* both of 1765, and the unabashedly erotic *Leda with the Swan* of 1764. They were typically small in size, measuring between 6 and 12 inches in height, so as to fit easily on a shelf of an étagère.[48] Larger pieces, however, were also made: Falconet's *Sweet Melancholy* is 28 inches high; the *Cupid* and the *Bather* were made in three sizes, 7½, 14, and 32½ inches; and Boizot's magnificent centerpiece *(surtout)* for the cameo service for Catherine the Great is 36 inches high.[49]

Some of Falconet's works from this period transcend the Rococo fluff of the Sèvres Manufacture and show that he remained faithful to his belief in not following blindly the precepts of either the Baroque or the ancient Greeks, but combining the heightened sensitivity and passion of the former with the clarity and simplicity of the latter. His ultimate goal was to express the natural without necessarily imitating it, and, above all, to avoid fanciful pretension and mannerist affectation. Three small marbles of the Sèvres period were especially successful. The *Bather* (fig. 1.7) exhibited at the Salon of 1757, shows a typically Falconetian adolescent girl testing the temperature of water with her toes before venturing in. Copies of it in marble, plaster, biscuit, bronze, and wood are so numerous that it is difficult to determine their chronology and the original size of the sculpture. If the one in the Louvre is its earliest marble version, then one would have to conclude that the original version measured no more than 34 inches.

The *Cupid* (fig. 1.8) commissioned by Madame de Pompadour was also shown at the Salon of 1757. It is one of rare examples of the habitually humorless Falconet being playful. The plump Cupid is preparing to perform his duties as the messenger of Venus. He has just alighted on a rock, for his wings are still extended. Fixing his next victim with his eyes and reaching with his left hand into his quiver, he puts the index finger of his right hand to his lips, as if to tell the viewer to be quiet so as not to scare away his quarry. It is a finely chiseled piece showing every crease in Cupid's baby flesh. The drama created by the implied triangular contact, linking Cupid by means of an arrow to his unseen victim and by means of a gesture to the unseen observer of the scene, makes the sculpture a veritable tour de force.

Fig. 1.7. Etienne-Maurice Falconet, *Bather*. Plaster, 1757. The State Hermitage Museum, St. Petersburg.

Fig. 1.8. Etienne-Maurice Falconet, *Cupid.* Marble, 1757. The State Hermitage
Museum, St. Petersburg.

Its success with the public was instantaneous. Falconet boasted to Diderot that Pigalle bid four thousand livres for the *Cupid* at the auction of Madame de Pompadour's estate, but lost out to an art dealer.[50]

In 1763 Falconet exhibited his enormously successful *Pygmalion and Galatea* (fig. 1.9). Pygmalion of the Greek myth is a sculptor who fashions a marble statue of a girl of remarkable beauty, the Galatea of later versions of the story. He falls in love with his creation and begs Aphrodite to bring the girl to life. His prayers are answered and Galatea, now with warm blood coursing through her veins, returns Pygmalion's love. In Falconet's composition the awakening Galatea is flanked by the kneeling figures of Pygmalion and Cupid, who as Aphrodite's messenger kisses her hand, imparting life to the stone, and pushes her gently toward the enraptured sculptor. In the Salon of 1763 Diderot waxed ecstatic over the statue:

> Nature itself and the Graces suggested the pose for the figure of Galatea. Her arms fall softly down her body, her eyes are on the point of opening. Her head is slightly inclined toward Pygmalion who is kneeling motionless at her feet. Life manifests itself in the delicate smile touching her upper lip. What innocence! She is having her first thought, her heart begins to stir but it will not be long before it starts pounding. What hands! What softness of flesh! No, this is not marble; press it with your finger and the stone will lose its hardness and yield to your touch. How much truth in her body! What feet! How sweet and delicate they are! A small Cupid has grasped one of the girl's hands—he is not kissing but devouring it. What liveliness! What ardor! How much playfulness in Cupid's head![51]

Diderot goes on and on with this breathless patter, which would be more appropriate in a sports broadcast than art criticism.[52] Catherine the Great's comment is less effusive, but more memorable. Looking at her own plaster cast of the statue, she said that it reminded her of the prayer *Ora pro nobis!* or "Pray for us!"[53] When Diderot saw the large model of the monument to Peter the Great, he thought back to the *Pygmalion* and, showing more restraint than before, wrote: "How could this astonishing work arise in the same head as the delicate image of the *Pygmalion!* These are two works of rare perfection, which, for that very reason, seem to exclude one another."[54]

Even before Falconet's association with Sèvres, a very large marble *Allegory of Music* was commissioned by Marigny's predecessor, Lenormant de Tournehem. It was slated to stand in the vestibule of Madame de Pompadour's château of Bellevue, as a counterpart to the allegory of *Lyric Poetry* by Lambert Sigisbert Adam. In Falconet's rendition of the theme, the statue is conceived as a tribute to the considerable vocal talents of the marquise. It shows a young, bare-breasted woman with slightly parted lips, crowned with a laurel wreath and draped in a loosely falling wrap. She holds a lyre in her right hand and extends her left hand, as she makes a step forward.[55] There seems to be no intent to achieve physical resemblance to the marquise. Instead, a page of the score of the opera *Aeglé* by Pierre de la Garde (1717–c. 1792) is

Fig. 1.9. Etienne-Maurice Falconet, *Pygmalion and Galatea*. Marble, 1763.
The Walters Art Gallery, Baltimore.

at her feet, alluding to the acclaim that the marquise received in the title role. Measuring about seven feet in height, it is the largest surviving work from Falconet's pre-Russian period. A plaster model of it was shown at the Salon of 1751, and the large marble, finished in 1752, was miraculously saved from the conflagration that destroyed the château of Bellevue during the Revolution.

Religious subjects were also prominent during Falconet's nine-year long employment at Sèvres. They form a continuum with his work on the interior of the church of St. Roch and include such superb examples of small-size sculpture as the terracottas of the *Expiring Mary Magdalene* and the *Temptation of St. Anthony,* both created in 1765. They are not signed, but their formal characteristics indicate Falconet's authorship.[56] Mary Magdalene, though at the point of death, symbolized by a skull next to her body, is shown as a typically Falconetian young woman. The inclination of her head to the left, the left arm resting on a rock, and the hand hanging down limply bring to mind Falconet's *Christ on the Mount of Olives* in the church of St. Roch and its inspiration—Bernini's *Ecstasy of St. Teresa.* The angel depositing Mary Magdalene resembles the angel of the *Annunciation* in St. Roch's, and the rebuffing gesture of *St. Anthony* is not unlike the defensive posture of *St. Ambrose,* on which Falconet was working at that time.

Falconet's appointment in Sèvres, though seemingly far below his talent and reputation, afforded him nine years of financial comfort, bridging the period between his work in the church of St. Roch and the St. Petersburg commission. His salary was twenty-eight hundred livres per year—a modest figure, especially when compared with the eight thousand livres per year (plus a percentage of sales) earned by the director of the Manufacture, Boileau de Picardie. Taken together, however, with the royal stipend of six hundred livres per year (increased to eight hundred livres in 1762), it was sufficient to give him the peace of mind needed to engage in his favorite occupations of reading and writing. Although the Sèvres routine did not require him to spend more than one day a week in the Manufacture, his duties there were far from light. Arriving from Paris on a horse-drawn barge (called a *chaise d'eau*), by way of the Seine, he would bring along models to be worked on during that week. "He was a demanding and strict boss, hard on himself as he was on others, controlling the whole process of production. His inspiration made of biscuit a precious substance and endowed the Manufacture with nobility and glory."[57]

It is generally agreed that the years of Falconet's association with Sèvres were the most brilliant and exciting in the history of the Manufacture, earning this period the appellation of *l'âge de Falconet.*[58] When the use of biscuit was severely curtailed in 1777, there were heavy hearts among those for whom the impersonal texture of hard-paste porcelain was no match for the delicately pliant qualities of biscuit. In the words of a French historian of the Sèvres Manufacture, "without the biscuits of Sèvres, French sculpture would have been poorer, just as painting would have been poorer without its gouaches and miniatures. Eighteenth-century society would have missed an important part of its own setting, a witness of its soul and taste, intimately involved in its history and pleasures."[59]

MAVERICK GENIUS

Apart from his genius as an artist, Falconet is a man of uncommon talents, erudition, and expansion of sentiment. . . . He is, however, said to possess, in a high degree, that *soreness,* as Pope expressed it, that impatience of unmerited censure and little peevishness, which men of fine parts often discover, on account of the erroneous judgment, which the multitudes form of their abilities and execution.
—Nathaniel Wraxall Jr. (1774)

Deprived of formal schooling in his childhood, Falconet was determined to make up for his deficiencies in general education during adolescence and continued scholarly pursuits as he moved on through life. As a result, he became the best-educated artist of his time. He knew the history of ancient Greek and Roman art and was acquainted with all the significant creations of the Renaissance and Baroque. Unable to travel, he had to rely on engravings, which fulfilled in those days the functions of photography. "His portfolios were filled and his walls were covered with the most beautiful engravings after the paintings of Poussin and other great masters."[60] Even so, throughout his life he was attacked for writing about works that he had not seen, especially the equestrian statue of Marcus Aurelius on the Campidoglio, which was the most serious cause of his frequent bouts with the "anxiety of influence" as he worked on the statue of Peter the Great.

The process of intellectual self-improvement took time away from Falconet's artistic endeavors and led to disagreements over his priorities in his financially strapped household. It was at least partly responsible for the strains which developed in his marriage, for his wife blamed her husband's addiction to reading for their straitened circumstances. She often scolded him for "wasting his time" with books instead of doing something "worthwhile." In the words of Lévesque: "In vain did his wife moan at seeing him with a book in hand instead of working with his modeling knife. With all the firmness of his character, he went on dividing his loyalties between sculpting and writing."[61]

Falconet's readiness to put his modeling knife aside and bury his head in books was due as much to intellectual curiosity as to his desire to free the artist from the dictates of the critics, whom he accused of setting the tone, taste, and fashion of art production, while ignoring its methods. Lemoyne's notorious inability to verbalize must have been a constant reminder that an artist who wished to safeguard his artistic independence must be armed with a knowledge of the history and theory of art.

His intellectual curiosity led him to a friendly exchange of letters and gifts with Sir Joshua Reynolds, whose work on the theory and history of painting gave him a standing equivalent to that of Falconet in sculpture. Falconet gave Reynolds a plaster model of his *Winter*. Reynolds had it engraved, and reciprocated by presenting Falconet with an engraving of *Count Ugolino in the Dungeon,* based on a scene from Dante's *Inferno.* It hung over Falconet's fireplace and, by his own admission, filled him with terror mingled with admiration each time he glanced at it.[62]

Long hours of study were not, however, the primary reason for Falconet's domestic problems. He was too stubborn, too quick-tempered, and too mercurial to provide a setting for a happy marriage. Many who were attracted to him because of his straightforward and uncompromising stands would eventually become estranged by his brusqueness. Here is how his friend Lévesque remembered him: "He was frequently annoyed, frequently grumbling, sometimes quick-tempered, always human. One could think of him as kind or nasty depending on the moment when one saw him. But when one knew him well, one realized that kindness under a rough surface was at the base of his character."[63]

Bourrée de Corberon, secretary of the French legation in St. Petersburg during a part of Falconet's stay there, liked the sculptor, but thought him "too sanguine about his own opinions, too caught up in his own interest, to be trusted blindly and uncritically."[64]

Diderot was devoted to him and willing to put up with his faults. Yet even his patience wore thin at times: "One could say that your habitual practice of addressing yourself to marble has made you forget that we are made of flesh. You are quick to take offense, easy to wound, you have sarcasm or irony perpetually on your lips. . . . It takes a very tough person, enthusiastic about your fine qualities, to remain your friend. I doubt that you are sincerely and truly loved by anyone except by me and your young disciple. You are a bizarre mixture of tenderness and harshness."[65]

With his philosophical turn of mind, straitened financial circumstances, upturned nose (so much in evidence in the *Milo of Crotona*), and scolding wife, Falconet found it natural to relate to Socrates, who, according to some accounts, was also a sculptor. Lévesque commented on that flattering self-identification: "Like Socrates, [he] took delight in drawing people out and then reducing their ideas to the absurd. For him, as for Socrates, irony as well as sarcasm were favorite rhetorical weapons, an attitude which made him enemies, as it did for Socrates. He didn't go around barefoot like the Athenian philosopher, but he wore the plainest of clothes and took pride in frugality. At a time when he was so well off that one could call him wealthy, I saw him allowing himself wine only once a week."[66]

Falconet's argumentative nature and frugal ways may justify a comparison to Socrates in personality, but on the religious plane he identified with the strict interpretation of the teachings of St. Augustine as preached by the Jansenists, whose books he encountered by chance in his eclectic reading.

Let us return to Lévesque: "Born with an extreme severity of character, he embraced with ardor the rigors of that sect, rendering his life, which was hard enough because of a lack of money, even harder. He added water to his soup and to the dishes that his wife prepared for him."[67]

A curious episode occurred when Falconet became friendly with John Ingram, an English engraver who belonged to the Reformed church. They lent religious books to each other and in the end, says Lévesque, "the Englishman was on the point of becoming a Jansenist and Falconet—Reformed."[68]

Later in life, Falconet became an atheist, but with a heavy admixture of puritanical Calvinist ethics, which manifested itself so strikingly in his proposed resolution of the "affair" of the statue of *France Embracing the Bust of Louis XV*. Finding the work too boring to complete it, he offered to return to the Treasury the nine thousand livres advance he had received for it.

Falconet was fiercely jealous of his artistic independence and interpreted any outside advice as an attempt to subvert and circumscribe his freedom. He liked to illustrate his point with Bouchardon's answer to the duc d'Antin, when the then director of the Bâtiments du Roi demanded that the sculptor remove a muscle from a clay model. "But, Sir," shot back the sculptor, "if I remove it now, I will have the problem of putting it back in, for this muscle controls facial movements."[69]

Constant interference in the artistic process by those who wield power to criticize and demand enraged Falconet, no matter how well intentioned it was. He felt, not without reason, that in that respect painters and sculptors were worse off than men of letters and complained bitterly about the difference: "Men of letters, how lucky you are that you do not have to deal with those gentlemen who would direct your ideas, with those dispensers of opinions, convinced that they honor you by making you their instrument with which, as they claim, they'll make beautiful things! . . . Gentlemen, leave them alone and you'll get human beings! If you lend them your glasses, they will see the way you do. Perhaps even worse."[70]

He also inveighed against artists who were cowed into surrendering their freedom of thought:

> Who can assure us that works whose high praise is thoughtlessly repeated, but whose weaknesses are apparent to those who look at them more carefully, . . . have not been the unspoken reason for the current opinion that our only business is to know how to hold a pencil, a brush, a sketchbook, or a chisel? That is, probably, the source of so many prejudices found in those eloquent but ignorant writings which victimize those of us who do not dare to think for themselves and speak out. . . . Pusillanimity destroys the courage to think and makes one accept mediocrity. Such a state of things makes people fall silent out of shame, fear, and weakness.[71]

Such opinions offered freely and eloquently show that sculpture, while being Falconet's métier, was not his all-consuming passion. One suspects, in fact, that he put more stock in his literary accomplishments than in the artistic ones. He may have been prescient, for Falconet is known in France more as a writer of programmatic and polemical pieces on art than as a sculptor. The sheer volume of his writings shows how difficult it was for him to commit himself fully to the chisel. He relished too much the fracas of debate, he was too stimulated by the strife of contention, to be satisfied with the silence of clay and stone. Having launched an idea in print, he would lie in wait for a response. If not fully satisfied with it, he would pounce on it and tear at its mistakes and inconsistencies till it lay bare, stripped of credibility.

His love of writing helped him fill the years of enforced leisure in St. Petersburg, when the large model of the monument was completed and the casting had not yet begun. Writing was also the only thing on his mind when he returned from Russia. Couched in a pungent style and laced with sarcastic wit, Falconet's publications had as many admirers as detractors. The Rev. William Tooke, chaplain to the British merchant colony in St. Petersburg and Falconet's first translator into English, belonged to the former: "The man capable of being one of the first sculptors of his age, if he had employed his genius that way, would have become one of the finest writers. How much he is of a scholar, every one is sensible that has read the pieces he has already published. His notes on the elder Pliny are sagacious and acute, and his remarks on the statue of Marcus Aurelius will remain a literary monument of his taste."[72]

Less awed by Falconet's writings was one of the most influential art critics in Europe, Friedrich Melchior Grimm (fig. 1.10), if one is to judge by the review of Falconet's *Réflexions sur la sculpture* which appeared in Grimm's *Correspondance littéraire* of July 1, 1761.[73] The review was anonymous, but if Grimm was not its author, he had to approve of its general tenor: "The author has no enthusiasm for his art, nor very profound views, nor a wealth of ideas. Several keen observations are the merit of this brochure. In the first part of his reflections, he discusses whether it is more difficult to be a painter or a sculptor. A pointless question. One could just as well wonder if there is more merit in being dark-haired or blond. It is obvious that the differences consist precisely in what is called talent or aptitude for something, and one either has it or does not."[74]

Diderot realized that Falconet was a rare phenomenon among artists, a well-educated man with a feel for a felicitous turn of phrase, a penchant for unorthodox views, and a pugnacious readiness to defend his positions in a literate and articulate way. Impressed by the sculptor's breadth of interests and the sophistication and independence of his critical judgments, Diderot let him be his guide in matters pertaining to the visual arts. In particular, he came to depend on Falconet for the evaluation of the works exhibited at the biennial salons in the Louvre, which Diderot undertook to review for the *Correspondance littéraire*. It was largely Falconet's doing that Diderot's account of the Salon of 1765 was more than six times as long as that of 1761 and more than four times as long as that of 1763. As the date of the opening

Fig. 1.10. Louis Carrogis de Carmontelle, *Friedrich Melchior Grimm in 1769*. Engraving by Lecerf (Sainte-Beuve and Paulin Limayrac, eds., 1854).

of the Salon of 1767 was approaching and Falconet was away in St. Petersburg, Diderot asked forlornly: "Who is going to take your place next to me? Who is going to point out to me the beautiful and the weak aspects [of a work of art]?"[75]

Diderot's high regard for Falconet's art began with his account of the Salon of 1761, where he singled out Falconet's bust of the nonagenarian physician of the king, Camille Falconet. He also praised highly the plaster maquette of *Sweet Melancholy*. In the Salon of 1763 it was the *Pygmalion* group which drew his raves. He judged it the most perfect work in the Salon and predicted that it would not be matched for a long time to come. In the Salon of 1765 Diderot admired particularly the *Figure of a Seated Woman* (*Winter*, see fig. 2.4) and the relief *Alexander the Great Offering Campaspe to the Painter Apelles*. The Salon of 1767 showed no work of Falconet, because the sculptor was already in St. Petersburg. Nonetheless Diderot managed to pay the sculptor a compliment in absentia. He noted that the salon was poor in sculpture because Pigalle was "too rich and too preoccupied with large monuments" to participate, while Falconet was far away.

Diderot's respect for intellectual achievement invariably evolved into feelings of personal affection. That is what happened in his relations with Falconet. The two became fast friends, even though Diderot's gushing joviality was worlds away from Falconet's misanthropic sobriety. In the Salon of 1765 Diderot gave proof of his closeness to Falconet. It was there that he pronounced the sculptor to be "a man who has genius and all kinds of character traits compatible and incompatible with genius."[76] By 1766, Catherine the Great had every right to proclaim Falconet "Diderot's *ami de l'âme*."[77]

Diderot's affection for Falconet extended also to Falconet's disciple and lifelong companion Marie-Anne Collot. Two years after the couple's departure for St. Petersburg, he was still unable to reconcile himself to their absence: "I love you with all my heart and I hasten to tell you, yes, I love you so much that I have not stopped being close to you."[78] And, as if to prove the sincerity of his declaration, he recounted his visits to Falconet's house on the rue d'Anjou, near the Faubourg St. Honoré, to which he had the keys. The small study where Collot used to work brought back memories of a young woman whom he loved "like his own child"; the scents of the garden, which Falconet himself cultivated, evoked "the sweet moments" that they all had passed there: "Won't we ever see each other there again? This year I have plundered all the flowers. Oh, the beautiful peaches! The beautiful plums! How many apples and pears I will have! It won't be the leaves but the profusion of grapes crammed together, one bunch pressed against the other, that will provide shade in the bower. Alas, I'll enjoy all of that alone."[79]

Nostalgic sentiments were helped on occasion by the wine that Falconet left in his cellar: "The sculptor's wine flows freely. I don't know if you feel better after so many toasts were raised to your health, but as for me, I feel on occasion somewhat uncertain on my feet (unlike the Prince [Golitsyn]). I often have the honor of having supper with him and sometimes there we are at two o'clock in the morning with a glass in hand and the names of the sculptor and his disciple on our lips."[80]

At the same time, Diderot was not blind to his friend's faults—his egotism, short temper, hasty judgments, and fits of professional jealousy. Here is how he summed up Falconet's personality: "He was harsh and tender, quibbling and confrontational, eager for praise and scornful of posterity, jealous of the kind of talent he lacked and caring little for the one he possessed, loving passionately and cruelly tyrannizing those he loved, rich in talent and a hundred, a thousand times more so in self-esteem, asking for advice and never following it, knowing everything, but always questioning and never learning anything; he was made up of all sorts of contradictions."[81]

Falconet's personality, it is true, cannot be hung on a single peg. He was "a bilious and misanthropic loner, who, in a sensual century, practiced extreme rigor and was attracted now by Jansenist austerity, now by Socratic simplicity."[82] He was, however, touched with genius and, unhappily for him, did not have enough sense of humor to deal with it. Yes, he could be sarcastic and cutting, but he lacked the ability to laugh at himself. That is why he took himself with such pompous seriousness, and that is why his cordial relations with the whimsical and droll Diderot and the rational and witty Catherine were of short duration.

Friendship with Diderot gave much more to Falconet than a sense of having a devoted and admiring friend. It provided him with an entry to the *encyclopédiste* clique, titillating his intellectual vanity and literary ambitions. Once admitted to that most exclusive club of the Age of Reason, he obtained an opportunity to participate in its intellectual ventures and could take pride in the fact that the entries on sculpture, relief, and draperies in the *Encyclopédie* came from his pen. The ultimate gift of his friendship with Diderot was the commission for the equestrian monument to Peter the Great in St. Petersburg. It fulfilled his most cherished dreams, giving him a chance to show his true mettle from a position of influence and prestige at one of the most resplendent courts of Europe.

Falconet's official title of sculptor of the king should not be taken as a badge of special distinction. It provided the artist with a royal pension, but held no promise of major royal commissions. In Falconet's case, they were practically nonexistent and, had it not been for the monument in St. Petersburg, his reputation would have had little to rest on. With his large religious statuary lost in the fires of the Revolution, posterity would have had to judge him by a dozen or so surviving marbles, mostly small in size, and close to a hundred clay models for the Sèvres Manufacture, designed to please the taste of Madame de Pompadour. Not much to build on for one's posthumous renown.

Catherine's idea of erecting a colossal equestrian monument to Peter the Great and entrusting Falconet with its execution turned out to be providential. Falconet made the most of the opportunity, creating a work that will forever remain an archetypal example of the equestrian genre. Without it, Falconet would have been remembered as one of the many very good sculptors of his generation, a Pigalle, Vassé, or Saly. With it, he laid claim to a place of eminence in the annals of eighteenth-century art. As one considers the totality of his oeuvre, it might, in fact, be more appropriate to think of Falconet as a sculptor of the empress rather than as a sculptor of the king. The problem with either designation is that Falconet was not cut out to be anybody's sculptor but his own, and that being his own master proved to be a much heavier burden than any a monarch could impose.

PRO AND CON

> Oh Posterity, holy and sacred, support of the oppressed unfortu-
> nate, you who are just and incorruptible, who avenge a decent
> man, unmask a hypocrite, condemn a tyrant, who offer security
> and consolation, don't ever abandon me!
> —Diderot (1766)

An important by-product of Falconet's friendship with Diderot was an epistolary debate that has come down to us under the name of *Le pour et le contre,* courtesy of Falconet.[83] As Diderot explained to his beloved friend Sophie Volland, he was provoked into the debate by a lighthearted remark of Falconet, who professed not to believe that artistic creation is stimulated by a drive to gain immortality in and through the eyes and minds of future generations.[84] Here is how Diderot characterized Falconet's position: "No man is more desirous of praise by his contemporaries and more indifferent to that of posterity. He carries this view to an unbelievable extreme, and has told me a hundred times that he wouldn't give a penny to guarantee eternity for his most beautiful statue."[85] Such a casual dismissal of the role of posterity was anathema to Diderot. Anticlerical but deistic, he viewed posterity as a kind of ersatz divinity and craved its applause as the key to life immortal. "To a philosopher," he told Falconet, "posterity is what the next world is to a religious man."[86] Falconet's rebuff to the future seemed to him nihilistic, almost sacrilegious. It had to be resolutely repudiated.

The ever realistic Falconet, a dogged champion of artistic freedom, could not be reconciled with the thought that his creativity should depend on so vague a factor as opinions beyond his ken and control. He agreed that "posterity, like eternal bliss, has its zealots," but refused to be hemmed in by such an irrational premise: "These two notions enlarge some souls, but other souls are large enough already and don't need an unwanted crown."[87] An artist, he claimed, must satisfy his own conception of truth and beauty and be responsible to himself alone, rather than to imaginary criteria of an imaginary audience.

Falconet's rejection of posterity as a factor in artistic creation had much to do with his general view of the creative process, which he thought ought to be fully independent of any stimuli other than the tension between the artist's idea and the matter on which he wanted to impose it. The future was outside the artist's field of vision, just as was the past, whose burden the artist was free to lay aside or incorporate in his conceit, as long as he did so consciously and freely. His was the program of an innovating artist who wished to be rid of the weight of tradition, especially the tradition of ancient art, which Falconet viewed without reverence. Antiquity was for him a mere period in history, nothing more and nothing less. Clearly, had he been engaged in the great Quarrel of the Ancients and the Moderns, which had been at the center of theoretical discussions on art and literature since the Renaissance, he would have sided with the moderns.

The *Le pour et le contre* debate started soon after Diderot's letter to Sophie Volland. At first he and Falconet met to discuss the issues viva voce, but they realized soon enough that their views had to be written down in order to avoid misunderstandings and memory gaps. Such was the beginning of the correspondence "from two corners." It lasted from the end of 1765 to the beginning of 1767 and involved an exchange of twenty-four letters. Diderot, a great polemicist himself, found in Falconet a worthy foil. Yet, no matter how divergent their views, the tone of the letters remained civil. One does, in fact, get the impression that the two adversaries were often engaged in friendly sparring, agreeing to disagree in order to better hone their rhetorical skills. Years after the debate, Falconet was happy to recollect only those moments which were free of rancor: "Diderot the *philosophe* and Falconet the sculptor, sitting by a fireplace in [Diderot's] house on the rue Taranne, discussed the question whether contemplating posterity makes one strive for more beautiful works and better deeds. They stated their positions, argued, and parted, each, as is normal, convinced that he was right. In the morning they would send each other notes with new arguments, keeping the dispute alive. When their patience was exhausted, they resorted to letters. . . . It is certain that Diderot has never treated any subject in a more interesting and amicable way."[88]

Catherine, to whom Falconet gave a copy of the text, was equally impressed by the courteous demeanor of the debaters: "It is a real pleasure to read a dispute so devoid of harshness and treated with as much fervor as politeness."[89]

Yet, not all of the debate was free of testiness and umbrage. Initially, Diderot assumed the pose of an experienced debater who sensed his intellectual superiority and counted on a quick surrender of his adversary. He described himself as "lying down calmly, like a big lion, showing his claws to his opponent and saying: 'If I only wanted to . . . ,' but instantly drawing his claws back in."[90] Falconet, however, was irritated by Diderot's condescending tone and by the vagueness of his sweeping humanistic arguments. His parries were swift, rapier-like thrusts of logical reasoning, liberally sprinkled with sarcasm.

The startled Diderot began to feel outmatched and, sensing a harder battle than he had anticipated, resorted to accusing Falconet of intentional misreadings and unfair debating tactics:

I'll present to you my ideas in isolation in order to spare you the bother of unraveling them. I'll present them to you in a brief, dry, and abstract way so that they might be less of a target for your sophistry. I'll strip them of all oratorical splendor because you are quick to take offense and my *cicéronnerie* could arouse your suspicions. . . . You are the most execrable adversary one can imagine. I wanted to see how you would act when one threw oneself on your mercy and whether you'd be enough of a coward to kick someone who is down. Because one is down, when one has to submit to your scholastic and sententious approach, knowing that what really matters are life, feeling, and enthusiasm.[91]

In his very first letter, Diderot defined the parameters of the debate: "Praise paid in cash is nearby, it is the praise of contemporaries. Praise presumed is heard in the distance, it is the praise of posterity. Why do you want, my friend, to accept but one half of what is due to you? It's not I, or Peter, or Paul who praise you. It's good taste, and good taste is an abstraction that does not die. . . . That voice . . . is immortal in spite of you. It is out there saying over and over again, Falconet, Falconet!"[92]

But Falconet would not be lured by a ticket to immortality on so flimsy a conveyance as the wings of memory: "How about all the great men whose works have been lost or destroyed? Or those whose works have been attributed to others? Or those whose works and names have equally perished?" For him the accolades of posterity were a lottery, whose drawing would not be held till after the players had died. As for the presumed role of posterity as an incentive to create, Falconet put no stock in it: "Fear of scorn, shame, and the humiliation that follows. . . . That's all the incentive I need."[93]

Fear of scorn, answers Diderot, is not sufficient to motivate an artist. It may help avoid mistakes, but it will never exalt the spirit and stimulate the artist to attempt great deeds. For that one needs "to burn with unquenchable thirst for praise. That is the sentiment which quickens your breath."[94] Not *my* breath, retorted Falconet, and to prove that the survival of a work of art and of the name of its creator may be due to sheer fortuity, he cited the case of the Hellenistic *Borghese Gladiator* by Agasias son of Dositheus, which survived by chance on the Italian seacoast, along with the name of its maker carved on the plinth. "Observe," Falconet told Diderot, "that Agasias, about whom we know nothing, could have been superior to Phidias!"[95]

And so it went, from letter to letter. Diderot kept questioning Falconet's disclaimers of interest in eternal glory and affected being shocked by anyone making fun of so serious a subject: "Joking is not in order, when one is concerned with the exhalations that fill the nostrils of gods, the fragrant vapors that embalm our temples, and the euphoria produced by chewing the sacred leaves of prophecies."[96] In his letter of February 15, 1766, which amounts to twenty-six printed pages, Diderot summed up his point of view: "I conclude that the sentiment of immortality and the respect for posterity move the heart and elevate the spirit, that they are at the root of great things."[97] But Falconet did not desist: "If a friend tells me his dream, I would be mad to argue with him about it. If he can draw from it practical benefits, it would be cruel of me to wake him up. But if he wants my dreams to be the color of his, I say, my friend, you're still asleep."[98]

For Diderot the most traumatic point in the debate came early on, when Falconet, deploring the disintegration and loss of Classical art, especially painting, advised Diderot not to put his trust in the testimony of men of letters because they were notoriously poor art critics and their praise was just as fragile as a work of art: "Couldn't eulogy and eulogist have turned to ashes many centuries ago?" Besides, their eulogies, even if they survived, were often wrong. "Beware of written testimonies handed down to posterity! If you only knew, my friend, the way a painter or sculptor knows, what puerile opinions are pompously served to us! If only I showed you what a driveling old fool *(petit radoteur)* Pliny was, you would agree with my not wanting ridiculously wrongheaded praise."[99]

To call Pliny the Elder, one of Diderot's favorite Roman writers, "a driveling old fool"! No, Diderot could not let Falconet get away with such sacrilege: "You were right in confiding this strange discovery to a friend's ear. Do you know him well, that Pliny about whom you speak so lightly? . . . Do you know that he was a man of the most profound knowledge and of the finest taste? . . . Do you know that only Tacitus was his equal?"[100] That was the defining moment of the debate, for it was one thing to argue about immortality, but quite another to have to defend the competence of one's professional confrère.

Falconet, seeing that he had to justify his condemnation of Pliny, wrote letter after letter citing and criticizing particular passages that showed that the Roman historian was a mere compiler, without his own point of view, without competence in art criticism, and without the right to pass judgment on art. The debate veered from posterity to antiquity. Diderot was not unhappy about that change because of his presumption that there existed a logical connection between these concepts, "two aspects of the same idea," linked by tradition and continuity.[101]

With the two adversaries becoming increasingly focused on the credentials of the men of letters of antiquity (for Falconet, *any* men of letters) as judges of art, the discussion began to lose its general theoretical character and turned instead to isolated passages and particular Greek and Roman works, some known only from literary descriptions. Thus, of the nine letters exchanged between May 10 and November 10, 1766, two deal with Pliny the Elder and seven with the Greek painter Polygnotus of Thasos (first half of the fifth century B.C.), whose frescoes in Delphi were described by the historian and geographer Pausanias (second half of the second century A.D.) before they were destroyed. The painting in question represented the embarkation of the Greeks after the capture of Troy. In the heat of battle, the two opponents did not stop to wonder whether discussing qualities of a painting known only from a literary description made any sense. They parsed the text of Pausanias, weighed his every word, examined it from all sides, peered into the Greek writer's subconscious, and came, naturally enough, to entirely different conclusions.[102]

What bothered Falconet most was Diderot's willingness to assume that "different kinds of art march in step" and that, therefore, Classical painting, which had almost totally perished except for vase decoration, had to be as good as the recognized masterpieces of Classical sculpture.[103] Here is how Diderot described that presumed interdependence in the Salon of 1765: "It is works of sculpture that convey to posterity the state of the fine arts in a nation. . . . What's left to us of Apelles? Nothing; but since the products of his brush equaled the sublime carvings of his time, [they] testify today to the extent of his gifts."[104] Such an assumption, says Falconet, is entirely unjustified: "You tell me that the *Farnese Hercules* by Glycon and the *Borghese Gladiator* by Agasias testify for Apelles and Phidias, . . . but when I read the nonsense on Apelles and see poor sculptures signed by Phidias, Praxiteles, or Lysippus, these testimonies become very feeble."[105]

The departure of Falconet for St. Petersburg put a virtual end to the debate, which had degenerated by then into a pedantic, if impressive, display of philological learning. But Diderot wanted to have the last word and, in order to do so, resorted to an evidently duplicitous device of painting his friend in overly optimistic hues and his object of travel in overly pessimistic ones, just to be able to pin on him the very notions that he had fought against so hard in the debate. Why, Diderot asked, would Falconet want to vanish "into the glacial North," leaving behind all the wonderful amenities of his life in Paris?

> Is it self-interest which takes you there? No, you have shown that you are above such considerations. Is it thirst for gold which torments you? No, you scorn gold. Are you seeking a greater fortune? No, you are wise and you have the riches of wisdom. Are you seduced by glory? No, you don't care about glory and, when you get it in full measure, your protracted and difficult task will bring you almost to the end of your career. You'll hardly have time to hear our praise, while in the subpolar regions you won't find the approbation to compensate you for it. Had you been vain, your statue of Winter executed in Paris would have better served your vanity. Tell me, who'll see your tsar? Who'll praise him? Who'll admire him? Almost no one.[106]

Constructing this image, Diderot must have known that it had little to do with reality—that Falconet looked assiduously after his own interests, that he was quite partial to money, and that he was very much concerned with his reputation. Nor did Diderot have any reason for making so gloomy a forecast of the reception of Falconet's monument in Russia. But Diderot's depiction denied Falconet rational reasons for making his decision, and allowed him to exclaim in the end: "What is it then that pulls you out of here? I'll tell you what it is, it is glory, my friend, and the sentiment of immortality and the respect of posterity."[107]

Falconet did not give Diderot the satisfaction of responding to this mysti-fication, whose aim was to put into question all of his arguments in the debate. He was clearly proud of holding his own in a head-on encounter with Diderot, and, even if the debate ended in a draw, he still wished to publish it as soon as possible. To do so he needed Diderot's consent and collaboration. The philosopher, however, was dragging his feet. He wanted to review and adjust the somewhat edited text that Falconet had sent him for his approval. But his heart was not in it. On the one hand, he must have been disappointed by the vagueness and diffuseness of his argumentation; on the other, he lacked Falconet's tenacity and will to carry on a debate which, he felt, could not be resolved. Falconet's plans to publish *Le pour et le contre* alone were of course a concern: "I received from [Falconet] the manuscript on the notion of immortality and the respect of posterity, which I was so afraid he might publish without my participation. In it there was a page with more additions. . . . You won't believe how much worry it has caused me."[108]

In the meantime, Falconet decided to show the text of the debate to Vol-taire and Catherine and ask for their judgments on the merits of the debate. Voltaire answered politely but, hiding as usual behind his real or imaginary maladies, declined to take sides, promising only to read everything that two men of such distinction had to say: "Even though I am on the point of losing my eyesight, my spirit will try to profit from your lessons."[109]

The appeal to Catherine alarmed Diderot: "Would you dare [*seriez-vous homme*] to leave the decision about our dispute to the judgment of my bene-factress? Take care, my friend. That woman is inebriated by the sentiment of immortality and I guarantee that she bows down before the image of posterity."[110] Undaunted, within a few months of arriving in St. Petersburg, Falconet sent a copy of the text to the empress and asked her to look it over.[111] She read it during her trip down the Volga in the spring of 1767, but not wanting to hurt the amour-propre of either combatant, refused to take sides in the dispute. She did, however, point out sensibly that the debate had all the aspects of an arid theological disputation and tried to make Fal-conet moderate his position: "You have found that your contemporaries are often wrong and that the same is true of posterity. Your pride and probity ask for the approval of a small number of connoisseurs. But why should they hail from your century only? What about all those who will come after them? What did they do to you that you don't want to please them? Is it because you don't know them? Should one treat kindly only those whom one knows? Would you hit someone you don't know? And why should you have so little regard for our grandchildren?"[112]

The empress did not wait for Falconet's answers, but wisely stroked his ego: "Your *Peter the Great* will demonstrate your good will to your contempo-raries and your kindness to posterity." That might have been enough, for Falconet never returned to the topic.

MADEMOISELLE VICTOIRE

To her talent she joins a splendid character and the highest moral principles. She does not lack in esprit. It is rendered most piquant by her purity, innocence, and lack of affectation.
—Friedrich Melchior Grimm (1766)

That Marie-Anne Collot (fig. 1.11) was a sculptor of great ability, one of the finest portraitists of her time, is evident from the many memorable works produced by her during a very short creative career. Yet, she is rarely mentioned in the annals of eighteenth-century sculpture, and her work is known today to but a few aficionados. There is no doubt that much of that neglect may be attributed to the powerful personality of Falconet which has made it difficult to place Collot in the limelight which is deservedly hers. Doing it for a woman in a field almost totally dominated by men makes this task even more daunting.[113]

The fact is that for all of the sixteenth and seventeenth centuries, only one woman-sculptor can be named, Properzia de Rossi (1490–1530), an artist of considerable skill, known chiefly for her bas-reliefs. She was nurtured in Bologna, a city whose artistic climate was particularly propitious for women. Nor does this situation improve much in the seventeenth and eighteenth centuries, when there were just the Spaniard Luisa Ignacia Roldán (1656–1704), who did much religious polychrome sculpture in wood and terracotta in Seville and Madrid, and Anne Seymour Damer, an English portraitist of some renown, who was Collot's exact coeval. This dearth of women sculptors was due in part to the physical demands that sculpture imposes upon the artist, in part to the perception of sculpture as manual labor and therefore unfeminine, and in part to the custom that prevented women from employing nude models, which was also the reason that the few women who tackled sculpture engaged in religious subjects and portraiture.

Marie-Anne Collot was born in Paris in 1748 into a dysfunctional family. Her father was an abusive drunkard, who mistreated his daughter and eventually caused her to flee the parental home. One gets a glimpse of his personality from an episode that occurred in Diderot's home soon after Monsieur Collot found out that his daughter had gone off to Russia with Falconet. Diderot described the outraged man's fulminations in a letter to "Mademoiselle Victoire," as he addressed Collot jokingly:[114] "Your father is a very strange man, indeed. Since he did not speak of you politely, Madame Diderot locked horns with him and they were not far from having a very violent scene right in my home."[115] A year and a half later Monsieur Collot disappeared from the scene: "Mademoiselle Victoire, I received the draft that was to assist your father. Despite all our efforts, neither I, nor his son, nor his parents could find him. All the indications are that he has died."[116]

Since Collot's mother is never mentioned in Diderot's correspondence, it is fair to assume that by the time of Collot's departure for St. Petersburg

Fig. 1.11. Pierre-Etienne Falconet, *Marie-Anne Collot*. Oil on canvas, 1773. Musée des Beaux-Arts, Nancy. Photograph G. Mangin.

she was no longer alive. We know, again on Diderot's authority, that Collot had a younger brother who, being illiterate, could not find employment and was essentially a charge of his sister. After Collot's departure, the ever solicitous Diderot had the boy learn to read and write and found him a job in the printing house of Le Breton.[117] He reported on the young man's progress in one of his messages to Collot: "Your brother is a good fellow, quite honest, quite simple, somewhat dense, somewhat limited. But he fulfills his duties, has standards, works hard, knows his profession, begins to make good use of his time, and quite soon will be able to manage without any support."[118]

Diderot also knew Collot's uncle, and liked him: "Mademoiselle Collot's uncle is a decent man and I respect him."[119]

Collot was barely fifteen when she presented herself to Jean-Baptiste Lemoyne and asked the sculptor to accept her as one of his pupils. The work that she brought to Lemoyne's atelier must have shown enough promise to make the aging maître take her on. She did not, however, spend much time with him—a few months perhaps, for in 1764 she was already in Falconet's atelier. She met him most probably at Lemoyne's, for Falconet visited his former teacher frequently.

Knowing Falconet's dislike of didactic work, one doubts that it was an offer to teach her sculpting that brought Collot into the house on the rue d'Anjou. It is more likely that he asked her to be his model, for her good looks and girlish figure qualified her as a typically Falconetian adolescent nude. The new situation must have seemed like paradise to this talented and intelligent teenager who had not had much opportunity to pursue formal education. Used to the rigors of a waif's existence, she found herself transported into the comforts of the home of a prominent sculptor, whom she could observe at work and leisure and whose professional advice she could profit from. She also met his learned friends, who treated her with affection and some of whom were to become her sitters.

Collot's artistic output, almost exclusively in portraiture, is surprisingly large for a sculptor active during a mere seventeen years, from 1765 to 1782. She was barely seventeen when she made a number of terracotta portraits of Falconet's friends, which impress by their maturity. In Grimm's opinion they were of sufficiently high quality to get her into the Académie "by a unanimous vote."[120] He blamed Falconet for not having done something about it before the two left for St. Petersburg. Others in the circle of Diderot were just as complimentary.

Not all of Collot's Paris work has come down to us, and some of it has been misattributed and misidentified—a function, no doubt, of her young age and inexperience. A case in point is a problem that has bedeviled Collot scholarship for years. It concerns three 1766 terracotta portraits by Collot, all of which received Grimm's highest marks.[121] The bust of the actor Préville in the role of Sganarelle in *Le médecin malgré lui* by Molière was, according to Grimm, astounding. Though its current location is unknown, we know what it looks like, for it was reproduced in a sale catalogue of 1928.[122] The bust of Diderot is known from a model of it, reduced in size for production in biscuit.[123] Diderot had this to say about it in his account of the Salon of 1767: "I forget to mention among the good portraits of me the bust by Mademoiselle Collot, especially the last one which belongs to my friend Monsieur Grimm. It is good, it is very good. In his home it has taken the place of another by her master Falconet, which was not good."[124]

The identification of the third bust, that of Prince D. A. Golitsyn, the Russian envoy in Paris, which Grimm considered "lifelike," has been complicated by three factors: the existence of two signed but unidentified busts by

Collot, the absence of any verifiable portrait of Golitsyn, and the following passage in a 1766 letter from Diderot to Falconet and Collot in St. Petersburg: "Our two busts have come back from the [Sèvres] Manufacture, the one of Damilaville baked superbly, that of Grimm with a burn on the forehead and nose. Mademoiselle, my forehead and nose are red, but that does not prevent me from looking very handsome. . . . The bust of Prince Golitsyn is perhaps a better likeness, but the one of me is more beautiful."[125]

Until 1998 this passage was taken to mean that Collot made the busts of Etienne-Noël Damilaville and Grimm, both friends of Diderot. At first, the unidentified bust dated 1765 was assumed to be a portrait of Golitsyn. When, however, it was realized that its middle-aged subject could not be a likeness of the young prince, it was suggested that it represented Damilaville.[126] The other unidentified bust was assumed to be a portrait of Grimm, despite its lack of resemblance to his other portraits, like the one by Louis Carrogis Carmontelle (fig. 1.10).[127]

Both of these identifications have now been disproved by the Paris art critic Marie-Louise Becker. She has pointed out that the habitual reading of Diderot's text is based on a misunderstanding of the French prepositional phrases *de Damilaville* and *de Grimm*. These phrases do not mean "representing Damilaville and Grimm," but "belonging to Damilaville and Grimm," that is, they are not used attributively but possessively.[128] Otherwise, why would Diderot identify one of these busts as his own likeness?

If, however, Collot did not make the busts of Damilaville and Grimm, whom do her two signed terracotta busts represent? The bust dated 1765 must now be considered unidentified, while the bust dated 1766 should be considered a likeness of Prince D. A. Golitsyn (fig. 1.12). This most plausible conjecture has been confirmed by Becker's discovery of a clearly identified portrait of D. A. Golitsyn, drawn by Falconet's son.[129]

Were Collot and Falconet lovers? There can be no unequivocal answer to that question, for whatever documentation that could have thrown some light on it fell into the hands of Collot's only daughter, Marie-Lucie, who destroyed it, presumably out of fear that divulging it could be injurious to her mother's memory. That action alone, while depriving us of a keyhole, provides a mute testimony to the existence of a compromising situation. Still, the absence of any direct testimony, and the natural reticence of those in the know, force the researcher to couch his answer in terms of probabilities rather than facts. This said, the probability that Collot and Falconet were linked by an intimate liaison before they left Paris, in Russia, and after they returned, is very high indeed. Indications that lead one to such a conclusion, while indirect, are too persuasive to be discounted.

Picasso used to say that love exists only in its outward manifestations. By that yardstick, all of Collot's life was one continuous manifestation of deep love for Falconet. For him she left Lemoyne's atelier. For him she left Paris, and followed him to an uncertain future in a faraway land, leaving behind a promising career and a probable election to the Paris Académie. For him

Fig. 1.12. Marie-Anne Collot, *Prince Dmitry Alekseevich Golitsyn.* Terracotta, 1766.
Present location unknown. Formerly in the collection of David Weill. Courtesy
Department of Sculpture at the Louvre and Ader-Picard-Tajan.

she thought nothing of putting up with evil tongues. She let him be not only her teacher, but also her manager and her spokesman. It is remarkable that whatever work Collot did for Catherine was arranged by Falconet. He spoke and wrote on her behalf, negotiated prices, brought her work to the empress, and on occasion asked for its return. One can say that Collot's life in art began and ended with Falconet. Except for two brief periods, when Collot was with Pierre-Etienne Falconet, the sculptor's son, the two were inseparable until Falconet's death in 1791 "did them part." The most touching was her devotion to the moody and irritable patient during the last eight years of his life, when he was laid low and incapacitated by a massive stroke.

An oblique but persuasive indication of Collot's feelings for Falconet is the bust she made of him in St. Petersburg (fig. 1.4), which is, by consensus, her best work. In this portrait, Falconet is not the tenacious, even obstinate, man who thrived on conflict and was ready to challenge the art establishment of Western Europe and eventually the whole political establishment of Russia. With a roguish smile playing on his lips, Falconet appears as a kindly if somewhat mischievous man, who looks younger than his age. It is an idealized portrait lovingly executed by a loving woman.

Diderot had a paternal affection for "Mademoiselle Victoire," and his chatty letters to her and Falconet in St. Petersburg leave little doubt as to the nature of their relationship. Here are a few examples of Diderot's banter, excerpted from his earliest letters. To Collot: "Mademoiselle Victoire, . . . I have often thought of Falconet, but not once without thinking of you, without missing you, without joining you to my heartfelt wishes for his health and happiness. May you be happy, one and the other. . . . Above all, one by the other." [130] "As you can guess, your name is often mentioned [in Paris] together with that of Falconet." [131] "He has only you and his genius. Don't spare him. Judge him sternly. If you are afraid of upsetting him, then you don't love him enough. Excuse his passing moods. Tomorrow he'll recognize the justice of your observation and he'll thank you with redoubled tenderness. . . . Does he take care of your happiness? Do you take care of his?" [132]

In the passages addressed to Falconet Diderot kept egging on his friend to marry: "My friend, if you don't give happiness to that child who has followed you to the end of the world, be careful! I won't forgive you as long as I live. I have almost had a hundred quarrels because I dared claim that you were not man and wife yet. They all wished it. They were sure of it." [133] Upon hearing that Collot made a bust of Falconet: "You must resemble yourself a lot if she made you in marble just as she knows you in the flesh." [134] "Aren't you married yet? Well, too bad for you, my friend, because I know the only woman whom you should have married. For two years you've been considered here husband and wife." [135] "I want you to bring happiness to Mademoiselle Collot because you are her master, her friend, her support, above all, her benefactor. Because no success, no honors can compensate her for domestic and private sorrow. Because, since she has attached her lot to yours, I have to wish for it to be a happy one." [136]

That Falconet and Collot lived like man and wife in St. Petersburg was openly maintained by some of those contemporaries who were privy to local rumors. Two travelers, the Frenchman Fortia de Piles, who visited St. Petersburg in 1792, and the Englishman John Carr, who was there in 1804, minced no words, as they referred to Collot as "the mistress of Falconet."[137] General Ivan Betskoi, who was in charge of the monument project, referred to the couple as Falconet and his Collot. Even Catherine dropped fairly transparent hints about their ménage. When Falconet asked her to lend him the bust of him so that Collot could improve it, the witty empress replied: "When I am away in the country, you can take your bust so that during the summer Mademoiselle Collot may caress it again."[138]

All this evidence suggests that Collot and Falconet had an intimate liaison during their stay in St. Petersburg, but were they lovers while still in Paris? Diderot's letters mention Collot's studio in Falconet's house and her frequent presence at the gatherings of Falconet's friends there. His extraordinary affection for Collot cannot be explained except by their frequent meetings, most likely together with Falconet in the house on the rue d'Anjou. The sculptor occupied it alone, his son Pierre-Etienne having gone off to live in London.

The strongest evidence, however, of the existence of a liaison between Collot and Falconet in Paris is provided by the circumstances of their going together to Russia. Indeed, if there had been no liaison, why would Falconet wish to take along an eighteen-year-old girl, no matter how talented she was? Why would she be so concerned about her reception in Russia? Why would Falconet be so reluctant to tell the Russians about her coming along? Why was her name not included in the official contract? Why did Falconet rely on his friends Diderot and Golitsyn to break the news to the Russians, instead of doing it himself? Why did they stress so much the impeccable morality of Collot's conduct?

Put off by the absence of evidence, authors tend to withhold judgment on the nature of Collot's relationship with Falconet. Some, like Kaganovich, avoid tackling the question altogether and prefer to think of it as professional collaboration and nothing else. Some, like Louis Réau, the most informed authority on the two sculptors, weigh the options, but find it difficult to make a pronouncement one way or the other. Writing in 1922, Réau suggested that "Mlle. Collot was perhaps [Falconet's] model, before becoming his pupil and his mistress."[139] Two years later, however, Réau rejected the view that the two had been lovers, although he found it credible that "in her young age Marie-Anne Collot felt love for her teacher Falconet."[140]

One wonders, however, on what evidence Réau concludes that Collot loved Falconet (platonically, presumably) in her young age only? Yes, she loved him when she was in her teens, but did she not love him when she was in her forties and was taking care of a paralyzed and wickedly irritable old man? Réau invokes Collot's character as a warrant of the purity of her behavior. But all we know about Collot's character is that she was independent enough to leave her parental home at the age of fifteen, uninhibited enough to take up a profession that was distinctly unfeminine, talented enough to win the friendship and admiration of such people as Diderot, Grimm, the Golitsyns, and Catherine, selfless enough to remain devoted to a man who refused to marry her and probably did not return her feelings, and brave enough to defy public opinion and go off with him to an exotic land. Such a person could easily take on Falconet as her lover. As for her youthful age, it need not signify anything beyond her need for a father figure after a childhood of parental abuse and indifference.

All this shows persuasively that Collot loved Falconet and loved him deeply. Whether Falconet loved Collot is another matter. One wonders, even, whether love for another person was a feeling which he could experience. Love is a binding, deeply committing, and forward-looking sentiment. Falconet had no use for the future, whether its name be God, Posterity, or Love. He was apparently content to treat his love affair with Collot as a fringe benefit of what he viewed as a professional association with limited responsibility.

Falconet's attitude points the way to the most tragic flaw of the sculptor's personality, his inability to sustain a deep personal relationship in which a mutual commitment is required. His life was a string of associations that wilted in his hands before attaining maturity. He managed to make his only surviving son, Pierre-Etienne, so miserable that the young man fled to England. Little is known about Falconet's treatment of his wife, but we do know that she died an unhappy woman, after nine years of married life. Diderot reports that he "made die of anguish" a woman with whom he was "madly in love."[141] Diderot himself fell victim to Falconet's mood swings, which transformed one of the warmest friendships imaginable into a feeling of genuine antipathy. Similarly, Falconet's relationship with Catherine, which began on a most auspicious note, foundered completely after several years.

The question whether Falconet and Collot had a durable liaison should not be passed over in silence, as it usually is in the puritanically decorous Russian works on the history of the monument. It is not a piquant episode introduced in order to enliven the narrative, nor is it an attempt to invade the couple's privacy. It is a matter of the greatest consequence in the biographies of the two artists. It dominated their personal lives, and in the end assumed the pathos of a Greek tragedy. It also provides the key to the personalities of its protagonists. Collot emerges as a selfless and generous person whose life was totally subordinated to the interests and wishes of the man she loved. Falconet, by contrast, comes through as a distant and narcissistic man, preoccupied with his work and image to the exclusion of all other concerns.

2

Between Paris and St. Petersburg

A BIT OF PREHISTORY

As to the design of the square, it should interact with the monument so that the two would compose a unified whole, which would delight the spectator. For the location lends splendor to the statue and is in turn adorned by the statue's artistry.
—Betskoi (1766)

Art serves many masters. On the one hand, it is a highly personal activity, extracting form and meaning from the disarray of individual experience, on the other, it is a social construct, whose goal is communication and interaction. As such, it has various goals and practical applications. It embellishes, advertises, teaches, intensifies religious experience, enhances politics or commerce. Each of these functions has its own characteristics, its own means of expression, and its own definition.

Political art may be defined as art that serves and promotes the interests of a particular polity, be it a state, town, party, or political program. In fulfilling that function, political art is akin to commercial art, for, like advertising, it aims to be quickly perceived and easily assimilated. That is why the most successful specimens of political art are large architectural objects and major outdoor monuments. Elaborate palaces, grandiose government buildings, triumphal arches, pyramids, columns, obelisks, and, of course, statues of individuals or allegories of abstract concepts such as the Statue of Liberty are all examples of political art.[1]

The equestrian monument is political art par excellence. Its visibility is guaranteed by its location on a hill or city square; by its height, the horseman being elevated by a double support, the horse and the plinth proper; and by its size, for it is practically always larger than life and, on occasion, colossal. The riding hero towers above the pedestrian and partakes of the strength and beauty of the mount, which helps project qualities of leadership, valor, endurance, and skill.

Technological progress has been inimical to the horse and, by extension, to the equestrian statue. It can no longer be taken for granted that equitation is in the portrayed hero's past, nor even that he or she knew how to ride. It may well be, in fact, that the equestrian genre in modern heroic and military statuary is on its way to the dustbin of history, even though attempts have been made to extend its limits. An instance of such a transmutation of genres is the monument to Lenin in front of the Finland Station in St. Petersburg, which portrays the Bolshevik leader on an armored car instead of a horse. The fact that Marshal Zhukov, the legendary Russian commander in World War II, was given an equestrian statue at the entrance to Moscow's Red Square bespeaks the strategic, albeit vestigial, role played by the cavalry in the Russian military effort.

There are many reasons for the prominent place occupied by the horse in art. Looking tame and placid when at rest, the horse becomes a thing of beauty and power when observed in motion. Speedy, strong, and graceful, the horse accompanied man at work and play, in peace and war, serving him obediently, patiently, and devotedly. Its importance in man's daily affairs made the horse enter the higher realms of mythology, religion, and art. We need only think of devotional paintings of galloping and rearing horses on the walls of Paleolithic caves in southern France, Spain, and northern Africa; images of sun gods circumnavigating the globe in chariots drawn by four winged horses in Greek mythology or a single horse in Scandinavian lore; the Dioscuri taming wild horses; and white silhouettes of Celtic horses cut into the limestone of mountainsides. Christianity added to that symbolism with images of the Four Horsemen of the Apocalypse, and the heroic figures of Archangel Michael the Warrior and Saint George leaning down from their mounts, one to pierce the deceiving tongue of Satan, the other to slay the bloodthirsty dragon.

From China across the steppes of Central Asia to the shores of the Mediterranean, images of horses with or without riders, single or yoked, loose or harnessed to chariots, have been engraved in stone, sculpted in bronze, or baked onto the sides of pottery. The Parthenon frieze in the British Museum, dated to the mid-fifth century B.C., represents a procession of mounted warriors. Another striking marble relief of a battle scene, portraying warriors on rearing or fallen horses, is the so-called Alexander's Sarcophagus, a Hellenistic monument from about 300 B.C. found in the Phoenician city of Sidon in today's southern Lebanon. The facade of the Basilica of San Marco in Venice is graced by a team of four horses in gilt bronze—part, no doubt, of a quadriga. Fashioned most probably by a Roman artist at the beginning of the Christian era, it was taken to Constantinople by Constantine the Great and brought to Venice in 1204 by the pillaging crusaders.

Ancient painting has not fared as well as stone or metal, but had it survived, it would have certainly brought us images of horsemen. The famous mosaic from the Casa del Fauno in Pompeii, showing Alexander the Great on horseback, charging into a host of Persian soldiers during the battle of Issus, is a second-century B.C. Roman copy of a Greek painting from 320 B.C.

Despite the popularity of the horse in art, the equestrian monument is attested by very few early specimens. This is due less to the inevitable decay of brute matter than to the frailty of an art form whose stability depends on four (actually, more often than not, three) thin legs and whose imperial symbolism and value as scrap metal present a tempting object for destruction and plunder. The earliest surviving equestrian statues are two almost identical marbles from the beginning of the first century A.D., excavated in 1746 in Herculaneum. The portrayed horsemen were identified as a Roman proconsul and his son, members of the noble Balbus family. The Balbus horses are graceful animals with one foreleg raised in a manège-like trot. Their bellies are supported by marble stumps. Somewhat younger than the Balbus statues, but never lost or buried and therefore much more famous, is the bronze statue of Emperor Marcus Aurelius (fig. 2.1), executed during his lifetime (ruled A.D. 161–180). Since Marcus Aurelius was pagan, his statue would not have survived the religious fervor of the early Christians had it not been misidentified as a likeness of Constantine the Great.

In late Rome, Byzantium, and the early medieval West, the equestrian statue was a monarchic prerogative, but all that has survived from that tradition are passing mentions, occasional written descriptions, or copies of uncertain attribution. We know that Julius Caesar had an equestrian monument in the Roman Forum, but not what it looked like. We also know that an equestrian monument of Emperor Justinian stood, before its destruction by the Ottoman Turks, on top of a column in front of the cathedral of St. Sophia in Constantinople. There were two equestrian monuments in Ravenna, thought to represent the Ostrogothic king Theodoric. One was moved by Charlemagne to Aachen and was not seen again. The other was moved in the eleventh century to Pavia in order to bolster that city's self-image. Known popularly as the *Regisole* (the Sun King), it used to stand on a high stone column in front of the cathedral, but was destroyed in 1796 by French troops under Napoleon. According to the traditional view, Charlemagne is the subject of a Romanesque gilt bronze statuette which shows a crowned rider holding the orb in his left hand, as a symbol of royal power.[2]

The decay of imperial authority and the rise of provincial centers and city-states at the end of the Middle Ages were reflected in monumental sculpture. In a return to the Roman republican tradition, equestrian monuments could be dedicated to any distinguished local military or political personage, not just to sovereign rulers. Such monuments grace the tombs of two north Italian noblemen, Cangrande della Scala in Verona (1330) and Barnabó Visconti in Milan (mid-fourteenth century).[3]

Peter the Great was aware of the European tradition of immortalizing sovereigns and military leaders by dedicating to them equestrian monuments. He knew of the *Marcus Aurelius* in Rome and referred to it as the "Capitoline horse."[4] From his art scouts in Italy he must have known of the magnificent Renaissance statues of two Venetian condottieri, the pensive Erasmo di

Fig. 2.1. Anonymous, *Marcus Aurelius.* Bronze, 2nd C. A.D. Piazza del
Campidoglio, Rome. Photograph by Anderson.

Narni, known as *Gattamelata,* in Padua by Donatello (1453) and the proud *Colleoni* in Venice by Verrocchio (1490), celebrated for the rider's contrapposto bearing. It is possible that Peter saw the engravings of the Farnese statues in Piacenza by Francesco Mochi (1620 and 1625). He may have heard of the *Philip IV* in Madrid by Pietro Tacca (1640), if for no other reason than that it was at that time the only bronze equestrian statue with a rearing horse. Its other claim to glory is the story, probably apocryphal, that its stability was assured by the calculations of none other than Galileo.

During his visit to Paris in 1717, Peter must have seen the monuments to Henri IV by Giovanni da Bologna and Pietro Tacca on the Pont Neuf (1614); to Louis XIII by Daniele da Volterra and Pierre Biard (1639) on the place Royale, now place des Vosges; and to Louis XIV by François Girardon on the place Louis le Grand, now place Vendôme (1699). During his visit to Versailles, he may have seen the marble equestrian statue by Bernini intended to represent the young Louis XIV (1675). The king took one look at the fanciful Baroque piece and ordered that it be scrapped. Girardon, however, in his capacity of royal sculptor and chief decorator of the palace and gardens at Versailles, refused to lend a hand to the wrecking of a work by Bernini. He replaced the king's head with one of his own making, changed the rocks on which the horse's belly rested into flames, refashioned a number of minor details, and presented the statue as a likeness of Marcus Curtius, the legendary Roman hero who jumped into a volcanic abyss that opened up in the Forum in order to save the Eternal City. The statue was then set up as a garden sculpture in Versailles and has remained there to this day.[5]

Finally, during a stopover in Berlin, Peter the Great saw the equestrian statue of the Great Elector of Brandenburg, Frederick William, by Andreas Schlüter (1703). The tsar knew the sculptor, who stayed briefly in St. Petersburg in 1713, joining forces with the Swiss architect Domenico Andrea Trezzini in designing Peter's summer residence in the Summer Garden. During his trip to St. Petersburg, Falconet stopped for a few days in Berlin to examine this dynamic and powerful riding composition.

This first-hand exposure to the best specimens of European monarchic statuary explains why Peter the Great conceived of the idea of commissioning a monument to himself in his own lifetime. One can date this with some precision to the year 1715, when, in the wake of the death of King Louis XIV, the tsar assumed, with good reason as it turned out, that during the period of the Regency many Parisian artists would become underemployed and might be willing to accept Russian invitations and commissions. The first major catch in the widespread Russian nets was Carlo Bartolomeo Rastrelli (1675–1744), a Florentine sculptor living in Paris. Job pickings had indeed become slim and Rastrelli was happy to accept an invitation to become the architect and city planner of St. Petersburg and its environs. The official signing of the contract took place in Paris in October 1715, and before the end of the year, Rastrelli was on his way to the new capital of Russia. Just a few months later, however, the Russians handed over the supervision of all urban construction in St. Petersburg to the celebrated French architect Alexandre-Jean-Baptiste Le Blond. Rastrelli refused to work under Le Blond, and, from that time on, devoted himself exclusively to sculpture, or, as it was phrased in his contract, to the making of "lifelike statues out of wax, plaster, marble, and metal."[6]

In 1716 Rastrelli began working on plans for a large bronze equestrian monument of the tsar. His sketch of the statue shows Peter the Great in a Roman toga and a flowing cape, astride a heavy charger. Hovering above the tsar and about to place a laurel wreath on his head is the winged goddess of Victory. On the lower level of the two-tier pedestal there is a bas-relief of the victory at Poltava, and, on the upper tier, figures of chained prisoners of war.[7] The statue is very much in the spirit of Baroque statuary of the period and is reminiscent of the equestrian statue of Louis XIV by François Girardon in Paris. Peter the Great approved Rastrelli's project and had a model of it in lead sent to Paris to the Académie des Belles-Lettres with a request that it be provided with appropriate Latin inscriptions.

In the meantime, however, the tsar had a change of heart and asked Rastrelli to draw sketches of him on a rearing horse. None of them has survived, but one was described in great detail by Henri Lavie, the French consul in St. Petersburg, in his report to the first minister, Abbé (later Cardinal) Dubois. It was a most outlandish production. The tsar is shown astride a rearing horse, set on a large pyramid-like hexagonal pedestal, with six lions lying crushed underneath. The horse is held up by three naked figures, representing the defeated powers of Sweden, Prussia, and Turkey. The two-tiered pedestal is surrounded by several mythological and allegorical groups: Hercules and Glory crown the tsar with a palm wreath, Mars is his sword bearer, Fame presents him with the laurels of victory, Mercury and Peace extend to him an olive branch. On the first step there is a large allegory of the Rhine, "surprised to see itself vanquished" and surrounded by several terrified children. On one side the Arts are at work for the greater glory of the tsar; on the other, allegories of Tranquility, Abundance, and Pleasure project a message that Peter's reign "is the happiest of all time." Three reliefs on the sides of the pedestal show Peter's moments of triumph: the victory at Poltava, the naval engagement at Hangö, and the triumphant entry into Moscow after Poltava. On the remaining three panels various war trophies are displayed. The whole, says the overawed Frenchman, "is the most superb and magnificent monument ever created."[8]

While Rastrelli was working on his designs in St. Petersburg, another possibility was being tried in Rome. In 1718 or 1719 Peter ordered a model of an equestrian statue of himself from the well-known Roman sculptor Camillo Rusconi. A wax model of the Rusconi statue arrived in St. Petersburg in 1720, but it has since disappeared. A badly damaged terracotta model of it is, however, preserved in the Hermitage. One can see that it aimed to show the tsar on a Bernini-like rearing horse, with a defeated warrior serving as the horse's support.[9]

Whether because the Rusconi statue was designed for execution in marble and was inappropriate, therefore, for a large political monument, or because Peter was displeased by the image of his horse trampling a fallen soldier, Rastrelli was asked to produce yet another model. That he did in 1720, replacing the trampled human figure with a snake symbolizing Envy. The new monument was more sparing in its allegorical content than the gushingly extravagant 1717 model. It was surrounded by "statues of the six virtues and below them an allegory of a river, and a globe supported by four Cupids. There were four bas-reliefs on the pedestal and another one encircling the socle."[10] The horse may have been rearing, and if it was, the presence of the snake makes one think of Falconet's later conceit.

A direct confirmation of the existence of Rastrelli's models may be found in three entries in the diary of Friedrich Wilhelm Bergholz.[11] In the entry for April 23, 1723, Bergholz reports that Rastrelli had in his studio models of two bronze statues of the tsar, one on foot and one on horseback; the latter was planned to be forty feet in height. Bergholz noted that the tsar had seen the models and liked them very much.

Peter the Great's death in 1725 put an end to these plans. During the short-lived and troubled reigns of his first four successors, Catherine I (1725–27), Peter II (1727–30), Anne (1730–40), and Ivan VI (1740–41), there was little incentive to commemorate Peter's rule. The situation changed with the accession of Peter's younger daughter Elizabeth (1741–61), who brought stability to the Russian throne. Wishing to put up a bronze statue of her father, Elizabeth remembered Rastrelli's models and decided to select one for casting. Since the last two projects were much too elaborate for a bronze statue, Elizabeth chose a somewhat simplified version of the 1716 design and ordered it cast.

Rastrelli died, however, before the cast could be done, and the task of finishing the monument fell to his assistant, Alessandro Martelli, and the sculptor's son, Bartolomeo Francesco Rastrelli, the celebrated architect of the Winter Palace and the Smolny Monastery. By 1747, however, when the cast was ready, Elizabeth's enthusiasm had waned and funding for the pedestal was not appropriated.[12] The statue was taken to an old barn near the Troitsky Bridge on the Neva and forgotten.

Elizabeth's death on Christmas Day 1761 ushered in the reign of her nephew Peter III, which was as brief as it was unpopular. On June 28, 1762, barely six months after ascending the throne, Peter III was toppled by his German wife, who passed into the history of Russia as Catherine II. Unable to claim consanguinity with the ruling house of the Romanovs, the new empress sought to establish a legitimizing ideological link to that dynasty's most illustrious representative, Peter the Great. Thus "no sooner had Catherine taken up the scepter of the Russian empire, . . . than she conceived of a noble desire to render well-deserved homage to the memory of her illustrious predecessor and to openly display the popular sentiments for the great

Founder with a public monument."[13] At the same time she resolutely refused to allow the erection of a monument to herself, realizing, no doubt, that she could not glorify herself more effectively than by linking her name to that of Peter the Great.[14] Despite her objections, Falconet made a model of a statue for a possible monument, a cast-iron copy of which may be seen in the State Russian Museum in St. Petersburg (fig. 2.2).

The Senate, not up to the manipulative subtlety of the empress's thinking, reminded her that languishing in its shed was Rastrelli's monument to Peter the Great. Why not take it out of mothballs, saving the treasury a great deal of money? Catherine gave the monument a casual look-over and declared it unworthy of "such a great monarch and the capital city of St. Petersburg." Her reasons for condemning Rastrelli's monument were most probably political. Had they been aesthetic, however, one would not be able to deny their justice. Rastrelli's equestrian statue is heavy and lifeless. The tsar, clad in elaborate Roman armor, with a wing-like cape flowing from his shoulders, sits stiffly on a graceless charger. An oversize laurel wreath, with leaves shooting up, gives his head a grotesque aspect. There is no inkling of the monarch's characteristic dynamism and natural simplicity.[15]

What Catherine wanted was an entirely new monument, one that would transcend a single human life and express the grandiose idea of an empire that endures. She wanted a monument that would impress the viewer with the scale of Peter the Great's vision and at the same time bear the stamp of her efforts to further that vision. The monument was to be more than a raw political statement. It had to be a thrilling work of art that would enhance her personal image as a leader in politics and culture. It was an ambitious and difficult program, one that could not be brought to fruition except by a highly accomplished sculptor. It was clear to everyone associated with the project that an artist of such a caliber would have to be brought in from the West.

Russia's inability to produce a sculptor who would be up to Catherine's challenge was not due to a lack of native artistic talent. Pre-Petrine Russia produced splendid icon and fresco painting, anonymous in the earliest period, but associated later with the names of such masters as Theophanes the Greek, Andrei Rublev, and the monk Dionisy.[16] Russian architects designed magnificent stone and wooden churches not only using imported Byzantine models but introducing their own ideas (such as the typically Russian tent-like roofs of wooden churches). The skill of Russian carpenters who built those structures, often with the most primitive tools, astonished foreign visitors. Russia also boasted a fine tradition of miniature painting and ornamental art, used in the illumination of manuscripts and in bookbinding. All these accomplishments, however, were generated by the needs of the Orthodox church, which called for the construction of places of worship, filling them with icons and holy books, and furnishing them with ornate liturgical objects.

Fig. 2.2. Etienne-Maurice Falconet, *Catherine the Great.* An 1804 cast-iron copy of a lost 1768 terracotta model for a monument to Catherine the Great. The State Russian Museum, St. Petersburg. Photograph by Mark Skomorokh.

While Russian architecture and painting benefited from the opportunities provided by the church, sculpture was not so favored. In sharp contrast to Western sensibilities, the Orthodox religious mind considered sculpture in the round too literal and corporeal to represent divinity, which by its very nature had to be immaterial and ineffable. During the Iconoclastic Controversy that shook Byzantium in the eighth and ninth centuries, even painted icons were considered a blasphemous violation of the spirit and letter of the Second Commandment. That the great battle over the use of graven images of "anything that is in heaven above" ended with the defeat of the Iconoclasts was due solely to the argument that two-dimensional images were sufficiently idealized and disembodied to allow the believer to intuit their third dimension, which is the divine essence. Such thinking allowed the Orthodox to think of icons not as products of human hands, but as epiphanies through which heavenly archetypes manifest themselves to man. Three-dimensional representations, however, did not allow such a leap of faith. Hence the Orthodox ban on sculpted sacred images, leading to the virtual absence of sculpture in the round in Byzantine art.

There was an additional consideration that made the Orthodox hierarchy frown upon sculpture in the round. It had to do with pagan practices of venerating idols, a problem that was as acute in biblical times, when the Israelites defended their monotheism against the lures of the Canaanite deities ("thou shalt not bow down thyself to them, nor serve them"), as it was in the newly converted Christian communities, with their vestiges of pagan idolatry. Medieval Rus' was such a community and the chronicle descriptions of the dumping of pagan idols in the Dnieper bespeak the importance accorded to the eradication of idolatry and the belief that sanctioning sculpture, however Christian in content, might open the way to idolatry's return. As a result, during the seven hundred years of Russia's history before Peter, sculpture, except for decorative architectural elements and ornamental carvings in wood and bone, remained a blank spot in Russian art.[17]

That was the reason that Ivan Ivanovich Betskoi, director of the Bureau of Buildings and Gardens and president of the Academy of Fine Arts, told the Senate in his 1762 report on the project for a statue of Catherine the Great that such an enterprise would require help of non-Russian masters: "It may be possible to find local people whose knowledge and art could serve us in a commendable way, but that is not enough for a work of such consequence. One must ask people who have gained greatest fame practicing these skills for their advice, help, ideas, projects, and models. . . . One must personally go to Italy and France, where such skills flourish, and use persuasion and conviction to bring their practitioners to Russia, because without their personal help such a monument cannot be properly executed."[18]

Catherine had an additional reason to welcome a prospect of importing a sculptor from the West. Always eager for closer and more lasting contacts with the best representatives of European culture, she thought that a renowned Western artist could become her liaison to the West, especially if he could be persuaded to stay in Russia for a fairly long time. Not interested in having her own monument, the empress decided to commission an entirely new monument to Peter the Great. In 1764 she communicated that decision to the Senate and asked Betskoi to oversee the execution of the project.

Betskoi sent his "program" for the monument to a number of French sculptors and art connoisseurs, along with his own very definite ideas about it. He stressed Russia's great physical size and extolled Peter's virtues as a sovereign, military commander, and lawgiver. He did not fail to mention that the project owed its existence to Catherine, a faithful follower of Peter's policies.

The emperor, he said, ought to be dressed *à la romaine ou à la grecque,* his hair should be short and natural, his cape should be besprinkled with imperial double-headed eagles, his arms should be about one foot apart and five or six inches thick, and he should hold the baton of a military commander. The horse "should produce the kind of enthusiasm that we feel looking at the horse of Marcus Aurelius," but there should not be any figures of crushed enemies under it because Peter himself would not have liked that. The bas-reliefs on the pedestal should represent the most important victories of the emperor, with the battle of Poltava occupying the central place. On smaller panels Betskoi suggested a representation of various nations inhabiting the immense expanse of Russia. Their identity was supposed to be assured by the addition of celestial constellations and, for those who were weak in astronomy, there would be explanatory labels in Latin or Greek. Among the inscriptions which Betskoi wanted to see, there should be one paying homage to the empress, who "faithfully follows in Peter's footsteps and shares in his glories and labors." The inscription should also recognize her merit in erecting a monument to her great predecessor.

One can imagine the mixture of mirth and horror with which these instructions were received in Paris. In particular, they must have colored Falconet's view of Betskoi in the darkest possible hues and must have filled him with grim forebodings about the nature of their future relations.

As for the location of the future monument, Betskoi asked his protégé and client Karl Leopold Bilistein (alias Bil'stein), an official in the Ministry of Trade and a member of the Imperial Trade Commission, to study the question and report on it.[19] Bilistein's report, dated December 1, 1766, lists five sites which at one point or another were under consideration: (1) the center of Palace Square; (2) the park adjacent to the Admiralty where Nevsky Prospect, Gorokhovaia Street, and Voznesensky Prospect come together; (3) the square between the Winter Palace and the Admiralty; (4) the right bank of the Neva, more or less across the river from the present site of the monument; (5) a large area between the Senate and the Admiralty, near the Isakievsky pontoon bridge on the Neva. The last site was the one that Bilistein considered the most suitable. The empress agreed and the area, enlarged by the lot left vacant after the demolition of the stone church of St. Isaac, was selected as the site for the future monument. Bilistein recommended that it be called Peter the Great Square.[20]

"Square," however, was a notion that this large space had to grow into. Prior to Falconet's arrival, it was an untended lot between the Admiralty and the Senate, crisscrossed by canals, which were eventually filled and transformed into city streets. Its only use was for the manufacture of ship riggings and boat lines for the Admiralty and for storage of building materials for the construction of the first St. Isaac's Cathedral at the crossing of the Vozne-sensky Prospect and Malaia Morskaia. The Admiralty itself was quite different from its elegant Neoclassical reconstruction (1806–23), planned by the architect Adrian Dmitrievich Zakharov (1761–1811). It was a functional but plain-looking building, designed by Ivan Kuzmich Korobov in the 1730s. On the western side of the square there was the modest building of the Senate, dating back to the days of Peter. It would be sixty years before it was replaced by the twin Neoclassical structures of the Senate and the Synod (1829–34). Further south, beyond Isakievskaia Street (later Galernaia), the future site of the manège of the Horse Guards (now Central Exhibition Hall), built in 1804–7 by Giacomo Quarenghi, was a storage space for ship tim-bers.[21] The Admiralty Canal, which was soon to be filled and become Novo-Isakievskaia Street (now Iakubovicha), was still a functioning waterway, spanned by the Lesser Isakievsky Bridge.[22]

The southern perspective of the square was not dominated yet by the grandiose golden dome of the second St. Isaac's, started in 1818 by Auguste de Montferrand and not completed until forty years later. The construction of the first St. Isaac's Cathedral, by Antonio Rinaldi, was at that time about to begin.[23] To the southwest of St. Isaac's, and diagonally from it, was the neoclassical mansion built in the 1760s for Prince L. A. Naryshkin. That was where Denis Diderot lived during his stay in St. Petersburg in 1773–74.[24] What is today Admiralty Garden (former Aleksandrovsky Garden), along the southern side of the Admiralty, was then part of the Admiralty Meadow. An early version of the Winter Palace existed already in its present location, but half a century would pass before the part of the Admiralty Meadow situated to the east of the Nevsky Prospect would become the beautiful Palace Square rimmed by the Winter Palace and the Neoclassical buildings of the General Staff designed by Carlo Rossi. Connecting Senate Square with the Vasilievsky Island and offering a view toward government and academy buildings lining the right bank of the Neva was the Great Isakievsky pontoon bridge built in 1727 and rebuilt in 1732. As the sole bridge across the Greater Neva, it served pedestrian and vehicular traffic between Vasilievsky Island and the Admiralty section of town.[25]

There is a passage in Bilistein's report that deserves special scrutiny, for Falconet selected it for ridicule. Bilistein recommended that the monument be placed "against the flow of the river" on a specially constructed promon-tory near the Great Isakievsky pontoon bridge. From that location, he ar-gued, Peter the Great would be able to survey "with his right eye the Admi-ralty, the left bank of the river, the imperial palaces with all their attendant monuments and palaces," and "the vast empire which he inherited from his fathers"; while "with his left eye" he would see "Vasilievsky Island, the citadel, the twelve colleges, the academies of science and fine arts, the great port filled with vessels," and various other objects and places on the right bank of the Neva, including "Finland, Karelia, Ingria, and other conquered provinces."[26]

This formulation was surely meant figuratively and referred to Peter's right and left sides, much as we speak of the right and left "hands" in describing sights along one's way. One could, however, give it a mercilessly literal reading and poke fun at Bilistein's apparent claim that human eyes are capable of unyoked vision. That is how Falconet, the monument's future sculptor, chose to interpret Bilistein's report when, three years after it was circulated, he fired a sarcastic salvo at Bilistein's ignorance of human physiology and made fun of his ascription of human attributes to inert matter: "I summon all the powers of my imagination . . . to understand how a statue can see ahead, on the right, on the left, behind, far away, and nearby, simultaneously or successively, and all of it without moving its eyes or its head, and I get lost."[27]

One gets the feeling that the object of Falconet's criticism was to score easy points against Betskoi, who was Bilistein's champion and protector. Bilistein may have been guilty of letting his metaphors run away from him, but certainly not of the sins against common sense which Falconet ascribed to him. What escapes the critics of Bilistein's unrestrained imagery, however, is that it presupposed the placement of the monument "*against* the flow of the river*," that is, parallel to the banks of the Neva and facing east. That such was Bilistein's intent is evident from the notes to his report in which he evaluates and rejects the other three possible orientations of the monument. He argues that if Peter were to face in the opposite direction (west), his left side would face his ancient empire and his right side the newly acquired territories, not a politically correct attitude. If he were to face south, he would be turning his back on Vasilievsky Island with its many edifices commissioned by himself, "an inadmissible position." If he were to face north, he would be turned toward Vasilievsky Island, but away from the empire, an attitude which "cannot be recommended."

The Senate, after some deliberation, agreed that the location between the Admiralty and the Senate was most appropriate. The planners, mindful probably of the fact that a leader must lead, disregarded Bilistein's strictures and allowed Peter the Great to turn his back on the old empire and face the river, with the Great Isakievsky pontoon bridge slightly to the right and the Vasilievsky Island straight ahead.[28]

Now the problem was to transform that half-empty space into a formal city square and the park that is adjacent to it today. In March 1769, the Academy of Fine Arts invited "architects, artists, and amateurs" to submit designs for the development of the square, accompanied by "an elucidating and detailed description of the project." The winners of the competition were to be rewarded according to the merit of their projects. The conditions of the competition contained various characteristics of the site and the monument, including the following explications of the monument's symbolism: "The rock, which is not decorated, denotes the difficulties surmounted by

Peter I, while the gallop of the charger symbolizes the pace of his deeds," and—a recurring refrain—the "fatherly hand needs no explanation."[29]

FRIENDSHIP WITH PRINCE D. A. GOLITSYN

His Excellency Prince Golitsyn was so skillful in securing the services of my Falconet . . . that there is almost no merit left for me in this affair. The charm and affability of the prince and the singular lack of mercenary instincts of the artist did it all.
—Diderot (1766)

When in 1764 Catherine decided to commission an entirely new monument to Peter the Great, France was the logical country to which to turn in search of its prospective sculptor. The many Baroque equestrian statues of the French kings, all destined to be destroyed by the zealots of the French Revolution, were still gracing the squares, streets, and bridges of French cities. In 1717, at the time of Peter the Great's visit to Paris, there were three royal monuments there: the *Henry IV* by Giovanni da Bologna, the *Louis XIII* by Daniele da Volterra and Pierre Biard, and the *Louis XIV* by François Girardon. Later a large *Louis XV* by Edme Bouchardon (1763) was erected on the place Louis XV, now place de la Concorde. In other cities, there was a *Louis XIV* by Martin Desjardins in Lyon, and another one by Charles Antoine Coysevox in Rennes. A *Louis XV* by Jean-Baptiste Lemoyne (1741) was in Bordeaux. Two statues of Louis XIV were not executed but models of them were known, one by Pierre Puget for Marseilles and one by Desjardins for Aix-en-Provence. Coysevox did *Fame* and *Mercury*, two large allegorical sculptures today topping the gate of the Tuilleries, while Guillaume Coustou I executed the rearing and riderless *Marly Horses*, which bracket the modern entrance to the Champs Elysées.

By the time Betskoi announced a competition for the monument to Peter the Great, a new generation of French sculptors had arrived on the scene. In 1750, an anonymous French art critic, in all likelihood La Font de Sainte-Yenne, compiled and published a list of living French sculptors favored by the public.[30] In order of their popularity, they were: Edme Bouchardon (1698–1762), Jean-Baptiste Lemoyne (1704–78), Jean-Baptiste Pigalle (1714–85), Lambert-Sigisbert Adam (1700–1759), Michel-Ange Slodtz (1705–64), Jacques-François Saly (1717–76), Etienne-Maurice Falconet, F. Ladatte (1706–87), Nicolas-Sébastien Adam (1705–78), Guillaume Coustou II (1716–77), and Paul-Ambroise Slodtz (1702–58).

Five sculptors entered the competition, of whom two did not make the list of La Font, but both were known in Russia. Augustin Pajou (1730–1809) was celebrated for his sculpted portraits, among them a superb bust of his teacher Jean-Baptiste Lemoyne (1758). He entered the highest bid of six hundred thousand livres, banking presumably on the success in Russia of his bas-relief for the tomb of Betskoi's half-sister, Princess of Hesse-Homburg (1759).[31] The other was Louis-Claude Vassé (1716–72), a pupil of Bouchardon and Pigalle. His Russian connection was Catherine's audience chamber designed in 1765. Vassé's price for the monument was four hundred thousand livres.[32]

Of the three sculptors who were on La Font's list, Saly alone had an equestrian statue to his credit, the *Frederick V* (1753) in Copenhagen. His bid was of 480,000 livres. Next was Guillaume Coustou II, who made the funerary monuments to the dauphin[33] and his wife Marie-Josephe de Saxe in Sens Cathedral (1777), but whose credentials for an equestrian monument were limited to the experience he got while helping his father make the *Marly Horses.* He asked for 450,000 livres. Finally, there was Falconet, who demanded 200,000 livres to be paid out over an eight-year period. His was by far the lowest bid and he emerged as the winner.

Falconet's lack of experience with major outdoor statuary makes one wonder what made Catherine place the monument to Peter the Great in his hands. The *Saint Ambrose* in the church of the Invalides and the statues for the chapel of Virgin Mary in St. Roch's were quite large, to be sure, but they were designed for church interiors. Otherwise, during the nine years preceding his departure for St. Petersburg, Falconet's artistic connection was with the porcelain manufacture of Sèvres, where he made models for Rococo figurines in biscuit and porcelain. These diminutive statuettes, no matter how subtle and elegant, could not inspire confidence in his ability to make a colossal heroic monument of the galloping Russian tsar.

It would be a mistake, however, to assume that Falconet's low bid tipped the scales in his favor. Money was never an issue in Russia when important projects were at stake. The Russians, in fact, were ready to pay him three hundred thousand livres, an offer that Falconet rejected as too high: "On this score we couldn't overcome the stubbornness of the sculptor. It's not our economizing, but his refusal," wrote Diderot.[34] Falconet's advantage lay in his excellent reputation in France and a fair amount of large religious statuary to his credit. Most important, however, Falconet's project, showing the emperor astride a galloping horse scaling a natural rock, must have struck Catherine as the most original and daring.

Considerations of political expedience were also very important. That was how Catherine chose her alliances, advisers, religion, and even her lovers. Falconet's reputation as one of the better French sculptors was, of course, important. But beyond that, the empress was aware of Falconet's connections with the Paris *philosophes* and realized that his appointment would help propagate her image not merely as a patroness of the arts but as a sponsor of the intellectual ferment of the Enlightenment. This was an image which she tried to cultivate by maintaining a friendly correspondence with Voltaire, Madame Geoffrin, and d'Alembert; by buying Diderot's library in order to help him financially, but leaving it with him for the duration of his life; and by offering to publish the *Encyclopédie* in Riga when it ran into political problems in

Paris.[35] She also knew that the appointment of Falconet would give her a more direct and better informed entry into the Paris art market, that it would allow her to come a step closer to emulating Frederick the Great's hosting Voltaire in Potsdam, and that it would show up Louis XV, who habitually neglected Falconet when royal commissions were distributed.

Such were reasons that made Catherine listen sympathetically to Diderot's recommendation of Falconet not only as a fine sculptor but also as a knowledgeable theoretician and historian of art, and his personal friend. When Prince D. A. Golitsyn, Russia's minister plenipotentiary in Paris, seconded Diderot's views, it was all she needed to empower him to draw up and sign the contract.[36]

Prince Golitsyn's active help in the matter of deciding the competition in favor of Falconet marked the beginning of a friendship which made the Russian diplomat one of the most ardent and devoted supporters of the French sculptor. As a man of great erudition and many-sided scholarly interests, Golitsyn appreciated the breadth of Falconet's interests and backed him unswervingly through the highs and lows of the sculptor's career, without ever bowing to the views of his St. Petersburg superiors, including the empress herself. He supervised the organizational problems of moving Falconet and Collot to St. Petersburg, hosted them during his later tenure as Russia's minister to Holland, and assisted Falconet in the publication of his writings. That alone, aside from the intrinsic interest of this important and complex but almost totally unknown figure of the Enlightenment, demands a vignette of Golitsyn's life and professional career.[37]

Prince Dmitry Alekseevich Golitsyn (fig. 1.12) was born on May 15, 1734, most probably on the family estate near Moscow.[38] His father, Aleksei Ivanovich Golitsyn, was killed at the age of thirty-two in the Russo-Turkish war of 1735–39, as an officer in the Moscow Butyrsky Regiment. His mother was Princess Daria Vasilievna Gagarina, reputedly one of the most striking Moscow beauties. After the death of her husband, Princess Golitsyn moved to St. Petersburg and enrolled her son in the Cadet Corps from which he graduated with honors in 1750.[39] Faithful to a family tradition, Golitsyn entered the Ministry of Foreign Affairs to train for a career in foreign service. His first foreign assignment was in the Russian embassy in Paris. He served there at the end of the 1750s in minor positions under several Russian ambassadors, including his cousin Dmitry Mikhailovich Golitsyn. In 1763, after D. M. Golitsyn's transfer to Vienna, D. A. Golitsyn was promoted to the rank of minister plenipotentiary, which at that time was Russia's highest diplomatic post in France.[40]

The chill in official relations between Russia and France limited Golitsyn's diplomatic functions to two weekly rituals, a formal visit to Versailles to pay his respects to Choiseul and a coded report to Count Nikita Panin, Russia's minister of foreign affairs.[41] As a man of broad scholarly interests, he could devote the rest of his time to reading, writing, and seeking direct contacts with French intellectuals, in particular, the group of the *Encyclopédie,* headed by the *philosophes* Denis Diderot in the humanities and Jean Le Rond d'Alembert in the sciences. Diderot described him as "a fine man who had the esteem of other fine people. He lived among men of letters and was loved and respected by them as much as he loved and respected them."[42] Voltaire called himself his friend.[43]

Prince Golitsyn's contacts in the intellectual circles of Paris were invaluable to Catherine, who, despite her absolute power, appreciated the significance of public relations. Through a skillful policy of maintaining contacts with the *philosophes,* she managed to neutralize the hostile attitude of French officialdom and project an image of a supremely enlightened monarch, fully in step with the most progressive ideas of the time. In building up this image, Golitsyn became her adviser and go-between, even though his pro-French sentiments were reflected in his conduct of official business, a fact which did not escape the attention of the empress and Panin.

Totally immersed in French culture, Golitsyn moved among the Paris artists and scientists with the ease of a native and appeared to be more at home in French than in his native Russian. He once complained to Diderot that he was having problems translating his own book on European painting from French into Russian because "Russian had not yet been fashioned and he had to fashion it."[44] Falconet transmitted Diderot's puzzled query about it to Catherine, who explained that "Golitsyn, like most Russian gentlemen, did not know his own language," which in her view, "had no equal in richness."[45]

In September 1767, a quasi-grammatical diplomatic impasse put in jeopardy Golitsyn's happy existence in the most exciting city of Europe, among friends who were at the forefront of European learning. It concerned the form of address used by Louis XV in his letters to Catherine. The empress insisted on the title "Your Imperial Majesty," while the French were not willing to go beyond "Your Majesty." At one point in the negotiations, Choiseul sought improbable succor of the "genius of the French language," which, he claimed, made it impossible to satisfy the demand of the empress.[46] If no compromise could be found, he warned Panin, a break in epistolary relations between the two sovereigns would necessarily follow. But was it worth it, he asked, to shatter that precious link because of a "grammatical difficulty"? The empress, however, herself a skillful user of French, was not persuaded by such a flimsy excuse and refused to back down. She resolved instead to send her communications through a chargé d'affaires, that is, through the lowest diplomatic channel available. To effect that change, Panin informed Choiseul that "Monsieur Khotinsky was being appointed the Russian chargé d'affaires in France and Prince Golitsyn was being recalled."[47] Choiseul confirmed the arrangement and reiterated his earlier point that thenceforth "the two sovereigns would not write to each other any more."[48]

Golitsyn found the prospect of returning to Russia mortifying. He applied for another diplomatic assignment, hoping that it would be close to Paris. His sights were set on The Hague, which had a vacant post of minister plenipotentiary. Suspecting that Panin might be reluctant to grant him his wish, he asked Falconet, then powerfully ensconced in St. Petersburg, to put in a good word for him with the empress. But the empress, angered partly by Golitsyn's pro-French sentiments and partly by rumors of his free-living style, answered Falconet's recommendation with a straightforward refusal: "The prince's wish to remain abroad in order to study and also because he likes it there, doesn't take into account his situation. He should leave Paris. He doesn't have sufficient means to travel. . . . I doubt that our government would be so kind as to spend its money on a subsidy for someone engaged in artistic and scientific pursuits. . . . To sum up, I think that in his homeland he will find plenty of opportunities to employ the talents given to him by Heaven."[49]

His last hope was his distant uncle and diplomatic predecessor in Paris, Prince A. M. Golitsyn, now vice chancellor. He thought that if his uncle supported his plea, his intercession might be able to sway the empress's mind. In the meantime, pleading poor health, he traveled to the waters in Aix-la-Chapelle (Aachen), which was then a popular spa and a fashionable place for the vacationing rich.

It was there that his fortunes turned for the better. At one of the balls, he met the young, beautiful, and intelligent Countess Amalie von Schmettau (1748–1806), a lady-in-waiting at the court of Prussia and daughter of the late Field Marshal Samuel von Schmettau. It was a *coup de foudre.* Within a few days Golitsyn proposed and was accepted. Upon his insistence the wedding took place practically on the spot, on August 16, 1768. He hoped, apparently, that the empress would like the young and vivacious fellow Prussian and would take his engagement as proof of his transformation from a carefree and somewhat dissolute bachelor into a serious family man.

Diderot reports that the prince had "some anxious moments about contracting a marriage without the consent of his family and the empress," but that he thought that "they would sulk for a time and then all would be fine."[50] Just in case, however, Golitsyn appealed for help to the vice chancellor: "The happiness of my days is completely in your hands. Countess Schmettau . . . has captured my heart and I don't desire anything as much as to unite my fate to hers. I have the consent of her mother, but it will mean nothing to me without the consent of our August Empress. I beg you to put me at her feet and get it for me. . . . As soon as she grants it, all my wishes will have been fulfilled."

He added a P.S., however: "How happy I would be if Her Imperial Majesty, in addition to granting me the favor which I am seeking from her, entrusted me with the post in The Hague."[51]

As it turned out, Golitsyn was quite right in expecting that his marriage would improve his image in the eyes of the empress. She gave her consent to the union and invited the young couple to come to St. Petersburg so that she could meet the princess personally. The visit was to be part of the honeymoon trip.

The newlyweds departed in the beginning of 1769 and stopped in Vienna, Prague, Dresden, and Berlin before arriving in St. Petersburg in late summer. By then the princess was visibly pregnant. If that was Golitsyn's ploy designed to strengthen his credentials as a family man, it worked as planned. The empress gave the couple her blessing and rewarded Golitsyn with the post in Holland. His annual salary was set at eight thousand rubles, more than enough for a comfortable, even stylish, life.[52] Diderot exclaimed: "Prince Golitsyn has just received the embassy in The Hague, the best of them all and the least troublesome. He can now be rich and lazy forever."[53]

On the way to Holland, the couple stopped for some time in Berlin, where on December 7 the princess gave birth to a daughter, Marianne. One year later a son, Dmitry, was born in The Hague.[54] Everything seemed to point to a happy marriage. Golitsyn's official duties in the embassy were light. The couple had time to entertain, remain in touch with the *encyclopédistes* in Paris, receive visitors from Russia, and make friends locally, in particular with the physician and medical researcher Petrus Camper and the philosopher Frans Hemsterhuis. Grimm came to visit, Diderot stopped in on his way to and from Russia, and Falconet lived in their house for two years after returning from St. Petersburg, to be joined there by Collot and her baby daughter Marie-Lucie. Above all, the Golitsyns had time to read and write, he on natural history, she on ethics and pedagogy.

But the marriage was not a happy one. The princess had streaks of odd behavior, which shocked the observant Diderot. "I'm afraid that Princess Golitsyn is not altogether there," he wrote, upon receiving a letter that she had purportedly written almost immediately after the wedding.[55] And after their first meeting, when he stayed with the Golitsyns on his way to Russia, he pronounced her "too sensitive for her own good."[56]

Diderot's forebodings turned out to be correct. The marital bonds began to come apart soon after he visited them on the return leg of his trip to Russia. Moved by a spirit of rebellion against her Catholic convent education and influenced by the freethinking ways of her husband, Amalie was initially indifferent toward religion. But the influence of Hemsterhuis, who became the house tutor and her lover, made her seek satisfaction in religion, meditation, and a fairly indiscriminate sex life. She moved out of the Golitsyn house in The Hague to a peasant cottage in the countryside and eventually settled with Hemsterhuis in Münster. There was no official divorce but for all practical purposes the marriage was dissolved.

That was a time of unusually intense diplomatic activity throughout Europe, brought about by the naval blockade of American ports declared unilaterally by Britain in its attempt to quell the rebellion in its American possessions. The British challenge pushed France to armed protection of its sea lanes in the West Indies, and eventually to an all-out war at sea, threatening the safety of normal trading activity in the European waters.

Most incommoded by the disruption were countries lying along the North Sea and the Baltic, such as Holland, Denmark, and Sweden, whose large merchant fleets, though flying a neutral flag, were becoming fair game for the British navy. Russia and France were also vulnerable, the former because its exports depended on free access of foreign merchant shipping to its ports, the latter because of its reliance on imports for the conduct of the war at sea. It was, therefore, to the benefit of all these countries to adopt a common policy that would force Britain to respect the right of the neutral countries to engage in free maritime trade. The principles of such a policy, championed most actively by Golitsyn, were first announced by Russia. They called for unfettered navigation of neutral vessels along the coasts of the nations at war and for their protection by force of arms. The Russian plan has come to be known as the policy of armed neutrality.[57]

Golitsyn's attempts to secure the participation of Holland in the League of Armed Neutrality were successful, but they earned him a reputation for having a pro-French bias. Sir Joseph Yorke, his British counterpart in The Hague, did not conceal his displeasure. He called him "all French, small and polite," and, referring to Golitsyn's interest in electricity, confessed that the two lacked a common subject of conversation: "I have no apparatus for electricity, nor any ambition to have my name enrolled as a natural philosopher."[58]

That Golitsyn had strong pro-French sympathies is unquestionable, but it is also true that he stood up for any cause which he considered just. Hence his contacts with the representatives of the United States of America before Russia's official recognition of the newly independent state. Among them were such luminaries as Benjamin Franklin, the American ambassador in Paris, and George Washington's future successor John Adams, when that diplomat came to The Hague to negotiate a peace treaty with Britain.

Such contacts constituted a breach of diplomatic protocol and brought upon Golitsyn official displeasure. Holland's recognition of the United States in 1782 prompted Count Osterman, A. M. Golitsyn's successor as vice chancellor of Russia, to instruct D. A. Golitsyn to "refrain from receiving visits from, or making visits to, either Mr. Adams or any other person accredited from the colonies which are breaking away from Great Britain."[59] Despite the warning Golitsyn used diplomatic pouch privileges to help John Adams transmit a portrait of George Washington to Francis Dana, the unofficial American representative in St. Petersburg. The indignant Catherine had the portrait returned to The Hague and issued a "very strong reprimand" to her independently minded diplomat.[60] A short time later Golitsyn was relieved of his duties in The Hague and was offered a much lesser position in the Russian legation in Turin. He preferred, however, to resign from foreign service and stay in The Hague as a private citizen.

Left to his own devices, Golitsyn devoted himself fully to the study of social and natural sciences. In philosophy, he edited and published the last work of Helvétius, dedicating it (over her objections) to Catherine.[61] In economics, Golitsyn was a follower of François Quesnay and his school of Physiocrats, who preached that natural resources, especially tillable lands, were the most reliable source of a country's national wealth. The Physiocrats met periodically to discuss applications of their theories in agriculture. Golitsyn participated in these meetings and, under their influence, conceived of a notion to increase the productivity of Russian agriculture through the emancipation of the serfs, an idea that was a hundred years ahead of its time.[62] Golitsyn's main publication in economics was *De l'esprit des économistes* (1796), a large treatise on the need to adopt Physiocratic teachings in their original Quesnayan form in order to stave off the danger of the spread of the French Revolution.

It was in the sciences, however, that Golitsyn worked most and hardest.[63] He built his own laboratory in The Hague, collected and studied minerals, and experimented with electricity. His publications demonstrate the range of his interests in the sciences. His naturalist's passions are reflected in the *Description physique de la Tauride, relativement aux trois régnes de la nature* (1788); the *Traité ou description abrégée et méthodique des minéraux* (1792); and the *Défence de M. de Buffon contre les attaques injustes et indécentes de MM. Deluc et Sage* (1793), in which Golitsyn defended Buffon's speculations on the possible solar origin of the Earth as a result of a cosmic collision. In 1799 Golitsyn was elected president of the Jena Mineralogical Society. His dictionary of mineralogy, hailed as one of the most important works in the taxonomy of minerals, came out in Brunswick (Braunschweig) in 1801, shortly before his death.

Golitsyn's research in the area of electricity is described in the *Lettre sur quelques objets d'électricité* (1778), a report addressed to the Academy of Sciences in St. Petersburg. One year earlier, Golitsyn wrote to Benjamin Franklin asking for comments on his views on the interaction of the positive and negative electrical fields.[64]

Golitsyn's interest in the fine arts was awakened and refined through his contacts with Diderot and Falconet and kept alive by his standing order from Catherine to buy paintings for her collections. Diderot watched the development of Golitsyn's connoisseurship and wrote about it to Falconet in connection with a new consignment of art acquired by Golitsyn: "The prince . . . has made incredible progress in his knowledge of fine arts. You yourself would be astounded by the way he sees, feels, and judges."[65] Equally impressed was E. A. H. Lehndorff, the chronicler of the Prussian court, who marveled at Golitsyn's knowledge of painting during the couple's honeymoon stopover in Berlin: "I frequently see Prince Golitsyn, who gives the impression of a very well educated man, especially in fine arts. In . . . a picture gallery he immediately recognizes each painter and talks about him as if he were reading from a book."[66]

Golitsyn's correspondence, and his exchange of publications and results of experiments with other scholars, made him one of Russia's most important links to the scientific and artistic community of Europe during the last third of the eighteenth century. He was elected member of the Scientific Society of Holland (1777); the academies of sciences of Brussels (1778), St. Petersburg

(1778), Stockholm (1788), and Berlin (1793); the London Royal Society (1798); the Free Economic Society of St. Petersburg (1798); and the Mineralogical Society of Jena (1799). In 1795 he was elected member of the oldest German scientific association, the Academy of Natural History, the Leopoldina in Halle.

In 1799 Golitsyn moved from The Hague to Brunswick for treatment of tuberculosis. He died there in 1803. His library and a rich collection of minerals were given to the Mineralogical Society of Jena. After the closing of the society at the end of the nineteenth century, the collection was transferred to the university, where it gradually lost its identity. His personal papers remained in Brunswick, but perished in World War II.[67] Also destroyed was the church of St. Nicholas, along with the churchyard where Golitsyn was buried.[68]

Various scientific publications carried notices of Golitsyn's death, praising his scholarly achievements. None, however, could approach the warmth of Diderot's earlier tributes to Golitsyn's personal qualities: "The prince is informality itself. Nobody has ever shown less hauteur about his birth and estate. His belief in equality of conditions is instinctive, and that is much more valuable than believing in it after reflection. He has never claimed any title but the most important one, that of a human being. . . . He does not know the difference between a castle and a peasant's hut, except by their facades. His habits are as simple as his clothes. I have never heard him say anything that was wicked in thought or feeling."[69] "[He] is one of the loveliest souls that heaven has ever made."[70]

TO RUSSIA WITH LOVE

What good is it to tell myself that he'll make a great thing, that he'll come back covered with glory! My heart aches. Adieu, Falconet, adieu, my friend.
—Diderot (1766)

Before leaving, Falconet had to attend to several matters. First of all, he had to apply for a leave of absence from his post as professor of sculpture at the Académie. On July 16, 1766, he wrote the marquis de Marigny asking his permission to accept the invitation of the empress of Russia, an opportunity "which undoubtedly would not be repeated in a lifetime."[71] On August 21 Falconet made an inventory of his books and possessions that would be left behind in his house on the rue d'Anjou.[72] A few days later Marigny transmitted to Falconet the king's consent and, referring to Saly's monument to King Frederick V in Copenhagen, expressed pleasure that another foreign nation showed confidence in a French artist.[73] That cleared the way for the signing of the contract, which took place on August 27, causing Golitsyn to exult excitedly: "The matter of Monsieur Falconet, the sculptor, has been concluded and the contract that I signed with him is enclosed herewith. I now ask you . . . to let me know if Her Imperial Majesty is satisfied with its terms. . . . Falconet is so noble and so unselfish that, though I offered him three hundred thousand livres as his honorarium, he refused to accept more than two hundred thousand. And the next least expensive competitor demanded four hundred thousand. That is the kind of man that I have the privilege of sending to our homeland."[74]

There was also the matter of Falconet's outstanding artistic commitments. On August 25 the four large statues for the church of St. Roch were delivered, but there were still four unfinished statues in Falconet's atelier: *Saint Ambrose,* the *Magnificence of the Princes* (also known as the *Sovereignty of the Princes*), the *Glory of the Princes,* and *Winter.*

Saint Ambrose of Milan was part of a large project initiated by the Ministry of War as custodian of the military hospital of the Invalides. The project envisaged fourteen larger-than-life marble statues to be placed around the upper gallery inside the dome of the church of the Invalides. The statues of various saints were commissioned from the best-known artists, offering a representative show of French sculpture of the eighteenth century, including works by such artists as Lemoyne, Pigalle, L.-S. Adam, Caffiéri, Allegrain, and Houdon.[75] A plaster model of *Saint Ambrose* was shown at the Salon of 1765, but the marble was only half-finished by the time Falconet left Paris. The statue was to be completed by Lemoyne, but it was not till 1769 that it was ready to be placed in its niche in the church. Diderot was ecstatic: "It's very beautiful. You yourself will be astonished by its power, should you see it again."[76]

The allegories called the *Magnificence of the Princes* and the *Glory of the Princes* were ordered in 1761 by Duke Charles Eugene of Württemberg for his castle in Stuttgart. After a series of misunderstandings concerning the availability and price of the marble and the terms of the contract with the duke, Falconet was in no hurry to complete the commission. With the date of his departure for Russia fast approaching, he thought that it might be wiser to offer the statues and the contract to Catherine. With the assistance of Prince Golitsyn and Diderot, the negotiations were promptly concluded and the unfinished statues were boxed for the trip to St. Petersburg. Although the statues are not to be found in any Russian collection, it is virtually certain that they arrived safely in Russia and were exhibited in the Hermitage. It is also highly probable that a marble statue in the Musée Jacquemart-André in Paris, known as the *Glory of Catherine the Great,* representing a young woman holding a medallion with the empress's profile (fig. 2.3), is a version of the *Glory of the Princes* as it appeared after Falconet finished it in St. Petersburg.[77]

The last major sculpture undertaken by Falconet before his trip to Russia was *Winter,* an allegorical figure ordered in 1763 by the marquise de Pompadour for her château of Bellevue (fig. 2.4). A terracotta model was exhibited at the Salon of 1765, eliciting enthusiastic comments from Diderot. He called

Fig. 2.3. Etienne-Maurice Falconet, *The Glory of Catherine the Great.* Marble.
A remake of *The Glory of the Princes,* executed in St. Petersburg in 1767.
Musée Jacquemart-André, Paris.

Fig. 2.4. Etienne-Maurice Falconet, *Winter*. Marble, 1771. The State Hermitage Museum, St. Petersburg.

it "a masterpiece of characterization, posture, and drapery."[78] Work in stone, however, ran into snags. One year was lost because an appropriate block of marble could not be found. Then, in the spring of 1764 Madame de Pompadour died and work on the statue stopped. The matter was brought to the attention of the marquis de Marigny, who suggested that the project should be taken over by the crown and that the statue should be placed in the botanical garden of the Petit Trianon in Versailles. That displeased Falconet, who wanted to give the statue greater prominence and easier access. Negotiations dragged on and the matter was still unresolved when Falconet was invited to Russia. This created a quandary, for Falconet claimed that work on the marble had "barely begun," even though he had received an advance of three thousand livres, as well as a block of marble from the royal store-house.[79] The problem was resolved by Prince Golitsyn, who, acting on behalf of the empress, bought the "future" of the statue for thirteen thousand liv-res.[80] A marble block with an outline of *Winter* joined the rest of Falconet's luggage, but work on it had to wait its turn until after the large model of the monument to Peter the Great was completed. Thus it was not till 1771 that the sculpture was delivered to Catherine.

In Baroque symbolic imagery, the seasons had their traditional representa-tions. Spring was a girl, summer a mature woman, fall a youth, and winter an old woman, bent and wrapped up. Falconet broke with that tradition by showing winter as a beautiful young woman, barefoot and scarcely protected from the cold by a flowing garment that leaves her right shoulder and right breast uncovered. With half-closed eyes and a light smile frozen on her lips, she seems to be in a peaceful trance, a state of dormancy that allows nature to survive the bitterness of the season. The woman is surrounded by wintry symbols—drooping flowers, which she tries to protect with a flap of her garment, and an earthen jar broken by frozen water. Winter signs of the Zodiac—Capricorn, Aquarius, and Pisces—are carved on the sides of the cube on which the woman is sitting. The cube itself could be associated with a chunk of ice cut out from a frozen lake or river. The statue is the most Neoclassical of all of Falconet's oeuvre and is the crowning glory of his French period.

Marigny's approval of Falconet's employment in Russia was relayed to the Russian minister of foreign affairs Count Nikita I. Panin and to Marig-ny's Russian counterpart Betskoi. Now that the choice had been made largely on the strength of Diderot's recommendation to Catherine, Betskoi consid-ered it his duty to inform Diderot of the preparations which were being made in St. Petersburg to receive Falconet. He assured Diderot that Falconet would be provided with comfortable working conditions and the needed materials and workers, expressed readiness to help with the transportation of Falconet's sculptures and models, promised to send someone to meet Fal-conet at the border and, in a delicately phrased reference to Collot, "those whom he will consider appropriate to bring along." He even invited Falconet to stay in his house "so that he would not feel alone in a country which he does not know."[81]

Having played so successfully the role of Falconet's impressario, Diderot felt that he had acquired proprietary rights to the sculptor and could repre-sent him in his dealings with Betskoi, in the capacity of business agent, artis-tic consultant, and attorney, all rolled into one. Thus, at the end of August 1766 Diderot sent Betskoi a letter, combining features of a promotional flier and a legal document, in which he referred to the sculptor not just as "mon ami," but as "mon Falconet, mon statuaire, mon artiste," and so forth.[82]

In this letter, Diderot took it upon himself to review the conditions of the contract and declared self-assuredly that he "saw nothing in it that could not be approved by Her Imperial Majesty." He dealt with the remuneration of Falconet and Collot, their quarters, their helpers, and their horses. He told Betskoi that since the Russian commission would not improve Falconet's financial situation, it was incumbent upon Betskoi to find other ways to gratify him. "Shower honors on my Falconet, make him happy, see to it that he enjoys his rest, that he is not being bothered, that there are no obstacles which might slow down his work!" He wanted Betskoi to shield the sculptor from professional jealousy and protect him from critics ("the buzzing and stinging of the wasps"). He told Betskoi that he had given Falconet certain assurances and that Betskoi now had to honor them. He painted the rosiest of pictures of Falconet's life in Paris, describing the sculptor's comfortable home, his excellent financial and social position, and all the other benefits which he was willing to sacrifice in order to accept the Russian commission.

Having thus prepared the ground for a favorable reception of Falconet in Russia, Diderot turned to the monument itself, and, sensing that Betskoi might object to the severity of its design, launched a preemptive strike:

> As soon as he arrives, my sculptor will present to you his model. He is a man who thinks and feels with grandeur. It seems to me that his concept is new, beautiful, and original. He is very much attached to it and has, I think, every reason to feel that way. He has great talent and at the same time is modest and not presumptuous. I am certain, however, that he would prefer to return to France despite the fatigue of a long and arduous journey than to be forced to make something ordinary and banal. The monument will be simple, but it will accord perfectly with the character of the hero. One could, of course, make it richer, but you know better than I do that overabundance is almost always a mortal enemy of the sublime. Our artists visited [Falconet's] atelier. They all congratulated him for having overcome the difficulties that faced him. I have never before seen a new idea so universally applauded by those in the arts and in society, by amateurs and connoisseurs alike.[83]

After this long list of demands, which might be considered bold even if Diderot had been Falconet's official representative, he warned Betskoi: "It is on these conditions that I am sending him to you." Then, as if to soften the negative impression that his letter was bound to create, Diderot added: "When my Falconet will be at the side of General Betskoi, he will need no one else. May he be left alone and he will do great things."[84]

As could be expected, Diderot's undiplomatically expressed wishes were not heeded by either party. Falconet was not eager to be at Betskoi's side, nor was Betskoi willing to leave Falconet alone. Disagreements, in fact, developed almost immediately after the sculptor arrived and lasted to the moment of his departure.

Diderot's letter was not at the root of the conflict between the high-strung and egocentric artist and the jealous and pedantic administrator, but it would not be far-fetched to assume that its tone heralded the troubles lying ahead. The French writer not only presumed to know what kind of sculpture would best express the essence of the hallowed ruler of Russia, but set the conditions for Falconet's stay, as if he was negotiating the *tournée* of a pampered prima donna. He also engaged in a none too subtle chiding of Betskoi's partiality to allegory when he told him, undoubtedly tongue-in-cheek: "you know better than I do that overabundance is almost always a mortal enemy of the sublime."

Whatever its intent, Diderot's letter was not an auspicious beginning to a relationship which placed two entirely different mind-sets in a confined arena. In one corner were two French freethinkers for whom Reason was the highest authority; in the other, a Russian conservative who venerated Tradition and Order. A tough fight was in the offing. The problem was that the august referee had other things on her mind and could not give the fight her undivided attention.

Betskoi's animus against the meddlesome *philosophe,* though carefully concealed from the empress, was generally known. When D. A. Golitsyn wished to obtain compensation for Diderot for his role in the acquisition of the art collection from the estate of Louis-Antoine Crozat (Baron de Thiers) for 460,000 livres, he thought it necessary to warn A. M. Golitsyn that Betskoi was not only "on bad terms with Falconet, but also bore a grudge against Diderot." In vain did he try to convince the vice chancellor, and through him Betskoi, that Diderot and Falconet could not be held accountable for each other's deeds and that "it would be an injustice to mix one in the faults of the other." Betskoi refused to give Diderot credit for the low price of the Crozat collection, insisting that the evaluation was made by François Tronchin, a Geneva lawyer, art connoisseur, and friend of Voltaire and Diderot.[85] Betskoi was technically correct in making that claim, but he conveniently forgot that it was Diderot who persuaded Tronchin to evaluate the paintings and the heirs of Crozat to accept Tronchin's evaluation.

One cannot fault Falconet for rejecting out of hand the role assigned to him by Betskoi, that of a mere artisan expected to fall into step with the Russian bureaucrat's habitually servile retinue. Having accepted Catherine's invitation on his own terms, he felt that he had the right to reject interference and directives from anybody, let alone a transmitter of orders, a fairly long way down in the chain of authority. Back in Paris he led the sedentary and comfortable life of a respected, if not inordinately successful, artist. He lived in a city he loved, enjoying a steady income from Sèvres, a pension from the king, occasional commissions from local nobility and clergy, his own new home with a garden on the rue d'Anjou, a young woman friend in Marie-Anne Collot, a large circle of friends from among the intellectual elite of the time, and all the books he needed to satisfy his scholarly needs. He was not ready to yield this independence to Betskoi's "table of ranks."

Falconet could foresee the problems lying ahead and hesitated whether to

accept the Russian commission. Diderot had to use all his powers of persuasion to convince him to go: "Remember the state of your soul when you
had to renounce all that surrounded you, those attacks of melancholy to
which you were subject from time to time and which I, with my constant
encouragement, found so hard to dissipate."[86] On the eve of Falconet's departure, however, when the sculptor's luggage was on its way to St. Petersburg and there was no danger that the sculptor would change his mind,
Diderot allowed himself the luxury of painting an idyllic picture of Falconet's
life in Paris: "You are leaving your country, your peaceful hearth, the house
which you built, the garden which you cultivated with your own hands. You
will no longer pick and offer to your friends the fruit of the trees which owe
their rich harvest to you. You will no longer make bouquets of the flowers
which you watered. You are renouncing meditation, study, and all the pleasures of retirement. You are leaving those who are dear to you. You are
sacrificing your rest and forgetting your health."[87]

What was it then that made Falconet exchange all these comforts for the
uncertainties of residence in a country which was leagues away from his home
and habitual experience? What gave him the courage to seek and accept so
difficult a task in totally unfamiliar circumstances? He had never before
sculpted a horse, never cast a bronze statue, never even traveled abroad. He
freely admitted to a dislike of portraiture. He knew as much about Russia
and about Peter the Great as the reading of Voltaire's biography of the tsar
could provide. In an age when allegory in art was de rigueur, his artistic credo
was to make the work of art speak for itself. Betskoi's letter about the monument should have sufficed to make him realize that the Russians might find
his design minimalistic. And yet, he was prepared to accept the challenge.
Why? Was it money? Falconet denied it and Diderot concurred. As he said
in his letter to Betskoi, "it is not a thirst for gold nor a desire for greater
fortune that make him take this decision. He despises gold. He is a wise
man, and his wisdom is his fortune."[88]

It is true that some actions of Falconet toward the end of his stay in Russia
may have put that claim in question. The fact remains, however, that the
remuneration he asked for was one-third lower than what the Russians were
willing to offer and at least one-half less than what other artists demanded.
As he explained to Diderot, if he could not be happy with twenty-five thousand livres a year, he would never be happy.[89] One must therefore accept
his and Diderot's claim that it was not money that made him take on the
Russian commission, and seek his real motives elsewhere.

Falconet was well aware of the trivial nature of his work in Sèvres and
was not happy with his larger works either: "My work in the church of St.
Roch was a trifle in comparison with the statue of Peter the Great," he wrote
to Catherine.[90] He was getting on in years, and now that an opportunity
was presenting itself to fulfill what he knew was his true potential, he was
desperate to seize it. As Diderot told Betskoi on the eve of Falconet's depar-

ture from Paris: "What motivates him is his talent and a desire to immortalize himself through something great and beautiful."[91]

One might think that Falconet's stubborn disclaimers of interest in the views of posterity would give a lie to such an assumption. Yet a lack of concern for posthumous acclaim does not rule out an ambition to be recognized by the living and to prove to himself that he could make an equestrian monument the like of which the world had not seen. To satisfy that desire he was willing to endure the hardships and heartaches of twelve years of exile, far from his Parisian haunts, his friends, and his books. His goal achieved, he never again felt the itch to lift his mallet and chisel.

Réau may have a point in speculating that by submitting the lowest bid, Falconet wanted to erase the memory of his partisan fight against the candidacy of Pigalle for the completion of the monument to Louis XV in Paris, after its sculptor Edme Bouchardon had died.[92] It was generally thought at that time that Falconet's support of Vassé was motivated by his personal animus against Pigalle, who was not only considered the better sculptor, but was also chosen by Bouchardon himself. Falconet defended his stand by pointing out that Vassé's price tag was far lower than that of Pigalle. Now, he had a chance to show that he was willing to do as he had preached. Yet, knowing Falconet's nature, one suspects that his ultimate motivation was not a wish to cleanse his conscience, but a secret hankering for recognition.

As for Catherine, whatever her motives for selecting Falconet, her decision proved once again her uncanny ability to find the winning combination. As the most distinguished Western artist to come to Russia for a protracted stay, Falconet helped build up Russia's image as an active participant in the cultural life of Western Europe. At the same time Russia got its most consequential work of visual art and a symbol of its historical and political identity, St. Petersburg was graced with an icon whose artistic and political refractions have guaranteed its living presence on the city's cultural landscape, and, almost as a footnote, the world gained its most dramatic equestrian monument.

On August 25, 1766, the luggage of Falconet and Collot was put aboard the packet boat *L'Aventurier* sailing from Rouen directly to St. Petersburg. Of the twenty-five cases and one smaller package, only one case contained private belongings. In the rest there were the three marble sculptures bought by the empress, plaster models of various sculptures by Falconet intended as gifts for the empress and the Academy of Fine Arts in St. Petersburg, tools, books, engravings, and a bust of Prince Golitsyn by Collot.

When in mid-September Falconet and Collot were boarding the stagecoach, a group of friends gathered at the city gate to bid them goodbye. Diderot and Collot were the most disconsolate. Collot was crying and Diderot, fearing that he would not be able to contain his emotions, had a note prepared beforehand, which he handed to the sculptor. It ended with the words: "Farewell, my friend! Be well and bon voyage! Remind yourself and think sometimes of the man who takes the most sincere and profound interest in your health, rest, honors, and success, whose heart has ached ever since it knew that it would lose you, and who sees the moment of our separation as the most painful in his life."[93]

The trip from Paris to St. Petersburg could have been made in four weeks, but Falconet and Collot were not in a hurry and spent six weeks on the road. They followed the habitual northern stagecoach route, going through Metz, Frankfurt, and Weimar. At the end of September they stopped in Berlin for a few days, for Falconet wanted to have a good look at Andreas Schlüter's equestrian statue of Frederick William, the Great Elector of Brandenburg. From there they continued via Königsberg and Memel, crossing the border of the Russian empire in Riga. The East Prussian leg of the trip was by far the most exhausting. Madame de Baurans, who one year later accompanied her lover Mercier de la Rivière and his wife on their trip to St. Petersburg, left a vivid description of the state of the roads there:

> Monsieur de la Rivière suffered as much as one can suffer in the sands of Westphalia, where we did eleven leagues in eighteen hours. Those of Pomerania are still worse. But all of that is nothing compared with the dreadful road we were on from Danzig to Courland. For sixty miles, one and sometimes two wheels of our coach were in the sea. We had twelve horses that pulled us with much difficulty and very frequently we would get stuck in the sand with nothing in view but the sea on one side and mountains of sand all the way to the horizon on the other. We were forever scared that our coach might break down because then we would have to stay in that place, there being no hut, not even a tree for ten or more miles. Those ten miles took us twenty-five hours. That horrible road is half in Prussia and half in Poland. Except for Königsberg and Mittau there is no inn, so the travelers bring along their beds and all necessary provisions.[94]

From Mittau it was only a few hours' ride to Riga, a seaport which the Russians had recently won from Sweden and the favorite gateway for overland travelers to St. Petersburg. A special dispensation allowed Falconet and Collot to cross the border without a customs inspection. Waiting for them on the Russian side was Captain Marin Carburi, Betskoi's aide-de-camp. He accompanied them the rest of the way via Revel (Dorpat) and Narva to St. Petersburg.[95] On October 25, 1766, the two travel-weary French sculptors descended from their coach at the Narva gate (*Narvskaia zastava*) in the southwestern section of St. Petersburg.[96]

Since their permanent lodging was not yet ready for occupancy, Falconet and Collot were offered a choice between staying in the house of General Betskoi or in rented quarters. They chose the latter and took up temporary residence in a house belonging to Jean Michel, a good friend of Betskoi and owner of a fashionable ladies' apparel store on Nevsky Prospect, the main thoroughfare of the Russian capital.[97] The house was on a lot on Admiralty Meadow occupied today by the building at 8 Malaia Morskaia Street. It was there that Falconet and Collot had their first atelier, where Falconet began working on the small plaster model of the monument, Collot worked on her first bust of the empress, and the two journeymen sculptors who came with Falconet transferred the *Winter* and the *Glory of Catherine II* (as remade from the *Glory of the Princes*) from plaster to marble.[98] In the courtyard of the house there was a specially made hillock whose slope was identical to that projected for the pedestal. There, in front of Falconet making hundreds of sketches, the best riders of the imperial stables modeled the stance of a galloping horse that is abruptly reined in and made to rear before coming to a full stop.[99]

According to the contract, Falconet's room and board were provided at the expense of the crown. That arrangement, by a special instruction of the empress, included "Mademoiselle Collot who came with [Falconet] from France and who is also knowledgeable in the art of sculpture."[100] The level of comfort provided for the couple may be seen from a letter that Michel sent General Betskoi in January 1767. The French merchant sought a raise in rent, explaining that the agreement between him and the Bureau of Buildings underestimated the cost of his lodgers' upkeep. "Your Excellency will see from the detailed bill which is attached . . . that I cannot provide for M. Falconet below 288.37 rubles per month. Since it is neither my estate nor occupation to take care of lodgers, in agreeing to this arrangement I was moved solely by the wishes of Her Imperial Majesty who wants M. Falconet to be well provided for. You will agree, Monsieur, that having a bachelor household, I am obliged to go to the same expense for one person as an innkeeper would for twenty. Moreover, M. Falconet wishes to take his meals separately and at times which are convenient for him, but not for me."[101]

An accounting, "For the monthly upkeep of M. Falconet," was attached to support Michel's claim:

Rent for a well furnished apartment with beds, glassware, chairs, tables, sideboards, wardrobes, heat, etc.	90.00
Meals, usually for three persons, morning and evening, silverware, linen and tableware, kitchenware, salary and food for one cook @ 3.50 per day	106.45
One bottle of Burgundy a day @ 1.30	
One bottle of Bordeaux a day @ .30	48.67
Candles	3.25
A comfortable two-horse carriage, upkeep and livery of a coachman	40.00[102]
	288.37

At the same time work was proceeding on a permanent lodging for Falconet and Collot on the grounds of the wooden Winter Palace, which Francesco Bartolomeo Rastrelli (son of the sculptor Carlo Bartolomeo Rastrelli), built in 1755 as a provisional residence for Empress Elizabeth. It was situated in the triangle bounded by Nevsky Prospect in the east, Kirpichny Alley in the west, and the embankment of the Moika in the south, and was built over Bol'shaia Morskaia (then known as Bol'shaia Gostinaia), turning it into a dead-end street. The stunted northern tip of the triangle reached a short section of Malaia Morskaia Street, then known as Bol'shaia Lugovaia. (For a plan of the Admiralty section of St. Petersburg in 1766, see below, pp. 312–15).

The provisional Winter Palace was used a mere seven years, until 1762, when Rastrelli's new Winter Palace on the embankment of the Neva was ready for occupancy.[103] At that time, Catherine, recently installed as the empress of Russia, declared the large wooden structure a fire hazard and had it taken down. While it is true that the site had a history of fires, the biggest in 1736 when the old Merchants' Hall burned down, it is much more likely that the real reason for Catherine's decision was a desire to erase the hateful memories of the years she had spent there in a loveless marriage to the heir to the throne, the future Peter III.

When Falconet and Collot arrived in St. Petersburg, the only remnants of the provisional palace were its two stone structures, the kitchen, toward the apex of the triangle, and the theater, toward its base. According to Jakob Stählin (1709–85), president of the art section of the Academy of Sciences, the kitchen became the private quarters of Falconet and Collot.[104] That left the theater, which according to the most plausible accounts, became Falconet's atelier.[105] Behind the theater, Carburi built a large shed and several workshops for the use of Falconet and his workers. That is where in May 1770 the large model of the monument was shown to the public. Falconet received furniture, dishes, houseware, and a carriage with horses, all valued at 178 rubles. The amount allotted for board was 150 rubles a month, which was increased to 175 rubles in 1773.[106]

Michel's house and Falconet's permanent lodgings were no more than a ten-minute walk from the site of the monument on Senate Square. That was an important consideration, because as soon as Falconet arrived, Senate Square came astir with the bustle of construction. The square was cleared of storage sheds and building materials, ditches along its sides were filled in, and piles were driven into the boggy ground to provide solid foundations for the monument and the new casting shed *(liteinyi ambar),* which for practical reasons had to stand as closely as possible to the site of the monument. Work on it began in mid-1767 under the supervision of Carburi.[107] It is likely that it was close to being finished in the first half of 1768, for an entry in the log of the Court Steward *(Kamerfur'erskii zhurnal)* for April 12 of that year reports Catherine's visit to "the portrait-casting house . . . located near Her Majesty's stone palace."[108]

Carburi made a very favorable impression on the French sculptors during their joint ride from Riga, and they were glad to see him assigned to them "for constant supervision and assistance and for the satisfaction of the needs of Professor Falconet and those with him in accordance with the contract."[109]

The enterprising Greek engineer was entrusted with the coordination of the search in the environs of St. Petersburg for a granite boulder to be used for the pedestal of the monument,[110] he made sure that Falconet's salary was regularly paid out, and he organized the supply of materials and workers for the various construction projects having to do with the monument.[111] He was employed in these capacities for almost seven years, from November 1, 1766—five weeks after the arrival of Falconet and Collot—until March 1773, when, much to the chagrin of Falconet, he left Russia for Paris. The French sculptor, who appreciated Carburi's technical skills and relied on his ability to get things done, had hoped to have him around during the casting of the statue. His attempts, however, to dissuade the Greek from leaving came to naught. There was a darker side to Carburi's personality, which cost him his credit with the empress and forced him to search for new pastures.

Upon their arrival in St. Petersburg, Falconet and Collot joined a large group of Western merchants, craftsmen, teachers, and artists who flocked to the Russian capital, tempted by the lure of higher earnings and better social status. Some of them, especially those involved in large urbanistic, architectural, and sculptural projects, had to stay in St. Petersburg for extended periods of time and would eventually settle in the city. The sculptor Carlo Bartolomeo Rastrelli and the architect Giacomo Quarenghi are examples of Western artists who decided to make Russia their adoptive homeland. The ever practical Diderot would even counsel Betskoi to make an effort to hire single young men in order to derive long-term benefits from short-term investments: "An old man arrives, renders the demanded services, trains several pupils who soon go to seed, receives the promised honorarium, and goes back. A young man takes a wife, acquires a family that remains [in Russia], and brings up his children the way he was brought up."[112]

At first blush, Falconet's stint in the service of Catherine the Great might appear to bear out Diderot's advice. Falconet was fifty when he arrived in St. Petersburg, an old man by the yardstick of his time. He came to render a specific service and he devoted whatever time was left from the performance of the task at hand to his own scholarly pursuits. As he himself admitted, his contacts with the local population were minimal: "The ignorance of the language, my sedentary occupations, and the little need I have to live with the Russians will always be an obstacle."[113] He trained no disciples, collected his honorarium, and left as soon as he felt that his usefulness had come to an end. And yet, however narrowly he chose to interpret the limits of his commitment, however obsessively he protected his right to be the sole master of his time, and however slight was his impact on the contemporary Russian art world, in the long run Falconet made a greater contribution to Russian culture than any expatriate artist could have hoped to make.

3

Sculptors of the Empress

GUEST OF HONOR

Monsieur Diderot . . . has made it possible for me to acquire a man who, I believe, is unique—Falconet. He will soon start making the statue of Peter the Great. There may be artists who are as talented as he is, but none, I dare say, is his match in intellect.
—Catherine the Great (1766)

Catherine had good reason to gloat over Falconet's arrival. She had a habit of treating architects and artists as skilled employees, whose usefulness ended with the completion of the project at hand. But Falconet was different. He was clearly much more than a craftsman coming to execute a commissioned work. The empress knew that she was hosting not only a major European artist but also an envoy from the land of the Enlightenment, a *philosophe,* an *ami de l'âme* of Diderot, and a contributor to the *Encylopédie.* She also realized that Falconet's intellectual interests and social and professional contacts could help her establish closer links to the artistic and literary circles in the West.

Intelligent and good-looking, witty and well-read, open to the most advanced ideas of the time, Catherine was, at thirty-eight, mature enough to exude the poise and self-assurance of an absolute ruler, yet young enough to be able to deploy her feminine charms whenever it suited her purpose. She wasted no time in putting Falconet under her spell, favoring him in every way, making him feel like her most cherished adviser and confidant, deferring to his judgment in artistic matters, inviting him to receptions in the palace, and showing him off as her latest and most precious acquisition. The special treatment accorded to Falconet was, of course, very much the topic of conversations at court and in diplomatic circles. One can detect a note of concern when the marquis de Bausset, the French minister plenipotentiary in St. Petersburg, informed the duc de Choiseul, Louis XV's minister of foreign affairs, that "the empress singles Falconet out on every occasion."[1]

Concern gave way to alarm when the marquis de Bausset got wind of the empress's intention to use Falconet as her "head hunter" in France. In his report to Versailles, Bausset warned that "the empress would like to attract into her empire many of our artists and scholars. . . . She has expressly asked [Falconet] to write to all his friends and assure them that they would be welcome here and to encourage them to come."[2] The duc de Choiseul fired back an angry dispatch in which he deplored the empress's attempt "to use Falconet as an instrument of seducing other artists," especially when the king was so accommodating in letting this one go.[3] Not that Choiseul was fearful of a "brain drain," for there was hardly any danger of a French run on employment opportunities opening up in Russia. Rather, known for his dislike of Catherine, he saw the empress as a culture vulture scavenging for prey from her perch above the waters of the Neva.

All this attention could turn anybody's head, especially that of someone like Falconet who craved praise and recognition. In France he was a respected sculptor, even a great one in the eyes of some, but he thought that the best part of his career was behind him. "I will soon be fifty," he said, "and I have done nothing yet that deserves to be known."[4] Without any hope of receiving major royal commissions, he could look forward to ending his life supervising the production of Rococo statuettes at the Sèvres Manufacture. Around him there arose a new generation of sculptors: Augustin Pajou (1730–1809), Pierre Julien (1731–1804), Clodion (1738–1814), and Jean-Antoine Houdon (1741–1828), a very able group that threatened to outshine his fading appeal. He may have been ready, in fact, to put away his chisel and mallet and devote himself fully to writing. It is no accident that the monument to Peter the Great was to be his last sculpture and that, during the years of enforced leisure in St. Petersburg, between the completion of the large model of the statue and the start of casting, he spent his time translating Pliny the Elder and writing art criticism.

But when the call came from St. Petersburg, as if with a wave of a magic wand, Falconet's somber world was bathed in all the hues of the rainbow. He found himself the focus of attention in one of the most resplendent courts in the world, received freely by the legendary woman who occupied the throne of All the Russias, conversing and corresponding with her and other personalities active in the political and cultural life of St. Petersburg, and being generally looked up to as a member of the Paris intellectual elite and a person of considerable influence in the Russian capital.

It was a totally novel and dizzying experience for a man who had never before had access to sources of power, let alone authority to influence political life around him. Falconet's special position allowed him to assist Russians as well. When it was time for the Russian sculptor Fedot Ivanovich Shubin to return to Russia after a stay of two years in Paris, from 1767 to 1769, the secretary of the Académie, Charles-Nicolas Cochin II, appealed to Falconet to help obtain for Shubin a year's extension of his Russian scholarship. Falconet's intervention was successful, and the Russian sculptor was allowed to stay longer and visit Rome. Even Prince Golitsyn, the Russian minister plenipotentiary in France, appealed to Falconet to support his plea for reassignment to Holland. At a time when France's foreign affairs were conducted by the openly anti-Russian duc de Choiseul and the French embassy in St. Petersburg was staffed by low-ranking chargés d'affaires, Falconet fulfilled the role of a French cultural attaché in Russia.

A narcissistic man by nature, Falconet was dazzled by the "enchantress of the North" and became thoroughly ensnared in her nets. Just three months after his arrival, he wrote Diderot that his greatest concern was how to respond to the "unexpected kindness" that the empress was showing him. "Diderot," he exclaimed, "you can't imagine how this unusual woman can elevate one's merits and talents. I'm working, I'm calm, nothing around me causes me any anxiety."[5] Catherine was indeed a guardian of Falconet's tranquility: "Whatever happens, let no one in Russia bother Monsieur Falconet, let his atelier and his quarters be his until he says, *I don't want them any more.*"[6] And, "the most important thing for you, for me, and for your work is that you be left in peace."[7]

Catherine stroked his vanity, played up to his sense of self-importance, and soothed his anxieties. She made him feel indispensable as her adviser in artistic affairs and her chief contact with the French intellectual elite. She was ready to fulfill his most demanding requests, as long as they were dictated by artistic needs. A case in point was the matter of the pedestal for the monument, where she persisted in a search for a monolith even when he himself had become reconciled to a pedestal composed of several smaller rocks, bound to each other by metal clasps. Falconet's habitual lack of sentimentality gave way to a melodramatic gushing of feelings: "Constant encouragement by the empress warms my spirit, ennobles and magnifies it to the point that had I come to Petersburg without a soul, this august wonder-maker would have created one especially for me."[8]

Too egocentric to wonder why a sovereign of a mighty empire should treat him as her equal, he misinterpreted the marks of Catherine's benevolence as signifying far more than their real intent. It never occurred to him that what he took for an expression of genuine friendship could be part of a calculated strategy to obtain a maximum of effort from a moody artist who had to be humored in order to deliver. Little by little the various chores with which the empress charged him made him believe that his standing with her was permanent and unassailable. That delusion bears in the final analysis the primary responsibility for the difficulties which arose in his relations with Betskoi and which would eventually destroy his friendship with Diderot.

In the meantime, however, honors were piling up. On December 23, 1766, Falconet was elected a foreign honorary associate of the Academy of Fine Arts and at the same session Collot was elected a foreign associate. It is remarkable that in the balloting, of fourteen votes cast, he obtained eleven for and three against, while she got thirteen for and one undecided.[9]

The enthusiasm with which Catherine welcomed Falconet's arrival gave rise to one of the most remarkable epistolary monuments of the time. An eager correspondent by nature, who once said that the sight of a blank page gave her an uncontrollable desire to fill it, Catherine threw herself with gusto into an animated exchange of letters with her French visitor. She touched upon a multitude of topics demonstrating the extent of her learning and of her fields of interest. She discussed the intellectual milieu of Paris, the *encyclopédistes,* art matters, and various tasks she wished Falconet to perform for her, such as help with art deals in the West and service as her liaison to the French intellectuals whom she wished to invite to St. Petersburg. Falconet responded to her questions and suggestions, adding his own concerns about the monument and everything that speeded up or delayed its progress.[10]

All in all the correspondence contains 198 letters, but the correspondents show varying degrees of epistolary activity. The first three years were by far the most active—letters were frequent, long, and cordial. By 1770 Catherine's letters begin to lose their personal touch and tend to become matter-of-fact messages of an informational or dispositional character. In 1773 the flow of letters from Catherine drops off dramatically and ceases altogether at the end of 1774. From then on Falconet is the sole letter writer and not a very faithful one at that. Table 3.1 shows how the letters were distributed during the twelve years of Falconet's stay in St. Petersburg.

One cannot be certain when Catherine met Falconet for the first time. It had to have happened soon after Falconet's arrival in St. Petersburg, that is, at the very end of 1766 or the very beginning of 1767, for in February of that year the empress left for an extended stay in Moscow to attend meetings of the commission debating the text of the new code of the rights of the nobility *(Ulozhenie).* At any rate, during that short span of two months they

Table 3.1   Correspondence of Catherine and Falconet

	From Catherine	From Falconet	Total
1767	8	10	18
1768	11	12	23
1769	12	17	29
1770	17	7	24
1771	11	17	28
1772	5	7	12
1773	17	28	45
1774	3	8	11
1775	0	2	2
1776	0	2	2
1777	0	1	1
1778	0	1	1

must have had several meetings, for her first letter to Falconet, sent from Moscow on February 18, shows a very friendly, even bantering, relationship. That letter must have been preceded by one from Falconet, perhaps overly polished and packed with courtly flattery, for she reacted to it by setting the tone for their future exchanges: "if you answer me, don't stand on ceremony, don't use any formalities, and above all, don't add any titles; I don't care about them."[11] Falconet, for reasons of his own, wanted on occasion to by-pass this interdict by lauding the empress indiscriminately in his letters to Paris and asking her to read them before he sent them out. Catherine saw through the scheme and reacted firmly against it: "Once and for all, I don't have and I don't want to have any right to see your letters. Since you have asked me to correct this one [to Diderot], I ask you to eliminate all the praise that you give me and that I don't deserve."[12]

The correspondence is, first of all, an invaluable source for the progress of the monument, for the empress was personally involved in all of its modifications. In her second letter to Falconet she showed her concern for Peter the Great's attire: "I hope that by my return, Peter the Great's toilette will have been done. They tell me that he is up already, but in a great deshabille."[13] The history of the addition of the snake writhing under the horse's hoofs may be fully reconstructed from the correspondence, beginning with Falconet's letter of June 28, 1768, and ending with Catherine's letter of August 7, 1769. Similarly, the matter of the casting of the statue is a constant topic of the correspondence, almost from the beginning of Falconet's stay in St. Petersburg.

By contrast, the feat of transporting the granite rock for the pedestal of the statue from the woods of Karelia to the center of St. Petersburg is mentioned but once in the correspondence, and obliquely at that, in connection with the contribution to it of the Greek engineer Carburi, a fact which testifies to Falconet's marginal role in that magnificent exploit.[14]

Marie-Anne Collot is, of course, a very frequent presence in the pages of the correspondence. Falconet took upon himself the role of agent/manager in all of her dealings with Catherine. The empress respected that arrangement and never addressed the sculptress directly. The arrangement extended also to Falconet's son, Pierre-Etienne, after his arrival in St. Petersburg in 1773. In matters not involving the empress, Collot carried on her own correspondence, of which, unfortunately, only one example has come to light, an exchange between her and Prince Alexander M. Golitsyn concerning a plaster copy of Collot's bust of the empress (fig. 3.1).

Another fixture of the correspondence was Ivan Ivanovich Betskoi, Falconet's nominal superior in St. Petersburg, but in fact his supreme tormentor. Throughout the correspondence, with increasing intensity and frankness, Falconet complains about the obstacles placed in his way by this jealous courtier of the empress. During the first six years, the empress acknowledged the complaints and took steps to rectify matters, but in a remarkable display of fidelity to Betskoi, she did not disavow him openly in any of her answers.

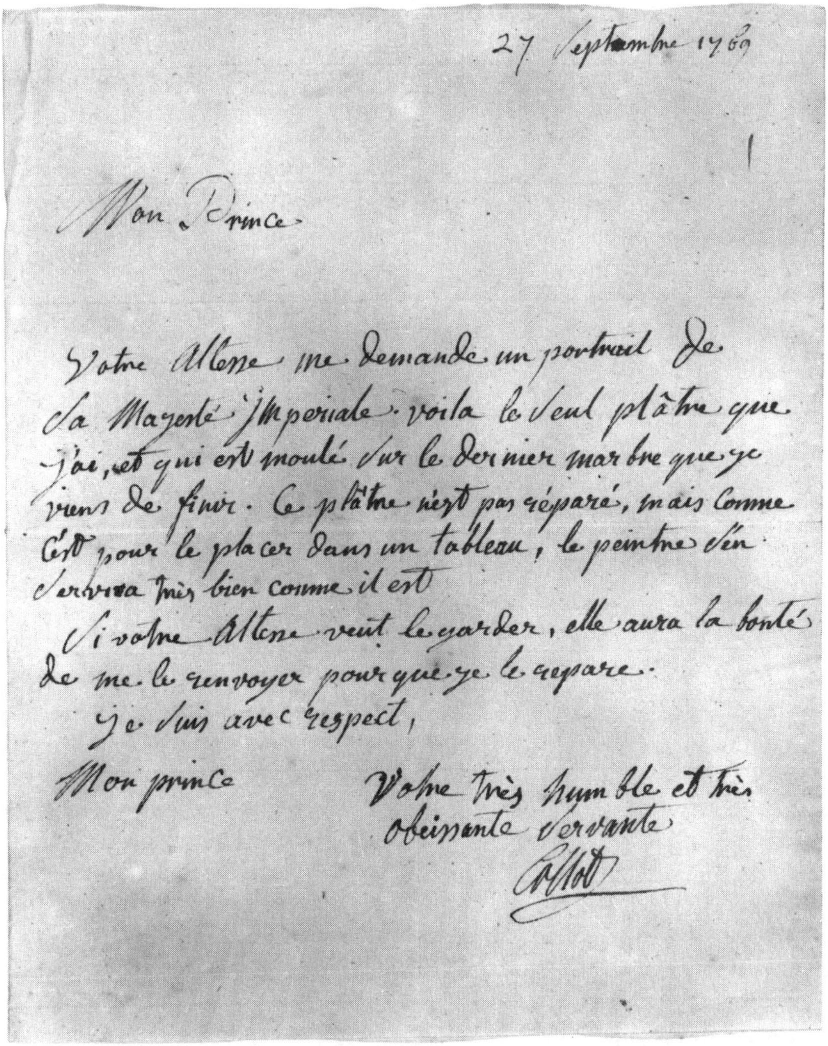

27 septembre 1769

Mon Prince,

Votre Altesse me demande un portrait de
sa Majesté Impériale. voila le seul plâtre que
j'ai, et qui est moulé sur le dernier marbre que je
viens de finir. Ce plâtre n'est pas réparé, mais comme
c'est pour le placer dans un tableau, le peintre s'en
servira très bien comme il est

Si votre Altesse veut le garder, elle aura la bonté
de me le renvoyer pour que je le répare.

je suis avec respect,

Mon prince

Votre très humble et très
obéissante servante
Collot

Fig. 3.1. Letter from Marie-Anne Collot to A. M. Golitsyn of September 27,
1769. RGADA, fond 1263, o. 1, no. 1746, f. 1. Collot informs Prince A. M.
Golitsyn that the bust of Catherine the Great which he asked for was not
touched up after coming from the mold, but that it was in sufficiently good
condition to be used for a painted portrait of the prince. The portrait in question
is by Dmitry G. Levitsky (1735–1822), now in the Tretiakov Gallery in Moscow.
It shows Prince Golitsyn standing at his writing table with the bust
of Catherine the Great by Collot in the background.

As the correspondence loses its vigor, Falconet's grievances remain unanswered, but not unheeded.

Not surprisingly, Falconet's association with Diderot occupies an important place in the correspondence. One of the first items that Falconet presented to the empress was the transcript of the "posterity" debate which had flared up in Paris in 1765 and 1766 between him and Diderot. In vain did he try to draw the empress into the argument, hoping that she would support him. The empress politely indicated that her sympathies were on the side of Diderot, but she preferred to stay on the sidelines, not wishing to offend the sculptor.

The correspondence reflects also Diderot's involvement in the neutralization of the feared effect of two eyewitness accounts of Russia. One was the visit of the astronomer Abbé Jean Chappe d'Auteroche in 1761–62 to view, from various observation sites in Siberia, the expected passage of the planet Venus across the face of the sun. In 1768 the learned abbé published a book entitled *Voyage en Sibérie,* an account of the primitive customs of the Russian and native population of Siberia. His harshly unadorned view was complemented by a critical evaluation of Catherine's reign, even though, having left Russia almost as soon as she assumed the throne, he had had practically no chance to observe it firsthand. The incensed empress sponsored a vitriolic attack on the book in a pamphlet, whose title, the *Antidote,* implies that Abbé Chappe's book was unadulterated poison. Here is what Sabatier de Cabre, the French chargé d'affaires in St. Petersburg, had to say about the incident in his report to the duc de Choiseul: "The late Abbé Chappe is still the object of execration and sarcasm on the part of Catherine II and her court. The Academy in this town received an order to discover errors in the astronomical part [of Chappe's book]. But, since science is not subject to an ukase and Chappe had to be refuted at any price without the use of a foreign pen (which was thought too dangerous or difficult to arrange), they concocted that miserable *Antidote,* assembled with little method and style, but filled with false and brazen accusations against France."[15]

The other such incident involved an account of Catherine's role in the murder of her husband, Peter III, during the coup of 1762. It is a story which passed into history under the name of the "affaire Rulhière," after the name of the author, a former secretary of the French legation in St. Petersburg, Claude-Carloman de Rulhière, who witnessed some of the events of the coup and knew many of its participants. His detailed account of the takeover, titled *Histoire ou anecdotes sur la Révolution de Russie en l'année 1762,* was completed in February 1768. The empress found out about its existence from a letter which Diderot wrote to Falconet in mid-June of that year. Although Rulhière assured Diderot that he had no intention of publishing the text, he did feel free to undertake readings of it in Paris salons. That, and the danger that the manuscript might eventually be published, made Diderot advise Catherine to try to buy Rulhière's silence.[16] Yet, despite the feverish efforts of her ministers, acting directly or through common friends, no deal was struck. Catherine's efforts to suppress the manuscript included offers of money and a threat of imprisonment in the Bastille. Rulhière responded that even if the manuscript were to be confiscated, it would do no good, for he carried it fixed in his memory.[17] The affair died down when it became clear that Rulhière would keep his word and refrain from publishing the account until after Catherine had died.

Much bile was spilled on the pages of the correspondence on account of the unsuccessful visit to St. Petersburg of the political economist Mercier de La Rivière, former governor of Martinique. The visitor was the author of *De l'ordre naturel des sociétés,* a political treatise expounding the economic doctrine of the Physiocrats. Diderot, who considered him the greatest man of the Enlightenment, recommended him to Catherine as the only Western scholar worthy of being appointed legal consultant to the new Russian Code, which was being prepared in Moscow. Falconet, impressed by Diderot's enthusiastic testimonials, took La Rivière under his wing, but was put off by his grand airs and exaggerated personal expectations. Nor was the empress pleased with the economist's ideas, especially after she realized that he lacked any knowledge of Russia.[18] After a fruitless stay of eight months (October 1767 till June 1768), La Rivière returned to Paris, much to the chagrin of Diderot, whose displeasure with Falconet's negative reaction to his protégé led him to exclaim: "Falconet keeps on tearing into de La Rivière with all his claws. His success [with the empress] has turned his head."[19]

Art purchases in Paris, with Diderot functioning as the empress's agent and Falconet as her middleman, fill many pages of the correspondence. The most important transaction was the purchase of the Crozat collection concluded by Diderot in 1772. It brought Catherine about five hundred paintings by the greatest European masters, among them works by Rubens, Titian, Poussin, Raphael, Correggio, Dürer, Leonardo da Vinci, Fra Bartolomeo, Giorgione, Van Dyck, Rembrandt, Watteau, and Chardin.[20]

During the early period of Falconet's visit, the informal bantering quality of the correspondence was truly remarkable. Barely arrived in Moscow, Catherine began the correspondence with a comment on the ruling style of King Louis IX: "Your king Saint Louis used to say that if he could divide himself in two, he would give one half to the Dominicans and the other to the Franciscans. As you can see, that would not leave that good king with much for his kingdom. I said *bon roi* ['good king'], but I should have said *bonhomme* ['simpleton'], because only a simpleton can tell such stories; a good king would do better to give all of himself to his kingdom, rather than dividing himself between mendicant friars."

A few lines farther she switched to the main topic of their interest and inquired about the progress of Falconet's work on the horse, which she must have seen before leaving for Moscow: "I espy from here that clever beast of yours, occupying the center of your atelier, and am afraid that you might give it too much brain. . . . I bet that your animal will speak and, if one doesn't understand what it is saying, it's only because the habit of hearing horses neigh will cause its speech to be taken for neighing."[21]

It took Falconet four weeks to reply, but when he did, he wrote the empress the most upbeat letter of his life (fig. 3.2).[22] Such was the power of Catherine's charm offensive that a habitually dour man began to see himself as a spirited bon vivant, who was able to cull enjoyment where others find disappointments: "if we stressed enjoyments, if we thought of them frequently and gratefully, our soul would be permanently happy." That self-image was totally out of character, but it seems to have briefly fooled the empress, and it certainly fooled Falconet himself, who proclaimed cheerfully: "the secret of the good Epicure . . . is my everyday philosophy. Stoicism is only for Sundays."

Falconet's euphoria may be sensed in every line of this first letter. In answer to Catherine's comments on Louis IX, he gave her a lecture in French history; he agreed with her characterization of Peter the Great's horse as a clever animal, and he even permitted himself a critical remark about her micromanagement of the project: "I would have never thought that Your Majesty would be so difficult in matters of sculpture. You are never out of my atelier and now you have asked me more than twenty times to redo things with which others were quite pleased." Finally, he proposed that the empress read the text of the dispute on posterity and judge whether it was worthy of being published in Russia; asked for her permission to give a plaster cast of Collot's bust of her to the British ambassador, Charles, Lord Cathcart; and, in a postscript, asked what she thought of his critique of the chevalier de Jaucourt's entry "Russia" in the *Encyclopédie.*

Catherine's response of March 28, 1767 (fig. 3.3), was couched in the same bantering tone.[23] She agreed with Falconet that Jaucourt's article was uninformed. She gave Collot her permission to dispose of the bust in any way she saw fit, adding in one of her sly, tongue-in-cheek references to the Falconet-Collot relationship, "I consent to it with pleasure, especially after reading [your] sentence: *Well, my friends, manufacture pleasures.*" She taunted Falconet about his protestations that he was not trying to create a masterpiece. She also commented on Falconet's complaint that she was too demanding a customer: "Don't say again that I am difficult and, above all, don't pay attention to what I'm saying, because I can be very wrong. Stick to your guns." An admission like that from the most powerful woman in the world could turn any man's head.

The perceptive Diderot realized very quickly that Falconet's chummy relationship with the empress had gone to his friend's head, turning his combativeness and self-assurance into aggression and arrogance. He told him so candidly, opening a chink in their relations that was soon to grow into a major fissure.

As for the reasons for the drastic reduction in the frequency of the correspondence in 1774 and its virtual cessation afterward, they were manifold.

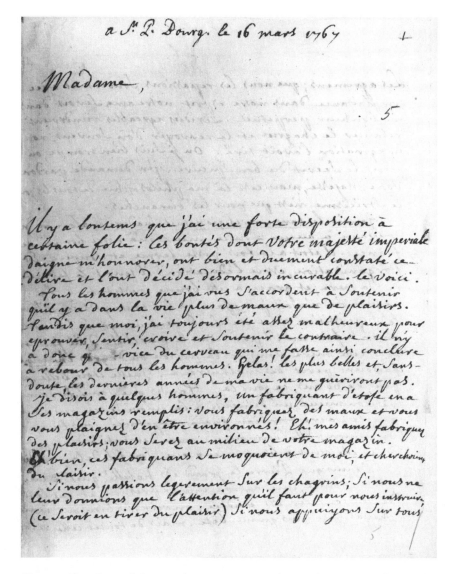

Fig. 3.2. First Page of the March 16, 1767, Letter from Falconet to Catherine the Great. RGADA, fond 5, no. 143, f. 5r. This is the beginning of the first surviving letter from Falconet to Catherine the Great (see p. 108).

External distractions of 1773–74, such as the Pugachev rebellion and the visit of Diderot, may have preoccupied the empress, but did not of themselves cause the cooling of her relations with the sculptor. Much more important was Catherine's realization that Falconet's self-portrait as a carefree bon vivant was merely an affectation. She saw Falconet's suspicious and combative

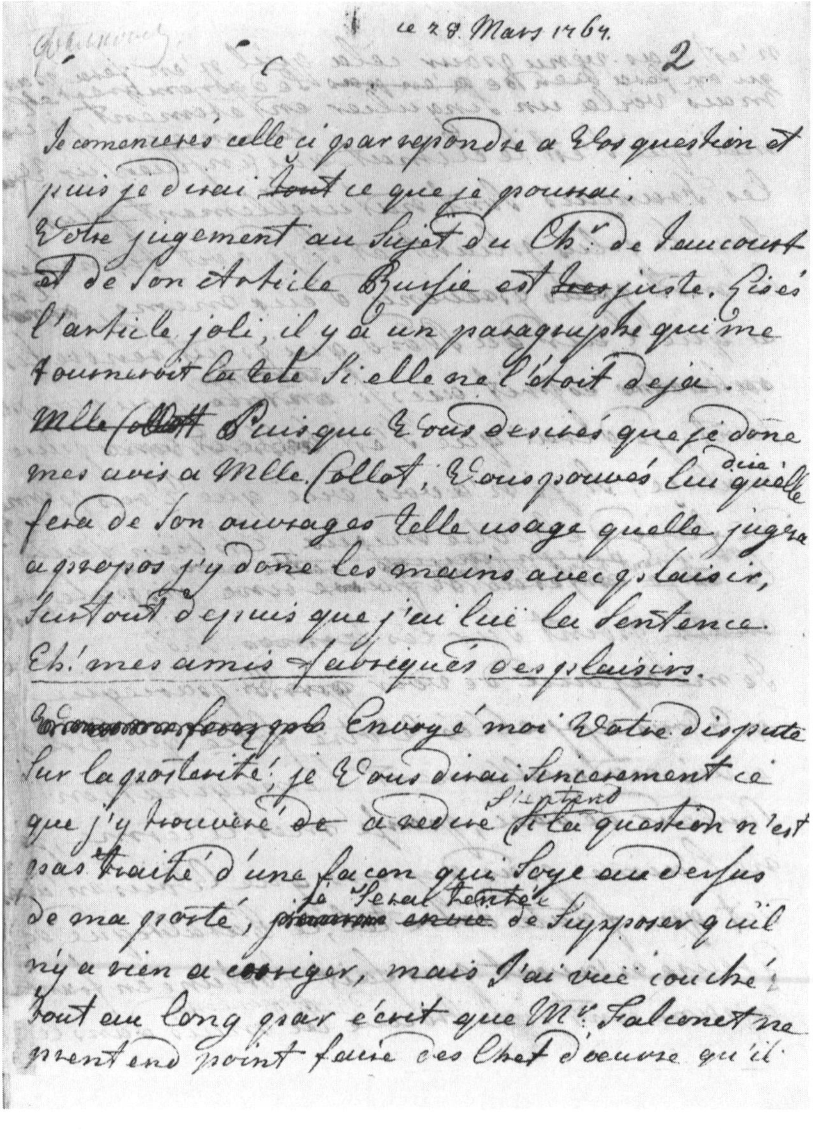

Fig. 3.3. First Page of the March 28, 1767, Draft of Catherine the Great's Answer to Falconet's Letter of March 16, 1767 (see fig. 3.2). RGADA, fond 5, no. 143, f. 2r. Reproduced in *SIRIO,* vol. 13, p. 6 (see p. 108).

nature as responsible for the setbacks with casting, which delayed the completion of the monument long beyond the planned deadlines. In addition, the image of Falconet spending years behind his desk, contesting the presumed perfection of the horse of the *Marcus Aurelius* and the reputation of Pliny the Elder's art criticism instead of working in the casting shed, must have been a powerful irritant. It was becoming ever more obvious that Falconet was fast approaching the point of exhausting the empress' patience.

THE CASE OF COLLOT

It is an exceedingly rare phenomenon to see a woman dedicate herself to that marvelous, but unsparing art, and who, by animating marble and bronze, helps perpetuate the memory of heroes and seems to partake of their glory.
—"Eloge de Mademoiselle Collot" (1772)

That the arrival in St. Petersburg of an unmarried man of fifty in the company of a young woman of eighteen might raise some eyebrows was clear to Falconet and Collot when they were still in Paris. Fear of public opprobrium was, in fact, the chief reason that Collot hesitated so long about whether to accompany Falconet to St. Petersburg. Diderot did all he could to convince her to go, but it was not easy. Three years later he recalled the tearful farewell scene: "O! Mademoiselle Collot, how you cried at the city gate and how difficult it was for me to stop your tears. But you are loved, respected, honored. So the arguments which I gave you then and which you found so difficult to accept, were good."[24]

The three attributes that Diderot mentions as proof that he was right in cajoling Collot into going to St. Petersburg may be easily deciphered. "Loved" alluded to a relationship that Diderot hoped would prosper in a foreign country, where Falconet and Collot would have to depend on each other to a far greater degree than back in Paris. "Respected" acknowledged the artistic and commercial success that Collot's work achieved both at the Russian court and in St. Petersburg's high society. "Honored" referred to the distinctions with which the art establishment of St. Petersburg marked its esteem for Collot. In the last two instances Diderot's expectations were fulfilled. As for love, perhaps even marriage, they turned out to be Diderot's wishful thinking.

The participants in the ceremony of contract signing, Diderot as its drafter, and Falconet and Prince Golitsyn as its two signatories, agreed not to include Collot in the official document, even though Falconet's right to bring along two journeymen sculptors and one molder was explicitly provided for. It seems that the widowed Falconet felt awkward about asking for an official permission to arrive in the company of a young woman whose presence could not be justified as indispensable to the execution of the project. He preferred to let Prince Golitsyn and Diderot pave Collot's way discreetly and unofficially. On August 31, 1766, Golitsyn did so in a letter to Count Nikita I. Panin, Russia's minister of foreign affairs: "Monsieur Falconet will bring along a young woman, his pupil. He takes a special interest in her because of her prodigious talent and her conduct. Many portraits that

I saw her make here are excellent and she cannot but be useful in our country. I consider her worthy of the protection of Her Imperial Majesty and I took the liberty of assigning her a salary of fifteen hundred livres a year on the recommendation of M. Falconet, but hope that you, Monseigneur, will raise it to two thousand livres."[25]

Even more discreet and roundabout was D. A. Golitsyn's letter of September 10 to his distant cousin, the vice chancellor Prince Aleksandr M. Golitsyn, characterizing Collot as a sculptress with "a real talent for portraiture." D. A. Golitsyn added: "She is as nice as she is gifted and your kindness will be well employed should you choose to do something for her."[26] In his response dated October 21, A. M. Golitsyn assured his cousin that he would seriously consider his recommendation: "She will find, I hope, opportunities to make portraits [for] there are few excellent artists here in that genre. She will soon begin one. It will be the proof of her skill and will get her as many commissions as she would want."[27]

Awareness of the potential awkwardness of the situation may account for Falconet's insistence that the head of the Bronze Horseman had been executed by Collot without his help. He may have hoped that such an assertion would constitute an unassailable proof of Collot's contribution to the monument and would remove whatever doubts people had about her role as his collaborator, rather than his paramour or companion.

The same motive must have prompted Diderot to wish to reassure General Betskoi about the totally respectable nature of Collot's association with Falconet. To do so he included four explanatory paragraphs in a draft of a letter to Betskoi two weeks before Collot's departure from Paris. Later, however, perhaps at Falconet's behest, he omitted most of the passage, leaving just a short sentence in which he informed Betskoi that Falconet would leave Paris "with a young person who is nineteen years old."[28] Nevertheless, whether actually received by Betskoi or not, Diderot's original lines show his, and what is even more significant, Collot's concern about the impression that her arrival together with Falconet might create:

> The young person who has the courage to accompany [Falconet] to the [North] Pole is one of his disciples, yes sir, one of his disciples. She is a child who did not hesitate to handle clay and chisel with her delicate hands. She is good-looking, but what you will find a greater prize are her excellent taste, good sense, and great talent, combined with morals of utmost uprightness and purity. . . . The one favor for which I beg Your Excellency is to succeed in convincing that young person that there is nothing untoward about her trip and that her presence and conduct will not leave an unfavorable impression in St. Petersburg.[29]

Diderot included a hint that was intended for the eyes of Catherine: "It would be natural for Her Imperial Majesty to honor with protection and shower favors upon women who dare elevate themselves above their sex." Upon reflection, however, he thought better of appealing to Catherine's gen-der loyalty and struck the passage out. He also took the responsibility for having promised Collot fifteen hundred livres a year for the duration of her stay in Russia. Hinting discreetly at Collot's liaison with Falconet, he added: "Your Excellence will readily understand that propriety has prevented me from including it as a separate article in the contract signed by Prince Golitsyn and Falconet. I thought, nonetheless, that I would not go beyond the prerogative which you have accorded me, and that my promise will be enforced as fully as if it had been expressly stated. Prince Golitsyn was forewarned about it and has consented to it, but we didn't have time to wait for your agreement and that of Her Imperial Majesty."[30]

There was probably no need for Betskoi to do Diderot's bidding and try to persuade Collot that "there was nothing improper in her coming to St. Petersburg and that her presence and conduct would not leave an unfavorable impression."[31] Contrary to Diderot's fears, in amorous matters St. Petersburg was as permissive as Paris, and the ambiguity of Falconet's relations with Collot did not cause any raised eyebrows.[32] The youthful sculptress was warmly welcomed and soon became the capital's favorite society portraitist. Within a few months of her arrival, she was elected foreign associate of the Academy of Fine Arts. She was the first woman to be so honored and was the Academy's youngest member.

The Bibliothèque Nationale in Paris possesses a manuscript testimonial, under the name of "Eloge de Mademoiselle Collot," detailing Collot's success in St. Petersburg during the first three years of her stay there:

Mademoiselle Collot . . . is equally commendable on account of the soundness of her judgment and the wisdom of her conduct as on account of her exquisite talent, which develops, expands, and grows stronger every day. Endowed with natural intelligence, a lively and fertile imagination, and an independent mind, she is entirely self-taught. Her personal qualities, her candor, her singular ability to sense what is true and beautiful and render it in her works, touched with genius, are appreciated by people of taste and knowledge and have earned her in Russia, as well as in France, the esteem and respect of those, who know how to appreciate modesty and virtue. What speaks most eloquently in her favor are the flattering testimonies of friendship and the special marks of distinction that she receives every day from a Sovereign who is as enlightened as she is beneficent.[33]

According to the "Eloge," those "marks of distinction" included a salary of one thousand rubles a year—that is, about five thousand livres—instead of the fifteen hundred or two thousand livres proposed by Diderot and Golitsyn. In addition, Catherine gave Collot various gifts, including a precious box, a gold watch, and cash, all amounting to about eleven or twelve thousand livres.[34] With her food and lodging expenses provided for and all of her works paid for separately, it is no wonder that in a fairly short time, Collot was able to amass a fairly large fortune, all of it kept in her Paris account.

The first work executed by Collot in St. Petersburg was a bust of Anastasia Sokolova, an illegitimate daughter of Betskoi and a favorite lady-in-waiting of Catherine. It was to be a test of Collot's sculpting talents. Satisfied with the result, the empress sat for Collot on several occasions. The "Eloge" lists two busts (1767 and 1769) and two medallions of the empress, the best known being the medallion of 1771 (fig. 3.4), but there certainly were more. The bust of 1767 pleased A. M. Golitsyn so much that he borrowed a plaster cast of it to place it in the background of the portrait of him by the painter D. G. Levitsky. He also asked Collot to make a bust of himself. It so happens that the exchange of letters between A. M. Golitsyn and Collot has given us the only extant text in Collot's own hand, the letter of September 27, 1769 (see fig. 3.1).[35]

Other sculptures of the St. Petersburg period mentioned in the "Eloge" include the head of Peter the Great for the monument (1767, fig. 8.7); three busts of 1768, Falconet (fig. 1.4), Peter the Great (fig. 8.8), and Mary Cathcart, daughter of the British ambassador to Russia; the head of a Russian peasant girl made in 1769; busts of Henry IV and his chief minister Sully, heads of Diderot (fig. 1.1) and Voltaire, medallions of Peter the Great, his daughter Empress Elizabeth, Jane Hamilton, Lady Cathcart, wife of the British ambassador, and Count Grigory Orlov, all of 1772; busts and medallions of Catherine's son, Grand Duke Paul, and his wife Grand Duchess Natalia Alekseevna, and a bust of the painter Pierre-Etienne Falconet, son of the sculptor, all of 1775; and bas-reliefs of the Stations of the Cross.[36]

Catherine's wish to have a gallery of famous people forced Collot to base some of her portraits on whatever likenesses she could obtain, without the benefit of live sittings. Such procedures entailed invariably a loss in quality. In the cases of Henry IV or Sully, that was unavoidable, but she also did the head of Voltaire without ever laying eyes on him. On the other hand, she was spectacularly successful with the head of Peter the Great for the monument, a circumstance which makes one wonder how independent a work it was, especially when one compares it with her uninspired portrait of Peter in the bust of 1768. In the case of the head of d'Alembert, she resisted the empress's proddings to rely on engravings and resolved to do it from life during her stay in Paris in the fall of 1775 and spring and summer of 1776. Whether she actually did so is not known, for a portrait of d'Alembert by Collot has not been identified.

The bulk of Collot's production in Russia coincides with Falconet's work on the large model of the monument; that is, it falls between the years 1766 and 1770. Then it slows down noticeably. One could say that Collot was energized by Falconet's active involvement in sculpting. The bust she did of him is without any doubt her best work. It is a candid and affectionate portrait, showing the sculptor at his most relaxed and lighthearted. Diderot knew enough about his friends' situation to write playfully to Falconet: "You must resemble yourself a lot if [Collot] made you in marble just as she knows you in the flesh."[37] Equally direct was the empress's tongue-in-cheek consent

Fig. 3.4. Marie-Anne Collot, *Catherine the Great*. Marble, 1771 (original version, 1769). The State Hermitage Museum, St. Petersburg.

to let Collot take Falconet's bust back for a while in order to improve it. "You may pick up your bust," she wrote Falconet, "so that during the summer Mlle Collot may caress it anew."[38]

Given the great mutual liking of Collot and Diderot, it is unfortunate that not one written word of Collot to Diderot has been preserved, whether in a letter of her own or added to one of Falconet's. All we have are Diderot's exceptionally warm messages to her, included with practically every letter to

Falconet. Here is one example: "Good day, Mademoiselle Victoire. I have always loved both of you equally. Keep the same sentiments for me. You wonder if your name is mentioned in the same breath as Falconet's. Shall I tell you? It is mentioned here with so much concern, so many tender feelings, that people often think that you are dearer to me than a daughter is to her father. There were times when I felt that I had to call upon the full force of my persuasion to disabuse people of that notion."[39]

Was it Madame Diderot or Sophie Volland, Diderot's mistress, who suspected him of unduly tender feelings for Mademoiselle Victoire? Most probably both.

THE FEUD WITH BETSKOI

If I don't manage to contain [Falconet] with all the trouble I've had before and after his arrival in St. Petersburg, it will be difficult to do so later. (Sometimes one may regret it when one's bride is too beautiful . . .)
—Betskoi (1767)

On November 20, 1700, beneath the battlements of Narva on the southern shore of the Gulf of Finland, Peter the Great suffered a humiliating defeat at the hands of the Swedish army under King Charles XII. Among the ten Russian generals taken prisoner by the Swedes was Prince Ivan Iurievich Trubetskoi (1667–1750), former governor of the province of Novgorod. Trubetskoi was sent to Sweden and kept there for eighteen years, but the terms of his internment were extremely mild. He was allowed to take part in the social life of Stockholm and enjoy the company of women, one of whom became the mother of his son. The boy was born in 1704 in Stockholm and was baptized there under the name of Johann (Ivan).

The mother's identity is not altogether certain. Some sources name the Swedish Baroness Wrede, others Baroness Skarre, and still others claim that she was a Polish noblewoman who happened to be in Stockholm at the time.[40] The stories that Prince Trubetskoi married the mother of Ivan in a secret ceremony are certainly unfounded, for left behind in Russia was his second wife, Irina Grigorievna Naryshkina, whom he had married in 1691. Their daughter Anastasia was born after he had been taken prisoner. When Princess Trubetskaia visited her husband on the eve of his release and learned of his Swedish-born son, she agreed to adopt the boy under the last name of Betskoi, in accordance with the custom practiced among the gentry of dropping the first syllable of polysyllabic family names of children born out of wedlock.[41]

It was as Ivan Ivanovich Betskoi that the boy grew up to occupy various government positions of influence, whose scope added up to the purview of a modern minister of arts and education. It included oversight of the construction of the monument to Peter the Great, a position from which he could facilitate or, as it happened more often than not, oppose Falconet's every move. Given the sculptor's argumentative frame of mind, fanned by his disdain for the opinions of nonspecialists, and the petty, obstinate, and jealous nature of Betskoi, battle lines were drawn as soon as the two met face to face. Catherine did her best during the honeymoon period of Falconet's stay in St. Petersburg to calm the sculptor down. Eventually, however, she assumed an anti-Falconet stance and took Betskoi off the leash, allowing the conflict to grow in intensity, until Falconet, defiant as ever, but without any succor in sight, left the battlefield. Negative as it was, the role played by Betskoi in the enterprise of the monument was of such importance that the man and his actions demand a closer scrutiny.

Not much is known about Betskoi's early career. It is assumed that after his father's release, he was in Denmark, where he received his early schooling and joined a cavalry regiment. He did not, however, stay long in the military service due to an accident in which he could have lost his life. During training exercises he was thrown off his horse and trampled by the squadron galloping behind him. Miraculously, he escaped without major injuries, but decided to dedicate himself to the civil service. He came to Russia around 1726 and joined the staff of his father, who by that time held the rank of field marshal and lived in Moscow. Although his duties were mainly administrative, he rose rapidly through the military ranks, undoubtedly aided by his father's connections. In the course of his work, he traveled widely in Western Europe, especially in Germany, preparing for a career in Russian diplomacy. His first appointment was as a diplomatic courier, a position which took him to several European capitals, including Paris.

Betskoi's first public role was at the side of Empress Elizabeth, to whom he was recommended by his half-sister, Princess Anastasia of Hesse-Homburg, the favorite lady-in-waiting of the empress. After Elizabeth's coup d'état in 1740, Betskoi acted as her liaison officer to foreign embassies in St. Petersburg, in particular to the French ambassador, the marquis de la Chétardie. Soon after her coronation, in accordance with the procedure established by Peter the Great, Elizabeth began making plans for her succession. Her choice fell upon the grandson of Peter the Great and her own nephew, Grand Duke Charles Peter of Holstein-Gottorp. His wife was to be Charles Peter's cousin, Princess Sophia of Anhalt-Zerbst.

When the grand duke came to Russia in 1741, Betskoi was appointed his lord chamberlain, a post which he held until 1744 when Princess Sophia arrived accompanied by her mother, Princess Johanna-Elizabeth of Anhalt-Zerbst. At that time Betskoi was assigned to the two ladies "for permanent service."[42] The following year the young couple married, he as Peter, she as Catherine. With their names extended by dynastic numerals, Peter III was destined to rule Russia for six months, while the reign of Catherine II was to last thirty-four years.

Princess Johanna-Elizabeth left Russia soon after the wedding, not, how-

ever, before befriending Princess Anastasia of Hesse-Homburg and in particular her handsome half-brother, who was also her own chamberlain. Their
friendship blossomed into an open liaison, flagrant enough to became the
talk of Moscow. Here is what the future empress Catherine II had to say
about it in her memoirs: "Little by little my mother took into her confidence
[in the original French *est devenue intime avec*] Monsieur Betskoi. . . . This
alliance displeased many, especially Count Lestocq and the lord marshal of
the grand duke, Brümmer, . . . but most of all Countess Rumiantsev, who
often tried to slander my mother to the empress [Elizabeth]."[43]

The affair was also responsible for a persistent rumor that Betskoi was
Catherine's natural father.[44] In the absence of any direct proof, the wagging
tongues had to rely solely on circumstantial evidence. Since the future empress was born on May 2, 1729, the alleged affair would have had to have
taken place in the late summer of 1728. Princess Johanna-Elizabeth, who
would have been seventeen at that time, did spend a part of 1728 in Paris,
and it is possible that Betskoi was there at the same time.[45] It is also true that
Betskoi visited the Anhalt-Zerbst principality during his European travels.

Although Catherine's parents were married in 1727, the possibility of an
affair of Princess Johanna-Elizabeth with Betskoi in 1728, though unlikely,
cannot be excluded. The princess was a vivacious and worldly woman, married to a man who was twenty-five years her senior and whose military career
condemned her to live in provincial Prussian garrison towns. Betskoi, on the
other hand, was just seven years older than the princess, a dashing six-footer
about to enter upon a brilliant political career (fig. 3.5). It has also been noted
that Betskoi and Catherine resembled each other physically and that there
was a strong and cordial bond between them. It showed particularly in Catherine's seemingly inexhaustible patience with Betskoi, who, by all accounts,
was a boring and difficult man. It was even said that Catherine would rise
from her chair whenever Betskoi entered the room and that when she visited
the aging man, "she would lean over his armchair and kiss his hand."[46]

By the time Catherine took over the reins of Russia, Betskoi was already
a highly placed civil servant, holding the post of director of the Bureau of
the Imperial and Public Buildings and Gardens to which he had been appointed by Peter III.[47] Yet, it was under Catherine the Great that he reached
the apogee of his power. She named him president of the Academy of Fine
Arts and director of the Cadet Corps. Besides, she took him as her adviser
in the field of education and appointed him as her personal reader, a position
which gave him daily access to her private chambers.

All these signs of imperial benevolence were observed and contributed to
the rumor mill. They need not, however, be ascribed to filial piety. It is
more likely that the empress found in Betskoi's fawning attitudes the kind
of parental warmth that was denied to her in her childhood. She herself
described her father, Prince Christian Augustus of Anhalt-Zerbst, as a retiring
and austere man who liked to read in his free moments and was often away
with his regiment. She saw him seldom, the last time in Stettin, when he bid

Fig. 3.5. Alexandre Roslin, *Ivan Ivanovich Betskoi*. Oil on canvas, 1777. The State Hermitage Museum, St. Petersburg.

her goodbye before her departure for Russia. Her mother, whom Catherine described as being "extraordinarily fond of amusement and society," was too self-centered to pay much attention to her daughter. Betskoi, on the other hand, was always there, a reliable and respectful courtier. His liaison with her mother made him, in a sense, a member of the family, while his frequent declarations of devotion to Catherine, whatever their ultimate motive, may have been perceived by her as manifestations of parental love. Besides, Catherine, intent on projecting an image of a truly Russian tsarina, may have adopted Betskoi as her surrogate father to demonstrate her successful Russification.

After the departure of Princess Johanna-Elizabeth, Betskoi, now in the rank of major general, remained behind in the entourage of Grand Duke Charles Peter and his wife. His career at the court was interrupted, however, by the ascendance of Count Aleksei Bestuzhev-Riumin, who in 1744 became Russia's chancellor, ushering in a period of anti-Prussian attitudes.[48] Betskoi, identified with the Prussian faction, had to resign his position. He left Russia in 1747 and stayed abroad for fifteen years, that is, until the moment when the death of Empress Elizabeth elevated Peter III to the Russian throne.

During his exile Betskoi visited Germany, Holland, France, and Italy. In Paris he was a guest in the salon of Madame Geoffrin, met many representatives of the French Enlightenment, notably Diderot and Grimm, and became acquainted with the educational views of Jean-Jacques Rousseau. He also visited many educational and charitable institutions, collecting information which he would later apply in Russia.[49]

Once back in favor, Betskoi threw himself with vigor into a variety of cultural ventures. He continued to direct the Bureau of Imperial and Public Buildings and Gardens, where he had the responsibility for the supervision of the construction and maintenance of the many building projects of the empress, wherever they were, but chiefly in St. Petersburg and its suburbs. His largest and most ambitious project was the drafting of plans for the reconstruction of the city of Tver after it had been devastated by fire in 1763.

In 1764 Betskoi was appointed president of the Academy of Fine Arts, founded seven years before by Empress Elizabeth. He revised its rules and persuaded the empress to start the construction of a permanent home of the Academy on University Embankment on Vasilievsky Island. Completed in the middle of the nineteenth century, it is an immense rectangular structure, with a circular courtyard and a symmetrically planned interior. A year later Betskoi took over the directorship of the Land Cadet Corps *(Sukhoputnyi Kadetskii Korpus),* founded in 1731 by Empress Anna Ioanovna as a counterpart to the Marine Cadet Corps, founded by Peter the Great in 1715. Its mission was to educate the sons of the nobility from age thirteen to eighteen and prepare them for military and civil duties. The corps was housed in the palace and grounds of the Menshikov estate on Vasilievsky Island, and its proximity to the Academy of Sciences facilitated appointments of senior scholars to the faculty. Under Betskoi's guidance the corps' structure and curriculum were revised, resulting in the expansion of the educational program to fifteen years of study. Renamed the Imperial Land Cadet Corps of the Nobility *(Imperatorskii Shliakhetnyi Sukhoputnyi Kadetskii Korpus),* it provided total education to boys of noble families from the age of five or six to twenty-one, divided into five age groups of three years each. The goal was to nurture a new kind of citizen, one fully prepared to advance the goals of a centralized state ruled by an absolute but enlightened monarch.

In addition to the regular curriculum, the cadets were taught military arts. Much attention was given to music and physical education, including dancing, horseback riding, and fencing.

Much to his credit was Betskoi's insistence on providing women with educational opportunities comparable to those of men, even though it is not entirely clear to what extent his thinking in this matter was shaped by the views of the empress herself. It is likely, however, that her *General Plan for the Education of Young People of Both Sexes* was drafted with his participation. It was a blueprint which resulted in the creation of the Imperial Society for the Upbringing of the Daughters of Nobility or the Smolny Institute.[50] It survived as the most prestigious institution dedicated to the education of young women until the revolution of 1917.

There is no doubt that Betskoi laid the foundation of the Russian national school system. He showed himself a humane and progressive educational reformer, aiming at the inculcation of moral and civil values. He stood up against corporal punishment in schools, explaining that beating intimidates children and "encourages servile and vicious thinking."[51] He once upbraided a Cadet Corps disciplinarian with the words: "You want to make serfs out of these boys, I want to make nobles."[52] He wanted to do away with the common practice of leaving the education of children to the care of French tutors and governesses, many of them poorly prepared to undertake such duties.

Betskoi, however, was not wholly successful. One of the difficulties he faced was societal in nature. The Cadet Corps, in spite of its protected character, was liable to drunkenness and dissipation. Count A. G. Bobrinsky, Catherine's illegitimate son, is often cited as one of the chief offenders.[53] Personnel was hired without a review process, resulting in unqualified and accidental appointments. In this area, Betskoi undermined his own efforts by the whimsical and self-serving way in which he ran the educational establishments entrusted to his care. One of the directors of the Cadet Corps was a former prompter of the French theater; the classroom inspector was a former valet of Catherine's mother; one of the teachers was a Monsieur Faber, former manservant of two professors of French; Madame Zeitz, "a woman of dubious morality," served as inspector; and Carburi, "a regular adventurer," was the chief of police of the Corps and eventually its acting director.[54]

The marquis de Bausset, French minister plenipotentiary in St. Petersburg, credited Betskoi with being alone in realizing that what Russia needed was "the third estate, as well as freedom, and that such was the goal of all his [educational] establishments."[55] That, in fact, was one of the goals of the foundling hospice created by Betskoi in Moscow. The hospice accepted babies with no questions asked, except whether the baby was baptized. The wards were then cared for, educated, and instructed in various crafts until the age of twenty, when they were assisted in setting up their own shops and businesses as free men and women. Betskoi's idea was that the wards of the hospice would gradually increase the ranks of the urban middle class.[56]

And yet, despite his obvious accomplishments and influence in the palace, Betskoi did not have a good name among those who knew him personally. He had, it is true, a sycophantic Russian following, but he was also reputed as being inordinately vain, stubborn, and dull-witted. One such opinion comes from the pen of Prince Mikhail M. Shcherbatov (1733–90), a worldly statesman, historian, and essayist, who pondered in his writings the problems of governance in Russia: "Betskoi was a man of small intelligence, but wily. . . . He pretended that all he was doing was for the greater glory of the empress, but on all his projects, printed in many languages, he flaunted his name as their primary author. He did not even let the empress appoint their directors, but he himself was their head and despot, until he fell from favor. To disguise this, he used every method of flattery."[57]

Betskoi's constant attempts to curry favor with the empress were often embarrassingly transparent, as shown by the following episode recounted by Princess Dashkova.

> On the fourth day after [Catherine's] accession to the throne, Monsieur Betskoi asked for and obtained a brief audience with her Majesty. I was the only other person in the room. Much to our astonishment he knelt before her and asked her if she knew to whom she owed her elevation to the throne. Her Majesty answered: "To God and to my faithful and good subjects." "Well then," Betskoi responded, "I must not wear this ribbon any longer," and he tried to take off the insignia of the order of St. Alexander with which he was decorated. The empress stopped him and asked him what was wrong. "I am," he answered, "the most wretched of men because you don't know that it was I who convinced the guards and gave them money." We thought, not without reason, that he had gone utterly mad. The empress extricated herself adroitly by telling him that she knew how much she owed him and that to him alone she would entrust the task of supervising the jewelers who were making a large diamond crown for the day of her coronation. He got up visibly happy and left us immediately, no doubt to communicate that wonderful news to his friends. We laughed wholeheartedly and I was full of admiration for her Majesty who got rid of an annoying fool.[58]

The amusement which followed Betskoi's declaration was understandable, for it was widely known that Betskoi showed great circumspection during the events of June 1762. The French diplomat Bérenger, who witnessed the coup from his post of chargé d'affaires in the French legation, joked that Betskoi's contribution to it amounted to his offering best wishes.[59] It may even be that Betskoi sided initially with Peter III.[60]

Betskoi had an especially poor press among the St. Petersburg French. Falconet had good reason to lead the chorus of criticism, but because of his dependence on the empress's goodwill could not be totally outspoken. By contrast, members of the diplomatic corps, such as Sabatier de Cabre and Bourrée de Corberon, both chargés d'affaires in the 1770s, felt free to leave behind frank accounts of the Russian courtier. Bourrée de Corberon in his memoirs never mentioned Betskoi's name without an unflattering comment. In the entry for April 9, 1778, he called him "an imbecile and ignorant old man whose base flattery is his only merit."[61] Sabatier de Cabre sent the minister of foreign affairs, the duc d'Aiguillon, a withering character sketch of Betskoi:

> There is here an illegitimate son of Trubetskoi, who under the name of Betskoi has reached the highest ranks and all the decorations. He is a friend, or rather a crony, of Catherine the Great. He is constantly around her, agitates her, listens to her, and has become indispensable to her. He deserves as little credit in large undertakings as in the toy departments which he directs, such as the Cadet Corps, a convent for young women modeled on St. Cyr, the fine arts, the buildings, and the like. He used to have tender feelings toward us, but has sacrificed them to keep his position. He stays afloat by flattery, discretion, the sense of tact of an experienced courtier, and always gladly accepts signs of reverence. He is not vicious. The greatest geniuses do not have as much pride or . . . so much plain vanity as this, the narrowest of minds. He has no point of view, no wit, no intelligence, and his limited capability has been dominated by sycophants and rascals in the administration of the two establishments which occupy him completely.[62]

On the hundredth anniversary of the unveiling of the monument, the Russian historian V. L. Mikhnevich wondered about the reasons which made Catherine entrust its supervision to Betskoi:

> The choice of Betskoi as the organizer and leader of that enterprise was most unfortunate. Catherine knew it herself, but for all kinds of delicate reasons could not bypass Betskoi, who was the chief administrator of and spokesman for the arts in Russia. Ivan Ivanovich Betskoi . . . was a simple-minded person, devoid of initiative, good taste, and talent, inordinately vain and pretentious in his drive for power and influence at the court and in government circles. . . . There was in him a great deal of pedantry and pettiness and that aspect of his personality came to the fore, often in the most comical manner, as he tried to direct the work on the monument to Peter, more often hindering its progress than helping it.[63]

There is no doubt that Betskoi considered the presidency of the Academy of Fine Arts as a license to meddle in the artistic aspects of the monument. But given the importance Catherine attached to the project, the question arises why she appointed Betskoi in the first place, and why, having seen that the differences between the general and Falconet were irreconcilable, she did not remove Betskoi from the project. The only answer is that she saw something positive in the heat generated by the permanent friction between the two adversaries.

In the early years of Falconet's stay in St. Petersburg, Catherine sided with the sculptor in the tug-of-war between the quintessential bureaucrat and the neurotic artist. A case in point was her ruling against Betskoi in the matter of freeing Falconet from the task of training Russian disciples. The empress agreed with the sculptor that his contract did not call for any teaching work at all. Betskoi was probably sent into a fit of rage, but there was nothing he could do about it because, as Diderot wrote to Mlle Volland: "Falconet has quarreled with General Betskoi, but he is so favored by the empress that the ministers fear him more than he does them."[64] Telling Falconet, "stick to your guns," the empress knew full well that such advice would not salve Betskoi's wounded pride. Falconet might have eased the situation had he taken into consideration Betskoi's alarmed state of mind, but confident of the support of the empress, he pushed his advantage with his habitual directness bordering on arrogance.

What the empress was saying to Betskoi, one can only guess at. She may have admonished him, but she never considered taking him off the job. "Delicate reasons," whatever they were, hinted at by Mikhnevich, never stopped the strong-minded empress from using the ax when important goals had to be reached. In this case, however, she must have reasoned that the conflict, without hurting the project, would put her in a stronger position vis-à-vis Falconet. Eventually she tired of having to rule on the disagreements and began to ignore the sculptor's grievances, letting Betskoi deal with Falconet in his own way. She underestimated, however, the sculptor's determination to defend his prerogatives, even at the price of shorting his personal circuit to her.

Wholly devoted to Catherine, Betskoi never married. As he said in one of his letters to the empress, "Your Majesty knows that I am nothing less than a courtier."[65] His natural daughter, Anastasia Sokolova, was known officially as a child adopted by him from the family of the painter Sokolov. Betskoi's half-sister, Princess Anastasia of Hesse-Homburg, took Anastasia to Paris to study with the celebrated actress Clairon.[66] Upon her return to Russia, Anastasia entered the service of Catherine and stayed with her for thirty-five years as her lady-in-waiting.[67] Late in life Betskoi took a romantic interest in Glafira Ivanovna Alymova (married name Rzhevskaia), a student in the Smolny Institute, but fear of public condemnation of a union with his own ward, fifty years his junior, prevented him from proposing marriage.[68]

In the last fifteen years of his life Betskoi lost his position as one of the preferred attendants of the empress. The cooling of their relations may be attributed to his poor state of health, as well as to Catherine's getting impatient with her rambling and vainglorious courtier, who staked his claims to the achievements of others, including her own educational initiatives.[69] Betskoi died in 1795, four years after Falconet and one year before Catherine. He was then ninety-one, forgotten and almost totally blind.

Falconet's relations with Betskoi were doomed from the start. Of the two protagonists of the feud, one was a stubborn and overweening bureaucrat, used to unquestioning obedience from his underlings, among whom he counted Falconet. The other was a headstrong artist, jealously safeguarding his freedom and insisting on having a direct and unfettered access to the empress. To Betskoi, a professional courtier and administrator and a believer in the established order of things, the existence of such a "special relationship" amounted to a gross violation of the sacrosanct principle of the "proper channels of communications," and a presumptuous invasion of his own traditional area of responsibility. He cringed each time Falconet would spring on him a decision of the empress of which he, until then the sole arbiter in matters of St. Petersburg's arts and architecture, had no prior knowledge.

Sparks began to fly at their very first meeting, one of the many occasions on which Falconet refused to grant Betskoi the premise that the monument project was their shared responsibility. The occasion was a courtesy call to which Falconet came bearing a personal letter of introduction from Prince Golitsyn. Here is how Ludwig Heinrich von Nicolaï, the tutor of the Grand Duke Paul, described the beginning of an association that was to last twelve years: "Betskoi immediately assumed an attitude which he deemed was consistent with his high position. He met Falconet with the benevolent look of a superior and said in a self-important manner: 'Well, my dear Sir, let us talk about our statue!'—'Our statue? Excuse me, Your Highness, you mean my statue?'—'Well, of course, you are going to make it, not I. But you and I still have some talking to do about it.'—'Not at all. The empress and I have already agreed on everything.' Whereupon Falconet turned around and left."[70]

During the first year of Falconet's stay in St. Petersburg, the empress was away from the capital and kept in touch with his affairs through reports from Betskoi and direct correspondence with the sculptor.[71] Events tended, however, to acquire a totally different twist depending on who was doing the telling. Thus, some six months into his stay Falconet declared that he would like to move from the house of Michel to the former kitchen on the grounds of the wooden Winter Palace.[72] That would allow him, he explained, to be closer to the big atelier which was then under construction, and in which the large model of the monument would be made. That is not, however, the way Betskoi described Falconet's motives in his report to Catherine of May 24, 1767:

> I have the honor to present to Your Majesty two letters that I have just received, one from Falconet, the other from Carburi. . . . I am the one in charge and I have borne the brunt of harassment and constant whims and fantasies, which I have handled nonetheless with the greatest patience. I may be wrong, but if the care that I have lavished on [Falconet] before and since his arrival in St. Petersburg does not bear fruit, it will be difficult to contain him. . . . The expense to which we are subjected every day because of his changing moods is all the more difficult to deal with, because there is no hope that it will ever end. . . . If I may say what I feel, Madame, I sense here one concern only—greed for money; that is evident from the Jesuitical subterfuges of his letter. . . . He will eagerly accept my last proposal. His calculations are all made. Instead of ten well-appointed rooms, he will lodge

in two or three miserable ones. He will not receive Burgundy wines every day, or the candles, not to speak of a respectable carriage, etc. But, before my proposal is accepted, I expect a number of face-saving tricks to elude the accusation of avarice, but I can prove it.[73]

Betskoi ended his letter with a crafty paraleipsis in which he hinted at a fire hazard created by Falconet's whims: "I do not mention a thousand interesting topics in order to save Your Majesty's precious time, such as the risk of placing the new casting shed *(liteinyi ambar)* in the center of the city, near the Palace and the Admiralty." What Betskoi did not say was that the proximity of the casting shed to the Admiralty and the Palace could not be avoided, since technical reasons required its location next to the emplacement of the monument.[74]

As one could expect at that early stage of Falconet's stay, Betskoi's representations did not have the desired effect on the empress. On June 18, 1767, he was obliged to agree to all the demands of Falconet and on July 26 the Bureau of Buildings allowed Carburi to spend six thousand rubles for furniture and carriage, and for the remodeling of the building to fit Falconet's needs.[75] In November Falconet was able to move into his new quarters.[76] There is little reason, however, to accept Betskoi's claim that Falconet's demand was motivated by greed. Falconet's expenses in St. Petersburg were paid by the Bureau of Buildings, and he did not stand to gain by moving out of Michel's house. Michel, however, had much to lose without his high-paying lodgers. It may well be, in fact, that Betskoi's explosion against Falconet was caused by his disappointment that Michel, who was his friend and confidant, would be deprived of a steady source of income. It may even be that Falconet, suspecting the existence of some under-the-table arrangement between Michel and Betskoi, demanded the change out of spite against Betskoi.

In the beginning of his stay, Falconet showed some understanding of Betskoi's complexes. "The general," he said, "is a good man. That is why it is important that I carefully keep away from him everything that, I think, might displease him."[77] He did not, for instance, show Betskoi a letter from Prince Golitsyn lest the courtier feel offended by a communication that bypassed his authority. Soon, however, Falconet's temperament pushed the feud into the open and kept it there during all of his time in St. Petersburg.

Having begun working on the large model of the monument, Falconet was surprised to hear Betskoi suggest that he would take care of the construction of the iron armature that was to hold up the horse on its hind legs. Here is how Falconet recalls his answer to Betskoi's suggestion:

"Are you a smith, Sir, for that is what I need now, a skillful smith. I designed the armature together with the rest of the sculpture in Paris when I, as you well know, received the commission from Her Imperial Majesty." . . . Monsieur Betskoi was displeased with my reply, but I went on: "Let me assure you, Sir, that a suggestion of that kind cannot be heeded except by inferior artists; only they would submit to it." I told him that everybody must stick to his profession, that no one should be robbed of what is his, and that in Paris the General Director does not come around to our ateliers to tell us: "I will do this or that for you," because he knows that this is our business and not his. Monsieur Betskoi became even more displeased and left immediately without responding. Count Carburi was present.[78]

Another instance of the Betskoi-Falconet tug-of-war was an incident involving the construction of a dwelling just a few yards from Falconet's atelier. Falconet, fearful for the safety of his work and knowing that any development of public land required the assent of the Bureau of Buildings, accused Betskoi, the bureau's director, of sanctioning the construction with malicious intent. Paranoid or not, this accusation appears unjust when confronted with Betskoi's many actions clearly intended to advance the enterprise of the monument. A more likely explanation is the obvious desirability of the empty lot left after the razing of the old wooden Winter Palace. Since its size and centrality were comparable to the area covered today by the Winter Palace and Palace Square, the lot attracted the attention of many land developers. One of them was a certain Monsieur Pochel, a theater entrepreneur, who wished to build a playhouse there. Using Michel's friendship with Betskoi, Pochel obtained the permission of the Bureau of Buildings to begin the construction.

Work on the foundations of the theater began in 1768. The ground shook in the immediate vicinity of Falconet's atelier and there arose the danger of a landslide. Falconet, who had just constructed the armature for the large model of the monument, became alarmed and complained to the empress. Her reaction was immediate:

Monsieur Falconet, no one has spoken to me directly or indirectly about Pochel's project. In any case, however, let me assure you that no one in Russia will bother Monsieur Falconet, that his atelier and his lodgings will remain his until he himself says: "I don't want them any more." In this particular case, I don't believe that the Pochels and Michels would dare suggest a project which cannot be executed without my say so. They have no illusions about my opinion—one is a professional schemer, while the other is a leech. . . . In any event, there is a plan signed by me five years ago and deposited with the police that no wooden building may be erected on that lot. It's all right to make a temporary exception to that plan for the sake of a statue of a great man which is being erected by an unusual artist, but not for a theater entrepreneur at the risk of burning down a whole section of town.[79]

Digging stopped, but not for long. Within two years Betskoi sent in more building crews, forcing Falconet to complain: "Monsieur Betskoi, who honors me with the most sincere hatred and who has given me proof of it on more than one occasion, has not even deemed it proper to tell me, if only to calm me down, what it is that he is building around my atelier and my lodgings."[80]

The following day the empress, clearly agitated, assured Falconet that she had expressly forbidden Betskoi to allow any work in the vicinity of his place of work and asked for more details.[81] These followed in two days: "The workers had orders to overturn the large forge where I am currently making the armature for the bronze cast. They had orders to dig the foundations and drive in the piles right up to my atelier. This little game was about to make everything tumble because piles being driven into unfortified ground causes shaking. All this was supposed to be done without my knowledge. Today at four o'clock in the morning, I stopped the workers who were pulling down the wall adjacent to the small courtyard of my lodging."[82]

To drive his point home Falconet used blackmail as his most powerful artillery: "Without your all-powerful protection, I would find it impossible to stay here another instant, especially since that man [Pochel] and his Michel spread as much hatred toward me as they can."[83]

Catherine was sympathetic, but expressed doubts about the validity of Falconet's complaints: "I must say that the edge of the building on which they were to work seems, according to the plan, rather far from your atelier."[84] That comment, showing a lack of total and unconditional support, was enough to make Falconet lose his cool. Accusing Betskoi of a conscious attempt to drive him out of his mind and force him thereby to resign, he concocted a nefarious scheme on Betskoi's part and unfolded it before the empress, putting it into Betskoi's own mouth: "F[alconet] is troublesome, he is not my creature, he does not want anything from me, he does not lower himself to ask for any favors from me. . . . Since the model is finished, we can do without him. I'll ask somebody else to continue the work. I'll publish and I'll make Michel publish a story that I had made changes and improvements [in the model] and I'll take away from him and many others the glory that I want so much and that he himself would not let me have. Thus the work will be finished by me, because I want to give the impression of having done it all."[85]

Continuing the letter in his own name, Falconet added: "If Your Majesty thinks that I've gone mad with all these visions, allow me to point out that, if I, after five years, didn't know that man and his ways of dealing with others, I would be an imbecile, who should be placed in a madhouse."

Intent on solving the problem once and for all, the empress paid Falconet an unannounced visit one morning. "[Falconet] greeted her in a frock of coarse cloth and a woolen bonnet. She took him by the hand, led him to the building site, and asked him to determine himself how far the workers might advance. An agreement was struck between the artist and the sovereign. Each side made concessions and the empress gave orders that the treaty which she had just negotiated and concluded be religiously observed."[86]

The successful completion of the transport of the granite boulder for the pedestal gave rise to another acidic exchange between the sculptor and the bureaucrat. It was occasioned by Betskoi's attempt not only to appropriate to himself all the glory of that operation, but also to present the pedestal as the most successful part of the monument, eclipsing even the sculpted figure of Peter the Great.

Betskoi's vainglory was also responsible for his maladroit attempt to organize his own publicity outside Russia. According to Nicolaï, he had his German secretary write a description of the transport of the granite boulder, lacing it with many references to his own all-important contributions. The article was then translated into French, but the translator, without Betskoi's knowledge, asked Falconet to look the text over and correct it. Falconet obliged and the article was sent for publication in the *Calendar of Gotha*. When the article appeared, Betskoi invited Falconet to his office and, pointing to the issue of the journal lying on the table, said:

"I am in awkward situation. Someone got an idea (God knows who he is) to publish in the *Calendar of Gotha* a long description of the transport of that large chunk of granite. I am a decided enemy not just of flattery, but of any public praise, and this author makes much too much noise. But the piece is not badly written. Would you like to take a look at it? You may take it with you." My rogue, writes Nicolaï, goes to the table with an innocent expression, takes the journal, reads a line, and puts it back. "Well, my dear Sir, aren't you curious at all?" "Oh, I know this piece very well," answers Falconet, "I worked on it before Your Excellency sent it off to Gotha."[87]

After such an exchange, can one be surprised that tormenting Falconet became Betskoi's obsession during the last years of the sculptor's stay in St. Petersburg?

LARGE MODEL

I invoke the help of our great artists. I invoke the help of those who have ceased to be. But try as I may, reality denies me the presence of either. I am alone . . .
—Falconet (1768)

In the beginning of February 1768 Falconet closed his atelier to the curious and began working on the large model of the monument. That summer he wrote Diderot that the model was taking shape and that he was doing his best to make it better than the small one, but that he felt oppressed by his loneliness—an artist face to face with his work, with no one to share his burden. "But don't pity me too much. I am energized by the importance of the task to which I devote all my time and which will be my last."[88]

Good friends were, of course, admitted and allowed to see the work in progress. One of the visitors was Prince Golitsyn. He and his wife of recent vintage, Countess Amalie von Schmettau, came to St. Petersburg in the summer of 1769 to pay their respects to Catherine and to visit with the prince's family. Golitsyn was enthralled by the large model and, upon his return, shared his admiration with Diderot, who was quick to write about it to Falconet: "I have just learned from Prince Golitsyn that your monument is sublime. You know how much pleasure this gives me."[89]

The large model was ready in the beginning of August 1769. "I redesigned it completely," said Falconet, "and finished it alone in eighteen months, although winter days allow just four working hours. . . . The two workers whom I had summoned worked no more than eight months. After their departure, I had to redo everything in order to assemble the parts."[90]

On May 9, 1770, Falconet wrote to Betskoi, inviting the members of the Academy of Fine Arts to view the finished model: "Sir, I believe that the model of the equestrian statue of Peter the Great is finished. My gratitude for it goes to the Academy and the nation. For several days before offering this model for public viewing, I ask the Gentlemen of the Academy of Fine Arts to see it, examine it, and point out any faults that may still be there, so that I can correct them. I beg you, Sir, to announce this in the Academy."[91]

Once the official visits were over, Falconet opened the doors of his atelier to the public. On May 21, 1770, the *St. Petersburg Gazette* carried a somewhat tardy notice that "for two weeks starting on May 19, between 11:00 A.M. and 3:00 P.M. and between 6:00 and 8:00 P.M., the model of the monument of Peter the Great will be on display in the building where the Winter Palace used to stand on Nevsky Prospect." As could have been expected, the atelier filled up with the curious. What they saw was a towering construction that occupied practically all of Falconet's sculpting shed. The anxious sculptor watched the crowds milling around the model and waited impatiently for some reaction, be it positive or negative. When none was forthcoming, he complained to the empress: "At last the curtain is raised. I am, as expected, at the public's mercy. My atelier is always full. But what I find somewhat peculiar is that not one of the local visitors has breathed a word; it is just as if I did not exist, even though I know that they are rather pleased with it. Whatever direct reactions I receive about my work are from sundry foreigners who come around. Such behavior is hardly known elsewhere."[92]

Catherine did her best to reassure her sculptor: "I know that the curtain is raised at your place and that people are in general very pleased. If they don't say a word to you, it is because they are tactful. Some don't consider themselves clever enough, some may hold back for fear of displeasing you with their comments, some finally cannot see anything there. Don't see the dark side in everything, the way so many Frenchmen do."[93]

What the empress did not tell her sculptor was undoubtedly the main reason for the diffident behavior of the visitors. They all knew that they were looking at a work that had the highest approval and they all suspected, most probably with good reason, that milling about were agents of the secret police, looking out for any criticism that could be interpreted as an expression of dissent and sedition. Thus, the only man who dared to harangue the crowd on the monument's shortcomings was a certain Mr. Iakovlev, who turned out to be mentally unstable. Here is how Falconet described his visit:

> There are no horrors that he did not find in the statue. That man, who claimed to have seen all statues, never saw a sculpted person with hair arranged in this way. He has forgotten, no doubt, that they are almost all alike, both ancient and modern. He found it awful that I had given the emperor the mustache that he had worn all his life. . . . He flew into a rage against the Russian cloak that is not Russian at all. He repeated that it was horrible and reprehensible for me to have given Peter the First a garment whose eradication cost the emperor so much effort. Since he probably has not seen the statue of Marcus Aurelius, he could not know that the garments of both emperors are alike. . . . Mr. Iakovlev shouted that my project had made more than five hundred members of the nobility indignant, that it was the talk of the town, and that only an ukase of the empress made people put up with it.[94]

The empress patiently tried to assuage Falconet's anguish. She explained that Iakovlev was a good-for-nothing mischief-maker who had been expelled from the army, pretended to be a nobleman, and constantly got into trouble. "Why, just the other day he molested two Jews." She gave Falconet her customary counsel: "Laugh at the fools and stay your course, just as I do."[95] But try as she might, it was not easy to reassure a paranoid artist who, according to some, would hide behind the curtains of his atelier to eavesdrop on private conversations and then suddenly jump out to dispute negative comments.[96]

Now that the model was completed, Falconet wanted to have a drawing of it so that it could be engraved.[97] Two painters were under consideration. One was Stéphane Torelli (1712–80), a well-respected artist, author of the ceiling frescoes in the palace of Oranienbaum and of allegorical portraits of Catherine the Great as Minerva, patroness of the arts, and as Victory triumphant in the war with Turkey. Torelli volunteered his services, but Falconet hesitated to entrust the task to him because of the painter's failing health. The second candidate was Anton Pavlovich Losenko (1737–73), an able Russian painter, whom Falconet befriended and on whose behalf he often interceded with the empress.[98] Since Losenko was already at work on a drawing of the model commissioned by Prince Golitsyn during his stay in St. Petersburg, Falconet suggested that both artists be allowed to proceed and then the better drawing could be selected.[99] As it happened, Torelli's drawing was not executed. Losenko's drawing (fig. 3.6) was completed in 1770.[100]

When Collot and Pierre-Etienne Falconet, the sculptor's son, traveled to Paris in 1775, Falconet *père* asked them to take the drawing along and show it at the Académie.[101] He reported later to the empress that the drawing was

Fig. 3.6. Anton Pavlovich Losenko, Large Model of the Monument to Peter the Great. Pencil and white pastel, 1770. The Latin inscription reads: "Stephanus Falconet, parisinus invenit et fecit, Maria-Anna Collot parisina Imperatoris similitudinem expressit, Antonius Lossenko ruthenus delineavit anno 1770." ("Conceived and made by Etienne Falconet of Paris, Marie-Anne Collot of Paris made the model of the [facial] likeness of the emperor, Anton Losenko of Russia made the drawing in the year 1770.") Musée des Beaux-Arts, Nancy. Photograph by G. Mangin.

a great success there and that there was an interest in having it engraved. Would she agree to his son finding an appropriate engraver?[102] There was no answer to that request, and for some reason Losenko's drawing, though highly praised by Falconet, was never engraved.[103] That fiasco left the Bronze Horseman as the only major equestrian monument without a contemporary engraving or a small model in bronze, terracotta, or wax. In one of his last letters to the empress, Falconet claimed that Collot was working on a small model, but it has not been found.[104]

The monument, as shown in Losenko's drawing, is strikingly similar to its final version in bronze. That circumstance should have put to rest the rumors that the finished monument differed in many details from the original design. It proves in particular the falseness of the widely circulated charge that the pedestal of the monument was made smaller by the sculptor than he originally intended. It also shows that the snake, which Falconet added in 1768 and which the Russian sculptor Fedor Gordeev completed after Falconet's departure from St. Petersburg, was faithful in all its tortuous convolutions to the design. As for the inscription, it was not in Losenko's drawing because at that time the text had not yet been agreed upon.[105] Thus, one may safely assume that what we see today in bronze and granite was, by and large, identical with the large model of the monument, which was open for public inspection in May 1770.[106]

Of all the equestrian statues known to Falconet, the *Marcus Aurelius* (figs. 2.1, 8.10) had a special meaning. For the critics and the public that was the prototypical equestrian monument and the gauge against which all other equestrian monuments should be measured. These comparisons were invariably decided in favor of the *Marcus Aurelius,* a circumstance which caused Falconet to make the classical statue his *bête noire.* The *Marcus Aurelius* along with its admirers became the butt of his ferocious attacks in a long disquisition called *Observations sur la statue de Marc-Aurèle.*[107] Significantly, he dedicated the booklet to Diderot, his opponent in the discussion on the virtues and faults of ancient art.

Falconet, however, should not have been bothered by such comparisons, for the two monuments express entirely different conceits. The Russian emperor galloping uphill is an apotheosis of engagement and action. The emperor of the *Marcus Aurelius,* as befits the author of the *Meditations,* is shown in a mood of contemplation and unclouded tranquility, as he slowly rides his high-stepping horse.

Assuming that Falconet's ideas about the monument to Peter the Great were formed before his arrival in St. Petersburg, there remains the question what these ideas originally were. Normally one would be able to reconstruct a sculptor's creative process from his sketchbook. In the case of Falconet, however, no drawings or sketches have survived. One has to rely instead on written testimony, of which there is fortunately a fair amount, mostly in the form of the sculptor's correspondence with Diderot and Catherine the Great.

The first known reference to the design of the St. Petersburg monument is in Diderot's farewell letter to the sculptor. It confirms that Falconet's original intention was to make the horse in the *pose bondissante* and to place it on a hill made of natural stone. Diderot's recollection is confirmed by Falconet in his *Observations sur la statue de Marc-Aurèle.* While discussing the need to combat one's ingrained prejudices and stereotypical reactions, the sculptor mentioned a conversation with an unidentified painter concerning the wisdom of using a natural rock for the pedestal of the statue. When the painter challenged the soundness of Falconet's decision to use natural stone in St. Petersburg where "there are no rocks," the sculptor countered, logically enough: "Does he think that square and polished pedestals grow there?"[108] That conversation, says Falconet, took place "right in front of the Palais-

Royal," that is, in the very heart of Paris, before the trip to St. Petersburg. In a footnote to this passage, Falconet recalls that he had used the corner of [Diderot's] table to "sketch the hero and his charger leaping onto the emblematic rock."[109]

All this leads one to conclude that, except for the later addition of the snake, the large model of the monument, as well as its final form in bronze, replicate faithfully Falconet's original design which he had sent to St. Petersburg from Paris.

4

Thunder Rock

ROLLING STONE

An awesome Russian mountain, by human hands not made,
Obeyed the voice divine that Catherine did utter,
To Peter's city came, across both land and water,
And at the feet of Peter was dutifully laid.
—Vasily G. Ruban (1770)

A Karelian forest in the dead of winter is the essence of peace and quiet.
No motion but for a wisp of snow floating down from a branch. No sound
but for an occasional crackle of wood snapping in the cold air. An immense
spider web, a nostalgic leftover of the summer, glistens in the first rays of
the sun. Stretched between two branches and surrounded by a dense growth
of pines, spruces, aspens, and white birches, it seems freshly spun, for no
gust of wind can reach it and disturb its perfect symmetry. Whiteness and
stillness all around. One can hardly imagine a more tranquil setting.

In the winter of 1770, however, a stretch of woods between the village of
Konnaia and the north shore of the Gulf of Finland, about an hour's ride
from St. Petersburg, was anything but tranquil. A wide road, freshly carved
from the forest and swept clean of snow down to the frozen ground, was
pulsating with life. There were the clanging of mallets, the rhythmic beat
of axes, the buzzing of saws, and the jumble of human voices. From a snow-
bank piled high along the roadside, a visitor could view a most unusual
spectacle. There in front of him, on a platform that looked like a sled, was
a granite boulder four times the height of man. Its contour was reminiscent
of a detached ship's prow. On top stood two drummers drumming. Behind
them dozens of stonecutters were busily trimming the boulder. And behind
the stonecutters, on a small ledge, there was a fired forge with two smiths
going about their business. But the most astonishing thing was that the boulder with all its hangers-on was slowly moving, "stern" first, in the direction
of the sea.

Joining that odd convoy were hundreds of people. Some walked alongside
the boulder shouting instructions; some were turning the capstans that pulled

the boulder along; some were checking the chassis on which the boulder rested, much as a modern railroad man checks the wheels on the train; some were dragging hollowed-out wooden beams from behind the boulder to the front; some were watching over a cortege of sleighs bringing up the rear; some were simply milling around, eager to see the sight that was the talk of the capital. What these people witnessed would eventually gain a reputation as one of the most spectacular technological accomplishments of the eighteenth century. And deservedly so, for never before had a mass of such dimensions been moved over land and sea for whatever purpose, let alone for art's sake.

The granite boulder that was making its way through the Karelian woods was destined to become the pedestal of the equestrian statue of Peter the Great, which the French sculptor Falconet was modeling at that time in St. Petersburg. It was to be given the shape of a cliff, gently sloping on one side and abruptly breaking on the other, resembling a large wave just before it washes ashore. The horse was to be shown rearing just short of the edge of the cliff in response to the restraining hand of the horseman. It was an entirely novel idea in heroic sculpture. Instead of the traditional pedestal, whose size and shape trivialize the horse's essential qualities of speed and grace and reduce it to the status of a horse-show or circus performer, Falconet intended to put his horse at the elevated end of a natural stone runway, climaxing an impetuous run to the top with the *pose bondissante.*

Falconet never expected to be able to obtain a sufficiently large boulder to work with and thought that he would have to assemble the cliff from several rocks. When, to everyone's surprise, such a massive boulder was found, it was generally believed that its size would make it impossible to transport it to St. Petersburg in one piece. The most obvious solution would have been to cut it up in the forest and reassemble it on Senate Square, the site of the monument. Most people, including Falconet, championed such a course of action, but not Catherine the Great. She wanted to bring the entire boulder to the city.

Was it an extravagant gift to a sculptor whom she admired and liked, or a wish to have him work on the pedestal under her watchful gaze? Most probably neither. Catherine the Great was a political animal through and through, and it was her political intuition that prompted her to stake money and reputation on an undertaking which she knew was adventurous, but whose potential political benefits were of such an order as to justify the risk. Later events proved the correctness of her gambling instincts. The incredible saga of the successful search for a natural stone for the pedestal and of its transportation to St. Petersburg caught the fancy of the world and brought Catherine's rule almost as much acclaim as the first sputnik brought to the Khrushchev regime.[1]

The events leading up to the finding of the boulder began to unfold in the spring of 1767, when Betskoi and his subordinates in the Bureau of Buildings were making plans for a pedestal assembled from several rocks, attached to each other by steel or copper clasps.[2] Several search expeditions were dispatched to the vicinity of St. Petersburg to look for rocks of appropriate size and color, but failed to find any usable stones. Betskoi, pushed undoubtedly by the empress, made the procurement of suitable rocks a matter of top priority. During the summer two new expeditions were organized. One, under Colonel Ivan Zverev, searched west of St. Petersburg; the other, under Sergei Vasiliev, was sent to Kronshtadt and regions south of the city. Again weeks passed without any success. On February 23, 1768, the Bureau of Buildings sent out the following announcement: "Needed, natural field stone in one or several pieces, for a mountain [i.e. pedestal] forty-two feet in length, twenty-one in height, and twenty-one in width. The Bureau asks the inhabitants of the St. Petersburg and Vyborg districts for information where such stones may be found, and to report their size, fissures, location, proximity to roads, and condition of the terrain. If found, please bring in chips from the southern and northern exposures for examination."[3]

When no finds were reported, the despairing Betskoi told the Senate on May 5, 1768, that there was no hope of finding a whole natural stone and that "even if it were found, its enormous weight would cause great difficulties in transporting it across the sea and rivers." He informed the senators that the total amount budgeted for the monument was 480,000 rubles, but that the cost of moving a solid rock could make that sum insufficient. Therefore, he said, it would be necessary to make up the pedestal from several smaller pieces.[4]

But those were not easy to find either. The twice-weekly *St. Petersburg Gazette* carried announcements, inviting anyone wishing to participate in the search for "six natural field stones" to come to the Bureau of Buildings and pick up specifications.[5] The locals were asked to form search parties. Orthodox priests and Lutheran pastors were asked to urge parishioners to be on the lookout for promising rocks. Rewards were offered. Still, no luck.

Fortune began changing when Captain Carburi, Betskoi's resourceful aide-de-camp, was appointed head of the search. He was the right person for the job. In his capacity as liaison officer between Betskoi and Falconet, he was in daily touch with the sculptor and was familiar with his plans and needs. His training as an engineer, his cosmopolitan background, and, most important, his energy, ambition, and talent for organization made him a highly valued member of Falconet's St. Petersburg enterprise. So much so, in fact, that he was the only man in Betskoi's entourage whom Falconet respected and trusted. In addition, he alone in the Bureau of Buildings remained stubbornly committed to the idea of having the pedestal made from a solid piece of granite. In a composite pedestal, he claimed, mechanical ligaments "wear out, get rusty and used up, they may be damaged in various accidents and poor weather, and soon what had seemed like solid stone takes on the appearance of a heap of rubble."[6] He had never lost hope that a solid rock of the dimensions required by Falconet's project would be found, and that a method could be devised to transport it to the city. At a time when all the search parties were coming back empty-handed, Carburi's optimism must have seemed utterly chimerical.

The first bit of good news came in early summer of 1768 when Sergei Vasiliev found a large granite rock off the island of Kotlin, some seventeen miles west of St. Petersburg, in the vicinity of the port of Kronshtadt. It was less than half the size needed for a solid pedestal, but it was certainly large enough to be the main component of a composite one. There was joy in Betskoi's camp, even though there were still formidable difficulties to overcome. There was no certainty that more rocks, matching the Kotlin rock in color and composition, would be found. Besides, the task of transporting the Kotlin rock to St. Petersburg turned out to be harder than originally thought, for the Admiralty, which was handling the job, lacked the necessary equipment and the requisite know-how. There was no crane to hoist the partly submerged rock, no seaworthy floating platform on which it could be moved, and the course to the city had not yet been charted. Realizing how much was at stake and fearing responsibility for failure, the Admiralty dragged its feet and, much to Betskoi's dismay, the whole summer passed in negotiations and preparations.[7] Then, just as the Admiralty seemed to be gearing up for action, all the plans for moving the Kotlin rock were suddenly aborted. Instead, the Bureau of Buildings turned its attention to the village of Konnaia[8] in the Vyborg region, on the north shore of the Gulf of Finland.

On September 8, 1768, one Semën Grigorievich Vishniakov, a local peasant and supplier of granite for various construction projects in the capital, walked into the Bureau of Buildings on Voznesensky Prospect and announced that he knew of a granite rock that seemed tailor-made for Falconet's needs. It was buried in a forest on the estate of Count Iakov Aleksandrovich Brius (Bruce), near the village of Konnaia, some four miles north of the shore of the Gulf of Finland, and about eight miles as the crow flies from the center of St. Petersburg, or about thirteen miles if one were to take it down to the gulf and continue via deep-water channels. Local peasants called it *Kamen'-Grom* or Thunder Rock, because there was a fissure in one corner, which, they believed, was caused by a bolt of lightning. There was also a legend that Peter the Great had once climbed the rock in order to survey the area. Vishniakov had hoped to use the rock as a quarry for his granite trade, but found it too big and too inaccessible. Now, lured by the promise of a reward of one hundred rubles, he was ready to show it to the officials of the Bureau of Buildings.

Not wasting any time, Carburi had Vishniakov conduct him to Konnaia so that he could take a look at the rock. What he saw exceeded his boldest expectations. Sticking out from the boggy floor of the Karelian forest was an enormous granite rock that was completely covered with thick moss. Except for the fissure, which was eighteen inches wide and had a sizable birch tree growing from it, the rock seemed solid (fig. 4.1). After some preliminary digging it was determined that it was a boulder, in other words, that it was

Fig. 4.1. Iury M. Fel'ten, The Thunder Rock as Found in the Karelian Forest. Engraving by Jakob van der Schley, 1768. The State Hermitage Museum, St. Petersburg.

detached. Six feet of the rock were above ground, while fifteen feet were buried below the surface. The top and the bottom were almost perfectly flat, a common feature of postglacial debris, which get polished by being pushed around by glaciers. The remarkable appearance of such a large granite boulder, so close to St. Petersburg, began to seem altogether miraculous when it was realized that the cleavage ran all the way to the bottom of the boulder, giving it the desired sloping shape. The local lore of its being due to a bolt of lightning added to a sense of supernatural intervention.

Falconet looked at that gift of Providence with mixed feelings. On the one hand, he did not believe that the Bureau of Buildings would be able or willing to lift the entire boulder from its forest bed and move it by land and sea to Senate Square. He was not alone in discounting such a possibility, for it was generally agreed that if "the sight of it caused wonderment, . . . the mere thought of moving it to another place evoked dread."[9] On the other hand, Falconet had to be overjoyed that there at last, within an hour's ride from the capital, was an immense mass of granite that could be cut up into five or six pieces, transported, and reassembled to form the pedestal, ending what until then had been a fruitless search. Yet the prospect of having to break up a solid granite boulder that, with some rearrangement, was big enough to make up the entire pedestal, must have been painful to countenance.

Not everybody, however, was willing to accept the pessimistic forecast that precluded the possibility of transporting the boulder in its entirety.

Carburi, for one, maintained all along that, after some preliminary cutting, the boulder could and should be moved. On September 10, he submitted to Betskoi a report on the find, accompanied by the following recommendation: "The rock should be transported six versts [about four miles] by land to the village of Lakhta and thence by boat, by way of the Lesser Neva, to its destination." Betskoi presented Carburi's views to Catherine and asked for her ruling. He did not have to wait long—an opportunity to score political points abroad by showing off Russia's technological potential was just too tempting to resist. Within a week, the empress announced her decision to go ahead with the project of transporting the Thunder Rock in its entirety, "first by land and then by water." As Carburi put it, "the sweep of her ideas, her wisdom, her exalted spirit placed her above the fears generated by mediocrity and the clamor dictated by envy."[10]

Falconet has sometimes been accused of unreasonable insistence on using a natural monolith for his pedestal. Reacting to these accusations with his customary touchiness, Falconet built up an elaborate case proving that such an idea had never entered his head. As he said in his answer to a Monsieur Linguet, who had made several critical remarks about the use of a monolith: "I played no part whatsoever in the choice of the rock, its transport, and the expense involved. I believed that the base of my statue would be fashioned out of well-matched, connected stones. In fact I had long kept in my atelier the models I had made of all the sections [of the pedestal]. Their existence proves that a monolithic rock was far from my thoughts."[11]

There is little doubt that Falconet was too pragmatic a man to entertain the pipe dream of finding a massive boulder, even though he may have spoken out on the advantages of a solid pedestal over a composite one. If he went along with the idea of moving the Thunder Rock in one piece, he did so without particular enthusiasm: "It wasn't I who had the rock transported. The operation was ordered by Monsieur Betskoi and was planned, directed, and very well executed by Count Carburi of Cephalonia. . . . I do not deserve the least credit for overcoming the difficulties."[12] And elsewhere: "It was proposed to me, I admired it, and said, 'Bring [the rock] over! It will make the base sturdier.'"[13] Not a very excited reaction from a sculptor who must have realized that Catherine the Great was handing him an opportunity that no other sculptor had ever had before. Was it a pose assumed after the rock had been moved? Probably not, for even during its transport, Falconet showed little interest in it. There is not a word about the move in his correspondence with Catherine the Great, not a word about it in his correspondence with Diderot. Given Diderot's effusiveness, it is likely that Falconet never brought up the subject at all. Perhaps he feared that the enormous effort put into the project by the Russians would make them feel more proprietary about the boulder and more critical of his decision to trim it down to the size projected in the model. Perhaps it was merely another example of Falconet's habit of accepting good fortune as his due and of showing emotion only when he felt wronged or threatened.

The empress's decision was communicated to the Admiralty, the Senate, and the Academy of Sciences together with the announcement of Betskoi's appointment as supervisor of the operation. The empress asked the Admiralty to assist him "in every way and without delay with tools and everything needed to lift [the rock] and move it by land, and provide [Betskoi] with men and boats properly outfitted to transport such a heavy stone to the pier at St. Isaac's [Senate] Square." She also ordered Admiral Semën Mordvinov, head of the Admiralty, to make a special effort to bring the stone over as soon as possible "fulfilling thereby our wishes."[14] By entrusting the direction of the operation to Betskoi, Catherine the Great was in fact appointing Carburi, whose technical skills, which served him well in several other projects, as well as his close ties to Falconet, made him especially well-suited for the job.[15]

Now that he knew the empress's wishes, Betskoi, her ever obedient courtier, put the machinery of the Bureau of Buildings into high gear. Almost every document in the archive of Admiral Mordvinov contains the qualifiers "immediately," "without delay," and other exhortations to prompt action. Work crews were told that machines, instruments, and supplies, if not immediately available, should be ordered from storage. "If they are not in storage, then they have to be manufactured without delay."[16] On September 26 excavation and construction work began in earnest.[17] The first order of business was to assemble teams of carpenters to construct housing for the work force of four hundred hired hands and five hundred soldiers. They cleared trees and shrubs, excavated around the boulder to a depth of 14 feet and a radius of about 100 feet, and built a road all the way to the gulf. For the first 1,428 feet, the road had a slight upgrade. In the first half of that segment, it was built to be 40 feet wide, but was widened later to about 70 feet. The larger width provided space for various maneuvers during the transport and ensured quicker drying and deeper freezing of the terrain. The bared boulder turned out to be 42 feet long, 27 feet wide, and 21 feet high.[18] Assuming that one cubic foot of granite weighs approximately 175 pounds, the weight of the rock was calculated to be about 4 million pounds or 1,800 metric tons.

By February 1769 the boulder was fully clear of earth, and Falconet could see that it would serve him best if the top and bottom were to become its sides. In other words, the boulder had to be flipped clockwise along its long axis, if one were to look at it standing behind the side with the fissure. In this new position the width would become the height and vice versa, so that the boulder would be 27 feet high and 21 feet wide.[19] The fissure must have been at least partly responsible for the decision to turn the boulder over, for the top of the boulder without the severed upper corner would have the sloping outline that was the distinctive feature of Falconet's design for the pedestal.

Before flipping the boulder over, Falconet decided to reduce it in size and weight. It was important, in particular, for the side that was to become the bottom, and on which the boulder was to ride into the city, to be made flat and straight. With that in mind, a team of stonecutters, directed by Falconet himself, lopped off almost 7,500 cubic feet of solid granite, trimming the boulder to about 2.7 million pounds or something over 1,200 metric tons, that is, more or less two-thirds of its original weight.[20] Falconet would have gone on had he not been stopped by Catherine, who wished to keep the boulder at its largest and most pristine in order to magnify the drama that the transport of the boulder was bound to create.

Falconet, to be sure, could not have cared very much how the corner was transported to St. Petersburg as long as it got there, for he had already determined its future use. It was to be split in half and the two pieces were to serve as the front and rear extensions of the pedestal, whose length was projected to exceed that of the trimmed-down boulder by about twelve feet (fig. 4.2).[21]

A prize of seven thousand rubles was announced for designing a mechanism to transport the Thunder Rock in one piece. It is difficult to know precisely how many bids were submitted and the nature of the different methods proposed. A court watchmaker was willing to move the rock provided all the smiths of the capital were put at his service. There was also a suggestion that the rock be moved on solid steel rollers ten inches in diameter. Both ideas were rejected out of hand. The project that was accepted was the "machine" submitted by Carburi. It was the only one that was professionally designed and that showed an appreciation of the magnitude of the task, the mass of the stone, the problems created by swamps and brooks along the way, the road turns, the transfer of the boulder to a raft, and its transport by sea and river to Senate Square.[22]

The machine of Carburi had two levels. The bottom was made up of two hollowed-out wooden beams forming gutters, each thirty-three feet long, fourteen inches wide, and twelve inches high. The hollow of each gutter was lined with copper two inches thick, and tapered from five inches across at the top to about three inches at the bottom. The two gutters, placed side by side, fifteen feet apart, and turned hollow side up, formed the guide rails of the machine. The top of the assembly consisted of two similarly hollowed-out wooden beams that were forty-two feet long, eighteen inches wide, and sixteen inches high and had their hollow sides down. The upper beams were connected by four wooden twelve-by-twelve crossbeams and three two-inch iron crossbars to form a sturdy fifteen-foot wide chassis for the boulder to rest on. Between the lower and upper gutters, on each side of the assembly, were placed fifteen evenly spaced five-inch copper balls that allowed the chassis to ride on the guide rails with a minimum of friction.[23] There were seven workers with crowbars on each side of the moving chassis to keep an eye on the functioning of the balls and be ready to adjust them as necessary. Six pairs of guide rails were built so that the rails over which the chassis had passed could be dragged to the front and reused. The motive power was provided by two, four, or six capstans, depending on the grade, using lines

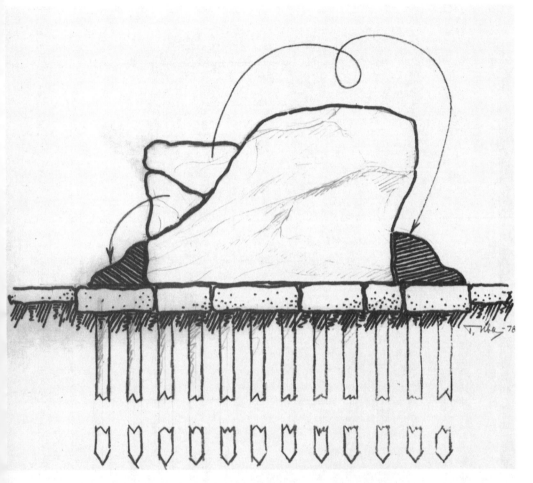

Fig. 4.2. Using the Split-Off Corner of the Thunder Rock to Extend the
Pedestal. Based on a reconstruction by Georgy Ivanovich Ivanov (1994, p. 66).
The original drawing by courtesy of the artist's wife,
Valentina Nikolaevna Ivanova.

that were an inch and a half in diameter. Each capstan was manned by thirty-
two workers (fig. 4.3).

Carburi assumed that the boulder placed on the chassis could be pulled
or pushed with relative ease. To put that assumption to a test, he had a small
model of the machine built and placed on it a proportionately smaller load.
The gathered scholars and military men saw that he could pull that load
effortlessly with one finger.[24] The demonstration of the model was apparently
persuasive, for Betskoi allowed Carburi to proceed with the development of

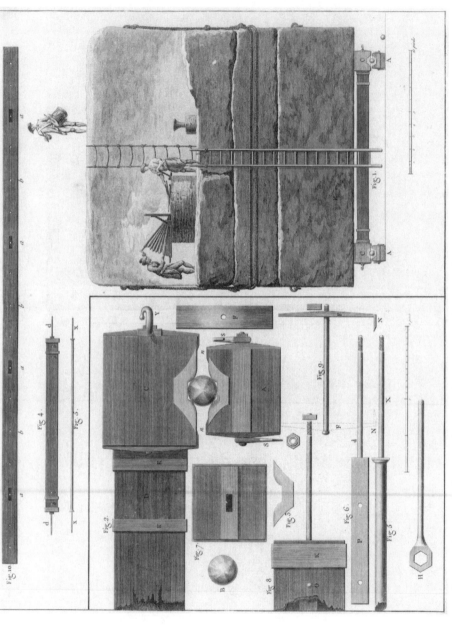

Fig. 4.3. Louis-Nicolas van Blarenberghe, Various Elements of Carburi's "Machine" and Rear View of the Thunder Rock Resting on Its Chassis and Guide Rails. Engraving by R.-H.-J. Delvaux (Carburi de Cephalonie, 1777). Courtesy Beinecke Rare Book and Manuscript Library, Yale University.

the full-size machine. There remained, however, many doubters for whom the model was no more than an abstract concept, whose practicality could not be tested until the boulder "was actually moved and lifted from its hole."[25] The skepticism of these "demi-savants," as Carburi called them, did not prevent him from proceeding with the first real test of his engineering skills—the turning of the boulder on its side.

The main force needed to upend the boulder was provided by twelve levers, each able to lift about two hundred thousand pounds. The levers were made of three sixty-five-foot poles and rested on a fulcrum placed close to the boulder. The lower end of the lever was inserted under the boulder, while its higher end was attached to a rope-and-pulley mechanism that was suspended from the top of a tall wooden derrick and connected to a winch below. Since the weight of the boulder was estimated at 3 million pounds and the lifting power generated by the twelve levers amounted to 2.4 million pounds, four supplementary pulling mechanisms had to be set up on the opposite side of the levers. They consisted of lines running from the top of the boulder to four capstans anchored a hundred feet away from the boulder. The upended boulder was to settle on a platform made of ten layers of criss-crossed wooden beams covered with a six-foot layer of moss and hay in order to cushion the shock of the landing (fig. 4.4).[26]

To the beat of a drummer, the workers operating the twelve winches on one side and the four capstans on the other slowly lifted one side of the boulder. After each foot of upward movement, wooden blocks were placed under the boulder to keep it in its new position, while the levers and fulcrums were adjusted for a repetition of the operation. At the same time wooden supports were placed on the other side of the boulder in preparation for the moment when its weight would be transferred to the other side and the problem would be how to slow down its descent onto the platform. The method devised by Carburi included six restraining lines on the upper side of the boulder and several huge jackscrews under it. As the wooden supports were gradually removed, the boulder descended slowly, and on March 12, 1769, after nearly two months of backbreaking and nerve-grating work, it came to a rest on the platform without making a dent in it.[27]

The next phase of the operations was to transfer the boulder from the platform to the chassis-and-guide-rail assembly waiting nearby. Since the chassis was seventeen feet wide and the width (former height) of the boulder was twenty-one feet, there were two feet of stone protruding on either side. Under these protruding parts of the boulder Carburi placed twelve large iron jackscrews, six to a side, made by Fügner, the best locksmith in St. Petersburg. With their help, the boulder was raised sufficiently to allow for the platform to be pulled out and replaced by the chassis.

Since the road leading to the Bay of Kronshtadt required four turns, Carburi had to design a special turntable that would allow the boulder to change its course. The turntable was based on the same principle as that used in the regular machine, except that it was circular and the lower and upper

Fig. 4.4. Louis-Nicolas van Blarenberghe, The Thunder Rock Being Flipped onto Its Platform. Note the twelve lifting levers on the left and four pulling capstans on the right. Engraving by R.-H.-J. Delvaux (Carburi de Cephalonie, 1777). Courtesy Beinecke Rare Book and Manuscript Library, Yale University.

parts were identical in size. The circle was twelve feet in diameter and there were fifteen copper balls in the assembly. At each turn in the road the boulder was raised by the method used in its transfer from the platform to the chassis-and-guide-rail assembly, which was pulled from under it and replaced by the turntable. Lines attached to the diagonally opposite corners of the boulder were pulled by two capstans, making the boulder turn on its axis. When the turn was completed, the boulder was raised again, the turntable was replaced by the chassis-and-guide-rail assembly, and the boulder was ready to roll on along its new path (fig. 4.5).

An assembly consisting of a metal casing filled with metal balls converting sliding friction into rolling friction was, for all practical purposes, a prototype of today's ball-bearing mechanism. Yet neither Carburi, who was not known for modesty, nor anyone else in his entourage was prescient enough to take credit for this revolutionary design. It took more than a hundred years for the ball-bearing mechanism to be reinvented so that modern civilization could prosper.

On April 1, with the boulder resting safely on the chassis-and-guide-rail assembly and its lower end pointed toward the sea, Carburi made the first attempt to move it. It ended in a fiasco. After an advance of a few feet, the guide rails sank in mud to a depth of eighteen inches. The two culprits of the accident were an unexpectedly early thaw and an insufficiently strengthened roadbed. The critics of the project gloated, seeing the mishap as a verification of their predictions of failure. All that Carburi could do to prove them wrong was to wait for the coming of next winter.

In the meantime, various preparatory works were carried out. A small forge was set up on a platform carved out of the upper front end of the boulder, allowing for instant repair and sharpening of tools. The back of the boulder, which was bigger and heavier than the front, was buttressed with thick beams of hard wood. The road was strengthened with stones and pilings, leveled with gravel, and cleared of vegetation so that nothing would interfere with its freezing to the greatest depth possible. A pier on the Gulf of Finland was built in expectation of the loading operations. It included a fifty-six-foot-wide jetty that was built on pilings driven into the bottom of the bay. The plan was to bring over a specially built barge and load the boulder onto it while the barge was submerged and lying on the bottom. To provide sufficient depth for such a maneuver, the jetty had to be extended twenty-eight hundred feet into the sea.

To the delight of Carburi, the winter of 1769–70 arrived early and the road, which was constantly being cleared of snow, froze to a depth of four feet. On November 15 the odd procession of the "mountain on eggs," as contemporary wits called it, was able to resume and advanced 160 feet. To get the boulder to move, Carburi used paired capstans attached to half-buried bundles of piles lining the two sides of the road at 350-foot intervals. On flat and horizontal segments of the road, two capstans were sufficient to

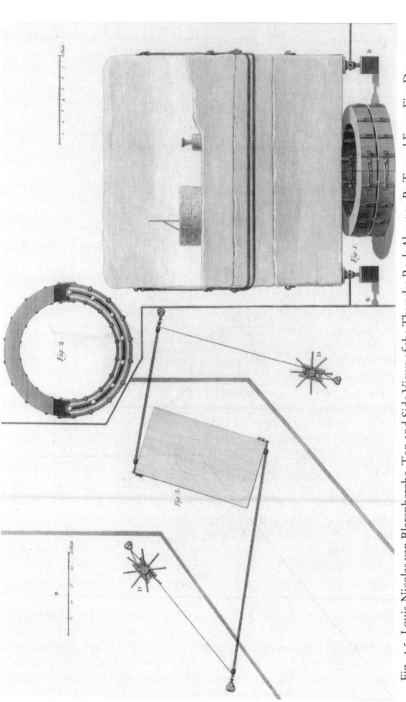

Fig. 4.5. Louis-Nicolas van Blarenberghe, Top and Side Views of the Thunder Rock About to Be Turned Forty-Five Degrees Clockwise on Its Turntable. Note the jackscrews which raise the boulder sufficiently for the turntable to be slipped under it. Engraving by R.-H.-J. Delvaux (Carburi de Cephalonie, 1777). Courtesy Beinecke Rare Book and Manuscript Library, Yale University.

move the boulder: "Once it got started, it advanced with the greatest of ease and the men could run while turning the capstans, almost without exerting themselves."[28] On upgrades, four or even six capstans had to be used. On downgrades, the capstans were placed behind the boulder to control its descent. With two drummers giving the beat, the workers reeled in the lines and the boulder was on its way, making between 500 and 1,300 feet a day (fig. 4.6).

The event was the sensation of the season for the St. Petersburgers, including the empress, who visited the site on January 20, 1770: "The forward progress of the boulder made for a rather curious sight. Forty stonecutters were continually working on top of the boulder to give it the desired shape. The forge kept on working. If one adds to this spectacle a cortege of sleighs, one can understand why, despite the rigors of the season, Her Imperial Majesty, the Grand Duke, and the whole court wanted to see it. Every day there was a crowd of spectators from all social stations and ranks, who came to view that mass in motion."[29]

The imperial visit was recorded by the St. Petersburg architect Iury M. Fel'ten in a drawing (fig. 4.7) which was adopted for the official medal commemorating the transport of the Thunder Rock. These images prove incontrovertibly that the split-off upper corner of the rock, tenuously attached to the mass of the stone, was transported separately to St. Petersburg. Such a conclusion should be self-evident had it not been for a set of drawings and gouaches made by the painter Louis-Nicolas van Blarenberghe for Carburi's account of the transport of the boulder, which show the corner attached by ropes to the main mass of the boulder and making the trip together with it. Fel'ten, however, was an eyewitness of the operation, while Blarenberghe's images were based on Carburi's account, which may have been exaggerated to magnify the scale of the feat and of his role in it.

Carburi's account is surprisingly brief, causing one to suspect that he was not present during most of the operation. We know that he combined his duties in Lakhta with the post of acting director of the Corps of Land Cadets in St. Petersburg.[30] We also know from his own account that he fell gravely ill during the initial stages of the operation. He complained of general tiredness, an upset stomach, and rheumatic pains in the joints, and diagnosed these symptoms correctly as scurvy, leading to a possible loss of all his teeth. High fever, he claimed, "brought him close to death's door." He blamed it all on his protracted exposure to unhealthy exhalations of the swamps that surrounded the boulder and urged that in the future the first order of business in similar situations be the draining and drying of the terrain.[31] He got better, but not before putting himself on a diet of citrus fruit, a strict regimen of exercise, and a cure in the south of the country.[32] Distraught by these ills, he could not follow closely the progress of the Thunder Rock, and his account of it is often sketchy and sometimes incorrect.[33]

More reliable, but far from exhaustive, are the data in the archives of the

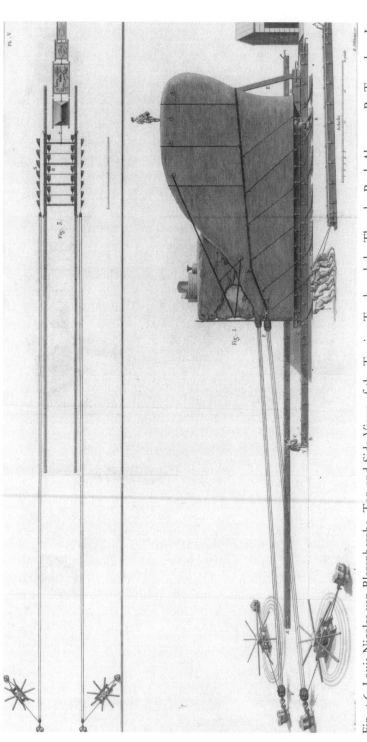

Fig. 4.6. Louis-Nicolas van Blarenberghe, Top and Side Views of the Towing Track and the Thunder Rock About to Be Towed on It. Blarenberghe, who did not witness the transportation, assumed that the split-off corner was moved together with the main mass of the boulder. The official medal issued to celebrate the success of the operation, however, uses Fel'ten's drawing, which shows that the corner was transported separately (see fig. 4.7). Workers at lower right are dragging a guide rail to the front of the assembly, while two workers are adjusting the position of the copper balls in a guide rail already in place. Two pulling capstans are shown at left. Engraving by R.-H.-J. Delvaux (Carburi de Cephalonie, 1777). Courtesy Beinecke Rare Book and Manuscript Library, Yale University.

Fig. 4.7. Iury M. Fel'ten, Catherine the Great Visiting the Site of the Thunder Rock on January 20, 1770. Engraving by Jakob van der Schley. The State Hermitage Museum, St. Petersburg. The empress is standing near the carriage at far left.

Bureau of Buildings. We learn from them that after a slow start due to the novelty of the procedure, the upgrade, and the turns in the road, the caravan with the boulder picked up speed. One document describes the route in terms of segments delimited by turns in the road and special occurrences along the way. After the start on November 15 the boulder advanced 160 feet to where the first turn took place. The next entry deals with the segment from December 21 to 24, when 336 feet were covered. No progress is reported for the next two and a half weeks while repairs were being made and there was a break for the Russian Orthodox Christmas. From January 9 to 16 the boulder made 931 feet, reaching the highest point on the road, some 20 feet above the level of the starting point. No progress was made for several days, while preparations were being made for Catherine's visit. On January 20 the empress witnessed the boulder advance 84 feet. In the next four weeks 3,584 feet were covered, a turn was then made, and by the beginning of March there was an advance of another 3,395 feet. The final segment of 17,409 feet was straight and all downhill.[34]

On March 27, 1770, the boulder arrived at the pier in Lakhta after covering the distance of close to five miles in four and a half months. That translates to an average of about one mile per month, not exactly breakneck speed, but still a very respectable rate of progress if one keeps in mind that during winter months, daylight in the northern latitudes allowed no more than five hours of working time. The overland portion of Operation Thunder Rock was over, and lying ahead were the waters of the Gulf of Finland followed by a voyage of six miles to the mouth of the Lesser Neva and another four miles to St. Isaac's Pier at Senate Square.[35] The problem was that the prospective maritime leg of the journey required a special transport vessel, and at the time of the boulder's arrival at the seashore, a vessel of that kind was not yet under construction.

The chief cause of the delay was the First Turkish War, which began in the fall of 1768, that is, about the time that the Thunder Rock was discovered. The war placed a heavy burden on the resources of the Admiralty. With the wharves of Kronshtadt fully engaged in the effort of building and outfitting ships in preparation for the planned naval expedition to the Mediterranean, the Admiralty showed little enthusiasm for the business of moving rocks, a project that it perceived as whimsical or, at best, inopportune. In this situation, the requests of Betskoi and the Bureau of Buildings, exhorting the Admiralty to act "immediately" and "without delay," were either ignored or did not make the Admiralty's short list. These attitudes were already in evidence in the summer of 1768, when preparations were being made for the transport of the Kotlin rock. Now, with Russia at war the Admiralty, faced with a much more difficult task of transporting the massive Thunder Rock, showed even less willingness to be distracted. In September 1768 Admiral Mordvinov informed Betskoi that all he could do was try to repair an old floating platform that was in the port of Kronshtadt, but that the two cutters demanded by Carburi to accompany it were not available.[36]

Seeing that his own authority would not suffice to compel Mordvinov to take prompt action, Betskoi enlisted the help of the empress. Only then did the admiral realize that the Thunder Rock project was a matter of the highest priority and that some show of activity was urgently needed to smooth Betskoi's ruffled feathers. With that in mind, he ordered Vice Admiral Grigory A. Spiridov, commander of the port of Kronshtadt, to send the old floating platform to St. Petersburg in order to check out its seaworthiness. In vain did Spiridov insist that the platform was in no condition to be taken off its mooring; he had no choice but to obey his superior. After some close calls at sea, the platform did make it to St. Petersburg, only to be pronounced too decrepit to be used for the transport of the boulder, which was what Spiridov had maintained all along.[37]

There being no appropriate vessel in Kronshtadt, the Admiralty had no choice but to agree to build an entirely new craft, designed specifically for the task at hand, that is, carrying a load of three million pounds concentrated on an exceedingly small area. The craft, moreover, could not draw more than eight feet in order to be able to negotiate the shallows of the Neva estuary. The design was entrusted to Grigory Korchebnikov, a very able shipbuilder specializing in the construction of small-size freighters used for merchant traffic on Russia's internal waters. Korchebnikov consulted with Carburi and by April 1770 his design was ready. It called for a rectangular barge whose sides were 17 feet high.[38] Its other measurements were 190 feet in length and 70 feet in width, along the top. Along the bottom these dimensions were reduced by several feet, giving the barge the shape of an inverted horizontal slice of an obelisk (fig. 4.8). For a load which occupied an area of 40 by 15 feet, these dimensions may appear exorbitant. Yet they were necessary in order to decrease the draft of the barge and to protect it against capsizing. The barge was to be moved along and steadied in rough waters by two cutters attached to its broadsides.

On April 8, while the Thunder Rock was waiting at the shore in Lakhta, the Admiralty approved Korchebnikov's project and began soliciting bids for the construction. Within the space of two weeks three bids were submitted, the winning one by Semën Vishniakov, the man who had found the Thunder Rock. He and his associate Anton Shliapkin, together with a crew of close to two hundred workers, mainly carpenters, obligated themselves to build the barge in three months for six thousand rubles. The greatest appeal of the bid was that Vishniakov and Shliapkin would provide their own materials, at a time when the Admiralty's reserves of shipbuilding timber were fully committed to naval construction. Work started in the beginning of May, and by mid-August the barge was ready to be towed to Lakhta, where Korchebnikov and First Lieutenant Iakov Lavrov were busy overseeing the preparation of the loading dock. Lavrov, an officer with much experience in shipbuilding, was given the overall command of the operation.

It was obvious that the boulder could not be loaded onto a free-floating barge, for the sheer weight of the rock would make it keel over and spill the

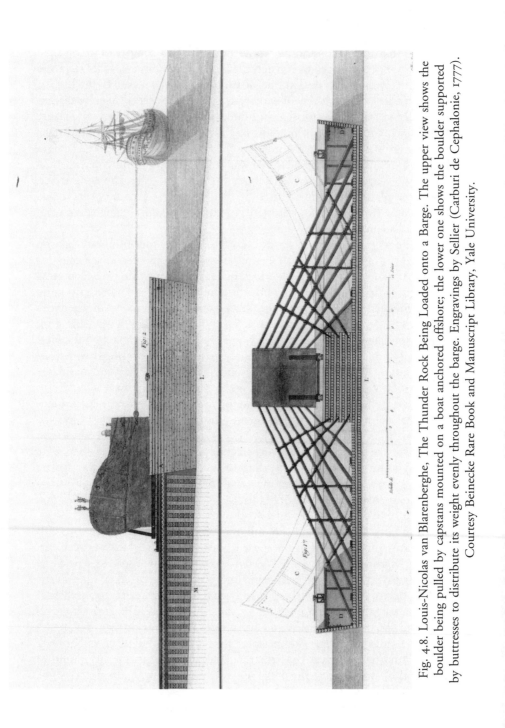

Fig. 4.8. Louis-Nicolas van Blarenberghe, The Thunder Rock Being Loaded onto a Barge. The upper view shows the boulder being pulled by capstans mounted on a boat anchored offshore; the lower one shows the boulder supported by buttresses to distribute its weight evenly throughout the barge. Engravings by Sellier (Carburi de Cephalonie, 1777). Courtesy Beinecke Rare Book and Manuscript Library, Yale University.

cargo. To preclude such a mishap the boulder had to be loaded while the barge was submerged and resting on the bottom of the bay, which in the area of the loading dock was eight feet deep. In anticipation of such a maneuver divers had leveled the sea floor and cleared it of rocks and debris. Since the boulder had to be rolled onto the barge on a level ramp and the landing dock was three feet above the surface of the sea, a platform had to be constructed in the center of the barge. It was made of crisscrossing wooden beams and was eleven feet in height and large enough to accommodate the chassis-and-guide-rail assembly on which the boulder rested. When the barge was filled with water and sank to the bottom, the platform became level with the landing dock. The upper boards of the barge's hull, being three feet higher than the landing dock, had to be opened so that a ramp could be thrown between the landing dock and the platform. The pulling power was provided by two capstans mounted on the deck of one of the cutters anchored out at sea. On August 28 the boulder was pulled aboard and came to rest on the platform. The closing of the gap in the side of the barge marked the successful conclusion of the first stage of the operation (fig. 4.8, upper view).

Now the barge had to be refloated, and here an unpleasant surprise awaited the planners. As the pumps sucked the water out of the barge, its prow and stern began to rise, while the middle, weighed down by the heavy cargo, refused to budge from the bottom of the sea. The timbers bent and began to creak, some of the boards broke, water poured back into the barge, and the refloating operation had to be stopped. There was speculation that if the boulder had been placed lengthwise on the barge, as planned by Korchebnikov, rather than sidewise across it, this mishap could have been avoided.

According to the account of Carburi, perhaps somewhat embellished by the boastful engineer, the Admiralty wasted two weeks searching for a way out, while reducing him to a role of a passive bystander. When the autumn winds picked up and the bottom of the barge was still dangerously curved, the Admiralty decided to return the boulder to the dock and postpone the move until the following year. Enter Carburi with a simple solution. The prow and stern had to be straightened out by weighing them down with rocks and forcing the whole barge to lie flat on the bottom. With the timbers returning to their original position, the cracks between them closed up and the barge became watertight again. The boulder was then raised slightly with jackscrews and surrounded with heavy wooden buttresses of different length. When the jackscrews were removed, the boulder settled on the buttresses and its weight was distributed evenly throughout the barge. The rocks serving as ballast were then removed, the water was pumped out, and the barge surfaced, keeping its original shape (fig. 4.8, lower view). Within a few days the barge with its precious cargo was on its way to Senate Square (fig. 4.9).[39]

Fig. 4.9. Louis-Nicolas van Blarenberghe, The Barge with the Thunder Rock Steadied by Two Cutters of the Imperial Navy en Route to St. Petersburg. Engraving by Sellier (Carburi de Cephalonie, 1777). Courtesy Beinecke Rare Book and Manuscript Library, Yale University.

Because of the shallows in the Gulf of Finland, the barge sailed south for about three miles and turned northeast for another three miles to the estuary of the Lesser Neva (fig. 4.10).[40] From there it proceeded to the spit of Vasilievsky Island, where the Lesser and Greater Neva separate. On September 22 (October 3 according to the Gregorian calendar) the barge passed in front of the Winter Palace, under the eyes of Catherine the Great, who was celebrating the eighth anniversary of her coronation. On the following day the barge sailed past the Admiralty and docked at night at St. Isaac's Pier at Senate Square.[41] Since the total distance from the landing dock at Lakhta to St. Isaac's Pier was only twelve versts or about nine miles (fig. 4.10), one may assume that the voyage took no more than one sailing day, especially since we know that the captain decided to sail continuously for fear of a change in weather. There was a west wind, as there often is in St. Petersburg at that time of the year, just enough to fill the cutters' sails, but not enough to cause trouble.[42]

To unload the boulder the barge had to be submerged to a depth of eight

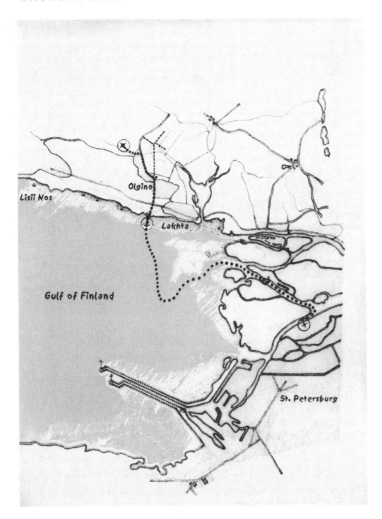

Fig. 4.10. Route of the Thunder Rock from Its Karelian Site to the Pier at Senate Square. Based on a reconstruction by Georgy Ivanovich Ivanov. Courtesy of the artist's wife, Valentina Nikolaevna Ivanova.

feet, just as had been done at Lakhta. Since the Neva at St. Isaac's Pier was quite deep, the landing area had to be made shallower by driving three hundred piles into the bottom of the river in advance of the landing. After the barge settled on the piling, it was attached by strong timbers to the pier on one side and a cutter standing at anchor on the other. Then a ramp was thrown and on September 26 the boulder was connected to two capstans, which pulled it off the barge (fig. 4.11). To witness the event the empress stood in the window of the Senate building, and a large crowd of onlookers gathered outside. Two weeks later, in the presence of the visiting Prince

Fig. 4.11. Louis-Nicolas van Blarenberghe, The Thunder Rock Being Moved from the Barge onto Senate Square. The building of the Admiralty is in the background, the Isakievsky Pontoon Bridge is on the left, and the northeast corner of the Senate building is on the right. Gouache, 1777. The State Hermitage Museum, St. Petersburg.

Henry of Prussia, the boulder was moved 145 feet to its final destination in the center of the square, which had been reinforced with piles and stone.

The year 1770 turned out to be a year of Russian triumphs. The Ottoman Turks were defeated on the Danube and in the Aegean archipelago, and now Russia was able to claim a technological achievement that excited people's imagination no less than would Lindbergh's flight across the Atlantic. The arrival of the Thunder Rock in St. Petersburg was greeted with enthusiasm and patriotic lucubrations, which described it as the culmination of a feat that surpassed the building of the Egyptian pyramids, the creation of the Colossus of Rhodes, and the transportation of the ancient obelisks.[43]

The woods between Konnaia and Lakhta were littered with chips of the Thunder Rock. They were collected and polished to make various keepsakes: jewelry, cufflinks, and knobs for walking sticks. Especially popular were pieces taken from a vein in the granite that became visible after the boulder had been flipped. It ran perpendicular to the base and, in contrast to the rest of the rock, which like all granite contained quartz, feldspar, and mica, it was practically all quartz, and had less density and more color.[44]

Catherine issued a medal commemorating her visit to the woods of Lakhta of January 20, 1770. On one side it bears her image and name and on the other the scene in the woods and the inscription "Daringly Performed." She also rewarded the "half-frozen" crewmen on the barge and on the cutters with wine and beer and five hundred rubles to be divided "proportionately."[45] Special bonuses of two to three hundred rubles were given to the barge designer, Grigory Korchebnikov, First Lieutenant Iakov Lavrov, and the rigging master, Captain Matvei Mikhailov. Carburi, however, is not mentioned in the archives as a recipient of any bonuses at that time, even though his role in the operation was undoubtedly crucial. As his friend and admirer, Falconet was shocked by this oversight and complained bitterly to the empress: "Let us simply admit that under the reign of Catherine, a man who achieved the most astonishing feat of its kind in the world was not compensated for it."[46] The injustice was quickly repaired by a gift of four thousand rubles "to Lieutenant Colonel Lascaris (Carburi) for his work connected with the Thunder Rock."[47]

Foreign reactions to Operation Thunder Rock were filled with superlatives. "Nothing equally great and marvelous is known in the history of the arts," said an anonymous writer quoted by Haigold.[48] The *Gazette de France* described the Russian effort as "incredible." It astonished "every beholder with a stupendous evidence of toil and enterprise, unparalleled since the subversion of the Roman empire," said the English traveler John Carr.[49] "The daring of this enterprise has no parallel among the Egyptians and the Romans," exclaimed the *Journal encyclopédique*.[50] Falconet wrote to Catherine that all Europe glorified "a feat so difficult to execute and so happily accomplished. . . . History will not forget it when it speaks of the greatest achievement of mechanics under the reign of Catherine II."[51] The awed *Mémoires secrets de Bachaumont* magnified the achievement by adding to it more than a thousand miles: "a rock of extraordinary size was transported at an immense cost from Siberia."[52]

With the boulder safely deposited on dry land and enclosed in a large wooden shed, it was now up to Falconet to direct its transformation into the pedestal he had designed. A simple matter, one would think, for all that he and his stonecutters had to do was to transfer the shape and dimensions of the plaster model of the pedestal standing in the sculptor's atelier to the boulder waiting on Senate Square. The problem, however, was that many of those who had breathlessly followed the spectacular struggle between man's wits and nature's recalcitrance became emotionally attached to the trophy snared from the woods of Karelia and did not want to see it diminished and become a piece of polished granite. Such a reaction could have been foreseen, and it is possible that Falconet did think about it when he seemed so nonchalant about the finding of the Thunder Rock. But he surely did not expect to be accused of having selfishly sacrificed the symbolism of the wild stone in order better to display his own work of art. Yet, such criticism was leveled against him, not only by Russians who had witnessed the heroic progress of the boulder, but also by foreigners who visited St. Petersburg after the monument had been set up.[53]

According to Charles Masson, a Swiss who lived in St. Petersburg at the time, "[The boulder] was deprived of its wild and primitive form to give it a more regular appearance, and what with hewing and polishing, was at last reduced in size by nearly one half, so that it is now a little rock under a great horse, and the tsar, who ought to be surveying from it his empire, more vast even than he had conceived, is hardly able to look into the first floor of the neighboring houses."[54]

Fortia de Piles, a French writer who visited Russia in 1792, agreed:

> By placing the statue on a block of granite, the sculptor intended to show the myriad of difficulties which the Russian legislator had to conquer in order to reach his goal. One could expect, therefore, to see Peter the Great on a steep rock that would be hard to climb so as to give an idea of his great effort. One sees instead a block of granite, trimmed and polished, whose incline is so gentle that the horse reaches the summit without much difficulty. The effect of this pedestal of such a novel kind is completely missed and the more one looks at it, the more one finds it detestable. Some people claim that M. Falconet did not wish to leave the rock in its original state for fear that the novelty and grandeur of the idea might detract from the work of art by attracting all the attention. If that is true, we would have to agree that great talent may be accompanied by much pettiness and unpardonable egotism.[55]

John Carr was also critical: "Filled as I was with admiration of this glorious work of art, I could not help regretting that the artist had so much reduced and polished the granite rock, which with great grandeur of conception forms the pedestal of the statue. So indefatigable has been the labour of the chisel upon [the stone's] enormous mass and rugged coating, that its history is its greatest wonder. Had this rock retained the size and shape which it bore . . . with only a few of its asperities removed, it would have increased the dignity and expression of the horse and its rider. . . . The genius of Falconet was evidently jealous of the rude but stupendous powers of nature, and was fearful that *her* rock might engage more attention than *his* statue; hence he reduced the former, until he rendered it disproportioned to the colossal figure which it supports; but he has thereby succeeded in bringing his work nearer to the eye of the beholder. Had he been content to share his homage with nature, he would not have been a loser."[56] Some even claimed that in his zeal to diminish the pedestal, Falconet corrupted his own design and was later forced to recover the original length of the boulder with a patch-up job of added pieces.

Stung by these criticisms, Falconet dedicated forty-five pages of his writings to self-defense.[57] He pointed out that the model of the pedestal had been approved as proposed, and that nothing he did to the stone was in any way new or improvised. He reminded his critics that the need to extend the pedestal in front and back was obvious to everyone and had been agreed upon when the boulder was still in the forest. As for reducing the size of the natural stone, he cited the self-evident truth that the pedestal ought to be for the statue, not the statue for the pedestal. All to no avail! The stories were repeated from one account of the monument to the next, even though

Falconet's explanations were explicitly supported by such witnesses as Carburi, Backmeister, and the French chargé d'affaires Bourrée de Corberon, and, most important, by Losenko's drawing of the large model.[58]

Catherine the Great, to be sure, was not among Falconet's detractors. Despite Betskoi's daily barrage of accusations against the French sculptor, she kept out of the fray, counseling Falconet to keep his cool and stay his course. An inveterate pragmatist, she was satisfied to have brought off her propaganda coup by transporting the Thunder Rock over land and water to the center of the capital "under Western eyes." Now what she wanted was the best equestrian monument in the world, and in matters of taste she wisely deferred to the artist.

What remains of the places that produced the drama of the Thunder Rock? The villages of Lakhta and Konnaia Lakhta have long been overtaken by suburban construction and are today within the city perimeter of St. Petersburg. Parks, dachas, and garden plots of Petersburgers have replaced the dense woods of the Lakhta region. If there remain trees that can remember "Operation Thunder Rock," they are few and far between.

The large hollow that was dug out around the boulder has gradually filled with water and is today a recreational pool used for swimming and skating by local youngsters. It is known appropriately as *Petrovsky prud* or Peter's Pond. As one walks from it toward the Gulf of Finland, one can still find pieces of granite, but they would have to be submitted to a chemical analysis in order to find out if they are in fact chips of the old block. There are no visible traces of the large pier at Lakhta, though there may still be remnants of the piles driven into the bottom of the Gulf of Finland. The successor to the old St. Isaac's Pier at Senate Square is now occupied by a stationary excursion boat that is used as a restaurant. The piles on which the barge came to rest were taken out in 1893 in order to allow larger ships to dock at the pier.

Only the pedestal bearing the Bronze Horseman rises above the river and the flat urban landscape on its other bank, as a constant reminder of the heroic days when the Thunder Rock was torn out of the Karelian forest floor and hauled to Senate Square to enter forever the history and myth of St. Petersburg.

MARIN CARBURI ALIAS CHEVALIER DE LASCARIS

The Greeks of Zante and Cephalonia . . . are notorious for stabbing with knives.
—William Eton (1798)

Marin Carburi, the Greek engineer to whose inventiveness the success of Operation Thunder Rock was attributed in the preceding section, was not, by most accounts, a man of sterling character and exemplary personal conduct. His personality, in fact, evoked so much criticism that doubts arose not only about Carburi's account of his role in the operation, but even about his professional skills. Upholding the opposite view was Falconet, who saw Carburi in action, both as an engineer in charge of the Thunder Rock operation and as a liaison with the Bureau of Buildings, in charge of materials, labor, and funds. He swore by Carburi's abilities and did all he could to persuade Catherine to keep Carburi in St. Petersburg until the completion of the monument.

Was Carburi fully responsible for the invention of the ingenious devices used in the transportation of the rock? While he himself claimed full credit for their design, some of his St. Petersburg contemporaries maintained otherwise. Whether their judgment was based on reliable or unreliable evidence, whether personal bias was involved, these doubts testify to Carburi's poor reputation in St. Petersburg. He was accused of deceit, extortion, moral turpitude, even murder. Some viewed him as a crafty seeker of riches in a land of opportunity, others saw in him a conniving criminal who came to Russia to escape punishment for some past misdeed. Mikhail I. Pyliaev, a popular nineteenth-century chronicler of St. Petersburg, called him "an adventurer and poisoner of three wives."[59] Even Catherine joined in the chorus of Carburi's detractors. She described him as "troublesome and ill-tempered, always demanding and never satisfied."[60]

On the other side of the spectrum were people who found the Greek engineer's skills personally useful. Falconet, who looked forward to Carburi's engineering skills in anticipation of the day when he might become founder of his own statue, called the Greek "one of the most honest, active, and intelligent people in Betskoi's employ."[61] Betskoi himself, who appreciated Carburi's resourceful and obedient execution of his wishes, used his services in tasks demanding intelligence and efficiency and recompensed him handsomely. The historian Antimo Masarachi, who was proud of the achievements of a fellow Cephalonian, saw in Carburi someone for whom "Russia was a splendid arena for glory, where he lived admired by the Petersburgers and surrounded by the magnificent gifts of the empress."[62]

Who was this man whose merits and personality evoked such contrasting assessments? Did he deserve to be known throughout Europe as the man "who had moved the rock," or was he just an able adventurer who exploited the skills of others? How did it happen that someone who arrived in St. Petersburg in 1761 as a penniless fugitive from justice left in 1773 as a retired lieutenant colonel in the Russian army, a former director of the prestigious Cadet Corps, and a prosperous double widower?[63]

Marin Carburi is a Venetian version of a name which in its original Greek was Marinos Kharvouris.[64] He was born in 1729 in Argostoli, the capital of the island of Cephalonia, the largest of a chain of seven islands (hence their name, the Heptanese Islands) lying off the western coast of Greece in the Ionian Sea.[65] Dominating the sea lanes between the eastern Mediterranean and the Adriatic, these islands, without forming a true archipelago, have a common history. They were given the status of a separate theme in the Byzantine Empire, but eventually fell under the dominion of Venice, thus escaping Ottoman rule, which was the fate of the rest of Greece. Lacking the stark, dichromatic beauty of the Aegean Islands, the Heptanese Islands are overgrown with lush vegetation and have a variegated economy, with vineyards, olive groves, and currant plantations supplementing the daily catch of local fishermen.

Like all who derive income from small-scale agriculture, the Ionian islanders are torn between centrifugal and centripetal forces, alternately leaving the land of their fathers when it cannot provide a livelihood for all the family and returning to it when it does not have to be relied upon as the sole source of income.[66] In the seventeenth and eighteenth centuries, the Venetian Republic and the Russian Empire were the countries of preference for islanders seeking employment and careers abroad. Venice was the political metropolis of the Ionians and a stepping-stone to Western Europe, while the Russia of the Romanovs had the allure of a military and economic power which, after the fall of Constantinople, was the strongest bulwark of the Orthodox faith.

There were five children in the Carburi family, four boys and a girl. In order of their birth, they were Giovanni Battista, Marin (Marino), Marco, Maria, and Paolo. The parents, Demetrio and Caterina, made their living selling vegetables in the Argostoli market square.[67] If that claim by André Grasset de Saint-Sauveur, the then French consul to the Ionian islands, is true, theirs must have been a much larger operation than a mere vending stall, for they were able to provide an excellent education for the older sons by sending them to the two great Venetian universities, Padua and Bologna.

Marin, defying his father's explicit wish that he devote himself to law at the University of Padua, followed a curriculum in pure and applied mathematics, aiming for a career in what today would be called civil engineering. His intelligence and enterprising spirit allowed him to range broadly into other lines of endeavor. Like so many inhabitants of the basin of the eastern Mediterranean, he had a cosmopolitan turn of mind and felt as much at ease in western and northern Europe as he did on his native island.

Marin's older brother Giovanni Battista was born in 1722. He received a degree in medicine in Padua and was appointed professor of medicine at the University of Turin. In 1770 he abandoned that position in order to become personal physician of Marie Thérèse of Savoy. When she married Duke Charles Philippe, Giovanni Battista followed her to Paris, where he became one of the favorite court physicians.[68] In 1795 Giovanni Battista left Paris and resumed his teaching career by accepting a chair in physiology at the university of Padua.

Marco, Marin's younger brother, was born in 1731. After receiving his medical degree at the University of Bologna, he was appointed professor of chemistry at the University of Padua, the first such appointment there and the second, after Bologna, in all of Italy. A distinguished scholar with many discoveries and publications in the field of metallurgy, he remained in Padua all his life, except for six years at the very beginning of his academic career, when the Venetian Senate dispatched him abroad to study more efficient methods of mining and refining copper, which was needed in the production of cannons for the Venetian navy. In the words of Italy's foremost Carburi scholar, it was a task that could be called "a mission of industrial spying."[69]

The Carburi family may have belonged to the Cephalonian nobility, but Marin Carburi did not possess the Venetian title of count at birth, as he and his Cephalonian biographers allege.[70] Documents preserved in the Venetian state archives show that the title of count was conferred on Marco and Giovanni Battista as late as 1760.[71] As for Marin, he obtained the title of count from the Venetian Senate when he was passing through Venice on his way back to Cephalonia.[72] The title was ratified in 1781, one year before Marin's death.[73]

Nor is there any reason to believe that Marin's use of the name Chevalier de Lascaris during his sojourn in Russia was justified by family connections, as he asserts in the *Avertissement* to his book on the transportation of the Thunder Rock, published in Paris in 1777:

Leaving behind his country, [Carburi] wanted also to leave behind a name which would have attached him to it forever, but in so doing he thought it fitting to take one which was not altogether strange to him. His family, which came from the Peloponnesus and before that from Candia, is honored to be related by marriage to the most ancient and most important families, among them to that of the Lascaris, who had to seek refuge from the revolutionary changes in the Eastern Empire. He felt entitled to borrow their name and resolved to bear it with dignity so as to earn the right to take back one day the name and the best example of his forefathers.[74]

The existence of marital alliances between the Carburi and Lascaris families is not supported by any documentary evidence. Without this, it is difficult to believe that a simple Cephalonian family, whether of Peloponnesian or Cretan origin, could have had anything to do with one of the most illustrious Byzantine families of Asia Minor, a family that produced the Lascarid dynasty, which was in power throughout most of the thirteenth century.[75] It is much more likely that Marin chose the name of Lascaris because he needed an identity which would not define him as an escaping subject of Venice, but would suggest instead a person of high birth seeking refuge from the Turks. As for the reasons that Marin had to escape from Venice, he himself tries to provide them in the *Avertissement* to his Paris booklet: "A passion, always reckless in one's young age, but a hundredfold more tyrannical in southern climes, made him commit an act of violence which could be excused by reason of age, but which was detestable to his heart, and which the law could not refrain from prosecuting. A necessary exile, certainly the cruelest price for someone who had the good fortune of being born subject of a wise and enlightened Republic, was the harsh punishment which he imposed upon himself."[76]

This grandiloquent apology leaves the reader wondering why Carburi does not divulge the precise nature of that act of violence which was serious enough to force him to flee the *Serenissima Repubblica.* Some thought that Carburi was angered by the infidelity of his mistress in Venice.[77] Given Carburi's attempt to justify his action as a crime of passion, that is a possible scenario, one for which he would have liked to blame his young age and the proverbial Mediterranean temper. But he could hardly claim immaturity as an extenuating circumstance, given that he was thirty at the time he committed his deed. The self-imposed "necessary exile" is surely no more than a euphemism for a quick getaway "to avoid criminal prosecution."[78] All in all, Carburi's text strikes one as a self-serving attempt to camouflage a crime rather than atone for it.

But what exactly was the nature of that crime? To find out, one has to consult the records of the Carburi case, resting among the documents of the *Avvogaria di comun,* in the vast state archives of the Venetian Republic.[79] They transport the reader to the Sestiere di Castello, about half a mile northeast of Piazza San Marco, where Venice loses its aspect of a crowded and noisy center of international tourism and becomes a quiet, almost somnolent, provincial Italian town. The bells on the campanile of San Francesco della Vigna, one of the tallest structures in Venice, provide the neighborhood with its loudest and most commanding call. A visitor proceeds from a little square called Campo delle Gatte and continues north to the Salizzada San Francesco or east to two other small squares called Campo di Santa Ternità and Campo della Celestia. From there it is only a few steps to the large Venetian shipyard, known as the Arsenale.

Today the Arsenale is a neglected and mostly abandoned facility, but in the heyday of the Republic it was the busiest and liveliest part of the city, employing up to sixteen thousand shipyard workers belonging to sixteen artisan guilds. In an emergency, the *arsenalotti,* as these workers were called, were capable of assembling and equipping a galley in twenty-four hours.[80] In those days the neighborhood of Santa Ternità was a bustling section of the city which, together with other neighborhoods along the perimeter of the shipyards, provided the *arsenalotti* with housing, trattorias, entertainment, and other necessary services. The streets around the Arsenale must have been then as animated and exciting as the waterfront of any major port city.

In November 1758 Demetrio Carburi and his son Marin took up residence on Campo delle Gatte in one of two houses with rooms to let, belonging to Stefano and Barbara Carara, both native Venetians. Stefano was a barber in the nearby parish of San Zulian, while his wife washed and repaired clothes for their single lodgers. The Greek visitors were among the many citizens of the Republic who flocked to the capital from the provinces in order to take care of business and legal matters. In the case of the Carburis there was some litigation to settle, a perfectly ordinary motive for the visit. Yet, within eight months of their arrival Marin Carburi stood accused of a brutal assault on Barbara Carara, which left her in a pool of blood. The files of a judicial inquest provide a solid basis for a reconstruction of the crime.[81]

Barbara's complaint against Marin was filed on July 17, 1759. She was at that time about twenty-four, mother of an eleven-month-old baby girl. Marin was a thirty-year-old bachelor.[82] The depositions taken by Antonio della Sala from the *Avvogaria di comun* reveal that, in addition to renting a room to the Carburis, Barbara consented to do Marin's laundry and sew on his collars. At Christmastime 1758, when their house had to have some masonry work done, the Cararas moved to their other house for the duration of the repairs. The Carburis had to move too, and rented a lodging in the house of Domenico Rossi, a coroner in the cul-de-sac of San Francesco.

Marin, however, continued to visit Barbara to drop off and pick up his laundry. When the carnival time came around, his visits became more frequent and it soon became clear to Barbara that laundry was not the only thing on his mind. One day he openly declared his love and tried to force himself on her. She resisted and Marin left, but not before threatening her with a knife. He also promised her "the life of a queen" if only she would consent to follow him to his Ionian home. Barbara wanted to complain to the police, but her priest advised her against it, so as not to provoke Marin to violence. She then told Marin that she would no longer be able to take care of his laundry and asked him not to visit her so frequently for fear of evil tongues. Marin left muttering "you'll pay me for that," and continued threatening her each time they met.

On July 15, at about eleven o'clock in the evening, Barbara, who was three months pregnant at the time, Stefano, and a couple of friends went out to seek relief from the oppressive heat on the Fondamenta nuove, a promenade along the northeastern embankment of the sestiere di Castello. The baby was left behind in the care of a servant girl. When they returned, Barbara hurried upstairs to see why the baby was crying, while Stefano stayed below talking to his friends. He heard, however, some noises inside the house and looked in to find out what was going on. He saw Marin Carburi standing on the landing and saying that he wanted to take leave of Barbara because he was about to go to the *terra ferma* (Venetian possessions on the mainland). Barbara wished him a happy trip and expected him to go, but Marin was in no hurry. He asked for a needle and thread so that he could sew a tassel onto the handle of his sword. Seeing that he did not know how to sew, Barbara helped him. Then she picked up her child and went to the door. At that moment, Marin turned toward her and said: "I'll be back in a month's time. Here's something to remember me by." With that he pulled out a razor, slashed Barbara on her face, and bolted out of the house. Stefano wanted to run after Marin, but Barbara held him back, fearing for his life.

A crowd gathered in front of the Carburi house and a surgeon arrived to tend to Barbara. Witnesses said that Marin ran in the direction of the church of San Antonin, a bared sword in his hand. They praised Barbara's modesty, testifying that she lived a life of a good Christian and was seldom seen outside her house and "never on the balcony." An old rusty razor, stained with blood, was found on the staircase. The slash from her right ear to her mouth maimed Barbara for life.

Giovanni Battista Constantini, the *avvogador di comun,* charged Marin Carburi with an unprovoked, premeditated crime, committed "scientemente, dolorosamente, deliberatamente, temerariamente, pensatamente." An order went out to detain Marin and bring him to trial. It was too late, however. Mattio Varutti, *capitan grande* of the police, reported that by the time he got to Marin's place, the accused had left the *Serenissima Dominazione.* Marin's goal was Trieste, which was then part of Austria. Armed with a letter of recommendation from his brother Giovanni Battista, he enlisted in the Austrian army, but did not stay long in service. In 1761 he left for Russia, spurred by "the example of his compatriots who found refuge there, and of other learned men who received protection, excelled in learning, were involved in politics, and acquired wealth and honors."[83]

Russia of the early sixties of the eighteenth century was a country on the move. The coup d'état of 1762 put an end to the preposterous, but mercifully brief, rule of Peter III and ushered in the age of Catherine the Great, arguably the most glorious thirty-two years in all of Russian history. Success followed success, in domestic and in foreign affairs, on the battlefield and in the legislative chamber, in learning and in the arts. It was Peter the Great who founded the new capital of the empire, but it was Catherine who gave St. Petersburg its shape and made it into a cosmopolitan city, a fitting center of her multinational empire, and a magnet for visitors from every corner of the world. Greeks were especially welcome, for at that time Russia was on the threshold of a war with Turkey in which the Greeks would figure as her natural allies. St. Petersburg offered Carburi all that he needed, a safe haven and an opportunity to put his talents to profitable use.

Carburi's first job in St. Petersburg was as a teacher in a pension belonging to a Frenchman, Monsieur Carbonet, with whom he had actually traveled from Warsaw. He did not stay long in Carbonet's employ, however, for he was soon introduced to General Ivan Ivanovich Betskoi, Catherine's steward of educational and artistic matters, who thenceforward became his chief employer and protector. It is not entirely clear who introduced Carburi to Betskoi, but it could have been Colonel Petr Ivanovich Melissino, an artillery officer of Cephalonian extraction, to whom Marin bore a letter of introduction from his brother Giovanni Battista.[84]

Impressed by the young Greek's abilities and ingratiating manner, Betskoi took him under his wing. He appointed him his personal aide-de-camp with the rank of lieutenant, and used him for a variety of services, including a mission to Riga to meet Falconet and Collot at the border crossing and accompany them to the capital.[85] By then Carburi was in the rank of captain. His advancement progressed rapidly, and within ten years of his arrival, he held the rank of lieutenant colonel and a position in the Cadet Corps, first as its chief of police and then as its acting director.[86]

Carburi's moment of glory came when Betskoi asked him to head the task force searching for a rock to serve as the pedestal for the statue of Peter the Great and, after the Thunder Rock was found, to move it to city center. Overcoming enormous technical difficulties, Carburi acquitted himself brilliantly in that task, garnering a reward of seven thousand rubles. Countering stories afloat in St. Petersburg that he had bought the design for the transporting apparatus from a local smith for a pittance, Carburi reaffirmed his sole responsibility for the invention and for devising the method of extricating the rock from its resting place in the Karelian bogs.[87] These claims appear to find support in one of Falconet's letters to Catherine: "Mr. Lascaris [Carburi] *alone* devised the way to transport the rock which is to serve for the pedestal of the statue and constructed the machine for that purpose. He directed that undertaking without any assistance whatsoever. If I allow this statement to stand unsupported by any examples, it is because they would be too numerous in a letter, because it would be difficult to cite them all without placing the most humiliating blame on some people, and because Your Highness knows that I am telling the truth."[88] The chief object of this testimony, however, was to discredit General Betskoi's attempts to present himself to the empress as the chief planner and coordinator of the rock-moving operation. It is Betskoi's name which lurks beneath Falconet's cryptic "some people."[89]

With the rock deposited safely on Senate Square, Carburi felt that the job which had earned him fame in every European capital deserved greater recognition than Betskoi was willing to offer. He may have had in mind the rank of general, but his later career would lead one to conclude that what interested him most was money. When his threat to resign and leave St. Petersburg did not produce the desired effect, Carburi turned to Falconet. He knew that the sculptor was impressed by his expertise in metallurgy and that he hoped to use it in the casting of the statue of Peter the Great.

If such were his calculations, they proved correct. Falconet, realizing Carburi's value to the project and having himself much reason to complain of Betskoi's behavior, launched an all-out offensive in support of Carburi's claims. At first the empress professed willingness to satisfy Carburi's demands, asking merely that she be informed why he wished to retire. Falconet's response contained unqualified praise of Carburi and several transparent allusions to Betskoi's malevolence:

[Carburi] was carefully kept in the background behind another person, who used all his ruses to make him appear as his assistant. That, of course, one can understand, but what I find less understandable is that a person to whom so much is owed should be so relentlessly harassed. . . . Under any other superior, [Carburi] would have been compensated in a manner commensurate with such an unusual undertaking, so difficult to execute, and so successfully accomplished. . . . History will not forget it when it speaks of the greatest achievement in the field of mechanics, accomplished during the reign of Catherine II. But posterity would never believe it if told that in the end its author was brought to the brink of despair. That is, Your Highness, the main reason why he is obliged to ask for permission to resign. There is no need, I believe, to list other reasons. A man who is hated and constantly persecuted for his good deeds cannot put up with such a patron.[90]

Betskoi, it is true, tried to garner all the credit for himself, but he was far from wishing to harm so useful a person as Carburi. He hastened to assuage his demands by appointing him acting director general of the Cadet Corps, a position which was normally reserved for a higher-ranking officer. Carburi served from July 1770 to February 1773, and would have served longer if Betskoi's initiative to appoint him to full directorship of the corps had not been thwarted by the unanimous opposition of all the corps officers, who "refused to take orders from a man whom they despised, one who gained a reputation for intrigues, dissipation, and corruption."[91] As a result, Carburi lost whatever support he had from the empress and was abandoned by Betskoi, who, with his courtier's sixth sense, realized that it was time to let go of his protégé.

The prospect of unemployment prompted Carburi to turn again to Falconet and offer him his services. The sculptor knew by then that he would have to cast the statue himself. Hence his second desperate appeal to the empress:

[Carburi] has stopped serving in the Cadet Corps. That is not my business and I am careful not to get involved in it. There is, however, one matter in this situation which does concern me. For over six years, since the moment when the monument to Peter the Great was started, [Carburi] has assisted in all our operations with rare conscientiousness, exactitude, and intelligence. He did it all without receiving one ruble in compensation, a circumstance which I have found difficult to believe.[92] Now, I am told, he will be leaving because the Cadet Corps will not retain him and one cannot expect that a prospect of nonsalaried employment would keep him. Should Your Majesty permit, desire, and command that he continue to assist me in my work, particularly in casting, where his activity would be especially needed, and should he receive a salary appropriate to his rank and duties, he would stay and would continue serving Your Majesty with the true zeal which I have always known him to have. There is really nothing personal in my intention. My only goal is the progress of my work and its quick completion. I have never been particularly friendly with [Carburi] and our closest relations have been professional in nature. But that does not keep me from seeing in him an honest man. I cannot think otherwise for I know of nothing to contradict such a belief. But that is not all, for I have much more proof of the benefits which he has continually brought to the work on the statue. In a word, he has been involved in everything, known everything, and assisted in everything from the very first step. Anyone taking his place would have to go through a stage of initiation, which he has passed long ago.[93]

If Falconet thought that his petulant recriminations would make the empress disavow General Betskoi and rule in favor of the cantankerous Greek engineer, he was sadly mistaken. His fervent pleas for Carburi succeeded merely in annoying the empress. They may, in fact, mark a watershed in her relations with Falconet. Her letters to him, once warm and personal, now become matter-of-fact and infrequent. At first she questioned the sincerity of Carburi's offer to work for Falconet: "I do not know how to reconcile [Carburi's] wish to take a leave and go to a spa with his desire to stay close to your work."[94] A few days later her puzzlement gave way to indignation:

I admit that I am not only astonished by the continually plaintive tone of [Carburi], but that I find it very odd indeed. Listening to him talk, one could think that he has been offended by everybody. Well, to learn the facts, find out how long ago it was that [Carburi] was a junior officer galloping after Monsieur Betskoi, who, having found him endowed with intelligence, talent, and other qualities, had him transferred from a field regiment, where he was, if my memory serves me, a lieutenant or at most a captain, to his own side as his battalion aide-de-camp. It must have been at most seven or eight years ago. His promotions were never awarded to him by seniority, as is normal, but always by special favor of his superior [Betskoi], or because he acquitted himself well in whatever he was asked to do. I have told his superior a hundred times that he has always been troublesome and ill-tempered, always demanding and never satisfied. It is possible that there are some in the army who advanced faster than he, but surely no one who did not pay for this advancement with his own blood. . . . I am not saying anything about other gifts which he received because he will tell you that he got them for services rendered. I would like to know if there is a country where he would receive not more, but as much. [Carburi] is hated in the Cadet Corps like a toad. It was necessary to give the corps a new commander in order to maintain harmony. I don't know what his superior has promised him, but I do know that there is no reason for him to complain of injustice.[95]

Catherine the Great's remarks reflect, no doubt, the opinion of many Petersburgers who began to see in Carburi an unprincipled social climber and shameless sycophant among his superiors, and an arrogant grandstander among his equals and subordinates. Scherer confirms the words of Catherine and charges Betskoi with indiscriminate support of Carburi:

All the honest people who were in that educational establishment [the Cadet Corps] together with [Carburi] fled his company. It seems, however, that Betskoi regarded his turpitude as a recommendation and advanced him . . . to higher and higher posts. When the chaplain publicized complaints of the gravest sort against him and accused him of no less a charge than corrupting the morals of young men and leading them into the kind of vice that is contrary to nature, [Carburi] hastened to bring vague charges against the chaplain who was then given leave and reassigned to a very demanding, unpleasant, and disagreeable position with the police. . . . [Carburi's] standing astonished all of St. Petersburg. The manner in which he used his position caused general indignation. One had to cringe before that parvenu, that most vicious of people, or be prepared to lose one's job.[96]

The Russian historian S. N. Shubinsky, one of Carburi's most severe critics, accused him of having acquired a considerable capital "through embezzlement and various affairs" and imputed to him a lack of any sense of morality: "Having made personal enrichment the only aim of his life, he worked toward that goal using any means, including criminal ones. A contemporary witness testifies that [Carburi] managed to marry three times in the space of two years and poisoned his wives in order to obtain their dowries. An indirect confirmation of such a serious accusation are the curious epitaphs preserved to this day on three tombstones in the cathedral of Alexander Nevsky."[97]

Shubinsky's accusation is repeated to this day by a number of writers, even though a visit to the St. Lazarus cemetery of the cathedral of Alexander Nevsky shows that only two graves of wives of Carburi are there. Their similar marble slabs are decorated with identical rampant lions supporting an elaborate coat of arms topped by a large crown. The highly ornate French epitaphs surprise by their similarity and depth of professed sorrow, even though the death of the second wife followed that of the first one by a mere sixteen months.

Both wives were of Greek descent. The grave of the first one bears an inscription in Russian which agrees with the French epitaph below it that the name of the deceased woman was Hélène, daughter of George Khrysoskouleo.[98] The epitaph provides the dates of Hélène's birth and death as May 27, 1749, and April 29, 1771, which means that she was not yet twenty-two when she died. Marin's correspondence with his brothers reveals that the couple had two children, Giorgio, born in 1768, and Sophia, born in 1770. According to the Greek historian Tsitselē, Hélène's father was a state counselor serving as one of Catherine's advisers on foreign affairs.

The second grave presents a puzzle. The French epitaph refers to the deceased as Agathe Karabusin, who was born on February 4, 1753, and died on August 16, 1772. The Russian inscription, however, calls her Gorodetskaia. Shubinsky's assumption that two different women were buried under the same slab is totally improbable. As for the cause of the demise of a nineteen-year-old woman, one would be led to suspect that she died in childbirth, were it not for Scherer's accusation that she had been poisoned by Carburi: "[She] died almost instantly. Jänisch, the doctor of the Cadet Corps, saw her only once, for when he visited her for the second time, she was already dead. Seeing this [Carburi] cried out, 'Good God! What kind of physicians we have today! You let my wife die. You are the cause of her death.' To which the doctor replied, 'Stop talking like that or I will speak out and reveal who the instrument of that death was by the symptoms which I have observed.'"[99] It is impossible to ascertain where and how Scherer came by this information.

In the spring of 1773, much to Falconet's regret, Carburi decided to take a one-year leave of absence, ostensibly to go to a spa. The empress, tired of his "incessant talking of being promoted or getting a leave," ruled that "he should be given a leave because one must not stand in anybody's way, nor must one accept anybody else's rules."[100] On March 30, 1773, the Bureau of Buildings announced that Carburi was no longer in its employ and transferred his responsibilities regarding the construction of the monument to the architect Iury Fel'ten and the accountant Karl Krok.[101] Their duties were to include the supervision of the working force, budget, and provision of building materials and tools. Freed from his obligations, Carburi entrusted his children to the care of his sister-in-law and left for Paris. He had then, by his own admission, one hundred thousand francs in savings, "including money obtained from the sale of his wife's jewelry."[102] He left it all in the care of his St. Petersburg financial agent.

Upon arrival in Paris, Marin was cordially received by his elder brother, the physician Giovanni Battista, who introduced him at court. He urged Marin to take advantage of his international renown as the "mover of the Thunder Rock" and publish a detailed description of its transportation. He promised to contribute to it a section on the chemical composition of the granite fragments which Marin brought with him to Paris. Marin agreed, but asked to defer the project until he could retrieve his notes and drawings left behind in St. Petersburg.

What occupied Marin at that time was a plan, hatched already in St. Petersburg, to go back to Cephalonia and start there an American-style plantation of rice, sugarcane, cotton, and indigo. First, however, he had to negotiate the conditions on which the Venetian Senate would agree to take him off the list of wanted criminals. His bargaining position must have been quite strong, for he not only obtained a pardon but was awarded the title of count, and received what he called a "vast terrain" on Cephalonia to realize his agricultural project.[103]

Masarachi's claim that Carburi's pardon was obtained with the help of the Russian consul in Venice would mean, if true, that it must have been arranged before Carburi's falling out with the empress.[104] For Carburi to receive such a pardon while still in Russia could have been a valuable bargaining chip in his financial negotiations. It is also possible that Giovanni Battista, at that time the most respected Ionian in Europe, could have helped his brother. Nor can one exclude the possibility that Marin did not need any outside assistance in gaining the pardon and other bounties to boot. Given his edge-of-the-volcano existence, one may surmise that he rendered some special services to the Republic during his exile. Several circumstances point in that direction. Marin's first connection in St. Petersburg was his compatriot Colonel Melissino, who, as Russia's best artilleryman, must have been of considerable interest to Venetian intelligence services. His younger brother Marco spent six years traveling throughout Europe at the behest of the Venetian Senate in search of more efficient ways to mine and process copper needed in the production of naval artillery. Carburi himself was well acquainted with the properties of copper. That is what helped him design the devices for the transportation of the Thunder Rock. It was also Carburi's knowledge of metals which Falconet found so useful.

However that may be, Paris offered Marin a welcome change of pace after so many years in the tense and stiff St. Petersburg. His search for female companionship amidst a variety of easily available pleasurable distractions brought him into the arms of a Stéphanie Vautez, whom he wooed away from her lover, a high-ranking officer in the French army.[105] To the dismay of other members of the Carburi clan, his affair with *la francese,* as they referred to Stéphanie, bore the hallmarks of a serious commitment.

Excited by the prospect of seeing his new possessions on Cephalonia, Carburi went back to St. Petersburg to pick up his children and arrange his personal affairs. That done, on August 28, 1776, he, his children, their governess, an Austrian music teacher, a Greek acquaintance, and a servant boarded a packet boat in Riga, bound for Le Havre.[106] Calamity, however, overtook them at sea. Battered by a vicious storm, the boat ran aground and sank. Giorgio drowned, but the rest of the party miraculously survived.[107] All of Carburi's personal belongings went to the bottom of the Baltic.

Without his notes and drawings, Marin had to rely on his memory to reconstruct Operation Thunder Rock. He titled it *Monument élevé à la gloire de Pierre le Grand*—a somewhat premature claim, for at the time of the book's publication in 1777, the casting of the statue had barely been completed and the monument was still in its shed, waiting to be transferred to the pedestal.[108] Since there was no longer any need to conceal the author's true identity, the title page bore the name of Count Marin Carburi of Cephalonia, followed by an impressive list of his Russian titles and functions. The book, whose value is perforce diminished by the loss of the original documentation, is a remarkable printing achievement, with twelve magnificent engravings by Delvaux and Sellier, based on the drawings by Blarenberghe and Fossier.

After the book appeared, Marin traveled to Padua to meet with his younger brother Marco. He then went on to Venice, where he left his daughter Sophia in the convent of St. George of the Greeks in the center of the Greek Orthodox community in the Sestiere di Castello. In May 1778 he hired a boat to take him to Cephalonia. Traveling with him were an Austrian musician from St. Petersburg, who came along because he thought that Carburi's Cephalonian venture promised to be a profitable investment for his savings, and a French agriculturist named Antoine Baudry, whom Carburi had met in Venice. Baudry had spent some years on a large plantation in the French West Indies and was familiar with the kinds of crops that Carburi intended to grow.[109] Persuaded by Carburi that the land given to him by the Venetian Senate could support a plantation, Baudry decided to join the operation to lend it the benefit of his experience. Stéphanie Vautez stayed behind in Paris, but eventually joined the group on Cephalonia, where she and Marin were married in a traditional Greek Orthodox ceremony.

Carburi and his companions met with their first disappointment immediately upon arrival in Cephalonia. The vaunted family possessions amounted to a house in Argostoli and a vegetable garden. There were other disillusionments in store. The land obtained from the Venetian Senate was in the swampy part of the island, called Livadi or "meadow," and had to be dredged. The climate of Cephalonia was not well suited for subtropical vegetation, especially indigo, whose cultivation is difficult and labor-intensive. The local work force was insufficient and did not possess the experience needed for such an exotic venture. There were also financial problems. The plantation was undercapitalized from the outset because Carburi either did not have sufficient funds to start a business venture on such a grand scale or was not willing to sink in it all of his money. By and by it was becoming clear that his plantation on Cephalonia was a pie in the sky.

Faced with these problems and not willing to quit, Carburi began to change his strategy. Instead of exotic crops, he turned to the more conventional corn and sorghum. Their cultivation, however, required land reclamation on a major scale and a larger work force than was available. Carburi had to resort to the importation of seasonal workers from the Greek mainland, mostly Morea in central Peloponnesus. The workers, twenty in number according to Grasset and the historian of Cephalonia Masarachi, were lured by a promise of easy work and good pay, and an assurance that they would soon be allowed to return to their families. But the pay was irregular, food and lodgings were poor, and working conditions were harsh. On top of it, Carburi, known for his short temper, and Baudry, accustomed to deal with slave labor on American plantations, did not treat the workers well. The Moreans grumbled and demanded to be sent home. Carburi, however, insisting that their contractual obligation was to complete the project, refused to let them go, and brought in a five-man detachment of guards from Argostoli to prevent an explosion of pent-up anger. The Austrian musician, sensing the danger of the situation, tried to leave the island, but Carburi placed constant obstacles in his way. One day he was found dead on the beach, felled by a single bullet. Though the murderer got away, an inquest pointed to one of Carburi's servants.

On the night of April 18, 1782, the Morean workers, taking advantage of a sudden recall of the armed guards, broke into Carburi's house in Livadi and stabbed him and Baudry to death. They pillaged the house and took their loot to a boat waiting offshore. Stéphanie was wounded, but managed to get away and hide under a bed, where she was given up for dead. In the morning she crawled out and summoned help. A sea pursuit was assembled and the Moreans, whose sailboat was becalmed between Cephalonia and

Ithaca, were apprehended, chained, and put in jail. The governor of the Heptanese Islands, residing on Corfu, was notified of the crime, but since the workers were all Ottoman subjects, the Porte demanded their extradition. A lengthy diplomatic exchange followed, but before things were sorted out, the leaders of the mutiny were summarily executed, while the rest were tried by the Venetian governor and sentenced to the galleys, where many of them died. The French occupation of the islands in 1797 mooted procedural issues.[110]

There is probably no need to see in the mutiny more than meets the eye, namely the Moreans' desire to get what they thought was rightfully theirs—overdue payments and reunification with their families. Yet the improbable international foursome—Carburi with his ties to Russia, his French wife of questionable virtue, a Frenchman running an unprofitable American-style plantation, and an Austrian musician—does invite questions. Should one believe Carburi's claim that his stay on the island would be devoted to meditation and enjoyment of "the most wonderful climate and the sweetest retirement"?[111] Did the authorities in Argostoli suspect him of working for Russia and using the plantation as a cover? Why were the armed guards so suddenly removed?

The unstable political situation in Greece at the end of the eighteenth century invites suspicions. With the Sublime Porte showing signs of decay, there loomed a possibility that Russia would team up with Austria in dismembering the Ottoman Empire and dividing the spoils.[112] The certainty of Russian victory in the imminent Russo-Turkish war lent greater validity to Catherine the Great's dream of liberating Greece and creating an Orthodox empire in the Balkans. In such a setting it is easy to imagine that the raging mob of workers on Carburi's plantation was unwittingly serving higher interests in the intricate game of local politics.[113]

In the aftermath of the massacre, Carburi's widow moved to the island of Corfu, where she married a naval officer of the noble Venetian family of Grimani. The couple traveled to Venice, but their union did not receive the blessing of either the officer's family or the Senate, and Stéphanie was forced to return to Corfu. When the settlement of property matters and other inheritance business demanded that she visit Cephalonia, she was accompanied there by the French consul general on the islands, André Grasset de Saint-Sauveur.[114] He came partly as his official duty and partly out of curiosity to see what remained of the plantation. This is how he described the spot where Carburi wanted to launch his plantation: "All I saw there was a deserted place surrounded by arid hills, imbued with the exhalation of swamps whose draining had barely begun. The memory of the tragic scene which took place there added to my horror and I hastened to leave the beach stained by the crime. The count's house remained empty, for the local peasants believed that devil dwelled there. . . . Such was the end of that imaginary plantation and of the unfortunate count who believed that it could become reality."[115]

One could say that Carburi received his just deserts after walking a crooked path all his life. And yet, when one stands before the monument to Peter the Great and gazes in wonder at the granite cliff, which paradoxically looks wilder after it was worked on by the sculptor's chisel than when it lay half-buried in the swamps, one cannot but feel grateful to the enterprising genius of that cosmopolitan Greek and to the circumstances, however detestable, that allowed him to employ it in such a cause.

5

Gathering Clouds

MADAME FALCONET

It's raining Falconets in St. Petersburg.
—Falconet (1773)

By the beginning of the seventies, Marie-Anne Collot had become the most sought-after society portrait sculptor in St. Petersburg. Young, good-looking, and by then independently wealthy, she could have struck out on her own if she had wished to do so. She preferred, however, to live and work by the side, and perforce in the shadow, of her *maître* and companion. The intimate nature of their relationship must have been common knowledge in St. Petersburg. Yet, if there were voices in St. Petersburg criticizing or gossiping about the informality of the joint ménage, they are yet to be discovered.

Diderot did not mince words as he kept urging Falconet to marry: "Falconet, keep the promise that I made to Mlle Collot one evening, several days before your departure! How uncertain she was! How she cried! And I was telling her that your staying alone in a foreign land will make you more indispensable to each other, more precious for each other."[1] On another occasion he told Falconet that Paris gossip had the couple married anyway: "For the last two years people here have thought that you two are husband and wife."[2] Falconet, however, turned a deaf ear to these entreaties. He had once described the institution of marriage as a bird-trap, and he was clearly unwilling to be caught in it.[3]

Collot loved Falconet, of that there can be no doubt. But did Falconet love her? No single act of the sculptor would suggest it. Duty, responsibility, even devotion, yes, but love, no. Letters would normally be the best gauge of the intensity of feelings, but unfortunately, there is practically no epistolary evidence to illustrate the many years of the couple's life together. Not a single letter of Collot to Falconet has survived the censorship of her daughter, Marie-Lucie. As for letters from Falconet to Collot, only two are extant, both written after their return from Russia and both a bit on the dry side, as if written in the knowledge that other eyes might one day gain access to them.

A bird-trap was how Falconet must have remembered his early marriage, which imposed upon him many constraints and little in the way of compensation. His wife had been a simple woman, concerned only with the material well-being of the family. Three of his four children had died at an early age, and with Pierre-Etienne, the one surviving son, he had no emotional rapport. He blamed family obligations for the late start of his artistic career, the delay with the *morceau de réception,* the deflection from his cherished writing pursuits, and the missed opportunity to be a fellow of the Académie in Rome. Painfully aware of his age, Falconet saw himself as a man who had an artistic mission to accomplish and too little time left to do it in. As he wrote Diderot at the beginning of his stay in St. Petersburg, "In my profession, when one is fifty, one must simplify the play, if one wishes to get to the last act."[4] Starting a second family with a wife who was thirty-two years his junior went squarely against that precept.

There were other reasons as well. Puritanically proper and scrupulously honest, Falconet was probably loath to give the lie to the official version, which his friends, Diderot and Golitsyn, broadcast on the eve of his departure for St. Petersburg. It was an image of a master sculptor accompanied by a disciple and collaborator who happened to be a very young and attractive woman.

Was he afraid that Collot in the role of Madame Falconet might steal some of his thunder? Such a possibility cannot be excluded, for Falconet, while proclaiming indifference to the opinion of posterity, was not immune to professional jealousy. It was envy that made him break a bust of Diderot of his own making when he thought that Collot had made a better one.

Vexations and irritations of daily life took their toll on the relationship as well. As the web of intrigues around the St. Petersburg monument grew tighter, as the casting of the statue suffered ever greater delays, as the friendly attitude of the empress began changing and Betskoi became emboldened in his hounding of the sculptor, as friends in the foreign colony of St. Petersburg departed, strains and stresses could not but overtake Falconet's personal life.

When it rains, it pours. On August 19, 1773, amidst preparations for the imminent arrival of Diderot, the door of Falconet's house opened and the dumbstruck sculptor saw before him his only son, Pierre-Etienne, just off a boat from London. It soon became obvious that the thirty-one-year-old painter expected to stay for some time. There was nothing for it but to let the young man occupy the room prepared for Diderot, and to accept Pierre-Etienne as a third member of the household, further complicating a situation that was awkward enough without him.

Pierre-Etienne Falconet was born in Paris on October 9, 1741. Early on he showed considerable gifts as a draftsman and, at the age of eighteen, enrolled in the Académie, probably in the class of Boucher. His artistic gifts, however, did not go hand in hand with diligence. His father, imbued with the Jansenist work ethic, did not hide his disapproval. Diderot reports a curious incident that took place in 1759, when unbeknownst to his father, Pierre-Etienne entered one of his canvases in a competition at the Académie. The father had Pierre-Etienne escort him to the exhibition hall and asked him to judge the exhibited paintings. The youngster lowered his head and remained silent. Thereupon the father turned toward his colleagues, and said: "This is not a wise entry, Messieurs, but the young fellow lacks the courage to withdraw it. If he won't take it away, I will." He then put his son's canvas under his arm and walked out.[5]

After that fiasco, Pierre-Etienne became interested in engraving, working under the guidance of John Ingram, an English engraver who came to Paris in 1755 to accept a position with the French Academy of Sciences. Pierre-Etienne's talent earned him a commission with the *Encyclopédie* for a series of eight engravings illustrating the article "Sculpture," authored in part by his father. They represented various sculpting tools and techniques used for work with clay, plaster, marble, and wood, as well as equipment needed to move and set up large sculptures. One of the engravings shows the transportation to the church of St. Roch of his father's large *Archangel Gabriel,* which was a part of the group of the *Annunciation* in the chapel of Virgin Mary (fig. 5.1).[6]

Falconet *père's* friendship with Sir Joshua Reynolds allowed Pierre-Etienne to go to London and work in Reynolds's workshop at about the same time that Falconet was leaving for St. Petersburg. The friendship and tutelage of the English painter stood the young man in good stead. Pierre-Etienne achieved success as a painter of children, animals, and still lifes and as a London society portraitist.[7] He was elected Fellow of the Society of Artists of Great Britain and the Free Society of Artists, the two groups which existed

Fig. 5.1. Pierre-Etienne Falconet, The Marble Statue of the Archangel Gabriel by Etienne-Maurice Falconet Being Moved to the Church of St. Roch in Paris. Engraving (*Recueil,* 1771). Courtesy Arts of the Book, Yale University Library.

before the foundation of the Royal Academy, and he regularly showed his works in their halls. A list of his works exhibited between 1767 and 1772 includes about two dozen portraits, most of them described merely as portraits of ladies of quality, gentlemen, and artists.[8] The portrait of Mrs. Macauley, however, is identified by name, as are drawings of King Christian VII of Denmark and Marie Antoinette. His genre painting *A Spaniel and a Cat at Play* and a portrait of a *Young Woman in a Straw Hat* are in the Musée des Beaux-Arts in Nancy. *Peter the Wild Man* (1767) gained popularity because its subject was a mute man who lived in the woods in the vicinity of Hanover. Surprised in his lair by King George I when out on a hunt, he was brought to England. He worked there as a porter and died without ever learning to speak.[9]

The seven years that Pierre-Etienne spent in London are not well documented. No letters to or from his father are extant, and it is quite possible that there were none, since the two had parted on bad terms. It was rumored that Pierre-Etienne married and divorced in England, but the story has not been confirmed.[10] Diderot's letters to Falconet show that Pierre-Etienne visited Paris from time to time during his father's stay in Russia and that he received rent for Falconet's house on the rue d'Anjou.[11] By 1770, however, despite his success in London and his Anglophile sympathies, Pierre-Etienne became tempted to cash in on his father's connections in the lucrative art market of St. Petersburg. He was wary, however, of making a direct approach and asked Diderot to test the waters for him. Here is what Diderot reported to Falconet: "I talked with your son. He could have been received in the Académie if he had followed the advice of the artists whom he had asked to judge some of his paintings. He seems to be a sensible, honest, and upright fellow. He wouldn't mind making a trip to St. Petersburg if he could be sure that in embracing him you would find at least a fraction of the pleasure that he would have from being in your arms. But he won't do anything without your consent. I promised him that I would tell you about it and that I would send him your response word for word. So tell me."[12]

Since Falconet's letters to Diderot after 1767 have not survived, one can only guess that the father did not show any burning desire to see his son, let alone hold him in his arms. Such an inference follows from Pierre-Etienne's decision to take the matter into his own hands and present himself on the threshold of his father's house without announcing his visit. The following day the surprised father wrote to the empress: "Last evening my son came suddenly from London, without a word of warning, without having written."[13] His reaction, however, was more indulgent than could have been expected. Since Pierre-Etienne had brought along some of his own works, Falconet suggested to the empress that he would check them out: "I'll see what it is and what kind of talent he has."[14] The empress was encouraging: "I won't mind seeing the work of your son. What I have seen engraved seemed very good to me."[15]

This friendly reaction reassured Falconet that his son might be able to make it on his own, without becoming a burden on his budget. It also helped reawaken his paternal instincts: "Every father is, after all, sensitive to the happiness of his son."[16] With these words of unaccustomed warmth Falconet *père* began promoting Falconet *fils* as a portrait painter, hoping, no doubt, that one day he might occupy a position analogous to that of Collot in sculpture.

Pierre-Etienne's first ambition was to paint a portrait of Catherine. The empress was interested, but demanded that he first show his mettle by painting a portrait of Marie-Anne Collot.[17] The three-quarter portrait is a fine likeness of a beautiful, pensive woman with high cheekbones, dark, expressive eyes, and a sensuous mouth (fig. 1.11). Pierre-Etienne also did a self-portrait, as a pendant to the portrait of Collot. He painted himself as a rather good-looking man with a diffident look, sporting a wide-brimmed hat and an elegant foulard (fig. 5.2). Looking at it, one might forget the harsh words of Chevalier Bourrée de Corberon, first secretary of the French legation and a good friend of Falconet *père:* "His appearance is so ordinary that one could take him for a fool. There are people here who willingly accord him that title."[18] Bourrée de Corberon's judgment is supported by a bust made at about the same time by Collot, showing Pierre-Etienne as a plain-looking man with a boyish and expressionless face.[19]

The empress was evidently pleased with the results of the test, for she asked Pierre-Etienne to make two portraits of her, a large official one and a smaller version for private use, as well as portraits of Grand Duke Paul Petrovich and Grand Duchess Natalia Alekseevna. Falconet *père* was overjoyed: "Neither he nor I could imagine that his arrival here would earn him such an honor."[20]

Pierre-Etienne began the large portrait of the empress immediately, but early in 1774 he had to call off the sittings in order to go to England to take care of some unspecified personal business. On May 5, 1774, Falconet *père* was able to inform the empress: "My son has just returned and this time it's to stay."[21] Work on the portraits resumed and by the end of 1774 all three portraits were ready. The empress liked the portraits of her son and daughter-in-law, but was not pleased with her own (fig. 5.3). Her displeasure led to a dispute about the price of the portraits. Pierre-Etienne insisted on being paid six thousand rubles, while Catherine, annoyed at the concurrent negotiations with Falconet *père* about his fee for the casting of the monument, was not willing to pay more than three thousand.[22] The negotiations dragged on and in early September 1775, when Pierre-Etienne made a year-long trip to Paris, the bill was still unpaid.[23]

Pierre-Etienne was not alone on the coach to Paris. Traveling with him was Collot, returning home to attend to family matters.[24] She had planned to make the trip since 1771, but was detained in St. Petersburg by her own commitments and the indefinite status of the casting of the statue. Now that

Fig. 5.2. Pierre-Etienne Falconet, *Self-Portrait*. Oil on canvas, 1773. Musée des Beaux-Arts, Nancy. Photograph G. Mangin.

the casting was definitely in the hands of Falconet, she felt free to absent herself from St. Petersburg. Along with family matters, she had several other reasons for undertaking the strenuous trip.

First of all, there was the matter of the drawing of the large model of the monument made in 1770 by Losenko (fig. 3.6) and presented to Falconet by the empress. The drawing was to be engraved, which was the usual way of making a work of art widely known before the advent of photography. The engraving could have been made in St. Petersburg, but for some reason never was. Now Falconet suggested to the empress that Collot take the draw-

Fig. 5.3. Pierre-Etienne Falconet, *Catherine the Great*. Oil on canvas, 1773.
The State Hermitage Museum, St. Petersburg.

ing to Paris and have it engraved there.[25] The empress agreed, but upon reflection Falconet thought that it might be better to have an engraving made from a drawing of the completed monument, rather than a plaster model. His plans, however, were dashed when he had to leave before the installation of the monument, which thus remains one of the few major works of art without a contemporary engraving.[26]

Collot did take the Losenko drawing to Paris and left it there. A good thing it was, for agents of Betskoi made an attempt to seize it from Falconet before his departure from Russia a few years later. As Falconet remembered the incident: "an instant before my departure, an official of the Bureau of Buildings [that is, an employee of Betskoi] wanted to take away the drawing, which I had received as a gift from the empress. The agent's bosses must have been somewhat disconcerted when they learned that for the last three years the drawing had been in Paris, quite beyond their reach."[27]

Falconet mentions another reason for Collot's going to Paris. Back in 1773, after receiving Collot's bust of Diderot, the empress expressed a wish to have a bust of d'Alembert as its "vis-à-vis."[28] Since there was no expectation that d'Alembert would come to St. Petersburg to sit for a clay model, Falconet told the empress that Collot would make the model in Paris and transfer it to marble after her return. It is doubtful, however, whether such a portrait was ever made.[29]

It has also been suggested that one of Collot's reasons for going to Paris was to gain the *agrément* and *réception* in the Académie. That goal would have been consistent with the high marks given to her early works by Diderot and Grimm, as well as with the acclaim she received in St. Petersburg. Paris, however, was always rife with rumors that Collot's artistic production benefited significantly from Falconet's assistance. Those rumors grew in intensity after the two sculptors left for St. Petersburg, allowing the Paris gossipmongers to spin their tales from the thin threads floating in from Russia. Falconet did what he could to deny these stories, insisting on the independence of Collot's work, but the presumption of his amorous liaison with Collot made that task difficult.

A way out of the impasse would have been for Collot to present herself in person to the Académie and be assigned a subject for the *morceau de réception*. By working on it in Paris while Falconet was in St. Petersburg, she would have been able to remove from herself the last shred of suspicion that her work was not fully independent. If that was her intention, she did nothing about it during her stay in Paris in 1775–76. In the proceedings of the Académie for those years, there is no mention of Collot, nor is there any indication that a process of her *réception* had been initiated. It is true that, while in Paris, Collot sculpted two busts, which Diderot thought "testified to her ability."[30] Both are lost, but one could have been of d'Alembert or Houdon,[31] while the other was most probably a bust of Godefroy de Villetaneuse, which Lévesque mentions as a "beautiful portrait made in Paris."[32]

It is possible, however, that malicious gossip in the salons of Paris was not alone responsible for Collot's failure to be elected to the Académie. The real reason may have been the narrow compass of her artistic production, which, though quite rich, included no narrative sculpture of any sort, be it mythological, religious, heroic, or funerary. In the eyes of the conservative judges of the Académie, used to the referential exuberance of Baroque statuary, Collot's exclusive interest in portraiture may have sufficed to preclude her *réception.*

Nonetheless, upon Collot's return to St. Petersburg, Falconet pronounced the trip a resounding artistic success. Here is how he reported on it to Catherine: "It is to your protection and kind encouragement that [Collot] owes the praise she received in a country where people used to think that I helped her in her work. They saw her sculpt and they believed. Our best artists and our best connoisseurs said and wrote the most flattering things about her work."[33]

While Collot was preparing for her trip to Paris, an unexpected complication put it in jeopardy. In the summer of 1775, while Falconet was wrapped up in preparations for the casting of the statue, there arrived the news from Paris that Charles-Jacques Collin, Falconet's trusted agent and manager of his house on the rue d'Anjou, had died. Collin, as the treasurer of the Royal Hunts, was an employee of the Crown. That meant that upon his death all his account books had to be sealed until examination of them revealed no shortfall or any other irregularity. That injunction automatically froze all of Falconet's and Collot's assets which were in Collin's custody. It so happened that Collot had just sent Collin the money that she would need in Paris. The alarmed sculptor informed Catherine about Collot's predicament and asked the empress to continue her salary while she was in Paris. The request was granted and Collot was able to leave as planned.[34]

Although Collot's visit to Paris lasted almost one year, no details about it have come down to us.[35] Diderot claims to have seen Collot frequently during that time, but the usually chatty *philosophe* does not say anything about the topics of their conversations or any other aspects of her stay in Paris.[36] We do not know whether Pierre-Etienne was with Collot throughout her stay or whether he spent some time in London. Since the house on the rue d'Anjou was presumably rented, where did she stay? Where was her atelier? Did she write to Falconet in St. Petersburg and did he write to her? If that correspondence existed, was it destroyed by her daughter?

Our ignorance of the particulars of Collot's and Pierre-Etienne's joint trip to Paris is all the more disturbing because during their absence from St. Petersburg Betskoi spread a story that the two "had been married incognito by the father," and that the marriage was contracted in spite of Pierre-Etienne's having a wife and two children in England. Betskoi quoted Falconet *père* as saying that his son's English marriage was null and void in France "because his English wife was Protestant."[37] Betskoi's story is especially intriguing in view of an astounding event that took place a year after the couple had returned to St. Petersburg. On July 29, 1777, Marie-Anne Collot and

Pierre-Etienne Falconet were actually married in a civil ceremony held in the chapel of the French legation, with the marquis de Juigné, the French plenipotentiary minister in Russia, officiating and several guests present. Although the event must have come as a total surprise to most of their acquaintances, there are just two extant echoes of it.

Lévesque mentions it in a few words, but his choice of them is most peculiar: "[Falconet] gave [Collot] his name by *making* her marry his son."[38] This odd formulation forces one to consider seriously the possible correctness of the story spread earlier by Betskoi.

The other reference to the marriage is much more extensive, for it comes from the pen of one of the witnesses of the ceremony, Chevalier Bourrée de Corberon:

> In the evening we signed the marriage contract between Falconet *fils* and Mlle Collot. I confess that I did it with repugnance, but since Monsieur de Juigné was in charge, I could not refuse. They say that Falconet was married in England. His marriage was dissolved, but that is not good enough for me. . . . Monsieur de Juigné, to whom I mentioned my doubts, tried to dispel them. So I signed, but that does not mean that I approve of what I couldn't prevent. . . . Money is the only reason for this marriage. . . . The Collot woman is worth forty thousand rubles or so they say. I don't know if the bans were posted in the Catholic church. I'll get some information on it later, as well as on this whole affair. It does not seem to be quite aboveboard, despite what Monsieur de Juigné is saying.[39]

Bourrée de Corberon was absolutely right in questioning the motives of Pierre-Etienne, who was known as a profligate wastrel. But Collot was nobody's fool either. Aware of her bridegroom's cupidity, she insisted on a carefully worded prenuptial agreement. It was signed on July 27, 1777, in the French legation and was witnessed by the marquis de Juigné, three employees of the legation, the Swedish-French portraitist Alexandre Roslin, and Falconet *père*. Emerging from the legal jargon is Collot's concern that her assets be protected from Pierre-Etienne: "There will be no joint estate between the above-mentioned future spouses. Consequently, one party will not be held responsible for the debts and mortgages of the other, which, no matter when contracted or incurred, will be paid by the debtor or borrower using his or her resources, while the other party and his or her resources will not be held responsible for such debts and mortgages."[40]

Collot's marriage to Pierre-Etienne poses, of course, a multitude of questions, most of them unanswerable for lack of documentation. When did the courtship begin? What were the sources of Betskoi's claim that the marriage was contracted privately before the couple left for Paris? Was it just a malicious rumor, or was Betskoi on to something, since his story anticipated the real event? Could it be that the trip to Paris was the premature honeymoon of a bigamist and an adulterous bride? And what did Lévesque mean by suggesting that Falconet *père* made Collot wed his son? Assuming that his charge is well-founded, was it because Falconet *père* wished to give Collot his name without having to marry her, which, as we have seen, he did not want to do? One can easily suspect Falconet *fils* of being unscrupulous enough to take part in such a wretched scheme, especially if it held a promise of financial gain. One might even suspect Falconet *père* of being unfeeling enough to organize it. But would Collot be willing to enter into a union with a man whom she did not love and who represented a threat to her financial security, solely in order to bear the name of the man she really loved? Such conduct seems totally out of character.

Pierre-Etienne's decision to stake a fairly successful career in England on the vague hope of a better life at the side of a difficult and unwelcoming father is also studded with questions. Was he running away from a marital entanglement in England? Did he have a special interest in renewing his acquaintance with Collot, whom he remembered from Paris as a penniless waif, but who had since become a well-to-do artist and a beautiful woman to boot? If Collot was the principal goal of his trip, was there any prior communication between them? Did he try to make his arrival in St. Petersburg coincide with Diderot's, so as to use him as a buffer in his first encounter with his father?[41]

A much more important question, however, is whether Pierre-Etienne was aware of Collot's relationship with his father as he was signing his name to the marriage contract. Faced with this quandary, Réau concluded that the problem was moot, for Collot was not a mistress of Falconet *père*, after all. In making this claim Réau changed his earlier stand, for he could not bring himself to believe that "knowing what we otherwise know about [Collot's] character, she would give her right hand to the son after giving her left hand to the father."[42] Implausibly, Réau finds support for his theory in the quick unraveling of the marriage and Collot's flight from her husband's side into the waiting arms of her father-in-law. "Had she really been a mistress of her father-in-law," he asks, "would she have dared to openly challenge public opinion by going off to rejoin him?" An odd question, considering Collot's history of braving public opinion—such as it was in eighteenth-century Paris and St. Petersburg—during all of her earlier life.

Réau gives much weight to the two surviving letters from Falconet *père* to Collot, written after the marriage had broken down and the old love affair was being resurrected. Their form of address, "Madame et chère fille," and their "respectful tone" do not, according to him, betray a man who had once been the addressee's lover. Speaking against that claim is the fact that these two letters happen to be the only ones which were not destroyed by Collot's daughter. Did they escape the fate of the rest of the correspondence precisely because of their "respectable tone?" What the tone of the destroyed letters was must be left to one's imagination. Another matter to keep in mind is that Collot and Pierre-Etienne were still officially man and wife and that

Falconet *père* had to consider the legal consequences of his actions, especially with regard to the status of his will, which appointed Collot executrix and principal heir of his estate.

Searching for a logically persuasive motive of Collot's decision to wed Pierre-Etienne, one may venture a guess that she wished to bear a Falconet child. When having it with Falconet *père* proved impracticable, she opted for the services of Falconet *fils*. If that was her plan, it was a total success. On April 24, 1778, within nine months of the marriage, Madame Falconet gave birth to Marie-Lucie or Mashenka, as the girl was called by her Russian nanny.[43]

As for the motives of Pierre-Etienne, one would think that Collot's virtues, celebrated in an anonymous poem found on an engraving of her portrait by him, should have sufficed to bring to her side not just him, but a whole bevy of other suitors:

> Grand homme, femme aimable, Elle excelle à la fois
> Dans l'art de Phidias et dans celui de plaire.
> Athène eut couronné ses talens autrefois;
> Elle auroit obtenu des autels à Cithère.[44]

Be that as it may, the sad fortunes of this ill-starred marriage make one suspect that the magnet that attracted Pierre-Etienne to his future bride is not to be found in an elegant poetic tribute, but in the dry prose of the prenuptial agreement.

IN THE SHADOW OF THE *MARCUS AURELIUS*

I incline with respect before Antiquity,
But not in reverence, nor with servility.
I look at the Ancients without bending my knee.
They are great, I admit, but not greater than we.
—Charles Perrault (1687)

The monument of Marcus Aurelius in Rome is the most important statue to survive unburied from antiquity (figs. 2.1, 8.10). Its history, in fact, is so long that the monument has acquired an aura of immortality and has become the epitome of its genre, an illustration of the establishment and transmission of a pattern, and a palpable proof of continuity in art. It was fashioned in the second century A.D., toward the end of the reign of Marcus Aurelius (A.D. 161–80), or shortly thereafter, by a sculptor whose name has not come down to us. The true identity of its subject was likewise lost during the upheavals of the barbarian conquests. In the Middle Ages and the Renaissance the rider was assigned various personae from the emperors Hadrian, Antoninus Pius, and Septimius Severus to Emperor Constantine the Great and King Theodoric the Great. It was even suggested that the horseman was the legendary Roman hero Marcus Curtius.

It was not till the sixteenth century that the rider was definitively identified as Emperor Marcus Aurelius. The monument was moved then from the vicinity of the Lateran to the Capitoline Hill, where it was placed on a marble pedestal designed by Michelangelo. It has since joined the list of the most popular Roman sights.[45] The fame of the *Marcus Aurelius* reached its peak in the seventeenth and eighteenth centuries. At that time it was frequently engraved, copied in bronze and plaster, and pronounced by such critics as Addison, Caylus, and Winckelmann to be one of the finest statues in existence, a standard of excellence against which all equestrian monuments should be judged.[46]

What is the essence of that standard? The horseman is astride a standing or slowly moving horse that raises one of its forelegs. In one hand he holds the reins (missing in the surviving statue), while the other may be clutching a sword, a baton, a hat, a roll of parchment, or may be extended in a pacifying or welcoming gesture. Whatever the original pedestal of the *Marcus Aurelius* was, the modern viewer has become used to the high, sculpted pedestal on which the statue was placed by Michelangelo. Except for Pietro Tacca's monument to Philip IV in Madrid, known as the *Buen Retiro,* the model of the *Marcus Aurelius* had been followed in all equestrian statues from the *Gattamelata* in Padua and the *Colleoni* in Venice to those of local dignitaries in Florence and Piacenza, and the French kings from Henry IV to Louis XV.

In this atmosphere of general acclaim, Falconet's programmatic disavowal of the Marcus Aurelius model created nothing short of a scandal. Instead of a decorous and sluggish horse, Falconet designed a spirited charger with an open mouth and distended nostrils, jumping onto a natural rock and rearing above its edge. The French and Russian critics did not expect such an explosion of raw naturalism and decreed almost unanimously that the sculptor was guilty of deliberately and arrogantly flouting the hallowed classical tradition exemplified by the *Marcus Aurelius.*

Catherine the Great was quite aware of these critical voices. Some of them, in fact, were heard in her immediate entourage, with Betskoi leading the chorus. But a fine taste in art and the courage to endorse untried ideas prompted her to side with Falconet and disregard the laments of the traditionalists. Having dismissed Rastrelli's heavy and pompous monument to Peter the Great as unworthy of its subject, she became entranced by the élan of Falconet's leaping horse and was happy to provide it with a prominent site in her capital, sensing that an event of major importance in the history of sculpture was in the making.

The support of the empress should have sufficed to reassure any artist in her employ—but not Falconet. He waited for support from other sculptors and well-trained critics, but such support was not forthcoming. The hypersensitive and irritable sculptor was so unsettled by the suggestions that he not stray too far from the classical proportions of the *Marcus Aurelius* that any mention, however veiled, of the Roman monument put him in the mood to do battle. An occasion presented itself soon enough. He had just begun working on the large model of the monument when Betskoi asked him to write up his views on Pietro Tacca's *Buen Retiro* and submit them to the empress for review.

Falconet suspected that the real interest of Betskoi was not the *Buen Retiro* but the *Marcus Aurelius.* The problem was the horse. Should it be the heroic image that Falconet conjured up, a forerunner of the flying steed of David's *Napoleon Crossing the Alps,* or the conventional mount on which Marcus Aurelius trotted into the annals of sculpture? Betskoi's request could be taken as either a vote of no confidence in Falconet's ability to be as good as Tacca, or a veiled exhortation to be more traditional in his design. Neither interpretation pleased him. He dismissed the *Buen Retiro* as a work not worthy of his concern and shifted the argument to the *Marcus Aurelius.*

His first move was, as usual, an appeal to the empress for help and guidance. On May 11, 1768, he wrote her a letter decrying Betskoi's meddling in matters which were not within his competence. It was in his view an assault on artistic freedom: "The statue of Marcus Aurelius is appropriate for Marcus Aurelius, as any statue should be appropriate for its subject. Different portraits should not resemble each other any more than different faces. . . . The Ancients are not our absolute masters, they did not do everything so well that the Moderns have nothing left to do. . . . To foist a *Marcus Aurelius* on a sculptor who chooses a different path that he knows will serve him well is wrong because there is more than one way to show the beauty of nature. What matters is that the choice be appropriate for the subject and be well executed."[47]

Falconet was preaching to the converted. Catherine had heard these arguments before and agreed with all of them. She did her best to calm the agitated sculptor: "Listen to me, forget the *Buen Retiro* and the *Marcus Aurelius,* forget the wrong advice of people who understand nothing in these matters, and stay your course. You'll do a hundred times better by being stubborn (excuse the term—I am not using it in a derogatory sense) than by paying attention to unsolicited advice and taking it too seriously."[48]

Neither combatant, however, would hang up his musket. As late as 1775, Betskoi asked Prince Alexander M. Golitsyn to have Count Otto Magnus Stackelberg, Russia's envoy to Spain, send him "at least three images of the equestrian statue that is in Buen Retiro with all the measurements." He wanted to know specifically whether the statue was supported by having the tail of the horse attached to the pedestal, and how widely spread were the hind legs. He insisted that the envoy get this information "with all diligence and as soon as possible."[49] All this was requested at a time when Falconet's statue was about to be cast!

That was clear interference, and Catherine's soothing words could do little to calm the sculptor's suspicions. He wanted the fight to get into the open so that the world would see the ignorance of those who criticized his project from the position of what was known then as *antiquomania,* that is, a belief that classical Greek and Roman art offered unparalleled models of excellence. One would have thought that Diderot was not to be counted among these critics, for he was a convinced believer in Falconet's artistic genius and an enthusiastic supporter of his design for the monument to Peter the Great. Yet, in the learned debate, which occupied the two friends from the end of 1765 to Falconet's departure for Russia, Diderot also had showed symptoms of antiquomania. To Falconet, who considered antiquity as just another period in the history of art, one in which good as well as bad works were produced, Diderot's pronouncements at that time called into question his credentials as an ally in the contest between him and the supporters of the Marcus Aurelius tradition.

While recognizing that many ancient works of art were worthy models for modern artists, Falconet showed no pity to those critics who praised a work of art simply because it was ancient. Here is how he summed up his feelings on antiquomania in the postscript to his *Passages de Pline,* first published in 1772 in Amsterdam and reissued the following year in The Hague: "Some of that prodigious veneration in which Pliny [the Elder] is held is due to our blind admiration of everything that is ancient and our contempt for everything that is modern. This should not amaze us. Antiquomania is a malady of all times. Horace, Pliny the Younger, and others complained about it. These two authors in particular were appalled by what was happening in their century, when a choice had to be made between the Ancients and the Moderns. It appears that Horace did not believe in the infallibility of the public. He was indignant to see blind preference accorded for no other reason than the virtue of being ancient."[50]

It was with Diderot in mind that Falconet decided to mount a counterattack on his critics in a booklet under the title *Observations sur la statue de Marc-Aurèle et sur d'autres objets relatifs aux beaux-arts.* Written in the winter and spring of 1770, when the large model of the monument was almost finished, it appeared in early 1771 in Amsterdam, with Prince D. A. Golitsyn assisting in its publication. It was a viciously sarcastic assault on the holiest idol of the "antiquomaniacs," making Goethe exclaim in horror: "Falconet is writing—with venom against everything."[51] Since the horse was central to his design of the statue, Falconet concentrated his attack on the horse of the *Marcus Aurelius.* He compared it to images of other horses, both ancient and modern, and concluded that its proportions were all wrong, that its gait was unnatural, and that it lacked grace: "The head, neck, thighs, legs, gait, the entire horse of the *Marcus Aurelius* do not merit their reputation at all."[52]

But the horse of the *Marcus Aurelius* was not the only target of Falconet's ire. The edge of his remarks was directed at its glorifiers: "I fling into fire the writings of all those people who repeat each other the way children repeat fairy tales after their nannies."[53] The people whose writings deserved to be so treated were, according to him, the *litterati,* that is, writers whose self-proclaimed authority and self-assurance lent their impressionistic divagations an air of genuine knowledge of art. It was they who were the veritable myth-makers, the false connoisseurs whose indiscriminate veneration of ancient art heralded the approach of Neoclassicism and would set the tone for art criticism for generations to come. Falconet's object was to derail Winckelmann's theoretical and archeological approach to the study of ancient art and to replace it with empirical connoisseurship which would lead to a more objective and detached analysis. As Dowley justly observes: "he wanted to judge an individual statue on what he took to be its own artistic and technical merits. Unlike Diderot, he would not defer to the authority of the traditional ancient sources, such as Pliny or Pausanias, unless confirmed by his own experience."[54]

Dedicating his *Observations* pointedly to Diderot, Falconet picked up some threads of the old debate and, mounting his moral high horse, upbraided his friend: "You are not going to tell me that one should rather be wrong with the crowd than right alone."[55] The response was not long in coming. Within three months of the publication of the *Observations,* Grimm's *Correspondance littéraire* carried a brief note announcing the event. It was as negative a reception as one could imagine.[56] It was couched, in fact, in terms of such vehemence and outright malice as to call into question the motives of its anonymous author. It branded Falconet's writings as "aggressive and arrogant" and declared that his character and talent were not worthy of admiration "because genius does not keep company with pettiness and narrowness of the mind and soul." The note continued with mounting derision: "Would you like to know the great discoveries of Etienne Falconet? (1) The much admired horse of Marcus Aurelius is bad because the horse of Peter the Great will not resemble it. (2) It is not necessary for an artist to go to Italy because Falconet did not go there. (3) It is better to judge the antiquities of Rome and Florence by their plaster casts than by the originals because Falconet did not see the originals. (4) The *litterati* do not understand anything at all in art because it is they who will judge the monument to Peter the Great."[57]

The note in the *Correspondance littéraire* was welcome news to those readers of Falconet's writings on art and art criticism who were often irritated, even scandalized, by the sculptor's iconoclastic opinions. Jacques-André Naigeon, Diderot's pupil and friend, called the *Observations* "a dull, insolent, and sullen work . . . which does not deserve to be read"[58] Voltaire's disapproval of the "irreverent way in which Falconet had treated the horse of the Marcus Aurelius" was mentioned by Théodore Tronchin, Voltaire's neighbor and physician, in a letter to Prince D. A. Golitsyn.[59] Golitsyn, who shared Falconet's distaste for antiquomania, answered: "I am surprised that your neighbor is angry with my friend Falconet for having slightly mistreated the horse of the *Marcus Aurelius.* I have thought him more tolerant and congenial with people who openly expressed their opinions, especially when they supported them with good arguments. . . . Your neighbor is a most respected man, deservedly very famous, and I would seek his advice in all matters except art, where I do not consider him a competent judge."[60]

One would have thought that Falconet would have been inured to criticism of his controversial views and, being a disputatious person by nature, might even relish it. Yet, the irrepressible malevolence of the note in the *Correspondance littéraire* was clearly beyond the pale. Falconet, who had access to it through Catherine, understandably exploded. His anger was directed primarily against Diderot, whom he must have suspected of the authorship of the note or, at the very least, of foreknowledge and tacit approval of its appearance.[61] He had good reasons to think so. Diderot was a frequent contributor to the *Correspondance littéraire,* especially in the area of the arts, and was responsible for covering the Paris Salons, a task in which he leaned heavily on Falconet's expertise. He also considered Grimm one of his closest friends and made no secret of his feelings.[62]

The affair of the note in the *Correspondance littéraire* was the first serious breach in the long friendship between Diderot and Falconet. It involved initially an exchange of three letters: one from Diderot, giving some explanation of what had happened; Falconet's incensed reaction to it; and Diderot's aggrieved answer, dated August 21, 1771, the only one of the three to have survived and the one whose testimony allows us to infer the existence of the other two letters. Falconet, eager to broadcast his point of view, sent the first two letters to Prince D. A. Golitsyn in the Hague, with a request to forward his reply to Diderot. Golitsyn complied, presumably retaining Diderot's first letter in his files. The reconstruction of this sequence of events rests on the last sentence of the first paragraph of Diderot's August 21 letter to Falconet: "You must have very little self-esteem or place very little stock in the judgment and respect of Prince Golitsyn to have sent him my letter and to have had him forward to me a torrent of venom and arrogance."[63] In the rest of the paragraph Diderot gave vent to his bitterness and his sense of impugned innocence:

This, my friend (for I can't stop myself from calling you so), is not an answer to the outrageous letter that you have written me. I am waiting for the indignation and pain to flow out of my heart and then I'll make you blush for your premeditated and meticulously ordered insults. I may have committed some grave sin of which my conscience is not aware. But I would never pardon myself for the sin you have committed by treating a man whose sentiments are beyond suspicion as shamelessly as you have done. Be careful! Your loneliness in St. Petersburg and the favors of the great sovereign are corrupting you. You are in danger of becoming mean. The first step to this is to find meanness where there is none, and you have taken that step.

The letter drew no response from Falconet, and on April 17, 1772, Diderot attempted to bury the hatchet:

It's been, it seems to me, a fairly long time since we, without ceasing to love each other, have actually said that we do. Falconet, you wounded me gravely and I was silly enough to repay pain with pain. You should be grateful for it, for with a somewhat cooler head, I could have been very cruel by letting you bear the weight of your wrongs. I could have answered you with the kindness and moderation that are absent from your letter, I don't recall any more which one. But this is all over, isn't it? Tell me then that our souls are as close as ever. I love you both. I send you regards and kiss you with all my heart.[64]

Since these avowals of friendship were not acknowledged, let alone reciprocated, and since the date of his departure for Russia was drawing closer, Diderot made another stab at reconciliation. On May 30, 1773, he sent Falconet and Collot an effusive letter, which was a veritable declaration of love:

. . . my friends. It's been a long time since you've had my news. It's been an eternity since I've had yours. I trust that the two of you are in good health. I trust that both of you are happy. I need that conviction, whether it is well founded or not, because without it, the past would be filled with too many regrets, while with it, I can arrange your domestic life as I please. I'll not be happy unless I go to St. Petersburg to see you, settle at your side, and verify my fiction. . . . What a day! What a moment for you and for me when I come knocking at your door, when I come in, when I fall into your arms, and when we exclaim confusedly: "It's you!—Yes, it's me.—Finally!—Yes, finally." How we'll babble! Woe betide the man who sees a friend after a long time and, without getting speechless, does not babble![65]

Diderot ended the letter with a question and answer: "But what if you don't love me any more? No, that can't be true. My heart is answering yours. You love me still." Little did he know that a few days before his letter reached St. Petersburg, Falconet was still seething: "All his beautiful promises are no more than fairy tales and I don't know their reasons and inner springs, . . . , Your Majesty is my witness that I have always served Diderot with the fervor of true friendship. He answered always with big words. In the end one gets tired of it and I have reached that point. Perhaps one day I will discover the true reasons for his behavior."[66] When Diderot's letter of May 20 arrived, Falconet sent it to the empress, who was impatient for news of the awaited visit. She returned it and, wishing to put Falconet in a more forgiving frame of mind, added: "It seems that his departure is no longer in doubt, his friendship for you is even less so."[67]

There were two more letters from Diderot to Falconet before the two "friends" parted company for good. Although the first one exists in a single copy only, there is no doubt about its authenticity. There are, however, good reasons to doubt that it was actually sent to Falconet and that it was written on May 2, 1773, as marked on the manuscript copy. It is couched in the form of a letter and contains a long and thoughtful review of Falconet's

Observations. Dieckmann and Seznec, editors of the letter, are probably right in their conjecture that Diderot hand-delivered it to Falconet when he saw the sculptor in St. Petersburg. The two critics have good reason to wonder about the odd timing of the letter. Why indeed would Diderot review Falconet's booklet more than two years after its appearance? Their explanation, however, that Diderot wished to resume the old *le pour et le contre* debate is too artless to be convincing.[68]

Diderot was coming to St. Petersburg to meet Catherine and discuss with her major problems affecting Russia and the world, rather than to argue with Falconet about fine points of interpretation of the critical writings of classical authors. The most probable reason for the review was to convince Falconet that an author of a serious and substantive critical article could not have had anything to do with the perfunctory note published in the *Correspondance littéraire.*[69] It is also possible that Diderot wanted the empress to see the letter in order to justify the published critique.

The last communication from Diderot to Falconet is dated December 6, 1773. It is definitely not a letter in the conventional sense of the word. By his own admission, Falconet himself solicited it when Diderot visited his atelier to examine the large model of the monument. Diderot's impressions, put down on paper right then and there, are the most enthusiastic endorsement of Falconet's conception that the sculptor had ever received: "I knew you to be a very able man, but let me die if I believed that you had anything like that in your head! How could I ever imagine that this astonishing image was lodged in the mind that conjured the delicate figures of the *Pygmalion?* Two pieces of such uncommon perfection, which, for that very reason, should exclude each other. . . . Your work, my friend, has indeed the true stamp of the finest creations. It appears beautiful the first time one sees it, and more beautiful the second time, and the third, and the fourth. One leaves it with regret and remembers it forever."

That was not all, however. Diderot found a way to flatter Falconet not only on his art, but also on his critical acumen. In a significant reversal of his earlier stand the philosopher admitted that

> the horse of the *Marcus Aurelius* is a very poor reflection of a poorly chosen animal. It is neither truthful in that simple and rigorous way that never fails to please, nor does it make up for it by being daringly deceitful. . . . The entire head is heavy. The details of the mouth, eyes, and neck lack finesse and elasticity. They look like gashes and flutings rather than folds of the flesh. In frontal view, one cannot tell to what sort of animal the lower part of the head belongs, . . . an ox or a bull. . . . The belly is swollen and heavy. . . . It's clear that this horse makes large steps with its hind legs and prances with its forelegs—an invalid and impossible motion. Your remarks on this issue, as well as all the rest, are just.

Diderot concluded: "Adieu, my friend, enjoy the satisfaction of having executed the noblest work of the kind in Europe, and enjoy it for a long time."[70]

There are three circumstances that make Diderot's complicity in the affair of the note in the *Correspondance littéraire* possible or, at the very least, thinkable. In the first place, a copy of the note is in the fonds Vandeul—a collection of writings by Diderot and concerning Diderot. Second, after an initial burst of outrage at Falconet's accusations, Diderot showed himself more than eager to forget the incident and in his three subsequent letters to Falconet displayed most tender feelings for his Parisian friend. Third, on May 10, 1774, barely five months after his last avowals of friendship and admiration for Falconet, Diderot stung the sculptor to the quick with a vicious and seemingly gratuitous attack on his *morceau de réception,* the *Milo of Crotona* of 1754 (fig. 1.3). Written under the guise of a letter addressed to Prince D. A. Golitsyn, in whose house in The Hague Diderot stopped for half a year on his way from St. Petersburg to Paris, it showed the true depth of Diderot's animus against Falconet.

The *Milo of Crotona,* with all its faults and virtues, was incidental to Diderot's letter. Its main object was Falconet's contention, made in the *Observations,* that men of letters are incapable of practicing meaningful art criticism, for they, unlike the artists, do not possess the technical knowledge necessary to understand the process of artistic creation. Diderot, with his passionate interest in art and a history of critical reports from the Salons, must have seen himself as the most obvious target of Falconet's criticism. He had yielded on the *Marcus Aurelius,* but he was not about to beat an all-out retreat. The note in the *Correspondance littéraire* had already made fun of Falconet's notions, by claiming that the sculptor wished merely to preempt the *litterati's* right to criticize his equestrian monument. Now Diderot set out to prove that he, as a paradigmatic member of the writing confraternity, could express himself knowledgeably and sensibly about a work of art. To do so, he selected an old sculpture by Falconet and subjected it to a critique in which he savaged Falconet's work as ferociously as the lion had dealt with Milo.

Diderot found fault with virtually every aspect of the sculpture. He accused Falconet of trying to imitate the *Laocoön* and of failing in that attempt because he did not show that one can suffer with dignity, an attitude so successfully displayed in the Hellenistic statue. The right arm of Milo, in Falconet's interpretation, was lifeless and showed no natural inclination to free itself from its trap; the abdomen had too many folds and cavities; the left arm was "stupidly stuck under the body" instead of being actively used in the struggle; the legs, "borrowed from the *Laocoön*" were misused and misplaced; there were ugly holes in the belly; and even the toes were not to Diderot's liking. Milo's head, which Diderot knew was a self-portrait of Falconet, bore the brunt of the critic's attack.[71] It was, he said, the head of a vile criminal, ignoble, vulgar, and plain: "The wild beast that sinks its claws and teeth in the thigh is less hideous than the man." The expression of pain was excessive and affected ("My poor Milo, scream less loudly and defend yourself better!"). It reminded Diderot of the suffering painted on the face of a criminal being tortured on the wheel.

The vehemence of Diderot's assault makes it clear that his ultimate motive was not a desire to prove Falconet wrong. A feeling of personal vendetta against the sculptor must have been at play. What else could have caused Diderot to inveigh against a work of art fully twenty years after it had earned its maker membership in the Académie? What else could have prompted him to couch his criticism in the form of a letter to a man in whose house he was staying and who was known for his friendly feelings toward Falconet? What else could have made Diderot interlace his critical judgments with assurances of feigned humility and sarcastic respect for the sculptor ("Let me ask with all the modesty appropriate for an ignoramus who is judging a work of a great master," or "Let me ask always with the same timidity")? It was not just an expression of art criticism, but a personal condemnation designed to hurt all the more for its being addressed to Falconet's best friend.

Waving the flag of the writing confraternity, Diderot delivered the coup de grâce to a friendship that the note in the *Correspondance littéraire* had already seriously tested: "And this is how a man of letters judges a piece of sculpture after he has examined it and decided to be sympathetic to the artist. And this is all that is needed to show the madness of the idea of giving the artist alone the right to judge a work of plastic art and impose silence upon those who write for and speak to posterity. Bronze decays, marble breaks, but our words stay forever. . . . There are half a dozen other sculptures by the same artist that could be subjected to criticism that would be more bitter and more deserved and," Diderot added ominously, "that judgment will be rendered if Falconet does not watch out."[72]

One may wonder why a long and fruitful friendship between a sculptor and a writer could drain away so suddenly, leading on the part of Falconet to obdurate silence and on the part of Diderot to an oscillation between fulsome praise and harsh censure. The note in the *Correspondance littéraire,* Falconet's condemnation of the horse of the *Marcus Aurelius,* his irreverent treatment of the critical acumen of the *litterati,* his unwillingness to respond to Diderot's repeated attempts to patch up their crumbling relationship, his refusal to offer Diderot hospitality in his home in St. Petersburg, Diderot's humiliation at having to concede the shortcomings of the *Marcus Aurelius*— all these factors contributed to the rupture. Yet the ultimate culprit is to be sought elsewhere.

While for various reasons, among them Falconet's own fussiness, the search for a founder of the statue proceeded at a snail's pace, the model languished, almost forgotten, in the sculptor's atelier. The ooh's and ah's which greeted its completion in May of 1770 were heard no longer, and in the suspicious mind of the sculptor a plot was being hatched by Betskoi and his confederates to let it stand unfinished beyond the eight-year term of his contract. The empress, so concerned and supportive in earlier years, was showing signs of getting tired of her cantankerous sculptor. It was becoming clear that the unfinished monument had begun sliding into the inner recesses of her mind, occupied as it was with such matters as the war with Turkey, which had taken a turn for the worse; the disruptive bickering between the Orlov and Panin factions at court; Pugachev's rebellion; Poland's gradual self-destruction; and the plague which attacked Russia's hinterland.

As enforced idleness made Falconet increasingly restless and impatient, exacerbating his innately combative nature, the pen, which he had always liked to wield, became his favorite tool. The chisel could be used to make an artistic statement, but it lacked the power to do battle against real or imaginary foes. It could neither explain nor defend. The pen, by contrast, could be turned into a formidable weapon, capable of wounding and disarming an opponent. Falconet, longing for a good fight, put the weapon to immediate use. The first salvo was blasted in the direction of the Ancients and the *Marcus Aurelius,* the second at his critics. Diderot may have viewed his argument with Falconet with utter seriousness, but in reality he was no more than collateral damage in a war which the despondent Falconet declared on anybody whose views he saw as harmful to the monument, the be-all and end-all of his existence.

There was, however, one matter in which Diderot played the role of the chief culprit. It was Catherine's anxious expectation of Diderot's visit to St. Petersburg and the warmth and enthusiasm with which she greeted the *philosophe* when he limped into her private chambers in the fall of 1773. Falconet, spoiled by his earlier success, could not but compare that reception with the cooling down of his own relations with the empress. Given his nature, he must have concluded that the two attitudes were causally connected. From then on he could not think of his erstwhile friend except as a successful rival in a competition for the favors of the one woman who mattered most in his life.

Falconet had no way of knowing that in this contest he was far from being the loser. Catherine may have enjoyed Diderot's entertaining company, she may have tried to charm him with her intelligence and wit, she may have lavished money and presents upon him, but at the end of the day it was Falconet on whom she bestowed the ultimate gift—the laurels of immortality.

DIDEROT IN ST. PETERSBURG

Catherine the Second came after Peter the First. But who will come after Catherine the Second? Such an extraordinary being may not come around for centuries.
—Diderot (1773)

Of all the French luminaries of the eighteenth century, Diderot was the one whom Catherine the Great admired most and whom she most wished to host in St. Petersburg. Her courtship of the *philosophe* began almost immediately after she ascended the throne, for on August 20, 1762—that is, a mere six weeks after the coup d'état—Catherine offered Diderot help with the publication of the *Encyclopédie,* which had run into censorship problems in France. The offer was announced to Diderot by Count Ivan Shuvalov, former chamberlain and favorite of Empress Elizabeth. Here is an excerpt of his letter: "The empress and my sovereign, a zealous protector of arts and sciences, has for a long time thought about the appropriate means to encourage the famous work to which you have contributed so much. It is on her orders, Monsieur, that I have the honor to write to you to offer you whatever help you will deem necessary to accelerate its publication. Should its printing face obstacles in other places, it can be done in Riga or in another city of this empire. The *Encyclopédie* will find here a safe haven against all the stabs of envy."[73]

If Catherine's gambit was designed to enhance her image in the West after her recent seizure of power in the coup of July 1762, it certainly succeeded. The offer, though declined by Diderot, was the first step in a campaign of self-promotion as a truly enlightened monarch, who had the will and the means to help worthy cultural projects develop and prosper.

Several years later, Diderot's financial distress gave Catherine another opportunity to come to his rescue. Hearing that the *philosophe* was putting his library on the block in order to raise money for the education and dowry of his daughter, the empress offered to buy it. General Betskoi announced the news in a letter to Grimm, dated March 16, 1765:

> The compassionate nature [of the empress] was moved by the news that this *philosophe,* so celebrated in the Republic of Letters, has found himself in a situation where fatherly love demands the sacrifice of the object of his delight, the source of his work, and the companion of his leisure. Therefore, Her Imperial Majesty, to show him a mark of her benevolence and encourage him to follow his career, has charged me to acquire that library at the price of fifteen thousand livres that you have proposed, the only condition being that M. Diderot should remain its holder until such time as it will please Her Majesty to ask for it.[74]

To sweeten the offer, the empress appointed Diderot the collection's salaried librarian. Upon hearing of the deal, Voltaire was moved to exclaim: "Who would have thought fifty years ago that one day the Scythians will so nobly reward virtue, science, and philosophy in Paris, while we treat them so ignobly?"[75] Grimm chimed in facetiously: "Her Imperial Majesty buys the library of the *philosophe* so that he may keep it, and she pays him a hundred pistoles [one thousand livres] a year to compensate him for the trouble of holding on to his books."[76]

Whatever the literary community in the West may have thought of it, Catherine's gesture was not a totally disinterested gift, the manna from heaven for a needy *philosophe,* but a shrewd business venture, an investment that could be counted upon to yield huge dividends. It enhanced Catherine's reputation throughout Europe as a protector and promoter of friendly intellectuals and made her an object of inordinate public flattery. It made Diderot her most active spokesman in France and her effective scout for Western art. It was he who negotiated some of the greatest acquisitions for the imperial art collections, bringing upon himself the ire of art aficionados throughout France: "I am the object of the most determined public hatred, and do you know why? Because I send you pictures. The art lovers make an outcry, the artists make an outcry, the rich make an outcry. In spite of all these cries and criers I always go my way and to hell with them. . . . The empress will get the collection of Thiers, while she is conducting a costly war. That's what humiliates and confounds them."[77]

It was now time for Diderot to render personal homage to his benefactress, who invited him repeatedly to visit her in St. Petersburg. She was ready to receive him with all the respect due to a teacher, shower him with gifts, and allow him hours upon hours of informal communion, hoping that upon his return, he would spread the word that in Europe's remotest northern corner there dwelt and ruled the most enlightened absolute monarch in history.

The slowness of Diderot's response suggests that he was reluctant to undertake such a journey. He would have preferred, no doubt, to express his gratitude to the empress with his pen, his most beloved and trusted conveyance, rather than by way of a stagecoach. Yet he was now morally obliged to throw himself at the feet of the fairy godmother of the *encyclopédistes,* whom Voltaire called "Catherine of the latter-day saints" and "the brightest star of the North." He was also looking forward to a reunion with Falconet, who, overwhelmed by the reception accorded to him by the empress, was urging Diderot to make the pilgrimage to St. Petersburg as soon as possible: "Why don't we kiss each other as guests of this august sovereign who wants you and loves you, whom I know better than I know you, because I see her, I hear her, because I find in her the principles of the sanest philosophy, even in her most informal conversation. . . . Come shed the tears of gratitude and pleasure in St. Petersburg. Catherine will bless them."[78]

In her letters to Falconet, the empress kept returning to the topic of Diderot's visit and was even making plans to keep him by her side for an extended stay: "As far as Monsieur Diderot is concerned, let me tell you that I would like him here out of a desire to protect him against future persecutions, which I always fear may befall him, and because one wants to host people of merit. I can't decide about his appointment. In the first place, I don't want to limit his own preferences. Besides I would like to know him better before offering him something. At any rate, I am certain that if he came here and if I followed my inclination, I would unquestionably keep him around me for my instruction."[79]

Diderot, however, temporized. Never before had he undertaken a major trip. He would not even emulate so many other prominent men of letters in making the traditional pilgrimage to Ferney on Lake Geneva to pay homage to the permanently ailing Voltaire. There was, first of all, the inevitable interruption of his daily routine in Paris and the prospect of five to six weeks of uncomfortable travel. There were also other, more important reasons. Diderot came to them in a long undated letter, written most probably in late spring or early summer of 1767.[80] Addressed to Falconet, but meant also for the eyes of the empress, its object was to justify what must have seemed to Catherine and Falconet as an unreasonably long delay in Diderot's travel plans.

Diderot began, as he usually did in situations when his emotions overwhelmed him, with a series of exclamations: "We will see each other. I'll take you yet in my arms. A wish of a sovereign, of an empress, of a benefactress, must be honored. One must see such a woman once in one's lifetime and I am going to see her." Not just yet, however. There followed a description of a seemingly ad hoc project that was certain to prevent his leaving Paris. It was to be a great dictionary of the French language on the scale of Samuel Johnson's dictionary of English. He presented a detailed account of its methodology and, as a sort of bait for Catherine, suggested that it could be used in producing an analogous Russian dictionary. It seems, however, that he had some doubts whether the compilation of a dictionary would be seen as a sufficiently persuasive reason for delaying the trip. He resolved, therefore, to own up to the "real" reasons for his temporization.

Yet, baring his heart in front of the empress was not an easy matter. He delayed it as long as he could with a series of preliminaries such as "Wait a moment, my friend. I feel that my soul will open, but the moment hasn't yet arrived" and dozens of unrelated topics, before he could announce: "Finally I am coming to the principal subject of your last letter. Here is my reply to it. Don't miss one word of what I am going to tell you." Marital and paternal duties were important, he said, but the main deterrent to travel was neither his wife nor his daughter, but his mistress. In a virtual love aria, Diderot described the depth of his affection for Sophie Volland and his inability to part with her: "I have two sovereigns," he declared, referring to Sophie Volland and Catherine the Great, "but my friend is the first and the oldest. . . . Heaven be my witness . . . that since the time I've known her, she has been the only woman in the world for me. And you want me to leave her one day, tomorrow, without telling her anything, in a stagecoach, to go a thousand leagues away from her, to leave her alone, desolate, perturbed, desperate?"[81]

Fulfilling his role of intermediary, Falconet showed Diderot's letter to the empress, who replied with her characteristic understanding of human foibles: "I esteemed Monsieur Diderot very much, but I esteem him even more after reading his twenty pages. His sincere confession is a heroic effort. He'll visit when he feels able to and he'll always be welcome. I wouldn't have the heart to advise him against his own happiness and that of *others*."[82] Diderot took advantage of Catherine's understanding attitude and delayed his trip to St. Petersburg for almost six years, by which time he felt less bound to Mlle

Volland. He welcomed, in fact, an opportunity to get away from Paris and, on the way to and from Russia, decided to pay extended visits to the Golitsyns in The Hague.

On August 20, 1773, after two months in The Hague spent writing, preparing for meeting Catherine, and discussing the virtues of spiritualism and materialism with the Dutch philosopher Frans Hemsterhuis, Diderot started the Russian leg of his trip. Much to his pleasure, he had an amiable traveling companion in the person of the young Aleksei Vasilievich Naryshkin, who had taken a water cure in Aachen and was now hurrying home to attend the wedding of Grand Duke Paul and Princess Wilhelmina of Hesse-Darmstadt, scheduled for October 9.[83]

There was an unfortunate delay at the very beginning of the trip, when Diderot was struck down with a severe case of food poisoning in the Ruhr district. The impatient empress checked frequently with Falconet and Golitsyn on the *philosophe's* whereabouts and was disappointed by his slow progress: "I was expecting Diderot at any moment, but I have just learned with great sorrow that he has fallen sick in Duisburg," she complained to Voltaire.[84]

When Diderot was well enough to resume the trip, he and Naryshkin took the southern route through Saxony, in order to bypass Berlin and avoid a meeting with Frederick the Great, which, diplomacy suggested, would have deprived Catherine the Great of a monopoly claim on Diderot. That took them to Dresden, where they stopped to inspect its famous art galleries. They then continued through Lower Lusatia to Frankfurt on the Oder, East Prussia, Königsberg, Memel, and Riga.

Another bout of intestinal poisoning overwhelmed Diderot near Narva. Despite severe cramps, he decided to continue on to St. Petersburg so that Naryshkin would not miss the imperial wedding. It was to be the most harrowing leg of the trip, as he confessed to his wife: "Try to imagine, if you can, the condition of a man tormented by a violent colic, traveling on the worst possible roads. At each bump, and they were pretty serious bumps, I was so much in pain that a knife thrust into my stomach and cutting my entrails in two could not have been worse."[85] The travelers arrived in St. Petersburg on October 8 (September 27, according to the Julian calendar), that is, on the eve of the wedding and of Diderot's name day, the feast of St. Denis. After more than seven weeks of travel on poor roads, with bad food and polluted water, Falconet's house and a prospect of a babbly reunion, camomile tea, syringe, and bed, must have seemed like the sight of an oasis in the desert.[86]

When, however, Diderot, "more dead than alive," presented himself at Falconet's door, the hoped-for oasis turned out to be a mirage. Sleeping in the bed that the *philosophe* had counted upon was Falconet's son, Pierre-Etienne, who had arrived unexpectedly a month before. The ailing and exhausted traveler was forced to accept the hospitality of Semën Kirillovich Naryshkin, uncle of his travel companion.[87] Mme Diderot became so incensed when she heard the news that her husband had to calm her down: "Try to make peace with Falconet and Mlle Collot. It is not the fault of the former and certainly not of the latter. [Falconet] knew what I didn't know . . . that Monsieur Naryshkin had prepared an apartment for me, and he thought that I had accepted it. Mlle Collot had nothing to do with it. She is not in her own place and I promise you that she was quite upset that I was staying at somebody else's, rather than at Falconet's."[88]

Diderot's arrival provided a finishing touch to the long list of distinguished guests arriving in the capital of Russia for the wedding of the Grand Duke Paul. Grimm, Diderot's friend and collaborator, was already there, having traveled in the suite of Christina Carolina, landgravine of Hesse-Darmstadt, Princess Wilhelmina's mother. The joint presence in St. Petersburg of the editor of the *Correspondance littéraire* and the editor of the *Encyclopédie* had the effect of promoting the Russian capital to the rank of one of the intellectual centers of Europe.

It also gave Catherine the Great a respite from her daily problems. Diderot and Grimm engaged her in sparkling conversation, flattered and distracted her, and above all complained about nothing and demanded nothing. "[Grimm's] conversation is a delight for me. We have so many things to say to each other that our meetings have so far been more emotional than orderly."[89] Diderot's visit exposed her to one of the liveliest minds of Europe, and his excitable manner, Gallic wit, and arm-waving and knee-slapping manner were a welcome change from the stilted court routine of St. Petersburg. As she said in one of her letters to Voltaire: "Monsieur Diderot, whose health is still precarious, will stay with us till February, when he will return to his homeland; Grimm also thinks of leaving at about that time. I see them very often and our conversations are endless. I don't know if they get very bored in St. Petersburg; but, as for me, I would speak to them all my life without getting weary. I find that Diderot has an inexhaustible imagination and I rank him among the most extraordinary people that have ever lived."[90]

In that atmosphere of general excitement, Falconet was very far from the empress's mind and his name came up but once (and that in the context of his son Pierre-Etienne) in her correspondence with Voltaire, in which she described the goings-on in St. Petersburg.[91] Shunted to a siding at the time when the large model of the monument had already been three years without a founder, Falconet must have felt abandoned. He was certainly jealous of the cordiality and frequency of Diderot's visits to the empress, during which the two discussed every issue under the sun: "in the palace of Her Imperial Majesty I am permitted to say anything that goes through my head. Sane things . . . when I feel crazy, and crazy ones . . . when I feel sane."[92] It is impossible to know whether Diderot, angry with Falconet after the *Marcus Aurelius* incident, said a few bitter words about his erstwhile friend to the empress, but it is almost certain that Falconet thought he did. What Falconet could not have known was that both Diderot and the empress were privately well aware that the ideas championed by the *philosophe* were quite unsuitable for Russian realities. "One thing is certain," said Diderot, "ideas transplanted from Paris get a very different coloring in St. Petersburg."[93] Catherine was equally skeptical:

> I had frequent and long conversations with [Diderot], more out of curiosity than with profit. Had I placed faith in him, every institution in my empire would have been overturned. Legislation, administration, politics, and finances would all have been changed for the purpose of substituting some impracticable theories. . . . "Monsieur Diderot," I said, "I have listened with the greatest pleasure to all that your brilliant genius has inspired you with. Yet all your grand principles, which I understand very well, will make fine books, but would not work well in actual practice. You forget in all your plans of reform the difference between our two positions. You work only on paper, which submits to everything, . . . while I, a poor empress, work on human nature, which is irritable and easily offended."[94]

It is quite possible that Catherine's courtiers realized that Diderot's advice was not being taken seriously by the empress, for they paid practically no attention to the visit of the "petty demon" from Paris, who preached liberalism and atheism. Diderot left behind a record of his conversations with Catherine the Great, but it evoked so little interest among his Russian hosts that it did not see the light of day until the very end of the nineteenth century, and that only because of the French interest in it.[95] His social philosophy, which Catherine the Great found unrealistic but fascinating, left no traces whatsoever in the writings of the witnesses of his five months in St. Petersburg, a fate not unlike Falconet's practically unobserved passage across the skies of the Russian capital.

Diderot left St. Petersburg on March 5, 1774. With his departure and the realization that he was too flighty and agitated to be of use in the serious enterprise of running an empire, with Voltaire beginning to justify his habitual references to himself as "the old and sickly man from Ferney," and with Falconet's fall from her grace, Catherine the Great's links to the West began to come apart. Searching elsewhere for a dedicated correspondent and a dependable executor of her errands around Europe, she found one in Grimm, who from 1774 until her death in 1796 became her trusted roving ambassador, an indulgent "father confessor," and an absolver of her absolutism.[96] The fawning flattery of his letters does not diminish their value as a virtual *Who's Who* and *What's What* of the last quarter of the eighteenth century. Grimm's added advantage was that, being of German extraction, he could be treated almost like a family member. In writing to him, Catherine enjoyed interspersing her elegant French prose with homey German expressions, intensifying thereby a sense of confidentiality and intimacy.

Parisian friends of Diderot and Grimm did not expect to learn much about Russia from either. They predicted that "Diderot would tell what he had not seen and Grimm would not tell what he had seen." This witticism was definitely true as far as Grimm was concerned. Diderot, however, could be mercilessly frank about his impressions, even to Catherine's face. Here is his remarkably incisive comment on the public behavior of the Russians, expressed during one of his encounters with the empress: "I think I've noticed a rather general circumspection, a lack of trust, which contrasts with that wonderful and loyal frankness of elevated, free, and self-assured spirits, such as those of our people or of the English. . . . I sense a trace of panicky fear, a probable consequence of many drastic changes and long despotism. People seem always as if they were on the eve or on the morrow of an earthquake and they appear to be testing the ground to make sure that it is firm under their feet."[97]

His opinion of Catherine as a person remained very high, but he permitted himself critical remarks about her political beliefs that ranged from the humorous ("The spirit of Brutus in the flesh of Cleopatra") to openly censorious when it came to the political treatise *Nakaz* ("Instruction") of 1767. Upon returning to France, he recounted in letters and private encounters that Russia was not exactly what his French friends had imagined: "St. Petersburg is nothing but the [imperial] court—a jumbled pile of palaces and thatched huts, grand lords surrounded by peasants and suppliers. Let me confess in a very low voice that our *philosophes,* who think that they know despotism best, have not seen it except through the neck of a bottle. What a difference between a tiger painted by Oudry and a tiger in the forest!"[98]

He preferred, however, to joke his way out of potentially embarrassing situations: "Concerning [Russian] climate, habits, laws, customs, practices, I'll follow Corneille's words about the famous cardinal: If I were to say bad things about them, I'd be ungrateful, if I were to say good things, I'd be a liar."[99]

FALCONET LE DIFFICILE

> You [Falconet] may be a great artist, but a work of literature translated and explicated in your fashion is as pitiful as a statue executed by a minor *littérateur* like myself.
> —Anonymous (1775)

Time was not on Falconet's side. As work on the monument dragged on, as his daily tiffs with Betskoi began to sound like a comic's tired routine, Falconet's demands, complaints, and accusations were getting less and less of a sympathetic hearing. By and by the empress began to think of her sculptor as an annoyance and an imposition. She was prepared to tolerate him for the sake of the monument, but the days when she treated him as a friend and confidant were definitely over.

Falconet's deteriorating relations with Diderot and Catherine the Great and his open feud with Betskoi were accompanied by more trouble brewing beyond Russia's borders. Taking the lead in attacks on Falconet was the influential *Journal encyclopédique,* a biweekly published in the town of Bouillon, the capital of a tiny Walloon domain of the dukes of Auvergne in southern Belgium. Some of its anti-Falconet articles may have been inspired by Betskoi, but some could have been the work of Diderot or people around him. Distasteful as this suggestion may be, it has to be contemplated, for Pierre Rousseau, the journal's founding editor, was on friendly terms with Diderot, and his journal, as its very name indicates, was the mouthpiece of the group of the *Encyclopédie.*[100] Among its regular contributors it counted several authors with well-known connections to Diderot, such as Voltaire, Jacques-André Naigeon, and Jean-Louis-Samuel Formey.

Although the anti-Falconet articles in the *Journal encyclopédique* may not have been designed as a deliberate campaign to blacken the sculptor's name, the fact remains that between 1775 and 1782 the journal carried several long pieces aimed against him. They were concerned with two issues: Falconet's annotated translation of books 34, 35, and 36 of Pliny the Elder; and the so-called Pomel affair, in which Falconet was accused by one of his helpers of reneging on his contractual obligations in the casting of the *Peter the Great.*[101]

The driving force behind the Pliny book was, as was often the case with Falconet's writing projects, an animus. This time his quarrel was with the chevalier de Jaucourt, a philosopher, mathematician, and physician who composed more than ten thousand articles for the *Encyclopédie,* among them a large number on art. To contest Jaucourt's opinions, Falconet decided to examine their cornerstone, Pliny the Elder's three books dealing with art matters. Having found no French translation in the libraries of St. Petersburg, Falconet undertook to translate the text himself and asked his acquaintance Ludwig Heinrich Nicolaï, the preceptor of Crown Prince Paul, to look the translation over and correct it as needed. Here is how Nicolaï remembered Falconet's translating methods:

> I did not pay attention to the stylistic qualities, but tried merely to restore the correct meanings of the misunderstood passages. The variant readings, however, caused us constant disagreements. Whenever, among the possible readings, one was nonsensical and absurd, Falconet invariably chose it and maintained that it was what Pliny had in mind. A long time afterward, he brought me a copy of the published translation . . . and left it on my table. I was wondering about the thickness of the book and found out that the notes, about which he hadn't told me, took up more than half of its length. I fell upon it eagerly. From the beginning to the end it was nothing but the bitterest satire on the ignorant, stupid Pliny. I understood then why he had always attacked the poor Roman and why he had always opted for the worst readings rather than the best.[102]

The *Notes sur trois livres de Pline l'Ancien, où il traite de la peinture et de la sculpture. On y a joint la traduction de ces mêmes livres,* was published in Amsterdam in 1772 and reissued a year later in The Hague. The precedence of the notes over the translation in title of the book is indicative of the relative importance the author assigned to these two parts. The translation was an impressive achievement, especially for someone like Falconet, who was a self-taught classicist, but the notes were clearly the chief object of the book. They are learned and copious, running sometimes over several pages. In the edition of 1781 they are provided with "second-generation" footnotes.

The book took up the two main themes of Falconet's earlier book on the *Marcus Aurelius*. Its first goal was to show that there was no reason to consider the ancients better than the moderns merely by virtue of their antiquity: "As for the trivial accusation that by bringing up errors of an almost universally admired ancient writer, I dared to stop waving the censer, I ask poor anti-quomania for this small favor: allow me to look at an idol before I kneel in front of it, and let me offer my venerations elsewhere if it turns out to be a fake. It is time to rip apart the veil which has covered the ancient phantoms, venerated most, when least known. Let us admire the greatness of the ancients when they have it and let us scorn the pedantry which obscures their faults from our view."[103]

The other aim of the book was to contest the assumption that any *littérateur* had an automatic right to be an art critic. Falconet lashed out against writers who had no qualifications to engage in art criticism, but berated all those who dared oppose their uninformed judgment: "They treat as spiteful nitpickers anybody who has the courage to go against the current, to show independence of judgment, to point out weaknesses where scholars find nothing but cause for ecstatic exclamations. The literary charlatans have too long accused of pettiness those whom they are unable to refute. . . . A false accusation and a swearword are easier to produce than a rational thought or admission of error."[104]

Falconet knew perfectly well that he was plunging a stick into an anthill. With a copy of his Pliny the Elder book sent to Voltaire, he enclosed these words: "Today I am doing the exact opposite of my profession. I am casting down an idol, adored for centuries. I send you both the idol and the tools which I have used to destroy it. I guess I am one of those *monsters* whose Patriarch you are, for I dare to use the powers of reasoning which God has given me and which, I know, he wants me to use."[105]

The reaction was not very long in coming. In 1775, in six installments spread over forty-four pages of consecutive issues of the *Journal encyclopédique,* there appeared an anonymous review of Falconet's book on Pliny the Elder (both its first and the second edition that came out in The Hague in 1773).[106] The attack was devastating. The reviewer found faults in Falconet's command of Latin, but the main thrust of his review was that Falconet had no business translating and analyzing an ancient text without being well versed in the methodology of textual criticism, that is, without being a trained philologist. Without such training Falconet could not know what was in Pliny's original text and what were the alterations and interpolations made by ignorant scribes who copied and recopied the text. Claiming that he could cite many examples of textual corruptions, the reviewer refrained from doing so because Falconet "would not be able to follow into the lands of which he is unaware."[107] The reviewer concluded his piece with a coup de grâce of his philological rapier: "Equal, then or surpass, if possible, my wishes [of success for your monument to Peter the Great] and the whole world will celebrate you as the greatest artist. Perhaps it will even forget your translation."[108]

Those words were echoed by other faithful followers of classical traditions: "While Falconet's sculptures have earned him well-deserved fame, his writings, in which he pokes fun at Pliny the Elder, have, by contrast, brought him discredit, for they are truly a contemptible mixture of false opinions, poor judgments, and insipid wit."[109]

Falconet was not one to ignore a challenge. The answer he sent to the *Journal encyclopédique* was even longer than the review, but when it appeared in 1776, it was drastically abbreviated.[110] The editor, Pierre Rousseau, claimed disingenuously that Falconet's defense was so successful and persuasive that it did not have to be published in full: "These citations, which constitute barely one third of Falconet's arguments, are sufficient to give an idea of the weapons with which he fights, repels, and vigorously presses his adversary." Unhappy about the cuts and Rousseau's explanation, Falconet took the matter into his own hands and in the 1781 edition of his works reprinted both the review and his full reply to it.[111]

Betskoi, who may have inspired the review in the *Journal encyclopédique,* relished every word of it.[112] His joy, however, would not have been complete, if the empress had not read it too. He made sure that this would not be the case. When he received from the empress the July 1, 1775, issue of the journal with the first installment of the review, he returned it promptly to the palace and attached a personal note to the empress: "It seems to me that the last *Journal encyclopédique* honors Falconet too much by publishing a critique of his writings. He is given there his just deserts. They even promise a continuation. Since the pages have not been cut, I've concluded that Your Majesty has not seen it yet. I am taking the liberty of sending it back to Her, for She might want to read it."[113]

One can imagine the malicious pleasure of the petty courtier, cutting the pages of the palace copy of the *Journal encyclopédique* and sniffing for Falconet's blood. If the empress, tired as she was of Falconet and the monument, did bother to ingest the tidbits of philological minutiae served up in the review, she probably did so to relieve insomnia.

The Pliny episode illustrates the lengths to which Betskoi was willing to go in his efforts to demolish the French artist in the eyes of the empress. Initially Catherine sided with the sculptor, but Betskoi's tireless campaign, accompanied by Falconet's complaints and accusations, made her reassess the utility of the French artist. On her scale of values, a servile and dependable Russian courtier was more valuable than this self-centered and ill-tempered man who kept to himself, refused to train disciples, and had by then fulfilled most of his artistic obligations. Paradoxically, she began to perceive Falconet as the main obstacle on the road to the completion of his monument.

The year 1773 may be said to be critical in Catherine's dealings with the sculptor. The empress was clearly getting tired of his biliousness and petulance and of having to adjudicate his unending quarrels with Betskoi. The novelty of the monument's design had worn off, the drama of the transport of the granite boulder had been successfully concluded, but the plaster model stood untouched, waiting to be cast. Instead of doing something about it, Falconet locked himself up in his study and wrote long and tedious commentaries on the *Marcus Aurelius* and Pliny the Elder. One can imagine that Catherine the Great was tempted to yell at him as his wife used to do: "Drop those books and start working!"

Besides, five years of absence from Paris and the rupture with Diderot had deprived Falconet of a direct link to the world of the Enlightenment, undermining his role as its unofficial envoy in Russia and dimming his nimbus as a fashionable Paris artist, a contributor to the *Encyclopédie,* and an expert on West European art markets. He could no longer be counted upon for the freshest news of the intellectual life in the French capital and was no longer privy to its latest gossip. *Falconet le difficile*—that is how Catherine the Great described the French sculptor in a 1775 letter to the ever-accommodating and well-informed Grimm, who had by then taken over Falconet's role as Catherine's chief link to the world of Western literature and art.[114]

As it happens, Falconet's being shunted to a side track may have turned out to be a blessing for the monument. Realizing that he could no longer dictate his conditions and that his stay in St. Petersburg might come to an abrupt end, the sculptor stopped stalling and set about the business of casting the statue, no matter how daunting a project it promised to be.

6

From Plaster to Bronze

PRELIMINARIES TO CASTING

Were I young enough to enter upon this career, I dare say, I could make a large cast, I won't say with my eyes closed, but as well as any founder.
—Falconet (c. 1780)

The matter of casting the *Peter the Great* was left open in the contract drawn in Paris by Prince D. A. Golitsyn and Falconet. The first clause specified merely that Falconet was being charged "with the composition and execution of the monument which will consist principally of an equestrian statue of colossal dimensions."[1] The question of who would choose the founder and decide on the details of casting was left to the good sense and good will of the participating parties, a presumption which, as it turned out, was all too optimistic.

The omission of an explicit mention of casting arrangements was due, no doubt, to the relative independence enjoyed by founders. Sculptors did not, as a rule, meddle in their business, chiefly because they knew little about it. This was not because of a lack of interest, but because successful founders guarded jealously the secrets of their profession, transmitted usually from father to son. It is, therefore, quite likely that, had Falconet's statue been of the conventional *Marcus Aurelius* design, casting would have been left to a founder hired by the Bureau of Buildings. The rearing horse, however, caused special problems and required, at least in the mind of Falconet, special solutions and a close collaboration between the sculptor and the founder. Without such collaboration, Falconet feared that the cast might fail.

Making a large bronze statue implied an ability to make a hollow cast. Ancient civilizations—Chinese, Egyptian, Greek, and Roman—knew how to do this, using the lost-wax method, which consists in making a wax model of the object to be cast between two layers of heat-resistant material. The form is heated until the wax melts and flows out, leaving an empty space, which is then filled with molten bronze. Ancient casts, however, were either small or done in segments so that the final product was an assemblage of separate pieces that had to be fused together. The *Marcus Aurelius,* for instance, was cast by such a sectional method. In the Middle Ages, when the erosion of strong central authority was not conducive to the erection of large monuments, hollow casting lost its usefulness and was replaced by small solid casts, such as the equestrian statuette, said to be of Charlemagne, in the Louvre. The rise of the small but powerful class of the condottieri in the Venetian Republic during the Renaissance reawakened an interest in large-size equestrian statuary, and the forgotten art of casting by the lost-wax method had to be reinvented. The technique of assembling larger statues from precast pieces was, however, preferred throughout the sixteenth century. It was used, for instance, in the *Cosimo I* in Florence (1594) and the *Henry IV* in Paris (1614), both by Giovanni da Bologna.

A major innovation in the practice of casting occurred when it was realized that molten bronze had the remarkable property of remaining uncongealed for sufficiently long periods of time to allow the casting of colossal statues in one pouring. This method of casting in one continuous operation became known as the single-jet technique. It was used in the casting of the equestrian *Gattamelata* (1453) by Donatello in Padua and the *Perseus Holding the Head of Medusa* (1553) by Benvenuto Cellini. Cellini's memoirs provide a brief account of the single-jet technique.

In the second half of the seventeenth century a new bronze alloy, containing zinc in addition to the traditional mixture of copper and tin, was developed in the Paris Arsenal by the brothers Keller from Zurich. Its strength allowed Johann-Balthasar, the younger of the Keller brothers, to try the single-jet technique in casting the equestrian statue of Louis XIV by François Girardon (1699), which used to stand on place Louis le Grand, today's place Vendôme. His attempt was successful and the statue of Louis XIV became the largest ever to be cast by that technique.

When, however, Jean-Baptiste Lemoyne hired the brothers Varin to cast his equestrian statue of Louis XV in Bordeaux, about forty years had elapsed since the casting of the *Louis XIV* and not one of the main participants in that operation was alive. In fact, Keller's single-jet technique would have been lost to posterity had it not been for the notes and drawings of the Keller process made by Germain Boffrand, a young Paris architect with a brilliant career ahead of him. Boffrand shared his notes with Lemoyne and eventually published them, producing the first substantial account of the process of casting by the single-jet technique.[2] The book came out in 1743, which was also the year of the unveiling of the *Louis XV* in Bordeaux. Varin's triumph, however, was not unqualified, for accidents interrupted the single-jet process and two additional castings were needed before the statue was completed. Falconet, who was one of Lemoyne's assistants, referred to the Bordeaux job when he experienced a similar mishap during the casting of the *Peter the Great* in St. Petersburg.

The next major project using the single-jet technique was Bouchardon's statue of Louis XV in Paris (1762). Its casting was done by Pierre Gore, the most respected founder of monumental statuary.[3] Every stage of the operation was witnessed by the painter and engraver Louis-Simon Lempereur in his capacity of the head of the Paris city council (*échevin*). His notes and drawings were edited by the engraver and art collector Jean-Pierre Mariette in a book that was published in 1768. It rivals and often surpasses Boffrand's work in its attention to detail and quality of artwork.[4]

The decision to place the *Peter the Great* on the left bank of the Neva between the Admiralty and the Senate was taken officially in the spring of 1768. The first order of business was to clear the cluttered space on future Senate Square of construction materials stored there by the Admiralty and the builders of the first St. Isaac's cathedral. As soon as the square was ready, work began on two large projects, the laying of the foundations for the monument and the construction of a special shed, where the statue was to be cast.[5] At the same time, Carburi, who was in charge of the operations on Senate Square, was ordered to prepare sufficient amounts of copper, lead, and wax. Betskoi's instructions to Carburi were invariably couched in terms of the greatest urgency: "as soon as possible," "without any loss of time," "at the earliest opportunity," as if the casting of the statue was imminent. His nervousness was contagious, and Carburi, afraid that he might not be able to finish his tasks by the end of 1768, requested a detachment of soldiers to help him and his workers bring all the facilities on Senate Square to a state of readiness.

The casting shed for the *Peter the Great,* as in other similar projects, was divided into two sections (fig. 6.1). One was the atelier with the furnace in which the bronze gets smelted, the other, to the side and below the level of the atelier, was the pit *(fosse),* large enough to accommodate the mold of the statue, enclosing a wax copy of the full-scale plaster model in the sculptor's atelier. The mold stood on a grill under which there was a series of small hearths *(galleries).* The production operation would proceed as follows.

All the preliminary work on the statue is conducted in the pit. An armature, or metal skeleton whose bearing parts will remain in the finished statue, is constructed according to the sculptor's design (fig. 6.2) and a plaster copy of the large model is re-created around it. The plaster model receives a thorough oiling so that a negative imprint of it, called a plaster mold *(moule de plâtre),* can be made. The plaster mold is then cut up into numbered segments (fig. 6.3) and its concave sides are thoroughly moistened and impregnated with a mixture of olive oil, rendered lard, and liquid tallow. They are then filled with wax to the desired thickness of the bronze, and the plaster mold, with its inner layer of wax forming a wax model, is assembled around the armature. The empty (except for the armature) inner space is then filled with a water-based heat-resistant investment, consisting of a mixture of plaster of Paris and ground brick (the so-called *grog*).[6] The investment is allowed

Fig. 6.1. Cross-Section of the Casting Shed for the Equestrian Statue of Louis XV by Edme Bouchardon. In the atelier (upper right) the furnace is burning and the molten bronze will soon be ready for pouring. It will then flow into the pit (lower left) and fill the mold. Engraving (Mariette, 1768). Courtesy Yale University Library.

to set, forming the core *(noyau)* of the mold. This done, the molder takes off the outer plaster mold, baring the wax model underneath, which is an exact copy of the original plaster model. At this time the sculptor may add or delete features, using a heated steel burin and a brush.

Once the wax model is finished, the molder and the founder envelop it with an intricate network of protruding wax rods which have three functions. The jets run from the funnel in the ceiling of the pit and branch out on their way down, ending buried in different places in the wax of the statue. The vents *(évents)* lead up from the wax, but are not connected to the funnel. The drains *(égouts)* point down from the bottom of the statue. They are used to conduct the melted wax out of the statue. The jets are the conduits through which the molten bronze flows to fill the space vacated by wax, while the gases produced by the heated bronze and the air which is pushed out by the gases escape through the vents (fig. 6.4).

Several pins, made of steel, which has a higher melting point than wax, are driven through the wax into the core and left protruding on the outside.

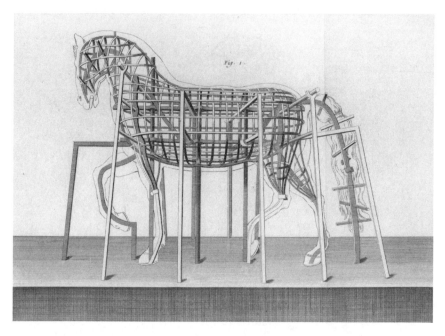

Fig. 6.2. Armature for the Equestrian Statue of Louis XIV by François Girardon.
Engraving by Benard (*Recueil*, 1771, first published in Boffrand, 1743).
Courtesy Arts of the Book, Yale University Library.

The whole statue is then wrapped in an outer mold *(moule de potée)* made
of grog or another heat-resistant investment (fig. 6.5, left). The pins, whose
protruding ends are now set in the outer mold, will help stabilize the core,
which has a tendency to shrink slightly when heated. The outer mold is
girt with iron bands and allowed to dry (fig. 6.5, right). Finally, the whole
construction is surrounded by a brick wall *(mur de recuit)*, and the space
between the wall and the outer mold is filled with bricks. A fire is made in
the hearths below the grill and is kept going until all the wax, including the
wax rods, is drained out and the core and the outer mold are well baked.
The bricks, whose function is to aid in the baking process, are removed and
their place is taken by well-packed earth mixed with sand.

At the beginning of the casting process a big fire is made in the furnace
to melt the bronze and collect it in a heated basin *(écheno)*. The preferred
fuel for the furnace is a well-dried hardwood, usually beech, which burns
with the greatest intensity and the least amount of smoke. Gore's casting of
the *Louis XV* used sixty thousand pounds of metal and took twenty-eight
and a half hours of very intense heat to melt it. The pouring itself took five
minutes and four seconds. The excess metal remaining in the basin was almost as liquid five minutes after the completion of casting as it was at the
start.

Fig. 6.3. Plaster Model and Section of Plaster Mold for the Wax Model of the Equestrian Statue of Louis XIV by François Girardon. Engraving by Benard (*Recueil,* 1771, first published in Boffrand, 1743). Courtesy Arts of the Book, Yale University Library.

The process of pouring molten bronze begins when its surface acquires a mirror-like sheen and smoothness and starts emitting white smoke. At that time, the stoppers in the basin are removed and the molten bronze flows down to the funnel in the ceiling of the pit, to be eventually conducted through a large number of openings to fill all the spaces vacated by the "lost" wax (fig. 6.6). The amount of bronze needed for the cast is calculated on

Fig. 6.4. The Wax Model of the Statue of Louis XIV by François Girardon
Standing in the Casting Pit. The network of wax rods will become jets, vents,
and drains. Engraving by Benard (*Recueil,* 1771, first published in Boffrand, 1743).
Courtesy Arts of the Book, Yale University Library.

Fig. 6.5. The Core and Outer Mold of the Wax Model of the Equestrian Statue of Louis XIV by François Girardon. At left is a cross-section of the core; at right is the outer mold (*moule de potée*) girt with iron bands. At bottom are the hearths (*galleries*) for baking the outer mold and melting the wax. Engraving by Benard (*Recueil*, 1771, first published in Boffrand, 1743). Courtesy Arts of the Book, Yale University Library.

the basis of the amount of wax used: one pound of wax to ten pounds of bronze.

When the cast cools off, the outer mold is removed and the core is taken out through openings in the bronze, which will be closed up later. This will protect the interior of the statue from moisture that could ooze into the statue's lower parts and freeze in winter, causing the metal to crack. The final stage of touching up the statue may now begin. The protruding bronze rods have to be sawed off, the surface has to be smoothed out, and fine details have to be chiseled and chased. Finally, the whole statue receives a coat of acids to give it a film of uniform dark patina.

TO CAST OR NOT TO CAST?

We'll carry on, you and I. You will make a beautiful horse despite the evil tongues of those who envy you. . . . Let them talk. Everything is as it should be and you have the tokens of their esteem. Overcome all obstacles and make fun of the rest! Obstacles exist in this world in order to be swept aside by worthy people.
—Catherine the Great (1769)

The idea of inviting an outside founder never appealed to Catherine, who sensed that Falconet would find it difficult to yield control over the only version of a work that would bear permanent testimony to his abilities. That is why she exhorted him from the very outset to be his own founder: "You won't just make a clay horse, but you'll finish the cast one as well."[7] But Falconet knew enough about the difficulty of the task to be unwilling to take it on. The statue meant too much to him to be entrusted to a beginner. He preferred to give it to a well-tested and cooperative founder, hoping that one could be found and hired.

The empress, however, persisted. Armed with her belief in the allied powers of "conjecture and conjuncture" and convinced that Falconet was blessed with both, she encouraged him to overcome his apprehensions, predicting that he could and would succeed.[8] She was right, as usual. But before her prediction was fulfilled, friendships had to be snuffed out, nerves had to be frayed, accusations and counteraccusations had to fly, and reams of paper

Fig. 6.6 (facing page). The Atelier of the Casting Shed for the Equestrian Statue of Louis XIV by François Girardon. The taphole (6) is about to be opened by shoving the door (5) into the furnace (1) so that molten bronze will pour into the basin (9). The stoppers (7) will then be broken, and the bronze will flow down through the jets to fill the space vacated by liquefied wax, which will have flowed out through the drains. Engraving by Benard (*Recueil,* 1771, first published in Boffrand, 1743). Courtesy Arts of the Book, Yale University Library.

had to be filled with claims, testimonies, explanations, and refutations. In other words, a typical Falconet affair.

Falconet had, it is true, some knowledge of casting, gained from personal observation of casting operations in Lemoyne's atelier and from extensive readings on the subject, but he also knew that theory alone would not suffice in so complex a task. What he lacked was that sixth sense which allowed an experienced founder to react instantaneously to unforeseen developments. Reading Mariette's account of the casting of the *Louis XV,* Falconet must have wondered whether he would have had the presence of mind of Pierre Gore, who saved the cast by shoving away the plug that threatened to stop the flow of the molten metal from the furnace into the basin.[9]

He knew also that inside Russia he would not be able to find a reliable specialist. Yes, there were foundries of artillery at the Arsenal, and church bell foundries existed in various parts of the country, but they were never employed in artistic casting. One of the locals who offered his services was Colonel Melissino, whose skill at casting cannons was well known. Melissino, however, had never cast a statue, and he wanted Falconet to be there to help him out. In addition, he demanded to be decorated for his labors. Falconet, incensed by this demand, told the empress that if the sculptor himself had no ambition to be decorated, "it would be bizarre for a founder, instructed and directed by the sculptor, to be so rewarded for a purely mechanical operation."[10]

Falconet did not wish, however, to appear uncooperative and decided to make a stab at casting his popular *Cupid.* He hired a master founder employed by the Arsenal, most probably Emelian Khailov, and the two set to work under the watchful eye the empress: "Your Majesty has asked me for the news of casting. Here is what I can say about it. The statue of the *Cupid* was cast, but failed. The founder did not understand anything, even though I did what I could to help him. I am trying to arrange for another casting with the help of one of my own workers. The casting of this small object will allow Your Majesty to judge my zeal in her service and my distaste for any kind of charlatanism."[11]

The failure of the first attempt could not but deepen Falconet's apprehensions, no matter who was responsible for it. The second attempt was successful, but it was not done till four years later.

Without any hope that a founder could be located on the domestic market, Betskoi began to look for one abroad. On April 26, 1768, he asked the Russian envoy in Sweden, Count I. A. Osterman, about the progress of Archevèque's statue of King Gustavus Adolphus in Stockholm. The reply was disappointing. The cast had failed because Archevèque experimented with a new casting method of his own invention and overheated the mold.[12]

France, with more equestrian statues than any other country, was next on Betskoi's list. Diderot kept recommending Pierre Gore as the best founder around.[13] Betskoi investigated this possibility, but balked at the price of four hundred thousand livres. Diderot bargained and claimed to have been successful in bringing the price down. Gore was, in fact, invited to visit St. Petersburg from Copenhagen, where he was finishing the equestrian monument to Frederick V by Saly. He dragged his feet, however, and the negotiations were broken off.[14]

Falconet's position during the search was ambiguous. On the one hand, he was wary of doing the casting himself. On the other, just as Catherine had thought, he could not bear the idea of yielding the responsibility for the fate of his statue to anybody else. In the meantime, he delayed the decision as much as he could.[15]

Two and a half years had gone by without any progress and Falconet was getting impatient. What was more, he began suspecting Betskoi of sabotaging the search in order to delay the completion of the monument. He was afraid that after the eight years specified in the contract had lapsed, Betskoi would offer him an extension of another eight years, knowing full well that he would not be able to accept it. The casting would then be turned over to someone who would treat it as a purely commercial proposition.[16] Having convinced himself that Betskoi was indeed going to enact that scenario, Falconet decided to launch a trial balloon. On August 1, 1769, he announced to Betskoi that he would be ready to cast the statue without any "pecuniary interest" on his part.[17]

Two weeks later Betskoi responded with what, one would think, was a gracious, though hardly ingenuous, acceptance of Falconet's offer:

> I know sufficiently well your way of thinking, Monsieur, and your lack of self-interest to be convinced that what you've suggested has no other motive than your zeal in the service of Her Imperial Highness and the most perfect execution of your task. It would be desirable if you yourself, Monsieur, directed the casting of the equestrian statue of Peter the Great. That work, guided by your care and your vigilance, cannot but inspire us with the greatest confidence. Rest assured, therefore, of our support in everything that would allow you to bring it to perfection. . . . It is true that there have been examples of skilled workers failing in important casts, but that should not discourage you. Those who were involved in them may not have had your knowledge or your skill.[18]

Betskoi's civil response did not, however, satisfy Falconet. Perhaps the touchy sculptor caught in it a note of condescension; perhaps the relations between the two men, though superficially polite, had reached the point of such tension that any request of the Russian courtier was certain to call forth a negative reaction; perhaps Betskoi's welcoming response convinced Falconet of the utter groundlessness of his suspicions; perhaps, once his offer was accepted, he again got cold feet. In any event Falconet beat a quick retreat:

> You know that the best intentions do not always have their desired effect when they encounter opposition. Diderot is not alone in his fears. Others

in Paris advise me not to undertake the casting, nor to allow anyone but a good founder to make it. That is more than enough reason for me not to get involved any further. I have shown some good will. There are obstacles. Let a professional do the rest. I was not charged with this obligation in my contract and now I would not pardon myself if I failed in so important an operation! . . . With a good founder, Her Imperial Majesty and you will be reassured, and I will avoid three or four years of continuous agony and trouble, . . . caused by what I suspect would be a lack of skillful help.[19]

Understandably puzzled by Falconet's response, the empress decided to revisit the matter a month later: "Please tell me why you don't want to cast the statue because, with all due respect, your letter to Betskoi gives no good reasons. You probably have better ones in your heart, but if it were possible to conquer these obstacles, you would be doing a very good and useful thing. What limits are there for a man of genius! Who has told you that a professional founder will do it better than you? . . . I am convinced that if you take it upon yourself to direct the casting, it will succeed and you will be less vexed by it than if it were to be done by some founder."[20]

Falconet answered with what was clearly a self-serving distortion of the meaning of Betskoi's words or, at the very least, a gross misinterpretation of them:

On August 1 I wrote Monsieur Betskoi that I was ready to cast the statue without any remuneration. This suggestion did not sufficiently excite His Excellence for him to deign to respond before the lapse of fifteen days, at which time I received four words [*sic*], neither clear nor satisfactory, because they do not seem to come from someone who understands the difficulties and importance of this operation. The nature of my suggestion prevented me from saying this outright in my letter [to Betskoi]. One has good reasons to be tired of a boastful braggart, but a simple man may find himself insufficiently encouraged when he is refused a just and honest request made to assure himself of no more than peaceful working conditions. A lack of response in this matter means a refusal.[21]

It did not occur to Falconet that Betskoi's "unacceptable" delay of two weeks could have been caused by the need to consult with the empress, who in August 1769 was preoccupied with the grand finale of the First Turkish War. He did not even think of it when the empress told him in plain French that until mid-September she was unreachable because of the *Te Deum* and other festivities in the capital following Rumiantsev's victorious campaign against the Turks, and "other distractions."[22] Falconet added, it is true, one substantive reason for his refusal—his own and his assistant's lack of experience in baking the mold, but all in all, his letter of October 10, 1769, marks one of the lowest points in the sorry history of his relations with Betskoi.

Negotiations with foreign founders dragged on through 1771. Ivan Shuvalov, the former curator of the Academy of Fine Arts, was drawn into the search during his stay in Rome, but he managed to find only two Italian metal workers, Gaetano Merchi and Carlo Richard. They came to St. Petersburg in late 1770, but turned out to be of no use to Falconet, for their specialty was chiseling and chasing a finished cast, not making one from scratch. Falconet refused to have anything to do with them and they returned to Italy within a few months of their arrival.[23]

Finally, in 1772, with the assistance of the Paris architect Philippe de la Guépière and Prince Dmitry Mikhailovich Golitsyn, the Russian ambassador in Vienna, Betskoi managed to sign up Benedict Ersmann, a reputable Swiss founder, who had cast the figures of the maidens supporting the pedestal of Bouchardon's monument to Louis XV in Paris and its two bas-reliefs. Ersmann agreed to conduct the casting of the *Peter the Great* for 140,000 livres.

In the contract, drafted in Paris at the beginning of 1772, Ersmann appeared mindful of Falconet's sensitivities, but careful to define his own area of responsibility and safeguard it against possible incursions by the sculptor:

> I know the fame and integrity of Monsieur Falconet sufficiently well to consider it not only my pleasure, but also my duty to consult with him. I am also convinced that this is the safest way for him and me to bring this important task to a successful conclusion. I will not disregard any advice from Monsieur Falconet, however negligible, for his wisdom guarantees the quality of his counsel. Logic dictates that I have full authority over the workshops. Only Monsieur Falconet may have a key to them. I will order, manage, direct, and choose all my workers. No one may interfere with and hinder this prerogative, whoever he might be. This, however, should not be taken literally by persons who by virtue of their position are beyond suspicion. His Excellency General Betskoi will decide who deserves to have access to the operations.[24]

Falconet, who was not involved in the appointment of Ersmann, must have viewed with anxiety the clause giving Betskoi peremptory authority over access to the casting site.[25] Yet, when on May 1, 1772, Ersmann arrived in St. Petersburg with his three assistants, peaceful collaboration between the sculptor and the founder seemed possible.[26]

As the first assignment for the newly arrived founder the empress asked Falconet to have him make a cast of the late Roman statue of a boy taking a splinter out of his foot, the famous *Spinario*, a plaster model of which was in the Academy of Fine Arts. What emerged from the mold was a beautiful cast that Backmeister found to be sufficient proof of the founder's casting skills.[27] Falconet was impressed as well and Ersmann was allowed to go ahead with preparations for the casting of the *Peter the Great.*

Among the first chores of the Swiss founder and his assistants was the preparation of a mixture of special soils, clay, and sand, which Ersmann had brought from France, in order to make the molds. One of his assistants began the building of a smelting furnace, "the likes of which had never before been seen in Russia."[28] Ersmann also supervised the construction of the armature for the statue, whose distinctive feature was a powerful metal assembly consisting of a transverse arc resting on a Y-shaped support, anchored in the hind legs of the horse and, through them, in the granite of the pedestal. The assembly, weighing more than ten thousand pounds, supports the croup of the horse and the horseman.[29] It was the work of Fügner, the very same locksmith who made the jackscrews for the lifting of the Thunder Rock. The building of the armature was accompanied by the making of the core over which the sections of the wax model and plaster mold were assembled. That done, the plaster mold was taken off, and the touching up work on the wax model began. It was at that moment that there arose a disagreement about the thickness of the walls of the bronze cast.

In order to assure the stability of the statue, whose immense weight was held up by no more than the two hind legs of the horse, its center of gravity had to rest squarely above that delicate support. In order to distribute the weight equally in front and rear, Falconet decided to vary the thickness of the walls of the cast, from twelve lines in the rear, to four lines in the center, and three lines in front.[30] In addition, the horse's haunches, thighs, rear legs, and tail were to be filled with iron and steel to make them heavier and sturdier.

Falconet voiced his concern about this matter soon after his arrival. "What should have been sent here," he wrote to Catherine the Great, "is an instruction about modulating the thickness of the bronze, the thickness of the iron supports in the legs, and the construction of the armature. Perhaps the Bureau of Buildings could provide that information."[31] But the Bureau of Buildings could not help, and Falconet had to rely on his own knowledge and the experience of local specialists in casting artillery pieces, recommended by the ever helpful Carburi. The advice of Colonel Melissino and his founders in the Arsenal was probably also very useful.

Ersmann was horrified when he was told of the planned variations in the thickness of the walls. He was especially concerned when told that the head, arms, legs, and clothes of the horseman, as well as the head and the forelegs of the horse, were to be only three lines thick.[32] His experience in casting told him that three lines was not sufficient in a statue of this size and that a cast featuring walls so thin was bound to fail.[33] Falconet, however, persisted, and in the end Ersmann gave in. In private, however, he kept repeating that Falconet must be out of his mind to insist on such a thin cast, one that had never been tried before.[34]

In spite of these doubts, Ersmann kept up with his duties. He helped touch up the wax model, attached wax rods for the jets, vents, and drains, and directed the preparation and pouring of the investment for the core, a mixture of plaster and crushed bricks made of the clay that Ersmann had brought from France. He also prepared the ingredients for the outer mold, including clay, lye, horse manure, and cow hair. After setting them aside for the hair and manure to rot, he dried, rinsed, and screened them several times, and mixed them with other binding substances. All these preparations were done in a peaceful and cooperative atmosphere. Nothing presaged the dramatic events that were to follow. Their sequence can be reconstructed, but not without a certain amount of speculation.

Betskoi, whose dislike of Falconet was growing by the hour, seems to have hatched a plot designed to entrap him. His accessory was Iury Matveevich Fel'ten (Georg Friedrich Velten), a St. Petersburg architect of German extraction, whose total devotion to Betskoi had earned him a high position in the Bureau of Buildings and, after Carburi's departure, the task of serving as liaison between the Bureau and the sculptor. Seeing Falconet's unwillingness to be his own founder and his deferential attitude to Ersmann, Betskoi and Fel'ten concluded that casting was the sculptor's Achilles' heel. What better way to destroy the remnants of his credibility with the empress than to force him do his own casting and thereby expose that weakness! The disagreement about the thickness of the walls provided a welcome pretext. Professing indignation over Ersmann's readiness to undertake a cast while saying openly that it was bound to fail, Fel'ten demanded that the Swiss founder be fired. Betskoi immediately concurred. Falconet, who had always said that he had had nothing to do with Ersmann's appointment, was in no position to object. On June 30, 1774, the order to release Ersmann was signed.[35]

The speed with which Betskoi decided to act against the founder of his own choice, one who was ably and diligently fulfilling the terms of his contract, makes this scenario plausible. It will be recalled that Betskoi had tried before to convince Falconet to do his own casting, but that the sculptor feigned offense at the "lateness" of Betskoi's offer and declined the invitation. This time, however, it was different. The empress was impatient about the constant delays, Falconet had quarreled with Ersmann and bragged of his own casting competence, and there was no founder around to undertake the chore. All Falconet could do was agree to undertake the casting of the statue and, being agnostic, place his trust in Fate and in his own abilities.

That is the background of his letter to Catherine the Great written in June or July 1774.[36] In order to reassure the empress that he was ready to undertake this assignment, Falconet began the letter by proudly announcing that the casting of the *Cupid* had finally succeeded.[37] He went on with a technical account of the various stages of casting, reassuring the empress that he and his molder knew how to do all the preliminary operations. The only area where he owned up to a lack of experience was the determination of the moment when the bronze would be ready to flow. To deal with that problem, he suggested hiring "for no more than two or three days," an artillery founder, most certainly Emelian Khailov again. As for the construction of the furnace, he could rely on plans obtained from Paris, presumably those published by Boffrand in 1743 and Mariette in 1768. His tone was so self-assured that, if one did not know the role played by Ersmann's teaching and preparatory work, one might wonder why he had been so reluctant to undertake the casting earlier on.

Falconet presented the casting operations as purely mechanical and expressed surprise that they should command fees as high as the two hundred thousand livres paid to Gore for casting the monument to Frederick V in Copenhagen. Sovereigns should be generous, he said, but not to the point of authorizing theft. The deal he proposed would be much cheaper. His molder's regular fee of four thousand livres should be raised to ten thousand, while he himself disclaimed any interest in remuneration: "Your Majesty knows me well enough to be certain that I want none of what is called money. . . . I put the continued benevolence of Your Majesty far above gold."

This profession of pecuniary disinterestedness was not as self-denying as Falconet made it sound. What he meant was that he would not claim for himself any payment above and beyond the 80,000 livres that remained from the 140,000 livres in Ersmann's contract. The empress promised to pay it to him, but did not give him an official contract to confirm that promise. This caused Falconet much anxiety, for he had obliged himself in writing to pay 15,000 livres each to two of Ersmann's assistants, Simon and Pomel, whom he had persuaded to stay behind and help him out. Suspecting that Betskoi would do all in his power not to abide by "the sacred word of the empress," Falconet went back to her to seek confirmation of her commitment. Her supply of benevolence for the sculptor had by then run practically dry and she cut him short with a haughty: "Do you think then that the crown does not keep its word?" One can only imagine the embarrassed response of the sculptor. There were no witnesses to this scene and Falconet had to live with his anxieties until just before his departure in 1778, when the payment was made.[38]

FIRST CASTING

Your Imperial Majesty has perhaps been notified that I find myself the founder of the statue of Peter the Great.
—Falconet (1774)

Thus, in the summer of 1774, practically by default, Falconet became his own founder. He blamed this development on the adverse forces that had conspired against him: "Because of having to deal with crude and simple people and because the good of my work demands it, I have finally been forced to disregard the considerations which, while exaggerated perhaps, have until now held me back. To put it briefly, I alone with my workers am doing my business as I see fit. And I will do my duty in spite of the indifference, not to say disdain that Monsieur Betskoi has always shown me and all those whom I respect. I'll do it in spite of his claims that he is the person in charge of the operation, which I alone direct and about which he is, naturally, altogether ignorant."[39]

"Doing his business as he saw fit" was a bit of an exaggeration. The duty that he took upon himself amounted to the adoption of Ersmann's technical know-how and his materials in the construction of the outer mold and the brick wall, filling the space between them with earth, melting out the wax model, baking the core and the outer mold, smelting the bronze and pouring it into the space vacated by the lost wax. Not a small order, to be sure, but one that without Ersmann's two years of work would have been incomparably larger.[40]

Falconet had hoped all along that Carburi would be around to help him solve various technical problems that might arise in the process of casting. But Carburi had left Russia a year before, and all the help that Falconet could muster were his French molder, the artillery founder Khailov, and Ersmann's two assistants, Simon and Pomel.

It took this crew about a year to reach the point of lighting the fires in the hearths in the pit and, four weeks later, in the smelting furnace. On August 7, 1775, Falconet reported to the empress: "The fire has been burning under the mold since July 20 and in about fifteen days the bronze will be ready to be poured."[41] Finally, on August 25 everything was ready and the operation of casting the *Peter the Great* could begin. Its success, however, was partial only. Betskoi must have experienced more than a touch of schadenfreude when he reported to the empress:

> In my last letter I had the honor to inform Your Majesty about the casting which was to take place the day before yesterday. [It did take place], but not in the way I would have wished, for the bronze pierced the form or the mold in many places. This despite the many warnings of our founder that the [outer] wall near the tail was too thin to withhold the impact of bronze and that buttresses should have been placed there. Falconet never wanted to listen, but when the mishap occurred, he was the first to lose his head, screaming that everything was lost. Seeing him and his Collot scamper up and down the scaffolding like mad, his panic-stricken assistants and workers ran for their lives, throwing themselves on each other. The lower part of the scaffold caught fire, but fortunately people got away with fractures and wounds only. Some are still in bed. Having given permission to open the furnace, . . . I left. Nobody will be able to say anything certain about the statue before we begin to open it up five or six days from now. There is little or no hope. Success is very much in doubt. Yesterday the younger Falconet made a probe from above, and instead of the head of the hero, found just a jumble of metal. It's not a total catastrophe, but one usually judges the whole by a sample. There is nothing to do but to remain patient. I will give more news to Your Majesty as soon as I can.[42]

Betskoi did so on the following day, but his assurances of personal despair about the failed cast sound just as disingenuous as his earlier description of the pouring accident is incorrect: "Your Majesty would not believe how saddened I am by it, but what can one do! Though patience is a poor solution, one has to resort to it and try again, but Falconet must not be involved in anything except his own business. Vile self-interest and sordid avarice made him attempt something that he never knew anything about." And with a suggestive innuendo that was characteristic of his modus operandi, he added darkly: "One could say a great deal about this, but I'll be silent."[43]

A few days later, when the cast was fully uncovered, the extent of the damage turned out to be less catastrophic than Betskoi had originally suspected: "The lower part has come out very well, without any flaw. The rest, that is, the inside of the horseman's [right] arm, his chest, shoulders, neck, and head, as well as the horse's neck, head, and the reins, together with the horseman's left hand, have failed completely. Your Majesty may see it all on the attached drawing which I ordered to be done in haste. It's true that it's something that can be redone. Falconet thinks that the second casting can be undertaken in six months. I give him a year."[44]

Betskoi described the casting as if he had been its eyewitness and, just as in the saga of the Thunder Rock, he portrayed himself as being in full command of the situation. There is, however, no evidence that he was in the casting shed when the mishap occurred or that he had anything to do with the technicalities of the operation, like "giv[ing] permission to open the furnace."

To know what actually transpired in the casting shed on August 25 one must contrapose Betskoi's reports to other accounts. Luckily, three of these have come down to us. Two are by persons intimately involved in the cast—Falconet himself and his chief molder Pomel—and the third is by Backmeister, who devoted nearly twenty pages to the cast in his book on the history of Falconet's monument. He was not an eyewitness, but as the librarian of the Academy of Sciences, he had an obligation to collect information and chronicle the sequence of events in as impartial a way as possible.

With over forty-four thousand pounds of metal to be smelted, the furnace was lit at noon on August 24, and twenty-four hours later, when the bronze reached the point of liquefaction, the stopper was knocked out and the stream of molten metal began its descent first into the heated basin and from there into the mold by way of five large jets and an intricate network of small conduits.[45] The initial stages of pouring went well and the lower part of the statue filled as expected. Suddenly, the top of the mold cracked open, and the molten bronze broke out and flowed onto the floor, which caught fire. Falconet, frightened and distraught, ran out of the shed, followed by his workers. The only person who did not succumb to general panic was Khailov. He stayed behind and managed to extinguish the flames. Some of the molten metal flowed into the courtyard and, according to Backmeister, could still be seen there in 1783.[46]

How did the crack occur? Falconet put all the blame on Pomel, accusing him of having fallen asleep on his watch, when the outer mold was being baked: "While Pomel was sleeping, the fire progressed so much that it burned the mold and that is what caused it to crack and spill the bronze."[47] Naturally, Pomel disagreed. According to him, Falconet was incapable of making and baking the outer mold and left it all to his care. His mold, he claimed, was "the most beautiful baking job possible, without any cracks."[48]

Backmeister confirms that Falconet made a midnight visit to the shed during the baking of the molds and found Pomel asleep, while the fire below raged almost out of control. Had Falconet not taken steps to reduce it, the mold could have burned down. The outer mold did develop a crack, but Backmeister is careful not to attribute it to excessive heat nor to blame it for the spillage of bronze that occurred during the actual pouring. The cause of the accident, he claims, was a cracked jet above the back of the horseman, due perhaps to poor design or faulty construction of the jet, which may have been too large, allowing too much bronze to flow through it too quickly. Alternatively, the jet may have been placed too close to a vent, which also broke. Falconet attached these conduits himself, making Backmeister doubt that he would be able to deny convincingly his personal responsibility for the mishap.

Falconet, however, tried to do just that in a version published in the *St. Petersburg Gazette* and reprinted by Backmeister. It contains much praise for the cast, but little in the way of substantive clarification of the accident:

> As may be seen after the removal of the outer wall, the casting of the statue went very well and according to plan, except in two places on top, about two feet in size. This regrettable accident was caused by a circumstance which could not be foreseen and, consequently, there was no way to prevent it. Considering, however, that the height of the total cast is thirty feet, that accident is not important and can be quickly corrected. Otherwise, this casting may be considered the best ever made, because there is no concavity or crack in either the horseman or the horse. Everything came out exactly as it was in the wax model. The accident mentioned above seemed so dangerous that there was a fear that the whole shed might burn down and the whole work might be ruined. All workers and assistants ran from their posts in fear, except for the Russian founder Khailov. This diligent man, who managed the furnace, remained steadfastly at his post and conducted the last drops of the molten bronze into the form, retaining his cheerful attitude, despite danger to his life. Monsieur Falconet was so touched by the founder's bold and selfless act that, when the work was done, he ran up to him, kissed him cordially, and as a token of gratitude, presented him with a sum of money out of his own purse, without prejudicing by that act any generosity of the empress.[49]

Nonetheless, the city was buzzing with rumors and questions, many of them spread and magnified by the triumphant Betskoi. If two feet of the cast had not come out, if the tsar had no head on his shoulders and perhaps no shoulders either, how could one say that everything "went very well"? What was the "circumstance which could not be foreseen?" What should be done now, after nine years of waiting and large sums of money spent? Would Falconet recast the missing part only or would he redo the whole cast? And, most important, could he be trusted as founder?

Falconet tackled these questions in a fairly detailed report to the empress dated August 31. The accident turned out to have been more complex than Backmeister had suspected. It consisted of two separate though concurrent events. One affected the core and the upper part of the outer mold, which were overbaked, perhaps even burned, during Pomel's nap and were breached in the upper part of the statue by the onrushing molten bronze. The other concerned the basin into which the molten bronze flowed directly from the furnace. It too was breached and some of the metal spread outside and set the wooden floor and two sacks on fire.[50] On the causes of the latter accident, Falconet is silent.

Although these two accidents made the head of the horseman and the whole upper portion of the statue fit for scrap only, Falconet did not give up: "I inform and assure Your Majesty that I will continue casting with the same degree of courage that I needed to undertake it." Falconet added an aside, directed at Betskoi: "I never knew my friends better than during those two nightmarish days. Kind people have felt sincerely sorry for me, while the villains (how can I call them anything else) were stupid enough to broadcast their joy as soon as they thought that the cast had failed and to recount what they could not have seen. That is how history gets written. A success of this kind has made me an even more favorite target for the malice and envy of those who wish to harm me. It is at this time that I have the greatest need of Your Majesty's support."[51]

Falconet's story was amplified in a letter which one Bérenger of Lausanne sent to his friend Dentan of Geneva in 1780. Bérenger confirmed that Pomel had fallen asleep during the baking of the molds and credited Falconet with having prevented potentially disastrous situations in both the baking and the casting episodes. It was, he said, Falconet's midnight visit to the shed that saved the molds from being burned or overbaked, and it was thanks to Falconet's "prompt action that the metal did not spill before reaching the mold and that the cast did not fail completely." To corroborate these facts, Bérenger claimed that he possessed copies of written attestations by other people employed in the casting. "Their testimonies, signed in front of the French minister plenipotentiary [marquis de Juigné], are in my hands and I am reading them as I write these words."[52]

The mishap with the first cast marked the nadir of Falconet's stay in St. Petersburg. With Catherine stubbornly silent and most of his friends looking away, Falconet must have felt like a caged animal, trapped by the unfinished monument and reduced to growling at Betskoi, who brought him his daily scraps.

THE POMEL AFFAIR

Let the public judge now between M. Falconet and his enemies, for Pomel in this affair is only a marionette in the hands of the latter. Let it reflect on how an honorable man may find himself in a

situation made more disagreeable because all that he has to reproach himself for is trying to do a good turn to an ungrateful
wretch.
—Prince D. A. Golitsyn (1780)

A quarrel with Pomel, played out before an international audience, was
the last thing that Falconet needed at a time when he was trying to live down
the partly failed cast of 1775 and was nervously preparing for the remedial cast
of 1777. Such, however, was the intensity of Falconet's and Betskoi's dislike
for each other and such was the petulant nature of the sculptor that an occasion for a good fight was not allowed to slip away.

The problem began with the arguments over the partial failure of the cast
of 1775. The foes of Falconet rejoiced, while his friends had no choice but
to agree that the cast was not entirely successful. Comments, offered either
in the spirit of censure and mockery or in that of concern and commiseration,
could not but make a dent in the amour-propre of the sculptor. Narcissis-
tically preoccupied with his image, Falconet countered his critics by allowing
the *Gazette des Deux-Ponts* of October 30, 1775, to reprint his letter to Prince
D. A. Golitsyn in which he tried to whitewash his reputation as founder by
shifting the blame to what he called an outside source: "The accident would
not have occurred had it not been for the bad conduct of one Pomel, a
worker now discharged."[53]

Pomel, worried that Falconet might retract his offer of payment, appealed
to the French minister plenipotentiary in St. Petersburg, Count de Juigné,
to help him receive his fifteen thousand livres even before Falconet himself
was paid the eighty thousand due to him from the Bureau of Buildings.
Bourrée de Corberon, dispatched by Juigné to clarify the matter, recorded
the outcome of his meeting with the sculptor: "Falconet asked Betskoi to
advance him the sum demanded of him against the payment of the total
owed to him. Betskoi answered rather disingenuously . . . that Falconet
would receive the promised sum after the casting is done and well done.
Besides, Falconet is too displeased with Pomel to accede to his wishes, even
if he could. I really believe that Pomel is guilty, but Falconet is too opinion-
ated and too self-centered to be believed blindly and unequivocally."[54]

Falconet's charges against Pomel started a war of words that lasted off and
on until 1780. Its battlefields were the pages of the *Journal encyclopédique,*
which had shown its anti-Falconet bias during the controversy over Falconet's translation of Pliny the Elder. Just as in that instance, the articles de-
fending Pomel and attacking Falconet were anonymous.[55] Common stylistic
features suggest that they were all written by one and the same person, but
who that person was is open to speculation. Although the use of the *Journal
encyclopédique* as the arena might suggest someone from Diderot's circle,
internal evidence points rather in the direction of Betskoi and his Russian
allies. That is also what Falconet suspected: "One can see that the factory
of all these iniquities is not in Paris."[56]

The first salvo in response to Falconet's accusations was fired in 1776 in the *Mémoire pour le Sr. Pomel*. Its version of the events in the casting shed could not have been at greater variance with Falconet's account. Pomel was presented as an enterprising and vigilant worker who saved the molds from being overheated. Falconet emerged as the villain who went home leaving his workers without any instructions to extinguish the fire in the hearths. Around midnight, Pomel noticed that the temperature in the pit was rapidly rising. Fearing that this might have disastrous consequences for the lower part of the molds, he took it upon himself to put out the fire.[57] As for the account of the actual pouring of the bronze, especially in Bérenger's version, the *Mémoire* suggested sarcastically that the only "prompt action" of Falconet was his speedy retreat from the shed. The mold cracked because the sculptor insisted on enveloping it with sand, against the advice of Pomel and the casting specialist, who recommended the use of *terre forte,* a kind of heavy clayish soil. The anonymous author added that even though Pomel was not a founder, he was sufficiently familiar with casting to know that had Falconet listened to his advice, "he would have enjoyed the glory of success that he had craved so much."[58]

Falconet's response was immediate. On August 1, 1776, he sent the *Journal encyclopédique* a two-page piece, *Ce que c'est qu'un écrit, intitulé Mémoire pour le Sieur Pomel.*[59] Intended to refute Pomel's charges, it was long on indignation, but short on facts. Falconet called the *Mémoire* a libelous defamation and promised to prove all his charges against Pomel when his work was finished, at which time he would turn the adjudication of the "libel" to appropriate courts. Most important, however, Falconet changed somewhat the conditions under which he would pay Pomel the promised fifteen thousand livres. The original agreement, confirmed by a promissory note which Falconet gave Pomel in 1775, called for the payment to be made as soon as Falconet himself received his eighty thousand.[60] Now, in a fit of pique, Falconet said that he would put the fifteen thousand livres in escrow and ask an appropriate judicial authority to decide whether Pomel should receive that sum or not. That change, even though Falconet was to repudiate it and pay Pomel in full in 1778, was used by Pomel and his supporters to accuse Falconet of looking for a legalistic loophole in order to dodge his obligation.

In a note accompanying Falconet's defense against the anonymous attack on his translation of Pliny, Pierre Rousseau stated the editorial policy of the *Journal encyclopédique:* "[The criticism we publish] is sometimes unfair and often harsh. In the former instance we do not take a stand, leaving the judgment to scholars. In the latter, we try, as far as we can, to soften the criticism. Clearly, despite this precaution, there always remain some remarks which are painful to their addressees. It is impossible in all instances to successfully oppose the mania for replacing rational arguments with sarcasm."[61]

In this instance, however, Rousseau took a definite stand against Falconet when he upbraided him for complaining that the *Mémoire* contained a libelous defamation: "I went back to the article about which the famous artist is complaining to make sure that I had not made a mistake about it. All I have found there is a well-founded complaint and a legitimate defense. "In fact," he added, "since exchanges of this kind, instead of contributing to the glory of the arts, degrade them, I would not have published [Falconet's] article, had I not received a request to do so from a *seigneur* as distinguished by his birth and position, as he is respected by his rare merits and the excellent use to which he puts his talents."[62]

The anti-Falconet forces struck their final blow in 1779 and 1780, in two articles published in successive issues of the *Journal encyclopédique* under the common title *Observations sur la fonte de la statue équestre.* An editorial note affirmed again the journal's complete impartiality: "We are adding another piece to these proceedings and, just as before, we are doing so without anger or prejudice."[63] The first of the two articles was concerned chiefly with a defense of Pomel. It repeated the arguments from the *Mémoire* and mentioned in addition a sum of fifty-two hundred livres which Falconet presumably owed Pomel for the "lost" year and for his travel expenses to Paris.[64] It also asserted again that, despite overheating, the molds had been excellently baked.

The second article, however, was a vicious personal attack on the sculptor. It began with an anonymous introduction: "We have followed step by step the sculptor who pretends to be a founder, during the whole course of various operations on the casting of the statue of Peter the Great. We have seen him, motivated by greed and pride, alternate between cunning and tyranny as a means of appropriating someone else's work and directing its progress."[65]

Not satisfied with an accusation of "ignorance, inattention, and stubbornness," the author continued: "After ten years of wearing the public down with a critique of a work that he had not seen, a tedious eulogy of a masterpiece that nobody had yet seen, and a barbarous translation of an author whom he did not understand, M. Falconet wanted to place himself above all his confrères by pretending that he possessed in equal measure the arts of sculpting and casting. But that phantom of conceit which he confidently proclaimed vanished suddenly when his cast had failed."[66]

It is important to keep in mind that by the time this passage appeared, the second casting had succeeded, and the statue was finished, though the monument was not yet unveiled, Pomel had received his fifteen thousand livres, and Falconet was back in Western Europe.[67] To launch so gross an attack in such circumstances shows that its anonymous author was out to get Falconet no matter what.

There were two documents cited in the article. One was a certificate drafted by Falconet himself immediately after the failed cast. Falconet wanted it to be signed in front of the Count de Juigné by the workers, who had had many opportunities to observe Pomel's behavior during the casting of the statue and would presumably support his criticism of his chief molder.[68] The other was a translation from Russian into French of a pro-Pomel certificate written by one Ivan Shpakovsky three years after the casting.[69]

Two pro-Falconet statements closed the dispute. The *Avis concernant la querelle qui s'est élevée entre M. Falconet et le Sr. Pomel* was contributed by Russia's envoy to Holland Prince D. A. Golitsyn, who stood up for Falconet with all the fervor of a devoted friend.[70] Golitsyn reviewed the disagreement step by step, refuting all the accusations of Pomel against Falconet and documenting the groundlessness of Pomel's additional monetary claims against Falconet. As for Shpakovsky, whom Falconet called "Pomel's crony," Golitsyn pronounced his certificate in defense of Pomel "very suspicious" and the man himself not worthy of trust and not entitled to use the formula "upon my honor" because "he is certainly not a gentleman." It is safe to assume that at the time of its writing, Golitsyn's resolute stand in support of Falconet was issued in defiance of his superiors in St. Petersburg and must have contributed to the empress's displeasure with him.

The second statement, called *Imposteurs démasqués et confondus,* was by Falconet himself.[71] It contained a rebuttal of the charges against him and a stinging rebuke to the editors of the journal for publishing unsigned and undated accusations, without so much as indicating the place from which they were sent. Using phrases like "insane impostors," "insolent deceit," "vindictive frenzy," Falconet threatened court action against the perpetrators of the campaign against him. Betskoi was his chief suspect, but he conceded that the libels could have been concocted not by the general himself, but by a Russian employed in Betskoi's office (Shpakovsky?): "The hate that Mr. Betskoi professes against me is no doubt total, but only the basest villain is capable of manufacturing a deception of such magnitude. . . . These people swear 'upon their honor' to things they know nothing about, and do so with impunity. And because they can tar the reputation of a man who is not stupid and does not let them get away with their deception, they don't care about the means they employ. They don't risk their honor for they are at a safe distance, but I don't advise them to try it in Paris."[72]

That was the final shot in the Pomel affair.

SECOND CASTING

> At last, my prince, it is done and well done, that cast about whose success you inquire. On July 15 at eight thirty in the morning my problems with this matter were over.
> —Falconet (1777)

All during the fall of 1775 work was proceeding on the preparation of the upper portion of the statue for the second casting or, what Falconet called *la petite fonte.* The missed parts and the protruding jets were sawed off and the statue was surrounded by bricks up to the height necessary for the new casting. That done, Falconet informed the empress that the casting shed was closed, and only he had the keys to it. What was now needed was to cut out a joint in the successfully cast lower part of the statue, in anticipation of its juncture with the new upper part.

In a massive statue like the *Peter the Great,* a simple butt joint, where two flat surfaces are brazed end-to-end, would have been much too weak. To strengthen the connection, the overlapping joint, or lap joint, is frequently used.[73] Falconet, however, referred to the joint used in the recast statue as the *queue d'aronde,* "dovetailing." Such a joint called for indentations in the walls of the lower part of the cast into which the liquid bronze for the upper part would flow. "It is a pleasure," as Falconet would write Prince Golitsyn, "to see how dovetailing allows the new bronze be joined to and meld with the old."[74]

Such work called for the services of someone who could work with solid bronze. One such person was the clockmaker Abraham Sandoz, who, while being employed in the construction of a large clock for the Fortress of Peter and Paul, touched up the casts of the *Cupid* and the *Spinario.*[75] Falconet liked his work and thought that he was an obvious candidate for the job. Betskoi, however, temporized, claiming that Sandoz's services were too expensive. Time passed and Falconet was getting more and more exasperated by his enforced leisure. He complained to the empress that for the last two months all work in the casting shed had stopped because of Betskoi's stubbornness. How can one talk about too high a price, he asked, when the cost of the *Peter the Great* was about two million livres (including the cost of transporting the Thunder Rock), while that of Bouchardon's *Louis XV* in Paris was five million livres and Saly's *Frederick V* in Copenhagen was three million?[76]

His arguments prevailed and in January 1776 a contract was signed between Sandoz and the Bureau of Buildings, calling for touching up the statue and bringing it to "the degree of perfection of the large model." Sandoz obliged himself to complete the work in two years for the sum of twenty thousand rubles, that is, just over one hundred thousand livres. The agreement was that he would be responsible to Falconet alone, thus avoiding Ersmann's dilemma of dual loyalty. Falconet gave him his total support: "I believe that Monsieur Sandoz has the abilities necessary for the job he is undertaking. I don't know anybody who would be better qualified overall than he to fulfill that goal. I also think that his price is reasonable."[77]

It took a year and a half for Falconet and his crew to prepare the statue for the second casting. It turned out to be much more than the *petite fonte* Falconet expected. As he wrote to D. A. Golitsyn, it was not merely a question of the heads of the tsar and the horse: "When it became possible to examine the bronze from inside, I realized that the upper part of the statue was so poorly done that I had to go down to the horseman's knees and recast almost half of the statue."[78] This time everything worked as planned and one can imagine the relief of the harried sculptor when on July 15, 1777, Peter the Great emerged from the outer mold, sitting bolt upright in his bronze splendor.

Despite all the precautions, the second casting was not free of mistakes, but this time, Falconet accepted full responsibility for them. Fortunately, they were minor and could be quickly repaired: "holes, small cracks on one side of the collar and in the harness of the horse."[79] On the outside Sandoz filed off the overflow of molten bronze, which formed a belt, not unlike the congealed glue at the juncture of two pieces of broken china. On the inside, he left it untouched. All in all, the second casting succeeded admirably, and a person looking at the statue would never suspect that it is composed of two separate pieces. Not even restorers working on the statue can see any outside traces of the seam between the two casts.[80]

On November 29, 1777, Falconet informed the empress that the second casting had been successfully completed and that in about four months' time the statue would be totally touched up. "Then I beg Your Majesty to be so kind as to take a look at my work, the fruit of eleven or twelve years of labor."[81]

There was no answer.

7

Denouement

FAREWELL TO RUSSIA

I wish for it to end once and for all, because Falconet is truly in-
supportable.
—Betskoi (1775)

By early 1778 the statue was cast, chiseled, and chased. The main section of
the pedestal had been shaped and hewn down to size. All that remained to
be done was to mold and cast the snake, transfer the two severed pieces of
the original Thunder Rock to the front and back of the pedestal in order
to give it the desired length of sixty feet (fig. 4.2), and install the statue. One
would think that there was every reason for Falconet to rejoice in the successful completion of a task which had consumed twelve years of labor at a cost
of almost half a million rubles.

But the sculptor was not in a celebratory mood. His work, it is true,
was almost done, but instead of cordiality and admiration, he found himself
surrounded by indifference, even hostility. Gone was the spirit of friendliness
and anticipation which had greeted him on his arrival in St. Petersburg.
Gone was the sense of being a cherished member of St. Petersburg's intellectual elite. Gone were many of his friends in the foreign colony of St. Petersburg. Diderot, once a faithful friend and regular correspondent, fell silent.
His son Pierre-Etienne left for Paris shortly before his wife's delivery. The
embarrassing story of the first casting and of the Pomel affair was making
the rounds of gossip mills in Russia and France.

Above all, his personal relations with the empress, the joy and pride of
his first years in St. Petersburg, had reached a dead end. Her terse letter of
December 4, 1774, dealing with what she thought was an exorbitant price
demanded by Falconet *fils* for his paintings, was her last personal message
to the sculptor. From that time on she did not acknowledge any of his letters,
nor answer any of his questions. The empress did not even visit the casting
shed to see the finished statue. The silent treatment was clearly meant to
impress upon the sculptor that he had overstayed his welcome.

Falconet's fall from grace could not escape notice in a city where every change in the empress's mood, every smile and frown on her face, was anxiously observed and commented upon. Betskoi was among the first to relish the sight of Falconet's falling star. Secure in the knowledge that the monument could now be completed without the troublesome sculptor, he engaged in a methodical campaign to get rid of him. "I see no obstacles to your leaving," he wrote the sculptor in mid-June 1778.[1]

Falconet, however, did see at least one obstacle. He expected the payment of the 80,000 livres, that is, the sum remaining from the 140,000 livres of Ersmann's unfulfilled contract for casting the statue. Although the payment had been promised to him by the empress, Betskoi was doing everything he could to avoid making a disbursement from the monument fund at the Bureau of Buildings. Accusing Falconet of predatory instincts, Betskoi ordered a detailed accounting of the sculptor's expenses, above and beyond those provided for in the contract, and deducted them from the 80,000 livres. The anonymous compiler of the account (presumably, Ivan Shpakovsky) looked into every nook and cranny to produce expenses which could be chargeable to Falconet, including his room and board during the four years which the sculptor spent in St. Petersbug beyond the contracted-for eight years, the cost of the second casting, and Sandoz's payment for touching up the statue after the second casting.[2]

After adding up these expenses, all that remained from the 80,000 livres was just about 1,266 livres, or 278 rubles. Not satisfied, the Bureau of Buildings asked Falconet to reimburse the 300 rubles which it had paid the painter Losenko back in 1771 for the drawing of the large model of the monument, choosing not to remember that the empress had offered it to Falconet as a gift.[3] In the final accounting, instead of owing Falconet 80,000 livres or about 16,000 rubles, the Bureau of Buildings decreed that the sculptor owed it 22 rubles.

This called forth an indignant protest from the sculptor. He reminded Betskoi that article 15 of his contract provided for his lodging and compensation beyond the term of eight years, if unforeseen circumstances prevented him from completing the monument within that time. The explanation offered by the Bureau of Buildings, that "it had run out of funds dedicated to the monument," was not a valid excuse, Falconet said. If there was a shortfall, it was not his fault, for his price for the monument was less than what other sculptors executing similar projects received. To prove his point Falconet compared the sum paid and owed him with the sums paid to Saly for the equestrian statue of Frederick V in Copenhagen and to Bouchardon for the equestrian statue of Louis XV in Paris. The comparison showed clearly that Falconet was not guilty of overcharging the imperial treasury.[4] Falconet ended the letter with a plea to Betskoi to recognize a job well done. He asked him to recall the praise which Catherine and Betskoi himself had heaped on the monument when it was still in its initial stages and much inferior to the finished product. "But who am I to sing praises of my works," he asked, "when it had been done earlier by Her Imperial Majesty, you Monsieur, enlightened artists, and the honest public?"[5]

Betskoi's accusation that "all [Falconet] wants is money, and money is all he is interested in,"[6] made the sculptor's retort angrily in a commentary to his letter, published several years later: "Let them accuse me as much as they wish. Well-educated and sensible people will not reproach me. They will see that I was unselfish as long as I could be, and that I carried that attitude to a fault. In the end I was obliged to stand up for my rights against those who did not want to grant them to me and who wished to rob me of what the empress in her sense of justice accorded to me."[7]

Falconet sent the empress a copy of his letter to Betskoi, hoping that she would not renege on her word. His expectations proved correct. Despite Betskoi's intrigues, the empress squared her accounts with the sculptor on August 23, 1778.[8] There were twenty-five hundred rubles deducted from the sum paid to Falconet, but he refused to blame the empress for that "low and mean action," which he knew was the work of Betskoi.[9]

There remained still one obstacle, but it was bigger and more alarming than any other facing Falconet. A story began to make the rounds of St. Petersburg that Betskoi wanted to scrap the statue and have it totally recast. That prospect sent a shiver down Falconet's spine. He had no way of knowing what Betskoi's real intentions were. Was it merely a malicious rumor, spread to rattle his composure, or a threat which should be taken seriously? Could he leave St. Petersburg and let his sworn enemy and cohorts from the Bureau of Buildings destroy his most cherished creation?

There was no sense in reasoning with Betskoi, who was so blinded by hatred of Falconet as to be capable of committing any act, however injurious, as long as its edge was turned against the sculptor. Nor could he stay on in St. Petersburg to monitor the situation, for he would have found himself with nobody at his side. Not even Collot could keep him company, for her husband kept urging her to join him in Paris as soon as possible. In this situation, there was nothing to do but appeal once again to the empress, knowing that she at least could be counted upon to act rationally.

How could one, he asked, use a trumped-up charge to destroy a successful cast? No casting venture was totally free of problems. Lemoyne's *Louis XV* in Bordeaux had had to be cast in two pourings. Saly's *Frederick V* in Copenhagen needed more than a thousand bronze patches to repair the cast. In neither case had the solidity and beauty of the finished work suffered. Falconet mentioned a number of changes he had introduced in the finished statue to improve it over the large model. They included a slight turn of the tsar's head, and the position of his legs and of the extended arm. He cautioned the empress that a new founder would not be able to duplicate the unique feature of his cast, namely the varied thickness of the walls, necessary to ensure the statue's stability: No modern founder would want to make a "thin cast" or would know how to make it.[10] He ended the letter with a warning: "Others than you, Madame, may consider me a dreamer, but those who think of recasting the statue would see how right I was when it would be too late. I cannot leave without telling Your Imperial Majesty this truth about the statue, even though She has not seen it yet. I should like to believe, however, that all this is no more than a rumor spread just to harass me."[11]

Shortly before leaving, Falconet addressed the following curt message to Betskoi as president of the Academy of Fine Arts: "Professor Falconet and his daughter-in-law beg you to kindly assure the gentlemen of the Academy of their respect. They also ask you, Monsieur, to accept their humble salutations on the eve of their departure."[12] The transparent wish to bruise Betskoi's ego by sending him a letter whose minimalism was more offensive than no letter at all shows the depth of Falconet's resentment. His intention was not lost on the addressee. Betskoi made sure that Falconet would not be present at the unveiling ceremony and that he, Betskoi, would garner all the laurels.

Nor did Falconet's letter to the empress, the last of 114, include any diplomatic niceties. There were no expressions of gratitude and no fond adieus. Just a brief first sentence: "Thanks to Your Imperial Majesty what has concerned me here is finished." A dry factual statement, or a double-entendre perhaps? Falconet reminded the empress of the trials and tribulations of his stay in St. Petersburg: "Amidst all the suffering to which I was subjected, I worked as an artist who knows how to put the good of the work with which he was entrusted above human whimsy. I disregarded words and deeds, just as Your Majesty counseled me so often, and thought only of fulfilling my duty."[13]

Back in July 1778, the *St. Petersburg Gazette* had run an advertisement: "Needed one manservant and one maid with good references, able to understand French or German, and wishing to travel to France. To apply see Madame Falconet in the house at the corner of Bol'shaia Morskaia Street, opposite the house of the Prussian envoy."[14] Now, a month later, the *St. Petersburg Gazette* announced the departure of "Professor Falconet with his daughter-in-law and her daughter, accompanied by the servants Anna Chibert and Johann Rosengrünn."[15]

As the party crossed the border at Riga, Falconet's Russian episode, one that occupied one quarter of his creative life and secured him a place of honor in the pantheon of French sculpture, came to a close. His relief was palpable: "When I got past Riga, I felt my chest expand and my blood course through my veins with an ease which I had almost ceased to know."[16] He was not the first and not the last visitor to Russia to experience that feeling.

The empress, too, must have heaved a sigh of relief at the news of Falconet's leaving, but she was clearly bothered by not having been properly taken leave of. A few weeks later she wrote to Grimm: "[Falconet] has left here without saying good-bye to me." And, as if to get even for the slight, she gently hinted that Falconet might have taken with him some letters of Voltaire which she had lent him.[17]

Consumed by a desire to transcend the traditional manner of executing the equestrian monument, Falconet spent twelve years in St. Petersburg as if in a dream. The monument became the focus of all his thoughts and actions. Even when he was not at his workbench, but at the writing desk, busying himself with correspondence or working on the translation of Pliny or the criticism of the *Marcus Aurelius,* his ultimate concern was with the monument. Events happened around him: wars were fought, friends died, neighborhoods burned, the Neva flooded the city in 1777, but one would look in vain for a flicker of reaction. He left no impressions of the country in which he lived, the city from which he never moved, or the houses in which he worked and slept. He never tried to come to know the qualities of the native population: "My ignorance of the language, my sedentary occupations, and the little need that I have to live with the Russians, will always be an obstacle."[18] He did make a few comments on the Russians' lack of understanding and appreciation of art, but nothing beyond that.[19]

Did he not care? He probably did, but he was preoccupied with the problems at hand, and had no time to pay attention to matters which seemed inconsequential. His correspondence dealt solely with business matters.[20] There exists no diary by Falconet. Perhaps it was his disdain for posterity, which convinced him that such a record was useless. Perhaps, aware of the aura of suspicion around him, he thought it potentially dangerous to commit his inner thoughts to paper. Perhaps such a diary existed, but was destroyed by Marie-Lucie along with other materials which she felt were injurious to her mother's memory.

Outside of Catherine the Great and Ivan Betskoi, Falconet's acquaintances in St. Petersburg were practically all foreigners—birds of passage, here today, gone tomorrow. With some of them he was on friendly terms. There was Pierre-Charles Lévesque (1736–1812), a French philosopher and historian with a teaching appointment in the Cadet Corps, whose stay in St. Petersburg (1773–78) partly overlapped with Falconet's. Lévesque is the author of a warm biographical sketch of Falconet, included as front matter in the 1808 edition of Falconet's writings.

There was Marin Carburi, the inventive Greek, without whom the Thunder Rock might never have exchanged its peace and seclusion in the woods of Karelia for the limelight of Senate Square. Until his departure in 1773, Carburi took care of all of the daily problems of both the sculptor and his work. During the course of that collaboration the two became good friends, if one is to judge by Falconet's repeated intercessions on Carburi's behalf before the empress.

There was Charles Lord Cathcart, the British ambassador to Russia from 1768 to 1772. He arrived in St. Petersburg eager to meet Falconet and Collot, about whom he had heard from George Macartney, his predecessor in the St. Petersburg post. Lord Cathcart, who was a patron of the arts and a fine horseman, took an active interest in Falconet and offered him advice on the stance of the horse during the sculptor's preparation of the large model of the statue.[21] Impressed by Collot's bust of Catherine, he commissioned from her a bust of his daughter, Mary, and a life-size marble medallion of his wife, Jane Hamilton.[22] Even after his return to London, Lord Cathcart corresponded with Falconet and sent him a Wedgwood medallion of Peter the Great, with a request that he pass it on to the empress.[23]

There was John Glenn King (1731–1817), the Anglican pastor of the British colony in St. Petersburg, whose knowledge of languages and interest in the arts and aesthetics helped Falconet in his dealings with both the Russians and the English. Reverend King specialized in commemorative medals and was Catherine the Great's consultant on that subject. He acted as a guide and interpreter for the Russian church delegation that visited Falconet's studio to examine the large model of the monument.[24]

Of Falconet's German friends one should mention Ludwig Heinrich von Nicolaï (1737–1820), an Alsatian with German cultural affiliations, hired by Catherine the Great as her librarian and teacher of Grand Duke Paul. Nicolaï visited Falconet in his atelier and described some of his early clashes with Betskoi. The Swabian art historian Jacob von Stählin (1709–85) was an important link to the scholarly community of St. Petersburg during the first half of Falconet's stay. A brilliant and multifaceted historian and engraver, Stählin was also secretary of the Academy of Sciences and director of its arts division. Seven letters of Falconet to Stählin have survived in the manuscript collection of the Russian National Library in St. Petersburg.[25] They deal chiefly with Falconet's requests for books from the library of the Academy and bits of bibliographical information for his research. Stählin claimed authorship of the initial version of the dramatically short inscription for the monument, *Petro I Catharina II posuit*, which is usually ascribed to Falconet.[26] That was the text which Falconet recommended to the empress and which she reduced further by eliminating the last word.[27]

Falconet kept his distance from the numerous Frenchmen living in St. Petersburg, finding them too mercenary and contentious. He did, however, develop a friendly relationship with Marie-Daniel Bourrée de Corberon, secretary of the French minister plenipotentiary, the marquis de Juigné. Bourrée de Corberon's stay in St. Petersburg from August 1775 to September 1778 was a period rife with problems for Falconet. They were commented on by Bourrée de Corberon in his *Journal intime,* which achieves thereby the status of a primary source on Falconet's Russian episode, especially on his attack on the *Marcus Aurelius,* on his annotated translation of Pliny the Elder,[28] and on the partly missed first cast. In his detailed account of the controversy about the presumed "overtrimming" of the Thunder Rock, Bourrée de Corberon resolutely supported Falconet's position.[29] We owe him a glowing description of the monument ("It is the most beautiful statue of this kind that I know"), an appreciation of the head of Diderot by Collot ("The resemblance is striking"), pro-Falconet comments on the Pomel affair, and a mention of Falconet's rich collection of engravings.[30] His portrait of Falconet is incisive: "[He] is quite a character, demanding and dangerous, once he gets you in his grasp. His great modesty is a cover for even greater airs. It is like the mantle of Diogenes, which did not disguise the philosopher's conceit."[31] Most importantly, Bourrée de Corberon provides an eyewitness account of the marriage ceremony of Falconet *fils* and Collot and owns up to distaste for its suspected motives and a sense of embarrassment for having had to take part in it.[32]

Of Falconet's Russian friends, the painter Anton Pavlovich Losenko (1737–73) was certainly the closest. Trained in Paris by Joseph-Marie Vien and Jean-Bernard Restout, he specialized in historical and mythological subjects. Losenko made the first drawing of the large model of the monument, which was supposed to be engraved, but never was.[33] Falconet took to heart the plight of Losenko, whose pedagogical and administrative duties in the Academy of Fine Arts were so demanding as to force him to abandon painting. In a dramatically phrased letter, Falconet called him "the first skilled painter of the nation"[34] and begged Catherine the Great to come to his rescue. The empress promised to help, but whatever she did came too late, for Losenko died just three years later.[35]

UNVEILING

The statue may be seen today in St. Petersburg. It stands there without any support and weighs upon all those who maligned me so stupidly, so perfidiously. Whether they be Russian or not, could I ask for a better revenge?
—Falconet (1779)

In September 1767 the Senate requested from the Bureau of Buildings a projection of the cost of the monument. Betskoi turned the request over to Carburi and Falconet, who came up with the figure of 480,000 rubles to be spent at the rate of 60,000 per year for the eight years during which Falconet obligated himself to finish the monument. This estimate was itemized as follows:

Falconet's salary, upkeep, and transportation	70,000
Six helpers	50,000
Locksmith, smith, and other workers	15,000
Construction of workshops, furnace, etc.	30,000
Materials (alabaster, iron, etc.)	10,000
Upkeep of workshops, heating, firewood	15,000
Copper and wax for casting	40,000
Binding large rocks for the pedestal, copper and lead, stone posts with chains, construction of the crane to lift the statue, scaffolding, etc.	250,000
	480,000[36]

This projection calls for a commentary:

1. The Falconet item of 70,000 rubles included Falconet's salary of 200,000 livres agreed upon in the contract, that is, 40,000 rubles, assuming an exchange rate of twenty Russian kopeks to a French livre.[37] This sum was transferred to France in annual installments of 25,000 livres. The remaining 30,000 rubles were for Falconet's expense account in St. Petersburg and travel costs from and to Paris.

2. The item for the binding of large rocks for the pedestal refers to the original plan to make the pedestal from half a dozen connected granite rocks. The discovery of the Thunder Rock made this procedure unnecessary. The cost of transporting the Thunder Rock was charged to the Admiralty budget.

3. In his August 1766 letter to Betskoi, Diderot asked that Collot's annual salary be set at 1,500 livres, that is, 300 rubles.[38] This sum was approved by the empress, but was not charged against the budget of the monument.[39]

4. Since casting was not mentioned in Falconet's contract, it may be assumed that the "etc." in the large item of 250,000 rubles included its cost. Actually, the special casting contract signed with the Swiss founder Ersmann called for an outlay of 140,000 livres or 28,000 rubles, of which Ersmann received 60,000 livres and Falconet took over the remaining 80,000 livres.[40]

This estimate was set up as an "idealized" monument fund in the budget of the Bureau of Buildings. The actual cost of the monument by March 1776 was 422,189 rubles and 3½ kopeks. Still to be done was the second casting, touching up the statue, and moving it to the pedestal, all estimated at 38,000 rubles. Thus, the total cost was just under 461,000 rubles or about 2,300,000 livres.[41]

The departure of Falconet was the fulfillment of Betskoi's most cherished dreams. After twelve long years of bitterness and contention he was getting rid of that ungovernable Frenchman who dared disregard court protocol and bypass his authority. Now Betskoi would be king of the hill, his primacy would not be challenged, he alone would have the ear of the empress. The architect Iury M. Fel'ten (fig. 7.1), who was to take over technical matters, was Betskoi's appointee and protégé and deferred to him in everything.[42]

An example of the freedom with which Betskoi could now operate was the matter of the grille around the monument. Rastrelli had wanted one around his monument and Betskoi assumed that there would be one around Falconet's monument. "No fence around Peter the Great," objected Falconet, "Why put him in a cage? If one has to protect the marble and the bronze against madmen and children, there are sentries for that in the empire."[43] A compromise was reached and the monument was to be encircled by chains suspended from low stone posts. Now that Betskoi alone was in charge, the idea of a fence was resurrected, and one was designed by Fel'ten and installed.

Fig. 7.1. Carl Ludwig Christineck, *Iury Matveevich Fel'ten*. Oil on canvas, 1786. The State Russian Museum, St. Petersburg.

It was Fel'ten who directed the monument's completion. He himself described his tasks in 1784 when he petitioned Betskoi to increase his pay retroactively from seventy-five rubles a month to a hundred rubles, on the grounds that had Falconet stayed on to complete the monument, he would have received 175 rubles for doing the same thing. According to him, his tasks included: (1) hewing the pedestal for the statue from a large rock with two rock attachments, to represent a natural hill; (2) transferring the statue to the pedestal and anchoring it securely; (3) attaching the inscription on both sides of the pedestal; (4) completing the molding of the snake, casting it, and affixing it on the rock; (5) paving a platform around the monument with large slabs of raw stone and surrounding it with a grille with appropriate ornamentation.[44]

These demands were partly justified and partly exaggerated. (1) The hewing of the main portion of the pedestal was completed before Falconet's departure. What Fel'ten had to do was supervise the shaping of two large chunks of the rock, split off by lightning, and attach them to the front and rear of the pedestal. (2) The transfer of the statue from the casting barn onto the pedestal required building a mechanism similar to the one used in the emplacement of the statue of Louis XV by Bouchardon in Paris (fig. 7.2). The statue was placed in a wheeled carriage and moved from the casting

Fig. 7.2. Emplacement of the Equestrian Statue of Louis XV by Edme Bouchardon. The statue has been moved from the casting shed in a wheeled carriage. It has then been lifted by a wheeled gantry, and will now be moved over the pedestal, lowered, and emplaced on the pedestal by inserting long iron pins, extending down from the two bearing hooves into pre-drilled holes. Engraving (Mariette, 1768). Courtesy Yale University Library.

barn to a point near the pedestal. The carriage and the pedestal were enclosed in a huge wooden gantry, whose crane lifted the statue from the carriage, moved it above the pedestal, and lowered it so that its three-foot-long iron pins, extending down from the hind hoofs of the horse and the snake, could be inserted into pre-drilled holes in the granite and made fast with liquid lead. (3) The bronze letters of the inscription were molded and cast while Falconet was still in St. Petersburg. All Fel'ten had to do was attach them. (4) The snake was designed by Falconet, but its head and tail "had to be molded on the rock itself after the statue had been emplaced."[45] That task was entrusted to the Russian sculptor Fedor Gordeevich Gordeev (1744–1810), in accordance with Falconet's specifications. The cast was made by Emelian Khailov, the local founder who worked for Falconet during Operation Thunder Rock and in the casting of the *Cupid,* the *Spinario,* and the *Peter the Great.* (5) Large flagstones and curbstones to pave the area around the pedestal had to be collected in the area of Lake Ladoga and brought by boat to St. Petersburg. The job was undertaken by the local peasant Obraztsov, who delivered the stones at the end of August 1780. The grille was cast by Vegner and Veber.[46]

Backmeister reports that many distinguished persons who witnessed the emplacement of the statue on the rock saw that it was so well balanced that "even before the openings were filled with lead, it stood perfectly erect."[47] To achieve this balance Falconet did not use any visible artificial devices, such as an over-long tail touching the ground, an unnaturally wide angle of the horse's *pose bondissante,* or an added figure behind the rider. He relied instead on equal weight distribution by varying the width of the walls of the cast, making them thinner in the forepart of the horse and thicker in its croup, and by filling the tail and hind legs with iron. Falconet's concern that this might not be enough to secure the balance made him insist on providing the statue with an unnoticeable additional point of contact with the pedestal. That is why in the beginning of 1768 he got the idea of putting an "allegorical" snake under the horse's hoofs and making it arch its body in the throes of agony so as to touch the tail of the horse. Neither the tail, however, nor any part of the snake is structurally connected to the bearing parts of the armature. The enormous weight of the statue rests on just two supports, the iron cores of the hind legs of the horse.

The monument was ready to be unveiled in the beginning of 1782, but the ceremony was delayed until Sunday, August 7, which was announced as the one-hundredth anniversary of Tsar Peter's coronation.[48] To the consternation of the organizers, the day began inauspiciously. It had been raining all night and rain continued into morning. The sky was covered with dark clouds and there was a strong wind. In the early afternoon, however, the wind subsided, the sun came out, and the thousands of spectators, who from morning had been flocking to Senate Square, renamed Peter's Square for the occasion, had good reason to expect that during the rest of the day good weather would hold.[49]

The Petersburgers thronging the large square between the Admiralty and the Senate knew that they were about to witness a historic event, the dedication of the first monument ever to be erected in Russia and a joint tribute to the only two monarchs in modern Russian history who were deemed worthy of the epithet "Great." Viewing arrangements corresponded to the rank of the spectator. The empress and the highest members of the government watched the proceedings from the balcony of the Senate. The highest two ranks of courtiers and civil servants and their families were assigned front windows in the Senate building.[50] The lower ranks occupied specially built stands on three sides of the square, leaving the view of the river unobstructed. Unranked people took whatever places they could find. They stood in the windows, on the balconies, and even on the roofs of nearby buildings, they climbed the parapets of the Admiralty, they filled boats in the river and the large pontoon bridge spanning it about twenty-five feet upstream from the monument. Even the opposite bank of the Neva, from which little could be seen, was teeming with people who wanted to get a sense of participation in the unusual event.

On the Neva, huge masts of imperial warships mingled with the masts of small private boats to form a virtual forest on the water. The square itself presented an unusual sight. During the sixteen years when work on the monument was going on, the Petersburgers saw there a fenced enclosure. Now the fence was gone and in its place there was a circular canvas screen with a view of a mountain on its sides.

In the early afternoon troops began to arrive to take up their assigned positions around the square. First to line up was the Preobrazhensky Guards regiment under Lieutenant-General Prince Grigory Aleksandrovich Potemkin. Other regiments followed—the Izmailovsky Guards, the Bombardiers, the Second Artillery, the Kiev Infantry, the Novotroitsky Cuirassiers, and finally two regiments of the Guards, the Cavalry and Semenovsky. All in all there were about fifteen thousand soldiers around the monument.

At four o'clock, Field Marshal Prince Aleksandr Mikhailovich Golitsyn, who had the overall command of the festivities, arrived on horseback. After receiving reports from regimental commanders, he rode down to the pier to await the arrival of the empress. Accompanying him were his staff officers and all the members of the Senate.

Catherine the Great, who was vacationing in her summer residence in Tsarskoe Selo, returned to the capital in the morning. She had lunch in the Summer Palace and in mid-afternoon boarded a naval launch to go to Peter's Square, less than a mile downstream. The symbolism of making the short trip by water rather than overland was not lost on the throngs of waiting Petersburgers. They knew that the empress wished to manifest her devotion to the ideals of the first tsar who sought to place Russia on equal footing with the great European powers and who appreciated the importance of the navy in that quest. Just as Peter's Baltic fleet opened up the sea lanes to the North European seaports and beyond, so would Catherine's Black Sea fleet unlock the Dardanelles and allow Russian ships free passage to the Mediterranean.

The most palpable proof, however, of Catherine's resolve to remain faithful to Peter's policies was the city of St. Petersburg, which was but a gleam in Peter's eye during his lifetime, but which had since become a mighty metropolis and one of Europe's jewels. It was glittering now in the bright sunshine of the summer afternoon.

The imperial launch docked at Peter's Pier at five o'clock sharp. After a welcome from the troops, the empress proceeded on foot to the building of the Senate, accompanied by her former favorite and now the commander of the operations against Turkey, Prince Grigory Potemkin. Walking behind them were the prosecutor general, the senators, and the whole court. The cortege ascended to the second floor and came out on the balcony. The ceremonies were planned with a fine sense for theatrical effect. The empress raised her hand and, as the screens surrounding the monument dropped to the ground, the spectators saw a real mountain replacing the painted one. On top of it, as if disgorged by the mountain itself, appeared the equestrian statue of Peter the Great (fig. 7.3). The emperor, riding a rearing horse, extended his right hand toward the river, its palm wide open and turned down in a peaceful gesture. Bronze letters, hammered into the rock below him, formed an inscription, remarkably brief for the density of its symbolic charge: "To Peter the First, Catherine the Second," in Russian on the eastern face of the rock and in Latin on its western face

As soon as the statue came into view, the troops presented arms and lowered their regimental colors, while the ships hoisted their flags. At the same time, the guns of the Admiralty, the Peter and Paul Fortress, and the warships anchored in the Neva gave a triple salute. Its rumble was accompanied by musketry, the throb of drums, martial music, and rocket flares.

That was the moment when Privy Councilor General Betskoi presented the empress with a set of medals and tokens minted for the occasion, while she honored him with a large gold medal in recognition of his services "in the erection of that great structure."[51] The master of ceremonies, Matvei Fedorovich Kashtalinsky, awarded additional gold and silver medals to those who had contributed most to the construction of the monument and to the most important personalities. Noncommissioned officers and privates received bronze tokens as mementos of their participation in the unveiling ceremony. Gold medals were handed to all foreign envoys, among them the French minister plenipotentiary marquis de Vérac, who reported to the French minister of foreign affairs, Count de Vergennes: "The courageous idea [of the monument] produces an admirable effect and does the greatest honor to the genius of Sieur Falconet. It is a flattering thought for our schools of sculpture that the most beautiful monuments of this kind in Northern Europe have been executed by French artists."[52]

After reviewing the troops, the empress boarded her launch and returned to the Summer Palace and later to Tsarskoe Selo. The Petersburgers, how-

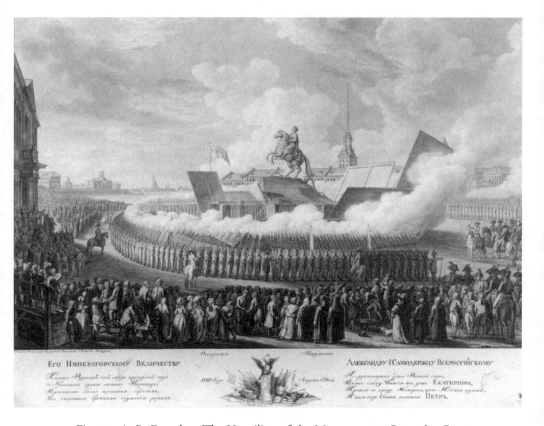

Fig. 7.3. A. P. Davydov, The Unveiling of the Monument to Peter the Great.
Engraving by A. S. Mel'nikov, 1782. The State Russian Museum, St. Petersburg.
Photograph by Mark Skomorokh.

ever, continued to celebrate late into the night, enjoying the music and the
splendid illumination of the city. Especially well lit were Peter's Square,
the buildings of the Admiralty and the Senate, and the ships in the river.
The small hut in the Petrograd section in which Peter had lived during the
first years of the construction of St. Petersburg was all ablaze with lights,
while "the monument itself was as clearly visible as in daytime."[53]

Catherine made certain that several acts of sovereign beneficence would
help mark the unveiling of the statue. Death sentences were commuted to
hard labor, and flogging sentences were commuted to deportation. There
were pardons for several categories of prisoners: convicts sentenced to hard
labor, provided they were not guilty of murder; soldiers absent without leave,
provided they returned to their units within a year or two and that the deser-
tion had occurred in Russia; and debtors to the Treasury who owed back
taxes up to five hundred rubles.[54]

Curiously, no description of the unveiling mentions the monument's consecration or indeed any participation by the dignitaries of the Orthodox church in the unveiling ceremony. If indeed they were not there, it would be a remarkable omission.

Amidst all the pomp and circumstance, the salvos from the Admiralty and the fortress, the music of the regimental bands, the fireworks from the spit of Vasilievsky Island, and the general merrymaking, it was easy to forget about the one man and woman who more than anybody else deserved to play a central role in these festivities. Falconet and Collot were not invited to the unveiling. More than that, theirs were not among the approximately five thousand names of persons awarded medals for their roles in the construction of the monument. Also missing from the list were the names of Diderot and Prince D. A. Golitsyn.[55] Carburi was not mentioned either, but he had been murdered not quite four months before. The list was prepared by Betskoi, who was basking in the limelight and savoring his revenge for years of mental torture at the hands of the obstreperous sculptor and all those who dared disregard his authority. He garnered most of the glory, with snippets distributed among inconsequential people and several of his protégés in the Bureau of Buildings.[56] It was a display of pettiness quite in keeping with the character of Betskoi.

As for Catherine, one could have expected from her some display of magnanimity and recognition for the work well done and for her friendly relations with Falconet during the first six years of his stay in St. Petersburg. But the gesture was not made, showing that the memories of the last six years had effectively overshadowed the earlier ones.

This wrong was partly redressed half a year later when, presumably upon D. A. Golitsyn's pleading, Catherine sent the sculptor two commemorative medals, one in gold for him, and one in silver for Collot. Golitsyn, who forwarded the medals to Falconet, included a citation from Catherine's secretary for cultural affairs, A. A. Bezborodko. It read among other things: "Her Imperial Majesty wishes to give Monsieur Falconet another proof of her esteem for his talents and of her appreciation of the beauty of his work here." This belated honor awakened bitter memories, and Falconet shared them ruefully with Collot: "You have not forgotten undoubtedly the covert and overt persecutions which I suffered during the whole duration of my work and you know how M. Betskoi distinguished himself in that area, how he tried to do his best to make me lose the favor of the empress. . . . Well, you see that despite so much spilled poison, she who knew us rather well has not forgotten us and at a moment when we least thought of it, we receive a token of her remembrance."[57]

Wishful thinking! Catherine was not in the habit of regurgitating the past, especially a past connected with so much bitterness. Thus, when she received the news of Falconet's death in 1791, her only comment, colored no doubt by the events of 1789, was: "I hardly paid it any attention."[58]

DENOUEMENT

LAST YEARS

> As for me, I have nothing to ask for from my native land when I
> visit it again, except a few feet of earth to cover my remains. It
> cannot refuse me that.
> —Falconet (1774)

From Riga, Falconet and Collot went to Berlin and The Hague, where
they parted company. He stayed behind, invited by Prince Golitsyn, while
she proceeded to Paris to join her husband. Falconet's program for The
Hague was to rest after twelve years of constant nervous strain and to work
on a full edition of his writings. Yet the atmosphere in the Golitsyn household was not as peaceful as Falconet might have wished. This was the time
when the Golitsyn marriage was unraveling. Princess Amalie with the children stayed much of the time in a small country house outside The Hague,
which she pointedly called *Niethuis:* "Not-at-Home." It was also a time when
strains began to develop between Golitsyn and his superiors in St. Petersburg,
chiefly because of his independent views on foreign policy, but also because
of his unfaltering loyalty to Falconet.[59]

The marriage of Collot and Pierre-Etienne Falconet was bound for the
rocks almost as soon as it was contracted. The first crack appeared in the
spring of 1778 when Pierre-Etienne went alone to Paris, leaving Marie-Anne
behind at a very advanced stage of pregnancy. The definitive rift, however,
came when Collot, with her infant Marie-Lucie, arrived in Paris in November 1778. Collot found her husband living at her expense in open concubi-
nage with a woman of ill repute. When she tried to put a stop to this conduct,
Pierre-Etienne brutally attacked her, threatening to kill her, destroy her work,
and prevent her from sculpting. He also demanded more money. Despairing
of ever being able to mend the relationship, Collot lodged a complaint with
the police, describing in graphic detail her husband's violent behavior. Here
is an excerpt of the report filed by Commissaire Gilles-Pierre Chenu on July
14, 1779:

> From that time on he made her suffer all sorts of wickedness, displaying the
> kind of violence of which she would have never thought him capable. He
> insulted her and even hit her without any reason. He tried to destroy her
> with calumnies that, in the opinion of decent people who take an interest
> in her, were shameful. He secretly traveled to Holland to visit his father and
> to warn him against her, after getting her to agree not to write to him about
> the problems in their household. Finally, he resorted to the most dreadful
> threats against her, he said that he would blow her brains out, but would
> put off her death just to make her feel the most cruel torments, that he would
> . . . chase away her visitors, break her work to pieces, etc. Three weeks ago
> he entered the apartment of the plaintiff in a fury and ordered her in the most
> frightening way to leave the house quickly or he would not be responsible for
> what might happen during the outbursts of anger that her presence called

forth. These words were followed by the most horrifying threats to poison or assassinate her, and she was lucky to be able to escape his violence by retreating to a room with a locked door.[60]

Jules-Jean Guiffrey, editor of the published text of Collot's complaint to the police, comments: "Need one look for another reason for the aversion of [Pierre-Etienne] Falconet for his wife, than the rumor . . . according to which intimate relations had existed between the teacher and his disciple before she married Pierre-Etienne Falconet? The latter's precipitous departure for France a short time before his wife's delivery, his strange conduct toward her, the separation, the menaces, the violent acts . . . would suggest that Falconet's son had become aware of the rumors circulating on the nature of the relations between his father and Mlle Collot."[61]

That would, of course, be the most obvious reason for the hostility with which Pierre-Etienne greeted his wife in Paris. Could it be possible, however, that he was not aware of the situation at the time of his marriage to Collot, when all of Paris and probably all of St. Petersburg had known and talked about it for years? Would not Pierre-Etienne's sudden realization that he did not have unlimited access to his wife's wealth offer a more persuasive explanation for this frightening explosion of rage? Unfortunately, we will never know for certain what it was that happened between the spouses in 1778, because the only document to survive from that period, outside Collot's police complaint, is a letter of June 8, 1779, from Falconet *père* to Collot which gives no additional revelations about their relationship.

That letter is, however, the only truly personal piece of correspondence between Falconet *père* and Collot to survive the annihilating purge of Marie-Lucie intended to protect her mother's reputation. That is why it possesses exceptional value for the history of the relationship and should be studied with special attention. A careful reading of the letter shows clearly that Réau was off the mark when he tried to prove the absence of a close relationship between Falconet *père* and Collot by characterizing the two surviving letters from Falconet as "very respectful and in no way betraying a former lover."[62] Quite the contrary! The letter of June 8 contains a number of indications attesting to the intimate nature of the relationship, including references to personal tidbits, a colloquial and informal style, and, above all, Falconet's effort to keep the letter confidential by sending it to his friend, the Paris notary Louis-Jacques Baron Jr., with instructions to hand-deliver it to Collot *(en mains propres à Mme Falconet).*[63]

The letter consists of eleven paragraphs

> Madame and dear daughter, I received your letter on May 4, upon my return from Amsterdam. We made a lovely trip a few days ago. We traveled through many places and stayed overnight in others. We also made a small voyage of about sixty to eighty leagues against the wind. I paid the tribute which you know so well. On the return leg, I had no trace of discomfort. Everybody felt wonderful.

The form of address "Madame and dear daughter" is the only part of the letter, which may be termed "very respectful." "Madame" need not, however, indicate anything beyond a usage practiced even between husband and wife. As for "dear daughter," this may be nothing more than a jocular form of address to his daughter-in-law thirty-two years his junior. The rest of the paragraph (indeed, of the whole letter) is anything but formal, especially the reference to Falconet's seasickness, presumably well known to Collot. The group traveling with Falconet was most probably the Golitsyn family, the prince and the princess and their two children Dmitry and Mimi.

> Those miserable trunks have finally arrived and here's how. Three were not soaked at all, and the books are all there, just as we packed them in St. Petersburg. But the others are in the most pitiful condition and their content is what may be called putrid. I've lost half of my books, including a box which has disappeared, I don't know where and how. But fortunately your coffee mill has not been damaged at all and you'll find it safe and sound. Your marble head has arrived and as for your plasters, it's curious to see how seawater has worked on them. You'll see them. As for your washstand, don't think about it any more. You'll burn it if you wish. Don't forget to bring whatever small keys you have. The medal case and its content have arrived in good condition. When you see M. Simon, tell him to follow my example and be content with his small package of books and not to count [on anything else]. I have some portfolios with drawings and engravings. The rest is either rotted or lost. And so, let's be content with our debris and the money which I'll have to throw after it.

Aside from its personal tone and total familiarity with the possessions of Collot, including her coffee mill and washstand, this paragraph shows that Collot's decision to join Falconet in The Hague was not taken on the spur of the moment, after an especially violent confrontation with her husband. A full month before Collot lodged her complaint with the police, Falconet was already prepared for her arrival. Their luggage, which had been shipped from St. Petersburg to Copenhagen, reached The Hague at the beginning of June 1779, but Collot placed her personal things in storage in Copenhagen, apparently because she was uncertain of her future in Paris. M. Simon was probably Falconet's molder who was with them in St. Petersburg.

> My advice is that you make light of the idea of my rumored marriage in The Hague. Pretend not to know anything about it. Pretend to be a simpleton who believes in everything and you'll have the pleasure to see how far the fools and idlers can push their nonsense. They are always the same and we won't remake them. When that is all the mischief they cause, they make us laugh and show themselves for what they are.

The reference to Falconet's presumed marriage in The Hague was certainly the oddest bit of gossip being spread about him in Paris. If its object was to upset Collot, it was clearly successful, for Falconet had to do his best to calm Collot down.

[Falconet describes the progress of the monument in St. Petersburg and the preparation of his writings for publication.]

Princess [Golitsyn] will probably leave around the beginning of August. She might only make one trip at that time. In any case, before she leaves, she'll take care of our concerns with the prince and princess of Orange. So be reassured, take care of your business, and don't delay long after that. Are you crazy with your fears and timidity about writing to Princess Golitsyn? Write to her without delay. Whatever you write will be fine and will be very well received.

Falconet's and Collot's common concerns most probably involved a commission for the busts of the Stadholder William the Fifth of Orange and his wife Frederica Wilhelmina of Prussia which Collot did in 1782.[64] Collot's unwillingness to write to Princess Golitsyn may have been caused by fears that her prospective reunion with Falconet *père* might appear shocking. Having spent a few months with the Golitsyns and having become aware of the princess's affair with Hemsterhuis, Falconet knew better and encouraged Collot to write her without any compunctions.

[Falconet describes his visit to Amsterdam to see two paintings by Bartholomeus van der Helst (1613–70) in City Hall.] I wished you were there, but we'll see them together.

[Falconet describes negotiations with the Lausanne publisher of his collected works. They appeared in 1781.]

No, I'll never believe that "you coddle yourself." I have seen enough of the opposite and more than once was angry about it. You need not exaggerate, but you should nevertheless take care of your health. You need it for many reasons, particularly to watch over the upbringing of your child, which, I'm sure, you won't neglect.

The personal concerns expressed in this paragraph show Falconet as more caring than his previous actions and writings would lead one to expect.

[Falconet instructs Collot how to transship her trunks from Copenhagen to The Hague.]

I have nothing more to tell you about your progress to the Académie for I see that you behave well and that you now see the differences in the people whom you meet on your way. Whether you achieve it or not, rest assured that my affection for you will always be the same. Do likewise and you'll make up for the annoyances which are otherwise troubling to me. We'll see if your Mashenka will be clever enough to recognize my round hat and my small wig. I don't think so, even though she played with it a lot during the trip. By the way, a letter from Madame Blemar was misunderstood in St. Petersburg and convinced people there that Mashenka died in Berlin.

This paragraph is couched in Aesopian language. Falconet connects Collot's attempts to be received in the Académie with some unidentifiable persons. Could one of them be Diderot, with whom Collot remained on friendly terms? Falconet assures Collot of his unalterable affection and asks for the same. Could the "annoyances" have something to do with Pierre-Etienne? The only concretely identifiable event is Mashenka's playing with Falconet's hat and wig during their trip together from St. Petersburg.

> Adieu, keep on getting better. Give my regards to Monsieur Baron. When you leave Paris, try not to be in a bad mood and, if you are, show it as little as possible to [your husband].[65]
> Your father and friend, Falconet.

That is hardly a letter that can be called "very respectful and in no way betraying a former lover."

The rift between Collot and Falconet *fils* was by then complete, and in July 1779 Collot and Mashenka left for The Hague, where they were reunited with Falconet *père*. Away from the cares of the failed marriage and the big-city bustle, Collot returned immediately to sculpting. By mid-August she had almost completed a bust of Princess Golitsyn which struck the philosopher Frans Hemsterhuis as being extraordinarily successful.[66] At about the same time, Collot did busts of Prince William V of Orange and his wife Frederica, and somewhat later produced a remarkable bust of Dr. Petrus Camper, in gratitude for his having inoculated Marie-Lucie against smallpox. Doctor Camper wrote her an effusive letter of thanks. Its last lines read: "Please give my respects to your father[-in-law]. Assure that esteemed *vieillard* of my regard and friendship. I'll never forget the pleasure of his conversation, always instructive, nor the honor of his friendship."[67] That esteemed *vieillard* was sixty-five at the time.

In October 1780 Falconet *père*, Collot, and Marie-Lucie returned to Paris. Falconet had given his old house on the rue d'Anjou to Pierre-Etienne and Collot as a wedding gift. Now that Collot was not willing to claim co-ownership with her husband, the trio had to look for a place to live. As their first domicile Falconet rented a house in the Paris suburb of Châtenay.

The following three years were certainly the quietest of Falconet's life. Although the monument to Peter the Great had not been engraved, enough people visited St. Petersburg to bear witness to its beauty and originality. They also brought along a multitude of stories about Falconet's accomplishments and adventures there. True or false, serious or piquant, they all helped to surround the sculptor with an aura of success and notoriety. His former colleagues in the Académie were quite willing to forget about his old image of a conceited grouch, while the new generation of painters and sculptors saw him as a venerable maître, whose artistic success and international reputation could only bring glory to the Académie.

Falconet, however, remained true to his vow that the monument to Peter the Great would be his last work of sculpture. Besides, as he had amply demonstrated in St. Petersburg, he had an aversion to teaching. Turning down an invitation to resume his former professorial post, he asked for, and, on December 2, 1780, was granted the status of professor emeritus.[68] He did, however, accept a largely honorary appointment as adjunct president *(adjoint-recteur)* of the Académie.

In retirement Falconet stayed in virtual isolation from the artistic milieu in Paris, living mostly in Châtenay and devoting himself to writing.[69] Collot, however, spent more time in Paris, where she and Falconet kept an apartment. The addresses changed frequently: rue de la Lune near Porte St. Denis, rue des Fossoyeurs (now rue Servandoni) in the Luxembourg section, quai des Théatins (now quai Voltaire), and rue Le Regrattier on the Ile Saint-Louis.

With the monument to Peter the Great finally installed and gathering international acclaim, Falconet was ready to make the trip he had dreamed of all his life—a visit to Florence, Venice, and especially Rome, where he would see at last the "real" *Marcus Aurelius,* the object of his most vehement critique and cause of interminable vexation and anguish. It was to be a trip of one year's duration, obliging Falconet to ask for a leave absence from the new director of the Bâtiments du Roi, Count d'Angiviller. The leave was granted on May 3, 1783, which was also the day when Falconet and Collot were to start their trip. The fates, however, ruled otherwise, as Falconet's good friend, the painter Jean-Baptiste Robin movingly describes:

> Since the casting of his colossal work, [Falconet] had announced that he would renounce sculpture forever and that he would busy himself solely with a revision of his writings. Yet, whatever he did, art alone warmed his heart and although he did not practice it any longer, his passion for it lost none of its power. He yielded to it by hoping to execute a project, long in planning—to travel through Italy in order to admire and examine the works of art in their sanctuary. Everything was prepared for the trip, which was supposed to begin with Switzerland. The carriage was ordered and the departure was set for Monday, May 3, 1783, when, two days earlier, as he was standing in front of the fireplace, [Falconet] collapsed into his armchair, stricken by paralysis, which deprived him of the use of half of his body.[70]

The massive stroke, which paralyzed Falconet's right side and seriously impaired his speech, left his intellect intact. He was able to read and learned to write and draw with his left hand. He was, however, unable to walk and was forced to give up his refuge in Châtenay and move to the very heart of Paris, to his house on the rue Le Regrattier where, according to Lévesque, he never left his room: "Others in his place would have gone out in good weather, especially since his resources permitted him to have a carriage. But he, who had always maintained that people get sick through their fault only and that they would enjoy unfailing health if only they followed the laws of nature, took simple meals, drank little wine, and no coffee or hard liquor.

Ashamed to be sick, he did not want to be seen, except by a small number of friends."[71]

And so, he stayed inside, more cranky and demanding than ever, with Collot sacrificing the prime years of her life and her artistic career in order to be at his side. Those who were allowed to visit the stricken man admired the extraordinary devotion with which she attended to Falconet's needs during the eight years of his slow extinction: "Let me . . . pay public tribute of admiration to Madame Falconet, his daughter-in-law. During the course of that long and debilitating sickness . . . she never ceased giving her maître, later father-in-law, the help that no one but servants and nurses can be expected to render, and that only the sensitivity and deftness of a woman can provide to the sick. She, who could have enjoyed in peace the fruit of her labors, sacrificed all in this honorable cause, animated by a spirit of attachment and gratitude whose ardor not even tears could extinguish."[72]

Much patience and even more affection were required to humor the moody patient: "The naturally difficult nature of the healthy Falconet became much worse during his sickness and he often seemed to derive malicious pleasure in demanding care that was not needed. One could be sure that he would have a pressing need of the services of his daughter-in-law whenever he suspected that she was receiving friends or that she allowed herself some distraction."[73]

After reading these passages, can one have any doubts about the depth and sincerity of Collot's affection for her beloved maître and companion?

In January 1790 Falconet's seniority entitled him to take over the post of *Recteur* of the Académie, but he had to decline the nomination.[74] Death came a year later, on January 24, 1791, when Falconet was seventy-five.[75] He was buried in the churchyard of the nearby Saint-Louis en l'Isle. The upheavals of the Revolution have effaced any trace of his grave.

AFTERMATH

> To the memory of Maurice Falconet, former *recteur* of the French Académie and member of the Academy of St. Petersburg, creator of the statue of Peter the Great; his son Pierre Falconet, amateur painter; and Marie-Anne Collot Falconet, his daughter-in-law, member of the Academy of St. Petersburg, owner of the estate of Marimont where she is buried.
> —Memorial plaque in the chapel of Marimont

Falconet's will favored Collot over Pierre-Etienne.[76] She received, as a separate bequest and thereby excluded from the estate, all of Falconet's books, drawings, engravings, and gold and silver medals, whose value was appraised at 4,660 livres.[77] The rest of the estate, appraised at 260,000 livres, was divided into two halves, one going to Pierre-Etienne, and the other to Collot, with a proviso that upon her death her inheritance would pass to her daughter, Marie-Lucie. Collot received also the rest of Falconet's personal belongings and was appointed executrix of the will. That left to Pierre-Etienne only that portion of the estate that could not have been withheld from him under French law, while Collot and Marie-Lucie became Falconet's principal heirs.[78]

Pierre-Etienne Falconet had but a few months to enjoy his inheritance. He died of unknown causes on June 25, 1791. In a space of a few months Collot became a double widow, losing the man she loved, but who would not be her husband, and the man who would be her husband, but whom she could not love.

The outbreak of the Revolution filled Collot with terror. Her long stay in Russia, and the favors shown to her by Catherine the Great, placed her unequivocally in the ranks of the "enemies of the people." Forced to stay in Paris by Falconet's affliction, she became an involuntary witness of the bloody excesses going on around her. The sight of the bloodied head of Princess de Lamballe, a friend of Marie-Antoinette, being carried at the tip of a pike by a band of sans-culottes in front of her windows must have made Collot fear for her own life. It may not have been enough to make her pine for the regimented order of St. Petersburg, but it certainly was enough to convince her that she had to get away from the frenzy sweeping Paris. She could have gone in the footsteps of the painter Elisabeth-Louise Vigée-Lebrun and chosen the difficult path of emigration, but with a thirteen-year-old daughter in her sole care, her options were limited. She set her sights on Lorraine, which, though formally a part of France, retained administrative and cultural autonomy. In 1791 she bought Marimont, an estate of more than twelve hundred acres about thirty miles northeast of Nancy. There she settled to lead a life of landed gentry, made comfortable by her personal fortune brought out of Russia and enlarged by her inheritance from Falconet.

As for sculpture, not since the bust of Dr. Camper in The Hague had she had an opportunity to work with the modeling knife. In former days it was Falconet's sickness which had occupied her thoughts and time. Now, without Falconet at her side, she lost all desire to take up her old calling. Her professional career had lasted a mere seventeen years, a remarkably short time for an artist who accomplished so much.

No sooner had Collot and Marie-Lucie settled in their new domicile than they became aware of a young man, Stanislas Jankovitz, who had recently returned from Paris to his native Lunéville.[79] Stanislas was then twenty-nine, a confirmed royalist with many political accomplishments to his credit. Lunéville being close to Marimont, the paths of Stanislas and Marie-Lucie crossed soon. Although Marie-Lucie had not yet turned fifteen, Stanislas asked for her hand in marriage. Given the young man's noble origins and Marimont's isolation during those most uncertain times, Collot consented to the match, and on New Year's Eve of 1792 the wedding was held in the chapel of Marimont. Stanislas, who until then had lived with his mother in Lunéville, moved to Marimont. On February 23, 1806, fourteen years after the marriage was contracted, a son, Anselme, was born. Despite Marie-Lucie's hopes for a large family, he was to remain the only child of the union, doted upon by his parents and two grandmothers.

In 1815 Collot, always a fervent supporter of the ancien régime, could rejoice in the return to normalcy. The Revolution had come and gone, the Empire had come and gone, and the reinstatement of the Bourbons carried with it a promise of peace and security. Her last years must have been the most serene of her entire life. She moved to Nancy, leaving the château of Marimont to Marie-Lucie and Stanislas, but visited them frequently, enjoying the political activities of her son-in-law, who served as a deputy from the department of Meurthe, and watching her grandson develop into a bright youth, devoted to the region and active in local charities. She died in Nancy on February 23, 1821, at the age of seventy-three.

Collot's death spared her the knowledge of a personal tragedy that was to befall Marie-Lucie and Stanislas. Anselme and a group of friends were out hunting on the grounds of Marimont. As Anselme was remounting his horse, a gun strapped to the saddle went off accidentally, shattering his knee. A tetanus infection set in and within thirteen days, on January 22, 1830, Anselme, not yet twenty-four, was dead. He was the last male descendant of Falconet.

Undoubtedly, because Anselme was the only child and his arrival was so eagerly awaited, his sudden loss left his parents emotionally ravaged. They could no longer stay all the time in Marimont, where every detail of the house and the grounds reminded them of their son. Versailles offered an escape. They bought a house there and made it their chief place of residence. The Revolution of 1830 gave Stanislas a pretext to withdraw from active politics and retreat into private life. At the age of sixty-seven, without a natural heir, he was concerned about finding a family member who could legally replace his son. The Polish line of the Jankovitzes having become extinguished with the death of Anselme, Stanislas turned his attention to his Hungarian relatives.

Hungary was not a strange country to Stanislas. Back in 1786, when Louis XVI imposed a high tax on commoners, he had traveled there to obtain a certificate of his family's nobility.[80] During that visit, he established ties with the Hungarian branch of the family. Now he was going to renew them and bring back a successor. His choice for an adopted son fell on his distant relative, Vincent de Jankovitz. At the time of his arrival in Versailles in 1842, Vincent was twenty-two.[81]

When Stanislas died in Versailles on June 15, 1847, at the age of eighty-four, it was assumed that Vincent de Jankovitz would be his sole heir. Marie-Lucie, however, who survived her husband by nineteen years, had other ideas. Vincent bore no physical or spiritual resemblance to her adored son. Unlike Anselme, who devoted his life to the region of Marimont and its peasantry,

Vincent moved to Paris, where he threw himself into the social whirlwind of receptions and balls. Bored by the capital, he traveled to Algeria, Switzerland, and Greece, took up painting, and got married as soon as he returned to Versailles. To Marie-Lucie he seemed a total stranger, especially when she compared him to another young man who lived nearby, Count François de Warren of Nancy. As Anselme's best childhood friend, François was a frequent visitor to Marimont and had come to be regarded as a family member. He now replaced Anselme in Marie-Lucie's heart, and upon her death in Versailles on January 1, 1866, at the age of eighty-seven, emerged as her main beneficiary and executor of her testament.[82]

Among the objects inherited by François were plaster casts of Falconet's *Cupid* and of Collot's bust of Falconet, made for Catherine the Great in St. Petersburg, as well as a marble of Collot's head of Mary Cathcart, also made in St. Petersburg. In the bequest there were several family portraits by Falconet *fils*, one of Collot (fig. 7.4), two of Marie-Lucie (fig. 7.5), and one of Falconet *père*. The objets d'art also included a wooden chest wrapped in a lattice of leather straps, identified as Peter the Great's own handiwork, and a heart-shaped black Chinese lacquer box in which Catherine the Great had kept her personal correspondence.

The remainder of the inheritance of Marie-Lucie was divided among three

Fig. 7.4. Pierre-Etienne Falconet, *Marie-Anne Collot*. Pencil and pastel, 1785. Private collection.

Fig. 7.5. Pierre-Etienne Falconet, *Marie-Lucie Falconet*. Pencil and pastel, 1785. On the obverse: "Mlle. Falconet en 1785, agée de 7 ans. Dessinée à Chatenay par son père. Elle fut plus tard la baronne de Jankowitz, morte en 1869" (actually, 1866). Private collection.

other beneficiaries. Copies of letters from Catherine and Betskoi to Falconet and most of the personal gifts from Catherine to Falconet were returned to Russia through the good offices of Baron A. F. Budberg, then ambassador of Russia in Paris. Most of the art collection, including the drawing of the monument to Peter the Great by Losenko (fig. 3.6), the terracotta busts of Falconet *père* and Falconet *fils* by Collot, the oil portrait of Collot by Falconet *fils* (fig. 1.11), and his self-portrait (fig. 5.2) were left to the Musée des Beaux Arts in Nancy. The bequest to Vincent de Jankovitz was modest, but it did include several drawings by Falconet *fils,* among them the all-important portrait of Prince D. A. Golitsyn.[83]

During the Allied offensive in the fall of 1944, the château of Marimont burned to the ground. The only structure left standing on the grounds of the estate is a chapel-mausoleum in the park with the tombs of Collot, Anselme de Jankovitz, and Marie-Lucie. A memorial plaque, whose text serves as the epigraph to this section,[84] provides the coda to the lives of Falconet *père,* Collot, and Falconet *fils,* the three French protagonists of the drama of the Bronze Horseman.

8

The Monument

CONCEIT

In this production [Falconet] has united the greatest simplicity with the truest sublimity of conception. No other statue, whether ancient or modern, gave him the design, which is singular in its kind, and is admirably adapted to express the character of the man and the nation over which he reigned.
—Nathaniel Wraxall Jr. (1776)

Before Falconet's monument to Peter the Great, there was only one free-standing bronze equestrian monument with a rearing horse, Pietro Tacca's *King Philip IV of Spain* (1640) in the royal park of Buen Retiro near Madrid. Being the first of a genre is, however, its only distinction. With an oversize tail hanging straight down and reaching the pedestal, the horse rears at a forty-five-degree angle, in a pose that resembles the mezair in equitation exercises. The rider is stiff and ramrod-straight in the saddle, and the baton in his outstretched right hand looks more like the equilibristic aid of a tight-rope walker than a symbol of royal power. The horse, in spite of its rearing stance and flowing mane, appears static. Its equilibrium, however, has proved secure, a tribute to Galileo, who, according to tradition, helped the sculptor with his calculations.

Other sculptors had, to be sure, plans for equestrian statues with rearing horses, but none was executed full-size. They exist in drawings or greatly reduced models. The best known among such projects are the sketches of Leonardo da Vinci for the equestrian monuments to Duke Francesco Sforza and the tomb of Gian Giacomo Trivulzio. Attributed to Leonardo is a terracotta model of an equestrian statue in the Budapest Museum of Fine Arts, dated to the beginning of the sixteenth century and said to represent the future King Francis I of France. It is a Baroque sculpture showing a helmeted but otherwise naked youth riding bareback on a wildly contorted stallion that recoils from some unseen danger. The crouching stance of the horse, with its hind hooves placed directly below the neck and head, assures the equilibrium of the statue. There exist also small bronze models of the equestrian statue of Louis XIV by Martin Desjardins, commissioned by the city of Aix-en-Provence. As shown in a model in the museum of Waddesdon Manor near London, the statue was secured by the overlong tail of the horse attached to the pedestal, and had a winged Victory fastened to the rider's back and the croup of the horse for counterbalance.[1]

Falconet, by contrast, was dedicated to the proposition that art, without copying nature, should not falsify it. As he said in his programmatic "Réflexions sur la sculpture," cited here in Tooke's translation of 1777,

> Whatever the imagination of the Sculptor can create of the most majestic, of the most sublime, of the most uncommon, ought to be only the expression of the possible appearances of Nature, of her effects, of her sports, of her accidents. . . . The Beautiful, even the ideal Beautiful in Sculpture as in Painting, should be nothing else than the result of the real Beautiful of Nature. . . . Above all things, Sculpture is the enemy of those forced attitudes which Nature disavows and which some artists have employed without necessity, and only to shew that they could sport with Design. . . . The more the efforts that are made to move us are discoverable, the less are we moved by them. Whence we are to conclude that the fewer means an artist employs to produce an effect, the greater is his merit in producing it, and the spectator delivers himself up the more implicitly to the impression which it was intended to make upon him.[2]

Hence Falconet's refusal to make use of unnatural and easily decipherable props to stabilize his equestrian monument. Hence his desire to come up not only with a novel artistic program, but with original engineering solutions: never before was a rearing bronze horse given such a small angle of inclination; never before was such an enormous mass of metal allowed to rest on two frail supports, the hind legs of the horse; never before was the pedestal designed as an integral part of the monument; never before did a sculptor, rather than a professional founder, successfully cast such a colossal bronze statue by the single-jet technique.[3] To cite the Russian art critic Vladimir Stasov, the monument "goes far beyond anything of this kind that was done before. . . . Looking at it one feels that . . . it is separated by peaks and chasms from contemporary eighteenth-century art."[4]

Important as these innovations are, they alone do not constitute the monument's guiding idea or its conceit, if one may use a somewhat archaic, but useful term. To understand what that conceit is, the existing documentation on the progress of the work on the monument—chiefly Falconet's correspondence with Catherine the Great—does not suffice. The monument materializes before our eyes like a jack-in-the-box, and the intended functions of its elements must be reconstructed from internal evidence, that is, from an analysis of their interdependence in the context of the completed work (see figs. 8.1–8.5, 8.9).[5]

Falconet's ideas on art were not beholden to a single style. His masters were the great artists of the Baroque, Bernini and Puget, and his first works,

Fig. 8.1. Etienne-Maurice Falconet, Monument to Peter the Great.
Photograph by L. Bogdanov.

especially the *Milo of Crotona* (figs. 1.2 and 1.3) and *Christ on the Mount of Olives* (fig. 1.5) bear a clear imprint of their influence. Later, however, in such works as the *Cupid* (fig. 1.8) and dozens of terracotta models which he did for the Sèvres Manufacture, Falconet worked in the idiom of the Rococo, in the manner of Boucher. At the same time, one can see in some of his work, especially the *Winter* (fig. 2.4), an anticipation of Neoclassicism. Though unwilling to accept Winckelmann's assumption of the necessary superiority of Greek art, Falconet heeded the call of the Ancients for simplicity and naturalness, for stripping art of the superfluous and affected. In the *Peter the Great,* Falconet's last and greatest work, the dignified Neoclassical posture of the tsar coexists with the Baroque restlessness of the rearing horse and the fluid wave-like shape of the pedestal.

To give his monument meaning, Falconet did not look to the hackneyed symbols of Baroque allegory, even though allegorical embellishments were still the fashion of the day and were urged on Falconet by all around him— except, significantly, the empress. In France, among the best-known examples of allegorical exuberance was Pigalle's monument to Louis XV in Reims. Falconet admired greatly the execution of the individual figures on that monument, but rejected their intended illustrative function. In Russia, Rastrelli's luxuriant projects for a monument to Peter the Great appealed greatly to Betskoi, a convinced fancier of allegory.

Even Diderot, who was known to be a severe critic of excessive symbolism in art, urged Falconet to turn his monument into a fountain, with water gushing from the pedestal into a pool surrounded by a full complement of crudely allegorical imagery: "Let me see Barbarity, her hair half-tousled and half-braided, her body covered with an animal skin, scared and almost trampled by your hero's steed, rolling her frantic eyes and threatening him. On one side, let me see the Love of the Peoples, her arms raised toward the legislator, following him with her eyes, and extending to him her blessings. On the other side, let me see a symbolic figure of the Nation, lying down and quietly enjoying comfort, rest, and security."[6]

But Falconet would have none of that. He envisioned a monument that would not be encumbered with allegorical imagery: "Barbarity, Peoples' Love, a symbol of the Nation will not be there at all. . . . Peter the Great is his own subject and his own attribute. All one has to do is show it. I insist, therefore, on my conception of this hero, whom I do not envision as a great military leader or a conqueror, even though he certainly was one, but more importantly, as a builder, a legislator, a benefactor of his country. A sculptor who knows how much a sovereign has deserved of his people should show all his virtues in a single image."[7]

"In a single image": that is one of the keys to Falconet's conceit of the monument. Here is how he phrased his views on allegory in a letter dealing with commemorative medals: "One should suppress, nay, eliminate totally if possible, those embarrassing, cold, ambiguous [allegorical] figures, that sterile abundance, which lays bare routine, but seldom genius. . . . Isn't history the subject of a medal? Make, then, a picture of history. Does one need allegory for that? Express it by emblems endowed with their own intrinsic meaning—there are so many of them! Draw them from your subject. It will always furnish them to you, if you know how to find them without an appeal to emblematic figures. . . . I love simple ideas, they often say more than complicated and far-fetched ones."[8]

That is not a denial of the role of allegory in art. It is a refusal to appeal to special props in order to express figurative meanings, to spoon-feed viewers with ready-made and easily assimilated imagery. Falconet designed his monument as a riddle, challenging the viewer to solve it and become thereby an active participant in the creative process. The discovered interpretations, whether intended or not, amplify and enrich the monument's symbolism. Falconet himself explicated some of the condensed and allusive ways of that kind of allegory: "My tsar holds no baton. He extends his benevolent right hand toward the land over which he gallops. He climbs the rock which is both his pedestal and the emblem of the difficulties he had to overcome. The fatherly hand, the gallop onto the steep rock—that is the theme assigned to me by Peter the Great. Nature and man placed in his way the most awe-some obstacles. He overcame them with the strength and tenacity of his genius."[9] (See figs. 8.1, 8.2, 8.9.)

Falconet's horse is usually described as galloping, even by the sculptor himself. Yet, it is shown in an attitude that has been referred to as rearing, although it does not raise itself high enough for the pose to fully qualify as such. More appropriate would be the French term *pose bondissante,* that is, a stance that resembles a levade in formal dressage (figs. 8.2, 8.3). Whatever the term, however, a horse standing on its hind legs cannot be said to be galloping. Nor is the position of the horseman compatible with a gallop.

Fig. 8.2. E.-M. Falconet, Monument to Peter the Great.
Photograph by L. Bogdanov.

Fig. 8.3. E.-M. Falconet, Monument to Peter the Great (detail).
Photograph by A. M. Schenker.

The tsar is sitting erect on a bearskin instead of a conventional saddle, he
has no stirrups to help him hold his balance, his legs are pushed forward
(fig. 8.4). The head is raised high and turned to the right, the right arm is
extended; his cape is not wind-blown, but falls gently off his shoulders (fig.
8.2). He holds the reins with his left hand, but is not pulling at them, for
the horse's head is also turned slightly to the right (figs. 8.3, 8.5). Had the
horse been galloping, the tsar's torso would have been leaning forward and
his legs would have been pushed back.

How then did the perception of a gallop arise? We know that Falconet
drew hundreds of sketches of accomplished horsemen riding up a mound
and making the horse stop suddenly on top. That combination of a sloping
runway and the horse in the *pose bondissante* allowed the sculptor to show
simultaneously the initial and final moments of an action, endowing a purely
static situation with a temporal dimension. By fusing these two fragments
into one image, Falconet obtained an illusion of continuous action, converting a single exposure into a moving picture. Seeing a rising path and the
horse's abrupt stop, the viewer is forced to conclude that he is witnessing
the culminating moment of a gallop when a horse must raise its forelegs in
order to stop without toppling head over heels. It is like an insect embalmed
in a piece of amber, its spread wings making it seem alive.

While lending the image a temporal dimension, the *pose bondissante* adds
also an element of instability and anticipation. The viewer wants to know

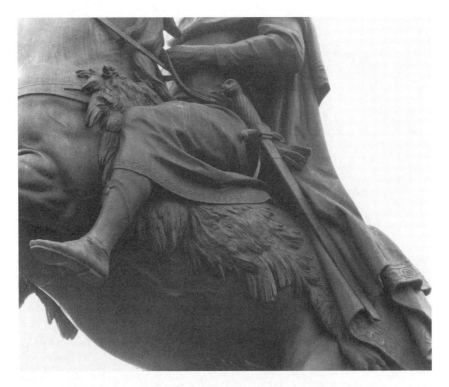

Fig. 8.4. E.-M. Falconet, Monument to Peter the Great (detail).
Photograph by L. Bogdanov.

not only where the impetuous run up the hill began, but, more important, where it will end. What will be the tsar's next move? The raised forelegs, hanging over the edge of the cliff, suspend the action and open up a large number of possible outcomes. Will the tsar turn his horse around and trot to the stable, will he guide it on, or will he let himself be taken toward an unknown future?

An unresolved action or situation, suspended literally and figuratively in midair—that is the principal idea of the monument, its conceit. To express it, the sculptor organized the monument on the principle of binary opposi-tions, contrasting freedom and constraint, rest and motion, passivity and activity, calm and agitation. Hence the monument's unstable equilibrium, endowing it with a sense of drama, ambiguity, and uncertainty.

The opposition between the horse and the horseman literally springs at the viewer. The horse, with its raised forelegs, open mouth, and wild gaze, is pre-Romantic in its agitation. The horseman, by contrast, in his classical mantle and a laurel wreath, is imperiously still. He is erect, his eyes fixed on distant horizons, undisturbed by the wild leap of the horse and uncon-cerned by the dangers which may be lying just beyond the lip of the crag.

Fig. 8.5. E.-M. Falconet, Monument to Peter the Great (detail). Photograph by L. Bogdanov.

The sharp precipice and the gentle slope, as well as the leaping animal and the impassive stone, provide another instance of the opposition between movement and quiescence. Spontaneity constrained, free will circumscribed by necessity—these contrasts are given shape when the seemingly limitless freedom of the horseman is suddenly checked by the cliff and the precipice looming beyond it. The tsar is free to gallop over his land, but his freedom is not total. There comes a moment when danger ahead forces him to rein in his horse.

Struggle between Earth and Water, so meaningful in St. Petersburg, is another instance of these binary oppositions. It manifests itself in the contrast between the matter of the pedestal and its shape. The granite rock may be perceived as condensed essence of the earth with which the pedestal forms an unbroken continuum.[10] Its shape, however, bringing to mind an immense sea wave about to break upon the shore, contrasts with the rock's solidity.

By endowing the monument with an aura of ambiguity, Falconet did more than enrich its internal semantic texture. He reached outside the monument and challenged the viewers to draw a parallel between the precariously balanced tsar and the Russia created by him, a community that had lost its sense of wholeness and social harmony in a contest between the forces of modernization and the staying power of conservatism, between an open and a closed society, between an autocrat and an enlightened ruler. These contending forces went on to play a major role in the social upheavals which befell Russia in the nineteenth and twentieth centuries and which unhappily remain unresolved to this day. In that sense, the binary structure of the monument exposed the rawest nerve of Russian sensitivity.

How did Falconet intuit the presence of these opposing forces? How did he sense that St. Petersburg was a foreign graft on the skin of Russia, a hothouse plant expected to take root in the acidic soil of the north? What was it that prepared him to comprehend the ambiguity of Peter's heritage and capture it in a single image? Was it the reading of Voltaire's *Histoire de l'empire de Russie sous Pierre le Grand,* and his conversations with Diderot and Prince D. A. Golitsyn? In the absence of memoirs or notes on work in progress, this quandary cannot be resolved. But even if it could, the answer would be of little consequence. What matters is that in his monument Falconet created a seismograph that registered the power of the earthquake that shook Russia to its core.

The monument has the shape of an acute-angled triangle, bisected into the trapezoid base and the smaller acute-angled triangle which is the bronze statue proper.[11] The long side of the triangle runs from the tsar's head at the apex, along the back of the tsar's mantle, the croup and the tail of the horse, and merges with the gentle slope of the granite rock. The short side has two large concavities. The upper one is formed by the indentation running from the horse's muzzle to the front hoofs. The lower indentation echoes the upper one by running from the lip of the granite rock down to its base.

As it appears today, the monument stands in the northwestern corner of Decembrists Square (formerly Senate Square), approximately three hundred feet from the Neva. On one side is the building of the Senate, on the other is the Admiralty with its celebrated golden needle, and behind it is the green backdrop of the Admiralty Garden, with the golden dome of St. Isaac's looming in the background. The area in front of the monument used to look different from its modern appearance. Just a few yards upstream, the Neva was spanned by the Isakievsky pontoon bridge leading to Vasilievsky Island. This wide and busy bridge was an important element in the monument's ensemble. It symbolized the conquest of the river and provided a large thoroughfare through which a steady stream of pedestrian and vehicular traffic gave the monument an aspect of centrality and connectedness to the right-bank sections of the city. It justified Peter's gallop and linked the tsar to his favorite buildings on University Embankment—the Kunstkammer, the Academy of Sciences, the Twelve Colleges, and the Menshikov Palace. It also extended the area from which the monument could be viewed. When, in the second half of the nineteenth century, the Isakievsky Bridge was moved to where the present Palace Bridge is located, well beyond the horseman's field of vision, the monument found itself deprived of its former active role in the daily life of the city.

Yet, being shunted a bit to the side has lent the monument greater majesty and has provided the viewer with a calmer environment from which to examine elements of its composition as they appear from different aspects. That is an important advantage, given Falconet's belief that "if [the sculptor] has well composed and well expressed one view of his work, he has only performed a part of his business, since that work has as many points of view as there are points of space which surround it."[12] Falconet lived up to this credo, and his *Peter the Great* displays a different individuality depending on the side from which it is approached.

From the right side, or the side of the Admiralty, the monument is at its most neutral. It is from here that one can concurrently see all its components: the horseman extending his right arm toward the river, palm down and fingers spread out, in a gesture of peace and authority, the horse in a mighty spurt forward and upward, just like the granite wave on which it stands, and the snake lying crushed under the horse's hooves (fig. 8.1).

Rightward is also the direction of the horseman's and the horse's gaze. But how differently they respond to what they see! The tsar's eyes are cold and impassive, while the horse's eyes are filled with primal fear (fig. 8.5). What is it that could cause such a reaction? Is it something that only the horse and the rider can see, something that lurks beyond the mortal's horizon and has enough dread in it to terrify the mount, while leaving the tsar unperturbed? Is it a vision of the future of Russia, which the ruler accepts with equanimity, but which makes the horse, seen by many as an allegory of Russia's social forces, recoil in fear? Continuing to the back of the monument, one is again faced with a triangular structure, but this time it is an isosceles cone with the head of the tsar at its apex. The long slope of the pedestal is fully in sight, and one's sense of the horse's motion is so real that one expects the horseshoes to have left imprints in the granite. Also fully visible is the contorted body of the snake, as it lies squashed under the right hoof. With the buildings of Vasilievsky Island visible across the river and the tsar's extended right arm outlined against the sky, Peter looks from this vantage point like the true master of his city (fig. 8.2).

The monument is at its most dramatic when viewed from the left, that is, the Senate side. The trees of the Admiralty Garden form a dark wall, against which the silhouette of the pedestal is clearly outlined. Piercing the sky from behind the trees is the golden needle of the Admiralty, which Peter the Great himself had projected. With the tsar looking away from the viewer and the snake totally out of sight, it is the horse that commands the viewer's attention. As one approaches the monument from the left-front side, the pedestal eclipses the hind legs of the horse and overwhelms the figure of the tsar. With the forelegs thrust ahead, the massive frame of the horse seems to be taking flight (fig. 8.3).

The closer one is to the front of the pedestal, the more oppressive are the hooves suspended above the viewer and the more immediate is their menacing outline. That is the angle from which the Russian viewer, whose eyes will always be below the hooves of the tsar's horse, senses most clearly the contrast between the ruler's exalted position and his own lowly station.

That also must have been the spot from which Evgeny, the humble foil to Peter the Great in Pushkin's *The Bronze Horseman,* looked up at the statue and through clenched teeth mumbled his deprecations against the "marvel-working builder," towering above him.

HORSE AND SNAKE

My friend, make them a beautiful horse. That will be the refrain of all my letters. Most importantly, a beautiful horse!
—Diderot (1769)

Given that the horse is the most dramatic element of the monument, one might assume that Falconet had a predisposition for sculpting horses, one of the favorite motifs of Baroque art. Such is not the case, however. Falconet was not "into horses" at all, and the monument in St. Petersburg was his first essay in that genre. Not even in Sèvres, where a horse would have been a perfectly natural subject for his pastoral scenes, did he show any inclination to make one. He was, however, eager to end his career in sculpting with a flourish, for which a major equestrian monument to one of the greatest European monarchs would certainly qualify.

Falconet knew enough about Peter the Great's personality and the political setting in which he operated to realize that a human figure alone would not provide sufficient opportunity to do them justice. He viewed the horse, therefore, not as a neutral bearer of the rider, but as an aid in his design to depict the complexities of the tsar's situation. He wanted to exploit the dual nature of the equestrian monument by endowing the horseman with the tsar's statesmanlike qualities and making the horse bear the traits of the tsar's tempestuous nature and of the turbulence which his reforms visited upon Russia.

Assigning dissimilar, nay, discordant notes to the horseman and the horse, while retaining the statue's conceptual unity, is one of Falconet's notable contributions to the equestrian portrait. In this respect the *Peter the Great* differs, in particular, from the *Marcus Aurelius,* whose sculptor gave the horse a deliberate and unruffled stance, paralleling the contemplative interests and manner of the emperor.[13] Falconet knew that a portrait of a monarch had to be a reflection of his realm; or, as he put it, "in order to magnify a Prince, one should not belittle a Nation."[14]

What Falconet wanted was not a ponderous appendage to the horseman, an extension of the pedestal providing the horseman with elevation, in the literal and figurative senses. He did not want the horse to be a mere attribute of authority and power. He wanted a horse that would become the focus of attention, a horse that would be caught in a burst of movement forward and upward, similar to the country Peter had created, overflowing with vitality and intensity, but often wild and unmanageable. That is what he set out to accomplish when he drew a project of the monument on the corner of Diderot's table, and that is how the viewers of the monument understood his artistic vision. "O, Russia! You are like that horse," as Andrei Bely exclaimed in his Symbolist novel *Petersburg.*

Diderot, eager to see his friend succeed in a venture tried but once before—a rearing horse in a colossal equestrian monument—kept sending him exhortations: "That horse, does he breathe yet? Does he fly out proudly against barbarous lands? Will he give us soon the sight of one of the most beautiful movements in nature, a leap into space by an animal that senses its master and responds to him?"[15] He continued his pleas as the large model was being finished: "Remember, Falconet, you have to die at your post or make a sublime horse. They haven't stopped screaming into my ears that your horse will come out poorly, that you won't be able to make it well. I'll kiss your feet if you prove them wrong."[16]

Whatever was the symbolic value of the horse, Falconet wanted its stance to reflect nature. In his "Observations sur la statue de Marc-Aurèle," he described at length the extraordinary pains he had taken to make sure of this.[17] To start with, he had an elevation built in the backyard of his atelier, which had the same degree of inclination as the pedestal. He then employed the best army horsemen and watched them gallop to its top and stop there abruptly. He had them do it repeatedly, more than a hundred times, with different horsemen riding different horses. Here is how he justified the need for so many rehearsals:

One's eye cannot grasp the effects of rapid movement except with the aid of very frequent repetitions, because reflection upon of what one has seen and its contemplation prepare one to see better on another occasion, and because only a repetition of experiments on different specimens allows one to determine with certainty how an animal moves in a specific situation. . . . I examined, drew, and modeled every part, looking at it from above and below, front and back, and the sides, because there is no other way to get to know an object intimately. Only after these examinations did I feel that I had seen and could render the movements of a horse climbing at a gallop, the true form of muscles and tendons at rest or in motion, and the effect of motion on the horse's skin.[18]

Realizing that the horse was the key to the success of his monument, Falconet sought confirmation of his observations among the best horsemen of St. Petersburg, in particular Colonel Melissino and the British ambassador Lord Cathcart. His efforts were rewarded by the plaudits of most contemporary viewers. Diderot, never in want of words, waxed rhapsodic when he saw the large model of the horse in St. Petersburg:

Well, my friend, let us leave that horse of Marcus Aurelius. Whether it's beautiful or ugly, what do I care! I don't know its sculptor and take no interest in his work. But let us speak of yours. You know well my friendship for you and will appreciate the anxiety with which I entered your atelier. But I saw it, I saw it well, and will never judge another piece of sculpture if yours is not a sublime monument and if its execution does not correspond in everything to the nobility and grandeur of the conception. I told you in the excitement of the first moment, and I repeat it having cooled off, that Bouchardon, before whose name you have the modesty to bow your head, saw horses, beautiful horses, studied them profoundly, and rendered them superbly. But he was in a manege and never entered the stables of Diomedes or Achilles and he did not see true steeds. It's you, my friend, who has brought them back to my imagination, just as the ancient poet had showed them to me.[19]

"I don't think that there exists another horse in marble or metal which could be compared to his. Falconet turned all his thoughts to the horse. So much so that Peter the First became for him of secondary interest," said L. H. Nicolaï, who saw the monument both as it was being created and when it was completed.[20] Fortia de Piles described the *pose bondissante* as "a novel and splendid conception."[21] John Carr ranked Falconet's horse "next its Venetian brethren, those matchless works of art which now adorn the gates of the Tuileries."[22]

Diderot realized that even if the details of Falconet's horse were portrayed with naturalistic exactitude, the whole was a creative and idealized amalgam: "You have rendered the truth of Nature in all its purity, but your genius knew how to blend it with the prestige of poetry which magnifies and surprises. Your horse is not a copy of the most beautiful horse in the world, just as the Apollo Belvedere is not an exact copy of the most handsome man."[23]

Not all viewers, however, were so perceptive. Some found fault with the angle of the horse's stance, some with the proportions of the horse's neck. Falconet countered that these critics relied on faulty observation or poor memory of the equine physique. He pointed out that those who had seen horses in mountainous terrain were not critical of him, for they knew that it was one thing to gallop in a country as flat as the environs of St. Petersburg and quite another to gallop up a hill. Falconet was also aware of the need to distort reality in order to counteract the effects of viewing a sculpture from a distance. That is why the front of the horse's neck is slightly thicker than average, just as the horseman's outstretched arm is longer than in nature.

Janson, while expressing his admiration for Falconet's horse, claimed that it is of a type "introduced by Bernini for his equestrian *Louis XIV*."[24] He could not have strayed farther from observable facts. Falconet admired Bernini, but his realistic portrayal of a horse is leagues beyond Bernini's unnaturally contorted animal with a fanciful head and undulating mane and tail. In his "Observations sur la statue de Marc-Aurèle," Falconet was very harsh in his criticism. Bernini, he said, "did not know how to make a horse. The one in Versailles [*Louis XIV*] is just a repetition of the horse of Constantine in Rome [at the head of the Scala Regia in St. Peter's Basilica]. Neither represents a fine horse, nor even a natural horse."[25]

As self-assured and sarcastic as he was in responding to his critics, Falconet was less confident when it came to the views of the empress, and anxiously sought her reassurance. She was, as always in the early stages of Falconet's work, protective and encouraging. In her very first letter to the sculptor, just three and a half months after his arrival, Catherine the Great made a joking reference to the horse in the small model: "I've been eyeing from here that clever animal that is in the center of your atelier and fear that you might give it too much brain. I simply think that you cannot make stupid animals, and bet that if your horse speaks and is not understood, that will be because one is used to hear a horse neigh and its speech will be taken for neighing."[26] A few months later, she described the horse as escaping from the fingers of the sculptor "straight into posterity."[27] She continued to reassure the sculptor during the last stages of his work on the large model: "You'll make a beautiful horse in spite of the aspersions of the envious."[28]

Falconet's emblematic use of the individual elements of the monument made it possible for him to deny Peter the Great the use of a saddle and stirrups. The emperor is shown riding on a bearskin, fastened with a belly band (fig. 8.4).[29] That, together with a bridle, is all the harness. The simplicity of this gear has been interpreted as an emblem of Peter's modest habits and unpretentious ways. As for the *pose bondissante*, its symbolism may be deciphered in different ways. If one sees in it an animal recoiling from danger, it may be interpreted as an allegorical representation of the conservative forces opposing Peter's reforms, a role reserved usually for the trampled snake.[30] If the rearing is viewed as a triumphant finale to a glorious ride, the horse may be said to be a mere instrument in Peter's hands, an ally in his mission to reform Russia. If the horse's stance is perceived as a moment of hesitation, which might end in a leap forward, a full stop, or a turnaround, it may express the Russians' doubts about the wisdom of Peter's attempt to steer the ship of state so abruptly onto a new course, with the winds high and the waters choppy. The latter view predominates in Russian thinking and has received expression in countless works of literature, above all in Pushkin's anxious question addressed to Peter's charger: "Where will you bring down your hooves?"

While the wild horse functions as an embodiment of untrammeled speed, beauty, and strength, and the domesticated one is seen as an obedient and faithful helper and friend in travel, hunt, battle, work, and leisure, the snake is as negative a symbol as the Judeo-Christian mythological bestiary has created. Representing ugliness, weakness, uselessness, secretiveness, danger, treachery, and damnation, it is, in fact, an easily legible foil to the horse.

Etched in collective memory are biblical images of the snake at the negative pole in the opposition of Good versus Evil, the most memorable ones being the punishment meted out to the snake for being the instrument of man's downfall in the Book of Genesis and the banishment of the dragon/serpent/beast in the Book of Revelation.[31] The latter is especially apt in the context of St. Petersburg, for St. John the Divine cites Water, the dragon's element, as a weapon of destruction against the Woman/Earth: "And the earth helped the woman, and the earth opened her mouth, and swallowed up the flood, which the dragon cast out of his mouth." The dragon/beast, which was the mount of the great whore of Babylon "that sitteth upon many waters," reminds us also that Babylon was a favorite simile for the "godless" St. Petersburg.

Early chronicles are just as colorful in their tales of fork-tongued snakes slithering treacherously to strike at unsuspecting victims. For the monument to Peter the Great, the tale of the death of the Kievan Prince Oleg (about 912) is particularly pertinent. Known to every educated Russian, if not from its original source in the *Primary Chronicle,* then from Pushkin's poem "The Tale of the Wise Oleg" (1822), the story contrasts the transience of the Good, represented by a particular horse, with the ever present Evil, symbolized by the generic snake. It tells of a magician's prediction that Prince Oleg would be killed by his favorite horse. Hearing it, Oleg decided never to ride the horse again, nor even to lay his eyes on it. After some years the horse died, and Oleg asked to be led to its remains. Upon seeing the horse's skull and bones scattered on the ground, Oleg laughed at the magician's prediction and, stamping on the skull, asked with derision: "Am I to find my destruction in *this? /* My death in a skeleton seeking?"

But the prediction found a way of getting fulfilled: "From the skull of the courser a snake with a hiss, / Crept forth, as the hero was speaking; / Round his legs, like a ribbon, it twined its black ring; / And the prince shrieked aloud as he felt the keen sting."[32] The poem ends with a wake for Oleg at the barrow where he was buried.

The opposition between a good horse and an evil snake or dragon is familiar to the Russians from Christian imagery as well. The mounted St. George,
the patron saint of Russia, is the heroic killer of the virgin-eating dragon, a
scene shown on countless icons and incorporated into the coat of arms of
Russia. The icons of the Archangel Michael the Warrior show him often
on horseback, piercing with his lance the Satan/Dragon's most dangerous
weapon—its tongue.

Adding a snake to the monument to Peter the Great was an idea that
occurred to Falconet late in the planning process, just after he had finished
working on the small model of the monument. He had confidence in his
calculations of equal front-to-back weight distribution of the statue and was
not thinking of adding a third point of support to the horse's hind legs. He
began to wonder, however, whether the crosswinds on Senate Square would
not upset the statue's lateral equilibrium, and began searching for some in-
conspicuous way to provide another point of contact between the horse and
the granite rock.

Lengthening the horse's tail so as to make it touch the pedestal, as Pietro
Tacca had done in the monument to Philip IV in Madrid, was too unnatural
a solution for a professed commonsense realist. He considered adding bronze
bushes along the horse's path and anchoring the tail in them, but rejected
that idea as artificial. Adding a snake, however, writhing in mortal agony
under the horse's hooves so that one of its coils would touch the horse's tail,
struck him as a perfectly acceptable component of a heroic monument. The
connection thus established between the horse and the pedestal would not
be very solid, but it would be sufficient to provide the statue with the necessary stability. The idea was, in fact, so happy a solution to Falconet's concerns
that he was willing to forswear his hostility to allegorical amplifications and
suggested that the snake be interpreted as a symbol of envy, which is being
defeated by the tsar.

From several exchanges between Falconet and the empress one may infer
that his idea of adding a snake was born in the spring of 1768. That is when
he talked about it to Betskoi, who reported the conversation to Catherine,
presenting the snake as a purely allegorical embellishment. When the empress, who liked the simplicity of the original design, took her time reacting
to the addition, Falconet decided to do his own lobbying. He met with the
empress on June 27, 1768, and followed up that conversation with a letter,
which marked the first appearance of the snake in correspondence: "I don't
know how the idea of the allegorical snake was presented to Your Majesty,
nor if it has earned scorn for its inventor. . . . As long as that allegory is not
wrongly interpreted, it provides the statue with a natural reinforcement,
which it lacked before. Not to use an emblem that is simple, clear, expressive,
and necessary would be to miss an opportunity."[33]

Falconet was right to take the matter into his own hands, for the empress,
knowing his dislike of allegory, suspected that the snake was Betskoi's suggestion and that it was being offered to her without the sculptor's approval.

Having learned that the idea was truly Falconet's and that the reason for incorporating it in the design was practical rather than allegorical, she gave it a lukewarm go-ahead: "I don't and I won't dislike the allegorical snake. It was proposed to me as an idea that you had thought of. But since one's own ideas are frequently attributed to someone else, I didn't want to agree to it without knowing what your thinking was. Once you told me, I wanted to know all the objections one could have against the snake. But I am not against it any longer."[34]

A year passed and the snake found its way into the large model of the monument. Falconet, however, was still unsure whether the empress was pleased with his idea:

> Some, who are perhaps too fastidious or perhaps not sufficiently sensitive to poetry that is both daring and simple, believe that the snake ought to be removed. They have told me so. But they don't know that without that fortunate addition, the balance of the statue would be most uncertain. They did not calculate, as I did, the strength that I need. They don't know that, if their advice were to be injudiciously followed, the statue would not last. It's not just a question of supporting the tail of the horse. My device and the way of using it support the legs and the legs support everything. . . . Submitting my reasons to Your Majesty, I beg her to decide whether a feature which brings no dishonor to the subject and is, in fact, in agreement with historical truth, should not be allowed to stand up to specious reasons for its removal. That Peter the Great met with envy along his way is certain. That he succeeded in conquering it is also certain. Such is the lot of every great man.
>
> P.S. I must not fail to tell Your Majesty that many of those who have seen the snake have called it a most ingenious idea, all the more so because it magnifies the conceit, supports the statue, and is constructed in such a way as to conceal the reason why it is necessary.[35]

A week later Falconet renewed his anxious requests for a clear signal of consent: "I forgot yesterday to ask Your Imperial Majesty if she is satisfied with my explanation of the snake. If you give me a sign of your approval, I will pay no attention to the buzzing around my ears and will go ahead without looking back."[36] The following day the empress gave him what he wanted: "There is an old song which goes: *S'il faut, il faut.* That's my response to the snake."[37]

Contrary to Falconet's fears, the reactions to the addition of the snake were invariably very positive. The view expressed by Diderot, who saw it on the large model of the monument during his visit to St. Petersburg, may be considered representative: "Leave that snake under [the horse's] hooves. Didn't Peter, didn't all great men have to crush them? . . . Besides, it looks good and has an indispensable and very secret mechanical application."[38]

What Falconet could not foresee was that the utilitarian snake would acquire a much greater part in the monument's symbolism than he had intended, and that its officially assigned allegorical interpretation as the embodiment of envy would come to be seen as banal and would soon be abandoned. As soon as the monument became a St. Petersburg fixture, other interpretations began capturing popular imagination, the most prevalent being that the snake symbolized the crushing of the conservative Muscovite attempt to reverse the course of Peter's reforms. Among the liberal, pro-Western segments of the population the snake exemplified backwardness in opposition to modernity.

In conservative communities, such as the Old Believers, in which Peter was viewed as Antichrist who had sold himself and Russia to the sinful West, there arose a different interpretation of the snake and its relationship to the horse and the horseman. Its roots may be sought in an early Christian eschatological composition, known in Byzantium as the *Apocalypse of Methodius of Patara*. Like other apocalypses, it is a collection of doomsday prophecies and visions. In one of the visions, ascribed to the patriarch Jacob, a roadside snake snaps at the hind leg of a horse and attaches itself to it. In Methodius's explication of this image, the horse symbolizes the world and its hind leg stands for the end of the world, while the snake represents Antichrist. This view was adopted by the Old Believers, except that in their cosmology, Methodius's "world" was equated with Russia.

According to Methodius, one of the features of the snake/Antichrist is its ability to move mountains, a trait whose topicality in the context of Peter's reforms, his founding of St. Petersburg, and particularly the moving of the Thunder Rock, was not lost on the Old Believers. "In such an interpretation," says the literary critic Iury Lotman, "the snake turns out to be an ally of Peter—who also presumes to reorder elements—rather than his enemy."[39]

Lotman does not suggest that this reading applies to Falconet's monument, if only because it predates it, and he leaves unexplained the death of the snake under the hooves of the horse. Yet the mere possibility of applying the symbolic imagery of the *Apocalypse of Methodius of Patara* to the interpretation of the monument is another example of its disquieting open-endedness.

HORSEMAN

[The tsar] sits on a bearskin, and is clad in a simple habit, not characteristic of any particular country, but such as may be worn, without violation of propriety, by an inhabitant of any. . . . His left hand holds the bridle, and his right is extended, as the artist himself expressed it, *en père & en maître*.
—Nathaniel Wraxall Jr. (1774)

To achieve authenticity, an artist trying to re-create the features of Peter the Great two generations after his death had to rely on portraits executed during the emperor's lifetime. Of painted portraits, there were the works of the Russians Andrei Matveev and Ivan Nikitin, the French Jean-Marc Nattier and Louis Caravaque, the Dutch Karel de Moor and Arnold Boonen, the German Johann Gottfried Tannauer, and the Englishman Sir Godfrey Kneller. Falconet could consult these portraits either in the original or in engravings.[40]

The few sculpted portraits that were accessible to Falconet were all executed by the tsar's court sculptor, the Italian Carlo Bartolomeo Rastrelli.[41] Especially important for Falconet were two wax masks, a life mask taken in 1721 and a death mask of 1725.[42] Rastrelli also made two portraits of Peter, a full-size Madame Tussaud–like wax effigy of the emperor in European garb sitting in a plain armchair as if it were a throne (1725),[43] and, more important, a bronze bust in armor (1723), which has deservedly been hailed as one of the best sculpted portraits of the period (fig. 8.6). The bust was in the imperial collection, and Falconet and Collot certainly saw it and used it in modeling the head of the tsar. It is not known, however, whether they were shown Rastrelli's bronze equestrian statue of the tsar, which Catherine had rejected as his official portrait.

In Rastrelli's bust, Peter is a military commander through and through. Clad in ornate, heavy armor, stiffly erect, with a proudly raised head and an angry, willful expression, the emperor's bust, though armless, is powerful enough to suggest the rest of Peter's six-foot-six frame. His high and broad forehead, bulging eyes, large nose, heavy jowls, and protruding chin give his face a feeling of strength, authority, and inflexibility. Its similarity to the life mask makes one confident that it faithfully renders the tsar's features.

Like any great portrait, the tsar's figure in Falconet's monument does not merely register external similarity. It identifies, but also explicates. In accordance with Falconet's conceit, instead of a soldier ready to do battle, one sees a monarch in a reflective mood. The slightly inclined head crowned with laurels, the firmly arched brow, the deep-set, inquisitive eyes turned in the direction to which the right arm is pointing emanate a sense of mental concentration, focused willpower, and calm self-assurance. It is the thinking face of a sovereign who peers into the future from his lofty perch and sees farther than any of his subjects.

According to a story that was making the rounds of St. Petersburg at the time, Falconet made a model of the head of Peter the Great and showed it to the empress, who rejected it out of hand. He tried again and again, with the same result. Collot, seeing the sculptor's distress, suggested that she would give it a try and in one night produced a likeness that the empress immediately accepted. The story, with its miraculous overtones of a hagiography, is most certainly apocryphal. It is indisputable, however, that it was Falconet who gave it currency. He insisted on Collot's authorship of Peter's head while they were still in St. Petersburg and after they had left. Here is how he expressed his debt to Collot: "I did not make the head of the hero. . . . That portrait, bold, colossal, expressive, and eloquent, is by Mlle Collot, my disciple (today my daughter-in-law)" (fig. 8.7).[44]

Fig. 8.6. Carlo Bartolomeo Rastrelli, *Peter the Great*. Bronze, 1723. The State Hermitage Museum, St. Petersburg.

Fig. 8.7. Marie-Anne Collot, Head for the Monument of Peter the Great. Plaster,
1767. The State Russian Museum, St. Petersburg. Photograph by
Mark Skomorokh.

Falconet's claim was accepted at face value by just about everybody who commented on the monument.[45] It would seem, at first blush, that it is supported by external evidence. Everyone knew that Falconet was not one to diminish his own merits and that Collot was at work at that time on a likeness of Peter the Great, resulting in the bronze bust in the Hermitage (fig. 8.8). One must also consider Falconet's self-confessed dislike of portraiture. Collot, on the other hand, was a recognized portrait maker.

Nonetheless, doubts about Collot's sole authorship of the head of the *Peter*

Fig. 8.8. Marie-Anne Collot, *Peter the Great*. Bronze, 1768. The State Hermitage Museum, St. Petersburg.

the Great arose in various quarters. As Diderot told Falconet: "You should know that in Paris and St. Petersburg, people find it peculiar that you should entrust to your disciple the execution of so important a part of your monument as the head of the hero."[46] Such doubts were in line with persistent questions about Collot's ability to work without Falconet's assistance. They had been voiced during the young sculptress's early years in Paris and they were still current during her stay in St. Petersburg.[47]

There are several reasons why Collot's sole authorship of the head of the *Peter the Great* could be questioned. In the first place, Falconet's unwillingness to engage in portraiture was not taken as a necessity imposed by artistic limitations but as a matter of the sculptor's personal choice. The two busts of Dr. Camille Falconet that garnered such high praise in the Salons give ample proof of his skill in modeling from nature. There is also Falconet's self-portrait in the 1754 *Milo of Crotona* (fig. 1.3) as well as Diderot's attestation to Falconet's ability to create profound psychological portraits in his account of the scene in which Falconet smashed to pieces Diderot's bust of his own making because he thought it inferior to Collot's. Writing of the Salon of 1767, Diderot regretted the sculptor's impulsive gesture: "I would say . . . that in this unfortunate bust there were traces of a secret inner wound which was devouring me when the artist made it. How is it that an artist may sometimes fail to duplicate obvious features of a face he has before his eyes, and yet manage to capture on canvas or in wet clay private feelings and impressions hidden deep in the soul?"[48]

More serious is the argument that Collot, aged twenty, did not have the intellectual and psychological maturity to create a portrait of such sophistication and subtlety as to stand out even in so fine a work as the monument itself. Her indubitable talent for portrait making notwithstanding, the head of the statue is exceptional among her works, together with the bust of Falconet.

It is significant also that despite mentioning Collot in various contexts as the author of the tsar's head, Falconet did not put her name next to his in the signature of the statue. Was it because, by the time he was signing the statue, all dissembling would have served no purpose? Puzzling also is the lack of any reference to Collot's collaboration on the monument in Falconet's correspondence with Catherine, which at that time was frequent and animated.

But if the head of the statue was not solely Collot's, why would Falconet insist that it was? Some suspected that Falconet tried to help the career of his disciple by attributing to her accomplishments which were not legitimately hers. That surmise, however, fails because of Collot's popularity as a St. Petersburg society portraitist. Everybody knew that she was in Catherine's good graces, and that was surely sufficient to advance her career. Was it love, then or, at the very least, Falconet's desire to be united with Collot in a work of sculpture, if not in marriage? Hardly, for there was nothing in Falconet's behavior to suggest that he loved Collot enough to deprive himself of sole authorship of a work which he considered his masterpiece and which he knew would be his last. The most plausible surmise is that Falconet wanted to demonstrate Collot's active participation in the enterprise of the monument in order to counteract scandalmongering in the salons of Paris and St. Petersburg. He may have thought that his social standing demanded proof that Collot was his bona fide collaborator, not just a paramour.

David Arkin, the most persuasive modern doubter of Collot's sole authorship of the head of the monument to Peter the Great, argues that Collot's bronze portrait of the tsar in the Hermitage (fig. 8.8) is a "respectable but completely ordinary representation," while the heads of Rastrelli's 1723 bust and of Falconet's monument are masterly in design and elaboration of decorative elements.[49] Rastrelli's portrait (fig. 8.6) is so "convincing, so acute in its characterization, that one need not compare it with the mask to believe in its fidelity. . . . The almost unnaturally tense, piercing and bulging eyes, the stuck-out chin, the nervous quiver that seems to be passing through the bronze, endow all the features of that unusual face with an expression of angry determination."[50] Similarly, the portrait of the tsar in the monument to Peter the Great is, in Arkin's view, an idealized image of an enlightened monarch, possessed of thought, power, and indomitable will: "The head of Peter, adorned with a crown of laurels and glowing with intelligence, is ready to absorb knowledge whose expanse is wider than the body of water spreading before the horseman's eyes."[51] The Hermitage portrait by Collot and the head of the monument to Peter the Great, concludes Arkin, "are two entirely different images, works by two artists who are totally unlike in their outlook and talent."[52]

While recognizing Collot's gift for faithfully rendering facial features, one cannot deny the justice of Arkin's argument that the Hermitage portrait, though competently rendered, lacks that spark of inspiration which separates great art from skillfully executed craft. If one were to ascribe to Collot the sole authorship of Peter's head, one would have to assume that she did two versions of it, an unremarkable one for the Hermitage bust and a superlative one for the monument to Peter the Great—an improbable scenario. It is more likely that Collot provided Falconet with a portrait of the tsar, but that he then altered it to suit his vision. If that is what happened, then the head came into being as a result of collaboration between two artists—a rare occurrence, to be sure, but as Diderot remarked, not without precedent in the annals of art: "All those who speak about it with so much inquisitiveness would rather condemn a very wise move than remember it as justified by the example of many ancient sculptors."[53]

A few months after the arrival of Falconet, Catherine wrote to the sculptor: "I hope that after I come back [from a visit to Moscow and the eastern provinces], the toilette of Peter the Great will be finished. . . . I was told that he exists already, but in a state of total deshabille."[54] The empress was referring to the earliest version of the small model of the monument in which the tsar was sculpted naked, while Falconet was mulling over the choice of the garments. It was not an easy decision, for everybody in the capital had an opinion on how the emperor should be dressed. Falconet settled on a neutral costume, a belted mid-calf-length shirt, draped with a flowing cape edged with a delicate ornament (fig. 8.4). The simplicity of the garment complemented the classical pose of the tsar, while defying identification with any national tradition. "It is"—to quote Diderot—"a simple and unpretentious garment, attractive without being overbearing. It is very tasteful and it suits the hero and the rest of the monument."[55] But the road to that garment was not nearly so simple as its cut.

The item which disturbed the critics most was the belted shirt. Some thought that it resembled a Roman tunic, while others that it was too much like a shirt of a Volga boatman—both clearly inappropriate.[56] Falconet defended himself by claiming that the tsar's garment transcended the fashions of a particular time and place. Being afraid, however, that his arguments might not convince Catherine, he decided to seek the succor of Diderot. His calculation was that the empress would be more likely to endorse his own point of view if she knew that Diderot was on his side. In accordance with this scheme, Falconet sent Diderot an account of the problem, couching it in the form of answers to imaginary questions posed by imaginary critics. He also sent the empress a copy of his letter.[57]

As Falconet saw it, there were four possible styles of dress available to him: Greek, Roman, Russian, and French. The Greek and French styles were ruled out, because there was no historical reason for the former, while the latter was too foppish to be appropriate in heroic sculpture.[58] Roman style implied a breastplate, which went against the sculptor's intention to present the emperor as a legislator rather than a military leader. Besides, had he wished to stress the emperor's valor, he would have presented him in Russian armor: "You know that I would not put Roman garments on him any more than I would put Russian garments on Julius Caesar, Pompey, or Scipio." As for purely Russian costume, it also was unacceptable because "Peter the Great did not like it and forbade it." Falconet acknowledged, however, that Russian garb would make more sense than any other because it was still being worn in the country and Peter himself used to wear in his younger days.

Falconet advised Diderot to tell the Paris critics that the garb of the Bronze Horseman was similar to that of the *Marcus Aurelius:* "His is a garment of all nations, all peoples, all times. In a word, it is a heroic garment." He ended his letter with his customary defense of the artist's right to make his own decisions and disobey the dictates of prejudice and the precepts of fashion: "When the statue is done, the preachers and teachers will either fall silent or, if they prefer, keep talking. That is their right."

When the critical voices persisted after a year and a half had gone by and Falconet was beginning to work on the large model of the statue, he made a direct appeal to the empress: "One often thinks that everything goes well, but everything does not go well. Your Imperial Majesty finds that the clothes of the statue are appropriate. . . . But very respectable persons have different views and spread them around. . . . Please tell me if I should diminish an idea of a genius [that is, of the tsar] or express it in a manner worthy of Peter the First and Catherine the Second."[59] To give this leading argument more substance, Falconet attached to the letter an expanded version of his February 28, 1767, discussion of the tsar's clothing. The new version was accompanied by a short preamble in which Falconet explained that its purpose was to give his views "greater clarity."[60] The empress patiently reassured her flustered sculptor of her continued support for his design of the garment: "Monsieur Falconet, I repeat what I've been telling you all along, disregard the blabbermouths, even though there may be respectable persons among them."[61]

In a brief description of the small model of the monument, the *St. Petersburg Gazette* declared that Peter's "fatherly arm needs no explanation."[62] Not all viewers, however, agreed. Count Grigory Orlov claimed that the arm was the most difficult and complex aspect of Peter's figure and that "[Falconet] alone could interpret it correctly."[63] Despite Falconet's assurances that the arm is raised with peaceful intentions, many found it aggressive or, at the very least, threatening. The accusation that it points menacingly at Russia's neighbors fails on geographical grounds, for Peter's arm is extended in the direction of the uninhabited expanse of the Arctic. The hand holds no sword and the fingers are not angrily knit together, but are spread out in a gesture that befits "a builder, legislator, and benefactor of his country" (fig. 8.9).

Fig. 8.9. E.-M. Falconet, Monument to Peter the Great (detail).
Photograph by L. Bogdanov.

Nor can one agree with those who found the emperor's gesture boastful: "His right arm, extended toward the Neva, the Admiralty, the Academy, and the Peter and Paul Fortress, reminds the spectator that the fleet, commerce, science, and the might of Russia were born and came of age under the emperor's protection. It seems to be saying: 'All these miracles were created by my hand.' "[64] No, there is no conceit in the tsar's gesture. He realized all too well the dangers of placing his capital on the banks of a wide and unpredictable river, which, in Pushkin's vivid description of the flood of 1824, could throw itself "like a maddened beast" upon the city and tear out its entrails.[65] The hand with the palm turned down is not a hand of a conceited monarch. It is the hand of a conjurer who is casting a spell over the waters below, hoping to pacify them and bind them to their bed, a hand that more than any other feature of the statue allies it with the *Marcus Aurelius* (fig. 8.10).[66]

If the Russians sense a threat in the extended arm, it is not because of the shape and function given to it by Falconet, but because it belonged to a tsar who, in addition to great political and military accomplishments, left behind a memory of dogged tenacity in implementing his vision of Russia. Not until Stalin, in fact, did Russia have a ruler who would be so unyieldingly dedicated to the proposition that the interests of the state transcend and eclipse the rights of the individual.

"The extended right arm of the tsar is completely devoid of nobility," said Fortia de Piles, adding to the voices claiming that it was unnaturally long.[67] Yet sniffing for technical errors in a work by an artist who spent much of his life in the study of proportions as practiced by ancient masters is a futile

Fig. 8.10. *Marcus Aurelius* (detail). Courtesy *Zeszyty Literackie.*

task. The presumed distortions of scale should be viewed, instead, in the context of the conventions of the Baroque. One of its main tenets was not to copy nature but to project it effectively to the viewer. Especially important in this regard were Bernini's ideas. He urged the artist to disregard objective measurements and deform, if necessary, realistic proportions in order to create a more convincing impression of reality. "A sculptor," he said, "makes a figure with one hand raised, the other placed on the breast. Practice makes one realize that the hand in the air must be made larger and broader than the other."[68]

Falconet was undoubtedly familiar with that view and that is why one should look at his statue instead of approaching it with a measuring tape in hand.

PEDESTAL AND INSCRIPTION

Instead of a pedestal adorned with inscriptions, or surrounded by slaves, [the tsar] appears mounted on a rock or stone of a prodigious size, up to the ascent of which the horse labors, and appears to have nearly reached its summit.
—Nathaniel Wraxall Jr. (1774)

Since the horseman and the horse form a conceptual unity, both have traditionally received the same amount of attention in the history of the equestrian monument. The pedestal, on the other hand, has been treated as an artistically separate element of the composition, serving merely to elevate the statue and provide a convenient surface for inscriptions and allegorical imagery.[69]

A description of the pedestal published in the *St. Petersburg Gazette* in the summer of 1768 is curiously lacking in any information on its shape: "The pedestal of the statue: A rock almost sixteen feet high; the horse and the horseman sixteen and a half feet [high]; the rock looks like an oblong rectangle, thirty feet long and fifteen feet wide. . . . Peter the Great is shown galloping onto the steep rock, which is the pedestal of the statue. . . . The rock is in its natural state, without any decorations, symbolizing the difficulties experienced by Peter the First."[70]

This description, if not a product of the author's guesswork, must have been based on the small model of the monument, the only one completed by the time of the description's publication.[71] But what did the small model look like? All we know about it is that the empress liked it: "You told me that you would make your small model ugly, but I insist that it is quite beautiful."[72] Had Falconet followed his impulse and sent a copy of the model to the Académie in Paris, we would still have it. But he gave up that idea when Diderot attacked it: "You must have a morbid craving for criticism and annoyance. And what do you want them to teach you, their *artiste mau-*

dit. Do they know more about it than you do? Don't you know them all? Don't you know that they will not mention its strong points, but will broadcast the smallest defect all over the city? . . . I beg you, work in peace and don't try to bring in the harvest before its time."[73]

As for the large model, we know from Losenko's drawing of 1770 (fig. 3.6) that its pedestal was identical to that of the finished monument. It is, therefore, probable that the pedestal sketched by Falconet "on the corner of [Diderot's] table" and the small model of the monument made in 1767 had essentially the same shape as the large model. Had there been any drastic changes in design, they would certainly have been reflected in Falconet's correspondence with the empress. It is certain, at any rate, that a conventional box-like pedestal, with its tiny surface on which to put the galloping horse, was totally antithetical to the sculptor's way of thinking. Eager, as always, to convey a naturalistic effect, he used instead a true-to-life setting of a gradually rising and abruptly plunging rocky outcrop.[74]

The natural rock, bearing the bronze statue, carried two immediate associations for the Russian viewer. One was with St. Peter, whose name the tsar bore, and to whom Jesus referred as the rock on which the edifice of the church would be built.[75] A link to St. Peter was especially dear to the tsar because Peter and his brother Andrew were fishermen and as such symbolized a connection with the sea.[76] A less obvious association of the rock is with the tsar's idea that his mission to shape the future of his country was not unlike the task of a stonecutter. Falconet wrote of his pleasure at seeing a seal, designed by Peter the Great, on which the tsar was shown as a sculptor carving Russia out of a rock.[77] He saw in that image a verification and confirmation of the correctness of his idea of incorporating the pedestal in the conceit of his monument by involving it in a network of binary oppositions so as to endow it with dialectical energy.

The contemporaries who blamed Falconet for having excessively trimmed the pedestal out of fear that the statue would be overwhelmed by the natural grandeur of untamed matter did not even try to understand the idea that guided the sculptor's hand.[78] Preoccupied with rubles and inches, they failed to see that Falconet's striving for a naturalistic setting for the monument forced him to design a slope with an incline that a horse ascending it at a gallop could negotiate. It is precisely the drastically trimmed rock that endows the statue with its dynamic energy and allows the viewer to imagine the horse having just galloped up to the top of the hill, rather than being placed there by the artifice of a crane or gantry. Above all, the critics failed to realize that in Falconet's design the pedestal ceased to be a utilitarian accessory to the statue and its artistically irrelevant appendage. It became instead the monument's essential element, complementing and enriching its conceit.

Across the two faces of the pedestal, in bold bronze lettering, is arguably the most ingenious monument inscription ever designed: "To Peter the First,

Catherine the Second," given in Russian and Latin versions. Who composed that terse inscription which established Catherine as Peter's successor through the logic of arithmetical progression? Falconet has traditionally been considered its author, even though he never expressly laid claim to it. He merely informed the empress that he had put the words "Petro Primo Catharina Secunda posuit" on Losenko's drawing of the large model and urged her to adopt them by pointing out that the ancients liked such a "lapidary style as the simplest and best suited for their monuments."[79]

Catherine the Great accepted the suggestion: "Don't be afraid that I would give in to the absurdity of inscriptions that never end. I'll stay with the one you know, in four words."[80] In so doing she earned Falconet's praise: "A labored panegyric would have been injudicious and unnecessary, since history has already performed that office with impartial justice, and held up the [tsar's] name to universal regard. And I must give her present majesty justice by saying that she had the taste and discernment enough to . . . prefer the present short inscription to any other which could be composed."[81]

"The one you know . . . " Does that mean that the idea for the inscription came from another source? That would indeed appear to be the case, if we accept what Jakob Stählin, director of the Arts Section of the Academy of Sciences, claimed in his *Notes on the State of Fine Arts in Russia*. What Stählin maintained was that in 1768 Falconet asked him for a text of the inscription he had composed for the project of a monument to Peter the Great in the Peter and Paul Cathedral.[82] Stählin obliged by giving the sculptor two variants of the inscription, one wordy and pompous, the other short and pithy. It was the latter that Falconet recommended two years later to the empress.[83]

The four-word inscription was a major departure from the reigning custom of composing long, frequently rhymed encomia of persons whose merits and deeds were rewarded by a monument. An example of a convoluted, though mercifully short, inscription is the one that Betskoi proposed to the sculptors entering the competition for the monument to Peter the Great: "If God had bestowed immortality upon one of the men he created, the hero represented on this statue would have been among us."[84] Much more elaborate were the five rhymed inscriptions proposed by Lomonosov in 1750 for Rastrelli's equestrian monument to Peter the Great. They described Peter's heroic deeds in verses whose length varied from four to fourteen lines.[85]

Contemporary reactions to Falconet's inscription were positive. According to the English traveler William Coxe, writing in 1784: "The simplicity of the inscription corresponds to the sublimity of the design, and is far preferable to a pompous detail of exalted virtues, which the voice of flattery applies to every sovereign without distinction."[86] Fortia de Piles commented that "the inscription is admirable because of its simplicity."[87] He claimed, however, that the name of Peter the Great was written in smaller letters than the name of Catherine the Great. If indeed there ever was such a difference, Falconet had nothing to do with it, for he left the country long before it was affixed. Today the inscriptions are of the same size and are clearly visible, for the monument, in accordance with Falconet's wishes, is no longer enclosed by a fence.

It is true that Grimm reported on some critical voices that considered the addition of the dynastic numeral an unnecessary encumbrance of the inscription. Catherine responded: "Let them criticize 'Petro Primo Catharina Secunda.' It's I who wanted it like that because I wanted people to know that it's I and not his wife."[88] She was referring to Peter's second wife and his successor on the throne, Catherine I.

The symbolism of the bilingual inscription is transparent—in Catherine's Russia the Byzantine East and the Latin West will be treated as equals. Even the geographical orientation of the two versions of one and the same message is appropriately symbolic—the Russian text faces east and the Latin one faces west.

We may never know who should be credited with the honor of devising the inscription. Its taste and political sense make Falconet and Catherine the most likely candidates for its authorship. As for Stählin, he seems to be too much a product of the Baroque to propose a text that is so simple and so unadorned. Ultimately, however, the question of authorship does not matter much. What is important is that the inscription on the monument to Peter the Great shows once again that in this work Falconet could do no wrong.

Epilogue

St. Petersburg has died and will not be resurrected. There is something insane in the idea of it, something that has predetermined its demise. . . . A monstrous rape upon Nature and Spirit was committed here. A Titan rose up against Earth and Heaven and is now suspended in space, poised on a granite rock. But what is the rock poised on? Is it not poised on a dream?
—Georgii P. Fedotov (1926)

Peter the Great dreamed a dream and called it St. Petersburg. He set it on spongy and oozy terrain, left it to the whims of a mighty river, and surrendered it to the mercy of winds which for the greater part of the year blow in rain, fog, and snow. Summer tries vainly to make up for St. Petersburg's climatic deficiencies. Its warmth has a way of turning into a fever of hyper-excitement, as the city, like a mayfly, wakes up from its benighted hibernation and steps into unending daylight. It was not a place meant for human habitation, and yet Peter the Great knew that a mighty city was necessary in precisely that spot, in order to propel Russia into the modern age. And so, armed with Reason and an imperious Hubris, he proceeded to defy God's design with his own Word. Where others saw wasteland, he saw Paradise; where others saw wilderness and rot, he saw a bright and halcyon future.

Hence the Petersburgers' manic-depressive reaction to their city. They accepted the notion of Paradise by ukase and even reaped benefits from it, but their subconscious told them that they were sharers in a sinful enterprise, that the fruit they were enjoying was forbidden, and that a place which has no divine protection is bound to become the hunting ground of Satan.[1] The very diaphanous beauty of St. Petersburg is suspect. It is not the earthy appeal of a Russian woman who can do, and often does, everything that is man's habitual province. It is the beguiling incandescence of a will-o'-the-wisp that lures men into a morass and dissolves in the morning mist.

This sense of impermanence has marked the history of St. Petersburg from the day of its birth, and it is a tribute to Falconet, a native of Paris, a city with deep and strong roots, that he was able to feel it and respond to it creatively. His is a monument to uncertainty and wonderment. Should one trust the imperiously calm tsar who is scanning distant horizons from his exalted height, or should one believe the instincts of the horse which recoils in terror before a peril it senses ahead? Should one fear the tsar's mighty arm or seek protection in its shadow? What is the true essence of the pedestal? Is it a piece of solid rock, a concentrate of Russian soil, or a wave, congealed for a time, but primed to smash one day against the shore, destroy it, and be gone forever? The very fact that such questions do not receive unequivocal answers may account for the generally held view that the monument captures the enigmatic essence of Russia, whether it be called its soul, fate, or curse.

Accepted enthusiastically at the moment of its creation, the monument has been gaining admirers ever since. Diderot saw it when he visited Falconet's atelier in 1773 and was astounded: "You have created the most beautiful work of this genre in Europe."[2] On the occasion of the one hundredth anniversary of the unveiling, the German critic Hermann Dalton wrote: "The monument to Peter the Great is unquestionably one of the most significant and forceful works of modern times. . . . Daring and self-confident, spirited yet tranquil, so stands the statue on its mighty rock, fused with it into a whole, a triumphant execution and realization of a great, brilliant idea by a great, visionary artist."[3] The twentieth-century art critic Louis Réau, author of the most thorough study of Falconet's oeuvre, declared that the monument "is an epoch-making work in the history of sculpture, one of which St. Petersburg can be as proud as Venice is of Verrocchio's *Colleoni*."[4]

Russian early reactions tended to be literal. Such, for instance, was the reading offered by the liberal political thinker and critic of absolute monarchy Aleksandr N. Radishchev (1749–1802). He saw the monument on the day of its unveiling and shared his impressions with a friend:

> The steepness of the hill symbolizes the obstacles lying in Peter's way. . . . The snake represents perfidy and malice which sought to punish Peter with death for the introduction of the new ways. His clothes of ancient cut, the bearskin, and the simplicity of the horse's harness and of the rider's attire point to the simple and coarse manners and the ignorance which Peter found in the populace and which he wanted to reform. . . . His spirited countenance shows the inner conviction of someone who has fulfilled his goals, while the extended arm is protective and betrays a man of strength, one who has overcome all the obstacles along his way and who is now offering refuge to those who would call themselves his children.[5]

Radishchev's commonsensical reading is still persuasive, but during the years which separate us from the day when it was proffered, it has given ground to a variety of other interpretations which view the monument not as a foreign body inserted into St. Petersburg's cityscape but as an integral part and parcel of it, a sharer of the city's dreamlike and spectral aspects, its vulnerability and indefiniteness. These interpretations have given rise to, or at the very least, have paralleled, the development of the St. Petersburg narrative strand which established itself firmly in Russian letters in the nineteenth and early twentieth centuries. Its practitioners count among their ranks some of the finest Russian writers, with Pushkin, Gogol, and Dostoevsky at the head.[6] In their attempts to pierce and penetrate the mists and shadows that shroud the city's secrets and enigmas, Falconet's monument hovers often in the distance as the hieroglyph of the St. Petersburg theme. Consider, for instance, this disturbing image conjured up by Dostoevsky in *The Adolescent* (1875): "And what if this fog dissipates and goes away? Won't this whole rotting and slimy city disappear also, float up with the fog, and vanish into thin air like smoke, leaving behind the old Finnish bog and, in the middle, for decoration perhaps, the Bronze Horseman on his feverish, weary horse?"[7]

How securely Falconet's monument has planted itself in the minds of the Petersburgers may be illustrated by a story dating back to the days when Napoleon's invasion of Russia was seen as a possible threat to the safety of the city. The authorities, mindful of the fate of the four horses of San Marco in Venice, considered sending Falconet's monument away for safekeeping. At that time, a certain Major Baturin told Prince A. N. Golitsyn, known for his interest in mysticism, that he had repeatedly had a dream in which the statue jumped off its pedestal and galloped to the summer residence of Emperor Alexander I. Once there, the bronze Peter addressed the reigning monarch: "Young man, what have you done to my country? But don't worry! As long as I remain in my place, the city has nothing to fear."[8] Needless to say, the statue stayed in St. Petersburg.

Moving from dream to reality, throughout the horror and misery of the nine hundred days of the German blockade of Leningrad in World War II, the Bronze Horseman stayed in its habitual place, wrapped in planks and sand, for no one, not even Stalin, could countenance the city's survival without it (fig. E.1). The lesson of these stories is clear—the true protector of St. Petersburg is not the ruler of Russia but "the local deity, a mythological patron of the sovereign capital."[9]

It is significant in this connection that during the ceremony of the consecration of St. Isaac's in 1858, it was proposed to combine the traditional procession around the cathedral with a circling of the Bronze Horseman. The procession was to stop in front of the monument and sing the threnody "Life Everlasting." The plan was canceled because the Moscow metropolitan, Philaret, objected to the sacrilegious character of such veneration.

Of a very large number of poetic reverberations of Falconet's monument, two works stand out: *The Monument of Peter the Great* by the Polish Romantic poet Adam Mickiewicz; and, written partly in response to it, Alexander Pushkin's *The Bronze Horseman*. The two poets lived in the first half of the nineteenth century and were, in fact, fast friends until their national loyalties placed them on opposite sides during the Polish uprising of 1830–31, the so-called November Insurrection. The Polish poem was written and published in 1832. Pushkin's *The Bronze Horseman* was written in October 1833, but its publication was delayed by Tsar Nicholas I, who read it in manuscript and found several passages objectionable.

Fig. E.1. The Bronze Horseman Being Dug Out from Its Protective Cover of Planks and Earth at the End of World War II. Photograph, 1945 (Brodskii, ed., 1973, p. 411). Courtesy "Khudozhnik Rossii," St. Petersburg.

The Monument of Peter the Great is one of a cycle of six poems appended to part 3 of Mickiewicz's play *The Forefathers' Eve.*[10] The cycle, which goes under the name of *Digression,* combines descriptive passages with features of a travelogue, a reconstitution of Mickiewicz's impressions of Russia during the initial phases of his six-year-long banishment from Wilno. Written under the impression of the recent defeats of the Russian liberals in the Decembrist movement and of the Polish patriots in the November Insurrection, the cycle is bitingly critical of Russian institutions, descending on occasion to the level of a political lampoon.

Mickiewicz sees Russia as a country stalled by an autocratic and bureaucratic regime. The pedestal of the statue, shaped like a frozen wave, makes him think of attempts at dissent immobilized by the despotic tsar. The granite rock, brought in from outside the city, reminds him of Russia's imperial ambitions: "But Peter cannot rest on Russian ground; / His native land is small for such as he." Yet, in a remarkable leap of faith for someone who had witnessed the sorry finale of Napoleon's Russian campaign of

1812, Mickiewicz predicts that authoritarian rule will not last: "But soon will shine the sun of liberty, / And from the west a wind will warm this land. / Will the cascade of tyranny then stand?"

The Monument of Peter the Great describes a meeting of two young friends at the monument's foot. It is raining and the young men must make do with one overcoat between them. One of them "was that pilgrim from a western land." That is how Mickiewicz introduces himself. The other was "the famous Russian bard, / Beloved through all the northland for his song." That is an unmistakable reference to Pushkin. Except for the authorial voice, Mickiewicz is silent; Pushkin does all the talking.

The narrator compares Falconet's monument to the monument of Emperor Marcus Aurelius in Rome and proclaims his preference for the latter:

Homeward he turns his steps to peaceful Rome.
Fair, calm, and noble is that brow, aglow
With thoughts of all his people's happiness.
He lifts with dignity his hand, as though
His thronging subjects he were now to bless.

The tsar, by contrast, is being carried headlong toward a catastrophic fall:

His charger's reins Tsar Peter has released.
He's been flying down the road. Perchance
A precipice arrested his advance.
With hoofs aloft now stands the maddened beast,
Champing its bit unchecked, with slackened rein.
You think that it will fall and be destroyed.

If Mickiewicz meant to suggest that Falconet's tsar is unable to check his horse's momentum or is indifferent to the forces which might carry him to perdition, he was guilty of a serious misreading of the monument's message and of the sculptor's intent. The composed and confident look on the face of Peter the Great should suffice to convince the viewer that the tsar releases his horse's reins not because he has lost control over his mount, but because he has reached the end of a difficult and often perilous ride. To quote Falconet himself, the legislator-monarch "has arrived, after finishing his gallop."[11] The rock was not an obstacle to be overcome, but the symbolic top of the hill. The horse, not knowing its rider's intentions, may wear a "maddened," feverish look. The tsar, however, having reached his destination, feels calm and satisfied as he surveys his domain. Falling down and being destroyed is surely not an option that would do justice to the monument's conceit.

Formally denser, stylistically more complex, and thematically more wide-ranging than Mickiewicz's poem is *The Bronze Horseman,* Pushkin's acknowledged masterpiece and one of the most consequential works of Russian literature. It is an ideal complement to Falconet's monument, and the two have coexisted fruitfully, enriching each other and sharing not only their name, but also their mysteries. The genesis of Pushkin's poem is closely tied to the appearance of the poem *To My Russian Friends,* which Mickiewicz appended to the *Digression* and in which he paid tribute to the Russian litterateurs who had befriended him during his stay in Russia and who were later executed or imprisoned for their part in the Decembrist movement. Mickiewicz included several bitter lines addressed to an unidentified writer who, "Perhaps seduced by the gifts of state, / Betrays his free soul to the tsar for hire / And bows today on threshold of the great."[12] It is likely that these lines were aimed at Pushkin, and virtually certain that Pushkin took them as such.

Pushkin had good reasons to feel that he was Mickiewicz's target. He knew that two of his 1831 poems, in which he condemned the November Insurrection and defended the Russian police action in Poland, had to be seen by Mickiewicz as a betrayal of the liberal cause espoused by the Decembrists. Besides, he must have had an uneasy conscience about receiving material gratifications upon the publication of these poems. The question was how to respond to Mickiewicz's charges. Since rationalizing his own nationalist stand as a patriotic gesture could have pigeonholed him as a loyalist poet, Pushkin decided to defend the new Russian capital against the Polish poet's angry and sarcastic description. He took up that task in the introduction to *The Bronze Horseman,* a stirring encomium to St. Petersburg and an apocalyptic vision of its founding.

In the opening lines we find ourselves at the beginning of time, witnessing the moment of Creation. The quasi-biblical demiurge, referred to merely by the capitalized form of the third-person pronoun, is standing on the bank of a river, surveying the vast panorama in front of him. In a scene that could have been lifted from the book of Genesis, everything is still formless, desolate waters, dense forests, and hazy, moss-covered marshes. "He" envisions a new city and explains that it should be founded precisely in that place as a bastion against Sweden, an "open window to Europe," and an outlet to the sea providing a harbor for ships of all nations. As his thought develops, Chaos gradually turns into Order.

A hundred years pass and we look at the Russian capital with Pushkin's own eyes. St. Petersburg has become the "glory and pride of Northern lands." Elegant palaces, gardens, and ships, streaming in from every corner of the world, have replaced the "marsh and overhung forest." In a glowing tribute to the new city, its beauty and its way of life, Pushkin takes issue with Mickiewicz's depiction of St. Petersburg as a city built by devils and for the first time mentions by name the founder of the city:

> I love you, Peter's own creation;
> I love your stern, your stately air,
> Neva's majestical pulsation,
> The granite that her quaysides wear.[13]

The Introduction ends, however, on a minor key. After an exhortation to the city to "stand steadfast as Russia, stand in splendor," Pushkin appeals to the Gulf of Finland's waves "not to trouble Peter's eternal sleep," a bid that is immediately invalidated by a somber warning that the tale about to be told will be a grievous one.[14] The effervescence of the earlier idyllic picture gives way to an ominous "A fearful time there was." The wide and sunny horizons of the introduction are replaced by murky darkness outside a basement window spattered with raindrops.

Part 1 begins with a portrayal of St. Petersburg on the eve of the great flood of November 7, 1824, when the waters of the Neva rose thirteen feet, inundating all of the river delta. It is here that the fictional part of the poem begins and its "young hero," a low-grade civil servant with modest expectations, makes his entry. He has been to a party and now returns, drenched, to his basement room. Pushkin does not divulge his last name, but his first name, Evgeny (Eugene), is richly suggestive. It is both "generic," having been used by Pushkin in his famous novel in verse *Eugene Onegin,* and "ennobling" if one considers its Greek origins.[15]

The howling storm makes Evgeny toss and turn on his cot. He thinks of his own meager personal resources and low station in life, but mostly of his beloved Parasha, who, he hopes, will one day become his wife. He worries that the rising waters of the Neva will cause the bridges to be taken down, thus separating him and Parasha for a few days.[16] The Neva's sudden interference with Evgeny's private life anticipates the river's dramatic role in the narrative, as Evgeny's adversary and the thwarter of his unpretentious dreams of a tranquil life.

Morning brings the first tidings of the "dreadful day" ahead. In gloriously sonorous lines, Pushkin describes the Neva bursting into the city, after it has been blocked from the Gulf of Finland by westerly head winds. Turned on its heels,

> Neva exploded, raging, yelling.
> In kettle-like outbursts of steam—
> Until, mad as a beast, the stream
> Pounced on the city. From its path
> Everyone fled, and all around
> Was sudden desert . . .

Evgeny, anxious about Parasha, wanders toward the Neva, whose "explosion" surprises him on Senate (Peter's) Square. Unable to retreat, he looks for a high perch to save himself from the rolling billows and finds it on one of the two marble lions guarding the entrance of a mansion. There he sits, hatless and wet, thinking about Parasha and her widowed mother in their "flimsy cottage, close to the seashore," while at the other end of the square, high above the billowing waters, rises the imperturbable granite mountain and on it the huge impermeable bronze of the *Peter the Great:*

> Looking out,
> With back turned to him, on the retching
> Waves of Neva in their wild course
> From his fast summit, arm outstretching,
> The Giant rides on his bronze horse.[17]

Thus, in a Wagnerian finale to part 1, the furious storm brings together the three protagonists of *The Bronze Horseman:* Evgeny, Peter the Great, and the swollen and untamable Neva.

Part 2 begins with the aftermath of the storm. The Neva has scarcely receded when Evgeny hails a ferryman to take him to Vasilievsky Island. The devastation exceeds his worst fears. Filled with dreadful premonitions, he rushes to where Parasha's cottage should be standing, but where is it? The familiar willow tree is there, but the cottage has disappeared. Overcome with grief at the realization of what has happened, Evgeny takes leave of his senses. He will never return to his room. Street nooks offer him shelter, kind people give him scraps of food, and children make fun of him as he wanders aimlessly around the city.

One autumn night, bad weather chases him from his beggar's shelter by the river. He walks a short distance and suddenly realizes that everything around looks familiar. There are the lions at the entrance to the mansion,

> And there, above the river's course,
> Atop his rock, fenced-off, defended
> On his dark summit, arm extended,
> The Idol rode on his bronze horse.

The events of the flood rise up before him "in frightful clarity." He looks at the Giant

> Who, motionless and without pity,
> Lifted his bronze head in the gloom,
> Whose will, implacable as doom,
> Had chosen seashore for his city.

Suddenly he understands everything. It is Peter the Great, the bronze idol rising high above him, who is to be blamed for his tragedy! The emperor and his unnatural creation, the city of St. Petersburg, are both guilty of what has happened! His blood seething, Evgeny squeezes his fists and whispers through clenched teeth: "All right then, you wonder-working builder. Just you wait! . . . " The threat is short and inarticulate, but sufficiently blasphemous to strike terror into Evgeny's heart. He recoils in panic and dashes away from the monument. But as he runs through the deserted streets of the city, he hears behind him the heavy clangor of the horse's hooves, resounding on the granite stones of the pavement:

> He had the impression
> That the grim tsar, in sudden race
> Of blazing anger, turned his face
> Quietly and without expression
> And through the empty square he runs,
> But hears behind him, loud as guns
> Or thunderclap reverberations,
> Ponderous hooves in detonation
> Along the shuddering roadway.

Afterward, whenever Evgeny passes by the monument, he doffs his cap, turns his eyes away, and sidles off. He dies a forgotten man. His body is found on the threshold of a flimsy cottage, presumably Parasha's, that has washed up during the flood on a tiny uninhabited offshore island. That is where he is buried.

Pushkin's *The Bronze Horseman* has been subjected to every parsing device known to literary criticism. Esthetic and ethical judgments have of late tended to yield to interpretations grounded in mythology. These often lead to interesting insights, but pose the danger of becoming a mechanical device, the critic's sleight of hand.

On its surface the poem is an idealized history of St. Petersburg since its founding in 1703, a description of the catastrophic flood of 1824, and a tale of a humble civil servant yearning for a crumb of personal happiness within Peter the Great's vast enterprise of modern state building. On a deeper level, however, it is a tragedy worthy of a Sophocles, a tale of an autocrat's hubris challenging God's design and of divine punishment meted out to future generations. It is also a subtle reclamation of the lessons of the Book of Genesis. Peter's arrogation of demiurgic prerogatives harks back to the story of the Fall of Man, while the flood of 1824 is a reminder of the Flood which was meant to cleanse the earth from the sins of its inhabitants. A biblical connection is made all the more persuasive by Peter's repeated references to the site of St. Petersburg as his Paradise.

The polemic with Mickiewicz in the introduction fades away in parts 1 and 2, and yields to a sense of bewilderment and anxiety about the aftermath of Peter's reforms, comparing them to Falconet's horse, whose rearing stance is remarkable for its unpredictability:

> what fire, what passion, and what force
> Are all compact in that proud horse!
> He gallops—to what destination?
> On the cliff-edge, O lord of fate,
> Was it not you, O giant idol,
> Who, pulling on your iron bridle,
> Checked Russia, made her rear up straight?

What is the proper balance between national and individual interests? Is there any limit to an autocrat's exercise of the privilege of eminent domain, when it impinges on the basic rights of his subjects? These questions have intrigued the interpreters of *The Bronze Horseman* from the moment of the poem's publication. Answers have dealt, on the whole, with the historical Peter, rather than with the hero of Pushkin's poem. Conservative Hegelian critics viewed Peter as History personified, and his reforms, including the founding of St. Petersburg, as an expression of the collective will of the nation. Peter, they said, understood historical necessity and fulfilled its bidding, despite the misguided protests of those—Evgeny is an exemplar—whose limited horizons prevented them from seeing and appreciating the inevitability of the process of change. Liberal critics had a much more critical view of Peter. They saw him as a rigid autocrat, unflinchingly pursuing his own vision of national interest, and stopping at no repressive measure in order to exercise his will.

Pushkin's own position is ambiguous, and his poem, just like Falconet's monument, has justifiably been called enigmatic. Next to providing one of the most exultant portrayals of Peter the Great as the builder of the empire and providential leader of his nation, Pushkin issues a warning to the despot that his reach is not without limit. The tsar may be able to crush any sign insubordination on the part of his subjects, but he is powerless before the forces of nature. Pushkin's Peter may show no concern about this limitation, but Pushkin's Alexander I, overwhelmed by the magnitude of the flood, would admit that "a tsar is no commander against God's elements."

The force of nature, however, is not the only threat to the despot. Even more serious is the dagger which Pushkin fashioned in the person of Evgeny, arguably the first dissident in Russian fiction. Evgeny's revolt may be inarticulate, but it is a revolt nonetheless—a revolt, moreover, that is calculated to gain the reader's sympathy. To Nicholas I it seemed serious enough to put him on guard. Acting as his own supreme censor, the tsar read Pushkin's manuscript and concluded that it was an attack on the rule of Peter the Great and, by extension, on his own autocratic prerogatives.[18] Especially objectionable to him were Pushkin's repeated references to Peter's bronze effigy as a pagan idol. Pushkin tried to meet Nicholas's objections, but eventually decided that the poem in a truncated version was not worth publishing. It finally appeared shortly after Pushkin's death, with cuts and changes made by the poet Vasily Zhukovsky. The original text was not published till the second half of the nineteenth century.

From the moment of its appearance, Pushkin's poem has lived side by side with Falconet's monument, engaging it in a dialogue that has enriched both works.[19] The monument was the inspiration for the theme of the poem, while the poem gave it in return its name and the réclame of Pushkin's poetic genius. To a Russian the two works have become unthinkable apart from each other, an unprecedented example of the creative symbiosis of visual and verbal arts. That is why the words which the poet Aleksandr Blok jotted down in his notebook, "*The Bronze Horseman*—we are all in the vibrations of its bronze," refer, in actual fact, to Pushkin's poem, but could apply just as easily to Falconet's monument.[20] That is also the reason that the question, which is sometimes asked in the West, whether Falconet's monument would have achieved its fame without the thunder of hooves behind the terrified Evgeny, can be countered with another question: whether Pushkin's poem would have ever been born if the only monument to Peter the Great in St. Petersburg had been Rastrelli's somber and heavily anchored statement which brooks no dissent and holds no enigmas.

The Russian penchant for the mystical, religious, and mythical has also opened the way to other decipherments of the symbolism of Falconet's monument. One such reading was offered by the Symbolist poet and religious philosopher Viacheslav Ivanov (1866–1949).[21] In Ivanov's vision, Russia is an arena of strife among three contending dominions. Holy or Christ's Russia, a land living in accordance with the Lord's commandments, is opposed by two Satanic powers. One of them is under the sway of Ahriman, so named after the Manichean demon of darkness; the other is ruled over by Lucifer, the rebel archangel of the Cabala. Ahriman's Russia is dominated by the spirit of destruction and putrefaction: it is a land of traditional, Byzantine ways, characteristic of old Muscovy. Lucifer's Russia, brought into being by Peter the Great, radiates its power from St. Petersburg. Its educated and freethinking proponents look for inspiration in the West and find it in the ideals of the French Revolution and Marxism.[22]

Here is how the art critic David Arkin adapted Ivanov's idea to Falconet's monument:

> The union of these two principles [Ahriman and Lucifer] is depicted with extraordinary force in the enigmatic monument which Pushkin made the hero of his inspired poem, a monument which, more than anything else in St. Petersburg, has struck the imagination of poets and artists. . . . The Russian creative genius . . . sensed in it something greater than a monument to the founder of the city and of the empire. It is a symbol of St. Petersburg and, at the same time, of the two elements, the two guises of Russia. The mark of Lucifer is in the figure of Peter, the founder of Lucifer's Russia, while the mark of Ahriman's Russia is in the Snake, coiling on the granite. . . . That is how the two of them rule in St. Petersburg, . . . two hypostases of [Satan], incarnate in St. Petersburg and shrouding the face of Christ's Russia.[23]

Arkin's interpretation would account for Evgeny's gesture of panic as he recoils from the "terrifying" visage of Peter under which he senses the image of Satan. It helps to understand the dismay with which a Russian looks at Pushkin's doodle, showing the monument without Peter in the "saddle" and with the snake dead or dying, a vision that leaves the viewer with nothing

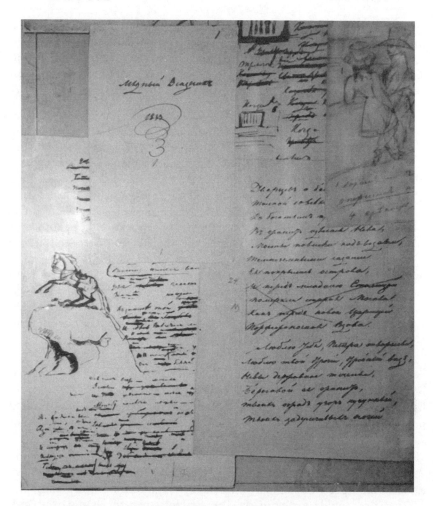

Fig. E.2. Pushkin's Drawing of the Riderless Bronze Horseman on the Margin of a Page from the Poem "Tazit." On top is the title page of Pushkin's *The Bronze Horseman;* on the right is an autograph excerpt from the introduction to *The Bronze Horseman.* Courtesy of the All-Russian Museum of A. S. Pushkin, St. Petersburg. Photograph by A. M. Schenker.

but the bewildered horse rearing above the precipice (fig. E.2). It connects also to the Old Believers' conviction that Peter's reforms of traditional Russian ways and values were the work of Antichrist.[24] Hence the Old Believers' identification of Falconet's monument with the apocalyptic image: "And I looked, and behold, a pale horse: and his name that sat on him was Death, and Hell followed him. And power was given unto them over the fourth part of the earth, to kill with sword, and with hunger, and with death, and with the beasts of the earth" (Rev. 6.8). This identification made Peter and, by extension, his effigy, responsible for every tragedy that afflicted Russia, whether it was brought about by war or by natural causes.[25]

Radishchev was the only observer of the unveiling of the monument who dared to use that solemn occasion to voice a remarkably frank and stern evaluation of Catherine the Great's regime:

> O Peter! When your resounding deeds caused amazement and respect, was there anyone among the thousands admiring the greatness of your spirit and intellect, who praised you out of the innocence of their hearts? Half of them were flatterers who secretly hated you and assailed your deeds. Others, seized by the terror of your total and absolute power, lowered their eyes slavishly before the radiance of your glory. Then, O tsar, you were alive and almighty. But today, sixty years after your death, when you can neither punish nor pardon, when there is no breath left in you, when you must yield to your lowest soldier, your glory is genuine, our gratitude is not pretended. But our recognition would have been truer and worthier of you if it did not have to follow the lead of your successor, who holds in her hand the life and death of millions of those who were created in her likeness. Our recognition would have been freer and the service at the dedication of your sculpted image would have been a service of grateful prayers which people, in their joy, offer to their primordial father.[26]

To this blend of loyalist and seditious sentiments, Radishchev added what is surely a first in Russian recorded history: "Let me say that Peter could have been greater if, while exalting himself and his country, he had affirmed personal freedom."

Was Falconet a great sculptor? There is a consensus that such surviving statuary as the *Christ on the Mount of Olives,* the *Bather,* and *Winter* have earned him a place of singular distinction in eighteenth-century sculpture. Most critics would also grant the Bronze Horseman the status of a work touched with genius. Does this entitle Falconet to be put alongside such sculptors as Girardon, Bouchardon, or Lemoyne? Many of his contemporaries, Diderot in particular, thought so. So does George Levitine, who calls him "the most engrossingly many-sided eighteenth-century sculptor before Houdon."[27] There are dissenting voices, however: "Have you ever heard of Falconet?" asked Stendhal sarcastically in 1828, recalling that sixty years earlier Diderot had promised the sculptor immortality.[28] This uncharitable view takes its cue, no doubt, from a contemporary Italian art historian who declared that, had it not been for the monument to Peter the Great, Falconet's name "would have perished along with the greater part of his works . . . without deserving to be rescued by the keepers of the country's patrimony."[29]

Tastes change, values go up and down, and the facts of one epoch may be confirmed or discredited by the facts of another. Myth, however, resists the ravages of time. It is like a dragon which regenerates its severed limbs, is immune to the lance of the skeptic, and, keeping close to the ground, does not feel the winds of circumstance and fashion howling above. But it is a voracious beast, assimilating fact and legend with equal facility. It had no problem ingesting Falconet's monument, for it found in it not only a feast for the eyes, but a luscious morsel on which it could satisfy its appetite for that which is concealed from the senses.

Falconet accomplished the dual feat of art-making and mythopoeia in such a spectacular fashion as to make one feel that all his earlier life served no other purpose than preparation for that final spurt of creativity, the monument to Peter the Great in St. Petersburg. One could even say that his road toward the monument had been paved with a sequence of quasi-miracles, or at the very least, a series of improbable events, all aiming to assure his creation immediate success and enhance its image in the eyes of posterity. One could count among these Falconet's self-transformation from an uneducated young man to a learned scholar; his selection to be the sculptor of the *Peter the Great* over a number of seemingly better-qualified candidates; the find of an immense granite rock in the midst of a northern swamp; the mind-boggling exploit of its transportation; his successful casting of the statue, a feat never performed by a sculptor on such a grandiose scale; and his fruitful, though posthumous, collaboration with the greatest Russian poet, Alexander Pushkin.

Even the selfless devotion of a beautiful and talented sculptress to a jaundiced and demanding artist thirty-two years her senior verges on the miraculous. Magical, at any rate, was Falconet's ability to make his sculptures anticipate the two milestones of that affair. For did not his famous *Pygmalion and Galatea* (fig. 1.9) presage the entry of Collot into his life? And did not his relief *Alexander the Great Surrendering Campaspe to the Painter Apelles* (fig. 1.6), showing the king of Macedonia presenting his concubine to the painter of her portrait, augur Falconet's urging his mistress to marry his son, who had just finished painting Collot's portrait?

Much has changed in Russia since the days when Catherine the Great had Radishchev arrested, terrorized with a commuted death sentence, and exiled to Siberia for his wayward thoughts. But much, also, has remained the same. Mickiewicz's dream that the west wind would bring to the peoples of Russia the glad tidings of freedom has not been fully realized. In the literal sense, the west wind subjected the inhabitants of St. Petersburg to devastation and human misery, described so poignantly in Pushkin's account of the flood of 1824. In the metaphorical sense, the west wind carried both good and bad seeds on its wings. Unhappily, the good seeds did not sprout well in Russian soil, while the bad ones flourished. Of the three slogans broadcast by the French Revolution, "fraternity" alone did well in Russia, simply because it was a familiar strand in the social fabric of the nation.

The questions posed by the two awestruck poets standing at the foot of the monument still keep resounding in the hollow spaces of the present-day

Decembrists Square. Some onlookers question the cold and cruel gaze of the tsar who gallops across his lands, oblivious of the fate of the little man and unmindful of the ultimate goal of his ride. Such is the tsar in Pushkin's *The Bronze Horseman,* a giant tsar "who, motionless and without pity, / Lifted his bronze head in the gloom," galloping, but "to what destination?" Others, looking at the horse, ask with dread whether its wild stance and bewildered look might be symbolic of Russia itself. One of these questioners was the Symbolist novelist and poet Andrei Bely in his darkly satirical novel *Petersburg:* "Will you break loose of the stone in which you are anchored, . . . will you fly unbridled through the air and plunge into the watery chaos? Or will you tear the mists apart, leap aloft, and . . . vanish in the clouds? Or, having raised yourself on your hind legs, will you be lost in perennial thoughts of the terrible fate that had tossed you here into this gloomy North? . . . Or, fearful of the leap, will you lower your hoofs again and, snorting, carry the great Horseman away from these lands of illusion to the vast expanse of the steppe?"[30]

Bely's "lands of illusion" seem even more illusory today. Gone is the city's status as the capital of the land, gone is the military power of Sweden, gone is the importance of a merchant port in the age of superhighways, pipelines, and airplanes. Gone, in other words, are the main reasons for the city's founding. What remain are ghosts of imperial splendor, churches turned into tourist sights, imposing government buildings which rent out space to offices and apartments, Baroque palaces housing archival collections and academic institutions.

Reading the enthusiastic accounts of the development of St. Petersburg in the eighteenth and nineteenth centuries, one is impressed by the city's aura of promise. A promise that it will be an open gate to Europe and will lead the rest of the country toward modernity and a prosperous future. Indeed, in order to help translate that promise into reality, a stream of master builders, city planners, painters, sculptors, and scientists, with Italian, French, Scottish, German, and Dutch names, rushed into the city in a virtual invasion by the West. They left behind beautiful avenues and spacious squares, magnificent buildings and lovely parks.

Yet, for all its unearthly beauty, for all its glorious two centuries as the capital and cultural center of the land, St. Petersburg has remained a dream, a gift of the West to Russia which has not fulfilled its promise. Instead of conquering the rest of the country with its achievements, it gradually succumbed to its encroachments. It grew like a lovely exotic flower planted amidst abundant and aggressive native vegetation. Pressed upon from all sides, it has become an isolated and puzzling phenomenon in its own country: "Don't believe St. Petersburg, it's all a deception, a mirage, a phantom, woven from opaque exhalations and mists, posed on marshlands. It is all obscurity, a fanciful dream, a lie, and an invention. It is fickle and faithless, a chimera, and a contradiction."[31] These words sum up the native reaction to St. Petersburg.

As a relatively recently founded city, St. Petersburg filled up with settlers from various provinces of the empire. Whether they were Russians or Ukrainians from the hinterland, Germans or Latvians from the Baltic regions, Greeks or Poles from their occupied lands, or mere fortune-seekers from various corners of the world, they enriched the city with their native experience and contributed a wealth of talent to its economic and intellectual development. They had too little time, however, to strike deep spiritual and emotional roots in the ethos of the country at large. They were the type of people whom Dostoevsky described so caustically in his short story "A Poor Joke": "He came from among the St. Petersburg Russians, that is, his father and his father's father were born, raised, and had government jobs in St. Petersburg. They never left St. Petersburg. That is an altogether special type among the Russians. They know almost nothing about Russia and that's fine with them. Their interests turn around St. Petersburg and especially their jobs. All they care about are a petty game of preference, the corner store, and their monthly salary. They don't know a single Russian custom, not one Russian song."[32]

This psychological isolation of the Petersburgers from the rest of the country may bear much responsibility for the spread of another unfulfilled Western promise to Russia, a promise to which Arthur Koestler gave the name of the "God that failed." For is it not possible that had it not been for the evangelization of Peter's spirit of revolt by the "rootless" Petersburgers, the "rootless" Marxist ideology would not have taken hold in Russia, sparing the country the national catastrophe which followed its inculcation?[33]

Catherine the Great did not show much gratitude to the man whose four words on the pedestal of the monument to Peter the Great have done more to perpetuate her glory than the massive statue in front of the Alexandrine Theater where she stands surrounded by her ministers, some of them also her bedfellows. And yet, it was she who paid Falconet the ultimate compliment, all the more precious for having been entrusted to the pages which come as close to a personal diary as any of her writings—a letter to Grimm. She recalled stopping at the monument, together with some of her closest associates, on the way to visit the ailing Betskoi: "When seen out in the open, Peter the First appeared alive and great. One could say that he was quite satisfied with what he had created. I could not look at him long for I felt an onrush of emotion and, when I looked around, I saw everybody with tears in their eyes. . . . He was too far to speak to me, but I thought that he gave me a look of approval. It gave me courage to try to do better in the future. I'll do what I can."[34]

Had Falconet been aware of these words, all the tribulations of his twelve years in St. Petersburg might have seemed inconsequential and, who knows, a tear of emotion might have glistened in his eye too.

There is no street or square in St. Petersburg dedicated to Falconet and Collot, the creators of the only monument in the world that has so captured the fancy of those who live in its shadow as to become their hallowed shield; a monument which is so Russian that it defies classification in the histories of French sculpture.[35]

In the Montmartre section of Paris, tucked in between the tiny passage Cottin and the rue du Chevalier de la Barre, which winds its way up to the Basilica of the Sacré-Coeur, there is a dead-end street that is only two houses long. No wonder that on most plans of Paris it is not even marked and that few people in the neighborhood know its name. It is the rue Falconet, the street which his native city dedicated to the memory of the sculptor who signed the greatest equestrian monument of all time *Falconet of Paris.*[36]

Could it be that posterity is paying Falconet back for the irreverence with which he treated it? Perhaps. But the monument on the Neva is beyond the mortal notions of remembrance and oblivion. It has become the flesh and soul of St. Petersburg and will stand as long as the city stands, embodying the dreams of its three conjurers, a Russian tsar, a German-born empress, and a French *maître-sculpteur.*

*The Admiralty District
of St. Petersburg in 1766*

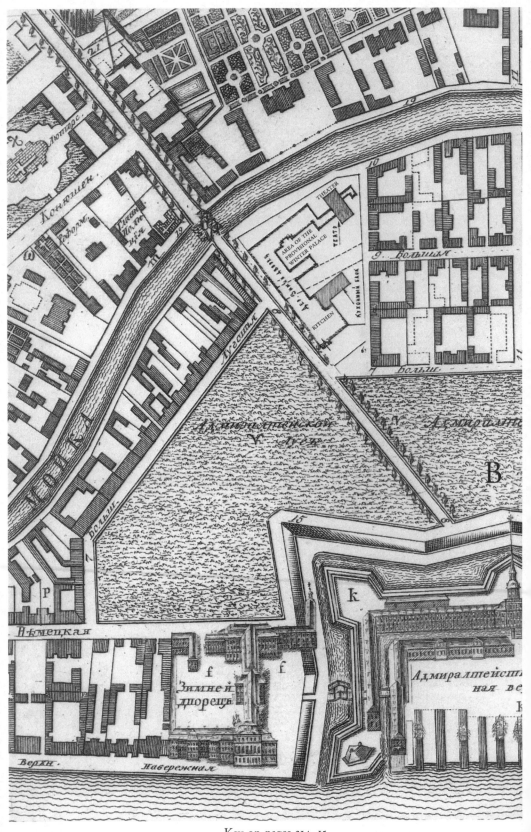

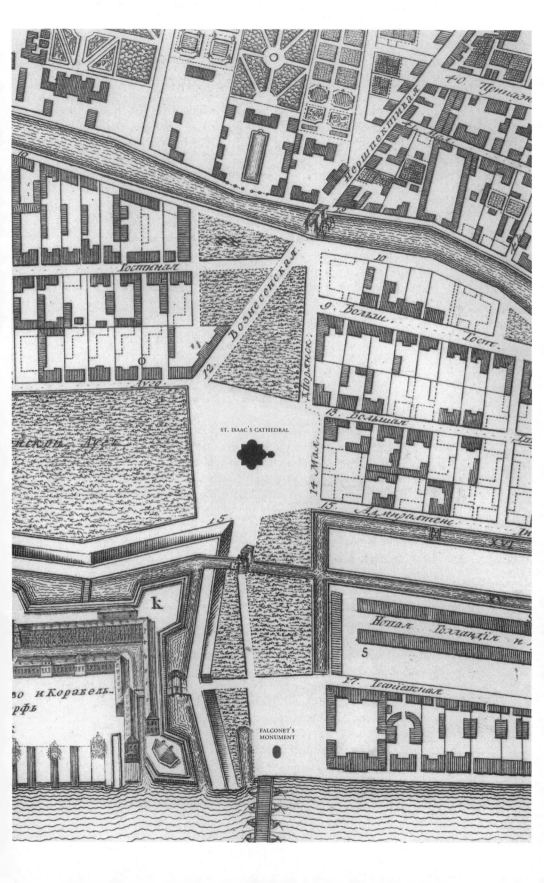

ST. ISAAC'S CATHEDRAL

FALCONET'S
MONUMENT

The plan shown on pages 312–13 is based on Mikhail Ivanovich Makhaev (1753), *Plan stolichnogo goroda Sanktpeterburga s izobrazheniem znatneishikh onogo prospektov,* St. Petersburg, map 5, and appears by courtesy of the Map Collection, Yale University Library.

This version of Makhaev's plan includes three changes which had occurred by the time of Falconet's arrival in St. Petersburg in 1766.

(1) The sites of the first St. Isaac's Cathedral (large black marker) and of Falconet's monument (oval black marker) have been added (after Kaganovich, 1982, p. 47).

(2) The stone structures remaining after the demolition of the provisional Winter Palace of 1755, at the corner of Nevsky Prospect and Moika Embankment, have been inserted (after Ivanov, 1994, p. 21).

(3) The second church of St. Isaac of Dalmatia on the Neva embankment between the Isakievsky Pontoon Bridge and the Senate, torn down in the early sixties, has been deleted.

Letter and numerical markings indicate the following buildings and landmarks (compass points in Makhaev's plan are reversed, north being at the bottom):

B: The Admiralty Meadow. To the southwest of the Admiralty, the first St. Isaac's Cathedral was being built. It was replaced in the first half of the nineteenth century by the current St. Isaac's Cathedral. A short distance to the east the Lobanov-Rostovsky Palace was erected between 1817 and 1820. In front of its entrance were the two guardian lions immortalized in Pushkin's *The Bronze Horseman.*

f: The Winter Palace

k: The Admiralty. The area occupied by the wharves and the Admiralty canal was replaced by Alexander (now Admiralty) Gardens.

S: Novaia Gollandia (now Konnogvardeisky Boulevard)

V: Eastern part of the Admiralty Meadow, partly replaced by Palace Square

6: Kirpichny Alley (linking 7 and 10)

7: Bol'shaia Lugovaia (east of Nevsky Prospect, now Bol'shaia Morskaia); Bol'shaia Lugovaia (west of Nevsky Prospect, now Malaia Morskaia)

8: Nevsky Prospect

9: Bol'shaia Gostinaia (west of Nevsky Prospect, now Bol'shaia Morskaia)

10: Gostinaia Embankment (now Moika Embankment)

11: Sredniaia (now Gorokhovaia)

12: Voznesensky Prospect

13: Bol'shaia Dvorianskaia (now Pochtamtskaia)

14: Malaia Dvorianskaia. The house at the corner of Malaia Dvorianskaia and Bol'shaia Dvorianskaia (now 9 Isakievsky Square) belonged to the Naryshkins. This is where Diderot stayed during his visit to St. Petersburg in 1773–74.

15:   Admiralteiskaia liniia (now Admiralteisky Prospect and Novo-Isakievskaia)
17:   Isakievskaia (now Galernaia)
19:   Koniushennaia Embankment (now Moika Embankment)
21:   Kazanskaia (now Plekhanova)
40:   Prikaznaia = Ofitserskaia (now Dekabristov)
228: Green bridge on the Moika (Politseisky most)
229: Blue bridge on the Moika
Black oval marker: Site of the monument to Peter the Great on Senate Square, slightly to the west of the Isakievsky Pontoon Bridge across the Neva. Farther west is the Senate building. The embankment of the Neva west of the bridge was called Beregovaia (now Angliiskaia) Embankment. The embankment east of the Admiralty was called Verkhniaia (now Dvortsovaia) Embankment.

In the area bounded by Nevsky Prospect, Malaia Morskaia Street, Kirpichny Alley, and Moika Embankment stood the provisional Winter Palace (1755–67), built for Empress Elizabeth. Its wooden parts were demolished by Catherine the Great, and the two remaining stone buildings were offered to Falconet and Collot. They resided in the former kitchen building, and their atelier was in the old theater (see pp. 97–98).

Note on Translations, Transliteration, Nomenclature, and Dates

Translations done by the author of the book are not attributed; translations by other persons are attributed in the notes. The latter include some of Falconet's writings on art, the poetry of Mickiewicz, almost all the poetry of Pushkin, Diderot's accounts of the Paris salons of 1765 and 1767, and several late-eighteenth-century texts.

Transliteration from Russian follows the Library of Congress system, with the exceptions recommended by the *Slavic and East European Journal*. This means that, except in bibliographic references, personal and place names are spelled as they are traditionally known in the English-speaking countries (e.g. Alexander Pushkin, not Aleksandr Pushkin; Bely, not Belyi; Dostoevsky, not Dostoevskii; Nevsky, not Nevskii). In similar circumstances the apostrophe for the soft sign is omitted (Mashenka, not Mashen'ka; Tver, not Tver').

The family name Golitsyn is a transliteration of its modern Russian spelling; in the West, however, this name is better known in its French version as Gal(l)itzin(e).

During his stay in Russia, the Greek engineer Marin Carburi assumed the name of chevalier de Lascaris. To avoid confusion, the name Carburi is used throughout the book.

Pushkin's poem *The Bronze Horseman* has lent its title to the monument of Peter the Great. The former is identified as *The Bronze Horseman,* and the latter as the Bronze Horseman.

Dates are given in accordance with the calendar of the region in question, Julian in Russia and Gregorian in Western Europe. In the second half of the eighteenth century, Gregorian dates fell eleven days after the Julian ones.

Abbreviations

AA	*L'Art et les artistes,* Paris
AAE, CP	Archives diplomatiques du Ministère des affaires etrangères, Corréspondance politique, Paris
AN	Archives nationales, Paris
AQ	*Art Quarterly,* New York
ASV	Archivio statale di Venezia, Venice
AVPRI	Arkhiv vneshnei politiki Russkoi imperii, Moscow
BCh	*Boldinskie chteniia,* Gorky
BM	*Burlington Magazine,* London
BMF	*Bulletin des musées de France,* Paris
BN(E)	Bibliothèque nationale de France, Cabinet des Estampes
BN, N. a. fr.	Bibliothèque nationale de France, Nouvelles acquisitions françaises, Paris
BSHAF	*Bulletin de la Societé de l'histoire de l'art français,* Paris
Chteniia	*Chteniia v Imperatorskom Obshchestve istorii i drevnostei slavianskikh pri Moskovskom universitete,* Moscow
CLT	*Correspondance littéraire, philosophique et critique par Grimm, Diderot et al.,* ed. by Maurice Tourneux, 16 vols., Paris, 1877–82
d.	*delo* (folder number)
DBI	*Dizionario biografico degli italiani,* ed. by Alberto M. Ghisalberti, Rome, 1960–99
DHS	*Dix-huitième siècle,* Paris
DNR	*Drevniaia i novaia Rossiia,* St. Petersburg
DOC	*Diderot: Oeuvres complètes,* ed. by Jules Assézat and Maurice Tourneux, 20 vols., Paris, 1875–77
DS	*Diderot Studies,* Geneva
Encyclopédie	*Encyclopédie, ou dictionnaire raisonné des sciences, des arts et des métiers par une société de gens de lettres,* ed. by d'Alembert and Diderot, 17 vols., 1751–66; see also *Recueil*
ESR	*European Studies Review,* London
f.	folio
FN	*Filologicheskie nauki,* Moscow
FO	*Oeuvres d'Etienne Falconet, statuaire,* 6 vols., Lausanne, 1781
FOC	*Oeuvres complètes d'Etienne Falconet,* 3 vols., Paris, 1808
GBA	*Gazette des Beaux Arts,* Paris
GdeF	*Gazette de France,* Paris
IstV	*Istoricheskii vestnik,* St. Petersburg
IZ	*Istoricheskie zapiski,* Moscow
JE	*Journal encyclopédique,* Bouillon

ABBREVIATIONS

JWCI	*Journal of the Warburg and Courtauld Institute,* London
LS	*Lotmanovskii sbornik,* Moscow
MRI	*Materialy po russkomu iskusstvu,* Leningrad
MSB	*Mémoires secrets de Bachaumont,* Paris and London, 1762–88
Mercure	*Mercure de France,* Paris
NYRB	*The New York Review of Books.* New York
o.	*opis'* (archival record)
PPSS	Aleksandr Pushkin, *Polnoe sobranie sochinenii,* Moscow and Leningrad, 16 vols. and Supplement, 1937–59
PSSZRI	*Polnoe sobranie Svoda zakonov Rossiiskoi Imperii,* St. Petersburg
PVA	*Procès-verbaux de l'Académie Royale de Peinture et de Sculpture, 1648–1793,* ed. by Anatole de Montaiglon, 10 vols., Paris, 1875–92
RA	*Russkii arkhiv,* Moscow
RBS	*Russkii biograficheskii slovar',* St. Petersburg/Petrograd, 1896–1918
RdeA	*Revue de l'art,* Paris
RdL	*Revue du Louvre et des musées de France,* Paris
RDM	*Revue des deux mondes,* Paris
Recueil	*Recueil de planches sur les sciences, les arts libéraux et les arts méchaniques avec leur explication,* Paris, 1771 (a collection of illustrations for the *Encyclopédie*)
RGADA	Rossiiskii gosudarstvennyi arkhiv drevnikh aktov, Moscow
RGAVMF	Rossiiskii gosudarstvennyi arkhiv voenno-morskogo flota, St. Petersburg
RGIA	Rossiiskii gosudarstvennyi istoricheskii arkhiv, St. Petersburg
RL	*Russkaia literatura,* AN SSSR, Institut russkoi literatury (Pushkinskii dom), Leningrad/St. Petersburg
RM	*Revue moderne,* Paris
RNB	Rossiiskaia Natsional'naia Biblioteka, St. Petersburg
RS	*Russkaia starina,* St. Petersburg
RUA	*Revue universelle des arts,* Paris and Brussels
SG	*Starye gody,* St. Petersburg/Petrograd
SGE	*Soobshcheniia gosudarstvennogo Ermitazha,* St. Petersburg
SHAF	*Société de l'Histoire de l'Art Français,* Paris
SIRIO	*Sbornik imperatorskogo russkogo istoricheskogo obshchestva,* St. Petersburg
SMAMID	*Sbornik Moskovskogo glavnogo arkhiva Ministerstva inostrannykh del,* Moscow
SORIaS	*Sbornik Otdeleniia russkogo iazyka i slovesnosti,* St. Petersburg
SPOARAN	Sankt-Peterburgskii otdel arkhiva Rossiiskoi Akademii nauk, St. Petersburg
SPV	*Sankt-Peterburgskie vedomosti,* St. Petersburg
Stampa	*Stampa della Nob[ile] Sig[noza] Co[ntessa] Sofia Carburi qu[erelante] Co[nte] Marin*
SZRI	*Sbornik zakonov russkoi imperii*
TsGALI	Tsentral'nyi gosudarstvennyi arkhiv literatury i iskusstva, Moscow
TsGAVMF	Tsentral'nyi gosudarstvennyi arkhiv voenno-morskogo flota
VF	*Voprosy filosofii,* Moscow
VL	*Voprosy literatury,* Moscow
ZfSlPh	*Zeitschrift für slavische Philologie,* Heidelberg

Notes

INTRODUCTION

1. Even in death the Petersburgers remain in touch with the monument: "Just as in Rome many graves are decorated with columns reflecting the motifs of the Forum, so the rock of the Bronze Horseman is frequently seen on Leningrad tombstones" (Antsiferov, 1926, p. 117).
2. When Peter the Great visited Paris in 1717, he was forty-five and Falconet was six months old. It was the only occasion when the future sculptor and the subject of his greatest work were in the same place at the same time.
3. A phrase attributed to Catherine's courtier, Ivan Ivanovich Betskoi.
4. Danilevskii, 1894, p. 58.
5. This ditty rhymes in Russian: "S odnoi storony—more, s drugoi—gore, s tret'ei—mokh, s chetvertoi—vzdokh."
6. Cited after Putnam, ed., 1952, p. 307.
7. Even today there are only five downtown bridges across the Greater Neva, accessible to pedestrian and vehicular traffic. They are the Lieutenant Shmidt (former Annunciation, 1850–55), Liteiny (1879), Trinity (1897–1903), Palace (1912–16), and Alexander Nevsky (1960–65).
8. In the modern period, the warmer winters and the discharge of industrial and human waste have significantly raised the temperature of the water, reducing thereby the period when the river cools off sufficiently to produce ice that is thick enough to support pedestrian traffic. The city discourages occasional risk-takers by cutting and maintaining an open channel in the middle of the river.
9. Catherine to Grimm, September 10, 1777: *SIRIO*, vol. 23, pp. 64–65, or *SORIaS*, pp. 52–53; cf. Pyliaev, 1990. pp. 114–17. The flood of 1824 was vividly described by Adam Mickiewicz in "Oleszkiewicz," and forms the central event in Alexander Pushkin's *The Bronze Horseman*. Neither the Polish nor the Russian poet witnessed the flood. Mickiewicz arrived in the city on the morrow, while Pushkin was away at his Novgorod estate.
10. Russia lost its access to the Baltic in 1617 when, according to the terms of the peace treaty of Stolbovo, Sweden took over the Finnic-speaking lands of Ingria and Karelia that had been part of the ancient patrimony of Novgorod Rus'. Peter's dream of having a nonfreezing harbor on the Baltic was not to be fulfilled until the end of World War II, when the Soviets took possession of the Lithuanian city of Klaipeda (Memel). When Lithuania regained independence in 1990, Russia was left with Baltiisk (former East Prussian Pillau) as its only nonfreezing Baltic port able to handle deep-draft shipping.

11. Russian waterways had lured the Swedes since the times of their Viking forefathers who, at the end of the first millennium, used the basins of the Volga and the Dnieper to foster trade with the Middle and Near East. A side effect of that commercial enterprise was the installation of the Viking Rurikide dynasty in the East Slavic principalities of Novgorod and Kiev.

12. The climatic conditions and geographic coordinates of the two cities—they are located on the sixtieth degree of northern latitude—are similar.

13. When Peter's trusted helper Menshikov suggested that the tsar's little house be built with the lumber of the Finnish huts from Nyenskans, a small Swedish fort a mile or so upstream, Peter objected because he did not want his own place to have any associations with the past. For Peter's demiurgic pretensions, cf. the first lines of the introduction to Pushkin's poem *The Bronze Horseman,* discussed in the epilogue.

14. In a letter to Lord Hervey, Algarotti says: "I am at length going to give you some account of this new city, of this window lately opened in the north, thro' which Russia looks into Europe" (Cross, ed., 1971, p. 183).

15. Ibid., p. 186.

16. Brodsky, 1985, p. 72. The Dutch pronunciation of *Sankt-Pieterburg* is *Sankt-Piterburkh,* and that is how it was originally spelled in Cyrillic. The name was too long and too foreign to suit the tastes of the population and was shortened to *Piter,* which has survived to this day in informal parlance. The Dutch name was first Germanized to *Sankt-Peterburg,* Slavicized to *Petrograd* at the outbreak of World War I in 1914, and Sovietized to *Leningrad,* following Lenin's death in 1924. After the dissolution of the Soviet Union it reverted to *Sankt-Peterburg.*

17. Peter must have favored such an association for he saw himself as the maker of Russia and had the sculptor C. B. Rastrelli represent him accordingly. On the right breastplate of his bust (1723) Peter is shown wearing the imperial crown and mantle with a mallet in hand, sculpting a standing female figure of Russia. Rastrelli projected a similar image for the top of a large column celebrating Peter's victories against Sweden, but never brought that idea to fruition.

18. Cf. the 1510 letter of the monk Philotheus to Grand Prince Vasily III which proclaimed that, after Rome turned against Eastern Christianity and Constantinople fell to Islam, Moscow assumed the role of the third Rome. "There will be no fourth," he predicted.

19. Nikolai M. Karamzin (1766–1826), author of a multivolume *History of the Russian State,* speaking at a meeting of the Russian Academy of Sciences in 1818, went so far as to claim that "Peter the Great transformed our country with his sovereign arm, making of us people similar to the Europeans. No point in ruing this. The link between the mind frames of ancient and modern Russians has been broken forever."

20. Peter's revolution has also left its imprint on Russian historiography by giving rise to the Eurasianist faction, which seeks connections and analogs to Russian cultural phenomena in Asia rather than in the West.

21. Tsar Peter was excommunicated by an ultraconservative branch of the Russian church.

22. Belyi, 1994, p. 98; italics added.

23. The two native Germans Catherine the Great and Friedrich Melchior Grimm corresponded in French. Similarly, Aleksandr Mikhailovich Golitsyn, vice chancellor of Catherine the Great, and his nephew Dmitry Alekseevich Golitsyn, the Russian envoy in Paris, used French in their correspondence.

24. Strange as it may seem, the lands of Kievan and Novgorod Rus', the two earliest political entities of the Eastern Slavs, had less of a problem with their European identity than did their Muscovite successors. Conscious of their Scandinavian origins, the Varangian

dynasty of the Rurikides of Kiev and Novgorod cultivated political and commercial ties to Western Europe. Particularly active in his relations with the West was the Grand Prince Yaroslav the Wise of Kiev (r. 1019–54), whose children married into the royal and princely families of France, Norway, Hungary, and Germany. Most interesting is the case of Yaroslav's daughter Anna, who married the French king Henri I in 1051. In 1063, acting on behalf of her eleven-year-old son Philippe I, Anna signed a charter for a monastery in Soissons using Cyrillic letters to render the Old French *Anna reina,* "Queen Anna." Anna's literacy is an oft-cited example of Kievan respect for learning. Novgorod, which escaped the Mongol yoke, retained self-government until its subjugation by Moscow in the second half of the fifteenth century.

25. How little the French knew of events in Russia in the seventeenth century is shown by the fact that Louis XIV wrote to Tsar Mikhail Fedorovich even after that first Romanov had died. The French dismissal of pre-Petrine Russia as a barbarous land differed from the matter-of-fact and tolerant attitude displayed by the British diplomats and merchants who visited Muscovy and left behind numerous accounts of their experiences. Captain Jacques Margeret's book on his experiences in the service of Boris Godunov is the lone example of a Frenchman's attempt to provide an unprejudiced picture of Russia. Margeret was, in fact, one of the few Frenchmen who learned to speak and read Russian very well. His knowledgeable account of Russia during the Time of Troubles has become a cherished source of information for scholars working on the Dmitry episode in Russian history (see Margeret, 1983, an English translation by Dunning). It is possible that the engraved portrait of Dmitry that Collot gave to the Russian playwright Aleksandr Sumarokov came from Margeret's collection (Ivanchin-Pisarev, 1842, p. 487). For a survey of the early contacts between France and pre-Petrine Russia, see the first chapter of Mohrenschildt, 1936.

26. "O nichtozhestve literatury russkoi," *PPSS,* vol. 11, p. 269. One may even claim that Peter's transfer of the capital to St. Petersburg changed the geographic coordinates of Russia in the eyes of the West, for throughout the eighteenth century and a good portion of the nineteenth, the country was viewed from Europe as the North rather than the East.

27. Ibid.

28. In his account of Peter's visit to Paris, Saint-Simon (1675–1755) did not shrink from the use of the term *barbarous* in describing Peter's habits. Yet, he was sufficiently sober-minded to see the dangers of the policy of dismissing Russia's importance in international affairs: "We have long had good reasons to reproach ourselves for yielding to the ill-fated charms of England, while treating Russia with insane contempt" (Saint-Simon, 1920, vol. 31, p. 390).

29. The French minister of foreign affairs, the duc de Choiseul, described the consequences of the French official coolness toward Russia in an instruction given on March 16, 1760, to the newly appointed French minister plenipotentiary at the court of Empress Elizabeth, Baron de Breteuil (1760–63): "For many years there have not been any relations between France and Russia. The king not only recalled from Russia his minister and consul who were posted there, but he did not even arrange for indirect lines of communication in St. Petersburg that are customarily maintained in other countries with which for political reasons we do not have public and open relations. That is why Versailles was completely ignorant of everything that had anything to do with the Russian government, with the instructions of the empress [Elizabeth], with the views of her ministers, when in 1755 she . . . informed the king [Louis XV] of her desire to reestablish perfect understanding between France and Russia" (Rambaud, ed., 1890, vol. 2, pp. 119–20).

30. Ibid., pp. 215 and 213. A month after the French minister of foreign affairs Choiseul was removed from his post in disgrace, Catherine the Great wrote to Mme Bjelke, an old friend of her mother and her frequent correspondent: "I bear so little grudge against M. de Choiseul that I am sorry he has been sacked. Wishing to cause me the greatest damage, he was always doing the wrong things. . . . He was as mad as they come and his employees here [from de Breteuil to Rossignol] were monsters of malice. But what is malice? In such persons it becomes ridiculous" (January 21, 1771, *SIRIO,* vol. 13, p. 63). A distrust of the West's intentions vis-à-vis Russia is a lingering presence in Russian politics.

31. December 18, 1763 (Rambaud, ed., 1890, vol. 2, p. 224). In fact, the king postponed marquis de Bausset's departure for St. Petersburg till 1765.

32. AAE CP Russie, vol. 85, f. 228r.

33. "Her informal *causeries* on any topic charm the reader by their simplicity and lack of pretense and her short notes, dry and abruptly broken off, are couched in a language of clarity, precision, measure, and accuracy which make up for their laconicism. This German-Russian empress was not only a great sovereign, but certainly one of the finest foreign writers in French in our eighteenth-century literature" (Réau, ed., 1921, p. xviii).

34. Voltaire to D. A. Golitsyn, December 31, 1766: Besterman et al., eds., 1968–, vol. 115, p. 187; to Catherine the Great, January 24, 1766: Besterman et al., eds., 1968–, vol. 114, p. 62; to Count Andrei P. Shuvalov, July 19, 1771: Besterman et al.. eds., 1968–, vol. 122, p. 31.

35. Catherine to Voltaire, March 15, 1767; *SIRIO,* vol. 10, p. 175.

36. Cf. Rambaud, ed., 1890, vol. 2, p. 264. In French diplomats' reports from St. Petersburg one finds numerous *mémoires* on Russia, all uniformly critical of the Russian political scene and of Catherine herself (see AAE, CP, Russie, especially vol. 85). Catherine was aware of these views and complained about them bitterly: "The French are funny people; some are absolutely out to harm me and they are the great majority; others wish to serve me, but they are few in number" (Catherine to Falconet, May 30, 1771: Réau, ed., 1921, p. 150). For surveys of Franco-Russian contacts in the eighteenth century, see Pingaud, 1886; Mohrenschildt, 1936; Lortholary, 1951; and [Angremy and Souslov], 1986–87.

37. Typologically, the pro-Catherine attitudes of Voltaire and the French *encyclopédistes* did not differ much from the Western liberals' indiscriminate praise of Stalin, even during the Soviet dictator's worst excesses.

38. Diderot to Falconet, April or May 1767: Roth, ed., 1955–70, vol. 7, p. 53.

39. Diderot to Falconet, May [30], 1773: Roth, ed., 1955–70, vol. 12, p. 229.

40. Brückner, 1885, vol. 1, p. 18.

41. Malinovskii, ed. and tr., 1990, vol. 1, pp. 167–68.

42. Two such cases were especially annoying to Catherine the Great. One was an eyewitness account of her personal involvement in the murder of her husband, Peter III, during the coup of 1762, written (not published till after Catherine's death, but widely known) by the former secretary of the French legation in St. Petersburg, Claude-Carloman de Rulhière. The other was the visit of the astronomer Abbé Jean Chappe d'Auteroche in 1761–1762 to view the expected passage of the planet Venus across the face of the sun from various observation sites in Siberia. The empress felt that Chappe's travelogue, published after his return, maligned Russia. The habit of writing such memoirs contin-ued in the nineteenth and twentieth centuries. The ones that showed disappointment with the local political situation caused similar outbursts of anger on the part of Russian officialdom, whether the writer was marquis Astolphe de Custine, who visited Russia under Nicholas I, or André Gide, under Stalin.

43. Le Blond's stubborn and haughty comportment in St. Petersburg led to disagreements with the sculptor Carlo Bartolomeo Rastrelli and his Russian patron, Prince Menshikov. Le Blond maligned Rastrelli before the tsar and tried to discredit his credentials as an architect in anonymous pamphlets. The mutual enmity of Le Blond and Rastrelli led to a *Romeo and Juliet*–like street brawl between the servants of the two households (see Arkhipov and Raskin, 1964, pp. 19–20).

44. The offer included a building lot and a house, freedom from taxation, and exemption from the obligation to give quarters to soldiers.

45. Le Prince may have accompanied Abbé Chappe on his visit to Siberia. His *Russian Baptism* was shown at the Salon of 1765 where it attracted favorable comments from Diderot.

46. The Imperial Academy of Painting, Sculpture, and Architecture was founded by Ivan Shuvalov (1727–97), one of the most learned protectors of the Russian arts and sciences and the founder of the University of Moscow. He presided over the Academy of Fine Arts until 1763 when Catherine replaced him with General Ivan Betskoi.

47. Réau, 1922, vol. 2, p. 329.

48. That is, since the ninth and tenth centuries, when the Varangians, an eastern offshoot of the Vikings or Norsemen, traded with the Orient via the Baltic, the Russian rivers, and the Black and Caspian seas. The name *Russia* is of Varangian origin, as was the first Russian dynasty of the Rurikides.

49. "Anekdoty proshlogo stoletiia," *RA*, 1877, a collection of eighteenth-century anecdotes. Apocryphal or not, this quotation is an apt illustration of the tsar's preoccupation with gaining access to the Baltic.

50. Antsiferov, 1922, p. 18.

51. The St. Petersburg theme in Russian literature is dealt with perceptively in Lo Gatto, 1960, and Ospovat and Timenchik, 1987. The two poems by Mickiewicz and Pushkin are treated briefly in the epilogue of this book.

CHAPTER 1. PARIS: THE EARLY YEARS

1. Falconet's early years have been reconstructed on the basis of documentation preserved in the Archives Nationales, the documents published in *BSHAF*, the biographical sketch by Lévesque which appears as front matter in *FOC*, vol. 1, the memorial eulogy by the painter Robin (1791), Jal's *Dictionnaire* (1872), and various writings by Louis Réau, especially his magisterial two-volume monograph on Falconet (1922). The name *Falconet* was frequently spelled with a double "n," even by Falconet himself. Such a lack of consistency in the spelling of last names was characteristic of the epoch, witness *Pigal/Pigalle* or *Le Moyne/Lemoine/Lemoyne*.

2. Here is an extract from the register of the parish of Saint-Sauveur in Paris, where Falconet was baptized: "Le premier décembre mil sept cent seize, est né, a été baptisé *Estienne Maurice*, fils de *Maurice Falconet*, bourgeois, et de *Françoise Guérin*, sa femme, rue de Bourbon" (Guiffrey, ed., 1876, p. 63).

3. Robin, 1791, p. 246.

4. Diderot complained facetiously about the choice of the allegorical figures on Pigalle's monument to Louis XV in Reims in the Salon of 1765. If the figures are intended to suggest the king's patronage over agriculture, commerce, and the population, what then, asks Diderot, is "the meaning of this woman pulling the lion's mane beside a dockhand stretched out on some sacks? The woman and the animal are heading toward the

sleeping dock-hand, and I am sure a child would cry out, 'Mommy, this woman is going to make her wild animal eat the poor sleeping man.' . . . Pigalle, my friend, pick up your hammer and smash this bizarre combination of beings" (Goodman, ed. and tr., 1995, vol. 1, pp. 223–24).

5. *FOC*, vol. 1, p. 4. The philosopher Pierre-Charles Lévesque (1736–1812) came to St. Petersburg in 1773 as a preceptor in the Cadet Corps. Diderot recommended him to Falconet as "an honest and fine man whose erudition and talent go hand in hand with rare kindness and modesty" (Diderot to Falconet, May 30, 1773: Roth, ed., 1955–70, vol. 12, p. 228). Lévesque spent seven years in the Cadet Corps, five of which coincided with Falconet's stay in St. Petersburg. Back in Paris, Lévesque taught history and morality at the Collège de France and wrote an *Histoire de Russie* (1782). His "Vie d'Etienne Falconet" is the main source of information on the sculptor's life.

6. BN, N. a. fr., 24932, fol. 115.

7. Falconet to Diderot, February 25, 1766: Benot, ed., 1958, p. 112.

8. Diderot describes Lemoyne's stammering but loving recollection of Falconet: "Falconet, my child, for he is my child. When his father brought him to me . . . No, it wasn't more than a year after I first saw him, I was saying to him: 'It's only up to you to be as simple as Bouchardon, as true as Pigalle, and as warm as I am . . . And that's where he is . . . He'll make a beautiful thing . . . '" (Diderot to Falconet, December 29, 1766; Roth, ed., 1955–70, vol. 6, p. 373). Falconet repaid his teacher's compliments: "You [Tronchin] don't know how long would be my story if I were to tell you of all my obligations to Monsieur Lemoyne. Tell him if you write to him that . . . I have more reason to boast of having him as a teacher, than he of having me as a pupil" (Tronchin, 1895 [cited after Réau, 1922, p. 57]).

9. Milo's story is told by several ancient writers: Herodotus, Strabo, Diodorus Siculus, Valerius Maximus. Among Milo's exploits was the feat of carrying a four-year bullock the length of the stadium in Olympia and then eating it in one day. Milo was also a successful field commander in the war between his native Crotona and Sybaris, both in southern Italy. Puget's *Milo of Crotona,* intended originally for the gardens of Versailles, is now the centerpiece of the sculpture court in the Louvre.

10. Other Baroque artists who worked on the theme of Milo of Crotona include the sculptors Nicolas-Sébastien Adam and Jean-Antoine Houdon and the painter Jean-Jacques Bachelier.

11. That condition was demanded by the Académie's book of rules, but it was usually disregarded (Robin, 1791, p. 248).

12. Réau, 1922, p. 130.

13. Levitine, 1972, p. 25.

14. It may be found in *A Leaf Turned Over (La feuille à l'envers), A Broken Clog (Le sabot cassé), Leda and the Swan,* and *A Knotted Tie (Le noeud de cravate),* as well as in the monument to Peter the Great in St. Petersburg.

15. Falconet told Lévesque (*FOC,* vol. 1, p. 5): "I am still quite happy with [*Milo*], but the head is worthless because I modeled it on mine." Inserting one's own likeness into a work of art was not unusual. Pigalle did it in his monument to Louis XV in Reims (1765), where the face of the allegorical figure of the Citizen is Pigalle's self-portrait.

16. Levitine's (1972) claim that a 1741 drawing by Lemoyne of a handsome and pensive youth with curls of hair falling down his shoulders represents Falconet aged twenty-six is not persuasive.

17. Levitine, 1972, p. 24.

18. Lévesque, *FOC,* vol. 1, p. 3. *Vysokorodie* was the equivalent of "right honorable," but literally means "highly born," a calque from the German *hochgeboren.*

19. Lévesque (*FOC*, vol. 1, p. 7) reports that during Falconet's frequent trips to Versailles he met a priest who agreed to tutor him in Latin, "an offer that was accepted with as much joy as gratitude." As a result, he became fluent in Latin and later in life translated into French three books of Pliny the Elder.

20. This episode is described in AN, O¹ 1073, docs. 66, 67, and 68. In 1762 Falconet's annual pension was increased to eight hundred livres to defray the costs of moving out of his atelier in the Louvre and building one elsewhere "in order to finish there the works for the church of St. Roch which lend so much glory to the arts and characterize so well his talents." (Cochin to Louis XV, August 24, 1762; AN, O¹ 1073, doc. 134).

21. Pigalle, Saly, and Falconet were virtual coevals. Also important, but belonging to a younger group identified more with the reign of Louis XVI than that of Louis XV, were Jean-Jacques Caffiéri (1725–92) and Augustin Pajou (1730–1809). Both, like Falconet, were pupils of Lemoyne and both became successful portrait sculptors. Caffiéri's best portraits are of the playwrights Jean de Rotrou and Molière, both in the Comédie Française. Pajou was the author of a fine bust of Lemoyne, but his best-known works are the voluptuous *Psyche Abandoned* (1791) and several large statues in the series of the great men of France, especially Bossuet and Pascal. Still younger were Claude Michel, known as Clodion (1738–1814), a sculptor of great poetic power, specializing in decorative sculpture, and Jean-Antoine Houdon (1741–1828) who was the last of the great portraitists of the period and to whom we owe busts of Voltaire, Rousseau, Buffon, Diderot, and Mirabeau, as well as Washington and Jefferson. All four of these sculptors contributed models for the porcelain factory in Sèvres.

22. The Order of Saint-Michel was established by Louis XI in 1469 to honor outstanding artists, initially painters alone. Pigalle was decorated with it after he had mounted a campaign for equal treatment of painters and sculptors.

23. Goodman, ed., 1995, vol. 1, p. 164.

24. Réau, 1927, p. 68.

25. During Falconet's twenty years of work in Paris, he received no more than six, mostly minor, official commissions, a fact which leads Réau to conclude that "among the great sculptors of the eighteenth century Falconet was certainly one of the least favored by official commissions" (Réau, 1922, p. 149–50; cf. Michel, 1984, p. 12).

26. The design was praised, however, by official critics, witness the following note in the *Nouvelles Littéraires* of Abbé Raynal: "Falconet . . . is working on a statue for Louis XV, representing France inclining before a sculpture of that king. . . . The model of that work has been much applauded and has earned the sculptor lodging [in the Louvre] in which to execute it." (*CLT*, vol. 1, p. 361).

27. AN, O¹ 1922^A1, doc. 2.

28. AN, O¹ 1922^A1, doc. 8. Work on the statue was taken over first by Edme Dumont and, after Dumont's death, by Augustin Pajou. It was completed in 1779. Falconet's letter to Marigny was published by Cournault in the *Gazette des Beaux-Arts* (1869).

29. AN, O¹ 1911, doc. 45.

30. The medallion of Madame La Live de Jully was part of a tomb designed by Falconet and destroyed during the Revolution. It was identified by Réau from a drawing of the ensemble preserved in the Musée Carnavalet in Paris.

31. For a history and description of the church of St. Roch, see Diderot's testy report in the *Correspondance Littéraire* for December 1760 (*CLT*, vol. 4, pp. 328–33) and Babelon, 1972. For an insightful treatment of Falconet's religious sculpture, see Scherf (2001a, pp. 31–37).

32. The scene of the arrival of the statue of the Archangel Gabriel at the church of St. Roch is shown in Pierre-Etienne Falconet's engraving illustrating the transportation of large marble statuary (see fig. 5.1).

33. The natural rocks and the snake presage the future monument to Peter the Great in St. Petersburg.

34. Falconet included Bernini among "the great modern sculptors" in his *Réflexions sur la sculpture* (*FOC*, vol. 1, pp. 49 (English tr. Tooke, 1777, pp. 37–38); cf. Janson's (1985, p. 35) puzzling claim that "Falconet hated Bernini."

35. Gaborit (1984, p. 448) considers it "unquestionably one of the best religious sculptures of the eighteenth century." On the other side of the spectrum are Diderot (*CLT*, vol. 4, p. 329), who criticized the statue for its purportedly different treatment of the upper and lower parts of the body; and Levey (1992, p. 135), who finds it "displeasingly rhetorical and sentimental."

36. Falconet to Marigny, June 4, 1765: AN, O^1 1911, doc. 45.

37. Goodman, ed. and tr., 1995, vol. 1, pp. 165–66.

38. Robin, 1791, p. 249. A successful representation of the folds in clothes or draperies was considered one of the supreme tests of a Baroque sculptor; cf. the section *Draperies* in Falconet's *Réflexions sur la sculpture* (*FO*, vol. 1, pp. 47–54; English tr. Tooke, 1777, pp. 36–41). Diderot's description of the model of *Saint Ambrose* appears in his account of the Salon of 1767 (Goodman, ed. and tr., 1995, vol. 2, pp. 165–66).

39. See the reproduction in Scherf (2001a, p. 35).

40. A plaster model of the *Sweet Melancholy* was shown in the Salon of 1761. Diderot loved *Friendship:* "this open mouth, these outstretched arms, this torso bent slightly forward are indescribably expressive. Her heart races, she's fearful, she's hopeful. . . . The arrangement of her hair is unusual; it's partly from the treatment of the hair, reminiscent of temple priestesses, that the figure derives its sacred character" (Goodman, ed. and tr., 1995, vol. 1, pp. 168–69).

41. Falconet's views on relief are summed up in the entry "Bas-relief" in the *Encyclopédie.* That entry was combined with the entries "Sculpture" and "Draperie" in the lecture "On Sculpture," given at the Académie in Paris. The lecture was published as the "Réflexions sur la sculpture" in *FO,* vol. 1, pp. 1–54. For an English translation see Tooke, ed. and tr., 1777, pp. 9–41, or Levitine, 1972, pp. 64–75 (where Tooke appears as Foote!); see also Dowley, 1968, for a discussion of Falconet's theory of reliefs.

42. Lévesque in *FOC,* vol. 1, p. 11.

43. The busts received very high marks in their respective Salons. In 1747 Abbé Leblanc writes: "It is striking in its resemblance; the sculptor is young and seems to be very able in his art" (*BSHAF,* 1907, p. 89). In 1761 Diderot says: "The bust of the physician Falconet is beautiful, very beautiful. There couldn't be a better likeness. When we lose this venerable old man, whom we all cherish, we'll ask for his bust and we'll go to see him again" (*BSHAF,* 1907, p. 90).

44. *FO,* vol. 1, pp. 190–91, fn. (o).

45. Italian *porcellána* ("cowrie" or "cowry") designated originally a marine gastropod mollusk with a thick and shiny oval shell. That term, according to tradition, was applied to Chinese ceramic by Marco Polo, who was reminded of the mollusk shell when he saw Chinese dishes at the court of Kublai Khan.

46. For accounts of the history of porcelain production in France and for the differences between hard and soft paste and the technology of the production of biscuit, see Eriksen, 1987, pp. 25–59; Pinot de Villechenon, 1997, 9–49; Albis, 2001, pp. 61–67; and Milande, 2001, pp. 77–87.

47. As for the *Flore* of 1761, which was also reproduced in biscuit, its authorship by Falconet has been questioned by Hawley (1994).
48. At Sèvres Falconet designed also such objects as jewelry, clocks, and silverware.
49. The blue-and-gold service in soft-paste porcelain was ordered by Catherine in 1777. Boizot's centerpiece, called the *Apotheosis of Catherine the Great* or the *Russian Parnassus,* shows a bust of the empress as Minerva, posed on a half-column and surrounded by twenty figures representing the various arts and sciences. The service was decorated in the classical style with white cameos on each of its 744 pieces. Its price was 331,217 livres, that is, 60 percent higher than what Falconet demanded for eight years of work on the monument to Peter the Great.
50. Falconet to Diderot, May 25, 1766: Roth, ed., 1955–70, vol. 6, p. 193.
51. Seznec and Adhémar, eds., 1957, vol. 1, p. 247.
52. Despite his passionate involvement with the arts and the "good read" that his accounts of the Salons offer, Diderot's credentials as an art critic have often been questioned.
53. Catherine to Falconet, 24 May 1768: Réau, ed., 1921, pp. 46–47.
54. Diderot to Falconet, December 6, 1773; *FO,* vol. 2, pp. 133–34.
55. Music's dancing step and a slight twist of her torso recur in Falconet's unused model for a statue of Catherine the Great in the Russian Museum in St. Petersburg (see fig. 2.2) and in the statue of the empress by the Russian sculptor Fedot Ivanovich Shubin (1740–1805).
56. Since the popularity of religious subjects was far less than that of their profane competitors, very few biscuit editions of the *Expiring Mary Magdalene* and the *Temptation of St. Anthony* were produced. The only extant examples are in the Victoria and Albert Museum in London. The terracotta originals are in the Musée national de céramique in Sèvres (Scherf, 2001a, p. 37). The *Expiring Mary Magdalene* is based on the account of her life in the *Golden Legend* by Jacobus de Voragine. According to it, Mary Magdalene spent the last thirty years of her life in Provence doing penance and missionary work. Close to death, she was borne by angels to the cathedral in Aix.
57. Terrasson, 1969, p. 104.
58. This is not to say that after Falconet's departure the company did not grow. In his day it employed 250 workers, while on the eve of the Revolution it employed close to 300.
59. Bourgeois, 1909, vol. 1, p. 23.
60. Robin, 1791, p. 250. The inventory of Falconet's estate, compiled on January 31, 1791, a week after his death, reveals a collection of engravings numbering over one thousand items; see *BSHAF,* 1918–1919, pp. 164–66.
61. *FOC,* vol. 1, p. 8.
62. Wraxall, 1776, p. 228, and Lévesque (*FOC,* vol. 1, p. 15); cf. Lord Cathcart's description of the painting cited by Falconet in his "Revision" (*FO,* vol. 2, p. 68).
63. *FOC,* vol. 1, pp. 9–10.
64. Bourrée de Corberon, 1901, vol. 1, p. 190.
65. Diderot to Falconet, September 6, 1768: Roth, ed., 1955–70, vol. 8, p. 132. The phrase "your young disciple" refers to Marie-Anne Collot.
66. *FOC,* vol. 1, p. 9.
67. Ibid., p. 8.
68. Ingram, trained in London, lived in Paris after 1755. He worked chiefly as a vignettist, collaborating with a number of well-known French engravers (Peloux, 1930, p. 68).
69. *FO,* vol. 5, p. 21.
70. Falconet to Diderot, March 6, 1766: Benot, ed., 1958, pp. 133–34.
71. *FO,* vol. 5, p. 20.

72. Tooke, ed. and tr., 1777, p. 6.

73. The *Correspondance littéraire* was a biweekly handwritten review of literary and artistic events in the major capitals of Europe, chiefly Paris, including reports from the Salons and sales of major art collections. It was at first an information bulletin for the use of Prussian royalty; its readership extended eventually to the heads of several other German states and the rulers of Tuscany, Sweden, Poland, and Russia, but it had no official circulation at the court of Versailles. It was founded and run by one of Diderot's closest friends, Friedrich Melchior Grimm (1723–1807) and appeared from 1753 till 1793 (after 1773 Grimm surrendered his responsibilities to his collaborators). Falconet's *Réflexions sur la sculpture* were destined for the *Encyclopédie*. Since the appearance of the *Encyclopédie* was delayed, Falconet published his text in a separate brochure in 1761. He also read it in the Académie on June 7, 1760.

74. *CLT,* vol. 4, pp. 431–32.

75. Diderot to Falconet, August 15, 1767: Roth, ed., 1955–70, vol. 7, p. 99.

76. Goodman, ed. and tr., 1995, vol. 1, p. 163.

77. Catherine to Mme Geoffrin, October 21, 1766: Réau, ed., 1921, p. 1.

78. Diderot to Falconet, July 18, 1768: Roth, ed., 1955–70, vol. 8, p. 71.

79. Ibid.

80. Diderot to Falconet, December 29, 1766: Roth, ed., 1955–70, vol. 6, p. 372. Occasionally, the two friends were joined by other *philosophes* happy to share the conversation and a bottle of good wine in the bower of the "chaumière de la rue d'Anjou." Such, for instance, was the get-together of Diderot and Prince Golitsyn with Mercier de la Rivière and Grimm on May 15, 1767.

81. Dieckmann, ed., 1952, p. 257.

82. Réau, 1922, vol. 1, p. 48. That judgment is much closer to the truth than Wrangel's outlandish claims of a sensual vein running through all of Falconet's art: "All subjects are the same to him, as long as he can depict what shimmers in his imagination. Saints and wise men, church fathers and ancient gods, all are to him the same gods of love. The *Cupid* sitting on roses is a ruler of the universe, the *Bather,* a sinful half-maiden, is washing her body in expectation of new amorous caresses" (Wrangel, in Grabar', 1909–14, vol. 5, p. 96).

83. That is also the title of the first full edition of the debate by Benot. He and other editors of Diderot face the same task of cleansing the correspondence of later accretions, added mainly by Diderot's friend Jacques-André Naigeon and his son-in-law Caroillon de Vandeul.

84. Diderot to Volland, November 21, 1759: Roth, ed., 1955–70, vol. 5, p. 190.

85. Goodman, ed. and tr., 1995, vol. 1, p. 164.

86. Diderot to Falconet, February 15, 1766: Roth, ed., 1955–70, vol. 6, p. 67.

87. Falconet to Diderot, January 27, 1766: Benot, ed., 1958, p. 69.

88. From an *avertissement* to an edition of the debate, planned by Falconet in 1780 but not published. BN, N. a. fr., 24983, fol. 113; cited after Dieckmann and Seznec, eds., 1959, p. 8.

89. Catherine to Falconet, June 7, 1767: Réau, ed., 1921, p. 17.

90. Diderot to Volland: Babelon, ed., 1930, vol. 3, p. 272.

91. Diderot to Falconet, February 15, 1766: Roth, ed., 1955–70, vol. 6, p. 59.

92. Diderot to Falconet, December 4, 1765: Roth, ed., 1955–70, vol. 5, p. 210.

93. Falconet to Diderot, December 25, 1765: Benot, ed., 1958, pp. 51 and 62–63.

94. Diderot to Falconet, January 10, 1766: Roth, ed., 1955–70, vol. 6 p. 14.

95. Falconet to Diderot, January 15, 1766: Benot, ed., 1958, p. 63. In saying this, Falconet

foreshadowed the conclusion drawn by Haskell and Penny (1981, p. 99) that the statues by the most famous artists of antiquity have not survived because "none of the names found on famous statues . . . were of men who had been singled out as great artists by Pliny or Pausanias."

96. Diderot to Falconet, January 27, 1766: Roth, ed., 1955–70, vol. 6, p. 37.

97. Diderot to Falconet, February 15, 1766: Roth, ed., 1955–70, vol. 6, pp. 624–25.

98. Falconet to Diderot, February 10, 1766: Benot, ed., 1958, p. 68.

99. Falconet to Diderot, January 15, 1766: Benot, ed., 1958, pp. 62–63.

100. Diderot to Falconet, February 15, 1766: Roth, ed., 1955–70, vol. 6, p. 84.

101. Dieckmann and Seznec, eds., 1959, p. 14.

102. They were not alone in their dogged attempt to unscramble the egg. Pausanias's descriptions were detailed enough to allow such eighteenth-century art historians and engravers as Count de Caylus, C. Robert, and L.-J. Le Lorrain to try to reconstruct the scenes painted by Polygnotus. Not surprisingly, such efforts ended up looking like reconstructions of different paintings.

103. Diderot to Falconet, May 28, 1766: Roth, ed., 1955–70, vol. 6, p. 195.

104. Goodman, ed. and tr., 1995, vol. 1, p. 175.

105. Falconet to Diderot, February 25, 1766: Benot, ed., 1958, p. 110.

106. Diderot to Falconet, beginning of September 1766: Roth, ed., 1955–70, vol. 6, pp. 327–28. Diderot was correct to prophesy that Falconet would get few laurels upon the completion of the monument. He was wrong, however, to fear that no one in the "subpolar regions" would see and appreciate it.

107. Ibid., p. 329. Note that Diderot finds Falconet thirsting for glory even though he claimed earlier that the sculptor "did not care about glory."

108. Diderot to Volland, September 1767: Roth, ed., 1955–70, vol. 7, pp. 133–34. Despite his concern, two years had passed and Diderot was still talking about "putting the last touches" on the text of his correspondence with Falconet (Diderot to Volland, September 11, 1769: Roth, ed., 1955–70, vol. 9, p. 138).

109. Voltaire to Falconet, December 18, 1767: Besterman et al., eds., 1968–, vol. 9, p. 213.

110. Diderot to Falconet, December 29, 1766: Roth, ed., 1955–70, vol. 6, p. 375. Basing themselves on this passage, both Polovtsov (*SIRIO,* vol. 17 [1876], p. 251, fn. 8) and Réau (ed., 1921, p. 10, fn.) claim that the idea of sending the text of the debate to the empress belonged to Diderot. The passage, however, shows clearly that Diderot was responding to an idea of Falconet and, if anything, was trying to dissuade him from it. Falconet must have told Diderot about his intention to send the text to the empress in a letter written in November 1766 from St. Petersburg that is lost (cf. Roth, ed., 1955–70, vol. 6, p. 369, fn. 2).

111. Falconet to Catherine, March 16, 1767: Réau, ed., 1921, pp. 9–10.

112. Catherine to Falconet, June 7, 1767: Réau, ed., 1921, p. 16.

113. In painting, one could argue, women had at least a token representation. Of those born between the mid-sixteenth and mid-eighteenth centuries one can name Sofonisba Anguissola (1540–1625) from Cremona; the Bolognese Lavinia Fontana (1552–1614), Barbara Longhi (1552–1638), and Elisabetta Sirani (1638–65); the Florentine Artemisia Gentileschi (1593–1652); the Dutch Clara Peeters (1594–1657) and Judith Leyster (1609–60); the German Maria Sibilla Merian (1647–1717); the Venetian Rosalba Carriera (1675–1757); the Swiss Angelica Kauffman (1741–1807); and the French Anne Vallayer-Coster (1744–1818) and Elisabeth Vigée-Lebrun (1755–1842). For studies devoted to women in the arts, consult Hess and Baker, eds., 1971; Heller, 1987; Krull, 1989, and Chadwick, 1990. Collot's output has been studied by Valabrègue, 1898; Réau, 1923; and Becker, 1998.

114. She must have reminded him of Madame Victoire (1733–99), the fifth daughter of Louis XV.

115. Diderot to Falconet, beginning of November 1766: Roth, ed., 1955–70, vol. 6, p. 344.

116. Diderot to Falconet, May 1768: Roth, ed., 1955–70, vol. 8, pp. 34–35.

117. Diderot to Falconet, July 11, 1769: Roth, ed., 1955–70, vol. 9, pp. 74–75.

118. Diderot to Falconet, March 20, 1771: Roth, ed. 1955–70, vol. 10, p. 249.

119. Diderot to Falconet, July 11, 1769: Roth, ed., 1955–70, vol. 9, p. 74.

120. Knowing full well that Catherine was a faithful reader of the *Correspondance littéraire*, Grimm ended his tribute with a plea to her "to let Marie-Victoire [*sic*] Collot make [the empress's] bust and send it to Paris to embellish the retreat of an obscure man, who is all filled with the glory of Catherine." He even promised to pray for that favor, making the sign of the cross according to the Russian Orthodox rite (*CLT,* vol. 7, pp. 107–8).

121. Ibid., p. 107.

122. Becker, 1998, p. 76.

123. Réau, 1922, vol. 2, p. 431.

124. Goodman, ed. and tr., 1995, vol. 2, p. 21. Falconet thought that Collot's bust of Diderot was so much superior to his that he broke his own piece with a hammer. In 1773 Collot, working from memory, made a head of Diderot for Catherine. The empress kept it in her study where she and Diderot met almost daily during the philosopher's visit to St. Petersburg. Diderot is said to have thrown off his wig in order to demonstrate to her the resemblance (Tourneux, 1970, pp. 75–76). Today it is in the Hermitage.

125. Diderot to Falconet, November 12, 1766: Roth, ed. 1955–70, p. 348.

126. Raymond, 1973. The fact that in 1756 D. A. Golitsyn was thirty-two, rather than twenty-seven as maintained by Raymond, does not invalidate the claim that he was too young to be the subject of the Louvre bust.

127. That is how it was identified at its last known sale in May 1975.

128. Becker, 1998, pp. 74–76. Becker's correction may be considered the most important recent contribution to Collot scholarship.

129. Included in Becker, forthcoming. An inscription in the painter's hand at the bottom of the drawing reads: "Prince Galitzin de La Haye." A terracotta head in the Louvre, once thought to be an early sketch for the head of Peter the Great by Falconet, is now ascribed to Collot, leaving two unidentified male portraits by her from the Paris period.

130. Diderot to Falconet, beginning of November 1766: Roth, ed., 1955–70, vol. 6, p. 344.

131. Diderot to Falconet, probably March 1767: Roth, ed., 1955–70, vol. 7, p. 41.

132. Diderot to Falconet, July 1767: Roth, ed., 1955–70, vol. 7, p. 86.

133. Diderot to Falconet, May 1768: Roth, ed., 1955–70, vol. 8, p. 43.

134. Diderot to Falconet, September 6, 1768: Roth, ed., 1955–70, vol. 8, p. 125.

135. Ibid., p. 128.

136. Ibid., p. 136.

137. Fortia de Piles and de Boisgelin, 1796, vol. 3, p. 193, and Carr, 1806, p. 42. Cf. also Versini, ed., 1994–97, vol. 5, p. 1376.

138. Catherine to Falconet, April 8, 1773: Réau, ed., 1921, p. 201.

139. Réau, 1922, vol. 1, p. 49.

140. Réau, 1924, p. 221.

141. The Salon of 1765 in Goodman, ed. and tr., 1995, vol. 1, p. 164. This may have been Mlle Mistouflet, who, according to Benot, ed. (1958, p. 7) possessed a "very handsome bosom." Réau (1922, p. 49) surmises that she might have been Falconet's model for the *Bather.*

CHAPTER 2. BETWEEN PARIS AND ST. PETERSBURG

1. Cf. Martin, 1986, 17–18. Of monographic studies of the equestrian statue one should mention Patte, 1765; Fleitmann, 1931; Friis, 1933; Keller, 1971; Artner and Kiadó, 1982; Martin, 1986; and Schumacher, 1994. Shorter treatments include Cicognara, 1823–24, vol. 6, pp. 337–438; Valentiner, 1946; Janson, 1967; and Cahill, ed., 1981. For a richly illustrated survey of extant equestrian monuments, see Liedtke, 1989. For observations on pagan and chivalric traditions in equine art, see Bethea, 1989, pp. 47–61.

2. It is in the Musée Carnavalet in Paris. In Germany there are two stone equestrian statues dating from the thirteenth century. The saintly *Bamberg Rider* occupies a niche in the Bamberg Cathedral, while a statue, probably of Emperor Otto I, stands in the market square of Magdeburg.

3. A well-known religious equestrian monument of the period is the exquisitely sculpted bronze statue of St. George killing the dragon, executed in 1373 by the Hungarian brothers Márton and György Kolozsvári. While the figure of the saint is fully within the Gothic idiom, the startled horse and the writhing dragon portend the advent of the Renaissance. Today a copy of the statue is in front of St. Vitus's Cathedral in Prague.

4. A marble copy of the riderless horse of the *Marcus Aurelius* stood in the Summer Garden until the middle of the nineteenth century. It was sent there from Venice by Peter the Great's agent Vladislavich-Raguzinsky (Andros[s]ov, 2000, p. 213).

5. Bernini fashioned the *Louis XIV* after his earlier *Vision of Constantine the Great,* which stands at the top of the grand staircase in St. Peter's in the Vatican. Falconet was contemptuous of both of these statues: "The Curtius of Bernini, mainly because of the horse, is one of the worst and most impertinent productions that one can see in sculpture" (Falconet, 1773, vol. 1, p. 70). A lead replica of the Versailles statue, misleadingly identified as a likeness of Louis XIV, stands in the Carousel courtyard of the Louvre. A small terracotta model of Bernini's original statue is in the Galleria Borghese in Rome.

6. Arkhipov and Raskin, 1964, p. 87. Peter's life mask in plaster, made by Rastrelli in 1721 (Hermitage), was used by Falconet and Collot when they were modeling the tsar's head. In 1723 Rastrelli made a magnificent bronze bust of Peter in full armor (Hermitage). It was preceded by a wax bust in armor (1719, Hermitage) and followed by a Madame Tussaud–like figure of the sitting tsar, dressed in his everyday garb (1725, Hermitage).

7. RGADA, fond 150, no. 1, f. 25. For a history of early projects for a monument to Peter the Great, see Morozov, 1965, pp. 102–8.

8. Lavie to Dubois, September 3, 1717: *SIRIO,* 1881, vol. 34, pp. 240–42. Lavie does not provide the sculptor's name, but identifies him as French, in the service of the tsar, and working on the tsar's statue. Since Rastrelli worked in Paris before coming to St. Petersburg, it seems safe to assume that Lavie had him in mind.

9. The attribution of the Hermitage terracotta model is due to an ingenious and convincing investigation by Andros[s]ov and Enggass (1994).

10. *SIRIO,* 1900, vol. 108, p. 239.

11. Bergholz (Russ. Berkhgol'ts) was in the entourage of Duke Charles Frederick of Holstein-Gottorp, Peter the Great's son-in-law and father of Charles Peter, who ascended the throne of Russia as Peter III. He recorded in his journal the events of the last four years of the reign of Peter the Great.

12. Backmeister, 1786, p. 8.

13. Ibid.

14. Within three weeks of the coup, I. I. Betskoi, the fawning and unimaginative director

of the Bureau of Imperial and Public Buildings and Gardens, introduced a resolution in the Senate to erect a monument to Catherine the Great (see *SIRIO,* vol. 17, Appendix I).

15. Some critics defend the artistic qualities of the Rastrelli monument. Thus V. N. Petrov (1965, p. 33) considers its rejection by Catherine "biased and incomprehensible." Rastrelli's monument was rescued from oblivion by Catherine's son and successor, Paul I, who acted more out of spite for his mother than out of genuine love of art. In 1800 he had it set up in front of the St. Michael's (Mikhailovsky) Castle where he resided. That is also its present location.

16. Theophanes was of Greek origin, but spent most of his life in Russia, mainly in Novgorod and Moscow. He may be considered a Russo-Byzantine painter.

17. Characteristically, the greatest number of wooden religious folk sculpture of the sixteenth to eighteenth centuries was found in the district of Perm' in the Urals, one of the last regions of European Russia to be converted to Christianity. Sculpting was practiced there despite an especially strict rule against religious statuary, testifying to the fear of the Orthodox church that the cult of wooden idols, practiced by the local Zyrian population before its conversion at the end of the fourteenth century, was being transferred to the effigies of Christian saints. In a similar vein, the modest influx of ancient and Western sculpture that began under Peter the Great (e.g., a Roman remake of a Greek Aphrodite, known in Russia as the *Tauride Venus,* and several works of the Italian Baroque) contributed to the tsar's image as a heretic.

18. SPOARAN, fond 3, o. 1, no. 277, f. 5.

19. Betskoi's earlier appeal for suggestions on the siting of the monument was made soon after the coup of 1762. The first respondent was the great Russian scientist Mikhail Vasilievich Lomonosov (1711–65), who proposed to place the monument on the stone bridge that was to be built across the Neva. He also took it upon himself to compose appropriate inscriptions, drawing on the material which, he thought, was "as abundant as the achievements of that hero were immense" (Pekarskii, 1873, pp. 798–99).

20. In his account of Bilistein's proposals, the usually dependable Kaganovich (1982, pp. 48–50) mistakenly ascribes to him a preference for siting the monument on Vasilievsky Island. Bilistein is quite explicit in favoring a location between the Admiralty and the Senate.

21. That area, known as New Holland, was replaced later by the Konnogvardeisky Boulevard.

22. Even seventy years later, Marquis de Custine commented that the square had enough buildings around it for a whole city, yet appeared insufficiently furnished: "It is a field, not of wheat, but of columns," in which the monument to Peter the Great disappears "like a pebble on the beach" (Letter 11, *La Russie en 1839,* 4 vols., vol. 1 (Brussels, 1843), p. 189).

23. The cathedral was so named in honor of St. Isaac, a fourth-century hegumen of a monastic community in Dalmatia, on whose feast day (May 30) Peter was born. The two successive cathedrals on Isakievsky Square were preceded by two earlier St. Isaac's churches on the Neva embankment. The first, wooden, version, close to the Neva and the Senate building, burned down in 1725 and was reconstructed as a much larger stone church by the German architect Georg Johann Mattarnowy. It was pulled down in the 1760s.

24. In the nineteenth century the mansion (9 Isakievsky Square) became the property of the Miatlev family. Today it houses the Prosecutor's Office.

25. There was a toll for using the bridge: five kopecks for a four-wheel carriage, three kopecks for a two-wheel cart, two kopecks for a wheelbarrow, and one kopeck for a pedestrian.

26. *SIRIO*, 1876, vol. 17, p. 342.

27. *FO*, vol. 1, pp. 55–57. Having read Falconet's retort, Catherine wrote to him: "The right and left eyes of Peter the Great make me laugh. It's more than stupid" (Catherine to Falconet, May 15, 1769: Réau, ed., 1921, p. 81). The empress had a very low opinion of Bilistein's intelligence, witness her description of him as "that fool and client of General [Betskoi]" (Catherine to Potemkin, prior to April 21, 1774: Lopatin, ed., 1997, p. 24). It is interesting that Falconet excluded his belated and unnecessarily harsh reaction to Bilistein's metaphor from later editions of his writings, when Betskoi's harassments had faded from his memory.

28. Kaganovich (1982, pp. 47–48) claims mistakenly that Bilistein wanted the monument to face the river, i.e., south, from the *right* bank of the Neva, a site and orientation explicitly rejected by Bilistein. He also misunderstood Bilistein's "left eye/right eye" figure of speech, making it even sillier than it actually was. Bilistein did not want Peter to rest his eyes on old and new Russia, but on the buildings on the left and right bank of the Neva!

29. RGIA, fond 789, no. 372, ff. 27–30.

30. *Nouvelles littéraires* of Abbé Raynal, *CLT*, vol. 1, pp. 469–72.

31. Princess Anastasia of Hesse-Homburg (1700–1755), née Trubetskaia, was the favorite lady-in-waiting of Empress Elizabeth. The bas-relief shows her as Minerva consecrating the order of St. Catherine on the altar of Immortality.

32. After Bouchardon's death in 1762, Vassé competed for the job of completing his equestrian statue of Louis XV in Paris. Falconet supported Vassé's bid, but the winner was Pigalle.

33. Son of Louis XV and father of Louis XVI.

34. Diderot to Betskoi, August 28–31, 1766: Roth, ed., 1955–70, vol. 6, p. 281.

35. In 1759, after Attorney General Omer Joly de Fleury described the *Encyclopédie* as an "impious book," Louis XV suppressed it altogether. One of the first acts of Catherine after she took over the throne of Russia in 1762 was to offer to publish the *Encyclopédie* in Riga, causing Voltaire to exclaim to Diderot: "What times are we living in! France persecutes philosophy, and the Scythians nurture it along." Catherine's offer was not accepted, for the *encyclopédistes* wished to keep the editorial office close by and were uncertain of the stability of Catherine's young regime.

36. Dmitry Alekseevich Golitsyn is referred to in this section by his last name only, except when it appears next to another bearer of that last name. Other Golitsyns are cited with their first name and patronymic—usually the initials only. For the transliteration of Golitsyn's name, see the note on conventions used in this book, p. 315.

37. Until recently, our ignorance of Golitsyn's appearance could not be dispelled because the only identifiable portrait of him was a tiny silhouette on the frontispiece of his 1780 booklet on electricity (reproduced in Köhler, 1993, and Schulz, ed., 1998, p. 154). In 2000, however, Marie-Louise Becker, the French biographer of Marie-Anne Collot, discovered a small portrait of Golitsyn by Pierre-Etienne Falconet. It supports Becker's and my conjecture that the terracotta head by Collot, previously identified as that of Grimm, is in fact that of Golitsyn (fig. 1.12; cf. above, p. 61).

38. The Golitsyns belong to the oldest stratum of Russian aristocracy. They trace their genealogy to the Grand Duke Gediminas (c. 1275–1341), the pagan founder of the Lithuanian dynasty of the Gediminides, who supplied rulers to a number of Eastern European countries in the fourteenth, fifteenth, and sixteenth centuries. As for Golitsyn's birthplace,

Tsverava (1985, pp. 12–13) favors Moscow, but Lemcke (1940, p. 24) thinks that it was St. Petersburg.

39. The Cadet Corps, located in the Menshikov Palace on Vasilievsky Island, was founded in 1731 by Empress Anne. At that time, it offered the only genuine secondary education in the country.

40. The Golitsyns had a family hold on important diplomatic assignments. D. M. Golitsyn's immediate predecessor was Aleksandr Mikhailovich Golitsyn, the future ambassador in London and vice chancellor of Catherine the Great (not to be confused with the field marshal bearing exactly the same name). He was D. A. Golitsyn's distant uncle.

41. The strains blighting Franco-Russian relations at the time of Golitsyn's posting in Paris were due to France's alarm over Russia's quest for political influence in central and southeastern Europe. Tensions grew with the accession of Peter III (1761), who replaced the Francophile policy of Empress Elizabeth with a period of rapprochement with Prussia. The coup of 1762, which placed a Prussian princess on the Russian throne, could not but deepen the malaise of the French foreign office, run in the sixties by the decidedly anti-Russian Etienne-François duc de Choiseul. As a result, during all of Catherine the Great's reign, France did not have any diplomatic representation in St. Petersburg above the rank of minister plenipotentiary. Since the diplomatic protocol required a quid pro quo, Russia had to answer in kind. In fact, D. A. Golitsyn was relieved of his duties in Paris so that his post could be lowered to that of a chargé d'affaires.

42. Diderot to Falconet, May 1768: Roth, ed., 1955–70, vol. 8, p. 27.

43. Voltaire to Golitsyn, January 25, 1769: Besterman et al., ed., 1968–, vol. 118, p. 262.

44. Diderot to Falconet, August 15, 1767: Roth, ed., 1955–70, vol. 7, p. 105.

45. Catherine to Falconet, October 12, 1767: Réau, ed., 1921, p. 25. Laudable as it was, Catherine's defense of her newly acquired but fully assimilated Russian language does not explain why an eighteenth-century educated Russian should experience difficulties writing in his native language. Golitsyn's problem, however, was real. It had to do with the late formation of a linguistic norm that could serve as an efficient instrument of secular written communication. That process, involving the merger of the "high" ecclesiastic language, known as Church Slavonic, with the "low" colloquial base was not completed until the end of the eighteenth century.

46. Choiseul to Panin, June 16 and June 18, 1767: SIRIO, vol. 141, pp. 313–18. These letters contain the fullest presentation of the French point of view in this matter. Choiseul attributed to the scribe's "slips of the pen" the three occasions when the adjective Imperial was actually used in French correspondence with Catherine the Great. He did not explain, however, why the "genius of the French language" did not prevent the French scribe's pen from slipping.

47. Panin to Choiseul (summary), August 27, 1767; SIRIO, vol. 141, p. 339. Nikolai K. Khotinsky, secretary of the Russian embassy in Madrid, was known to the French because he had served in the Paris embassy under D. M. Golitsyn: RGADA, fond 1263, o. 1, no. 193, tetr. 2, f. 23. Khotinsky's appointment lasted till 1778.

48. Choiseul to Panin, October 29, 1767: SIRIO, vol. 141, p. 355; cf. also another version of this letter (ibid., pp. 358–61). Jean-Baptiste-François Rossignol was appointed as the new French chargé d'affaires.

49. Catherine to Falconet, November 29, 1767: Réau, ed., 1921, p. 34.

50. Diderot to Volland, August 24, 1768: Roth, ed., 1955–70, vol. 8, p. 95.

51. D. A. Golitsyn to A. M. Golitsyn, August 2, 1768: RGADA, fond 1263, o. 1, no. 1116, ff. 72r–73v. I am grateful to Professor Georges Dulac for sharing with me copies of several letters from the A. M. Golitsyn archive in RGADA.

52. RGADA, fond 1263, o. 1, no. 194, f. 11.
53. Diderot to Volland, September 22, 1769: Roth, ed., 1955–70, vol. 9, p. 150.
54. Dmitry Dmitrievich Golitsyn became a Catholic priest in America. He was trained in the Baltimore seminary under Bishop John Carroll, taking his vows as Father Demetrius Augustine Gallitzin. His parish was in Loretto, Pennsylvania. He died there in 1840.
55. Diderot to Volland, August 24, 1768: Roth, ed., 1955–70, pp. 94–95. Diderot continued: "Can you imagine that her letter is anonymous and that it contains a most ferocious satire by her, most intemperate and most indecent. . . . The letter is incredible. One has to see it. Grimm, to whom I've shown it, doubts that she had written it, contrary to the unequivocal opinion of the prince."
56. Diderot to Volland, July 22, 1773: Roth, ed., 1955–70, vol. 13, p. 36.
57. Golitsyn has been credited by some with the formulation of this policy; see his letter to Panin of March 3/14, 1780 (Bolkhovitinov, 1975, pp. 3–29).
58. Yorke to Harris, March 21, 1780 (cited after Madariaga, 1962, p. 151, fn. 37).
59. Osterman to Golitsyn, May 6, 1782: Bashkina et al., eds., 1980, p. 149.
60. Bezborodko to Osterman, June 21/July 2, 1782: Bashkina et al., eds., 1980, pp. 158–59.
61. *De l'homme, de ses facultés intellectuelles et de son education,* 2 vols., (The Hague, 1772).
62. Golitsyn outlined his ideas in a number of letters to Vice Chancellor A. M. Golitsyn. These letters, preserved in the huge Golitsyn archive in RGADA (nos. 1111–25), were partly published in Rachinskii, ed., 1881, and Shchipanov and Svetlov, eds., 1952, pp. 33–45. Analyses of his views may be found in Bak, 1948, and O'Meara, 1988. Diderot, who was also influenced by Quesnay, recommended the services of a Physiocrat economist, Paul Mercier de la Rivière, to Catherine the Great. La Rivière, however, failed to impress in St. Petersburg and had to leave Russia under a cloud. The La Rivière incident caused a tiff between Falconet and Diderot.
63. For a survey of Golitsyn's work in the natural and exact sciences, see Tsverava, 1985, chaps. 3, 4, and 5.
64. Golitsyn to Franklin, January 17/28, 1777: Bashkina et al., eds., 1980, pp. 41–43.
65. Diderot to Falconet, May 15, 1767; Roth, ed., 1955–70, vol. 7, p. 57.
66. Lehndorff, 1921, p. 141.
67. Schlafly, 1997, p. 716.
68. Tsverava, 1985, p. 172.
69. Diderot to Volland, September 24, 1767: Roth, ed., 1955–70, vol. 7, p. 146.
70. Diderot to Falconet, December 29, 1766: Roth, ed., 1955–70, vol. 6, p. 370.
71. Falconet to Marigny, July 16, 1766: AN, O^1 1911[(1)], doc. 101.
72. The house itself was rented to Prince Golitsyn, who, as Diderot informed Falconet, used it as a place of assignation to meet with his mistress Mlle Dornet (Diderot to Falconet, July 11, 1769: Roth, ed., 1955–70, vol. 9, p. 72).
73. Marigny to Falconet, August 26, 1766: BN, N. a. fr., 24983, f. 328.
74. Golitsyn to A. M. Golitsyn, August 31, 1766: *SIRIO,* vol. 17, p. 378. An indisposition of Golitsyn and the absence of Marigny from Paris caused a month's delay in the signing of the contract. Aware of Catherine the Great's impatience to see Falconet in St. Petersburg, Golitsyn in Paris had to reassure A. M. Golitsyn and Betskoi in St. Petersburg that the delay was not due to his negligence (RGADA, fond 1263, op. 1, no. 1114, ff. 242, 246, 250, 253). An executed copy of the contract reached St. Petersburg on September 11 (see Betskoi's report to the Senate of September 15, 1766: RGADA, fond 248, no. 5482, f. 317). For the text of the contract, see *SIRIO,* vol. 17, pp. 375–77.
75. All but two of the statues in the Invalides, the *Virgin* by Houdon and the *Saint Jerome* by L.-S. Adam, were smashed during the Revolution.

76. Diderot to Falconet, July 11, 1769: Roth, ed., 1955–70, vol. 9, p. 73.
77. Réau, 1922, pp. 312–317. Réau's identification of the Jacquemart-André statue with the *Glory of the Princes* is validated by Diderot's description of the original statues in his 1766 letter to Betskoi (*DOC,* vol. 6, p. 632): "One represents *Sovereignty* leaning on the fasces; the other, *Glory* placing a garland around a medallion on which an image of Catherine would be most appropriate." Marie-Louise Becker surmises that Catherine's profile on the medallion was made by Collot.
78. Goodman, ed. and tr., 1995, vol. 1, pp. 164–65.
79. The payment was made on August 12, 1765: AN O¹ 1922^{A1}, doc. 7.
80. Golitsyn to Panin, August 31, 1766: *SIRIO,* vol. 17, p. 374.
81. Betskoi to Diderot, May 1766: Roth, ed., 1955–70, vol. 6, p. 182. Betskoi's letter was written in response to Diderot's letter of April 16, which is not extant.
82. The text of the letter comes from a draft of it that is not dated. Several dates were later suggested, ranging from 1765 (which is most certainly a mistake) through April 16, 1766, to August 1766. The date that is generally accepted is late August 1766, on the strength of Diderot's assertion in the letter that the contract with Falconet, dated August 27, 1766, had already been signed. The late dating of the contract, however, need not be an insurmountable obstacle to an earlier dating of the letter, if one assumes that a short preliminary agreement preceded the final contract, and that Diderot referred to the former. Such a scenario is probable for, according to Diderot, "the agreement with Falconet was completed in one quarter hour and was written on half a page," while the final contract, signed on August 27, is a thoughtful document with nineteen paragraphs on three quarto pages.
83. Diderot to Betskoi, August 28–31 (?), 1766: Roth, ed., 1955–70, vol. 6, p. 284. The French word translated here as 'model' is *ébauche,* which is a general term for any rough version of work in progress. Thus it could also mean a sketch or a draft. It is, however, safe to assume that what Diderot had in mind was a three-dimensional model. First of all, there would be no reason to mention a sketch, for Betskoi must have seen a drawing of the monument before Falconet's selection was approved. Second, Diderot's claim that the Parisian artists admired Falconet's project in the artist's atelier means that what they saw was a model, for they would not have been impressed by a drawing. Third, Diderot's letter includes praise of the model uttered by one of the *workers,* which implies a three-dimensional model. Fourth, in his farewell letter to the Paris Academy Falconet recalled his wish to execute the monument "under the very eyes" of his colleagues, which surely suggests a plaster or clay model, not a sketch. I am grateful to Marie-Louise Becker and Vincent Giroud for helping me interpret this term.
84. Ibid, pp. 285–86.
85. RGADA, fond 1263, o. 1, no. 1121, ff. 177, 196, 226. The Crozat collection was the most famous private collection of paintings in Europe; Golitsyn, who co-signed with Diderot the act of sale, was quite right when he insisted that Diderot managed to save the empress at least two hundred thousand livres (cf. p. 107).
86. Diderot to Falconet, July 1767: Roth, ed., 1955–70, vol. 7, p. 88.
87. Diderot to Falconet, beginning of September 1766: Roth, ed., 1955–70, vol. 6, p. 327.
88. Diderot to Betskoi, August (?) 1766: Roth, ed., 1955–70, vol. 6, p. 278.
89. Benot, ed., 1958, p. 282.
90. Falconet to Catherine, 21 June 1767: Réau, ed., 1921, p. 17.
91. Diderot to Betskoi, late August 1766: Roth, ed., 1955–70, vol.. 6, p. 278.
92. Réau, 1922, vol. 1, p. 84.
93. Diderot to Falconet, beginning of September 1766: Roth, ed., 1955–70, vol. 6, p. 332.

94. RGADA, fond 11, no. 1035, ff. 3 v and 4 r. Apart from the fact that there surely were inns before Mittau, in such towns as Memel or Palanga, other accounts of travel woes in East Prussia support the tale of Mme de Baurans. Thus the British ambassador Sir James Harris, traveling along the same road ten years later, echoed her observations: "We found the roads very bad before we got [to Danzig], but they have been still worse since then. For these last four days we have had one of our wheels in the Baltic" (Putnam, ed., 1952, p. 197). The poor segment of the road to which both writers refer was on the Curonian Spit (Russ. *Kurskaia kosa*], a narrow sandbar jutting into the Baltic from the Sambian peninsula, north of Königsberg. It was the preferred route for stagecoaches between Königsberg and Memel, for it avoided the longer and slushier road via Tilsit. At the tip of the Curonian Spit, the coaches had to take a ferry across the Curonian Straits to Memel.

95. On Carburi's mission to meet Falconet and Collot, see Betskoi's September 21, 1766, instruction to the Bureau of Buildings to issue the sum of four hundred rubles to Captain Lascari [Carburi] of the Engineering Battalion "for the expenses incurred in connection with his mission to accompany Professor Falconet from Riga to St. Petersburg": RGIA, fond 470, o. 103/537, no. 5, f. 7; also fond 467, o. 2, no. 101, ff. 54, 56, 57.

96. A press release by the French embassy in St. Petersburg for the *Gazette de France* notes under the dateline of October 26, 1766: "Sieur Falconnet, chosen by the Empress to execute the Equestrian Statue of Peter the Great, arrived yesterday in this city" (AAE, CP, Russie, vol. 80, f. 110).

97. Jean Michel was the son of a merchant from Rouen, who had been brought over by Peter the Great. Michel's store provided him with valuable local contacts among members of St. Petersburg's high society.

98. Malinovskii, ed. and tr., 1990, vol. 1, p. 181. Sources on the first residence of Falconet and Collot in St. Petersburg include Falconet's letters to the empress, Jakob Stählin's *Notes on the Fine Arts in Russia,* and archival materials in RGIA, fond 470, op. 103/537. According to Malinovskii's edition of Stählin, the house was built at the end of the 1730s for Major General Johann von Albrecht and was later acquired by Major General V. V. Fermor, director of the Bureau of Buildings. In the 1760s it was leased and eventually bought by Jean Michel (Malinovskii, ed. and tr., 1990, vol. 1, p. 192, fn. 104).

99. Unfortunately, not a single sketch by Falconet is extant.

100. November 1, 1766: RGIA, fond 467, o. 2, d. 101, ff.. 69.

101. RGIA, fond 470, o. 2 (103/537), no. 5, ff. 30–31.

102. Michel claimed that the price for the carriage was quite reasonable considering that it was "very clean and came with a German coachman in a livery, while even a plain coach would usually cost two rubles a day."

103. Rastrelli's new Winter Palace, which houses the main portion of the Hermitage collection, abutted the location of Peter the Great's winter residence on the Zimniaia Kanavka canal. Catherine the Great had Giacomo Quarenghi redo it as the Hermitage Theater (1783–87).

104. Malinovskii, ed. and tr., 1990, vol. 1, p. 181.

105. There exist other versions of the disposition of the land left after the dismantling of the wooden Winter Palace. According to Petr Stolpiansky's history of the city (1918, [reissue 1995, pp. 175–76]), the theater was given to Falconet as his private quarters and a large atelier was built next to it, while the part of the lot fronting on Nevsky Prospect and including the kitchen and the throne chamber was bought by the chief of police N. I. Chicherin, who in 1768 started building a large private house there. According to Broitman and Krasnova (1997, pp. 33 and 47) Falconet received the reconstructed kitchen for his residence, while the throne chamber became his workshop.

106. RGIA, fond 470, o. 2 (103/537), no. 14, ff. 1–4, August 4, 1778.
107. RGIA, fond 470, o. 2 (103/537), no. 9, f. 1, April 25, 1768.
108. Cf. Krasnova, 1985, p. 3. All directives issued by Betskoi in the first years of Falconet's stay, ended with the ritualistic admonition "without any waste of time."
109. RGIA, fond 467, o. 2, no. 101, f. 60; cf. fond 470, o. 2 (103/537), no. 9.
110. RGIA, fond 467, o. 2, no. 101, f. 73. For the story of the search and delivery of the granite boulder, see chapter 4.
111. The monies for these expenses came from the budget of Betskoi's Bureau of Buildings. The great expense of bringing the granite boulder from Lakhta to Senate Square was covered from the budget of the Admiralty. Carburi's quarterly reports and accountings for the Bureau of Buildings provide much information on the initial phase of the work on the monument; see RGIA, fond 470, o. 2 (103/537), nos. 6 and 7.
112. Diderot to Betskoi, August (?), 1766: Roth, ed., 1955–70, vol. 6, p. 287. A similar idea was expressed by I. I. Shuvalov in his 1757 project for an Academy of Fine Arts: "[its] fruit, when it ripens, will not only glorify this empire, but will be of great value to state and private projects for which we now pay big money to foreigners of modest abilities, who take it and depart" (quoted after Semenova, 1998, p. 67).
113. Falconet to Diderot, February 26, 1767: Roth, ed., 1955–70, vol. 7, p. 3.

CHAPTER 3. SCULPTORS OF THE EMPRESS

1. Bausset to Choiseul, December 16, 1766: *SIRIO,* vol. 141, p. 212.
2. Ibid.
3. Choiseul to Bausset, January 23, 1767: *SIRIO,* vol. 141, p. 231. Fear of Russian competition, especially in the manufacture of textiles and furniture, made French traders and diplomats recommend that Choiseul make it more difficult for skilled French workers to leave for Russia. They were clearly concerned that French specialists, lured by lucrative offers, would teach the Russians their skills and help them set up their own manufacturing facilities. See Raimbert to Choiseul, December 5, 1767 (*SIRIO,* vol. 141, p. 374), and Jean-Baptiste Rossignol to Choiseul (AAE, CP, Russie, vol. 82, ff. 143–46).
4. Falconet to Marigny, June 4, 1765: AN, O[1] 1911, doc. 45.
5. Falconet to Diderot, February 26, 1767: Roth, ed., 1955–70, vol. 7, p. 33.
6. Catherine to Falconet, February 14, 1769: Réau, ed., 1921, p. 71.
7. Catherine to Falconet, May 15, 1769: Réau, ed., 1921, p. 81.
8. Falconet to Diderot, July–August 1767: Roth, ed., 1955–70, vol. 8, p. 82.
9. RGIA, fond 789, no. 297, ff. 18–19. On the same day Diderot also became foreign honorary associate of the Academy, but the results of the balloting were not given; news of the election was printed in the *Gazette de France* for March 9, 1767, no. 20, p. 79.
10. The correspondence between Catherine the Great and Falconet has appeared in two excellent editions. In 1876 A. A. Polovtsov, president of the Russian Historical Society, published an annotated French-Russian edition (*SIRIO,* vol. 17). Another edition was put out in 1921 by the French art historian Louis Réau, under the auspices of the Institut Français de Petrograd. All quotations from the correspondence are based on Réau's edition.
11. Catherine to Falconet, February 18, 1767: Réau, ed., 1921, p. 6. Diderot commented: "the haughtiness of rank is always due to the pettiness of the person who displays it" (Diderot to Falconet, May 15, 1767: Roth, ed., 1955–70, vol. 7, p. 61.)

12. Catherine to Falconet, May 10, 1769: Réau, ed. 1921, p. 77.

13. Catherine to Falconet, March 10, 1767: Réau, ed. 1921, pp. 7–8.

14. Falconet to Catherine, June 23, 1771: Réau, ed. 1921, p. 159.

15. AAE, CP, Russie, vol. 85, f. 226. This criticism of the *Antidote* was echoed even by Diderot, who said that it was "the worst book possible for its tone, the meanest for its content, and the most absurd for its pretensions. . . . He who refuted Chappe is more contemptible for his sycophancy than Chappe is for his errors and lies." Diderot to Grimm, March 4, 1771: Roth, ed., 1955–70, vol. 10, pp. 236–37. Sabatier de Cabre's disclaimer of foreign participation in the composition of the *Antidote* should put to rest the frequently voiced suspicion that it was edited by Falconet.

16. Diderot to Falconet, May 1768: Roth, ed., 1955–70, vol. 8, pp. 32–33.

17. Rulhière, 1797, p. ii.

18. There exists no unanimity on how to refer to Mercier de La Rivière: *de la Rivière* (Diderot and Falconet in their correspondence); *La Rivière* (Roth, ed., 1955–70); *Mercier* (Madariaga, 1981); *Rivière* (Alexander, 1998). I follow Roth, whose edition of Diderot's correspondence is used in this book. The La Rivière affair figured prominently in many exchanges between Falconet and the empress, beginning almost immediately after his arrival. La Rivière was also the topic of several letters between Diderot and Falconet in which Diderot defended the French economist and accused Falconet of sowing discord between the empress and La Rivière. Diderot to Falconet, May 1768: Roth, ed., 1955–70, vol. 8, pp. 34–37; Falconet to Diderot, July–August 1768: ibid., pp. 79–81; and Diderot to Falconet, September 6, 1768: ibid., pp. 110–22. Madame de Baurans's account of La Rivière's long and uncomfortable journey to St. Petersburg was cited above, p. 96.

19. Diderot to Volland, August 24, 1768: Roth, ed., 1955–70, vol. 8, p. 95.

20. The act of sale was signed by Diderot and Prince D. A. Golitsyn on January 4, 1772: Roth, ed., 1955–70, vol. 12, pp. 11–12. See also Diderot to Falconet, April 17, 1772: ibid., p. 49. Cf. above, p. 93.

21. Catherine to Falconet, February 18, 1767: Réau, ed., 1921, pp. 4–5.

22. Falconet to Catherine, March 16, 1767: Réau, ed., 1921, pp. 9–10.

23. Catherine to Falconet, March 28, 1767: Réau, ed., 1921, pp. 12–14.

24. Diderot to Falconet, September 7, 1769: Roth, ed., 1955–70, vol. 9, p. 133.

25. RGADA, fond 1263, o. 1, no. 1114, published in *SIRIO*, vol. 17, p. 374.

26. RGADA, fond 1263, o. 1, no. 1114, ff. 263 to 264r., published in *SIRIO*, vol. 17, p. 381.

27. RGADA, fond 1263, o. 1, no. 4174, f. 3, published in *SIRIO*, vol. 17, p. 379. The portrait to which A. M. Golitsyn referred was a bust of Anastasia Sokolova, an illegitimate daughter of General Betskoi.

28. Diderot knew that Collot was barely eighteen when she went to St. Petersburg. Was it his concern with propriety that made him age her by one year?

29. Diderot to Betskoi, draft, end of August, 1766: Roth, ed., 1955–70, vol. 6, p. 283.

30. Ibid.

31. Ibid., p. 284.

32. Similarly, the arrival in St. Petersburg in 1767 of La Rivière, accompanied by his wife and his mistress Madame de Baurans, a trio that Grimm compared to Abraham, Sarah, and Hagar, passed almost unnoticed in the annals of St. Petersburg society.

33. The anonymous and fragmentary "Eloge de Mademoiselle Collot" is to be found among the Falconet papers (BN, N. a. fr., no. 24983, f. 405 r.) where it is marked "Chapter Nine," forming presumably a part of larger work on Russia whose other parts have not survived. According to a plausible suggestion of Marie-Louise Becker (forthcoming), its author was the French doctor Noël Girard, who was in St. Petersburg from 1766 till

1769 as personal physician of the president of the Academy of Sciences Count Kirill G. Razumovsky. Since Falconet mentioned Girard as author of a short history of contemporary Russia (Falconet to Catherine, November 9, 1769: Réau, ed., 1921, p. 108), Becker surmises that the "Eloge" was part of that work. Girard may have given the "Eloge" to Falconet, which would account for its survival.

34. Ibid. The box mentioned in the "Eloge" is presumably the large heart-shaped Chinese lacquer box with mother-of-pearl incrustations mentioned in Réau, 1922, vol. 1, p. 119. Its shape suggests that it was meant to be used for love letters.

35. RGADA, fond 1263, o. 1, no. 1746, f. 1.

36. Some of these works are reproduced in Becker, forthcoming. Both Cathcart portraits were identified by Opperman, 1965.

37. Diderot to Falconet, September 6, 1768: Roth, ed., 1955–70, vol. 8, p. 125.

38. Catherine to Falconet, April 8, 1773: Réau, ed., 1921, p. 201.

39. Diderot to Falconet, March, 1767: Roth, ed., 1955–70, vol. 7, p. 41.

40. This rumor may be due to the fact that the young man passed himself off on occasion as a Polish gentleman (Maikov, 1908, p. 5).

41. Cf. Pnin for Repnin, Litsyn for Golitsyn, Rontsov for Vorontsov, and Bokov for Nabokov.

42. Catherine the Great, 1927, p. 44.

43. Ibid. Count Jean-Germain Lestocq was a personal physician of Elizabeth and the grand duke; Count Otto von Brümmer was the lord marshal; and Maria Andreevna Rumiantseva was the chief lady-in-waiting.

44. Bil'basov (1890, p. 3, fn. 1) thinks that the rumor was first mentioned in a footnote to the German translation of Masson's *Mémoires secrets sur la Russie.*

45. Betskoi, according to Maikov (1904, pp. 14–15), his only serious biographer, was stationed in Russia as his father's aide-de-camp during all of 1726, 1727, and the first half of 1728. Maikov cannot, however, account for Betskoi's whereabouts in the second half of 1728.

46. Waliszewski, 1893, p. 3.

47. The Russian name of the office translated here as 'bureau' was *kantseliaria,* "chancery," till 1769, when it was changed to *kontora,* "office."

48. The chancellorship was the highest civil post in Russia, corresponding to that of chief minister.

49. For surveys of Betskoi's administrative duties, see Maikov, 1904; Lappo-Danilevskii, 1904; and Eroshkina, 1993. Betskoi's correspondence is scattered among various archives.

50. From the name of its location in the Smolny Monastery.

51. Dukes, 1967, p. 193.

52. [Chistovich and Gorgolia], 1863, p. 153.

53. Zaichkin and Pochkaev, 1996, p. 239. Betskoi sent Catherine regular reports on Count Bobrinsky, but never referred to his misbehavior.

54. Waliszewski, 1893, pp. 486–87.

55. Bausset to Choiseul, January 6, 1767: *SIRIO,* vol. 141, p. 226.

56. Maikov, 1908, p. 8.

57. Shcherbatov, "On the Decline of Morality in Russia" (written in 1786 or 1787), in Iukht, ed., 1996, p. 267.

58. Dashkova, 1999, p. 63.

59. Polovtsov, 1876, p. vii.

60. Maikov, 1904, pp. 65–67. One may also be led to that conclusion by the servile tone of the letter (in German, dated January 11/22, 1762) that Betskoi sent from Vienna to

Peter III upon his ascension to the throne. Here is the first paragraph: "My joy at the auspicious ascension of Your Imperial Highness to the hereditary throne of All the Russias is as sincere and heartfelt as my fidelity to Your August Majesty which I have harbored during all my life and which is becoming ever stronger. Added to it is the deepest obedience which I owe to my August Monarch as His subject. The happiness of old Betskoi [he was fifty-eight at the time], who for such a long time has benefited from the generous bounty of Your Imperial Highness, could not be more complete at this ascension" ([Chistovich and Gorgolia], 1863, p. 82).

61. Bourrée de Corberon, 1901, vol. 1, p. 153.
62. July 31, 1772, AAE, CP, Russie, vol. 85, f. 237r. The "two establishments" are the Bureau of Buildings and the Cadet Corps.
63. Mikhnevich, 1882, pp. 168–69.
64. Diderot to Volland, September 1767: Roth, ed., 1955–70, p. 133.
65. Betskoi to Catherine, May 3, 1775: RGADA, fond 11, op. 1, no. 983, f. 124 r.
66. The artistic pseudonym of Claire-Josèphe Léris.
67. [Chistovich and Gorgolia], 1863, p. 152. The believers in Betskoi as Catherine's father might take her devotion to Anastasia as support for their views. Anastasia married Major José de Ribas of the Cadet Corps, variously referred to as a "Neapolitan adventurer" (Réau, 1923, p. 168; Madariaga, 1981, p. 415) and a brilliant naval officer who routed the Turks in the delta of the Danube in 1790. Anastasia and her husband inherited most of Betskoi's considerable estate.
68. For an account of the failed romance, see the memoirs of Rzhevskaia (RA, 1871, no. 1).
69. As Catherine said, Betskoi "arrogates to himself the sovereign's glory" (Zaichkin and Pochkaev, 1996, p. 240).
70. Heier, ed., 1965a, pp. 142–43.
71. In 1767 eight letters from the empress and ten letters from Falconet were exchanged.
72. Report of Carburi, July 19, 1767, RGIA, fond 470, o. 2 (103/537), no. 6, f. 32; cf. Stählin in Malinovskii, ed. and tr., 1990, vol. 1, p. 181.
73. May 24, 1767, RGADA, fond 11, o. 1, no. 983 (Letters and reports of Ivan Betskoi to Empress Catherine II), ff. 27r–29v.
74. To avoid the danger of fire spreading to the Admiralty during casting, many special precautions were taken, detachments of soldiers were placed on watch, storage sheds were closed, water cisterns were prepared, and all gunpowder was moved out of the building.
75. Betskoi to Carburi, June 18, 1767: RGIA, fond 467, o. 2, no. 101, ff. 74, 76; July 26, 1767, RGIA, fond 470, o. 2 (103/537), no. 6, f. 33.
76. RGIA, fond 470, o. 2 (103/537), no. 14, f. 1.
77. Falconet to Catherine, November 12, 1767: Réau, ed. 1921, p. 32.
78. FO, vol. 5, pp. 21–23, fn. g. Falconet's self-righteous indignation may have been totally unjustified if Betskoi's suggestion was made after Falconet had appealed to the Bureau of Buildings to supply him with information on "the construction of the armature" (Falconet to Catherine, May 11, 1768: Réau, ed., 1921, p. 41).
79. Catherine to Falconet, February 14, 1769: Réau, ed., 1921, p. 71. The wooden building that was allowed there as an exception was the atelier of Falconet. The mention of plans deposited with the police indicates that Stolpianskii (1918, pp. 175–76) was right in claiming that the part of the lot fronting on Nevsky Prospect was promised to the chief of St. Petersburg's police, N. I. Chicherin.
80. Falconet to Catherine, May 29, 1771: Réau, ed., 1921, p. 148.
81. Catherine to Falconet, May 30, 1771: Réau, ed., 1921, p. 150.

82. Falconet to Catherine, June 1, 1771: Réau, ed., 1921, p. 151.

83. Ibid., p. 152.

84. Catherine to Falconet, June 4, 1771: Réau, ed., 1921, p. 153.

85. Falconet to Catherine, June 16, 1771: Réau, ed., 1921, pp. 155–56.

86. Lévesque, FOC, vol. 1, p. 17.

87. Heier, ed., 1965a, pp. 144–45. A manuscript copy of the article in the Calendar of Gotha is preserved in BN, N. a. fr., 24983.

88. Falconet to Diderot, July–August 1768: Roth, ed., 1955–70, vol. 8, p. 82.

89. Diderot to Falconet, September 7, 1769: Roth, ed., 1955–70, vol. 9, p. 132.

90. Observations sur la statue de Marc-Aurèle (FO, vol. 1, p. 178, fn. G). Falconet had, in fact, four helpers during the first six months of work: the carvers Fontaine and Richard, the molder Simon, and the sculptor Vandendrisse. Fontaine and Richard were dismissed in August 1768. See Bubnov, 1941, pp. 20–21.

91. Falconet to Betskoi, May 9, 1770: RGIA, fond 789, o. 1 (p. 1), no. 297, f. 9.

92. Falconet to Catherine, May 28, 1770: Réau, ed., 1921, pp. 125–26.

93. Catherine to Falconet, May 29, 1770: Réau, ed., 1921, p. 127.

94. Falconet to Catherine, June 1, 1770: Réau, ed., 1921, pp. 128–30.

95. Catherine to Falconet, June 2, 1770: Réau, ed., 1921, p. 131. Among other comments that made Falconet cringe was one by P. P. Chebyshev, a procurator of the Holy Synod, who complained that the statue was twice the size of Peter the Great. He thought that there should be an injunction against making people and horses bigger than they actually were.

96. According to Nicolaï, in Heier, ed., 1965a, p. 147.

97. Engravings helped popularize works of art, fulfilling the role of today's photographs.

98. From 1760 till 1769 Losenko lived in Paris and Italy. After his return to Russia, he was elected academician and, in 1772, director of the Academy of Fine Arts. He died in poverty.

99. Falconet to Catherine, May 7, 1770: Réau, ed., 1921, p. 124. Losenko's drawing for Golitsyn (without the pedestal) is possibly the one which was said to be in the Research Museum of the Academy of Fine Arts (Nauchno-issledovatel'skii Muzei Akademii Khudozhestv), but I failed to find it there.

100. The drawing was presented by the empress to Falconet.

101. Falconet to Catherine, March 8, 1775: Réau, ed., 1921, p. 250.

102. Falconet to Catherine, July 10, 1776: Réau, ed., 1921, p. 257.

103. The drawing was left in Paris, which turned out to a good thing because Betskoi made an attempt to sequester it from Falconet on the eve of his departure from St. Petersburg.

104. Falconet smashed the original small model to pieces in a fit of anger.

105. In the letter in which Falconet informed the empress of Losenko's finished drawing, he suggested also that the text of the inscription read Petro Primo Catharina Seconda [sic] posuit and that it not be made longer (Falconet to Catherine, August 14, 1770: Réau, ed., 1921, pp. 133–34). Catherine made it shorter.

106. Falconet did introduce some changes into the final cast, but they were minor (see Falconet to Catherine, September 1, 1778: Réau, ed., 1921, p. 268).

107. See pp. 191–92.

108. FO, vol. 1, p. 264.

109. Ibid., fn. (ddd). In a later edition that passage is changed from "on the corner of your table" to "before leaving for Russia" (FOC, vol. 3, p. 114). It may be argued that Falconet borrowed his idea from Bernini, who placed Louis XIV's horse on a pile of stones, claiming that it symbolized the peak of the reign of the Sun King. In Bernini's equestrian

monument, however, stones are not used as a pedestal. They are there to support the marble of a bounding horse.

CHAPTER 4. THUNDER ROCK

1. Catherine's yearning for international acclaim made her insist that the boulder be moved as little whittled down as possible, even though Falconet urged that its size be reduced to the dimensions required by his design.
2. Primary sources used in the reconstruction of the operation Thunder Rock include: Falconet's responses to his critics; Carburi de Cephalonie, 1777; Backmeister, 1786; and the collections of the Russian State Historical Archive and the Central State Archive of the Navy, and the French Bibliothèque Nationale. Of these, the account of Carburi deserves special attention, for the Greek engineer, despite his reputation as one given to bombast and self-promotion, was closer to the search than anyone else and played a crucial role in the venture of transporting the boulder to the city. I have also used several secondary sources: Bubnov's 1941 typescript account of the history of the monument prepared by him for the Office for Preservation of City Monuments; Kaganovich's 1982 book on the monument; and G. I. Ivanov's 1994 book on the Thunder Rock. I was also fortunate to have access to Ivanov's research notebooks, designs, reproductions, and photographs.
3. RGIA, fond 467, o. 2 (73/187), no. 101, f. 93.
4. RGIA, fond 467, op. 2, no. 101, f. 110. Betskoi's original plans called for a pedestal made up of twelve stones.
5. *SPV,* no. 55, June 6, 1768.
6. Carburi de Cephalonie, 1777, p. 8.
7. The chronicle of the dealings between the Bureau of Buildings and the Admiralty is recorded in the archive of the naval minister, Admiral Semën Mordvinov (TsGAVMF, fond 173, year 1768).
8. Konnaia (or Konnaia Lakhta) belonged to Count Grigory Orlov, one of Catherine the Great's favorites.
9. Backmeister, 1786, p. 15.
10. Carburi de Cephalonie, 1777, p. 12.
11. *FOC,* vol. 3, p. 361. The existence of Falconet's model, showing how several stones would be assembled to form a pedestal, is confirmed by Carburi (1777, p. 8).
12. *FO,* vol. 6, p. 205.
13. *FOC,* vol. 3, p. 361.
14. Ukase of Catherine the Great of September 15, 1778, TsGAVMF, fond 173, op. 1, d. 39 (papers of Admiral Mordvinov), f. 156.
15. Carburi claimed credit for the vast atelier in which Falconet made the model of the statue. It was built in 1767 and, according to Carburi (1773, p. 10), was strong enough to survive several severe squalls and the flood of 1777.
16. TsGAVMF, fond 173, op. 1, no. 39, f. 155 (1768).
17. For the chronology of the operations, see RGIA, fond 467, o. 2 (73/187), no. 101, ff. 263–64.
18. Ivanov (1994, p. 43) cites these dimensions in leagues instead of feet—an obvious misprint.
19. The flipping of the stone is probably responsible for the puzzling discrepancies in reporting the boulder's dimensions. The figures of 27 feet wide and 21 feet high (Carburi)

were probably taken before the boulder was turned over, while the figures of 22 feet wide and 27 feet high (Backmeister and Schley) were taken afterward. Later authorities (see Ivanov 1994, p. 42) tend to follow the figures of Backmeister and Schley. Ivanov, however, errs when he claims that Backmeister's figures agree with Carburi's.

20. The trimmed boulder weighed three times more than the giant Egyptian obelisk that was brought to Rome in A.D. 37 by Caligula and erected in St. Peter's Square in 1586 with the help of 900 workers and 75 horses.

21. This is an important detail, for Falconet would later on be accused of overtrimming the boulder and having to repair his own mistakes with a patch-up job.

22. There was a persistent rumor in the capital that the method proposed by Carburi was actually devised by an anonymous smith who was paid a pittance by the wily Greek. There is, however, no way to substantiate that story. It is likely that it was born after the fact, one of the many examples of a tendency to pin every kind of sin on the generally disliked Carburi.

23. Carburi tried using iron balls, but they were crushed by the weight of the boulder. All metal parts of his machine were made in Tula, the center of Russian copper manufacture.

24. Carburi de Cephalonie, 1777, pp. 13 and 15. The French travelers Fortia de Piles and de Boisgelin (1796) report having seen the model in the Academy of Fine Arts in St. Petersburg. Later on, it was reported to be in the Museum of Transport.

25. Carburi de Cephalonie, 1777, p. 17.

26. In his description of this operation Carburi (1777, p. 19) expressed great admiration for the manual skills of Russian workers: "Almost all Russian peasants and soldiers are carpenters, which was of no mean help to me in doing my work promptly. They are so skilled in handling the ax that there is no job of carpentry which they could not do with merely an ax and a chisel."

27. Ibid. Carburi reports that the six days of lying under the boulder transformed the six-foot layer of moss and hay into a compact four-to-five inch sheet that was completely bulletproof.

28. Ibid., p. 24.

29. Ibid., p. 25.

30. See above, pp. 169–70.

31. Carburi de Cephalonie, 1777, p. 16. Carburi's concern for the draining and drying of swamplands was connected, no doubt, with his having received a swampy tract of land in his native Cephalonia from the Venetian Senate.

32. Carburi had a streak of hypochondria and in letters to his brothers, the physician Giovanni Battista in Paris, and to the chemist Marco in Padua, he complained incessantly of various ills, most often affecting his digestive tract. Marco sent him a crate of lemons and oranges.

33. Such, for instance, is his claim that the overland segment of the journey took a mere six weeks, when, as we know from Backmeister (1786, p. 28), it was at least three times as long. This is one of the few instances where Backmeister shows himself better informed than Carburi. In most cases, Backmeister relied on the data provided by Carburi.

34. RGIA, fond 467, o. 73/187, no. 101, f. 264. Ivanov (1994, p. 73), basing himself on the Russian translation of Backmeister's book (1786, pp. 26–27) and on archival sources, was able to plot the overland route of the boulder (see the adaptation in fig. 4.10).

35. Not the Lesser Nevka, as claimed by Kaganovich (1982, p. 121).

36. For a reliable reconstruction of the planning and execution of the maritime leg of the transportation of the Thunder Rock, based chiefly on the archives of the Admiralty and the Bureau of Buildings, see Kaganovich, 1982, pp. 113–24 and 185–86.

37. In the summer of 1769, that is, soon after the incident of the barge, Admiral Spiridov was given command of the first naval squadron to be sent from Kronshtadt to the Mediterranean. He distinguished himself in the naval battle at Chesme in 1770.

38. Carburi de Cephalonie, 1777, p. 28; Backmeister, 1786, p. 30. By the terms of the contract, the height of the barge was eleven feet (Kaganovich, 1982, p. 118). That would have sufficed if the loading dock had been at sea level and not, as is more likely, three feet above it, as reported by Carburi and Backmeister.

39. Carburi de Cephalonie, 1777, pp. 29–30.

40. The course of the barge in the Gulf of Finland was re-created by Ivanov (1994, p. 65) on the basis of secret eighteenth-century maps drawn by Captain Nogaev and preserved in TsGAVMF.

41. St. Isaac's Pier was so named because the church of St. Isaac used to be nearby.

42. Russian sources do not provide the date of the barge's departure, but *Gazette de France* (no. 90, November 9, 1770) confirms that the barge left on October 3.

43. The official versifier, Vasily Grigorievich Ruban, wrote an ode celebrating the event. It was printed on leaflets and freely distributed. A translation of its final stanza supplies the epigraph to this section.

44. See the first chemical analysis of the rock in Carburi de Cephalonie, 1777, pp. 34–46, made by Giovanni Baptista Carburi, Marin's older brother. Falconet confirmed the existence of the vein in his *Entretien d'un voyageur avec un statuaire,* and described it as composed of "poorly amalgamated particles and some rough and imperfect crystalline matter." The vein disappeared when the boulder was hewn down. The rumor that the vein contained semiprecious stones such as topazes, amethysts, garnets, and carnelians (Backmeister, 1786, p. 14) spread, according to Falconet, from St. Petersburg to a 1770 issue of the *Almanach of Gotha* (*FO,* pp. 210–11). According to Fortia de Piles and de Boisgelin (1796, p. 195), the geographer and explorer Peter Simon Pallas claimed that "the granite of this pedestal is of a kind which does not ever reach the hardness of other granites, that it crumbles and becomes dust, and that the rock will suffer the same fate in two or three centuries." Fortia de Piles agreed with this verdict. Clearly, neither Pallas nor Fortia de Piles realized that the Thunder Rock had lain in its location since the glacial period.

45. RGADA, fond 468, o. 1/2, no. 3885 (1771).

46. Falconet to Catherine, June 23, 1771: Réau, ed., 1921, p. 159.

47. RGADA, fond 468, o. 1/2, no. 3886 (1771). Falconet's accusation, however, was not altogether fair, for two years earlier, soon after the boulder had been brought to the pier at Lakhta, Carburi was promoted to the rank of lieutenant colonel. Falconet himself thanked the empress for that advancement (Falconet to Catherine, July 1, 1769: Réau, ed., 1921, p. 87).

48. Haigold, 1770, p. 214.

49. John Carr (1806, p. 41), traveled in Russia during the reign of Paul I.

50. October 15, 1773, vol. 7, part 2, p. 327.

51. Falconet to Catherine, June 23, 1771: Réau, ed., 1921, p. 159.

52. *Mémoires secrets de Bachaumont,* vol. 21, September 22, 1782, p. 115.

53. Betskoi said that every stroke of Falconet's hammer felt like a dagger plunged into his heart (*FO,* p. 207).

54. Masson, 1800 to 1803, p. 73.

55. Fortia de Piles and de Boisgelin, 1796, p. 194.

56. Carr, 1806, p. 41.

57. *FO,* vol. 6, pp. 202–47. At one point Falconet writes: "The stone was thirty-seven feet long when it entered my atelier and those are still its dimensions. My model is fifty feet

long at the base. It is necessary, therefore, to add to the base a dozen or so feet if one does not want the statue to appear sullen and stiff on its block, without grace, grandeur, truth, and solidity" (p. 214).

58. Bourrée de Corberon (1901, vol. 1) defended Falconet against accusations of pursuing selfish goals in reducing the boulder in size: "I don't think that he is capable of such petty motives" (p. 138). He also expressly denied the rumor that Falconet had to retrace his steps by adding two extensions which he had previously cut off. He attributed the rumor to Betskoi and added: "This is how people get calumniated every day, especially in this country" (pp. 153–54).

59. Pyliaev, 1990, p. 473, fn. 145. Pyliaev's characterization of Carburi echoes the views of Chantreau (1794, p. 22) and of the Russian historian Shubinskii (1871, pp. 246–47). The Polish-French historian Waliszewski (1894, pp. 258 and 310) called Carburi "an adventurer of the worst kind."

60. Catherine to Falconet, March 14, 1773: Réau, ed., 1921, p. 198.

61. Falconet to Catherine, July 1, 1769: Réau, ed., 1921, p. 87.

62. Masarachi, 1843, p. 65.

63. Scherer (1792, p. 233), who was an employee of the French legation in St. Petersburg, described him as arriving in St. Petersburg in tatters.

64. A sketch of Carburi's life may be found in Dendrinos, 1976.

65. From the north, the Heptanese Islands are Corfu, Paxos, Santa Maura, Ithaca, Cephalonia, Zante, and Cerigo (French name, Cythère).

66. Odysseus of Ithaca was certainly the most famous and the most peripatetic Ionian of all time.

67. Grasset Saint-Sauveur, Year 8 (1800), vol. 3, p. 38. Although Grasset claims to have known Carburi well, his testimony is seriously impugned by the Cephalonian historian Antimo Masarachi (1843), who includes a chapter on Carburi in his book on notable Cephalonians. Masarachi accuses Grasset of "having accumulated uncorroborated and easy to refute slanders . . . in order to denigrate Carburi and our whole nation" (p. 53). One obvious mistake in Grasset's account is his replacement of the name Marin with Giorgio, the name of Marin's son.

68. Charles Philippe, count of Artois, was Louis XV's grandson and brother of Louis XVI. He became king of France in 1824 under the name of Charles X but was forced into exile by the revolution of 1830. Giovanni Battista counted among his patients Benjamin Franklin and Thomas Jefferson, during their tenures as U.S. ministers to France. Yale's Benjamin Franklin Papers contain a 1765 note in which G. B. Carburi, acting on behalf of the Duke of Marlborough, invites Benjamin Franklin to perform electrical experiments in the Marlborough residence in London. (I am grateful to Karen Duval of the Yale Benjamin Franklin Papers for this information.) Jefferson later met and befriended Giovanni Battista Carburi, calling him "Dr. Carberry" (Foss, 1969, p. 81). For more details on Giovanni Battista and a bibliography, see Baldini, 1976, pp. 723–25.

69. Giormani, 1989, p. 388. Since the trip came after Marco's inaugural lecture at the University of Padua and lasted six years, a legend was born that it marked the beginning of the institution of sabbatical leaves. Aside from the fact that such a "sabbatical" would have produced a most unusual repartition of teaching time versus leave time, Marco's trip must have been more demanding than his lectures at the university.

70. A list of noble Ionian families, known as the Golden Book (Libro d'Oro), compiled at the turn of the sixteenth century, is often used to settle such matters. All the original copies of the Golden Book, however, were destroyed during the Napoleonic invasions and what we have today is a reconstruction of it by Rankabē (1926). Tsitselē's (1904,

p. 800) claim that the Carburis were in the original Golden Book at the time of its compilation "between the years 1593–1604" is supported by Rankabē (p. 11).

71. Marco justified his petition by a claim that during his official mission abroad he would have to associate with persons of high birth and that the title of count would facilitate the establishment of personal contacts necessary to ferret out industrial secrets and gain easier access to mines and smelting works. He attached copies of two documents which showed that in 1650 his Cephalonian ancestors possessed the title of count "deriving from public favor," but was unable to produce the originals of these documents. Giovanni Battista received the title a few months later in recognition of his achievements in medicine (Giormani, 1989, pp. 383–86).

72. Grasset Saint-Sauveur, Year 8 (1800), vol. 3, p. 41.

73. ASV, Senato Mar, reg. 240, March 29, 1781.

74. Carburi de Cephalonie, 1777, pp. 3–4.

75. Here is what Scherer (1792, p. 237) had to say on this matter: "[Carburi] had the effrontery to announce everywhere that he was the last offspring of the famous dynasty of the Lascarides. Unfortunately for him, the envoy of Ragusa in St. Petersburg, whose wife was truly that last offspring, found out about that gasconade while visiting the Academy of Fine Arts. . . . He made [Carburi] come to that public place and in front of several other officials berated him for his impudence and forbade him to use that name in the future."

76. Carburi de Cephalonie, 1777, p. 3.

77. Tsitselē, 1904, p. 801, fn. 1.

78. Ibid, p. 801.

79. The office of the *Avvogaria di comun* consisted of three *avvogadori di comun,* state prosecutors attached to the doge. They functioned as his legal advisers and advocates for the legal rights of the citizenry.

80. The Arsenale was started at the beginning of the twelfth century and grew over the years into a complex network of wharfs, workshops, and boathouses, occupying an area of more than a hundred acres. The conveyor-like technology of the Arsenale shipbuilders so impressed Dante that he used it in the *Inferno* (*Canto* XXI, verses 7–18).

81. The documents used in the following reconstruction include the depositions of the plaintiff, Barbara Carara, and three witnesses: her husband Stefano, a pork curer, Zuzanne-Maria Lisignol, and a scale inspector, Candido Zitolo, as well as the text of the indictment against Marin Carburi (ASV, Avvogaria di comun, Processi, Files 100.4, 100.5, and 468.11).

82. Marin's father does not appear in the documents concerning the case, and it is likely that by that time he had left Venice.

83. Tsitselē, 1904, p. 801. The most striking example of the bond between the Ionians and the Russians is the case of the Corfiote count Giovanni Capo d'Istria. From 1809 to 1822 Capo d'Istria was chief foreign policy adviser of Alexander I. His greatest contribution was in the area of Russo-Prussian and Russo-Austrian affairs, notably at the Congress of Vienna.

84. Colonel (Major General from 1769) Petr Ivanovich Melissino was a son of a Cephalonian physician who had emigrated to Russia from Venice in the days of Peter the Great. It was also reported that Melissino was one of the riders who modeled for Falconet during his work on the horse of Peter the Great. According to Scherer (1792, pp. 233–34), the go-between was a certain Jelmatschainoff, who agreed to help Carburi obtain employment with General Betskoi in exchange for a promise that Carburi would marry his sister.

85. Carburi's allowance for the trip was four hundred rubles in silver (RGIA, fond 470, o. 103/537).

86. For a detailed description of the corps's progressive educational program, see Georgi, 1794, pp. 278–95.

87. This story is told by Scherer (1792, p. 239) and repeated by Chantreau (1794, Appendix, p. 22) and Shubinskii (1903, p. 248). Its denouement, according to Scherer (1792, pp. 240–41), was tragic: "The smith who had invented the procedure employed in moving the rock claimed in vain his reward, crying that he had been robbed. The ruthless Lascaris [Carburi], feeling secure under the protection of Betskoi, let him spend his strength in useless efforts until the unfortunate man died of sorrow and despair. After his death, Lascaris, fearing that the widow and the children might reach the empress with the tale of this injustice and its consequences, agreed to pay her a little less than a half of what her husband had legitimately earned."

88. Falconet to Catherine, June 23, 1771: Réau, ed., 1921, p. 159.

89. Backmeister (1786, p. 16), as librarian of the Academy of Sciences, was obliged to accept the "official" version of events, and in his history of the monument, published soon after the unveiling, he accorded chief credits to Betskoi as the man who directed the operation "with the assistance of Count Carburi."

90. Falconet to Catherine, June 23, 1771: Réau, ed., 1921, p. 159.

91. Shubinskii, 1871, p. 246.

92. Falconet evidently was not aware of Carburi's treatment by Betskoi, which, if one may trust Scherer's testimony, was not all that shabby. It seems that at one point Carburi complained to Betskoi that four thousand rubles in bank notes were picked from his pocket during work. Betskoi reimbursed him for the loss and, in addition, gave him a bonus of five thousand rubles and an expensive box.

93. Falconet to Catherine, March 10, 1773: Réau, ed., 1921, pp. 195–96.

94. Catherine to Falconet, March 10, 1773: Réau, ed., 1921, p. 196.

95. Catherine to Falconet, March 14, 1773: Réau, ed., 1921, pp. 197–98.

96. Scherer, 1792, p. 235.

97. Shubinskii, 1871, pp. 246–47; Shubinskii, 1898, pp. 74–75.

98. Scherer's story cited above that Carburi's first wife in St. Petersburg was a Mlle Jelmatschainoff is not supported by other sources.

99. Scherer, 1792, p. 235.

100. Catherine to Falconet, March 14, 1773: Réau, ed., 1921, p. 198.

101. March 30, 1773: RGIA, fond 467, o. 2, no. 101, f. 231.

102. Marin Carburi to Giovanni Battista Carburi, February 18, 1773: *Stampa*, c. 1786, p. 3. This collection of documents supporting Sophia's contestation of her father's last will is a valuable source of information on the last years of Marin Carburi. I am grateful to the librarian of the Hellenic Institute of Byzantine and Post-Byzantine Studies in Venice for allowing me to consult this publication.

103. Carburi mentions the award, seemingly oblivious of having used that title for years in Russia.

104. Masarachi, 1843, p. 75.

105. Tsitselē, 1904, p. 801.

106. Marin Carburi to Giovanni Battista Carburi, August 26, 1776: *Stampa,* c. 1786, p. 6.

107. Marin Carburi to Marco Carburi, January 1, 1777: ibid., p. 7.

108. To be fair, the book's subtitle says in smaller print: *ou Relation des travaux et des moyens mechaniques qui ont été employés pour transporter à Pétersbourg un Rocher de trois millions pesant, destiné à servir de base à la Statue equestre de cet Empereur.*

109. Tsitselē, 1904, p. 805.

110. Asanēs, 1818, pp. 653–54. Curiously, the memory of the Carburi murder was still alive in Cephalonian folklore at the beginning of the twentieth century when Tsitselē (1904, p. 808) recorded a stanza of a Cephalonian folk ballad re-creating the events of that fateful night: "That man Carburi, that wild beast, / Brought in the Moreans from Anatolikó / To dig up swamps and dredge them, / To plant flax and sugarcane. / They decided one Saturday night / To kill Carburi and take his money."

111. Carburi accompanied this lyrical effusion by a homage to his Russian and Venetian rulers, in which he ascribed the laws of Venice to its lagoons—a metaphor that bogs down in obsequiousness—and moved the birthplace of Catherine the Great a hundred miles to the west: "It is on Cephalonia, warring and unhappy in the past and now peaceful and rich, that he [Carburi] will enjoy the most wonderful climate and the sweetest retirement, and will have frequent occasions to meditate, remembering that while the lagoons of Venice give laws to a part of Greece, a Princess, born on the banks of the Elbe, makes the Laws of Rome and the arts of Athens flourish among the Hyperboreans" (Carburi de Cephalonie, 1777, p. 4).

112. "The Turkish Empire is crumbling day by day," as Napoleon was to say in 1797, while the Russians had already agreed to the Austrian annexation of several Venetian islands in the Kvarner Archipelago in the Adriatic.

113. It is interesting that a few months after Carburi's murder, some Cephalonian patriots fought under Russian command in a naval skirmish against the Turks and that their participation in that affair was thought to have been inspired by Carburi (Chiogna, in *DBI*, p. 727). A few years later the Heptanese Islands became a Russian protectorate.

114. Carburi left the bulk of his property to Stéphanie Vautez, but his will was contested by his daughter Sophia, leading to a lengthy trial and the private printing of various documents and letters pertaining to her case in *Stampa*.

115. Grasset Saint-Sauveur, Year 8 (1800), vol. 3, pp. 48–49.

CHAPTER 5. GATHERING CLOUDS

1. Diderot to Falconet, July 18, 1768: Roth, ed., 1955–70, vol. 5, p. 71.

2. Diderot to Falconet, September 6, 1768: Roth, ed., 1955–70, vol. 8, p. 128.

3. Falconet to Catherine, November 19, 1769: Réau, ed., 1921, p. 111.

4. Falconet to Diderot, February 26, 1767: Roth, ed., 1955–70, vol. 7, p. 32.

5. Reported by Diderot in his account of the Salon of 1775: Goodman, ed. and tr., 1995, vol. 2, p. 330. Yet, during his father's tenure as director of sculpture at the Sèvres Manufacture, some of Pierre-Etienne's designs were accepted for biscuit production.

6. *Encyclopédie*, vol. 8, pp. 834–37. Compare Pinault (1984, pp. 27–29): "A crowd of spectators is gathered on rue Saint-Honoré and on the balconies, while a team of horses pulls [a sled with] the marble figure. It will be lifted later up the twenty-two steps of the church, whose two columns and left-side entrance are visible. The fact that Falconet [*fils*] left the center of the scene empty and highlighted the steps by giving them chiaroscuro relief, alludes to the difficulty of the operation." Falconet's *Annunciation* was lost during the reconstruction of the nave of St. Roch's in the nineteenth century.

7. He also did a series of portraits of the members of the Royal Academy, engraved in 1768 by Pariset (BN, [E], Oeuvre de P. E. Falconet, AA3).

8. Graves, ed., 1969, s.v. Falconet.

9. The portrait of Peter the Wild Man by P.-E. Falconet was eventually acquired by Catherine the Great. Its present whereabouts are unknown. An engraving by Valentine Green is in the British Museum.

10. Bourrée de Corberon, 1901, vol. 2, p. 174.

11. Diderot to Falconet, July 11, 1769: Roth, ed., 1955–70, vol. 9, p. 72.

12. Diderot to Falconet, December 29, 1770: Roth, ed., 1955–70, vol. 10, p. 197. The characterization of Pierre-Etienne as an "honest and upright fellow" bespeaks Diderot's kindheartedness, but is way off the mark. Pierre-Etienne was in fact reputed to be a venal and unscrupulous man.

13. Falconet to Catherine, August 20, 1773: Réau, ed., 1921, p. 213.

14. Ibid.

15. Catherine to Falconet, August 22, 1773: Réau, ed., 1921, p. 214.

16. Falconet to Catherine, September 19, 1773: Réau, ed., 1921, p. 222.

17. The choice of Collot as Pierre-Etienne's model was probably dictated by convenience rather than by malice, as suggested by Denis Roche (1920, p. 244).

18. Bourrée de Corberon, 1901, vol. 2, p. 90.

19. Reproduced in Becker, 1998, p. 82. Bourrée de Corberon's characterization of Pierre-Etienne was recorded in a meticulous diary which this observant young diplomat kept during 1775–80, the period of his posting in St. Petersburg, first as secretary of the French minister plenipotentiary marquis de Juigné, then as the French chargé d'affaires. The diary contains perceptive vignettes of prominent members of St. Petersburg's society, while his dispatches to Versailles show that he was an intelligent observer of Russian institutions, especially its finances and commerce.

20. Falconet to Catherine, September 19, 1773: Réau, ed., 1921, pp. 221–22.

21. Falconet to Catherine, May 5, 1774: Réau, ed., 1921, pp. 235.

22. Falconet to Catherine, August 7, 1775: Réau, ed., 1921, p. 252. A. M. Golitsyn to Catherine, May 26, 1775: RGADA, fond 17, o. 1, no. 280, f. 1v.

23. In the absence of Pierre-Etienne, Vice Chancellor Aleksandr M. Golitsyn tried to give the three thousand rubles to Falconet *père,* but the latter refused to accept the payment, claiming that he had no right to meddle in his son's affairs. A. M. Golitsyn to Catherine, December 10, 1775: RGADA, fond 17, o. 1, no. 280, f. 3. For the fate of the three portraits, see Roche, 1920, p. 246.

24. Falconet to Catherine, March 8, 1775: Réau, ed., 1921, p. 249.

25. Falconet to Catherine, March 8, 1775: Réau, ed., 1921, p. 250. An example of a fine engraving made at the time in St. Petersburg is Collot's monument version of the head of Peter the Great. It was drawn by Losenko and engraved in 1772 by Benoît-Louis Henriquez, professor of engraving at the Academy of Fine Arts.

26. In 1821, the year of Collot's death, Marie-Lucie Falconet and her husband, Baron Stanislas de Jankovitz, published a lithograph of the monument and dedicated it to the memory of Marie Lucie's grandfather Etienne-Maurice and her parents, Marie-Anne and Pierre-Etienne. The credits below the lithograph attribute the drawing to Pierre-Etienne, even though it appears well below his talent. It follows by and large the outlines of the Losenko drawing, but is inferior to it in technique, proportions, and facial features. Its most striking flaws are the absence of the rider's left foot, which should have been plainly visible from the vantage point of the draftsman; the placement of the Latin text of the inscription on the right side of the monument rather than on the left; and making it read *Petro Magno Catarina* instead of *Petro Primo Catharina Secunda.* The Losenko drawing has no inscription; at the time of its making the text was not yet agreed upon.

27. "Réponse," *FO,* vol. 6, p. 303.
28. Catherine to Falconet, April 8, 1773: Réau, ed., 1921, p. 201.
29. Réau (ed., 1921, p. 249, fn. 1) does not think that Collot made such a bust. Becker (1998, p. 81) allows a possibility that of the two busts which, according to Diderot, Collot made in Paris during her stay there, one was of d'Alembert.
30. Diderot to Grimm, end of August 1776: Roth, ed., 1955–70, vol. 14, p. 217.
31. Becker's (1998, p. 81) suggestion that one of the busts was of Houdon would be more persuasive if it could be shown that Collot worked in Houdon's atelier while in Paris.
32. Lévesque, *FOC,* vol. 1, p. 18. Charles-Théodore Godefroy de Villetaneuse (1718–96) was a Paris jeweler and banker and a noted art and book collector. As for the date of his portrait by Collot, Valabrègue (1898, p. 30) and Réau (1922, vol. 2, p. 519) assume that it was made in 1779, that is, during Collot's stay in Paris immediately after her return from Russia. It is unlikely, however, that Collot could work professionally at a time when she was trying to cope with serious personal and marital problems. Nor can one agree with Becker's (1998, p. 81) opinion that the portrait was executed after 1780, that is, after Collot and Falconet returned to Paris from The Hague, given Lévesque's testimony that Collot worked on the portrait "far from Falconet"—a circumstance which, according to him, silenced all those who claimed that she was unable to work without Falconet's help.
33. Falconet to Catherine, July 10, 1776: Réau, ed., 1921, p. 257. If such pronouncements were made, they are no longer extant, except for Diderot's phrase cited above.
34. Falconet to Catherine, August 7, 1775: Réau, ed., 1921, pp. 251–52. This was not the first time that Falconet asked the empress to treat a trip by Collot as a paid leave of absence. He had done so before her two unrealized trips, one in 1771 and one in the spring of 1775. (Falconet to Catherine, April 26, 1771, and March 8, 1775: Réau, ed., 1921, pp. 145–46 and 249.) Such requests, coupled with the disagreement about the price of the portraits by Falconet *fils,* must have strengthened Betskoi's argument that the trio was inordinately venal.
35. Collot and Pierre-Etienne did not leave St. Petersburg until after the first casting of the monument, which took place on August 24, 1775. Becker (1998, p. 81) antedates their departure by several months by assuming that it took place in the spring of 1775. Collot returned to St. Petersburg in the summer of 1776, presumably together with Pierre-Etienne.
36. Diderot to Grimm, end of August, 1776: Roth, ed., 1955–70, vol. 14, p. 217.
37. Betskoi to Catherine, September 10, 1775: RGADA, fond 11, op. 1, no. 983, f. 124v.
38. Lévesque, *FOC,* vol. 1, p. 17. The italics are mine.
39. Bourrée de Corberon, 1901, vol. 2, p. 175. According to the marriage contract, Collot had then about 110,000 livres of savings. That is about one half of Bourrée de Corberon's estimate, but twice as much as Falconet *père* had (Réau, ed., 1919, p. 160).
40. The full text of the prenuptial agreement may be found in Réau, ed., 1919, pp. 158–59.
41. Had Diderot not been detained by sickness in The Hague and Duisburg, the two would have arrived at about the same time.
42. Réau, 1924, p. 221.
43. Mashenka is a Russian nickname for Maria. The French spelled it phonetically as Machinka.
44. "Eloge de Mademoiselle Collot": BN, N. a. fr., no. 24983, f. 411. Translated literally, the poem reads: "A remarkable human being and a lovely woman, / She excels in the art of Phidias as well as in the art of pleasing. / In times of yore, her talents would have

been crowned by Athena / And she would have had her altars on the isle of Cythera [the birthplace of Aphrodite]."

45. The monument displayed today is a copy; the original, placed in a glass case, is inside the Capitoline Museum.

46. The history of the *Marcus Aurelius* is outlined in Haskell and Penny, 1981, pp. 252–55.

47. Falconet to Catherine, May 11, 1768: Réau, ed., 1921, pp. 40–41.

48. Catherine to Falconet, May 16, 1768: Réau, ed., 1921, p. 42.

49. Betskoi to A. M. Golitsyn, 1775: RGADA, fond 1263, o. 1, no. 590, f. 3.

50. *FO*, vol. 5, p. 457. Falconet buttresses his arguments by extended citations from Horace.

51. Goethe, 1973, p. 518.

52. *FO*, vol. 1, p. 161. In saying this, Falconet had a powerful ally in the person of Charles Perrault, the opponent of Boileau in the dispute between the Ancients and the Moderns, which raged in France and England in the seventeenth century: "The horse raises its foreleg higher than it should, it walks in such a way that its neck seems dislocated. . . . The first time I saw that statue, I thought that the emperor was sitting on a brood mare, because the horse's flanks were so broad and swollen, forcing this good emperor to sit with his legs spread wide apart" (1688, vol. 1, pp. 185–86). Perrault was also the author of the poem "Le Siècle de Louis le Grand" whose first quatrain is cited in the epigraph to this section. It reads in the original: "La belle Antiquité fut toujours vénérable; / Mais je ne crus jamais qu'elle fût adorable. / Je vois les Anciens sans plier les genoux; / Ils sont grands, il est vrai, mais hommes comme nous."

53. *FO*, vol. 1, p. 161.

54. Dowley, 1968, p. 185.

55. *FO*, vol. 1, p. 163.

56. The *Correspondance littéraire* is described briefly in chapter 1, n. 73.

57. *CLT*, July 1, 1771, vol. 9, pp. 344–45.

58. Dieckmann, ed., 1951, p. 105.

59. Tronchin did not have to worry that Voltaire would alter his friendly feelings toward Falconet. He thanked Falconet for sending him the book on Pliny and, referring to the copious notes on the translation, added: "the frame is worth more than the picture." (Voltaire to Falconet, June 17, 1772: Besterman et al., ed., 1968–, vol. 10, p. 1061).

60. See Voltaire to Golitsyn, June 17, 1772: Besterman et al., ed., 1968–, vol. 10, pp. 1062, fn., and 1580, fn.

61. Most modern critics share Falconet's suspicions. Maurice Tourneux, editor of the *Correspondance littéraire,* was the first to suggest it (*CLT,* vol. 9, p. 345). Herbert Dieckmann, editor of the *Inventaire du fonds Vandeul,* a collection of writings by and concerning Diderot which was originally in the possession of Diderot's daughter, found that the tone and style of the note betrayed the pen of Diderot (Dieckmann, ed., 1951, p. 122). Jean Seznec appears to share the view of Dieckmann (Dieckmann and Seznec, 1952, p. 199). Yves Benot, editor of the correspondence between Diderot and Falconet, allows a possibility of Diderot's complicity and, therefore, "one can easily understand that the relations between the two friends suffered their first crisis around 1771–72" (Benot, ed., 1958, p. 235). Georges Roth, in his edition of Diderot's correspondence, suggests that the note "was perhaps due to Diderot himself" (Roth, ed., 1955–70, vol. 12, p. 1015). On the other hand, Jean de Booy, reviewing Diderot's contributions to the *Correspondance littéraire,* assumes that a phrase in the note referring to Diderot in the third person (suppressed in the edition of Tourneux) makes Diderot's authorship unlikely (1969, p. 375). On the basis of de Booy's skepticism, Ulla Kölving and Jeanne Carriat, editors

of the *Inventaire de la Correspondance littéraire,* claim that "specialists hesitate to attribute this article to Diderot." But in the very next sentence they suggest that Diderot and Grimm could have collaborated on it (1984, vol. 1, p. 272).

62. Here is how Diderot addressed Grimm a few months after the incident: "You who have always been and always will be my dearest and only friend, so that even if you were to kill me with your own hand, I'd rather think that it was for my own good than to impute to you the least malice. . . . I feel so powerfully united to you that I have never separated your actions, good or bad, from mine" (Diderot to Grimm, May 15, 1772: Roth, ed., 1955–70, vol. 12, pp. 62–63).

63. Diderot to Falconet, August 21, 1771: Roth, ed., 1955–70, vol. 11, p. 128. It is possible to understand the words "my letter" and "a torrent of venom and arrogance" as referring to one and the same letter of Falconet to Diderot. In that interpretation, there would be no reason to posit the existence of an initial letter from Diderot to Falconet.

64. Diderot to Falconet, April 17, 1772: Roth, ed., 1955–70, vol. 12, p. 50.

65. Diderot to Falconet, May 30, 1773: Roth, ed., 1955–70, vol. 12, pp. 227–28. Some editors accept the date of May 20 given in Diderot's autograph (ibid., fn. 2); cf., however, Diderot announcing the imminence of his departure: "Tomorrow, yes tomorrow, I'm leaving for The Hague" (ibid., p. 229), despite indications that he was still in Paris in early June (Dieckmann and Seznec, eds., 1952, pp. 199–200, fn. 7).

66. Falconet to Catherine, July 1, 1773: Réau, ed., 1921, pp. 206–7.

67. Catherine to Falconet, July 8, 1773: Réau, ed., 1921, p. 208.

68. Dieckmann and Seznec, eds., 1952, pp. 199–200 and 203.

69. Whatever its date and mode of delivery, there is no way of knowing whether the letter reached its addressee. Dieckmann and Seznec, eds. (1952, pp. 198–99), suggest that Falconet's note on Diderot's letter of December 6, 1773, refers to the letter of May 2, proving that the letter reached him. That postscript, which reads: "Mr. Diderot did not sink his teeth into the *Observations sur la statue de Marc-Aurèle* while in Paris. He has even explained it himself rather frankly" (*FO,* vol. 2, p. 140), could however, refer to Diderot's letter of August 21, 1771, which has not survived (see above).

70. Diderot to Falconet, December 6, 1773: Roth, ed., 1955–70, vol. 13, pp. 117–21.

71. See chapter 1, n. 15.

72. Diderot to Golitsyn, May 10, 1774: Roth, ed., 1955–70, vol. 14, p. 24.

73. *CLT,* January 1, 1763, vol. 5, pp. 199–200.

74. *CLT,* April 15, 1765, vol. 6, pp. 265–66. In 1785, one year after the death of Diderot, the library, consisting of three thousand volumes, was shipped to St. Petersburg. It has unfortunately lost its integrity and has been scattered among several libraries and collections.

75. Voltaire to Damilaville, April 24, 1765: Besterman et al., ed., 1968–, vol. 113, p. 66.

76. *CLT,* April 15, 1765, vol. 6, p. 266.

77. Diderot to Falconet, March 20, 1771: Roth, ed., 1955–70, vol. 10, p. 250. The exceedingly rich collection of Pierre Crozat (Baron de Thiers) forms the golden core of the Hermitage.

78. Falconet to Diderot, November 10, 1766: Benot, ed., 1958, pp. 236–37.

79. Catherine to Falconet, March 10, 1767: Réau, ed., 1921, p. 7. Given the special treatment she accorded to Diderot, it is surprising that Catherine, who thought nothing of initiating a lively correspondence with Voltaire and other personalities of the French Enlightenment, should prove so reticent about writing to him herself. In fact, she never communicated with him directly, relying on such intermediaries as Voltaire, Grimm, Betskoi,

D. A. Golitsyn, and Falconet. The persecutions mentioned by the empress refer no doubt to Diderot's three-month-long detention by the police in 1749 and the problems he was having with French officialdom about continuing the publication of the *Encyclopédie*.

80. Roth, ed., 1955–70, vol. 7, pp. 56–72, 85–96, as well as Lewinter, ed., 1970–73, vol. 7, pp. 512–25, 537–48, and Versini, ed., 1994–97, vol. 5, pp. 730–37, 741–48, divide this letter into two autonomous letters, one dated arbitrarily by Vandeul, Diderot's son-in-law, to May 15, the other dated by an unknown hand to July. The text of this letter in Diderot's hand appears in BN, N. a. fr. 24983, ff. 23–35, as a single letter, with the "July" letter on ff. 23–27v (bottom) and on ff. 33–35, while the "May 15" letter appears on ff. 27v (bottom)–33. The reason for this division is that a somewhat different and abbreviated version of this letter appears also in BN, N. a. fr. 13781, ff. 149–154, as two letters. The edition of Assezat-Tourneux (1875–77) adopts the unified version of BN, N. a. fr. 24983. That is also the approach here, with the proviso that the "July" letter is assumed to antedate the "May 15" letter. All references to these letters follow the Roth edition, but are left undated.

81. Roth, ed., 1955–70, vol. 7, pp. 60–69.

82. Catherine to Falconet, October 12, 1767: Réau, ed., 1921, p. 24.

83. The Naryshkins were a noble Russian family related to the Romanovs through Peter the Great's mother, Nataliia Kirillovna Naryshkina.

84. Catherine to Voltaire, September 11/22, 1773: Besterman et al., ed., 1968–, vol. 124, p. 127.

85. Diderot to Mme Diderot, October 9, 1773: Roth, ed., 1955–70, vol. 13, p. 65. Back in Paris, when asked if it was true that roads in Russia were poor, Diderot answered: "Absolutely not. There are no roads in Russia."

86. Ibid., pp. 65–66.

87. In the nineteenth century the Naryshkin mansion belonged to the family of the humorist poet Miatlev and was visited, among others, by Pushkin. Its current address is 9 St. Isaac's Square (corner of Pochtamtskaia Street). A marble plaque commemorates Diderot's visit.

88. Diderot to Mmes. Diderot and Vandeul, December 30, 1773: Roth, ed., 1955–70, vol. 13, p. 145. There was, in fact, no cause for alarm. The Naryshkins had reckoned with Diderot's visit and made sure that he had all the comforts of home during his stay in St. Petersburg.

89. Catherine to Voltaire, September 27, 1773: *SIRIO,* 1874, vol. 13, p. 358.

90. Catherine to Voltaire, December 27, 1773: *SIRIO,* 1874, vol. 13, p. 377.

91. Catherine to Voltaire, September 11/22, 1773: Besterman et al., ed., 1968–, vol. 124, p. 127.

92. Diderot to Dashkova, December 24, 1773: Roth, ed., 1955–70, vol. 13, pp. 135–36. Falconet was not alone in feeling jealous of Diderot. Grigory A. Potemkin, the freshly accredited favorite of Catherine the Great, exploded in rage when the empress and Diderot stayed up talking till midnight (see her March 19, 1774, answer to Potemkin's letter which has not come down to us: Lopatin, ed., 1997, pp. 17–18).

93. Diderot to Dashkova, December 24, 1773: Roth, ed., 1955–70, vol. 13, pp. 135–36.

94. Ségur, 1825–27, vol. 3, pp. 34–35.

95. The original is in the collections of the Manuscript Section of the Winter Palace Library (No. 728).

96. Serving the empress of Russia was a full-time job; it forced Grimm to transfer his mantle as editor of the *Correspondance littéraire* to his Swiss collaborator Jakob Heinrich Meister.

97. Diderot in Vernière, ed., 1966, p. 67.

98. Diderot to Mme Necker, September 6, 1774: Roth, ed., 1955–70, vol. 14, pp. 72–73. Jean-Baptiste Oudry (1685–1755) specialized in painting animals.

99. "Du climat septentrional / Ma prose ni mes vers ne diront jamais rien. / Je serois un

ingrat si j'en disois du mal; / Je serois un menteur si j'en disois du bien." Diderot to Mme Necker, September 6, 1774: Roth, ed., 1955–70, vol. 14, p. 75. That was a remake of Corneille's ditty about Cardinal Richelieu: "Du fameux Cardinal / Ma prose, ni mes vers n'en diront jamais rien. / Il m'a fait trop de bien pour en dire du mal. / Il m'a fait trop de mal pour en dire du bien."

100. For a history of the *Journal encyclopédique,* see Charlier and Mortier, 1952.

101. The Pomel affair is dealt with below, pp. 230–34.

102. Nicolaï in Heier, ed., 1965a, p. 144.

103. *FO,* 1781, vol. 3, p. xxviii.

104. Ibid., pp. xxx–xxxi.

105. Falconet to Voltaire, March 27, 1772: Besterman et al., ed., 1968–, vol. 122, p. 312.

106. "Examen de la traduction des Livres 34, 35 & 36 de Pline l'ancien, avec des Notes," *JE,* 1775, vol. 5, part 1, pp. 135–42; part 2, pp. 327–35; part 3, pp. 504–10; and vol. 6, part 1, pp. 122–26; part 2, pp. 326–34; part 3, pp. 523–28. Reprinted in *FO,* vol. 6, pp. 63–126.

107. *JE,* 1775, vol. 5, part 1, p. 139.

108. *JE,* 1775, vol. 6, part 1, p. 126.

109. Meyer, 1974, p. 267.

110. "Lettre de M. Falconet à M. * * *, ou réponse à un prétendu examen de la traduction de trois livres de Pline," *JE,* 1776, vol. 3, part 1, pp. 100–109.

111. *FO,* vol. 6, pp. 62–201.

112. The review may have been written by a St. Petersburg classical philologist. What makes this conjecture probable is the cringing reference to the two Russian monarchs: "I revere too much the memory of my hero, Peter the Great, in order not to desire ardently that you fulfill the expectations of the august and admirable empress" (*FO,* vol. 6, p. 101).

113. Betskoi to Catherine, August 20, 1775: RGADA, fond 11, o. 1, no. 983, f. 116.

114. Catherine to Grimm, June 30, 1775: *SIRIO,* 1878, vol. 23, p. 27 (*Pis'ma Imp. Ekateriny II k Grimmu*).

CHAPTER 6. FROM PLASTER TO BRONZE

1. For Falconet's contract, see BN, N. a. fr., 24983, ff. 334–35, and AVPRI 50/6, no. 216; it was published in *SIRIO,* vol. 17, pp. 375–77.

2. Boffrand, 1743. The French text of Boffrand's bilingual French and Latin narrative forms the kernel of the entry "Bronze" in the *Encyclopédie,* 1752, vol. 2, pp. 436–43. For the plates, see *Recueil,* 1771, vol. 8.

3. Pierre Gore (spelled also Gaure or Gor) was *commissaire* of artillery foundries in the Paris Arsenal and the successful founder of several large works, including Bouchardon's *Fountain of the Rivers* on the rue de Grenelle in Paris. Gore also did the monuments to Louis XV by Pigalle in Reims and the equestrian monument to Frederick V by Saly in Copenhagen.

4. In addition to Boffrand, the *Encyclopédie,* and Lempereur and Mariette (listed as Mariette, 1768), the single-jet method is dealt with in Backmeister (1786) and in Chekalovskii (1810) in his description of the casting of bronze statuary for the Kazan Cathedral in St. Petersburg. There are also summaries of the single-jet technique in a letter from Falconet to Catherine (undated, but presumed to have been written in the middle of May 1774: Réau, ed., 1921, pp. 236–38), and in his "Sur les fontes en bronze" (*FO,* vol. 6,

pp. 264–94). All these sources were used in compiling the necessarily brief account of the process in this chapter. Janson's (1985) summary of the single-jet method is unsatisfactory.

5. RGIA, fond 470, o. 2 (103/537), no. 9, ff. 1–17.

6. That was what was used for the core of the thinner parts of Girardon's statue of Louis XIV. For the massive body of the horse, the founder used clayish and sandy soil, mixed with horse manure.

7. Catherine to Falconet, June 7, 1767: Réau, ed., 1921, p. 16.

8. Catherine to Falconet, September 18, 1769: Réau, ed., 1921, p. 101.

9. Mariette, 1768, p. 109.

10. Falconet to Catherine, May 8, 1769: Réau, ed., 1921, p. 74.

11. Ibid. Emelian Khailov cast copper parts for the machine used in the transport of the Thunder Rock and worked with Falconet on the castings of the statue in 1775 and 1777.

12. Betskoi to Osterman, April 26, 1768, and Osterman to Betskoi, June 17, 1768: RGIA, fond 467, o. 2, no. 101, ff. 103 and 115. Meier had been called to Copenhagen to cast Saly's *Frederic V,* but because of his disagreements with the French sculptor, did not receive the commission.

13. Diderot to Falconet, July 11, 1769: Roth, ed., 1955–70, vol. 9, p. 74: "Trust me, take Gore instead of leaving the fate of the monument to some apprentice founder because of your misguided notion of economizing."

14. Diderot to Falconet, August 21, 1771: Roth, ed., 1955–70, vol. 11, p. 129; and April 17, 1772: Roth, ed., 1955–70, vol. 12, p. 50. Diderot was also in touch with two molders, Simon and Vandendrisse (Diderot to Falconet, March 1767, April or May 1767, and May 15, 1767: Roth, ed., 1955–70, vol. 7, p. 39).

15. As evidenced by his letter to Catherine in which he proposed to spend four years "supervising operations leading to casting," but not specifying what these operations were (Réau, ed., 1921, p. 73). The letter is undated, but Réau, extrapolating from Falconet's mention that the large model of his statue would not be finished for another year, concludes that it was written between the letters of February 14 and May 8, 1769.

16. Ibid., p. 73.

17. *FO,* vol. 6, p. 280.

18. Betskoi to Falconet, August 14, 1769: Réau, ed., 1921, p. 93.

19. This letter, dated September 3, 1769, was omitted from *FO,* but included in *FOC.* It was reprinted in Réau, ed.. 1921, pp. 94–95.

20. Catherine to Falconet, September 18, 1769: Réau, ed., 1921, p. 101.

21. Falconet to Catherine, October 10, 1769: Réau, ed., 1921, p. 103.

22. Catherine to Falconet, September 17, 1769: Réau, ed., 1921, p. 97.

23. Kaganovich (1982, p. 138) errs in claiming that they left in January 1771. Merchi's exit visa was issued on May 23, 1771 (RGIA, fond 470, o. 2 (103/537), ff. 184–85).

24. Draft of the contract dated January 21, 1772: RGADA, fond 248, vol. 5482, ff. 345–46.

25. "Sur les fontes en bronze" (*FO,* vol. 6, p. 283).

26. Catherine's request to the Senate for the funds to bring Ersmann from Paris is dated May 13, 1772 (RGADA, fond 248, vol. 5482, f. 343).

27. Backmeister, 1786, pp. 61–62. Backmeister is correct in thinking that the *Spinario* was in the Hermitage—it is still there. The description of Ersmann's duties in St. Petersburg is based on Backmeister's testimony and *Observations sur la fonte de la statue equestre* in *JE,* 1779, vol. 8, part 3, pp. 505–9. See also the letters of Falconet to Catherine of April 3, 1773, July 28, 1773, and May 1774: Réau, ed., 1921, pp. 200, 210, 239.

28. August 4, 1778: RGIA, fond 470, o. 2 (103/537), no. 14, f. 2.

29. I owe the description of the shape of the assembly to Viacheslav Semënovich Mozgovoi, who participated in the 1976 restoration of the monument. He entered the statue through a hatch concealed in the croup of the horse and inspected its interior. According to Mr. Mozgovoi, the tail of the horse is not connected to the weight-bearing assembly. Its role is to provide a third point of contact with the pedestal, ensuring better stability of the monument, which is especially important in high winds. Cf. also Kudriavtsev and Shkoda (1982, p. 36) who confirm Mr. Mozgovoi's report and reproduce a photograph of the shank of a hind leg of the horse, on which the solid cast-iron core is clearly visible under a slice of bronze removed during the 1976 restoration work.

30. A line equals $1/12$ of an inch or 2.5 mm.

31. Falconet to Catherine, May 11, 1768: Réau, ed., 1921, p. 41.

32. Backmeister, 1786, pp. 80–81.

33. The article "Bronze" in the *Encyclopédie* (vol. 2, p. 438) recommends that the thickness of the walls of figures two feet in height should be two lines and that of the walls of figures of human size should be six lines, while the bronze walls of larger figures could be of varying thickness. Boffrand reports that the horse in the equestrian statue of Louis XIV by Girardon in Paris had solid legs up to the shank, while the walls of the thighs were twelve lines thick, those of the tail six lines, and the rest of the body ten lines.

34. See Falconet "Sur les fontes en bronze" (*FO*, vol. 6, p. 284).

35. This sequence is re-created on the basis of Falconet's testimony in footnote (f) to his "Sur les fontes en bronze" (*FO*, vol. 6, pp. 284–85).

36. The letter is undated. Polovtsov places it in the beginning of 1774 (*SIRIO*, vol. 17, pp. 218–21), while Réau lists it between Falconet's letters of May 5 and 19, 1774 (Réau, ed., 1921, pp. 236–38). Neither, however, gives any reason for such dating. Since the letter contains Falconet's offer to become his own founder, it would follow that it was written after or shortly before Ersmann's dismissal on June 30, 1774, and before August 31, 1774, when Falconet announced to Catherine his appointment as founder (Réau, ed., 1921, p. 241).

37. His helper was again the artillery founder Khailov. Falconet's claim that he had hired him for a mere six hours is most probably an understatement.

38. "Sur les fontes en bronze," *FO*, vol. 6, note (e), pp. 280–81. Falconet's justifiable claim on the eighty thousand livres remaining from Ersmann contract was used by Betskoi and his associates as an example of Falconet's greed. Diderot, by then soured on Falconet, agreed that money was the only reason why Falconet agreed to conduct the casting.

39. Falconet to Catherine, August 31, 1774: Réau, ed., 1921, p. 241.

40. Falconet's skillful use of Ersmann's groundwork was quite unreasonably held against him by Pomel, one of Ersmann's workers retained by Falconet (*JE*, 1779, vol. 8, part 3, p. 503).

41. Falconet to Catherine, August 7, 1775: Réau, ed., 1921, p. 251. The fire in the furnace was lit just twenty-four hours before the actual pouring of the bronze.

42. Betskoi to Catherine, August 26, 1775: RGADA, fond 11, o. 1, no. 983, ff. 118–19.

43. Betskoi to Catherine, August 27, 1775: RGADA, fond 11, o. 1, no. 983, f. 120.

44. Betskoi to Catherine, August 30, 1775: RGADA, fond 11, o. 1, no. 983, ff. 121–22.

45. The sources which give August 25 as the date of the operation count from the moment of pouring, rather than of lighting the fire.

46. For an account of the casting, see Backmeister, 1786, pp. 62–80. The year 1783 is when the original German version of his book was published.

47. *JE*, 1779, vol. 8, part 3, note 1, p. 505.

48. Ibid, p. 509.

49. *SPV,* September 1, 1775, No. 70.
50. For "sack" Falconet uses the term *couloque,* a French transcription of the Russian *kulëk.*
51. Falconet to Catherine, August 31, 1775: Réau, ed., 1921, pp. 253–54.
52. *FO,* vol. 6, pp. 313–14. Bérenger and Dentan were members of the Society for the Advancement of the Arts in the City and Territory of the Republic of Geneva. Falconet was elected its Honorary Associate during his 1780 stay in Geneva, when he was preparing the first edition of his collected works.
53. The letter was reprinted in *JE,* 1776, vol. 5, part 1, pp. 132–33.
54. Bourrée de Corberon, 1901, vol. 1, p. 190.
55. All in all the journal published three articles against Falconet: *JE,* 1776, vol. 5, part 1, pp. 132–40; 1779, vol. 8, part 3, pp. 500–510; and 1780, vol. 1, part 1, pp. 129–35.
56. *JE,* 1780, vol. 5, part 1, p. 139.
57. *JE,* 1776, vol. 5, part 1, p. 135.
58. Ibid., pp. 138–39.
59. *JE,* 1777, vol. 1, part 2, pp. 333–35.
60. Falconet said in the promissory note: "Although I have good reasons to be very displeased with the conduct of Mr. Pomel during his work on the statue, I will give him the sum of fifteen thousand livres that I had promised him in accordance with the conditions stated above"; i.e., after the receipt of eighty thousand livres from the crown.
61. "Lettre de M. Falconet à M. ***": *JE,* 1776, vol. 3, part 1, pp. 108–9.
62. *JE,* 1777, vol. 1, part 2, p. 333. Rousseau referred no doubt to Prince D. A. Golitsyn, who stood resolutely behind Falconet in the Pomel affair.
63. *JE,* 1779, vol. 8, part 3, note 1, pp. 500–501.
64. Four thousand livres for one year of "lost time" in St. Petersburg and twelve hundred livres to defray the costs of his return trip.
65. *JE,* 1780, vol. 1, part 1, p. 129.
66. Ibid, p. 130.
67. Pomel acknowledged receipt of the final payment due to him by Falconet (*JE,* 1780, vol. 5, part 1, pp. 136–37).
68. According to Bérenger, the testimonies critical of Pomel were executed before the French ambassador by a molder, two students of the Academy of Fine Arts who were employed by Falconet, and other workers. Falconet's footnote to Bérenger's letter in the 1808 edition of his works explains that the two Russian soldiers, Osip and Rodion, who woke Pomel up, had not been permitted by their superiors to testify about this. Conscience-stricken, they came to Falconet's carriage to bid him goodbye and bless him before he left Russia (*FOC,* vol. 3, pp. 428–29).
69. Shpakovsky was actually one of Betskoi's associates in the Bureau of Buildings. His citation for a medal awarded on the day of the unveiling of the monument credited him with being "from the very beginning of the monument in charge of the building materials and the budget both in the construction of the monument and the transportation of the rock" (RGIA, fond 470, o. 2 [103/537], no. 14).
70. *JE,* 1780, vol. 3, part 1, pp. 128–32, and RNB, fond 871 (Stählin papers), no. 842, ff. 1–2.
71. *JE,* 1780, vol. 5, part 1, pp. 135–40. Falconet sent it from Prince D. A. Golitsyn's residence in The Hague, where he was staying for a time after his return from Russia.
72. Ibid., p. 137.
73. A lap joint looks like the joint between a box and an overlapping cover. By providing an area of overlap between the two parts, the lap joint makes it possible to drive in connecting pins. A variant of the lap joint is the bevel joint, in which the two surfaces

are cut at identical complementary angles. Their juncture looks like two right-angled triangles put together to form a rectangle.

74. Falconet to D. A. Golitsyn, July 25, 1777: *JE,* 1777, vol. 7, part 1, p. 141.

75. Sandoz was a Swiss watchmaker whose watch factory on Vasilievsky Island was destroyed in the great fire of May 1771. Forced to live in a deserted section of the island, Sandoz appealed to Betskoi for a teaching position in the Academy of Fine Arts. He was unwise, however, to mention his friendship with Falconet, for Betskoi's answer was certainly colored by his ill will toward the sculptor: "Watchmaking is a useless skill here. We have no need for it nor for those who teach it. We will instead import watches from abroad." Falconet to Catherine, May 29, 1771: Réau, ed., 1921, pp. 148–49.

76. Falconet to Catherine, December 30, 1775: Réau, ed., 1921, pp. 254–55.

77. January 27, 1776: RGADA, fond 248, vol. 5482, ff. 366 and 376–78, and RGIA, fond 470, o. 2 [103/537], no. 12, f. 5.

78. Falconet to D. A. Golitsyn, July 25, 1777: *JE,* 1777, vol. 7, part 1, p. 141.

79. *FO,* vol. 6, pp. 278–79.

80. The joint, however, is clearly visible on the inside (oral communication kindly provided by Mr. V. S. Mozgovoi).

81. Falconet to Catherine, November 29, 1777: Réau, ed., 1921, p. 261.

CHAPTER 7. DENOUEMENT

1. Betskoi to Falconet, July 13, 1778, cited after "Petit différend," *FO,* vol. 6, p. 259.

2. August, 4, 1778: RGIA, fond 470, o. 2 (103/537), no. 14, ff. 1–4.

3. Unable to collect this payment, Betskoi's agents attempted to seize the drawing from Falconet, not knowing that Collot had taken it to France in 1775 (*FO,* vol. 6, p. 303).

4. Falconet to Betskoi, June 21, 1778, reprinted in "Petit différend" (*FO,* vol. 6, pp. 248–63).

5. Ibid., pp. 257–58.

6. Ibid., p. 260. The empress was just as irritated by Falconet's presumed venality. Here is how she remembered Falconet *père* and *fils* and Collot ten years later in a letter to Grimm: "those people are so greedy for money that they will gladly sell you [my] portrait for an insane price that you would not want to pay" (Catherine to Grimm, April 6, 1787: Grot, ed., 1878, p. 405).

7. *FO,* vol. 6, p. 263.

8. Ibid., p. 258.

9. Ibid., p. 259. That sum was to be used as payment to the Russian artillery founder Emelian Khailov for his help in the casting.

10. A thin cast *(fonte mince)* is one with thinner walls on the non–load-bearing parts of the statue.

11. Falconet to Catherine, September 1, 1778: Réau, ed., 1921, p. 268.

12. Falconet to Betskoi, September 1, 1778: RGIA, fond 789, o. 1 (part I), no. 297, f. 20.

13. Falconet to Catherine, September 1, 1778: Réau, ed., 1921, pp. 267–68.

14. *SPV,* July 27, 1778: no. 60, p. 798.

15. *SPV,* August 24, 1778: no. 68, p. 928.

16. "Petit différend," *FO,* vol. 6, p. 259, note (o).

17. Catherine to Grimm, October 1, 1778: Grot, ed., 1878, p. 104.

18. Falconet to Diderot, February 28, 1767: Benot, ed., 1958, pp. 240–41.

19. Ibid., p. 240. Diderot took him to task for that: "You have populated St. Petersburg with idiots and rascals thinking apparently that two or three winters were enough to kill them off in Paris, like caterpillars" (Diderot to Falconet, September 6, 1768: Roth, ed., 1955–70, vol. 8, p. 111).

20. This may be partly due to his realization that letters sent through the mails were subject to censorship. Because of that all his correspondence with Diderot was sent through friends or the diplomatic pouch.

21. Backmeister, 1786, p. 46.

22. For reproductions and identification of Mary Cathcart's portrait and of Lady Cathcart's medallion, see Opperman, 1965.

23. Catherine to Falconet, August 22, 1773: Réau, ed., 1921, p. 214. The medallion turned out to be an inferior copy of a much better original which Falconet knew. Since it was made of black basalt, Catherine the Great referred to it as "Lord Cathcart's Negro."

24. The delegation included the Archbishop Gavriil of St. Petersburg, Bishop Gavriil of Tver, and the Archimandrite Platon of the monastery of the Holy Trinity near Moscow (Falconet to Catherine, June 1, 1770: Réau, ed., 1921, pp. 129–30).

25. RNB, fond 871 (Stählin papers), no. 709.

26. Malinovskii, ed. and tr., 1990, vol. 1, p. 183.

27. Falconet to Catherine, August 14, 1770: Réau, ed., 1921, p. 134.

28. Bourrée de Corberon, 1901, vol. 1., pp. 137 and 157–58.

29. Ibid., pp. 141 and 153–54.

30. Ibid., pp. 141, 157, 189–90, 315, and 215.

31. Ibid., p. 152.

32. Cf. p. 186.

33. Losenko's drawing of the head of the *Peter the Great* was engraved by Benoît-Louis Henriquez, a Paris engraver who worked in St. Petersburg in the early 1770s.

34. Falconet to Catherine, October 25, 1770: Réau, ed., 1921, pp. 137–38.

35. Catherine to Falconet, October 27, 1770: Réau, ed., 1921, pp. 138–39.

36. September 25, 1767: RGIA, fond 467, o. 2, no. 101, ff. 86, 87. Betskoi confirmed this figure in his report to the Senate of May 12, 1768: RGADA, fond 248, no. 5482, f. 322.

37. That was the rate at which Michel was paid for Falconet's room and board; see RGADA, fond 248, no. 5482, f. 302 (March 19, 1767). The accounting of 1778 used the exchange rate of twenty-two kopeks to one livre.

38. Diderot to Betskoi, August 1766: Roth, ed., 1955–70, vol. 6, p. 283.

39. December 26, 1766: RNB (Manuscript Section), fond 708 (Sobko), no. 426, f. 18r.

40. RGADA, fond 248, no. 5482, ff. 345–46.

41. March 4, 1776: RGIA, fond 467, o. 2, no. 101, ff. 260, 261 and, RGIA, fond 248, no. 5482, ff. 376–78 and 380v–81r. Backmeister's figures for the total cost are somewhat lower—424,610 rubles.

42. RGIA, fond 470, o. 2 (103/537), no. 14, ff. 1–4. It will be recalled that Fel'ten had taken over Carburi's duties after the latter's departure in 1773.

43. Falconet to Diderot, February 26, 1767: Roth, ed., 1955–70, vol. 7, p. 33.

44. RGIA, fond 470, o. 2 (103/537), no. 14, f. 71. Fel'ten's request was granted and he received 4,720 rubles for three years, eleven months, and six days of work at one hundred rubles per month. The success of Fel'ten's petition prompted others to ask for similar tokens of Betskoi's beneficence. Thus, Karl Krok complained that that he had not received any pay at all for nine years of work as a groom, a task for which Carburi used to get forty rubles a month. His petition was successful as well and he received ten rubles a month as back pay (RGIA, November 4, 1778, fond 470, o. 2 (103/537), no. 14, f. 77).

45. "Petit différend;" *FO,* vol. 6, p. 249.
46. RGIA, fond 475, o. 1, no. 1903, d. 123. The document calls them "peasants."
47. Backmeister, 1786, p. 85.
48. It is not clear how that date was selected, for the double coronation of the brothers Ivan and Peter took place on June 25, 1682. The medals minted for the occasion of the unveiling bear the date of August 6. The change from the 6th to the 7th was dictated probably by the preference for Sunday over Saturday.
49. Like so many places in Russia, the square changed its name to reflect changing historical realities. Called initially Senate Square, it was renamed Peter's Square, reverted to Senate Square, and is now Decembrists Square, in memory of the failed insurrection against Tsar Nicholas I, which started and ended on December 14, 1824, on Senate Square. The description of the unveiling ceremony is based on several sources: RGIA, fond 470, o. 2 (103/537), no. 14, ff. 25, 26r; the *Kamerfur'erskii zhurnal* for August 1782; Backmeister 1786, pp. 91–100; Alexander Radishchev's personal impressions, shared with a friend in Tobolsk; a report from the French minister plenipotentiary marquis de Vérac to the French minister of foreign affairs Count de Vergennes; correspondence from St. Petersburg in the *MSB,* no. 21, September 22, 1782; and the surprisingly late description of the ceremony in the *St. Petersburg Gazette,* no. 79, of Tuesday, October 4, 1782.
50. There were fourteen ranks of civil servants and court officials, corresponding to the ranking scheme of the army and navy officers. It was a classification introduced by Peter the Great in his Table of Ranks.
51. *SPV,* no. 79, October 4, 1782, pp. 625–28.
52. That is, Falconet in St. Petersburg, Saly in Copenhagen, and Archevèque in Stockholm (Vérac to Vergennes, August 23, 1782; AAE CP, Russie, vol. 109, f. 136).
53. *SPV,* no. 79, October 4, 1782, pp. 625–28.
54. *SZRI,* August 7, 1782.
55. The names of the winners of medals are listed in the file "On the Award of Medals for the Construction of the Monument," RGIA, fond 470, o. 2 (103/537), no. 14.
56. Including Iury Fel'ten for the transfer of the statue from the foundry to the rock and the beautification of the site, Ivan Shpakovsky for supervising the budget and building materials, Ivan Khozikov for assisting in the transport of the Thunder Rock, and Timofei Nasonov for supervising the hewing of the Thunder Rock.
57. Falconet to Collot, January 31, 1783: Réau, ed., 1921, p. 270.
58. Catherine to Grimm, December 7, 1792: Grot, ed., 1878, p. 579.
59. These strains led to Golitsyn's dismissal from his post in The Hague in 1782.
60. File 878, Commissaire Chenu: *BSHAF,* vol. 3, October 1877, pp. 160–61.
61. Ibid, pp. 158–59.
62. Réau, 1924, p. 221. Falconet's second letter, that of January 31, 1783, was indeed semi-official in tone, for it dealt with the official matter of transmitting to Collot a silver medal marking the unveiling of the monument.
63. Bracketed sentences in extracts summarize omitted text. Falconet's letter of June 8, 1779, is reproduced in full in Valabrègue, 1898, pp. 49–52.
64. They are in the City Museum of The Hague.
65. The words "your husband" were restored by Valabrègue, because the corner of the page was torn off, presumably by Marie-Lucie.
66. On August 15, 1779, Hemsterhuis wrote Princess Golitsyn in Münster: "I was struck by the resemblance of your bust. That work, which is about to be finished, is being done with a great deal of taste" (Fresco, 1998, p. 37). Unhappily, the bust has not been located.
67. Camper to Collot, July 11, 1781: *BN, N a. fr.* 24983, ff. 403–4.

68. *PVA,* vol. 9, pp. 42–43.

69. "[Falconet] left Russia several years ago and is said to be in France, living in retirement. It is also said that he no longer works as a sculptor, but, being a writer as well, has bought a small house in the country, not far from Paris, and writes there about his profession" (*MSB*, vol. 21, September 22, 1782, p. 116). It was from Châtenay that Falconet sent Collot in Paris the silver medal commemorating the unveiling of the monument (Falconet to Collot, January 31, 1783: Réau, ed., 1921, p. 270).

70. From Robin's funeral oration, (1791, p. 255.) The letter informing Falconet of the granting of his leave of absence bears a few words scribbled by the secretary: "At the moment that I was sending out this leave, word came that Monsieur Falconet was paralyzed. Adieu to the trip" (AN, O^1 1095, cited after Réau, 1922, vol. 1, p. 112). Robin's friendship with Falconet makes one accept the date of the stroke as May 1, 1783, but the minutes of the Académie give the date of May 3 (*PVA,* vol. 9, p. 151).

71. Lévesque in *FOC,* vol. 1, p. 20.

72. Robin, 1791, p. 256.

73. Lévesque in *FOC,* vol. 1, p. 21.

74. *PVA,* vol. 10, p. 42.

75. January 24 is generally accepted as the date of Falconet's death, but the minutes of the Académie for January 29 give January 25 (*PVA,* vol. 10, pp. 91–92).

76. The will was made in The Hague in 1779 and confirmed in Paris in 1784. Excerpts of it are given in Réau, ed., 1919, pp. 161–63.

77. For the inventory of them, see Réau, ed., 1919, pp. 164–67.

78. *Légataires universels,* in French legal terminology. Falconet's wish not to leave to his son more than absolutely necessary was made explicit in his last will: "I reduce my son's share to what is prescribed by law" (Réau, ed., 1919, p. 161). In other words, Pierre-Etienne Falconet was quasi-disinherited.

79. Jankovitz or Jankowitz are the spellings favored in France. The family is of Croatian origin but, displaced by Turkish invasions, one branch established itself in Slovakian Hungary, another in Poland. Because of these peregrinations, other spellings have also been used, Hungarian Jankovics and Croatian Jankovich (for modern Janković). Stanislas Jankovitz was the son of Joseph Jankovitz, who arrived in Lorraine as a consequence of two failed political ventures. In 1711, when Rákóczy's insurrection against the Austrians was defeated, Joseph Jankovitz, still as a child, was taken to Poland, where he was raised. There he allied himself with the cause of King Stanislas Leszczynski in his struggle for the throne of Poland against the Saxon dynasty. After his defeat, Leszczynski fled to France to claim the dukedoms of Lorraine and Bar, which his son-in-law, Louis XV, had offered him, along with the right to bear the title of king. In Leszczynski's suite was Joseph Jankovitz. (This account is based on the "Souvenirs de famille," a Jankovitz family history, compiled by Baron Louis de Jankovitz in 1959. His daughter, Madame Elisabeth Nénert, was kind enough to make this fascinating handwritten document available to me.)

80. In addition to becoming a member of the nobility of Lorraine, Stanislas received in 1820 the title of "hereditary baron." From that time on, his full name was Stanislas baron de Jankovitz de Jeszenicze (the family estate in Slovakian Hungary).

81. Vincent was the great-grandfather of Louis de Jankovitz, the compiler of the "Souvenirs de famille" (see above, note 79).

82. Marie-Lucie was buried in the funerary chapel of Marimont, next to Stanislas and Anselme. Her testament was drawn on April 25, 1854, and deposited after her death with Maître Besnard, a notary in Versailles. Louis de Jankovitz, in his 1959 history of the family, transcribed the pages containing the repartition of the inheritance. He also noted

the coolness of the relations between Marie-Lucie on the one side and Vincent and his wife on the other. After a brief attempt to live together in Versailles failed dismally, they saw each other as seldom as possible.

83. Réau, ed., 1919, pp. 167–68. The head of Mary Cathcart by Collot and the drawings by Falconet *fils* are reproduced in Becker, forthcoming.

84. Jankovitz, 1959, p. 74a.

CHAPTER 8. THE MONUMENT

1. For a discussion of Desjardins' models, see Martin, 1986, pp. 178–88.

2. Tooke, ed. and tr., 1777, pp. 12–13.

3. Benvenuto Cellini's *Perseus Holding the Head of Medusa* (1553) was a much smaller statue.

4. Stasov, 1877, p. 342–43.

5. Figs. 8.1–8.2, 8.4–8.5, and 8.9 are the work of the St. Petersburg photographer Leonid Bogdanov. It is a pleasure to acknowledge here his contribution.

6. Diderot to Falconet, ca. September 10, 1766: Roth, ed., 1955–70, vol. 6, p. 329. Cf. Diderot's critical remarks on allegorical compositions in the Salon of 1765 (Goodman, ed. and tr., 1995, vol. 1, pp. 223–24) and in a letter to Volland (Diderot to Volland, January 27, 1766: Roth, ed., 1955–70, vol. 6, p. 33). In his account of the Salon of 1767, Diderot admonished the painter Lagrenée: "Be advised that an ordinary allegory is a bad one, even if it is new, and that a sublime allegory should only be used once. Otherwise it becomes the equivalent of a witticism deadened by retelling" (Goodman, ed. and tr., 1995, vol. 2, p. 48). He also criticized the engraver Cochin for using "too much over-cooked allegory that spoils everything, jumbles everything, almost rendering captions useless. I'll never change my mind. I'll never cease to regard allegory as the expedient of a weak, sterile mind, one that's incapable of turning reality to account and so calls allegory to the rescue" (ibid., p. 314).

7. Falconet to Diderot, February 28, 1767: Roth, ed., 1955–70, vol. 7, pp. 32–33.

8. Falconet to Catherine, June 30, 1768: Réau, ed., 1921, pp. 55–56.

9. Falconet to Diderot, February 28, 1767: Roth, ed., 1955–70, vol. 7, p. 33.

10. That continuum allows the horse and the rider to partake of the myth of Antaeus, who found an inexhaustible source of strength in an unbroken connection with Mother Earth.

11. The monument stands 10.44 m (34′ 3″) from ground level to the tips of the horse's ears. The bronze statue alone is 5.34 m (17′ 6″) high and 6.20 m (20′ 4″) long, and weighs 20.5 tons. The pedestal is 5.10 m (16′ 9″) high, 8.50 m (27′ 11″) wide at the bottom, and 14.50 m (47′ 7″) long. (I am grateful to S. O. Androsov for communicating to me these measurements.) The angle of inclination of the rearing horse is 35°–40° from the line of the horizon, but only 10° from the brow of the pedestal. The latter measurements exceed somewhat the figures given by Falconet: "The gallop of my horse is at 10° (an elevation encountered in natural gallop), and the line of the horse's body parallels the line of the terrain, whose inclination is also 10°" (*FO*, vol. 1, p. 179). The monument's triangular structure was Falconet's favorite; it can be seen in a number of his works, beginning with the *Milo of Crotona* (1754).

12. "Réflexions sur la sculpture," *FO*, vol. 1, p. 7, quoted here in Tooke's translation (p. 14).

13. For Falconet's detailed criticism of the *Marcus Aurelius,* see his "Observations sur la statue de Marc-Aurèle" (*FO*, vol. 1, pp. 157–348); "Parallele des proportions du cheval de Marc-Aurèle et de celles du beau naturel" (*FO*, vol. 2, pp. 1–28); and "Révision,"

(*FO,* vol. 2, pp. 39–90). Diderot's reaction to Falconet's analysis of the horse of the *Marcus Aurelius* may be found in Diderot to Falconet, May 2, 1773: Roth, ed., 1955–70, vol. 12, pp. 235–63.

14. *FO,* vol. 2, p. 184, fn. (a).

15. Diderot to Falconet, July 1767: Roth, ed., 1955–70, vol. 7, pp. 85–86.

16. Diderot to Falconet, July 11, 1769: Roth, ed., 1955–70, vol. 9, p. 76.

17. His claims are supported by Backmeister, the librarian of the Academy of Sciences and eyewitness of the events surrounding the construction of the monument.

18. Falconet, "Observations sur la statue de Marc-Aurèle," (*FO,* vol. 1, pp. 305–6). According to Backmeister (1786, pp. 44–45) Falconet used two of the finest stallions from the imperial stables, Brillant and Capricieux. Falconet praises especially the prowess of one of the riders, Afanasii Telichnikov (Falconet to Catherine, [beginning of 1775]: Réau, ed., 1921, p. 70).

19. Diderot to Falconet, December 6, 1773: Roth, ed., 1955–70, vol. 13, pp. 115–16. The poet in question is probably Homer, but he could also be Euripides, who, in his play *Heracles,* mentioned the capture of Diomedes' man-eating mares as one of the hero's twelve labors.

20. Heier, ed., 1965a, pp. 148–49.

21. Fortia de Piles and de Boisgelin, 1796, vol. 3, p. 193.

22. Carr, 1806, p. 42. The reference is to the horses over the entrance to St. Mark's basilica, which Napoleon brought from Venice to Paris, but which were returned to Venice after his downfall.

23. Diderot to Falconet, December 6, 1773: Roth, ed., 1955–70, vol. 13, p. 116.

24. Janson, 1985, p. 35.

25. *FO,* vol. 1, p. 209.

26. Catherine to Falconet, February 18, 1767: Réau, ed., 1921, p. 5. The empress was writing the letter from Moscow. The reference to "stupid animals" is a word play on the French *bête,* meaning "animal" and "stupid."

27. Catherine to Falconet, June 7, 1767: Réau, ed., 1921, p. 12.

28. Catherine to Falconet, September 17, 1769: Réau, ed., 1921, p. 97.

29. Backmeister (1786, pp. 47–8) mistakes the bearskin for a tiger skin.

30. Recalcitrant Russia, rising against the speed of Peter the Great's reforms (*SPV,* Supplement, No. 58, July 18, 1768) or the "boyars whom the tsar tried to rein in" (Dumas, 1881, p. 32).

31. "Thou art cursed above all cattle and above every beast of the field; upon thy belly shalt thou go, and dust shalt thou eat all the days of thy life" (Gen. 3.14). "And the great dragon was cast out, that old serpent, called the Devil and Satan, which deceiveth the whole world" (Rev. 12.9).

32. Translation by Thomas B. Shaw in *Blackwood's Edinburgh Magazine,* vol. 58, July–December, 1845, pp. 146–48.

33. Falconet to Catherine, June 28, 1768: Réau, ed., 1921, pp. 53–54.

34. Catherine to Falconet, July 1, 1768: Réau, ed., 1921, p. 57.

35. Falconet to Catherine, July 31, 1769: Réau, ed., 1921, pp. 88–89.

36. Falconet to Catherine, August 6, 1769: Réau, ed., 1921, p. 90.

37. Catherine to Falconet, August 7, 1769: Réau, ed., 1921, p. 93.

38. Diderot to Falconet, December 6, 1773: Roth, ed., 1955–70, vol. 13, p. 118.

39. Lotman, 1984, p. 35.

40. An unsigned oval portrait of Peter the Great, attributed to Caravaque or Nikitin, was actually presented to Falconet by Catherine. It was returned to the Gatchina palace in

1865 as part of the bequest of Baroness Marie-Lucie de Jankovitz, Falconet's granddaughter. In 1925 it was transferred to the Russian Museum in St. Petersburg. On the backside of the stretcher there is an inscription: "venant de M^de falconet" (Andros[s]ov, 1998, p. 181).

41. According to Backmeister (1786, p. 37), Falconet received a copy of an anonymous bust of Peter from Bologna.

42. Rastrelli used the life mask in making a plaster head of Peter, which Falconet later borrowed from the Academy of Sciences. Backmeister (1786, p. 37) reports also that Falconet had free access to the Academy, where he could examine Peter's wax mask, which, in all probability, was the death mask.

43. The sitting tsar in the wax effigy by Rastrelli may have given Mikhail Shemiakin the idea of showing Peter sitting down in his 1990 statue in the Peter and Paul Fortress.

44. Footnote to the "Observations sur la statue de Marc-Aurèle": FO, vol. 1, p. 178.

45. Here is a selection of the earliest opinions. "Not the artist himself but Mademoiselle Collot, who accompanied him here, made the head of the horseman. [Falconet] did not wish to conceal that in any way. He praised it freely and confessed that [Mlle Collot] was superior to him in the art of making a model of the head" (Backmeister, 1786, pp. 38–39). "The hero's head is not by Falconet, but by Mademoiselle Collot" (Fortia de Piles and de Boisgelin, 1796, vol. 3, p. 193). "The head of Peter, which is very fine, was modelled by Madame Collot" (Carr, 1806, p. 42). Collot is also mentioned as the sculptor of the head in the 1772 engraving by Henriquez after a drawing by Losenko.

46. Diderot to Falconet, December 6, 1773: Roth, ed., 1955–70, vol. 13, p. 120.

47. Falconet's best friend in St. Petersburg, the philosopher Pierre-Charles Lévesque, mentioned these doubts, but found them without substance (Lévesque in FOC, vol. 1, p. 18).

48. Goodman, ed. and tr., 1995, vol. 2, p. 21.

49. Arkin, 1958, p. 31.

50. Ibid., pp. 29–30.

51. Ibid., p. 34.

52. Ibid., p. 32.

53. Diderot to Falconet, December 6, 1773: Roth, ed., 1955–70, vol. 13, p. 120.

54. Catherine to Falconet, March 10, 1767: Réau, ed., 1921, p. 8.

55. Diderot to Falconet, December 6, 1773: Roth, ed., 1955–70, vol. 13, p. 117.

56. Peter's garment appeared native even to such a fine specialist in the early history of St. Petersburg as Svin'in (1816, p. 27): "The emperor wears a mantle and has a laurel wreath on his head. His clothing is Russian."

57. Falconet to Diderot, February 28, 1767: Benot, ed., pp. 239–40. Showing Catherine drafts of his letters to Diderot became Falconet's favorite ploy. He used it to resolve real and imaginary problems, as well as to pay the empress indirect compliments; cf. p. 104.

58. Diderot agreed on the inappropriateness of the French attire. Here is what he wrote of it in a critique of a painting by Roslin: "One should see the nonsense of our close-fitting jackets, tight breeches, . . . cuffs, buttonholes" (account of the Salon of 1761).

59. Falconet to Catherine, August 22, 1768: Réau, ed., 1921, p. 64.

60. The expanded version was published in the 1781 edition of Falconet's writings, as a separate piece entitled "Extrait d'une lettre à Mr. Diderot": FO, vol. 2, pp. 181–92. All the above citations dealing with Peter's garb are taken from the "Extrait."

61. Catherine to Falconet, August 27, 1768: Réau, ed., 1921, p. 65.

62. SPV, Supplement, No. 58, July 18, 1768.

63. Quoted in Catherine to Falconet, March 28, 1767: Réau, ed., 1921, p. 14.

64. Svin'in, 1816, pp. 27–28.

65. During the flood of 1777, the home and atelier of Falconet and Collot must have been under water.

66. Cf. Andros[s]ov's (2000, p. 215) perceptive observation that the two mounted emperors are linked "not only by the quasi-classical convention of their clothing, but also by the pointing gesture of the right hand" and, one might add, the wide-spread fingers suggesting peaceful intentions.

67. Fortia de Piles and de Boisgelin, 1796, vol. 3, p. 193.

68. Bernini as quoted by his French companion and guide Paul Fréart de Chantelou (1985, pp. 16–17). Compare the view of Guarino Guarini in *Architettura civile* (1737): "In order to serve the appearance of the required proportions, architecture is obliged to depart from the rules and from the real proportions" (Kaufmann, 1955, p. 242).

69. Since the horseman and the horse were usually done in the *Marcus Aurelius* manner, the pedestal could become the sculptor's chief opportunity to display his inventiveness. A case in point is the 1716 project for a monument to Peter the Great by Rastrelli. The horse and rider follow the model of Girardon's Louis XIV, but the shape and ornamentation of the pedestal are Rastrelli's own.

70. Announcement for the competition for the beautification of Senate Square in *SPV,* Supplement, No. 58, July 18, 1768.

71. Note that these measurements understate the actual size of the monument by one-third as regards the height of the pedestal, by one-fourth for the height of the bronze statue, and by half for the length and width of the pedestal.

72. Catherine to Falconet, May 16, 1768: Réau, ed., 1921, p. 131.

73. Diderot to Falconet, May 1768: Roth, ed., 1955–70, vol. 8, pp. 38–39.

74. Falconet followed the same idea in the chapel of the Crucifixion in the church of St. Roch in Paris, where the cross was surrounded by several natural rocks.

75. Matthew 16.18. Jesus was referring to Simon's sobriquet *Cephas* ("rock"), calqued in Greek as *Pétros* ("rock").

76. Peter "appointed" St. Andrew the patron of the Russian navy.

77. *FO,* vol. 1, p. 264. The seal referred to by Falconet was probably a version of the image of the tsar on the right breastplate of the 1723 bust of Peter the Great by Rastrelli (fig. 8.6) (see Matveev, 1981).

78. See above, pp. 159–61.

79. Falconet to Catherine, August 14, 1770: Réau, ed., 1921, p. 134. Yet Losenko's drawing of the large model does not bear any inscription. It is possible that Falconet put the five-word inscription directly on the large model, for its existence was reported by a number of visitors to Falconet's studio, including Wraxall (1776, p. 225) who saw it in 1774, bearing the provisional date of "177 ."

80. "Four words" means, no doubt, that the empress decided then and there to drop the superfluous verb *posuit* (see Catherine to Falconet, August 18, 1770: Réau, ed., 1921, p. 136).

81. Quoted by Wraxall, 1776, pp. 226–27.

82. The monument was planned by Empress Elizabeth to honor the memory of her father; who was the first Romanov to be buried in the cathedral.

83. Malinovskii, ed. and tr., 1990, vol. 1, pp. 181–83. Malinovskii (ibid., p. 190, fn. 112), the editor of Stählin's *Notes,* observed that Falconet corroborated Stählin's account when he confirmed the existence of the long version of the inscription in his letter to the empress of August 14, 1770 (Réau, ed., 1921, p. 134). Falconet characterized it as a *kyrielle,* that is, a long and incomprehensible sequence of words.

84. *SIRIO,* vol. 17, p. 366.
85. Lomonosov's inscriptions are exhaustively discussed in Morozov, 1965.
86. Coxe, 1785, vol. 1, p. 425.
87. Fortia de Piles and de Boisgelin, 1796, vol. 5, pp. 194–95.
88. Catherine to Grimm, March 9, 1783: Grot, ed., 1878, p. 272.

EPILOGUE

1. Almost immediately after Peter the Great's death in 1725, there was a mass flight from the city, reducing its population by half in less than five years.
2. Diderot to Falconet, December 6, 1773: Roth, ed., 1955–70, pp. 116 and 121.
3. Dalton, 1882, p. 153.
4. Réau, 1913, p. 37. Some Western critics are less generous: "[Falconet's horse] will soon be covered with snow on the banks of the Neva and no one will talk about it anymore," said the painter Jacques-Louis David in 1793 (Wildenstein and Wildenstein, 1973, no. 477, p. 56). Lida Louise Fleitmann maintained that the monument is "remarkable only for its colossal size and situation" (1931, p. 257). "A typical Petersburg monstrosity," declared Aileen Kelly in her review of Solomon Volkov, *St. Petersburg: A Cultural History* (*NYRB,* February 20, 1997, p. 43), disputing his view that the monument is "one of the great European sculptures of the eighteenth century" and St. Petersburg's "most important and popular representation" (Volkov, 1995, p. 21).
5. Radishchev, 1949, pp. 12–13.
6. For a survey of literary reactions to Falconet's monument, see Ospovat and Timenchik, 1987.
7. Dostoevskii, 1972–90, vol. 13, p. 113.
8. Prince A. N. Golitsyn was a high official of the Holy Synod and minister of education. In some versions of the story, the major's name is given as Bakhmetev (see Stolpianskii, 1918, p. 5). It has also been attributed to Prince Golitsyn directly, hence its name "Golitsyn's Dream." The story is said to have fascinated Pushkin with its poetic potential.
9. Pumpianskii, 1939, p. 91.
10. The titles of other poems in the cycle are indicative of their content: *The Road to Russia; The Suburbs of the Capital, St. Petersburg; The Review of the Army; The Day Preceding the Inundation of St. Petersburg in 1824. Oleszkiewicz.* They were translated by Marjorie Beatrice Peacock (Noyes, ed., 1944, pp. 337–66; Lednicki, 1955, pp. 109–39).
11. *FO,* vol. 2, p. 34.
12. Translation by Watson Kirkconnell (Noyes, ed., 1944, pp. 367–68).
13. Translation by Sir Charles Johnston (1983). His is the only English translation of *The Bronze Horseman* that keeps Pushkin's rhyme and meter. It is a pleasure to thank his niece Shervie Price for the United Kingdom rights to quote from that translation.
14. One should bear in mind that the phrase "not to trouble Peter's eternal sleep" could be translated as "not to trouble Peter's eternal dream," since Russian *son* means either "sleep" or "dream." The latter interpretation, if allowed, would be one of the many references to St. Petersburg's dreamlike aspect.
15. From *eugenēs,* "well born." Pushkin bemoans Evgeny's decline on the social ladder by recalling his noble ancestry. In so doing, he may be settling a personal grievance against Peter the Great, who curtailed ancestral privileges of noble families, causing many of

them to lose their economic and social standing. This is just one of the several instances in the poem in which Pushkin identifies with the sorry lot of his hero.

16. Evgeny lives on the left bank of the river in Kolomna, a poor section of the city inhabited chiefly by low-ranking functionaries and small-time merchants and artisans, while Parasha lives on the right bank, on Vasilievsky Island, the lowest-lying section of St. Petersburg. In Peter the Great's unrealistic scheme for St. Petersburg's growth, Vasilievsky Island figured as the city center.

17. In Pushkin's day the large Senate Square afforded unobstructed vistas from the Lobanov-Rostovsky mansion, where Evgeny was sitting, to the Neva. Today the trees and plantings of the Admiralty Garden obscure the view of the monument and, much to its detriment, give the area the aspect of a playground (cf. Spasovich, 1889, p. 240).

18. That the concerns of Nicholas I were not altogether idle is shown by the critics' repeated attempts to see in the drama of *The Bronze Horseman* a reflection of actual historical events, such as the Decembrists' uprising against Alexander I (Vernadsky, 1923–24).

19. See Bethea's (1993) ingenious study of the equine symbolism in Pushkin's *The Bronze Horseman*.

20. Blok, 1965, p. 169.

21. Ivanov, 1995, pp. 322–23.

22. Ivanov wrote his essay just before the Bolshevik takeover in October 1917. Writing a century later, he might have replaced Marxism with another import from the West, such as globalization.

23. Arkin, 1991, p. 266. If one were to extend Arkin's metaphor to later times, Stalin would undoubtedly qualify as the embodiment of Ahriman. The absence of Christ's Russia from the monument accords with the popular belief that many of Peter's innovations did not have the benefit of divine presence and protection.

24. Representations of Antichrist in the guise of man or God, as in Luca Signorelli's mural of the *Last Judgment* in the Orvieto cathedral, are especially terrifying.

25. Peter's foes explained his reign as a scourge brought about by the unpopular church reforms introduced in the seventeenth century by Patriarch Nikon. The Moscow scribe Grigory Talitsky (end of the seventeenth century) found a justification for Peter's identification with Antichrist in Rev. 17. Talitsky's comparison of Muscovy with Babylon and his call for civil disobedience to Peter cost him his life.

26. Radishchev, 1949, pp. 11–12. Radishchev's book *A Journey from St. Petersburg to Moscow* (1790), which was passionately and openly critical of the Russian social system, was blacklisted and its extant copies were destroyed, so that it had to be circulated in handwritten copies. Pushkin recalls borrowing the book from one of his Moscow friends, who had to reach behind other books on the shelf to get it out of its hiding place ("A Journey from Moscow to St. Petersburg" (1834), *PPSS*, vol. 11, pp. 244–45). The persecutions to which Radishchev was subjected led eventually to his suicide.

27. Levitine, 1972, p. 62.

28. Stendhal, 1938–40, vol. 1, p. 223.

29. Cicognara, 1823–24, vol. 6, p. 324.

30. Belyi, 1994, p. 98

31. Arkin, 1991, pp. 260–61. Arkin's verdict is indebted to Gogol's memorable coda to his short story "Nevsky Prospect": "O, don't you believe that Nevsky Prospect! . . . It's all a lie, it's all a dream, it's all not the way it seems to be. . . . It lies to you all the time, that Nevsky Prospect, but most of all, when night descends upon it with its condensed bulk and brings out white and yellowish house walls, when the whole city turns into thunder and lightning, carriages by the myriad descend from the bridges, couriers shout

and jump on their horses, and when the devil himself turns on street lights, for no other reason than to show everything not the way it is."

32. Dostoevskii, 1972–90, vol. 5, p. 26

33. The "rootlessness" of St. Petersburg/Leningrad made Stalin doubt the city's loyalty to his leadership and caused him to engage in periodic purges of its party apparatus.

34. Catherine to Grimm, December 10, 1782: Grot, ed., 1878, vol. 23, p. 265. The visit in question took place on August 31, 1782, a few weeks after the unveiling of the monument. Accompanying the empress were her former favorite Prince G. A. Potemkin, her current favorite General A. A. Lanskoi, and her lady-in-waiting A. S. Protasova (Lopatin, ed., 1997, p. 723). The visit is recorded also in the log of the Court Steward (*Kamerfur'ersky zhurnal*).

35. The monument's "Russianness" explains why it is so little noticed outside Russia's borders. In France "still today the name of Falconet evokes for the 'general public' the clock of the *Three Graces,* rather than the Bronze Horseman. Yet, the attribution of the clock is uncertain." (Benot, ed., 1958, p. 7, fn. 1).

36. The Latin inscription engraved on a fold of the rider's cape on the left side of the monument reads "fecit et fudit stephanus falconet parisiensis mdcclxxviii" "Executed and cast by Etienne Falconet of Paris, 1778."

Bibliography

BOOKS ON THE MONUMENT

There are only three books and one book-length manuscript that deal exclusively with the history of the creation of the monument to Peter the Great by Falconet: Johann-Konrad Backmeister, *Historische Nachricht von der metallenen Bildsäule Peter des Großen*, Riga, 1783, translated into Russian by Nikolai Karandashev as *Istoricheskoe izvestie o izvaiannom konnom izobrazhenii Petra Velikogo*, St. Petersburg, 1786; David Arkin, *Mednyi vsadnik: Pamiatnik Petru I v Leningrade*, Leningrad, 1958; and Avraam Kaganovich, *"Mednyi vsadnik": Istoriia sozdaniia monumenta*, Leningrad, 1975 (2nd ed., 1982). In 1940–41 L. A. Bubnov authored "Nauchno-istoricheskii pasport na pamiatnik Petru Velikomu (Fal'kone)," a typewritten history of the monument, prepared for the St. Petersburg Bureau for Preservation of City Monuments. In addition, two books deal specifically with the transportation of the granite boulder which serves as the plinth of the monument: Marin Carburi de Cephalonie, *Monument élevé à la gloire de Pierre-le-Grand*, Paris, 1777; and Georgii I. Ivanov, *Kamen'-Grom*, St. Petersburg, 1994.

Falconet's art and writings have given rise to a somewhat larger number of separately published titles: Hermann Dalton, *Falconet und das Denkmal Peter des Großen in St. Petersburg (1782–1882): Eine Secularerinnerung*, Heidelberg, 1882; Georges Constantin Pélissier, *Falconet: His Life and His Work*, New York, 1907 (a facsimile handwritten edition); Edmund Hildebrandt, *Leben, Werke und Schriften des Bildhauers E.-M. Falconet, 1716–1791*, Strasbourg, 1908; Louis Réau, *Etienne-Maurice Falconet, 1716–1791*, 2 vols., Paris, 1922; Fernand Vallon, *Falconet: Falconet et Diderot, Falconet et Catherine II*, Grenoble, 1930; Anne Betty Weinshenker, *Falconet: His Writings and His Friend Diderot*, Geneva, 1966; and George Levitine, *The Sculpture of Falconet*, Greenwich, Conn., 1972. Of these only Hildebrandt, Réau, Weinshenker, and Levitine offer exhaustive monographic treatments. In addition, the catalog of the exhibit *Falconet à Sèvres, 1757–1766, ou l'art de plaire*, edited by M.-N. Pinot de Villechenon, held from November 2001 to February 2002 in the Musée national de céramique in Sèvres, Paris, 2001, contains several valuable contributions on Falconet.

There exists no book-length study of Collot.

I am aware of three novelistic treatments of the topics discussed in this book. Of those in Russian, Nataliia L. Nutrikhina, *Mademuazel' Viktuar,* St. Petersburg, 1996, is concerned chiefly with M.-A. Collot, while Elizaveta Topalova, *Milon Krotonskii,* Moscow, 1991, deals with Falconet and his ideological background. An English novel, Petrie Harbouri, *The Brothers Carburi,* London, 2001, was inspired by the careers of three older Carburi brothers. In so far as it deals with Marin Carburi, the main character in chapter 4, it offers a blend of fact and fiction in an interesting cocktail that tends to be alternately headier and flatter than reality.

GENERAL REFERENCES

Albis, Antoine d' (2001), "Providence ou fatalité? Les heureuses coincidences qui, l'une après l'autre, guidèrent Vincennes vers Sèvres," in [Pinot de Villechenon, commissaire], 2001b, pp. 61–67.

Alekseeva, T. V., ed. (1979), *Russkoe iskusstvo vtoroi poloviny XVIII–pervoi poloviny XIX v.: Materialy i issledovaniia,* Moscow.

Alexander, John T. (1998), *Catherine the Great: Life and Legend,* New York.

Algarotti, Francesco (1769), "Letter to Lord Hervey of June 30, 1739," in Count Francesco Algarotti, *Letters to Lord Hervey and the Marquis Scipio Maffei Containing the State of the Russian Empire,* London.

Andros[s]ov, Sergei (1996), "Gli scultori carraresi e la Russia del settecento," in Bertozzi, ed., pp. 39–67.

———— (1998), *Zhivopisets Ivan Nikitin,* St. Petersburg.

———— (2000), "O statue Petra Velikogo raboty Fal'kone," in Bespiatykh, ed., pp. 209–18.

Andros[s]ov, Sergei O., and Robert Enggass (1994), "Peter the Great on Horseback: A Terracotta by Rusconi," *BM,* vol. 136, pp. 816–21.

[Angremy, Annie, and Vitaly Souslov] (1986–87), *La France et la Russie au Siècle des Lumières: Relations culturelles et artistiques de la France et de la Russie au XVIII siècle* (catalogue of exhibition, Grand Palais, Paris, November 20, 1986–February 9, 1987), Paris.

[Anonymous] (1770), "Description d'une pierre trouvée en Russie et destinée pour servir de piédestal à la statue équestre de Pierre le Grand," in Haigold, pp. 209–14.

Antsiferov, Nikolai P. (1922), *Dusha Peterburga,* St. Petersburg.

Arkhipov, Nikolai I., and A. G. Raskin (1964), *Bartolomeo Karlo Rastrelli, 1675–1744,* Leningrad and Moscow.

Arkin, David E. (1958), *Mednyi vsadnik: Pamiatnik Petru I v Leningrade,* Leningrad.

———— (1991), "Grad obrechennyi," *Novyi zhurnal* (New York), nos. 184–85, pp. 256–69. (Reprint from *Russkaia svoboda* [Petrograd], nos. 22–23.)

Artner, Tivadar, and Corvina Kiadó (1982), *Horse and Horseman in Art,* translated by Maria Steiner, Budapest.

Asanēs, Spyridōn (1818), letter to Count Theodoros Negrēs, in *Hermēs ho Logios,* 1990, vol. 6, pp. 652–55.

Assézat, Jules, and Maurice Tourneux, eds. (1875–77), *Diderot: Oeuvres complètes,* 20 vols., Paris.

Babelon, André, ed. (1930), *Diderot: Lettres à Sophie Volland,* 3 vols., Paris.

Babelon, Jean-Pierre (1965), "Les Falconets de la collection Thiroux d'Epersenne," *BSHAF*, 1964, pp. 101–11.

────── (1972), *L'Eglise de Saint-Roch à Paris*, Paris.

Bachelier, Jean-Jacques (1781), *Mémoire historique de l'origine, du régime et des progrès de la Manufacture Nationale de porcelaine de France*, Paris (ed. by Gustave Gouellain, 1878).

Backmeister, Johann-Konrad (1786), *Istoricheskoe izvestie o izvaiannom konnom izobrazhenii Petra Velikogo*, translated from German by Nikolai Karandashev, St. Petersburg.

Bak, I. S. (1948), "Dmitrii Alekseevich Golitsyn," *IZ*, vol. 26, pp. 258–72.

Baldini, Ugo (1976), "Carburi, Marco," *DBI*, vol. 19, pp. 723–25.

Bartenev, Petr I., ed. (1869), *Osmnadtsatyi vek: Istoricheskii sbornik*, vol. 1, Moscow.

Bashkina, Nina N., et al., eds. (1980), *Rossiia i SShA: Stanovlenie otnoshenii 1765–1815: Sbornik dokumentov*, Moscow.

Batiushkov, Konstantin, N. (1977), *Opyty v stikhakh i proze*, Moscow.

Beaulieu, Michèle (1992), "Les 'écrits' de Falconet sur la sculpture (1716–1791)," *BSHAF*, 1991, pp. 173–85.

Becker, Marie-Louise (1998), "Marie-Anne Collot (1748–1821): L'Art de la terre cuite au féminin," *L'Objet d'art*, no. 325, June 1998, pp. 72–82.

────── (forthcoming), "Marie Collot à Pétersbourg (1766–1778)," in *La Culture française en Europe au XVIIIe siècle et les archives russes*, Collection Archives de l'Est, Centre International d'Etude du dix-huitième siècle à Ferney-Voltaire.

Belyi, Andrei (1994), *Peterburg*, Moscow.

Benot, Yves, ed. (1958), *Diderot et Falconet, Le pour et le contre: Corréspondance polémique sur le respect de la posterité, Pline et les anciens auteurs qui ont parlé de peinture et de sculpture*, Paris.

Bernoulli, Johann (1780), *Reisen durch Brandenburg, Pommern, Russland und Pohlen in den Jahren 1777 und 1778*, 4 vols., Leipzig. (The Russian episode translated and annotated by P. I. Bartenev in *RA*, 1902, vol. 1, no. 1, pp. 5–30).

Bertozzi, Massimo, ed. (1996), *I marmi degli zar: Gli scultori carraresi all' Ermitage*, Milan.

Bespiatykh, Iu. N., ed. (2000), *Fenomen Peterburga*, St. Petersburg.

Besterman, Theodore, ed. (1956), *Studies on Voltaire and the Eighteenth Century*, vol. 2, Geneva.

Besterman, Theodore, et al., eds. (1968–), *The Complete Works of Voltaire/Oeuvres complètes de Voltaire*, Geneva and Toronto.

Bethea, David M. (1989), *The Shape of Apocalypse in Modern Russian Fiction*, Princeton, N.J.

────── (1993), "The Role of the *eques* in Puškin's *Bronze Horseman*," in Bethea, ed., pp. 98–118.

Bethea, David M., ed. (1993), *Puškin Today*, Bloomington and Indianapolis.

Bil'basov, Vasilii A. (1884), *Didro v Peterburge*, St. Petersburg (Reprint with an introduction in English by A. Lentin, Cambridge, England, 1972; one chapter in *DNR*, vol. 17, no. 5 (May 1880), pp. 330–52).

────── (1890), *Istoriia Ekateriny Vtoroi*, vol. 1, St. Petersburg.

────── (1901), "Ekaterina II i Didro," *Istoricheskie monografii*, vol. 4, pp. 239–377, St. Petersburg. (First published in *RS*, 1884.)

Blok, Aleksandr (1965), *Zapisnye knizhki 1901–1920*, Moscow.

Boffrand, Germain (1743), *Description de ce qui a été pratiqué pour fondre en bronze d'un seul jet la figure équestre de Louis XIV, élevée par la ville de Paris dans la ville de Paris dans la place de Louis le Grand en 1699,* Paris.

Bolkhovitinov, Nikolai N. (1975), *The Beginnings of Russian-American Relations, 1775–1815,* translated from Russian by Elena Levin, Cambridge, Mass.

Booy, Jean Th. de (1969), "Inventaire provisoire des contributions de Diderot à la *Correspondance littéraire,*" *DHS,* vol. 1, pp. 353–97.

Bourgeois, Emile (1909), *Le biscuit de Sèvres au XVIIIe siècle,* 2 vols., Paris.

Bourrée de Corberon, Marie-Daniel (1901), *Un diplomate français à la cour de Catherine II, 1775–1780: Journal intime du chevalier de Corberon,* annotated by L.-H. Labande, 2 vols., Paris.

Brière, Gaston (1907), "Note sur les bustes de Camille Falconet par Etienne Falconet," *BSHAF,* 1907, pp. 87–92.

Brodskii, I. A., ed. (1973), *Khudozhniki goroda-fronta: Vospominaniia i dnevniki leningradskikh khudozhnikov,* Leningrad.

Brodsky, Joseph (1985), *Less Than One,* New York.

Broitman, Larisa I., and E. I. Krasnova (1997), *Bol'shaia Morskaia,* St. Petersburg.

Brückner, Aleksandr (1885), *Istoriia Ekateriny Vtoroi,* 5 vols., St. Petersburg.

Brunet, Marcelle, and Tamara Préaud (1978), *Sèvres des origines à nos jours,* Fribourg.

Bubnov, L. A. (1941), "Nauchno-istoricheskii pasport na pamiatnik Petru Velikomu (Fal'kone)," typescript in Biblioteka Otdela okhrany pamiatnikov, St. Petersburg.

Butler, Kira (1975), "Sèvres for the Imperial Court," *Apollo* (June), pp. 452–57.

Cahill, Patricia, ed. (1981), *Glorious Horsemen: Equestrian Art in Europe, 1500–1800,* exhibition catalogue, Springfield, Mass.

Campardon, Emile (1877), "Pierre-Etienne Falconet, et sa femme Marie-Anne Collot, sculpteur," *BSHAF* (October 1877), pp. 158–61.

Carburi de Cephalonie, Marin (1777), *Monument élevé à la gloire de Pierre le Grand ou relation des travaux et des moyens mécaniques qui ont été employés pour transporter à St. Pétersbourg un rocher de trois millions pesant, déstiné à servir de base à la Statue équestre de cet Empereur,* Paris.

Carr, John (1806), *A Northern Summer or Travels round the Baltic, through Denmark, Sweden, Russia, Prussia, and Part of Germany in the Year 1804,* in *A Collection of Modern and Contemporary Voyages and Travels,* London.

Catherine the Great (1927), *Memoirs of Catherine the Great,* translated by Katharine Anthony, New York and London.

———, *see also* Gamburger, ed., 1867; Grot, ed., 1878; Lopatin, ed., 1997; Polovtsov, ed., 1876; Réau, ed., 1921; Réau, Lundberg, and Weigert, eds., 1932; Vernière, ed., 1966.

Caylus, Anne-Claude-Philippe de (1910), *Vies d'artistes du XVIIIe siècle: Discours sur la peinture et la sculpture. Salons de 1751 et de 1753,* Paris.

Chadwick, Whitney (1990), *Women, Art, and Society,* London.

Chantelou, Paul Fréart de (1985), *Diary of the Cavaliere Bernini's Visit to France,* edited by Anthony Blunt, translated by Margery Corbett, Princeton, N.J.

Chantreau, [Pierre Nicolas] (1794), *Philosophical, Political, and Literary Travels in Russia, during the Years 1788 & 1789,* anonymously translated from the French, 2 vols., Perth.

Chappe d'Auteroche, l'Abbé Jean (1770), *A Journey into Siberia,* translated from the French, London. (Reprinted in New York, 1970.)

Charlier, Gustave, and R. Mortier (1952), *Le Journal Encyclopédique (1756–1793): Notes, documents et extraits réunis,* Paris.

Chekalovskii, Petr P. (1810), *Opyt vaianiia iz bronzy, odnim priemom, kolossal'nykh statui,* St. Petersburg.

Chiogna, Sergio (1976), "Carburi, Marino," *DBI,* vol. 19, pp. 725–27.

[Chistovich, Ilarion A., and Ivan S. Gorgolia] (1863), "Materialy ob Ivane Ivanoviche Betskom," *Chteniia,* vol. 47, no. 4 (October–December), pp. 81–156.

Cicognara, Leopoldo (1823–24), *Storia della scultura dal suo risorgimento in Italia fino al Secolo di Canova,* 2nd. rev. and enl. ed., 7 vols., Prato.

Cournault, Charles (1869), "Etienne-Maurice Falconet et Marie-Anne Collot," *GBA,* 2e pér., pp. 117–144.

Cournault, Charles, ed. (1866–67), "Lettres inédites de Diderot au sculpteur [statuaire] Falconet (1766–1773)," *RM,* vol. 39 (November), pp. 288–319; (December), pp. 381–99; vol. 40 (January), pp. 50–80; (February), pp. 303–25.

Coxe, William (1785), *Travels into Poland, Russia, Sweden and Denmark,* 2 vols., 2nd ed., London.

——— (1809), *Travels in Russia,* in John Pinkerton, ed., *General Collection of the Best and Most Interesting Voyages and Travels in All Parts of the World,* vol. 6, London.

Cross, Anthony G. (1972), "Chaplains to the British Factory in St. Petersburg, 1723–1813," *ESR,* vol. 2, pp. 125–42.

——— (1997a), *Anglo-Russian Relations in the Eighteenth Century: Exhibition Devised and Catalogue Compiled by Anthony Cross,* Norwich.

———, (1997b), *By the Banks of the Neva: Chapters from the Lives and Careers of the British in Eighteenth-Century Russia,* Cambridge.

Cross, Anthony G., ed. (1971), *Russia under Western Eyes, 1517–1825,* London.

Dalton, Hermann (1882), *Falconet und das Denkmal Peter des Großen in St. Petersburg (1782–1882): Eine Secularerinnerung,* Heidelberg.

Danilevskii, Nikolai, Ia. (1894), *Rossiia i Evropa,* 5th ed., St. Petersburg. (Reprinted by Johnson Reprint Corporation, New York, 1966.)

Dashkova [Dachkova], Ekaterina R. (1999), *Mon histoire: Mémoires d'une femme de lettres russe à l'époque des lumières,* edited by Alexandre Woronzoff-Dashkoff et al., Paris.

Dendrinos, Kleovoulos (1976), "Marinos Kharvourēs, o mēkhanikos kai physikomathēmatikos me ta aksiologa erga tou stē Rōssia kai Kephallēnía (1729–1782)," in *Prōtoi Hellēnes tekhnikoí epistēmones periodou apeleutherōsēs,* edited by Paulos Kyriazēs, Athens.

Diderot, Denis (1760), "Les embellissements de l'église Saint-Roch," *CLT,* vol. 4, pp. 328–33.

———, see also Assézat and Tourneux, eds., 1875–77; Babelon, ed., 1930; Benot, ed., 1958; Cournault, ed., 1866–67; Dieckmann and Seznec, eds., 1959; Goodman, ed. and tr., 1995; Lewinter, ed., 1970–73; Roth, ed., 1955–1970; Versini, ed., 1994–97, vol. 5.

Dieckmann, Herbert, ed. (1951), *Inventaire du fonds Vandeul et inédits de Diderot,* Geneva.

——— (1952), "An unpublished notice of Diderot on Falconet," *JWCI,* vol. 15, pp. 257–58.

Dieckmann, Herbert, and Jean Seznec (1952), "The Horse of Marcus Aurelius: A Controversy between Diderot and Falconet," *JWCI,* vol. 15, pp. 198–228.

Dieckmann, Herbert, and Jean Seznec, eds. (1959), *Diderot et Falconet: Correspondance, Les six premières lettres,* Frankfurt am Main. (*Analecta Romanica,* no. 7).

Dilke, Lady Emilia Francis Strong (1900), *French Architects and Sculptors of the XVIIIth Century,* London.

Dostoevskii, Fedor M. (1972–90), *Polnoe sobranie sochinenii v tridsati tomakh,* 30 vols. edited by V. G. Bazanov et al., Leningrad.

Dowley, Francis H. (1968), "Falconet's Attitude towards Antiquity and His Theory of Reliefs," *AQ,* vol. 31, pp. 185–204.

Dukes, Paul (1967), *Catherine the Great and the Russian Nobility: A Study Based on the Materials of the Legislative Commission of 1767.* London and Cambridge.

Dumas, Alexandre (1881), *Le maître d'armes,* Paris.

Dussieux, Louis et al. (1854), *Mémoires inédits sur la vie et les ouvrages des membres de l'Académie Royale de Peinture et de Sculpture,* Paris.

Eriksen, Svend (1974), *Early Neo-Classicism in France: The Creation of the Louis Seize Style in Architectural Decoration, Furniture and Ormolu, Gold and Silver, and Sèvres Porcelain in the Mid-Eighteenth Century,* translated and edited by Peter Thornton, London.

———— (1987), "The Early Years," in Eriksen and Bellaigue, pp. 25–98.

Eriksen, Svend, and Geoffrey de Bellaigue (1987), *Sèvres Porcelain: Vincennes and Sèvres, 1740–1800,* London and Boston.

Eroshkina, Alla N. (1993), "Obshchestvenno-politicheskaia i administrativnaia deia-tel'nost' I. I. Betskogo v 60–90 gg. XVIII veka," avtoreferat dissertatsii, Moscow.

Eton, William (1798), *A Survey of the Turkish Empire,* London.

———— (1807), *A Letter to the Right Honourable the Earl of D*** on the Political Relations of Russia, in Regard to Turkey, Greeece, and France,* London.

Ettinger, Pavel (1915), "Risunok A. P. Losenko s Falkonetovskogo pamiatnika Petru Velikomu," *SG,* March, pp. 45–48.

Falconet, Etienne-Maurice (1773), *Traduction des XXXIV, XXXV et XXXVI Livres de Pline l'Ancien, avec des notes par Etienne Falconet,* The Hague.

———— (1781), *Oeuvres d'Etienne Falconet, statuaire; contenant plusieurs écrits relatifs aux Beaux-Arts, dont quelques-uns ont déjà paru, mais fautifs; d'autres sont nouveaux,* 6 vols., Lausanne.

———— (1785), *Oeuvres choisies de Falconet,* Paris.

———— (1787), *Oeuvres diverses de Falconet concernant les arts,* 3 vols., Paris.

———— (1808), *Oeuvres complètes d'Etienne Falconet,* 3rd ed., 3 vols., Paris. (Reprinted Geneva, 1970.)

————, *see also* Benot, ed., 1958; Cournault, ed., 1866–67; Heier, ed., 1965a, 1965b; Hoyt and Cassirer, eds. and trs., 1965; Platonova, ed., 1928; Polovtsov, ed., 1876; Réau, ed., 1921; Tooke, ed. and tr., 1777.

Fedotov, Georgii Petrovich (1988), "Tri stolitsy," in *Litso Rossii: Stat'i 1918–1930,* 2nd ed., Paris, pp. 49–70. (Reprint from *Versty,* no. 1, 1926.)

Fleitmann, Lida Louise (1931), *The Horse in Art from Primitive Times to the Present,* New York.

Fortia de Piles, Alphonse, and de Boisgelin (1796), *Voyage de deux Français en Allemagne, Danemarck, Suède, Russie, et Pologne, fait en 1790–1792,* 5 vols., Paris.

Foss, Arthur (1969), *The Ionian Islands: Zakynthos to Corfu,* London.

Fresco, Marcel F. (1998), "Amalias Jahre in den Niederlanden: Ihre Freundschaft mit dem Philosophen Frans Hemsterhuis," in Schulz, ed., pp. 28–42.

Friis, Hjalmar (1933), *Rytterstatuens historie i Europa fra oldtiden indtil Thorvaldsen,* Copenhagen.

Gaborit, Jean-René (1984), "Les sculpteurs," in *Diderot et l'art de Boucher à David: Les Salons 1759–1781,* exhibition catalogue, Paris.

Gallitzin [Golitsyn], Demetrius von (1780), *Sendschreiben an die kaiserliche Akademie der Wissenschaften zu St. Petersburg über einige Gegenstände der Elektrizität,* Münster and Leipzig.

Gamburger, A. F., ed. (1867), "Pis'ma Imperatritsy Ekateriny II k G-zhe Zhoffren," *SIRIO,* vol. 1, pp. 253–91.

Garrard, John G., ed. (1973), *The Eighteenth Century in Russia,* Oxford.

Georgi, Johann Gottlieb (1794), *Opisanie rossiisko-imperatorskogo stolichnogo goroda Sankt-Peterburga i dostopamiatnostei v okrestnostiakh onogo,* St. Petersburg. (Reissued in 1996.)

Giormani, Virgilio (1989), "Marco Carburi," *Praktika tou Diethnous Panioniou Synedriou (Hetareia Kefallēniakōn Historikōn Ereunōn),* vol. 1, pp. 381–88.

Goethe, Johann Wolfgang von (1973), *Schriften zur bildenden Kunst,* edited by Siegfried Seidel (*Berliner Ausgabe,* vol. 19), Berlin.

Golitsyn, Dmitrii Alekseevich (1952), "Pis'ma," in I. Ia. Shchipanov, ed., *Izbrannye proizvedeniia russkikh myslitelei vtoroi poloviny XVIII veka,* vol. 2, Moscow.

———, *see also* Gallitzin, 1780; Rachinskii, ed., 1881.

Goodman, John, ed. and tr. (1995), *Diderot on Art,* vol. 1: *Salon of 1765 and Notes on Painting,* vol. 2: *Salon of 1767,* New Haven, Conn.

Grabar', Igor' E. (1909–14), *Istoriia russkogo iskusstva,* 6 vols., Moscow.

Granville, Augustus B. (1829), *St. Petersburgh: A Journal of Travels to and from that Capital,* 2nd ed., vol. 1, London.

Grasset Saint-Sauveur, André jeune, (Year 8 [1800]), *Voyage historique, littéraire et pittoresque dans les isles et possessions ci-devant Vénitiennes dans le Levant,* 3 vols., Paris.

Graves, Algernon, ed. (1969), *The Society of Artists of Great Britain, 1760–1791, The Free Society of Artists , 1761–1783: A Complete Dictionary of Contributors and Their Work from the Foundation of the Societies to 1791,* Bath. (Reprint of the 1907 edition.)

Grimm, Friedrich Melchior, *see* Grot, ed., 1885; Réau, ed. 1932; Sainte-Beuve and Limayrac, 1854.

Grot, Iakov K., ed. (1878), *Pis'ma Imperatritsy Ekateriny II k Grimmu (1774–1796),* *SIRIO,* vol. 23.

——— (1880), "Ekaterina II v perepiske s Grimmom," *SORIaS,* vol. 20, pp. 1–130.

——— (1885), *Pis'ma barona Mel'khiora Grimma k imp. Ekaterine II, SIRIO,* vol. 44.

Guiffrey, Jules-J., ed. (1876), "Actes d'état civil d'artistes français tirés des Archives Nationales," *BSHAF* 1876, p. 63.

Haigold, Johann Joseph (1770), *Beilagen zum neuveränderten Rußland,* Riga and Leipzig, pp. 209–14.

Haskell, Francis, and Nicholas Penny (1981), *Taste and the Antique: The Lure of Classical Sculpture, 1500–1900,* New Haven, Conn., and London.

Haumant, Emile (1913), *La Culture française en Russie (1700–1900),* 2nd. ed., Paris.

Hawley, Henry (1994), "Tassaert's *Venus,* not Falconet's *Flora,*" in *Studi sulla Scultura in onore di Andrew S. Ciechanowiecki,* Antologia di Belle Arti, n.s. 48–51, Turin, pp. 100–106.

Heier, Edmund (1981), *Ludwig Heinrich von Nicolay (1737–1820) as an Exponent of Neo-Classicism,* Bonn.

Heier, Edmund (1965a), *L. H. Nicolay (1737–1820) and His Contemporaries,* The Hague.

——— (1965b), "Vospominaniia A. Nikolai o E. M. Fal'kone," *Iskusstvo,* no. 4, pp. 69–71.

Helbig [Gel'big], Georg von (1900), *Russkie izbranniki,* translated and edited by V. A. Bil'basov, Berlin.

Heller, Nancy G. (1987), *Women Artists: An Illustrated History,* New York.

Henry, C., ed. (1880), *Mémoires inédits de Charles-Nicolas Cochin,* Paris.

Hess, Thomas B., and Elizabeth C. Baker, eds. (1973), *Art and Sexual Politics,* New York and London.

Hildebrandt, Edmund (1908), *Leben, Werke und Schriften des Bildhauers E.-M. Falconet, 1716–1791,* Strasbourg.

Hill, Emita B. (1981), "Diderot's Letter to Falconet, Summer 1767," *DS,* vol. 20, pp. 125–41.

Hoyt, Nellie S., and Thomas Cassirer, eds. and trs. (1965), *Encyclopedia: Selections, Diderot, D'Alembert,* Indianapolis (Falconet's article "Sculpture").

Iukht, Aleksandr I., ed. (1996), *Ekaterina II i ee okruzhenie,* Moscow.

Ivanchin-Pisarev, Nikolai (1842), "O redchaishem gravirovannom portrete Lzhedimitriia," *Moskvitianin,* part 2, no. 4, p. 487.

Ivanov, Georgii I. (1986), "Kamen'-Grom," *Pamiatniki nauki i tekhniki,* 1985, Moscow.

——— (1994), *Kamen'-Grom: Istoricheskaia povest',* St. Petersburg.

Ivanov, Viacheslav I. (1995), "Lik i lichiny Rossii: K issledovaniiu ideologii Dostoevskogo," *Lik i lichiny Rossii: Estetika i literaturnaia teoriia,* Moscow (Originally published in 1917 in *Russkaia mysl'.*)

Ivinskii, Dmitry P. (1993), *Aleksandr Pushkin i Adam Mitskewich v krugu russko-pol'skikh literaturnykh i politicheskikh otnoshenii,* Vilnius.

Izmailov, Nikolai V. (1975), *Ocherki tvorchestva Pushkina,* Leningrad.

Jal, Augustin (1872), *Dictionnaire critique de biographie et d'histoire; errata et supplément pour tous les dictionnaires historiques d'après des documents authentiques inédits,* 2nd ed., Paris.

Jankovitz, Louis de (1959), "Souvenirs de famille: Lorraine/Hongrie." (Manuscript.)

Janson, Horst Woldemar (1967), "The Equestrian Monument from Cangrande della Scala to Peter the Great," in Archibald R. Lewis, ed., *Aspects of the Renaissance, A Symposium,* Austin, Tex., pp. 73–85. (Reprinted in Janson, *16 Studies,* New York, 1973.)

——— (1985), *19th-Century Sculpture,* New York.

Johnston, Charles, tr. (1983), *Narrative Poems by Alexander Pushkin and by Mikhail Lermontov,* New York and Toronto.

Kaganovich, Avraam L. (1982), *"Mednyj vsadnik": Istoriia sozdaniia monumenta,* 2nd ed., Leningrad.

Kahn, Andrew, *Pushkin's "The Bronze Horseman,"* London. (Extensive bibliography.)

Kaufmann, Emil (1955), *Architecture of the Age of Reason,* Cambridge, Mass.

Keller, Ulrich (1971), *Reitermonumente absolutistischer Fürsten,* Munich and Zurich.

Kleiner, Juliusz (1948), *Mickiewicz,* vol. 2, pp. 449–57, Lublin.

Knabe, Georgii S. (1993), *Voobrazhenie znaka: Mednyi vsadnik Fal'kone i Pushkina,* Moscow.

Knigge, Armin (1984), *Puškins Verserzählung "Der eherne Reiter" in der russischen Kritik: Rebellion oder Unterwerfung,* Amsterdam.

Köhler, Mathilde (1993), *Amalie von Gallitzin: Ein Leben zwischen Skandal und Legende,* Paderborn.

Kölving, Ulla, and Jeanne Carriat, eds., 1984, *Inventaire de la Correspondance littéraire de Grimm et Meister,* 3 vols., *Studies on Voltaire and the Eighteenth Century,* nos. 225–27, Oxford.

Kor, E. (1990), "Monument kak pamiatnik kul'tury," in E. Romanenko, ed., *Skul'ptura v gorode,* Moscow, pp. 23–30.

Korshunova, Militsa, F. (1982), *Arkhitektor Iury Fel'ten: Katalog vystavki,* Leningrad.

Kosareva, Nina (1975), "Masterpieces of Eighteenth-Century French Sculpture," *Apollo,* June, pp. 443–51.

Kovalenskaia, Natal'ia N. (1940), *Istoriia russkogo iskusstva XVIII veka,* Moscow and Leningrad.

Krasnov, Georgii V. (1984), "Miatezhnaia Neva, Evgenii i kumir na bronzovom kone," *Pushkin: Boldinskie stranitsy,* Gorky, pp. 143–72.

Krasnova, E. I. (1985), "Masterskaia Fal'kone," *Vechernii Leningrad,* no. 168 (17658), July 25.

Krull, Edith (1989), *Women in Art,* London.

Kubacki, Wacław (1951), *Palmira i Babilon,* Wrocław.

Kudriavtsev, A. I., and G. I. Shkoda (1982), "Pervyi monument Rossii: Mednomu vsadniku—dva veka," *Leningradskaia panorama,* no. 8 (August), pp. 33–36.

Kupriianov, S. A., and N. A. Kondrat'ev (1950), *Izgotovlenie bronzovoi skul'ptury,* Moscow and Leningrad.

La Lande, Charles de (1783), "Compte rendu des *Oeuvres d'Etienne Falconet," Journal des Sçavants,* February.

Lami, Stanislas (1910), *Dictionnaire des sculpteurs de l'école française au dix-huitième siècle,* vol. 1, Paris, pp. 335–38.

Lappo-Danilevskii, Aleksandr S. (1904), *I. I. Betskoi i ego sistema vospitaniia,* St. Petersburg.

Larivière, Charles de (1909), *La France et la Russie au XVIIIe siècle,* Paris.

Lebit, D. A. (1967), "Fal'kone—khudozhnik-myslitel," *VF,* vol. 21, no. 1, pp. 140–49.

Lednicki, Wacław (1955), *Pushkin's Bronze Horseman: The Story of a Masterpiece,* Berkeley, Calif., and Los Angeles.

Lehndorff, Reichsgraf Ernst Ahasverus Heinrich (1921), *Des Reichsgrafen E. A. H. Lehndorff Tagebücher und seine Kammerherrenzeit,* edited by K. E. Schmidt-Lötzen, Gotha.

Lemcke, Peter Henry (1940), *Life and Work of Prince Demetrius Augustine Gallitzin,* translated from German by Joseph C. Plumpe, London.

Leonov, Aleksei I., ed. (1952), *Russkoe iskusstvo. Ocherki o zhizni i tvorchestve khudozhnikov: Vosemnadtsatyi vek,* Moscow.

Lévesque, Pierre-Charles (1808), "La vie de Falconet," in FOC, vol. 1, pp. 3–21.

Levey, Michael (1992), *Painting and Sculpture in France, 1700–1789,* New Haven, Conn., and London.

Levitine, George (1972), *The Sculpture of Falconet,* Greenwich, Conn.

Lewinter, Roger, ed. (1970–73), *Denis Diderot: Oeuvres complètes, édition chronologique,* 15 vols., Paris.

Librovich, Sigizmund F. (1916), *Istoriia mednogo vsadnika,* Moscow.

Liedtke, Walter (1989), *The Royal Horse and Rider: Painting, Sculpture, and Horsemanship, 1500–1800,* New York.

Lo Gatto, Ettore (1960), *Il mito di Pietroburgo: Storia, leggenda, poesia,* Milan.

Lopatin, V. S., ed. (1997), *Ekaterina II i G. A. Potemkin: Lichnaia perepiska, 1769–1791,* Moscow.

Lortholary, Albert (1951), *Les "Philosophes" du XVIIIe siècle et la Russie: Le Mirage russe en France au XVIIIe siècle,* Paris.

Lotman, Iurii M. (1984), "Simvolika Peterburga i problemy semiotiki goroda," in Lotman, ed., 1984.

Lotman, Iurii M., ed. (1984), *Semiotika goroda i gorodskoi kul'tury: Peterburg,* Trudy po znakovym sistemam, 18, Tartu.

Madariaga, Isabel de (1962), *Britain, Russia, and the Armed Neutrality of 1780,* New Haven, Conn., and London.

——— (1981), *Russia in the Age of Catherine the Great,* New Haven, Conn., and London.

Maikov, Petr M. (1904), *Ivan Ivanovich Betskoi: Opyt ego biografii,* St. Petersburg.

——— (1908), "Betskoi, Ivan Ivanovich," *RBS,* vol. 3, pp. 5–12.

Maistre, Joseph de (1993), *Les Soirées de Saint-Pétersbourg,* edited by by Jean-Louis Darcel, vol. 1, Geneva.

Makarovskaia, Gera V. (1978), *"Mednyi vsadnik": Itogi i problemy izucheniia,* Saratov.

Malinovskii, Konstantin V., ed. and tr. (1979), "Zapiski Iakoba Shtelina o skul'pture v Rossii v XVIII v.," in Alekseeva, ed., pp. 108–36.

——— (1990), *Zapiski Iakoba Shtelina ob iziashchnykh iskusstvakh v Rossii,* 2 vols., Moscow.

Margeret, Jacques (1983), *The Russian Empire and Grand Duchy of Muscovy: A 17th-Century French Account,* translated and edited by Chester S. L. Dunning, Pittsburgh.

Mariette, Pierre-Jean (1768), *Description des travaux qui ont précédé, accompagné et suivi la fonte en bronze, d'un seul jet, de la statue équestre de Louis XV le Bien-Aimé, dressée sur les mémoires de M. Lempeureur, ancien échevin,* Paris.

Martin, Michel (1986), *Les monuments équestres de Louis XIV: Une grande entreprise de propagande monarchique,* Paris.

Masarachi, Antimo [=Antimos Mazarakēs] (1843), *Vite degli uomini illustri dell' isola di Cefalonia,* translated from Greek by N. Tommaseo, Venice.

Masson, Charles François Philibert (1800–1803), *Mémoires secrets sur la Russie,* 4 vols., London.

Matsulevich, Zhannetta (1959), "Neizvestnoe proizvedenie Mari Anny Kollo," *SGE,* no. 16, pp. 20–21.

——— (1962), *"Milon Krotonskii* E.-M. Fal'kone," *Iskusstvo,* no. 12, pp. 64–67.

Matveev, V. Iu. (1981), "K istorii vozniknoveniia i razvitiia siuzheta *Petr I, vysekaiush-chii statuiu Rossii,"* in B. V. Sapunov and I. N. Ukhanova, eds., *Kul'tura i iskusstvo Rossii XVIII veka,* Leningrad.

Meyer, Johann Heinrich (1974), *Geschichte der Kunst,* Weimar. (Originally published in 1824.)

Michel, André (1923), Review of Louis Réau, *Etienne-Maurice Falconet (1716–1791), GBA,* July–August, pp. 127–28.

Michel, Christian (1984), "Les conseillers artistiques de Diderot," *RdeA,* no. 66, pp. 9–16.

Mickiewicz, Adam (1995), *Dzieła,* vol. 3 *(Dramaty), Ustęp,* pp. 265–316, Warsaw.

———, *see also* Lednicki, 1955, pp. 109–39; Noyes, ed., 1944.

Mikhnevich, V. A. (1882), "Istoriia mednogo vsadnika," *IstV,* vol. 9, pp. 164–84.

Milande, Véronique (2001), "Du modèle en terre au biscuit de porcelaine: Les terres cuites du Musée national de céramique—La réalisation d'un biscuit de porcelaine," in [Pinot de Villechenon, commissaire], 2001b, pp. 77–85.

Mohrenschildt, Dimitri S., von (1936), *Russia in the Intellectual Life of Eighteenth-Century France,* New York.

Morozov, A. (1965), "K istorii nadpisei M. V. Lomonosova 'K statue Petra Velikogo,'" *RL,* no. 4, pp. 102–14.

Nekliudova, Mariia S., and Aleksandr L. Ospovat (1997), "*Okno v Evropu:* Istochnikovedcheskii etiud k *Mednomu Vsadniku,*" *LS,* vol. 2, pp. 255–72.

Nikolaï [Nikolay], L. H., *see* Heier.

Noyes, George Rapall, ed. (1944), *Poems by Adam Mickiewicz,* New York.

O'Meara, Patrick (1988), "Prince D. A. Golitsyn and His Proposals for Social Reform," in R. P. Bartlett et al., eds., *Russia and the World of the Eighteenth Century,* Columbus, Ohio, pp. 273–87.

Opperman, Hal N. (1965), "Marie-Anne Collot in Russia: Two Portraits," *BM,* vol. 107, no. 749, August, pp. 408–15.

Ospovat, Aleksandr L., and R. D. Timenchik (1987), "*Pechal'nu povest' sokhranit'* . . . ," Moscow.

Panfilowitsch, Igor (1995), *Aleksandr Puškins "Mednyj vsadnik": Deutungsgeschichte und Gehalt,* Munich.

Patte, Pierre (1765), *Monumens érigés en France à la gloire de Louis XV précédés d'un tableau du progrés des arts et des sciences sous ce régne, ainsi que d'une description des honneurs et des monumens de gloire accordés aux grands hommes . . . ,* Paris.

Pekarskii, Petr P. (1873), *Istoriia imperatorskoi Akademii nauk v Peterburge,* vol. 2, St. Petersburg.

Pélissier, Georges Constantin (1907), *Falconet: His Life and His Work,* New York.

Péloux, Charles du (1930), *Répertoire biographique et bibliographique des artistes du XVIII siècle français,* Paris.

Perrault, Charles (1688), *Parallèle des Anciens et des Modernes en ce qui regarde les Arts et les Sciences,* Paris.

Petrov, Petr N. (1886), *Istoriia rodov russkogo dvorianstva,* vol. 1, St. Petersburg.

Petrov, Vsevolod N. (1965), "Konnaia statuia Petra I v Leningrade, 1720–1724," in Rogachevskii and Baltun, eds., pp. 47–60. (Reprinted in Petrov, 1978, pp. 19–42.)

——— (1972), *Equestrian Statue of Peter I by Carlo Rastrelli,* Leningrad.

——— (1978), *Ocherki i issledovaniia,* Moscow.

Pinault, Madeleine (1984), "Diderot et les illustrateurs de l'*Encyclopédie,*" *RdeA,* no. 66, pp. 27–29.

Pingaud, Léonce (1886), *Les français en Russie et les russes en France,* Paris.

Pinot de Villechenon, Marie-Noëlle (1997), *Sèvres: Porcelain from the Sèvres Museum 1740 to the Present Day,* translated by John Gilbert, London.

——— (2001a), "Un sculpteur au royaume de la porcelaine," in [Pinot de Villechenon, commissaire], 2001b, pp. 11–29.

[Pinot de Villechenon, Marie-Noëlle, commissaire] (2001b), *Falconet à Sèvres, 1757–1766, ou l'art de plaire* (catalog of exhibition, Musée national de céramique, Sèvres, November 6, 2001, to February 4, 2002), Paris.

Platonova, Nina, ed. (1928), "Pis'ma skul'ptora E. M. Fal'kone k akademiku Shtelinu," *MRI,* vol. 1, pp. 137–42.

Polovtsov, Alexandr A., ed. (1876), *Perepiska imperatritsy Ekateriny II s Fal'konetom,* *SIRIO,* vol. 17, St. Petersburg.

Posada, Maurice (1973), "An Introduction to the Textual Problem of the Diderot-Falconet Correspondence on Posterity," *DS,* vol. 16, pp. 175–96.

Pouqueville, François-Charles-Hugues-Laurent (1806), *Travels through the Morea, Albania, and other parts of the Ottoman Empire to Constantinople during the years 1798, 1799, 1800, and 1801,* London.

Pumpianskii, L. V. (1939), "Mednyi vsadnik i poèticheskaia traditsiia XVIII veka," in *Pushkin: Vremennik Pushkinskoi komissii,* pts. 4–5, pp. 99–124.

Pushkarev, Ivan I. (1839), *Opisanie Sankt-Peterburga,* St. Petersburg.

——— (1843), *Putevoditel' po S-Peterburgu i okrestnostiam S-Peterburga,* St. Petersburg.

——— (1846), *Istoricheskii ukazatel' dostoprimechatel'nostei S-Peterburga,* St. Petersburg.

Pushkin, Aleksandr S. (1937–59), *Polnoe sobranie sochinenii,* edited by various hands, 16 vols. in 20 and supplement, Moscow and Leningrad.

———, *see also* Johnston, tr., 1983.

Putnam, Peter, ed. (1952), *Seven Britons in Imperial Russia, 1698–1812,* Princeton, N.J.

Pyliaev, Mikhail I. (1990), *Staryi Peterburg,* Leningrad. (Reprint of the 1889 edition.)

Rachinskii, A., ed. (1881), "Piat' pisem kniazia D. A. Golitsyna vitse-kantsleru kniaziu A. M. Golitsynu," *SMAMID,* no. 2, pp. 81–117, Moscow.

Radishchev, Aleksandr N. (1949), *Izbrannye sochineniia,* Moscow and Leningrad.

Rambaud, Alfred (1877), "Catherine II et ses correspondants français d'après les recentes publications de la Societé imperiale d'histoire de Russie," *RDM,* vol. 19, January, pp. 278–90, February, pp. 570–604.

Rambaud, Alfred, ed. (1890), *Recueil des instructions données aux ambassadeurs et ministres de France depuis les traités de Westphalie jusqu'à la révolution française,* vol. 9: *Russie,* vol. 2, Commission des archives diplomatiques, Paris.

Rankabē, Eugenios Rizos (1926), *Livre d'or de la noblesse ionienne,* vol. 2: *Céphalonie,* Athens.

Raymond, Agnès G. (1973), "Le buste d'Etienne-Noël Damilaville par Marie-Anne Collot," *RdL,* vol. 23, nos. 4–5, pp. 255–60.

Réau, Louis (1913), *Saint-Pétersbourg,* Paris.

——— (1922), *Etienne-Maurice Falconet, 1716–1791,* 2 vols., Paris.

——— (1923), "Une femme-sculpteur française au XVIIIe siècle: Marie-Anne Collot (Madame Falconet)," *AA,* vol. 6, pp. 165–71.

——— (1924), "Une femme-sculpteur française au XVIIIe siècle: Marie-Anne Collot (1748–1821)," *BSHAF* 1924, pp. 219–29.

——— (1927), *Les Lemoyne,* Paris.

——— (1929), *Catalogue de l'art français dans les musées russes,* Paris.

——— (1938), *L'Europe française au siècle des lumières,* Paris.

——— (1952), *L'Art au XVIIIème siècle en France: Style Louis XVI, 1760–1789,* Paris.

Réau, Louis, ed. (1919), "Documents inédits sur Falconet," *BSHAF* 1918–19, pp. 152–68.

——— (1921), *Correspondance de Falconet avec Catherine II, 1767–1778,* Paris.

——— (1932), "Correspondance artistique de Grimm avec Catherine II," in Réau, Lundberg, and Weigert, eds., pp. 1–206.

Réau, Louis, G. Lundberg, and R.-A. Weigert, eds. (1932), *L'Art français dans les pays du Nord et de l'Est de l'Europe (XVIIIe–XIXe siècles),* Archives de l'art français, *SHAF,* n.s., vol. 17, Paris.

Reimers, H. (1931), "Les bustes de Marie-Anne Collot," *La Renaissance,* vol. 14, pp. 306–12.

Robin, Jean-Baptiste-C. (1862), "Eloge de Falconet, sculpteur," *RUA,* vol. 15, pp. 245–56. (Reprinted from *Tribut de la Societé nationale des Neuf-Soeurs,* Paris, 1791.)

Rocca, Ignazio (1780), *Lettera ed epigrafe al. Sig. Conte Marino Carburi di Cefalonia ora dimorante in Venezia,* Piacenza.

Roche, Denis (1920), "Le fils de Falconet," *La Renaissance de l'art français et des industries de luxe,* June 3, pp. 240–49.

Rogachevskii, V. M., and P. K. Baltun, eds. (1965), *Iz bronzy i mramora: Kniga dlia chteniia po istorii russkoi i sovetskoi skul'ptury,* Leningrad.

Romm, Abram [Aleksandr] G. (1944), *Pamiatnik Petru I v Leningrade; Skul'ptor E.-M. Fal'kone, 1716–1791,* Moscow and Leningrad.

———— (1952), "Pamiatniki Petru I: K.-B. Rastrelli (1670–1744), E.-M. Fal'kone (1716–1791)," in Leonov, ed., pp. 171–90.

———— (1965), "Pamiatnik Petru I v Leningrade, 1765–1782," in Rogachevskii and Baltun, eds., pp. 83–94.

Roth, Georges, ed. [with Jean Varloot from vol. 13] (1955–70), *Diderot: Correspondance,* 16 vols., Paris.

Rovinskii, Dmitrii A. (1895), *Podrobnyi slovar' russkikh graverov XVI–XIX vv.,* 2 vols., St. Petersburg.

Rulhière, Claude-Carloman de (1797), *Histoire ou anecdotes sur la Révolution de Russie en l'année 1762,* Paris. (English translation: *A History or Anecdotes of the Revolution in Russia in the Year 1762,* London, 1797.)

Rzhevskaia, Glafira I. (1871), "Pamiatnye zapiski Glafiry Ivanovny Rzhevskoi," *RA,* no. 1, pp. 14–33.

Sainte-Beuve, and Paulin Limayrac, eds. (1854), *Gazette littéraire de Grimm: Histoire, littérature, philosophie, 1753–1790,* Paris.

Saint-Simon [Louis de Rouvroy] (1920), *Mémoires de Saint-Simon,* edited by A. de Boislisle, vol. 31, Paris.

Savill, Rosalind (1982), "Cameo Fever: Six Pieces from the Sèvres Porcelain Dinner Service Made for Catherine II of Russia," *Apollo,* November, pp. 304–11.

———— (1988), *The Wallace Collection: Catalogue of Sèvres Porcelain,* 3 vols., London.

Scherer, Jean-Benoit (1792), *Anecdotes intéressantes et secrètes de la cour de Russie, tirée de ses archives . . . Pub. par un voyageur qui a sejourné treize ans en Russie,* 6 vols., Paris.

Scherf, Guilhem (2001a), "Les sculptures religieuses de Falconet," in [Pinot de Villechenon, commissaire], 2001b, pp. 31–37.

———— (2001b), "Problèmes d'attribution: Marbres de Falconet, Tassaert et Broche," in [Pinot de Villechenon, commissaire], 2001b, pp. 39–45.

Schlafly, Daniel L., Jr. (1997), "Father Demetrius A. Gallitzin: Son of the Russian Enlightenment," *Catholic Historical Review* 83: 716–25.

Schulz, Petra, ed. (1998), *Amalia Fürstin von Gallitzin (1748–1806): "Meine Seele ist auf der Spitze meiner Feder,"* Ausstellung zum 250 Geburtstag in der Universitäts- und Landesbibliothek, Münster, vom 28. August bis zum 2. Oktober 1998, Münster.

Schumacher, Birgit (1994), *Pferde: Meisterwerke des Pferde- und Reiterbildes,* Stuttgart and Zurich.

Ségur, Louis-Philippe (1825–1827), *Memoirs and Recollections,* 3 vols., London.

Semenova, Lidiia N. (1998), *Byt i naselenie Sankt-Peterburga (XVIII vek)*, St. Petersburg.

Seznec, Jean (1956), "Falconet, Voltaire et Diderot," in Besterman, ed., pp. 43–59.

——— (1957), *Essais sur Diderot et l'antiquité*, Oxford.

——— (1965), "Falconet, Diderot et le bas-relief," in *Mélanges W. Friedländer*, Berlin, pp. 151–57.

Seznec, Jean, and Jean Adhémar, eds. (1957), *Diderot: Salons*, vol. 1.

Shalabaeva, Vera N. (1958), "Pamiatnik i ego sozdatel'," *Iskusstvo*, no. 12, pp. 33–39, 80–82.

Shchipanov, Ivan Ia., and L. B. Svetlov, eds. (1952), *Izbrannye proizvedeniia russkikh myslitelei vtoroi poloviny XVIII veka*, vol. 2, Moscow.

Shubinskii, Sergei N. (1871), *Rasskazy o russkoi starine*, St. Petersburg.

——— (1898), "Istoriia mednogo vsadnika," *Literaturnoe prilozhenie "Nivy,"* St. Petersburg.

——— (1903), *Istoricheskie ocherki i rasskazy*, 4th ed., St. Petersburg.

Shugurov, M. F. (1869), "Didro i ego otnosheniia k Ekaterine II-i," in Bartenev, ed., vol. 1, pp. 333–78.

Smirennyi, I. I. (1987), "Perevozka *Grom-kamnia*—unikal'naia transportnaia operatsiia XVIII veka," *Promyshlennyi transport*, no. 6, pp. 34–37.

Spasovich, V. D. (1889), *Sochineniia*, vol. 2, St. Petersburg.

Stählin, Jakob, *see* Alekseeva, ed., 1979, pp. 180–211; Malinovskii, ed. and tr., 1979, 1990.

Stampa della Nob[ile] Sig[nora] Co[ntessa] Sofia Carburi qu[erelante] Co[nte] Marin [Letters and documents pertaining to Sophia Carburi's contestation of Marin Carburi's last will and testament], c. 1786.

Stasov, Vladimir V. (1877), "Tri frantsuzskikh skul'ptora v Rossii," *DNR*, vol. 1, January–April, pp. 329–52.

Stendhal (1938–40), *Promenades dans Rome*, 3 vols., Paris.

Stolpianskii, Petr N. (1918), *Peterburg: Kak voznik, osnovalsia i ros Sankt-Piterburkh*, Petrograd. (Reissued in 1995.)

——— (1924), *Staryi Peterburg: U mednogo Petra*, Leningrad.

Surgères, de Granges de, ed. (1893), "Artistes français des XVIIe et XVIIIe siècles (1681–1787): Extraits des Comptes des Etats de Bretagne," *BSHAF*, 1893, pp. 74–75.

Svin'in, Pavel P. (1816), *Dostoprimechatel'nosti Sanktpeterburga i ego okrestnostei*, 5 vols., St. Petersburg. (Russo-French bilingual edition.)

Ternovets, B. N. (1941), "Et'en-Moris Fal'kone (1716–1791)," *Iskusstvo*, no. 2, pp. 80–82.

Terrasson, Janine (1969), *Madame de Pompadour et la création de la "Porcelaine de France,"* Paris.

Timiriazev, V. (1895), "Frantsuzskaia khudozhnitsa pri dvore Ekateriny II," *IstV*, vol. 59, pp. 913–23.

Tooke, William, ed. and tr. (1777), *Pieces Written by Mons. Falconet and Mons. Diderot on Sculpture in General and Particularly on the Celebrated Statue of Peter the Great, now finishing by the former at St. Petersburg*, London.

Toporov, Vladimir N. (1995), "O dinamicheskom kontekste trekhmernykh proizvedenii izobrazitel'nogo iskusstva (semioticheskii vzgliad): Fal'konetovskii pamiatnik Petru I," *LS*, vol. 1.

Tourneux, Maurice (1970), *Diderot et Catherine II*, Geneva. (Reprint of the 1899 Paris edition.)

Tretiak, Józef (1906), *Mickiewicz i Puszkin: Studia i szkice,* Warsaw.

Tronchin, Henry (1895), *Le Conseiller François Tronchin et ses amis, Voltaire, Diderot, Grimm, etc.* D'après des documents inédits, Paris.

Tsitselē, Elias A. (1904), "Kephallēniaka Symmikta," in *Symvolai eis tēn historian kai laographian tēs nēsou Kephallēnias,* 3 vols., Athens, 1980, vol. 1, pp. 800–808.

Tsverava, Grant K. (1985), *Dmitrii Alekseevich Golitsyn,* Leningrad.

Uspenskii, Boris A., ed. (1987). *Iazyki kul'tury i problemy perevodimosti.* Moscow.

Valabrègue, Antony (1894), "Madame Falconet: Une artiste française en Russie," *La vie contemporaine,* August, pp. 326–44.

———— (1898), *Une artiste française en Russie, 1766–1778: Madame Falconet,* Paris.

Valabrègue, Antony, ed. (1895), "Etienne-Maurice Falconet. 1779: Lettre à sa belle-fille Marie-Anne Collot," *Nouvelles Archives de l'art français,* 3d ser., vol. II, p. 20.

Valentiner, Wilhelm R. (1946), *Origins of Modern Sculpture,* New York.

Vallon, Fernand (1930), *Falconet: Falconet et Diderot, Falconet et Catherine II,* Grenoble.

Vereshchagina, Zh. F. (1995), "Fal'kone. Mednyi vsadnik," in *Sankt-Peterburg: Kul'tura i traditsii: Lektsii po kursu "Istoriia russkoi kul'tury,"* St. Petersburg.

Verlet, Pierre, et al. (1953), *Sèvres,* Paris.

Vernadsky, Georgii V. (1923–24), "*Mednyi vsadnik* v tvorchestve Pushkina," *Slavia,* vol. 2, pp. 645–54.

Vernière, Paul, ed. (1966), *Mémoires pour Catherine II,* Paris.

Versini, Laurent, ed. (1994–97), *Diderot: Oeuvres,* 5 vols., Paris.

Vitry, Paul (1936), "La sculpture française classique de Jean Goujon à Rodin," *BMF,* vol. 8, pp. 140–42.

Volkov, Solomon (1995), *St. Petersburg: A Cultural History,* translated by Antonina W. Bouis, New York.

Voltaire, *see* Besterman et al., eds., 1968– .

Vrangel' [Wrangel], Nikolai N. (1909–14), "Istoriia skul'ptury," in Grabar', ed., 1909–14, vol. 5.

———— (1911), "Inostrantsy v Rossii. Les peintres étrangers en Russie," *SG,* July–September, pp. 5–94.

Waliszewski, Kazimierz (1893), *Le Roman d'une impératrice: Catherine II de Russie,* Paris. (English translation: *The Romance of an Empress: Catherine II of Russia,* New York, 1894.)

———— (1894), *Autour d'un trône,* Paris.

Weihrauch, Hans R. (1967), *Europäische Bronzestatuetten: 15–18. Jahrhundert,* Braunschweig.

Weiner, Petr P. (1915), "*Zima,* statuia Fal'kone," *SG,* December, pp. 26–36.

Weinshenker, Anne Betty (1966), *Falconet: His Writings and His Friend Diderot,* Geneva.

Wildenstein, David, and Guy Wildenstein (1973), *Documents complémentaires au catalogue de l'oeuvre de Louis David,* no. 477, Paris.

Wilson, Arthur M. (1972), *Diderot,* New York.

———— (1973), "Diderot in Russia, 1773–1774," in Garrard, ed., pp. 166–97.

Wraxall, Nathaniel William (1776), *A Tour through Some of the Northern Parts of Europe, Particularly Copenhagen, Stockholm, and Petersburgh, in a Series of Letters,* 3rd corrected ed., London.

———— (1845), *Historical Memoirs of My Own Time, from 1772 to 1784,* 4 vols., London.

Zaichkin, Ivan A., and E. N. Pochkaev (1996), *Ekaterininskie orly,* Moscow.

Zaretskaia, Z. V. (1970), *Fal'kone,* Leningrad.

Zhivov, Viktor M., and B. A. Uspenskii (1987), "Tsar' i bog: Semioticheskie aspekty sakralizatsii monarkha v Rossii," in Uspenskii, ed., pp. 47–153.

Zick, Gisela (1975), "Amor-Harpokrates: Zur Wirkungsgeschichte und ikonographischen Herleitung einer Skulptur von Etienne-Maurice Falconet," *Wallraf-Richartz Jahrbuch,* Cologne.

Zinner, Johann (1783), *Empfindungen über das Denkmal welches Peter dem I Katharina die II feierlich errichtet hat,* Vienna.

Index

Note: Page numbers in **bold type** indicate illustrations.

INDEX